Statistics
for Advanced Level

Statistics
for Advanced Level

Second edition

JANE MILLER

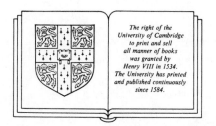

The right of the
University of Cambridge
to print and sell
all manner of books
was granted by
Henry VIII in 1534.
The University has printed
and published continuously
since 1584.

CAMBRIDGE UNIVERSITY PRESS

CAMBRIDGE

NEW YORK   PORT CHESTER

MELBOURNE   SYDNEY

Published by the Press Syndicate of the University of Cambridge
The Pitt Building, Trumpington Street, Cambridge CB2 1RP
40 West 20th Street, New York, NY 10011, USA
10 Stamford Road, Oakleigh, Melbourne 3166, Australia

First published 1983
Reprinted four times
Second edition 1989

Printed in Great Britain at the
University Press, Cambridge

Library of Congress catalogue card number: 82-4550

British Library cataloguing in publication data
Miller, J.C. (Jane C.), *1944–*
Statistics for advanced level – 2nd ed.
1. Statistical mathematics – For schools
I. Title
519.5

ISBN 0 521 36772 7

(ISBN 0 521 28930 0 first edition)

Contents

Contents

Preface to the first edition

Recent years have seen the increasing application of statistics in many fields, for example the physical and social sciences, biology, medicine, geography and economics. The number of students of statistics at GCE Advanced level has also grown but few books have been written specifically for this group. The GCE examining boards in England and Wales have different A-level syllabuses but I hope that this book will cover all their requirements. My intention has been to provide a book for class use. The introduction to each new topic is fairly brief but could be extended according to the interests of the teacher and his or her pupils. Some suggestions for general background reading are given in the bibliography as are references for further reading on specific topics.

It is assumed that students using this book will be familiar with various topics in pure mathematics. These are the summation of series (which first appears in Chapter 2), the exponential function (Chapter 7) and the calculus (Chapter 9). Appendix 1 gives some relevant theorems and examples on Σ-notation.

Some sections are marked with an asterisk, either because they are more demanding and/or because they appear in only a few syllabuses. These can be omitted without affecting the continuity of the text. This apart, the book should in general be worked through in the order given. A possible exception is Chapter 11 which is concerned with theoretical probability distributions other than the Binomial, Poisson and Normal ones. The sections of this chapter could be taken later, either together or separately. The Normal distribution is the first continuous distribution introduced (Chapter 9) because I have found that students readily understand the use of the Normal distribution function table but often lose sight of the statistical implications of other continuous distributions when faced with the integration involved.

Exercises are placed after each new topic and the student should aim to work through most of these. At the end of each chapter is an exercise on all the topics (including those in sections marked with an asterisk). These exercises do not follow the order of the material in the chapter and so are designed to test the student's ability to select the correct approach to a particular problem. Most of the questions set by examining boards are from A-level papers although some are from O-level and Additional Mathematics papers. There are also a few harder questions from Special papers to test the most able pupils.

Most chapters incorporate one or more project ideas for practical work. Students enjoy these and I hope that the projects will emphasise the practical relevance of abstract statistical concepts. (Although the projects on a chapter are placed at the end of it, they can be done during the work on that chapter.)

I gratefully acknowledge the permission of the following examining boards to use questions from their past papers: Associated Examining Board (AEB), Cambridge Local Examination Syndicate (C), Joint Matriculation Board (JMB), University of London

University Entrance and School Examinations Council (L), Oxford Local Examinations (O), Oxford and Cambridge Schools Examination Board (O & C), Southern Universities Joint Board (SUJB), Welsh Joint Education Committee (W). I am indebted to Messrs D. V. Lindley and J. C. P. Miller and to Cambridge University Press for permission to reproduce Tables A1, A3, A4, A5, A6, A7 and A8 from tables in *The Cambridge Elementary Statistical Tables*; to Dr H. R. Neave and George Allen and Unwin Ltd for permission to use material taken from *Elementary Statistical Tables* (1981) in Tables 17.14 and 17.24; the *Sunday Times* for permission to use material adapted from *Planet Earth*; Penguin Books Ltd for permission to use material adapted from *Facts in Focus* (2nd edition 1974) compiled by the Central Office of Information (Crown copyright © 1972, 1974), the Controller of Her Majesty's Stationery Office for permission to use material adapted from *A Century of Agricultural Statistics* and *The General Household Survey, 1973* (Crown copyright © 1976) and the Statistical Office of the European Communities for material from *Employment and Unemployment*.

Finally I must thank my husband, James, for all his help and encouragement, Marie Kirkland, of Loughborough Technical College, for reading the manuscript and checking my arithmetic, and Phillipa Doidge for patiently transforming my scrawl into typescript. My own students, past and present, have given immeasurable if sometimes unwitting help in testing ideas and examples. In the end, however, any errors or omissions are mine and I should welcome the comments and criticisms of fellow teachers.

J.C.M.

Preface to the second edition

In the years since the first edition of this book was published there has been a significant increase of interest in statistics as an A-level subject, and this has encouraged me to prepare a revised and slightly expanded second edition.

The principal changes are the inclusion of some new topics: the geometric mean, weighted averages, price indices, and the Geometric distribution. The section on time series has been amplified to include trend lines, seasonal variation and estimation. Three chapters on topics which often cause difficulty to students have also been expanded: Chapter 4 on *Probability*, Chapter 11 on *Other theoretical distributions* and Chapter 15 on *Significance testing*. In these and other places extra exercises, mainly containing simpler problems, have been added. At the end of each chapter the reader will now find a summary of the main points of the chapter.

The sections on projects at the end of each chapter now include references to *Advanced Level Statistics Software*. This is a comprehensive package of computer programs designed by myself and five other teachers of A-level statistics, which is published by Cambridge University Press. The programs include demonstrations, simulations and utilities which are designed to enhance the teaching of statistics in ways which would be difficult, if not impossible, without a desktop computer.

In general the examination questions included in the first edition are also included in this edition. Since syllabuses are constantly being revised each question may not always be indicative of a current syllabus. In particular the Oxford Local Examinations Board wish it to be noted that the questions of theirs which are used in this book relate to a previous syllabus.

I gratefully acknowledge permission of Her Majesty's Stationery Office to print the material in Tables 1.8 and 2.12 which is taken from *Key Facts* (1986).

Finally I am most grateful to those people who have made comments on or pointed out errors in the first edition. I hope for the continued interest of these and other readers.

J.C.M.

1 Presentation of data

1.1 Introduction

The word 'statistics' can be used in several different ways. The first definition of it given by the Concise Oxford Dictionary is 'numerical facts systematically arranged'. The importance of statistics in this sense can be gauged from the fact that there are few organisations, from governments down to small firms, who do not collect and make use of statistics. For example, in Great Britain there is a Government Statistics Office whose concern is the collection and analysis of data, which cover a wide range of fields including education, industry, trade, employment, population and social services. Some of this data is available in a series of books *Facts in Focus*, published by Penguin Books in association with HMSO, and more recently in *Key Data*, compiled by the Government Statistical Service and published by HMSO. These compilations make fascinating reading and illustrate well one aspect of the subject – descriptive statistics – which is concerned with presenting numerical information in a convenient, usable and understandable form.

There is, however, little purpose in the collecting of data unless we make use of them. Of course, the data mentioned above are used in planning and decision making. Another aspect of the subject statistics is mathematical statistics, which is concerned with the interpretation of data. It seeks to answer such questions as 'Is the standard of driving really worse on Bank Holidays than at other times?' 'Are the unemployment figures this month significantly higher than last month's?' 'Is a new vaccine more effective in protecting against a disease?' Statistics cannot usually give a *definite* answer to such questions, and it is probably for this reason that the subject has acquired a rather dubious reputation with the public. What statistical theory, correctly used, *does* do, is give an unbiased answer which makes the fullest use of the information available. Mathematical statistics is also of fundamental importance in the design and analysis of scientific experiments: with it we can make the best use of our resources and define the accuracy of the final experimental result.

1.2 Some basic terms

In order to introduce some of the terms commonly used in statistics we will consider a particular investigation: how many brothers and sisters does a sixteen year old in a particular town, Siblington, have? The sixteen year olds of Siblington form a **population**: that is a collection of people about whom we require information. In a statistical sense, the term 'population' need not refer to people, as it does here. It can be any set of items under consideration which we define by some shared characteristic. We could for example have the population of the pages in this book or the population of road accidents last year.

1

The sixteen year olds of Siblington form a **finite** population since, at any one instant, there is a definite number of them. However, **infinite** populations are also possible, for example the score when a die is thrown repeatedly. In this case there is theoretically no limit to the number of times the die can be thrown and so the population consisting of the scores is infinite.

In this particular investigation we are interested in the number of siblings (i.e. brothers and sisters) of each member of the population. This quantity, which we observe, is called a **variate** as it varies from member to member of the population. In the present example it is **quantitative** because it has a numerical value for each member of the population. Variates can also be **qualitative** which means that they describe some quality or attribute of an item such as colour.

If it were possible to obtain the value of the number of siblings for each member of the population then we could calculate exactly the average (or mean) number of siblings for a sixteen year old in Siblington. This quantity is called a **parameter** of the population and its value depends on the distribution of the variate in the population.

In practice, it is not usually possible to obtain values of the variate for all members of a finite population and obviously impossible for an infinite population. Instead values of the variate are obtained for a subset of the population known as a **sample**. We can use the values of the variate for the sample members to obtain an estimate of the mean number of siblings in the population, and this estimate, calculated from the sample, is called a **statistic** (the third way in which the word 'statistics' may be used). To distinguish between a parameter and the corresponding statistic, the parameter is usually denoted by a Greek letter and the statistic by the corresponding English letter.

1.3   Presentation of data: frequency tables and bar charts

Table 1.1 gives the number of siblings for a sample of 30 sixteen year olds from Siblington. (How a sample should be chosen so that it is representative of its population is the subject of Chapter 12.) Presented in this form the data are confusing but they can be summarised by finding the frequency with which each value occurs and presenting the results in a table, as in Table 1.2. This gives the **frequency distribution** of the variate. Tally marks are a

Table 1.1 *Number of siblings of 30 sixteen year olds*

3	1	3	2	2	1	1	3	1	1
5	3	3	2	0	4	2	1	2	5
3	1	2	2	1	1	2	4	2	1

convenient way of doing this. The column labelled **relative frequency** is obtained by dividing each frequency by the total frequency. The total of the relative frequency column should, of course, be 1 (if there are no rounding-off errors).

In this example the variate is **discrete**. This means it can only take particular values and not the values between them, e.g. 2.5 is meaningless. Such data are best represented by a bar chart as shown in Figure 1.1.

Table 1.2 *Frequency table for data in Table 1.1*

Value of variate	Tally marks	Frequency	Relative frequency
0	1	1	0.033
1	~~HHH~~ ~~HHH~~	10	0.333
2	~~HHH~~ 1111	9	0.300
3	~~HHH~~ 1	6	0.200
4	11	2	0.067
5	11	2	0.067
		30	1.000

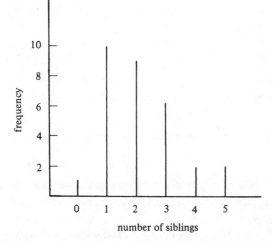

Figure 1.1 Bar chart for the data in Table 1.2, showing the number of siblings of 30 children

1.4 Presentation of continuous variates: histograms and frequency polygons

Table 1.3 gives the concentration of an antibody in blood serum taken from 50 donors. Here the variate takes so many values that little insight is gained by listing the frequency for each value. Instead the data are divided into groups with a suitable **class interval**. Suitable class intervals for the data above are 4.0–5.9, 6.0–7.9 g/l etc. (Choice of class interval is discussed in Section 1.5.) The class intervals must be chosen so that each value can be assigned unambiguously. The concentration of an antibody is a **continuous** variate: that is it may take any value in a particular range. However, it is important to realise that our measurement of it is discrete because of the accuracy with which we make the measurement. The class described above as 6.0–7.9 g/l includes all samples whose antibody concentration, c, lies in the range $5.95 \leqslant c < 7.95$ and these values are called the **true class limits**. Note that the top true class limit of one class coincides with the bottom true class limit of

Table 1.3 *Concentration of antibody in blood serum (g/l)*

11.6	15.8	17.0	14.2	16.2	17.3	15.7	17.3	12.0	11.5
8.4	13.2	12.5	15.7	14.0	10.8	9.9	14.0	15.0	10.2
19.2	12.0	8.2	13.8	12.6	9.6	16.0	13.7	11.5	14.8
17.5	15.2	7.2	17.0	5.2	9.4	7.5	15.5	10.7	14.2
15.3	7.8	11.2	10.0	12.1	10.5	12.2	8.6	9.9	16.1

Table 1.4 *Grouped frequency table for data in Table 1.3*

Class interval (g/l)	True class limits (g/l)	Mid-class value (g/l)	Frequency
4.0– 5.9	3.95– 5.95	4.95	1
6.0– 7.9	5.95– 7.95	6.95	3
8.0– 9.9	7.95– 9.95	8.95	7
10.0–11.9	9.95–11.95	10.95	9
12.0–13.9	11.95–13.95	12.95	9
14.0–15.9	13.95–15.95	14.95	12
16.0–17.9	15.95–17.95	16.95	8
18.0–19.9	17.95–19.95	18.95	1
			50

the class above. The **width** of a class is the difference between its upper and lower true class limits. Using these true class limits we can make a grouped frequency table, Table 1.4, for the antibody concentrations of serum samples.

Results for continuous data such as these can be represented by a **histogram** as shown in Figure 1.2. The divisions between the bars fall on the true class limits and the heights of the bars, and consequently their areas, are proportional to frequency. The data may also be represented by a **frequency polygon** which is constructed by joining the mid-points of the tops of the histogram blocks using straight lines. These mid-points are called the **mid-class values** and are the average of the upper and lower true class limits. The frequency polygon for the data in Table 1.4 is also shown in Figure 1.2. This method of representation is of value when two or more sets of data are to be compared.

1.5   Choice of class interval

It is important that the class interval is chosen so that the histogram gives a clear representation of the data. Choice of too large a class interval will lead to loss of detail: thus in the previous example the choice of the two large intervals 4.0–11.9 and 12.0–19.9 would summarise the results to an absurd degree. On the other hand too small a class interval would destroy the original point of grouping. A convenient rule of thumb is to choose a class interval so that the average frequency is about 5, i.e.

number of classes $\simeq \frac{1}{5}$(total frequency)

For the example in Section 1.4 this gives about 10 classes: in fact 8 classes were used since this gave a convenient choice of class interval.

1.6 Histogram with unequal class intervals

Grouped frequency tables are sometimes given with unequal class intervals because a particular range of the variate may be of especial interest. An example is given in Table 1.5.

Care has to be exercised in calculating the true class limits as age is measured differently from other variates; for example, the class 18–20 includes people who are just 18 to those one day less than 21.

Since the eye compares areas and not heights in a histogram the areas of the blocks must be proportional to class frequency. That is: height of block $\times$ class width $\propto$ class frequency, giving

$$\text{height of block} \propto \frac{\text{class frequency}}{\text{class width}}$$

This ratio, class frequency/class width, is known as the **frequency density** and Table 1.5 shows its calculation for each class. The limit for the last class has been taken (arbitrarily) as 75 so that a frequency density can be calculated for it. The corresponding histogram is shown in Figure 1.3.

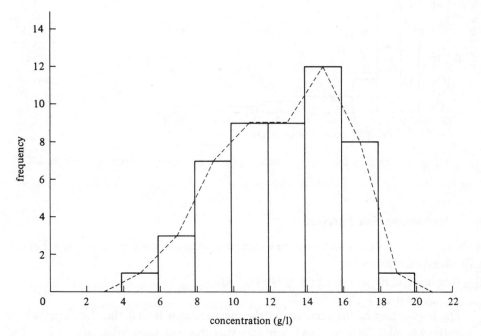

Figure 1.2 Histogram and frequency polygon for the data in Table 1.4, showing the concentration of an antibody in blood serum taken from 50 donors

Table 1.5 *Age at marriage for males in UK 1972*. (Source: *Facts in Focus*, 2nd edition, 1974, reprinted by permission of Penguin Books Ltd)

Class interval (yr)	True class limits (yr)	Class width (yr)	Frequency (thousands)	Frequency density (thousands per yr)
16–17	16–18	2	4	2.0
18–20	18–21	3	73	24.3
21–24	21–25	4	185	46.3
25–29	25–30	5	104	20.8
30–34	30–35	5	34	6.8
35–44	35–45	10	33	3.3
45–54	45–55	10	22	2.2
55 and over	55–75	20	26	1.3

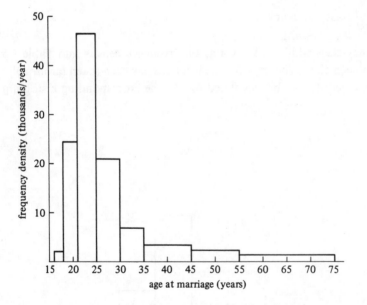

Figure 1.3 Histogram for the data in Table 1.5, showing the age at marriage for men in the UK

1.7   Interpreting class intervals

In published statistics class intervals are sometimes given in forms different from that used above. Some examples are:
  (i) Weight of adult men in kg (to nearest 0.1 kg)
       40–, 50–, 60–, 70–, 80–, 90–120.
       The implication of the accuracy of the measurement is that the class intervals are 40.0–49.9, 50.0–59.9 etc., and therefore that the true class limits are 39.95–49.95, 49.95–59.95 etc.

(ii)   Weekly income in £s
       0-, 100-, 200-, 300-, 400-
       or 0 and under 100, 100 and under 200 etc.
       In this case no indication of accuracy is given and we must state our own interpreta-
       tion. One possibility is that 0- means 0 to as near as 100 as we like to make it, so that
       the true class limits will be 0-100, 100-200 etc. Another is that measurements are to
       the nearest £. In this case true class limits are 0-99.50, 99.50-199.50 etc.
(iii) Distance to take-off in metres of a certain aircraft
       320-330, 330-340 etc.
       In this case the class limits coincide and can be taken as the true class limits. However,
       this form of class interval is not to be recommended since there are two possible
       classes to which a value of 330, say, could be allocated.

1.8   Cumulative frequency diagrams

This is another way of representing data graphically. The cumulative frequency for a
particular value of the variate is the frequency of observations below that value of the
variate. A cumulative frequency table can easily be made from a frequency table as shown
in Table 1.6.

   In calculating the upper true class limit it has been assumed that the incomes are given
to the nearest £0.01. The cumulative frequency curve is shown in Figure 1.4 where cumulative frequency is plotted against upper true class limit. The last point has been omitted
since the top income limit is unspecified. The cumulative frequency curve has uses which
are described in Sections 2.4 and 3.3.

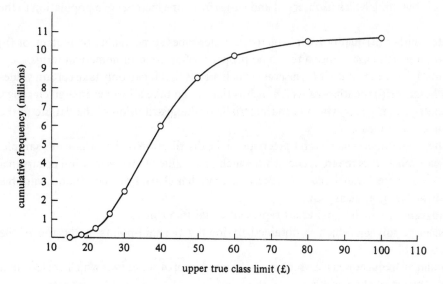

Figure 1.4 Cumulative frequency curve for the data in Table 1.6, showing the weekly income of men in
Great Britain in 1973

1 Presentation of data

Table 1.6 *Weekly earnings of male adults in full-time employment in Great Britain in 1973* (Adapted from *Facts in Focus*, 2nd edition, 1974, p. 121, reprinted by permission of Penguin Books Ltd)

Income (£)	Frequency (millions)	Cumulative frequency (millions)	Upper true class limit (£)
less than 15	0	0	14.995
15 and less than 18	0.1	0.1	17.995
18 and less than 22	0.4	0.5	21.995
22 and less than 26	0.8	1.3	25.995
26 and less than 30	1.2	2.5	29.995
30 and less than 40	3.5	6.0	39.995
40 and less than 50	2.6	8.6	49.995
50 and less than 60	1.2	9.8	59.995
60 and less than 80	0.8	10.6	79.995
80 and less than 100	0.2	10.8	99.995
more than £100	0.2	11.0	unspecified
	11.0		

Summary

A **population** is the total set of items under consideration and is defined by some characteristic of those items.

A **sample** is a finite sub-set of a population.

A **variate** is the thing which is observed and varies from one member of a population to the next.

A variate is either (a) **qualitative** in which case it describes some quality of an item, or (b) **quantitative** in which case it measures some property of an item in numerical terms.

A quantitative variate is either (a) **discrete** which means that it can only take certain values in a given range, or (b) **continuous** which means that it can take all values in a given range.

A **parameter** is a number which is characteristic of the distribution of the variate in the population, e.g. the mean.

A **statistic** is a number which is characteristic of the distribution of the variate in a sample.

A **frequency table** gives the frequency with which each value of an observation occurs in a sample. For a discrete variate it can be represented by a **bar chart**. For a continuous variable it can be displayed graphically by:

(a) a **histogram** in which equal areas represent equal frequencies,
(b) a **frequency polygon** which is obtained by joining the mid-points at the top of the histogram blocks,
(c) a **cumulative frequency** curve which gives the number of observations which are less than a stated value of the variate.

Relative frequencies express frequencies as a fraction of the total frequency.

Project

Obtain 100 values of a discrete variate from one of the following sources. Draw up a
frequency table and illustrate by a bar chart.
(a) The results of 100 throws of a die.
(b) The number of brothers and sisters of 100 of your contemporaries.
(c) Using four-figure tables the last digit of the sines of the angles from 0.1° to 10.0°.
(d) The number of letters in the first 100 words of this chapter.

Exercise on Chapter 1

(1) Which of the following variates are discrete and which continuous?
    (a) The throw on a die.
    (b) The height of a person.
    (c) The number of people on a bus.
    (d) The length of a train journey.
    (e) The weight of an egg.
    (f) The number of rooms in a house.
    (g) The age of a car.

(2) For the following classes, give the true class limits and mid-class values.
    (a) Length in mm (measured to nearest 0.1 mm)
        20.0–20.4, 20.5–20.9, 21.0–21.4, 21.5–21.9.
    (b) Length in mm (measured to nearest 0.01 mm)
        20.00–20.49, 20.50–20.99, 21.00–21.49, 21.50–21.99.
    (c) Age in years
        1, 2, 3, 4, 5.
    (d) Weight in kg (to nearest 1 kg)
        58, 59, 60, 61, 62, 63.
    (e) Height in cm (to nearest 1 cm)
        140–, 150–, 160–, 170 and less than 180.
    (f) Height in cm (to nearest 0.1 cm)
        140.0–, 150.0–, 160.0–, 170.0 and less than 180.0.

(3) For the data in Table 1.7, give the true class limits, mid-class values, and relative
    frequencies. Illustrate by a histogram and by a cumulative frequency curve.

(4) Table 1.8 gives the population of the United Kingdom analysed by sex and age at 30
    June 1985. (Source: *Key Data*, 1986, p. 8, reprinted by permission of HMSO.) Compare
    the figures for males and females graphically.

(5) The lives of 50 electric lamps in hours, to the nearest hour, are given in Table 1.9.
    Form a grouped frequency table and illustrate by (a) a histogram, (b) a cumulative
    frequency curve.

Table 1.7

Height in cm (to nearest cm)	Frequency
120–129	2
130–139	12
140–149	17
150–159	18
160–169	7
170–179	1

Table 1.8

Age (years)	Population in thousands	
	Female	Male
0–4	1753	1842
5–14	3599	3803
15–24	4547	4737
25–34	3857	3924
35–44	3699	3733
45–54	3120	3107
55–64	3311	3068
65–74	2732	2117
75–84	1865	1016
85 and over	504	152

Table 1.9

724	695	716	730	689	700	689	726	662	681
676	732	676	697	710	694	715	738	696	696
682	699	714	707	697	710	660	703	717	692
698	684	695	682	721	708	722	692	717	656
697	701	699	705	680	702	690	663	695	670

(6) (i) Nests of the Blue Tits are observed in two localities, (a) East Anglia and (b) Wales, and the number (x) of eggs in completed nests are counted. The observed frequencies (f(a), f(b)) are given in Table 1.10.
Draw a suitable diagram to show all this information.

Table 1.10

x	5	6	7	8	9	10	11	12	13	14	15
f(a)	2	0	4	10	15	18	21	24	12	8	6
f(b)	0	1	4	9	16	22	26	20	16	5	2

(ii) The number of surviving bacteria in a culture at various times after the start of an experiment is given in Table 1.11. Draw a suitable diagram to illustrate the numbers of deaths in the intervals between consecutive observations.   (C)

Table 1.11

Time (minutes)	0	1	2	4	8	16
Number of bacteria	384	306	235	168	92	20

(7) The numbers of pupils on the registers of grant-aided schools in England and Wales are as in Table 1.12. Show this information on a histogram.   (SUJB)

Table 1.12

Age (yr)	Number (thousands)
2–4	197
5–10	3677
11	596
12	572
13	595
14	172
15–18	276

(8) A large motor company, Xbar Ltd, produce their popular family saloon, Hiawatha, in two different countries. They have one factory in Pinkland and one in Blueland, each having a production target of 5000 vehicles per month. Table 1.13 gives actual production figures for these factories during 1978.
Summarise these data graphically. Comment.   (AEB)

Table 1.13

Month	Jan.	Feb.	Mar.	Apr.	May	June
Pinkland	5200	4100	6000	6900	6050	7000
Blueland	2100	1050	2950	5000	6300	5200

Month	Jul.	Aug.	Sep.	Oct.	Nov.	Dec.
Pinkland	8050	5900	4950	7100	6000	4900
Blueland	5100	nil	3300	5900	6800	6000

(9) Present the following information in a table and represent it graphically in a form suitable for reproduction in a popular newspaper.

Out of 3 720 000 males employed in non-manual occupations in 1951, 450 000 were employed in professional jobs, 1 290 000 in administration, 500 000 were shopkeepers, 690 000 were clerical workers, 480 000 shop assistants and the remainder in personal services. Of the 3 870 000 women employees in non-manual occupations in 1951, 40 000 were in professional jobs, 780 000 in administration, 160 000 were shopkeepers, 1 090 000 were clerical workers, 560 000 shop assistants and the rest in personal services.

In 1961, the number of male employees had gone up by 850 000. There were increases of 210 000 in professional jobs, 80 000 in shopkeepers, 120 000 in clerical workers and 20 000 in personal services. The number in administration was then 1 620 000. In 1961, the female total was 4 730 000. Female clerical workers were 1 540 000, in personal services 1 360 000 and in administration 920 000. Female shop assistants increased by 110 000 in 1961, and professional women by 10 000.

These figures are taken from the Census of Population Occupation Tables, 1951 and 1961, published by the General Register Office.   (O)

2 Measures of central tendency

2.1 The median

The frequency distributions in the previous chapter tended to cluster about a central value. For example the number of siblings in Figure 1.1 clusters about 1 to 2, and the blood serum protein concentrations in Figure 1.2 about 13.95 to 15.95 g/l. It is useful to have a single value which measures this **central tendency**, both to condense the information contained in a sample and for the purposes of comparison.

To introduce the ideas of this chapter we will use the example of the word lengths in two short passages. The first is from a child's reading book and the second from *Gulliver's Travels*.

'Once there was a boy who lived on a farm. Every day he had to take his father's sheep to a hill a long way off. He did not like being there on his own.'

'My gentleness and good behaviour had gained so far on the emperor and his court and indeed upon the army and people in general that I began to conceive hopes of getting my liberty in a short time.'

Arranging the values for the number of letters in each word in ascending order we have, for the child's book:

1, 1, 1, 1, 2, 2, 2, 2, 2, 2, 3, 3, 3, 3, 3, 3, 3, 3, 3, 3, 3, 3, 4, 4, 4, 4, 4, 4, 5, 5, 5, 5, 5, 5, 7

A simple way of measuring the central tendency is to take the middle value, which is called the **median**. In this case there are 35 values and the middle one is the 18th, which is 3.

Repeating this procedure for the excerpt from *Gulliver's Travels*, the word lengths are:

1, 1, 2, 2, 2, 2, 2, 2, 2, 2, 3, 3, 3, 3, 3, 3, 3, 3, 3, 4, 4, 4, 4, 4, 5, 5, 5, 5, 6, 6, 6, 7, 7, 7, 7, 8, 9, 10

In this case there are 38 values giving two middle values, the 19th and 20th. The median is taken to be half of their sum. In the example above this gives a median of $\frac{1}{2}(3+4)$ which is 3.5.

In general the median, M, of n observations is defined as follows: if the observations are arranged in order according to size, then, for odd values of n, the median is the $\frac{1}{2}(n+1)$th observation; for even values of n, the median is half the sum of the $\frac{1}{2}n$th and the $(\frac{1}{2}n+1)$th observations.

Although the second passage considered above contained many more long words than the first, the value of the median was nearly the same in both cases. This is an unsatisfactory property of the median: it is completely insensitive to values at the extremes of a sample.

To obtain a measure of central tendency which gives equal weight to all values we need to turn to the arithmetic mean.

2.2   The arithmetic mean

The **arithmetic mean** (normally called the 'mean') is what is usually meant in everyday language by the 'average'. It is the sum of the observations divided by the number of observations. Using the examples in the previous section the mean number of letters per word for the two passages are

$$\text{mean (child's book)} = \tfrac{113}{35} = 3.23$$
$$\text{mean } (Gulliver's\ Travels) = \tfrac{158}{38} = 4.16$$

Notice that although the original observations were all integers there is no reason why the mean should also be an integer.

In general the mean is more useful as a measure of central tendency than the median since it can be treated theoretically much more easily. There are, however, cases where the median is more useful as a representative value. Consider, for example, the following figures, which are the weekly wages of the employees of a small firm:

£130, £130, £130, £130, £140, £160, £160, £200, £200, £200, £240, £440, £500

for which median = £160
       mean = £212 (to the nearest £)

A prospective employee, who had been told that the 'average' wage was £160, would almost certainly be disappointed when he learnt *he* would earn, since ten out of thirteen employees earn less than the mean wage. In this case the mean is much higher than the median because of the much higher salaries of £440 and £500. The median gives a better idea of a representative wage *because* it is insensitive to these high salaries.

2.3   Median from a frequency table for a discrete variate

If the data are not grouped the median can be easily found from the cumulative frequency table. Table 2.1 gives the scores obtained for 50 throws of a die. The 25th and 26th values are both 3, giving a median of 3. (For a discrete variate for which the data are grouped the median can be found by using a cumulative frequency curve as described for continuous variates in the following section. In such cases the upper class limits are calculated *as though the variate were continuous*.)

2.4   Median of a continuous variate

Table 2.2 gives the data from Table 1.4 together with the cumulative frequency and upper true class limit. Figure 2.1 shows the cumulative frequency curve for these data, in which cumulative frequency is plotted against the upper true class limit. This is a 'less-than' curve since for any value of the variate, x, we can read off a corresponding value of the

Table 2.1 *Cumulative frequency table for 50 throws of a die*

Score	Frequency	Cumulative frequency
1	7	7
2	15	22
3	10	32
4	3	35
5	9	44
6	6	50

cumulative frequency which gives the number of values below x. To obtain the median we read off the value of the variate corresponding to half the total frequency. Half the values lie below this value of the variate and half above. From Figure 2.1 the median is 13.

If preferred the median can be found using linear interpolation between the two points on the curve on either side of the median. These points are labelled A and B in Figure 2.1. They and the point E corresponding to the median are shown schematically in Figure 2.2.

Table 2.2 *Cumulative frequency table for data in Table 1.4*

Class interval (g/l)	Frequency	Cumulative frequency	Upper true class limit (g/l)
4.0– 5.9	1	1	5.95
6.0– 7.9	3	4	7.95
8.0– 9.9	7	11	9.95
10.0–11.9	9	20	11.95
12.0–13.9	9	29	13.95
14.0–15.9	12	41	15.95
16.0–17.9	8	49	17.95
18.0–19.9	1	50	19.95

If we assume the curve is linear between A and B, then $\triangle ABC$ and $\triangle AED$ are similar. Thus,

$$\frac{AD}{AC} = \frac{ED}{BC}$$

Therefore

$$\frac{M-11.95}{13.95-11.95} = \frac{25-20}{29-20}$$

$$M = 13.06 \text{ g/l}$$

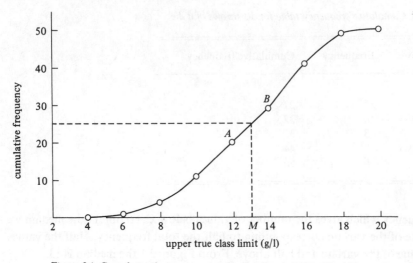

Figure 2.1 Cumulative frequency curve for the data in Table 2.2, showing the median

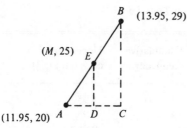

Figure 2.2 Schematic diagram to illustrate interpolation on a cumulative frequency diagram

2.4.1 Exercise

(1) Find the median for the data in Table 1.2.

(2) Find the median for the data in Table 1.5.

(3) Construct a cumulative frequency curve for the data in Table 2.3 and use it to find the median.

(4) Table 2.4 gives the numbers of deaths occurring in various age-groups during one year in a certain community.
     The age recorded for each person is the number of complete years lived.
     Construct a cumulative frequency table and use it to estimate the median age of death.

(C)

Table 2.3 *Annual income of 180 employees in a factory (to the nearest £) in 1972*

Annual income (£)	Frequency
500–	9
1000–	25
1500–	47
2000–	43
3000–	30
4000–	15
5000–	7
10000–15000	4

Table 2.4

Age-group	0–4	5–14	15–29	30–39	40–49	50–59	60–69	70–99	100–
Deaths	7	2	4	6	6	15	24	31	0

2.5   Calculation of the mean from a frequency table

Table 2.5 shows again the scores obtained for 50 throws of a die. Rather than add each score individually, a column has been added showing each score multiplied by its frequency. The total of this column is the total of the scores, and the mean is given by

$$\text{mean score on die} = \tfrac{160}{50} = 3.2$$

For a grouped frequency table such as Table 2.2, the mid-class value is taken to be representative of the whole class. This table is reproduced as Table 2.6 showing the calculation of the mean. The error introduced by using the mid-class value as representative of the class is usually negligible. In this case the mean calculated using the original data in Table 1.3 is 12.74 g/l.

Table 2.5 *Calculation of the mean from a frequency table*

Score	Frequency	Score × frequency
1	7	7
2	15	30
3	10	30
4	3	12
5	9	45
6	6	36
	50	160

Table 2.6 *Calculation of mean for data in Table 2.2*

Class interval (g/l)	True class limits (g/l)	Mid-class value (g/l)	Frequency	Frequency × mid-class value
4.0–5.9	3.95–5.95	4.95	1	4.95
6.0–7.9	5.95–7.95	6.95	3	20.85
8.0–9.9	7.95–9.95	8.95	7	62.65
10.0–11.9	9.95–11.95	10.95	9	98.55
12.0–13.9	11.95–13.95	12.95	9	116.55
14.0–15.9	13.95–15.95	14.95	12	179.40
16.0–17.9	15.95–17.95	16.95	8	135.60
18.0–19.9	17.95–19.95	18.95	1	18.95
			50	637.50

$$\text{mean} = \frac{637.5}{50} = 12.75 \text{ g/l}$$

2.6   Notation

The preceding calculations can be conveniently summarised using the following notation. If a variate takes n values $x_1, x_2, \ldots, x_n$, then the mean $\bar{x}$ is given by

$$\bar{x} = \frac{\sum_{i=1}^{n} x_i}{n} \tag{2.6.1}$$

(Those unfamiliar with Σ-notation should consult Appendix 1.)

For data in a frequency table where $x_1, x_2, \ldots, x_n$ occur with frequencies $f_1, f_2, \ldots, f_n$ respectively, the mean is given by

$$\bar{x} = \frac{\sum_{i=1}^{n} f_i x_i}{\sum_{i=1}^{n} f_i} \tag{2.6.2}$$

2.6.1   *Exercise*

(1) Find the mean for the data in Table 1.5. (Take the true limits of the last class as 55–75.) Compare this with the median, calculated in Exercise 2.4.1, question 2.

(2) Calculate the mean for the data in Table 1.12.

2.7   Aids to calculation

It will be evident from Table 2.6 that such calculations may become extremely tedious even
with the aid of a calculator. Fortunately there are means by which the calculation may be
simplified. Suppose we have to find the mean of 73, 72, 70, 71, 71, 69 and 74. Rather than adding these values we can add their deviations from (say) 70, which is known as an **arbitrary
origin**. The deviations are 3, 2, 0, 1, 1, -1, 4. The sum of these deviations is 10 and their mean
is $\frac{10}{7} = 1.4$. So the mean of the original data is $70 + 1.4 = 71.4$.

In some cases it is also convenient to change the **unit**. For example, let us find the average
of 980.8, 981.1, 980.7, 980.3, 981.8, 982.5. Measuring from 980 in units of 0.1, we have
deviations of 8, 11, 7, 3, 18, 25. Their sum is 72 and their mean is $\frac{72}{6} = 12$. The mean of
the original data is $980 + 12 \times 0.1 = 981.2$.

This method can be generalised as follows. If we have observations $x_1, x_2, \ldots, x_n$,
which are converted to $u_1, u_2, \ldots, u_n$, using A as arbitrary origin and B as unit

then $x_1 = A + Bu_1, x_2 = A + Bu_2, \ldots, x_n = A + Bu_n$

and $\bar{x} = A + B\bar{u}$ (2.7.1)

Proof of equation (2.7.1)

$$\bar{x} = \frac{\sum_{i=1}^{n} f_i x_i}{\sum_{i=1}^{n} f_i} = \frac{\sum_{i=1}^{n} f_i(A + Bu_i)}{\sum_{i=1}^{n} f_i}$$

$$= \frac{\sum_{i=1}^{n} f_i A + \sum_{i=1}^{n} Bf_i u_i}{\sum_{i=1}^{n} f_i}$$

$$= \frac{A \sum_{i=1}^{n} f_i + B \sum_{i=1}^{n} f_i u_i}{\sum_{i=1}^{n} f_i}$$

$$= A + \frac{B \sum_{i=1}^{n} f_i u_i}{\sum_{i=1}^{n} f_i}$$

$$= A + B\bar{u}$$

The u_is are sometimes called **coded data.** To show how use of an arbitrary origin and unit
simplify calculation, Table 2.7 repeats the calculation of Table 2.6 using this method. The

values have been coded using arbitrary origin $A = 12.95$ and unit $B = 2$. (Although taking $B = 2$ in this case does little to simplify the calculation it will be seen in the next chapter that it is useful to keep the coded values as small as is conveniently possible.)

Table 2.7 *Calculation of the mean using coded data*

Class interval (g/l)	True class limits (g/l)	Mid-class value x_i (g/l)	Frequency f_i	Coded value u_i	$f_i u_i$
4.0– 5.9	3.95– 5.95	4.95	1	−4	−4
6.0– 7.9	5.95– 7.95	6.95	3	−3	−9
8.0– 9.9	7.95– 9.95	8.95	7	−2	−14
10.0–11.9	9.95–11.95	10.95	9	−1	−9
12.0–13.9	11.95–13.95	12.95	9	0	0
14.0–15.9	13.95–15.95	14.95	12	1	12
16.0–17.9	15.95–17.95	16.95	8	2	16
18.0–19.9	17.95–19.95	18.95	1	3	3
			50		−5

$$\bar{u} = \frac{-5}{50} = -0.1$$
$$\bar{x} = A + B\bar{u}$$
$$= 12.95 - 2 \times 0.1$$
$$= 12.75 \text{ g/l}$$

(This is identical with the value obtained previously in Section 2.5.)

2.7.1   *Exercise*

(1) Find the mean for the data in Table 1.2. Compare this with the median, calculated in Exercise 2.4.1, question 1.

(2) A sample of 50 sixth-form students, who had part-time paid jobs, were asked how many hours a week they worked. The results are shown in Table 2.8. Calculate the mean number of hours worked per week.

Table 2.8

Number of hours worked	5–6	7–8	9–10	11–12	13–14	15–16	17–22
Number of students	3	21	6	8	5	4	3

(3) Table 2.9 gives the number of shoots produced by 50 plants in a botanical research

establishment. Taking the middle of the class 20–24 as arbitrary origin and a unit of 5, calculate the mean number of shoots per plant.   (C)

Table 2.9

Number of shoots	0–4	5–9	10–14	15–19	20–24	25–29	30–34	35–39	40–44	45–49
Frequency	1	1	1	6	17	16	4	2	1	1

2.8   The mode

Another measure of central tendency is the **mode**. For ungrouped data this is the most frequently occurring value of the variate. For example in Table 2.1 the mode is 2. For a grouped frequency distribution the **modal class** is appropriate and this is the class with the greatest frequency. It is possible for a frequency distribution to have more than one mode: distributions with one mode are called **unimodal**, those with two modes **bimodal**, and those with more than two modes **multimodal**.

2.9   Skewness

The frequency distribution shown in Figure 2.3 is **symmetrical** and the mean, median and mode are equal. The distribution in Figure 2.4 is said to be **positively skewed** and its median is less than the mean. The distribution in Figure 2.5 is **negatively skewed** and the median is greater than the mean. The effect of skewness was shown in the example of the salaries in Section 2.2 where the median was less than the mean.

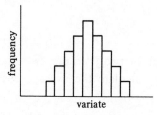

Figure 2.3 A symmetrical frequency distribution

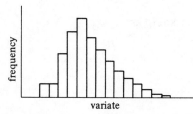

Figure 2.4 A positively skewed frequency distribution

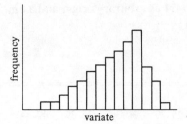

Figure 2.5 A negatively skewed frequency distribution

2.10   The geometric mean

If a variate takes n values $x_1, x_2, \ldots, x_n$, then the **geometric mean** is the nth root of the product of these values:

$$\text{geometric mean} = \sqrt[n]{(x_1 x_2 \ldots x_n)} \qquad (2.10.1)$$

Like the arithmetic mean, the geometric mean utilises all the information available. It can be shown that the geometric mean is always less than the arithmetic mean.

As a result of some of its properties the geometric mean is not much used as a measure of central tendency. For example, if even a single value of the variate is zero, then the geometric mean will necessarily be zero. Also, negative values of the variate will lead to imaginary values of the geometric mean. However, it has some advantages when dealing with a quantity whose rate of change depends on the quantity itself, e.g. population. Suppose a certain population was 1 million in 1960 and doubled to 2 million in 1970. The geometric mean, 1.4 million, gives a better estimate of the population in 1965, i.e. the middle of this period, than the arithmetic mean, 1.5 million. This is because the former assumes that the population increases by a fixed percentage each year while the latter assumes that the population increases linearly.

2.11   Weighted means

Table 2.10 gives details of the cost and distance travelled for two journeys, with the last column giving the cost per kilometre. How should we calculate the average cost per kilometre?

Table 2.10

Journey	Distance (km)	Cost (£)	Cost per km (p/km)
A	120	12.48	10.4
B	150	17.25	11.5

At first sight we might assume that we could take the arithmetic mean of the two figures in the last column to give 10.95 p/km. However, a little thought shows that this is misleading because the journeys are of different lengths: more weight should be given to journey B, the longer of the two journeys. We do this by calculating a **weighted mean**, in which the costs per km are weighted in the ratio of the journey lengths, in this case in the ratio $120:150$. The weighted mean is calculated as follows:

$$\text{weighted mean} = \frac{120 \times 10.4 + 150 \times 11.5}{120 + 150}$$
$$= 11.01 \text{ p/km}$$

In effect this method calculates the overall cost per kilometre.

In general if the values x_1, x_2, etc. are given weights w_1, w_2, etc. then

$$\text{weighted mean} = \frac{w_1 x_1 + w_2 x_2 + \ldots + w_n x_n}{w_1 + w_2 + \ldots + w_n} = \frac{\sum\limits_{i=1}^{n} w_i x_i}{\sum\limits_{i=1}^{n} w_i} \qquad (2.11.1)$$

An application of weighted means is described in the following section.

2.12 Price indices

A price index is a number which gives the cost of a commodity or service as a percentage of its cost in one particular year, known as the base year. Table 2.11 shows how the cost of renting a holiday flat for a particular week in the year varies over a period of years.

Table 2.11

Year	Cost (£)	Price index
1982	90	$100 \times \frac{90}{90} = 100$
1983	105	$100 \times \frac{105}{90} = 117$
1984	115	$100 \times \frac{115}{90} = 128$
1985	130	$100 \times \frac{130}{90} = 144$
1986	145	$100 \times \frac{145}{90} = 161$
1987	170	$100 \times \frac{170}{90} = 189$

The third column shows the calculation of the price index taking 1982 as the base year, using the formula

$$\text{price index for year } A = 100 \times \frac{\text{cost in year } A}{\text{cost in base year}} \qquad (2.12.1)$$

We can, if we wish, change the base year. For example, the price indices for Table 2.11, with 1984 as the base year, are found by multiplying the current indices by $\frac{100}{128}$.

Price indices are valuable for comparing the change in price of different commodities. Table 2.12 gives the price index for a number of household commodities and services in the

United Kingdom taking 1974 as the base year. It shows, for example, that the cost of tobacco has increased more rapidly than that of food over the period in question.

Table 2.12 *Price indices for a number of household commodities in the UK* (Source: *Key Data 86*, HMSO.)

Year	Tobacco	Housing	Transport	Food
1974	100.0	100.0	100.0	100.0
1976	147.8	135.3	149.5	150.7
1978	195.2	163.9	186.7	192.1
1980	250.3	254.7	260.1	241.2
1982	356.6	338.7	309.5	282.1
1984	421.9	378.7	337.6	307.4

The concepts of weighted mean and price index are combined in the calculation of the General Index of Retail Prices. This monitors the level of the prices of goods and services purchased by households in the United Kingdom. In calculating the index a weight must be given to each price which reflects its relative importance in the household budget. The following example gives a simple illustration of the principles involved.

2.12.1   Example

In a manufacturing process four different raw materials A, B, C and D are used. The masses required are in the ratio $1:2:4:5$. Table 2.13 shows the cost (in £) per tonne of these materials in 1980 and in 1987. Calculate a price index for the cost of the process in 1987 taking 1980 as the base year.

Table 2.13

Material	A	B	C	D
Cost in 1980	123	154	76	98
Cost in 1987	143	213	89	112

First we need to calculate a weighted average of the cost per tonne for each year.

$$\text{weighted average for 1980} = \frac{1 \times 123 + 2 \times 154 + 4 \times 76 + 5 \times 98}{1 + 2 + 4 + 5}$$

$$= \frac{1225}{12}$$

$$\text{weighted average for 1987} = \frac{1 \times 143 + 2 \times 213 + 4 \times 89 + 5 \times 112}{1 + 2 + 4 + 5}$$

$$= \frac{1485}{12}$$

Now the price index can be calculated:

$$\text{price index for } 1987 = 100 \times \frac{\frac{1485}{12}}{\frac{1225}{12}} = 121.2$$

2.13 Time series and moving averages

Table 2.14 gives the quarterly unemployment figures for the UK over a period of nearly three years, and the data are indicated by the crosses in Figure 2.6. Many time series show a similar form: a seasonal variation produces a zig-zag effect which to some extent masks any general trend, in this case a downward trend.

Table 2.14 *Quarterly unemployment figures* (*in thousands*)
(Source: *Employment and Unemployment,*
published by the Statistical Office of the
European Communities)

	Month	Number unemployed
1977	July	1622
	October	1518
1978	January	1549
	April	1452
	July	1586
	October	1430
1979	January	1456
	April	1341
	July	1464
	October	1368
1980	January	1471

The seasonal variation can be removed by calculating the **four-quarterly moving average**. This is found by averaging the values over four quarters and plotting the average obtained in the middle of the range used. For example, the average for the first four quarters in Table 2.14 is

$$\tfrac{1}{4}(1622 + 1518 + 1549 + 1452) = 1535.25$$

which is plotted mid-way between October 1977 and January 1978.

The next moving average can be found most simply from $1535.25 + \tfrac{1}{4}$ (value for July 1978 − value for July 1977) and similarly for subsequent values of the moving average. Table 2.15 shows the calculation of the differences and moving averages. The values are shown in Figure 2.6 by the circles.

For data given monthly the twelve-month moving average is calculated using a similar method. In the same way for data, such as the birth rate, which may show a cyclical variation over a number of years, a five- or ten-year moving average may be used to reveal the general trend.

Table 2.15 *Calculation of moving averages*

	Month	Unemployed	Difference	Difference ÷ 4	Moving average
1977	July	1622			
	October	1518			1535.25
1978	January	1549	−36	−9	1526.25
	April	1452	−88	−22	1504.25
	July	1586	−93	−23.25	1481.00
	October	1430	−111	−27.75	1453.25
1979	January	1456	−122	−30.5	1422.75
	April	1341	−62	−15.5	1407.25
	July	1464	+15	+3.75	1411.00
	October	1368			
1980	January	1471			

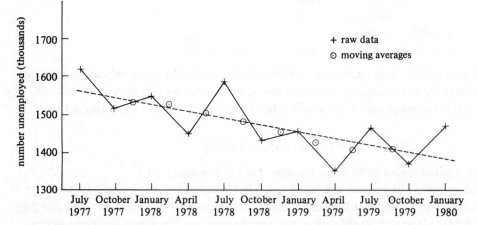

Figure 2.6 Graph showing the raw data and the moving averages for the unemployment figures given in Table 2.14

The moving averages in Figure 2.6 show a downward trend and a straight line has been drawn by eye to fit the moving averages as closely as possible. This line is called a **trend line**. (A statistical method for fitting such a line to the original points is described in Chapter 18.)

The discrepancies between the trend line and the individual points allow us to estimate seasonal effects. For example, all the points for July are above the trend line, suggesting that unemployment increases in July irrespective of the general trend. (Can you give a reason?) One way of measuring the discrepancy is by expressing the observed value as a percentage of the value predicted by the trend line. For example, for July 1977 the value predicted by the trend line is 1567, and the observed value (1622) is 104% of this. Table 2.16 shows the value for each quarter expressed as a percentage of the predicted value for that quarter, and at the bottom of the table the averages for each column. Percentages are used rather than differences since it is likely that the seasonal effect will not give a constant difference but depend on the general level of unemployment at that time.

Table 2.16

Year	January	April	July	October
1977			104	98
1978	101	96	106	97
1979	100	93	103	97
1980	106			
Average	102.3	94.5	104.3	97.3

The trend line and the estimates of seasonal effects can be combined to forecast future figures. For example the trend line predicts a value of 1371 for April 1980 which, when corrected for the seasonal effect by multiplying by $(\frac{94.5}{100})$ gives a figure of 1296. Extrapolation of this kind should be used very cautiously. There is no reason to suppose that variables like unemployment follow easily quantifiable scientific laws and, as the data in question 6 at the end of this chapter show, the trend in unemployment was upwards from 1983 to 1986.

2.13.1 *Exercise*

(1) Table 2.17 gives the quarterly sales in thousands of pounds at a large store for the period 1975–77.
Calculate a set of moving averages which removes the effects of seasonal variation.
Illustrate on one graph both the original figures and the moving average values.
Use your moving average graph to estimate the sales in the first quarter of 1978. (C)

Table 2.17

	1975	1976	1977
1st quarter	168	171	178
2nd quarter	182	188	190
3rd quarter	189	193	198
4th quarter	210	213	218

(2)   Table 2.18 gives the quarterly fuel and lighting costs for a large building during three successive years.

Plot these results on a graph.

Calculate the four-quarterly moving averages and plot these on the same graph. Draw a straight line to fit these averages as closely as possible and use the graph to estimate the rate at which the costs increased over the three years.   (C)

Table 2.18

	1st quarter	2nd quarter	3rd quarter	4th quarter
1st year	£103	£76	£62	£87
2nd year	£115	£86	£70	£95
3rd year	£127	£92	£76	£109

(3)   Table 2.19 shows the numbers of births (in thousands, to the nearest thousand) in a certain country in the years 1918 to 1929.

Calculate five-year moving averages. Plot both the original figures and the moving averages on the same graph and analyse the results briefly.   (C)

Table 2.19

1918	1919	1920	1921	1922	1923	1924	1925	1926	1927	1928	1929
65	62	78	84	80	75	72	71	72	74	72	70

(4)   State briefly the circumstances under which you would use moving averages and the advantages of doing so.

Table 2.20 shows the average numbers of hours of sunshine per day which occurred at a certain town.

Draw a graph to illustrate these figures.

Calculate a suitable set of moving averages and plot these averages on the same graph.   (C)

Table 2.20

	Jan./Feb.	Mar./Apr.	May/June	July/Aug.	Sept./Oct.	Nov./Dec.
1976					2.9	2.0
1977	2.0	4.1	7.1	8.3	3.5	3.2
1978	4.4	3.5	8.3	8.3	4.1	3.8

Summary

For a set of n values of a variate, $x_1, x_2, \ldots$, the arithmetic **mean** $\bar{x}$, is given by

$$\bar{x} = \frac{\sum_{i=1}^{n} x_i}{n}$$

or, if values are repeated, by

$$\bar{x} = \frac{\sum_{i=1}^{n} f_i x_i}{\sum_{i=1}^{n} f_i}$$

where f_i is the frequency of value x_i.

The **geometric mean** is

$$\sqrt[n]{(x_1 x_2 \ldots x_n)}$$

The **weighted mean** is

$$\frac{\sum_{i=1}^{n} w_i x_i}{\sum_{i=1}^{n} w_i}$$

where the value x_i is given a weight w_i.

The **median** of the values is the middle value when they are arranged in order of increasing size or, if there is an even number of values, the mean of the two middle values. For grouped data the median can be found from a cumulative frequency curve and is the value of the variate corresponding to half the total frequency.

The **mode** is the most commonly occurring value.

A **moving average** is used to smooth out seasonal variations and show an overall trend.

Projects

(1) *Bisecting a line by eye*

Ask 100 people to mark the mid-point of a line 20 cm long by eye (i.e. without measuring or folding). The line should be presented so that it is vertical on the paper as seen by the subject. Obtain attempts on two separate lines for each person, making sure that the attempts are labelled 'first' and 'second'. Measure the distance of each mark from the centre of the line taking the distance as positive for marks above the centre and negative for marks below. Draw up suitable frequency tables for the measuring lengths for the first and second attempts and calculate the mean in each case.

(2) *Comparing authors*

For each of two authors, make a frequency table of the number of words in a sentence for a sample of 100 consecutive sentences. Compare the results graphically and calculate the mean sentence lengths.

(3) *Advanced Level Statistics Software*

The *Economic statistics* section contains programs to demonstrate price indices, weighted means and moving averages. The calculations for the first two are displayed in tabular form and the effect of altering the base year or weightings can be investigated. The moving average is displayed graphically and group size can be altered to find the one which gives the best smoothing of seasonal variations. Examples of suitable data are included on the data disc.

Exercise on Chapter 2

(1) Give the mean, median and mode(s) for the following values. Which gives the best measure of central tendency?

2, 4, 6, 3, 1, 2, 1, 1, 5, 4, 4, 2, 5, 6, 8, 15, 7

(2) Calculate the mean for the data in question (3) of the Exercise on Chapter 1.

(3) The mark distributions in Table 2.21 were obtained from two groups of children taking the same school examination.
  (a) Plot these distributions, in the way that seems best to you, in order both to illustrate them separately and to show up the differences between them.
  (b) Estimate the median marks for the two groups.   (C)

Table 2.21

Mark range	0–29	30–49	50–59	60–69	70–79	80–100	Total
Group P	4	2	4	11	7	6	34
Group Q	2	4	4	5	11	8	34

(4) The sunshine figures for a certain town in England for the years 1975–77 are given in Table 2.22, each figure representing the mean hours of sunshine per day over the month.
  (a) Draw a graph to illustrate this information.
  (b) Superimpose a second graph showing the twelve-month moving average.(SUJB)

Table 2.22

	Jan.	Feb.	Mar.	Apr.	May	June	July	Aug.	Sept.	Oct.	Nov.	Dec.
1975	1.2	2.8	5.0	5.6	6.6	5.4	8.5	6.4	5.2	3.8	1.8	1.4
1976	1.8	2.5	4.5	5.5	7.8	5.1	5.1	4.9	3.3	3.6	1.9	0.7
1977	1.5	2.7	3.1	5.2	6.7	9.6	4.5	4.7	3.7	2.7	2.1	1.7

(5) Table 2.23 shows the cumulative distribution of gross weekly earnings of male full-time workers in Great Britain in April 1976.

Estimate for the distribution

(a) the median earnings of a manual worker,

(b) the median earnings of a non-manual worker,

(c) the proportion of manual workers earning less than the median earnings of non-manual workers.

Construct the grouped frequency distribution of the gross weekly earnings of manual workers and represent it as a histogram.

Estimate the mean weekly earnings of manual workers.

The figures in the table were obtained by means of a sample survey. Men whose pay for the survey period was affected by absence were not included in the tabulated results. If these men had been included, comment briefly on the expected effect on the distributions.

(JMB)

Table 2.23

Gross weekly earnings (£) under	35	40	45	50	55	60	70	80	100	200
Manual workers (millions)	0.1	0.3	0.7	1.3	2.0	2.7	4.0	4.9	5.7	6.1
Non-manual workers (millions)	0.1	0.2	0.4	0.6	0.9	1.2	1.8	2.4	3.2	4.1

(6) Table 2.24 gives further unemployment figures for the United Kingdom. Draw a graph to illustrate this information and superimpose the four-quarterly moving average.

Table 2.24 *Unemployed people in the United Kingdom. Figures in thousands*
(Source: *Key Data 1986*, HMSO)

Year	January	April	July	October
1983			3021	3094
1984	3200	3108	3101	3225
1985	3341	3273	3235	3277
1986	3408			

(7)   Calculate the mean mark for the groups in question (3).

(8)   Table 2.25 is a frequency table for the number of words in a sentence for a paragraph in a book. Calculate the mean number of words in a sentence.

Table 2.25

Number of words	Number of sentences
5–9	9
10–14	10
15–19	8
20–24	11
25–29	8
30–34	4
35–39	4
40–44	1
45–49	1

(9)   For a project a student collected data on the hair-care habits of fellow students. She asked 50 boys and 50 girls how many times they had washed their hair in the previous week. The results are shown in Table 2.26.

Table 2.26

Number of washes	1	2	3	4	5	6	7
Number of girls	2	22	22	4	0	0	0
Number of boys	0	10	19	13	2	2	4

Find the mean, median and mode for each group.

(10) A factory uses five raw materials A, B, C, D, E to manufacture a flash-gun. The masses of the materials used in its production are in the ratios $1 : 1 : 4 : 3 : 1$ respectively. The prices of the materials, in pounds sterling per tonne, in the years 1978 and 1980 are given in Table 2.27.

Table 2.27

Raw material	A	B	C	D	E
1978	4	3	2	5	3
1980	8	5	3	9	8

Taking 1978 as the base year, calculate an index number for the total cost of the raw materials used for the manufacture of the flash-gun in 1980.

(L, part question)

3   Measures of dispersion

3.1   The range

Returning to the examples of word lengths used in the previous chapter (see Section 2.1), we obtained for the extract from the child's book a mean word length of 3.23 letters. For *Gulliver's Travels* extract, a mean word length of 4.16 letters was obtained. Besides the difference in mean word lengths between the two passages, the words in the second extract are evidently more variable in length and less closely clustered about the mean. This spread in values is known as **dispersion**. How can we measure it?

The simplest possible method is to take the difference between the highest and lowest values of the variate. The result is known as the **range**. We have

range for extract from child's book $= 7 - 1 = 6$ letters
range for extract from *Gulliver's Travels* $= 10 - 1 = 9$ letters

The obvious disadvantage of this method is that it uses only two values of the variate.

3.2   Interquartile range

This is a measure of dispersion which extends the idea of the median. Below are the word lengths for the extract from the child's book with the median circled:

1, 1, 1, 1, 2, 2, 2, 2, 2̲, 2, 3, 3, 3, 3, 3, 3, 3, ③, 3, 3, 3, 3, 4, 4, 4, 4, 4̲, 4, 5, 5, 5, 5, 5, 5, 7.

The median divides the data into two equal halves. If we now find the middle value of each half we have for the lower half 2 (which is underlined) and for the upper half 4 (also underlined). These two values are called the **lower quartile**, Q_1, and the **upper quartile**, Q_3, respectively since they divide the distribution into quarters. The difference between them, $Q_3 - Q_1 = 2$, is called the **interquartile range** and $\frac{1}{2}(Q_3 - Q_1)$ is called the **semi-interquartile range**.

We can see that the quartiles are the $\frac{1}{4}(n+1)$th and $\frac{3}{4}(n+1)$th values. These can be simply found when $n+1$ is a multiple of 4. However, for the extract from *Gulliver's Travels* there are 38 values so that the $\frac{1}{4}(n+1)$th value will be the 9.75th value. We take this to lie between the 9th and 10th values, which are underlined in the list below.

1, 1, 2, 2, 2, 2, 2, 2, 2̲, 2̲, 3, 3, 3, 3, 3, 3, 3, 3, ⟨3, 4,⟩ 4, 4, 4, 4, 5, 5, 5, 5, 6̲, 6̲, 6, 7, 7, 7, 7, 8, 9, 10

Since these values are both 2, the lower quartile is also 2. Similarly the upper quartile is the 28.25th value which lies between the 28th and 29th values and is therefore 6. This gives

34

interquartile range $Q_3 - Q_1 = 6 - 2 = 4$

As we would expect the interquartile range is greater for the extract from *Gulliver's Travels*.

When a quartile lies between two values which are not equal it can be found by linear interpolation. For example, if the 9th and 10th values were 2 and 3 respectively then the 9.75th value could be given as 2.75. The method of finding the quartiles which is described here is one of a number of different conventions which lead to slightly different results: for practical purposes these differences are unimportant, especially for large samples.

3.3   Interquartile range for grouped data

Figure 3.1 reproduces the cumulative frequency curve shown in Figure 1.4 for the earnings of male adults. The median is found by reading off the income corresponding to a cumulative frequency of one-half the total frequency, i.e. $\frac{11}{2} = 5.5$, and is £38.50. The lower quartile is found by reading off the income corresponding to a cumulative frequency of one-quarter the total frequency, i.e. $\frac{11}{4} = 2.75$, and is £31. The upper quartile is found by reading off the income corresponding to a cumulative frequency which is three-quarters of the total frequency, i.e. $\frac{3}{4} \times 11 = 8.25$, and is £48.

interquartile range $= £48 - £31 = £17$
semi-interquartile range $= £8.50$

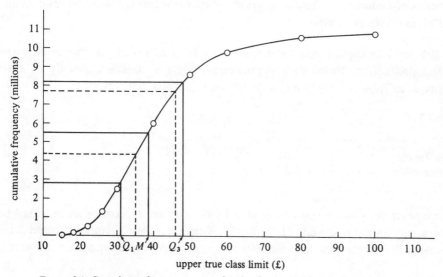

Figure 3.1 Cumulative frequency curve for the data in Table 1.6, showing the median, the quartiles and the 40th and 70th percentiles

3.4   Percentiles

The lower quartile, the median and the upper quartile give the values of the variate below which lie 25%, 50% and 75% of the total frequency respectively. It is sometimes useful to have values below which other cumulative frequencies lie, e.g. from the cumulative frequency curve we see that 40% of the incomes (i.e. 4.4 million) lie below £35. This is called the 40th **percentile**. The 40th percentile can also be referred to as the 4th **decile**, i.e. the value of the variate below which $\frac{4}{10}$ of the total frequency lies. From the graph the 7th decile is £46. Quartiles, percentiles and deciles are referred to collectively as **quantiles**.

One use of percentiles is in the standardisation of examination results. A cumulative frequency curve can be used to find the pass mark which will allow a certain proportion of candidates to succeed.

As measures of dispersion, quartiles are subject to the same disadvantages as the median as a measure of central tendency: they do not give equal weight to each member of the sample.

3.4.1   *Exercise*

(1) In Table 3.1 x is the number of grams of impurity in one-litre containers of a chemical solution.

Table 3.1

x	0–25	26–50	51–75	76–100	101–125	126–150	151–175	176–200
f	20	73	85	114	106	54	36	12

By means of a cumulative frequency graph estimate the median impurity content and the 10th and 90th percentiles.   (C)

(2) 120 girls send in applications for employment as members of the chorus in a new musical production. From their applications they are classified initially by their heights, as in Table 3.2. (155– means 155 or more but less than 161.)

Table 3.2

Height (in cm)	155–	161–	164–	167–	170–	173–	176–	179–	182–	191–
Number of girls	4	6	12	17	28	22	16	9	6	0

The manager decides that they must reject girls who are 175 cm or more in height. Draw a cumulative frequency curve (scale: 2 cm represents 5 cm height and 2 cm represents 20 girls) and use it to estimate the percentage of girls who are not rejected.   (C)

(3) An inspection of 34 aircraft assemblies revealed a number of missing rivets as shown in Table 3.3.

Table 3.3

Number of rivets missing	0–2	3–5	6–8	9–11	12–14	15–17	18–20	21–23
Frequency	4	9	11	6	2	1	0	1

Draw a cumulative frequency curve. Use this curve to estimate the median and the quartiles of the distribution. (O+C)

(4) Every day at 08.28 a train departs from one city and travels to a second city. The times taken for the journey were recorded in minutes over a certain period and were grouped as in Table 3.4. (The interval −90 indicates all times greater than 85 minutes up to and including 90 minutes.)

Table 3.4

Time	−80	−85	−90	−95	−100	−105	−110	−115	−120	−125	over 125
Frequency	0	6	12	22	31	15	7	4	2	1	0

From these figures draw a cumulative frequency curve and from this curve estimate
(a) the median time for the journey,
(b) the semi-interquartile range,
(c) the number of trains which arrived at the second city between 10.00 and 10.15. (C)

(5) Easyadd Ltd manufactures electronic desk calculators. One of the electronic components in the calculator is available in two types, A and B. In order to decide which to use in the calculator the company obtains a sample of 100 of each type and tests these to failure. The results of these tests are summarised in Table 3.5.

Table 3.5

Time to failure (hours)	Number of components	
	Type A	Type B
Less than 10	10	1
10–19	10	2
20–29	9	3
30–49	9	9
50–99	7	23
100–149	8	18
150–199	6	11
200–299	8	13
300–399	5	8
400–499	3	5
500 and over	25	7
Total	100	100

Compare these two distributions (a) graphically, (b) numerically.
What is your interpretation of the differences, and which type of component would you recommend the company to use? (AEB)

3.5   The mean deviation

This is a measure of dispersion which uses all the values of the variate. It is found by finding the deviation of each value of the variate from the mean, without regard to sign, and calculating the mean of these deviations. In Σ-notation,

$$\text{mean deviation} = \frac{\sum_{i=1}^{n} f_i|x_i - \bar{x}|}{\sum_{i=1}^{n} f_i}$$

The calculations of the mean deviations for the samples from the child's book and *Gulliver's Travels* are given in Table 3.6. The second column gives the deviations from the mean. The final column gives the sum of the deviations for each value of the variate. As we would expect the mean deviation is greater for the *Gulliver's Travels* extract.

The disadvantage of this measure of dispersion is that information is lost by ignoring the signs of the deviations, making it difficult to treat it theoretically.

Table 3.6 *Calculation of mean deviation for samples from the child's book and* Gulliver's Travels

Child's book $\bar{x} = 3.23$

x_i	$|x_i - \bar{x}|$	f_i	$f_i|x_i - \bar{x}|$
1	2.23	4	8.92
2	1.23	6	7.38
3	0.23	12	2.76
4	0.77	6	4.62
5	1.77	6	10.62
7	3.77	1	3.77
		35	38.07

Gulliver's Travels $\bar{x} = 4.16$

x_i	$|x_i - \bar{x}|$	f_i	$f_i|x_i - \bar{x}|$
1	3.16	2	6.32
2	2.16	8	17.28
3	1.16	9	10.44
4	0.16	5	0.80
5	0.84	4	3.36
6	1.84	3	5.52
7	2.84	4	11.36
8	3.84	1	3.84
9	4.84	1	4.84
10	5.84	1	5.84
		38	69.60

mean deviation for extract from child's book
$= \frac{38.07}{35} = 1.09$

mean deviation for extract from *Gulliver's Travels* $= \frac{69.6}{38} = 1.83$

3.6   The standard deviation

The **standard deviation (s.d.)** overcomes the problem of the signs of the deviations by using their squares. The mean of the squares of the deviations is called the **variance** and the square root of the variance is the standard deviation. An elementary example will make the method clear.

3.6.1   *Example*

Calculate the mean and s.d. of 6, 7, 8, 9, 10.

Table 3.7

x_i	$x_i - \bar{x}$	$(x_i - \bar{x})^2$
6	−2	4
7	−1	1
8	0	0
9	1	1
10	2	4
40		10

The first column of Table 3.7 gives the values of the variate. The total is 40 so that the mean, $\bar{x}$, is given by

$$\bar{x} = \tfrac{40}{5} = 8$$

Using this value of $\bar{x}$, the deviations have been calculated in the second column and the squares of the deviations in the third column. The sum of the squares of the deviations is 10, giving

variance = mean of the squared deviations
$$= \tfrac{10}{5} = 2$$
$$\text{s.d.} = \sqrt{(\text{variance})}$$
$$= \sqrt{2} = 1.414$$

Using Σ-notation we have, if the variate takes the values $x_1, x_2, \ldots, x_n$, the standard deviation, s, given by

$$s = \sqrt{\left\{ \frac{\sum_{i=1}^{n} (x_i - \bar{x})^2}{n} \right\}} \qquad (3.6.1)$$

3.6.2   *Exercise*

Find the mean and standard deviation for each of the following sets of data.

(a)   1, 2, 3, 4, 5.
(b)   55, 56, 57, 58, 59.
(c)   10, 20, 30, 40, 50.
(d)   2, 56, 57, 58, 112.

3.7   A useful relationship

The calculation of standard deviation in Section 3.6 was relatively simple because the values of the variate, the mean and consequently the deviations were whole numbers. Had the mean not been an integer the calculation would have been more tedious. There is a useful identity which can be used to simplify the calculation of s in such cases. It is

$$s = \sqrt{\left\{ \frac{\sum\limits_{i=1}^{n} (x_i - \bar{x})^2}{n} \right\}} = \sqrt{\left\{ \frac{\sum\limits_{i=1}^{n} x_i^2}{n} - \left(\frac{\sum\limits_{i=1}^{n} x_i}{n} \right)^2 \right\}} \qquad (3.7.1)$$

Proof of equation (3.7.1)

$$\sqrt{\left\{ \frac{\sum\limits_{i=1}^{n} (x_i - \bar{x})^2}{n} \right\}} = \sqrt{\left\{ \frac{\sum\limits_{i=1}^{n} (x_i^2 - 2x_i\bar{x} + \bar{x}^2)}{n} \right\}} \qquad \text{(expanding the term } (x_i - \bar{x})^2)$$

$$= \sqrt{\left\{ \frac{\sum\limits_{i=1}^{n} x_i^2}{n} - \frac{2\bar{x} \sum\limits_{i=1}^{n} x_i}{n} + n \times \frac{\bar{x}^2}{n} \right\}} \qquad \text{(separating terms)}$$

$$= \sqrt{\left\{ \frac{\sum\limits_{i=1}^{n} x_i^2}{n} - 2\bar{x}^2 + \bar{x}^2 \right\}} \qquad \text{since } \frac{\sum\limits_{i=1}^{n} x_i}{n} = \bar{x}$$

$$= \sqrt{\left\{ \frac{\sum\limits_{i=1}^{n} x_i^2}{n} - \bar{x}^2 \right\}}$$

$$= \sqrt{\left\{ \frac{\sum\limits_{i=1}^{n} x_i^2}{n} - \left(\frac{\sum\limits_{i=1}^{n} x_i}{n} \right)^2 \right\}}$$

3.7.1 *Example*

Find the mean and s.d. of 1, 2, 4, 6, 8, using equation (3.7.1).

The calculation of the required summations is shown in Table 3.8.

$$\text{mean} = \frac{\sum_{i=1}^{n} x_i}{n}$$

$$= \frac{21}{5} = 4.2$$

Table 3.8

x_i	x_i^2
1	1
2	4
4	16
6	36
8	64
21	121

Standard deviation,

$$s = \sqrt{\left\{ \frac{\sum_{i=1}^{n} x_i^2}{n} - \left(\frac{\sum_{i=1}^{n} x_i}{n}\right)^2 \right\}}$$

$$= \sqrt{\left\{ \frac{121}{5} - \left(\frac{21}{5}\right)^2 \right\}}$$

$$= 2.56$$

3.7.2 *Exercise*

Repeat exercise 3.6.2 using the method of Example 3.7.1.

3.8 Calculation of standard deviation for a frequency table

If x_1 occurs with frequency f_1, x_2 with frequency f_2 etc., the formula for standard deviation becomes

$$s = \sqrt{\left\{ \frac{\sum_{i=1}^{n} f_i(x_i - \bar{x})^2}{\sum_{i=1}^{n} f_i} \right\}} \tag{3.8.1}$$

and the alternative form corresponding to (3.7.1) becomes

$$s = \sqrt{\left\{\frac{\sum\limits_{i=1}^{n} f_i x_i^2}{\sum\limits_{i=1}^{n} f_i} - \left(\frac{\sum\limits_{i=1}^{n} f_i x_i}{\sum\limits_{i=1}^{n} f_i}\right)^2\right\}} \tag{3.8.2}$$

3.8.1   Example

Calculate the standard deviation of the data in Section 3.5, Table 3.6 for the word lengths for the extract from the child's book.

The calculation of the required summations is shown in Table 3.9. Using equation (3.8.2),

Table 3.9

x_i	f_i	$f_i x_i$	$f_i x_i^2$
1	4	4	4
2	6	12	24
3	12	36	108
4	6	24	96
5	6	30	150
7	1	7	49
	35	113	431

$$s = \sqrt{\left\{\frac{\sum\limits_{i=1}^{n} f_i x_i^2}{\sum\limits_{i=1}^{n} f_i} - \left(\frac{\sum\limits_{i=1}^{n} f_i x_i}{\sum\limits_{i=1}^{n} f_i}\right)^2\right\}}$$

$$= \sqrt{\left\{\frac{431}{35} - \left(\frac{113}{35}\right)^2\right\}}$$

$$= 1.37$$

3.8.2   Exercise

Calculate the standard deviation for the *Gulliver's Travels* extract.

3.9 Use of arbitrary origin and unit

Standard deviation calculations can also be simplified by coding the data as described in Section 2.7. If we use arbitrary origin A and unit B so that $x_i = A + Bu_i$, we have

$$s = B \sqrt{\left\{ \frac{\sum_{i=1}^{n} f_i u_i^2}{\sum_{i=1}^{n} f_i} - \left(\frac{\sum_{i=1}^{n} f_i u_i}{\sum_{i=1}^{n} f_i} \right)^2 \right\}} \qquad (3.9.1)$$

Proof of equation (3.9.1)

From (3.8.1),

$$s = \sqrt{\left\{ \frac{\sum_{i=1}^{n} f_i (A + Bu_i - A - B\bar{u})^2}{\sum_{i=1}^{n} f_i} \right\}} \qquad \text{(since } x_i = A + Bu_i \text{ and } \bar{x} = A + B\bar{u}\text{)}$$

$$= \sqrt{\left\{ \frac{B^2 \sum_{i=1}^{n} f_i (u_i - \bar{u})^2}{\sum_{i=1}^{n} f_i} \right\}}$$

or

$$s = B \sqrt{\left\{ \frac{\sum_{i=1}^{n} f_i u_i^2}{\sum_{i=1}^{n} f_i} - \left(\frac{\sum_{i=1}^{n} f_i u_i}{\sum_{i=1}^{n} f_i} \right)^2 \right\}} \qquad \text{(using equation (3.8.2))}$$

For a grouped frequency table, the mid-class value is taken as representative of each group, as in the calculation of the mean.

3.9.1 *Example*

Calculate the standard deviation for the data in Table 2.7.

The calculation of the required summations is shown in Table 3.10. As before the values have been coded using $A = 12.95$ and $B = 2$.

Table 3.10

Class limits (g/l)	True class limits (g/l)	Mid-class value x_i (g/l)	Frequency f_i	Coded value u_i	f_iu_i	$f_iu_i^2$
4.0- 5.9	3.95- 5.95	4.95	1	-4	-4	16
6.0- 7.9	5.95- 7.95	6.95	3	-3	-9	27
8.0- 9.9	7.95- 9.95	8.95	7	-2	-14	28
10.0-11.9	9.95-11.95	10.95	9	-1	-9	9
12.0-13.9	11.95-13.95	12.95	9	0	0	0
14.0-15.9	13.95-15.95	14.95	12	1	12	12
16.0-17.9	15.95-17.95	16.95	8	2	16	32
18.0-19.9	17.95-19.95	18.95	1	3	3	9
			50		-5	133

$$\bar{u}=\frac{\sum\limits_{i=1}^{n} f_iu_i}{\sum\limits_{i=1}^{n} f_i}=\frac{-5}{50}=-0.1$$

$$\bar{x}=A+B\bar{u}=12.95-2\times0.1=12.75 \text{ g/l}$$

$$s=B\sqrt{\left\{\frac{\sum\limits_{i=1}^{n} f_iu_i^2}{\sum\limits_{i=1}^{n} f_i}-\left(\frac{\sum\limits_{i=1}^{n} f_iu_i}{\sum\limits_{i=1}^{n} f_i}\right)^2\right\}}$$

$$=2\sqrt{\left\{\frac{133}{50}-\left(\frac{-5}{50}\right)^2\right\}}$$

$$=3.26 \text{ g/l}$$

The advantage of taking $B=2$ should now be apparent, since the values of $f_iu_i^2$ are kept as small as possible (see Section 2.7).

3.9.2   Exercises

(1) Find the mean and s.d. for the following.

   7, 10, 15, 22, 35, 71

(2) Calculate the range, mean deviation and standard deviation of the eleven numbers
   0, 8, 4, 6, 5, 9, 3, 7, 6, 2, 5.
   (a) Choose a twelfth value from the numbers 2, 6 and 10 which will increase the range, and state this new range.

(b) Choose another twelfth value from the numbers 2, 6 and 10 which will decrease the standard deviation, and state this new standard deviation. (L)

(3) Calculate the mean and s.d. for the data in Table 3.11 using an arbitrary origin and unit.

Table 3.11 *Shoe sizes of a group of 50 women*

Shoe size	Frequency
3	1
$3\frac{1}{2}$	2
4	4
$4\frac{1}{2}$	6
5	10
$5\frac{1}{2}$	12
6	9
$6\frac{1}{2}$	5
7	1

(4) The distribution of goals scored by an amateur football team during two seasons is shown in Table 3.12.
Verify that the mean number of goals per match is 5 and calculate the standard deviation. (C)

Table 3.12

Number of goals	1	2	3	4	5	6	7	8	9	10
Number of times	2	3	8	4	4	3	6	3	2	1

(5) (a) Two novices at shooting fired eight shots each at a target. The figures in Table 3.13 show how far (in mm) from the centre of the target each shot went.
Find the mean and the standard deviation for each set of results and state which novice was the more consistent.

Table 3.13

Novice *A*	53	21	12	38	6	67	26	41
Novice *B*	12	5	21	62	32	18	25	9

(b) If the figures had been as in Table 3.14, state, *without doing any further calculation*, what the standard deviations would have been, giving brief reasons.   (C)

Table 3.14

Novice A	5.3	2.1	1.2	3.8	0.6	6.7	2.6	4.1
Novice B	1.2	0.5	2.1	6.2	3.2	1.8	2.5	0.9

(6) Every day for four weeks a man runs round a park and records his time to the nearest second. Table 3.15 shows his times in minutes and seconds for the 28 runs. For example 24,17 indicates a time of 24 minutes 17 seconds.

Construct a frequency table using a class interval of 20 seconds beginning at 23,00. Use this frequency table to estimate

(a) the mean time of a run, (b) the standard deviation.   (C)

Table 3.15

24,17	25,18	24,17	24,55	24,10	23,38	24,02
23,52	24,13	24,06	24,03	24,22	24,33	24,05
24,38	23,52	24,11	23,57	24,28	24,24	23,55
23,35	23,48	23,23	23,42	24,06	23,01	23,28

(7) Calculate the mean and standard deviation for the data in Table 3.3.

(8) A student measured the time in seconds taken for a trolley to run down a slope and obtained the following values.

$$34.2, \ 32.7, \ 29.8, \ 31.5, \ 30.6, \ 30.9$$

Calculate the mean and standard deviation of these results.

(a) Without further detailed calculation, give the mean and standard deviation for the time taken in minutes.

(b) After she had made these measurements the student realised the stop-clock she had used was faulty: its second hand started from the one second mark instead of from zero. Without further detailed calculation, find the correct values for the mean and standard deviation of the time taken in seconds.

3.10   Finding the mean and standard deviation of a combined sample

Sometimes we have information about the mean and standard deviation of two or more samples and wish to find the mean and standard of the sample formed by combining these samples. This obviously presents no problem if the original data are available but it is also possible if only the means and standard deviations of the individual samples are known, as is shown in the following example.

3.10.1 *Example*

The values in Table 3.16 show the mean and standard deviation of the marks obtained by two classes in a test. Calculate (a) the mean and (b) the standard deviation for the two classes combined.

Table 3.16

	Mean	Standard deviation	Class size
Class A	67	5	15
Class B	58	8	18

The method is based on finding Σx and Σx^2 for each sample and hence finding Σx and Σx^2 for the samples combined.

(a)   From equation 2.6.1

$$\bar{x} = \sum_i x_i/n$$

we have

$$\sum_i x_i = n\bar{x} \tag{3.10.1}$$

Using subscripts to distnguish the two samples, we have

$$\Sigma x_A = n_A \bar{x}_A = 15 \times 67 = 1005$$

$$\Sigma x_B = n_B \bar{x}_B = 18 \times 58 = 1044$$

Combining the samples

$$\Sigma x = 1005 + 1044 = 2049$$

$$n = 15 + 18 = 33$$

giving a mean for the combined sample of

$$\bar{x} = 2049/33 = 62.1 \text{ (to 3 significant figures)}$$

Note that in effect we have calculated a weighted mean (see Section 2.11).

(b)   From equation (3.7.1)

$$s^2 = \sum_i x_i^2/n - \bar{x}^2$$

which can be rearranged to give

$$\sum_i x_i^2 = n(\bar{x}^2 + s^2) \tag{3.10.2}$$

For the two samples separately

$$\Sigma x_A^2 = n(\bar{x}_A^2 + s_A^2) = 15(67^2 + 5^2) = 67\,710$$

$$\Sigma x_B^2 = n(\bar{x}_B^2 + s_B^2) = 18(58^2 + 8^2) = 61\,704$$

and for the samples combined

$$\Sigma x^2 = 67\,710 + 61\,704 = 129\,414$$

The variance for the combined sample is given by

$$s^2 = \Sigma x^2/n - \bar{x}^2 = 129\,414/33 - (2049/33)^2 = 66.355$$

and the standard deviation for the combined sample is 8.15 (to 3 significant figures).

3.10.2   *Exercise*

A third class, with 17 pupils, took the test described in example 3.10.1. The mean and standard deviation of their marks were 61 and 7 respectively. Calculate the mean and standard deviation of the marks for all three classes combined.

Summary

For a set of values of a variate x_1, x_2 etc. which occur with frequencies f_1, f_2 etc.

the **mean deviation** is $\left\{ \dfrac{\sum\limits_{i=1}^{n} f_i |x_i - \bar{x}|}{\sum\limits_{i=1}^{n} f_i} \right\}$

the **standard deviation**, s, is $\sqrt{\left\{ \dfrac{\sum\limits_{i=1}^{n} f_i (x_i - \bar{x})^2}{\sum\limits_{i=1}^{n} f_i} \right\}}$

$$= \sqrt{\left\{ \dfrac{\sum\limits_{i=1}^{n} f_i x_i^2}{\sum\limits_{i=1}^{n} f_i} - \left(\dfrac{\sum\limits_{i=1}^{n} f_i x_i}{\sum\limits_{i=1}^{n} f_i} \right)^2 \right\}}$$

The **variance** is the square of the standard deviation.

If the values are arranged in order of increasing size the $\frac{1}{4}(n+1)$th value is the **lower quartile**, Q_1, and the $\frac{3}{4}(n+1)$th value is the **upper quartile**, Q_3.

The **interquartile range** is $Q_3 - Q_1$.

The **semi-interquartile range** is $\frac{1}{2}(Q_3 - Q_1)$.

For grouped data the quartiles can be found from the cumulative frequency curve. The lower and upper quartiles are the values of the variate corresponding to one quarter and three quarters of the total frequency respectively.

Projects

(1) *Variation in accuracy at bisecting a line by eye*

For the data obtained in Project (1), Chapter 2, calculate the standard deviation for the measured lengths for the first and second attempts at bisecting a line by eye. Does accuracy appear to improve with practice?

(2) *Variation in sentence length*

For the data obtained in Project (2), Chapter 2, calculate the variances of the sentence length for the two authors and compare them.

Exercise on Chapter 3

(1) 100 pupils were tested to determine their intelligence quotient (IQ), and the results were as in Table 3.17. All IQs are given to the nearest integer.

Table 3.17

IQ	45–	55–	65–	75–	85–	95–	105–	115–	125–134
Number of pupils	1	1	2	6	21	29	24	12	4

(a) Calculate the mean, and the standard deviation.

(b) Draw a cumulative frequency graph, and estimate how many pupils have IQs within 1 s.d. on either side of the mean.   (SUJB)

(2) Table 3.18 gives the heights of 100 trees measured to the nearest metre. Assemble them into a frequency table, and use it to calculate the mean height and the standard deviation. Represent the information graphically.

The mean height of all the 100 individual trees is 69.43 metres. Explain any discrepancy between your answer and this.   (O)

Table 3.18

68	70	61	82	54	84	51	74	64	45
77	80	52	62	63	70	69	55	68	66
60	60	88	67	84	87	77	66	69	61
47	85	66	94	57	71	58	87	78	64
71	72	50	57	95	88	64	70	73	56
62	83	90	63	73	55	61	72	61	74
65	67	74	69	65	92	67	54	83	68
64	69	56	75	89	48	79	85	63	67
54	76	65	59	70	64	72	82	83	75
68	86	51	92	69	86	62	73	56	70

(3) A class of 40 male students were weighed and the results, recorded to the nearest kilogram, were grouped as in Table 3.19.
By using an assumed mean of 66.5 kg, estimate
(a) the mean mass, (b) the standard deviation of the masses.
If two additional students of masses 53 kg and 78 kg were included would you expect the value of the standard deviation to increase, decrease, or remain the same?   (C)

Table 3.19

Mass (kg)	53–56	57–60	61–64	65–68	69–72	73–76	77–80
Frequency	3	5	10	11	5	4	2

(4) In a fishing competition, the total catches of 50 anglers had masses (to the nearest 0.1 kg) as given in Table 3.20.

Table 3.20

Mass (kg)	0–0.2	0.3–0.7	0.8–1.2	1.3–1.7	1.8–2.2	2.3–3.7	3.8–5.2
Frequency	8	8	12	8	8	4	2

Draw a histogram to represent the frequency distribution.
State formulae for the mean and standard deviation of a frequency distribution, explaining the symbols used.
Prepare a table for the given data, showing the mid-values of the class intervals and all the terms in the summations that have to be calculated to obtain the mean and variance. Calculate the mean, variance and standard deviation of the distribution.
Given the additional information that all eight anglers placed in the first class interval caught nothing at all, obtain a revised value for the mean.   (JMB)

(5) A tyre manufacturer conducts trials on a particular type of tyre. A sample of 100 tyres is put on test and the distances travelled by the tyres before reaching the legal limit of tyre wear are shown in Table 3.21.

Table 3.21

Distance (km)	Number of tyres
5000–25000	8
25000–35000	14
35000–45000	24
45000–55000	26
55000–65000	16
65000–85000	12

(a) Plot these data as a histogram.
(b) Calculate the mean distance.
(c) Obtain the cumulative frequency distribution and estimate the median and interquartile range.

These data were collected by fitting the tyres to the front wheels of a fleet of hire cars of the same model. Suppose that the manufacturer had, instead, tested the tyres by running them on constant speed rollers in a simulated wear trial. Describe the effect you think this would have had on the distribution of distances travelled by the tyres. Discuss briefly the relative merits of the two methods for examining tyre wear.   (JMB)

(6) Given that the mean and standard deviation of a set of figures are μ and σ respectively, write down the new values of the mean and standard deviation when
(a) each figure is increased by a constant c,
(b) each figure is multiplied by a constant k.
A group of students sat two examinations, one in algebra and one in biology. In order to compare the results the algebra marks were scaled linearly (that is, a mark of x became a mark of $ax - b$ where a and b are constants) so that the means and standard deviations of the marks in both examinations became the same. The original means and standard deviations are shown in Table 3.22.

Table 3.22

	Algebra	Biology
Mean mark	48	62
Standard deviation	12	10

Find a and b.

The original marks of a particular student are 36 in algebra, 48 in biology. In what sense, if any, has he done better in algebra than in biology?   (C)

(7) Prove the formula
$$\sum (x - \bar{x})^2 = \sum x^2 - n\bar{x}^2$$
In a middle school there are 253 girls whose ages have a mean 11.8 yr and a standard deviation 1.7 yr. There are also 312 boys whose ages have a mean 12.3 yr and a standard deviation 1.9 yr. Calculate the mean and standard deviation of the ages of all the 565 pupils.   (AEB)

(8) The times taken by a group of people to solve a puzzle are shown in Table 3.23.

Table 3.23

Time (s)	10–14	15–19	20–24	25–29	30–34	35–39	40–44	45–49
Frequency	1	3	7	10	15	12	6	2

(a) Calculate the mean and standard deviation of these times.
(b) Draw a cumulative frequency curve and from it find the median and interquartile range.
(c) From the cumulative frequency curve estimate the proportion of times which lie within one standard deviation on either side of the mean.

(9) A teacher has marked a large set of examination papers and has then done some statistical work on the marks, obtaining the following results:

mean mark $= 36$
median mark $= 42$
standard deviation $= 12$
interquartile range $= 15$
greatest mark $= 72$

The teacher then decides to scale the marks by means of the formula $y = cx + d$, where x is the original mark, y the new mark, and c and d are positive constants chosen so that the new marks, y, have a mean of 50 and a standard deviation of 8. Calculate the values of c and d, and hence find the new values for the median, the interquartile range and the greatest mark.

(L, part question)

(10) A population consists of n_1 males and n_2 females. The mean heights of the males and females are μ_1 and μ_2 respectively and the variances of the heights are σ_1^2 and σ_2^2 respectively. Show that the mean height of the whole population is $w_1\mu_1 + w_2\mu_2$ and

the variance is $w_1\sigma_1^2 + w_2\sigma_2^2 + w_1 w_2(\mu_1 - \mu_2)^2$ where $w_1 = n_1/(n_1 + n_2)$ and $w_2 = n_2/(n_1 + n_2)$.

Hence, or otherwise, show that, if a single observation taking the value x is added to a population of size n with mean μ and variance σ^2, the new variance will be larger than the old if

$$|\mu - x| > \left(\frac{n+1}{n}\right)^{1/2} \sigma \tag{O}$$

4 Probability

4.1 Empirical probability

Probability theory forms the basis of inferential statistics. It had its origins in games of chance such as dice and card games. Many card players know from experience (even if they know nothing of probability theory) that certain types of hands turn up more frequently than others. Relative frequency can be used to define **empirical probability**. If we are interested in the occurrence of an event A, we could perform a large number of trials and define the empirical probability of A occurring at any one trial, $P(A)$, as

$$P(A) = \frac{\text{number of trials in which } A \text{ occurs}}{\text{total number of trials}}$$

Ideas about probability rest on the intuitive assumption that this ratio will in fact tend towards a particular value as the number of trials increases.

4.1.1 *Exercise*

Throw a coin 100 times, keeping running totals of the number of heads and the number of throws. Plot a graph of fraction of heads against number of throws.

4.2 Theoretical probability

In practice we do not derive all our values for probabilities from experiment. Suppose we toss a die and want to know the probability of throwing a 2. There are six ways the die can fall, of which only one is a 2. We can define a **theoretical probability** by

$$P(2) = \frac{\text{number of ways of getting a 2}}{\text{total number of possible outcomes}} = \frac{1}{6}$$

This does not, of course, mean that each sequence of six throws will contain one 2, but that in a long series of throws the proportion of 2s tends towards the value $\frac{1}{6}$.

The set of possible outcomes is called the **sample space**, S. In the example above S is the set $\{1, 2, 3, 4, 5, 6\}$. Each possible outcome is called a **sample point**. An **event**, E, is a set which consists of one or more of the sample points. In the example above $E = \{2\}$. Using this terminology we can define the theoretical probability $P(E)$ of an event E as follows: if a sample space, S, consists of $n\{S\}$ *equally probable* sample points then

$$P(E) = \frac{\text{number of sample point in } E}{\text{number of sample points in } S} = \frac{n\{E\}}{n\{S\}} \tag{4.2.1}$$

This definition is only true if the sample points are equally probable: in the example above, if the die had been loaded, it would not apply.

It follows from this definition that probabilities lie between 0 and 1. If an event cannot occur, its probability is 0: if it must occur, its probability is 1. Probabilities are sometimes expressed as percentages. For example the probability of throwing a 6 with a die is 0.167 or 16.7%.

$P(\bar{E})$, sometimes written $P(E')$, denotes the probability that E does *not* occur. $\bar{E}$ is known as the **complement** of E and $P(\bar{E})$ can be calculated from $P(E)$ as follows

$$P(\bar{E}) = \frac{n(\bar{E})}{n(S)} = \frac{\{n(S) - n(E)\}}{n(E)}$$

$$= 1 - \frac{n(E)}{n(S)}$$

$$P(\bar{E}) = 1 - P(E) \tag{4.2.2}$$

4.2.1 *Exercise*

(1) Give the probabilities of
   (a) getting a head when a fair coin is tossed,
   (b) picking a red card from a pack of 52 cards,
   (c) picking a king from a pack of cards,
   (d) picking a diamond from a pack of cards,
   (e) tossing a 1 or a 6 with a die.

(2) In a given circle of radius r we are to construct a chord. The following three methods of construction are suggested:
   (a) Let AB be a fixed diameter in the circle. Draw the chord from A at an angle α to this diameter, where α is a value chosen at random between $-\frac{1}{2}\pi$ and $\frac{1}{2}\pi$.
   (b) Again let AB be a fixed diameter in the circle. Choose a point C at random on the diameter AB. Draw the chord perpendicular to AB through C.
   (c) Choose a point at random within the area of the circle. Make this the centre of the chord.
   For *each* method of construction evaluate the probability that the length of the chord is greater than r.   (AEB)

Probability problems often involve the enumeration of possible outcomes and the following examples illustrate two convenient methods of doing this.

4.2.2 *Example*

What is the probability of throwing a total score of 6 with two dice?

Here the points of the sample space are best found by making a table (see Figure 4.1)

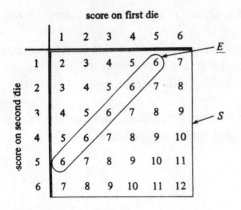

Figure 4.1 Sample space for the total score when two dice are thrown

showing the score on each die and the total scores. All the points in the sample space are equally likely.

$$S = \{\text{total score on two dice}\}, \qquad n\{S\} = 36$$
$$E = \{\text{total score on two dice} = 6\}, \qquad n\{E\} = 5$$
$$P(\text{score of 6}) = \tfrac{5}{36} = 0.1389 \text{ or } 13.89\%$$

4.2.3 *Example*

What is the probability of obtaining two heads and one tail when three coins are tossed?

Where three (or more) objects are involved the layout of the previous diagram is not possible. Instead the possible outcomes can be found by using a tree diagram as in Figure 4.2. The first 'branches' of the tree give the possible outcomes of tossing the first coin, the next branches the outcome of tossing the second coin and so on.

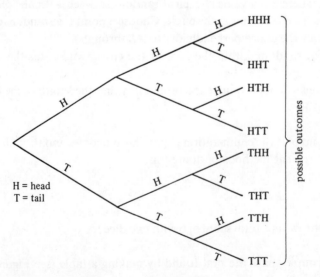

Figure 4.2 Tree diagram showing the possible outcomes when three coins are tossed

There are eight equally likely outcomes:

HHH, HHT, HTH, HTT, THH, THT, TTH, TTT

of which three contain two heads. So we have

$S = \{\text{outcomes of throwing three coins}\},$ $\qquad\qquad n\{S\} = 8$

$E = \{\text{outcomes of throwing three coins in which two are heads}\},$ $\quad n\{E\} = 3$

$P(\text{two heads}) = \dfrac{n\{E\}}{n\{S\}} = \dfrac{3}{8}$

4.2.4 *Exercise*

(1) Use Figure 4.1 to find the probabilities of the following outcomes when two dice are thrown.
 (a) A double.
 (b) A total score greater than 9.
 (c) A score of 6 or less.

(2) Two tetrahedral dice, with the faces of each labelled 1, 2, 3 and 4, are thrown. The total score is the *product* of the numbers on the bottom faces. Construct a sample space of the possible outcomes and from it find the probability that the total score is
 (a) greater than 8,
 (b) 6 or less,
 (c) a multiple of 3.

(3) Extend the tree diagram in Figure 4.2 so that it represents the results of tossing four coins. From your diagram find the probability of an equal number of heads and tails.

(4) A box contains three 'Scrabble' tiles, one with A on it, one with E and the third with T. A tile is taken at random, the letter noted and the tile replaced. This is repeated once. Draw a tree diagram to find the possible outcomes. What is the probability of getting two vowels?

 The experiment is modified so that the first tile is not replaced before the second tile is chosen. Modify your tree diagram and find the new value for the probability of getting two vowels.

4.3 The addition law

How is the probability that one of several events occurs related to the probabilities of the individual events? To take a specific example, what is the probability in Example 4.2.3 that we throw two or more heads and how is it related to $P(\text{two heads})$ and $P(\text{three heads})$?

Figure 4.3 shows the sample space for this problem where $E_1 = \{\text{outcomes with three heads}\}$ and $E_2 = \{\text{outcomes with two heads}\}$. In this case E_1 and E_2 are **mutually exclusive**. This means that they cannot both occur at the same time.

From our definition of probability (equation 4.2.1)

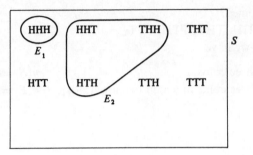

Figure 4.3 Sample space for the possible outcomes when three coins are tossed

$$P(\text{two heads or three heads}) = \frac{n\{E_1 \cup E_2\}}{n\{S\}}$$

$$= \tfrac{4}{8} = \tfrac{1}{2}$$

This value can be related to the individual probabilities as follows:

$$P(\text{two heads or three heads}) = \frac{n\{E_1 \cup E_2\}}{n\{S\}}$$

$$= \frac{n\{E_1\} + n\{E_2\}}{n(S)} = \frac{n\{E_1\}}{n(S)} + \frac{n\{E_2\}}{n(S)}$$

$$= P(E_1) + P(E_2)$$
$$= \tfrac{1}{8} + \tfrac{3}{8} = \tfrac{4}{8} = \tfrac{1}{2}$$

The probability that E_1 or E_2 occurs is denoted by $P(E_1 \cup E_2)$ so that we have for two mutually exclusive events

$$P(E_1 \cup E_2) = P(E_1) + P(E_2)$$

This can be generalised for n mutually exclusive events to

$$P(E_1 \cup E_2 \cup \ldots \cup E_n) = P(E_1) + P(E_2) + \ldots + P(E_n) \tag{4.3.1}$$

This is the **addition law for mutually exclusive events**. The following example shows how it must be modified for events which are not mutually exclusive.

4.3.1 *Example*

What is the probability of drawing an ace or a spade from a pack of 52 well-shuffled cards?

Here
$$E_1 = \{\text{card is a spade}\}$$
$$E_2 = \{\text{card is an ace}\}$$
but the events are not mutually exclusive since a card can be both a spade *and* an ace. Figure 4.4 shows the sample space. In this case

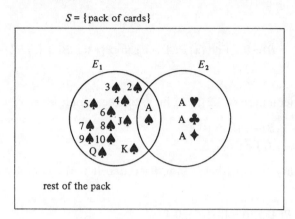

$S = \{\text{pack of cards}\}$

Figure 4.4 Sample space to illustrate Example 4.3.1

$$P(\text{spade or ace}) = \frac{n\{E_1 \cup E_2\}}{n\{S\}} = \tfrac{16}{52}$$

This probability can be related to individual probabilities as follows:

$$P(\text{spade or ace}) = P(E_1 \cup E_2)$$

$$= \frac{n\{E_1 \cup E_2\}}{n\{S\}}$$

$$= \frac{n\{E_1\} + n\{E_2\} - n\{E_1 \cap E_2\}}{n\{S\}}$$

$$= \frac{n\{E_1\}}{n\{S\}} + \frac{n\{E_2\}}{n\{S\}} - \frac{n\{E_1 \cap E_2\}}{n\{S\}}$$

$$= P(E_1) + P(E_2) - P(E_1 \cap E_2)$$
$$= \tfrac{13}{52} + \tfrac{4}{52} - \tfrac{1}{52}$$
$$= \tfrac{16}{52}$$

$P(E_1 \cap E_2)$ denotes the probability that *both* E_1 and E_2 occur. This probability must be subtracted so that the ace of spades is not counted twice, once as a spade and once as an ace.

In this example, we have established the general addition law for two events

$$P(E_1 \cup E_2) = P(E_1) + P(E_2) - P(E_1 \cap E_2) \qquad (4.3.2)$$

which is applicable whether or not the events are mutually exclusive. If they *are* mutually exclusive then the last term on the right-hand side of the equation is zero.

It is worth pointing out that the expression 'E_1 or E_2 occurs' is somewhat ambiguous in the English language but is taken in probability problems to mean that 'E_1 and/or E_2 occurs', as is indicated by the way the probability is expressed in set notation.

Set notation for probabilities can be extended to embrace complements. For example, $P(E_1 \cup \bar{E}_2)$ is the probability that E_1 occurs and/or E_2 does not. The following example illustrates how such probabilities may be simply calculated from a Venn diagram.

4.3.2   *Example*

If $P(A)=0.3$, $P(B)=0.4$ and $P(A \cap B)=0.1$, find (a) $P(A \cup B)$, (b) $P[(A \cup B)']$, (c) $P(A \cup B')$, (d) $P(A' \cap B)$.

(a)   The general addition law (equation (4.3.2)) can be used to calculate $P(A \cup B)$.

$$P(A \cup B)=P(A)+P(B)-P(A \cap B)$$
$$=0.3+0.4-0.1=0.6$$

(b) $P[(A\cup B)']$ is the probability that neither A nor B occurs. It is the complement of $A \cup B$ so

$$P[(A \cup B)']=1-P(A \cup B)=1-0.6=0.4$$

The Venn diagram in Figure 4.5 shows the probability associated with each region of the diagram. Each probability represents the fraction of events falling in a region and so the sum of the probabilities for all the regions must be 1. From this diagram the remaining probabilities can be found.

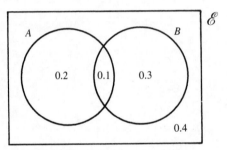

Figure 4.5 Venn diagram to illustrate Example 4.3.2

(c) $P(A \cup B')$ is the probability that A occurs and/or B does not occur. Using the general addition law

$$P(A \cup B')=P(A)+P(B')-P(A \cap B')$$
$$=0.3+0.6-0.2=0.7$$

(d) $P(A' \cap B)$ is the probability that A does not occur and B does occur.

$$P(A' \cap B)=0.3$$

Two or more events are said to be **exhaustive** if at least one of them must happen. Expressed in set notation this condition is met by

$$P(E_1 \cup E_2 \cup E_3 \cup \ldots \cup E_n)=1$$

By their nature an event and its complement must be exhaustive.

4.3.3 *Exercise*

(1) For each of the following pairs of events A and B say whether or not they are (i) mutually exclusive, (ii) exhaustive.
- (a) A child is chosen at random from a class. $A = \{$child has blue eyes$\}$, $B = \{$child has brown eyes$\}$
- (b) A die is thrown. $A = \{$result is a multiple of 3$\}$, $B = \{$result is a multiple of 2$\}$
- (c) A card is drawn from a pack of cards. $A = \{$the card is a picture card$\}$, $B = \{$card is a king$\}$
- (d) A coin is tossed. $A = \{$toss gives a head$\}$, $B = \{$toss gives a tail$\}$.

(2) C and D are two events such that $P(C) = 0.1$, $P(D) = 0.2$ and $P(C \cup D) = 0.3$. Are C and D mutually exclusive events? Justify your answer. Find the values of (a) $P(\bar{C})$, (b) $P(\bar{C} \cap \bar{D})$.

(3) In a group of 50 pupils, 30 study chemistry and/or physics. If 20 study chemistry and 15 study physics, what is the probability that a pupil chosen at random studies (a) chemistry, (b) physics, (c) chemistry and/or physics, (d) chemistry and physics?

(4) A and B are two events such that $P(A) = 0.2$, $P(B) = 0.9$ and $P(A \cap B) = 0.1$. By finding $P(A \cup B)$ show that the events A and B are exhaustive.

(5) E and F are events such that $P(E) = 0.7$, $P(F) = 0.6$ and $P(E \cup F) = 0.8$. Find
- (a) $P(E \cap F)$
- (b) $P(E' \cap F)$
- (c) $P(E \text{ or } F \text{ but not both occurs})$
- (d) $P(E' \cap F')$

4.4 Conditional probability

Suppose we have a group of 30 students of whom 15 are blue-eyed, 5 left-handed and 2 both blue-eyed and left-handed. This information is shown in Figure 4.6 where the numbers in the diagram refer to the number of sample points in each part of the sample space. Obviously

$$P(L) = \tfrac{5}{30} = \tfrac{1}{6} \quad \text{and} \quad P(B) = \tfrac{15}{30} = \tfrac{1}{2}$$

If we know that a student is blue-eyed, does this alter the probability that he is left-

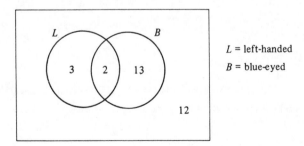

L = left-handed
B = blue-eyed

Figure 4.6 Sample space to illustrate the example in Section 4.4

handed? Out of 15 blue-eyed students 2 are left-handed, so that the probability that a student is left-handed *given that he is blue-eyed* is

$$\frac{\text{number of sample points in } L \cap B}{\text{number of sample points in } B} = \frac{2}{15}$$

This is the **conditional probability** of the event L (left-handedness) given that the event B (blue-eyed) has occurred. It is written $P(L|B)$. We have

$$P(L|B) = \tfrac{2}{15}$$

Dividing top and bottom of this fraction by the total number of points in the sample space, i.e. 30, we have

$$P(L|B) = \frac{2/30}{15/30} = \frac{P(L \cap B)}{P(B)}$$

This is a general result. If we have two events E_1 and E_2 then

$$P(E_1 | E_2) = \frac{n(E_1 \cap E_2)}{n(E_2)}$$

Dividing top and bottom of the fraction by $n(S)$ gives

$$P(E_1 | E_2) = \frac{n(E_1 \cap E_2)/n(S)}{n(E_2)/n(S)}$$

so

$$P(E_1|E_2) = \frac{P(E_1 \cap E_2)}{P(E_2)} \tag{4.4.1}$$

and similarly

$$P(E_2|E_1) = \frac{P(E_1 \cap E_2)}{P(E_1)} \tag{4.4.2}$$

4.4.1   *Example*

If A and B are two events such that $P(A) = \tfrac{1}{3}$, $P(B) = \tfrac{1}{2}$ and $P(A|B) = \tfrac{1}{4}$, find (a) $P(A \cap B)$, (b) $P(A \cup B)$, (c) $P(B|\bar{A})$

(a)   Since

$$P(A|B) = \frac{P(A \cap B)}{P(B)}$$

we have

$$P(A \cap B) = P(A|B) \times P(B) = \tfrac{1}{4} \times \tfrac{1}{2} = \tfrac{1}{8}$$

(b)   From the addition law

$$P(A \cup B) = P(A) + P(B) - P(A \cap B)$$
$$= \tfrac{1}{3} + \tfrac{1}{2} - \tfrac{1}{8} = \tfrac{17}{24}$$

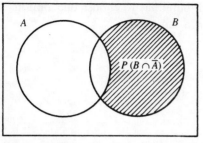

Figure 4.7 Diagram to illustrate Example 4.4.1

(c)   The Venn diagram in Figure 4.7 shows that

$$P(B \cap \bar{A}) = P(B) - P(A \cap B) = \tfrac{1}{2} - \tfrac{1}{8} = \tfrac{3}{8}$$

and

$$P(\bar{A}) = 1 - P(A) = 1 - \tfrac{1}{3} = \tfrac{2}{3}$$

so

$$P(B \mid \bar{A}) = \frac{P(B \cap \bar{A})}{P(\bar{A})} = \frac{(3/8)}{(2/3)} = \tfrac{9}{16}$$

In many cases conditional probabilities can be calculated without equation (4.4.1), as in the following example.

4.4.2   Example

Two cards are drawn from a well-shuffled pack of 52 *without replacement*. If the first card is an ace, what is the probability that the second card is also an ace?

   The term **without replacement** means that items, once drawn, are not replaced. If the first card is an ace, of the remaining 51 cards, 3 are aces so the probability that the second card is also an ace is $\tfrac{3}{51}$.

4.4.3   Exercise

(1)   If A and B are two events which are exhaustive, such that
$$P(A \cap B) = \tfrac{1}{4}, \quad P(A \mid B) = \tfrac{1}{3}$$
find (a) $P(B)$, (b) $P(A)$, (c) $P(B \mid A)$.

(2)   What is the probability that the second card drawn from a well-shuffled pack is a heart if (a) the first card drawn was a heart, (b) the first card drawn was not a heart?

(3)   The probability that a person plays billiards is $\tfrac{1}{10}$.
The probability that he smokes if he plays billiards is $\tfrac{14}{15}$.
The probability that he plays billiards if he smokes is $\tfrac{3}{10}$.
What is the probability that a person smokes?

(4) In the third year of a certain school each pupil has to choose one 'option'. Table 4.1 shows the results with boys and girls listed separately.

Table 4.1

Option	Boys	Girls
The theatre	19	23
Healthy living	21	22
Sport for all	29	17
Total	69	62

A pupil is chosen at random. If

$G = \{\text{pupil is a girl}\}$
$B = \{\text{pupil is a boy}\}$
$T = \{\text{pupil chooses 'The theatre'}\}$
$H = \{\text{pupil chooses 'Healthy living'}\}$
$S = \{\text{pupil chooses 'Sport for all'}\}$

give the values of (a) $P(G)$, (b) $P(B)$, (c) $P(T)$, (d) $P(H)$, (e) $P(S|B)$, (f) $P(G|T)$, (g) $P(H|G)$, (h) $P(T'|G)$, (i) $P(H'|G')$.

4.5   The product law

Rearranging formulae (4.4.1) and (4.4.2) we have

$$P(E_1 \cap E_2) = P(E_2)P(E_1|E_2) = P(E_1)P(E_2|E_1) \qquad (4.5.1)$$

This is the **product law for joint events**.

4.5.1 *Example*

What is the probability that if two cards are drawn from a pack without replacement (a) they are both aces, (b) neither is an ace, (c) at least one is an ace?

(a) $E_1 = \{\text{first card an ace}\}$ $E_2 = \{\text{second card an ace}\}$

$P(E_1) = \frac{4}{52} = \frac{1}{13}$ $P(E_2|E_1) = \frac{3}{51} = \frac{1}{17}$ (see Section 4.4)

$P(E_1 \cap E_2) = P(E_1)P(E_2|E_1) = \frac{1}{13} \times \frac{1}{17} = \frac{1}{221}$

(b) Similarly

$$P(\bar{E}_1 \cap \bar{E}_2) = P(\bar{E}_1)P(\bar{E}_2|\bar{E}_1) = \frac{48}{52} \times \frac{47}{51} = \frac{188}{221}$$

(c) Since the events 'neither is an ace' and 'at least one is an ace' are exhaustive and mutually exclusive, this probability can be found by subtraction.

$$P(\text{least one ace}) = 1 - \tfrac{188}{221} = \tfrac{33}{221}$$

The product law can be extended to multiple events if each probability is calculated assuming the occurrence of previous events.

4.5.2 *Example*

A box contains six red and ten black balls. What is the probability that if four balls are chosen without looking they are all black?

$$P(E_1 \cap E_2 \cap E_3 \cap E_4) = P(E_1)P(E_2|E_1)P(E_3|E_2 \cap E_1)P(E_4|E_3 \cap E_2 \cap E_1)$$
$$= \tfrac{10}{16} \times \tfrac{9}{15} \times \tfrac{8}{14} \times \tfrac{7}{13} = 0.115$$

4.5.3 *Example*

A certain rare genetic condition affects 0.01% of the population. A test has been developed which can detect the condition, if it is present, with a probability of 95%. Unfortunately, when the condition is not present, there is a probability of 0.05% that the test will still give a positive result. Calculate the probability that (a) a person has the condition and the test gives a positive result, (b) the test gives a positive result, (c) a person has the condition given that the test gave a positive result.

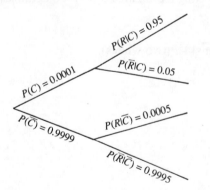

Figure 4.8 Tree diagram to illustrate Example 4.5.3

A convenient way of solving problems of this type is with a tree diagram as shown in Figure 4.8. Let C be the event that a person suffers from the condition and R the event that a person shows a positive reaction. The first branches show the possibilities that a person does or does not have the condition followed by the possibilities that they give a positive or negative reaction to the test. The branches must be in this order because the probability of R depends on whether or not the person has the condition rather than vice versa.

(a)   The probability required is

$$P(C \cap R) = P(C) \times P(R|C) = 0.0001 \times 0.95 = 0.000\,095$$

(b)   We can use the addition law for mutually exclusive events to find the required probability, $P(R)$.

$$\begin{aligned} P(R) &= P(C \cap R) + P(\bar{C} \cap R) \\ &= P(C) \times P(R|C) + P(\bar{C}) \times P(R|\bar{C}) \\ &= 0.0001 \times 0.95 + 0.9999 \times 0.0005 = 0.000\,594\,95 \end{aligned}$$

(c)   This asks for the value of $P(C|R)$ which can be calculated from the answers to parts (a) and (b).

$$P(C|R) = \frac{P(C \cap R)}{P(R)} = \frac{0.000\,095}{0.000\,594\,95} = 0.16 \text{ (to 2 d.p.)}$$

Consequently the probability that a person has not got the condition when a positive result is obtained is 0.84 (i.e. $1 - 0.16$), which suggests that the test may be of little practical value.

4.5.4   *Example*

A box contains ten green and six white marbles. A marble is chosen at random, its colour noted and it is not replaced. This is repeated once more. What is the probability that the marbles are of the same colour?

This is another problem which may be conveniently represented by a tree diagram as shown in Figure 4.9.

$$\begin{aligned} P(\text{marbles are the same colour}) &= P(\text{two greens}) + P(\text{two whites}) \\ &= \tfrac{10}{16} \times \tfrac{9}{15} + \tfrac{6}{16} \times \tfrac{5}{15} \\ &= \tfrac{1}{2} \end{aligned}$$

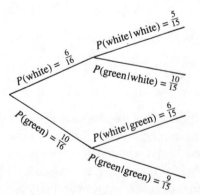

Figure 4.9 Tree diagram to illustrate Example 4.5.4

4.6   Independent events

If $P(E_1|E_2)=P(E_1)$ then the fact that E_2 has occurred does not affect the probability of E_1 occurring. E_1 and E_2 are then said to be **independent**. Equation (4.5.1) becomes

$$P(E_1 \cap E_2)=P(E_1)P(E_2) \tag{4.6.1}$$

This is called the **product law for independent events**. It can be generalised to several events as

$$P(E_1 \cap E_2 \cap \ldots \cap E_n)=P(E_1)P(E_2)P(E_3)P(E_4) \ldots P(E_n) \tag{4.6.2}$$

4.6.1   *Example*

A coin and a die are tossed. What is the probability of getting a 6 and a tail?

$$E_1=\{\text{a tail}\} \qquad E_2=\{\text{a 6}\}$$
$$P(E_1)=\tfrac{1}{2} \qquad P(E_2)=\tfrac{1}{6}$$
$$P(E_1 \cap E_2)=\tfrac{1}{2}\times\tfrac{1}{6}=\tfrac{1}{12}$$

4.6.2   *Example*

A coin is tossed five times. What is the probability that all the throws are heads?

$$H=\{\text{a head}\} \qquad P(H)=\tfrac{1}{2}$$
$$P(\text{five heads})=P(H)\times P(H)\times P(H)\times P(H)\times P(H)$$
$$=1/2^5=1/32$$

4.6.3   *Example*

A die is thrown three times. What is the probability of getting (a) exactly one 6, (b) at least one 6?

(a) $P(\text{exactly one 6})=P(6)\times P(\bar{6})\times P(\bar{6})+P(\bar{6})\times P(6)\times P(\bar{6})+P(\bar{6})\times P(\bar{6})\times P(6)$
$$=\tfrac{1}{6}\times\tfrac{5}{6}\times\tfrac{5}{6}+\tfrac{5}{6}\times\tfrac{1}{6}\times\tfrac{5}{6}+\tfrac{5}{6}\times\tfrac{5}{6}\times\tfrac{1}{6}$$
$$=\tfrac{25}{72}$$

(b)   Since the events 'at least one throw results in a 6' and 'no throws result in a 6' are exhaustive and mutually exclusive, the required probability can be found by subtraction

$$P(\text{at least one 6})=1-P(\text{no 6s})$$
$$=1-(\tfrac{5}{6})^3$$
$$=\tfrac{91}{216}$$

4.6.4   *Exercise*

(1) A and B are two events such that $P(A)=\frac{1}{2}$, $P(B)=\frac{1}{3}$ and $P(A \cup B)=\frac{2}{3}$.
   (a) Find (i) $P(A \cap B)$, (ii) $P(A|B)$, (iii) $P(B'|A)$.
   (b) Are the events A and B (i) independent, (ii) mutually exclusive? Justify your answers.

(2) Repeat Example 4.5.4 for the case when the first marble *is replaced* before the second marble is taken.

(3) For Example 4.5.3, calculate the probability that a person (a) has the condition, (b) does not have the condition, given that the reaction to the test is negative.

(4) I try to catch the bus to work each day but if I miss it I have to walk. The probability that I catch the bus is 0.7. If I catch the bus the probability that I arrive on time is 0.98 but if I walk this probability falls to 0.84. What is the probability that (a) I catch the bus and I am on time, (b) I am on time, (c) I caught the bus given that I arrived on time?

(5) (a) Given that, for two events R and S,

$$P(R)=0.3, \qquad P(R \cup S)=0.6$$

   find $P(S)$ and $P(\bar{R} \cap S)$ when R and S are (i) mutually exclusive events, (ii) independent events.
   (b) A company selling wines has two methods of customer sales approach, the current method A and a new method B which is being introduced. Each salesman uses either method A or method B but not both. Only 25% of salesmen are using method A. The probability of success is $\frac{2}{3}$ for A and $\frac{3}{4}$ for B. One sales success is chosen at random from all the company's sales successes. Using a tree diagram, or otherwise, find the probability it was achieved by method B.   (L)

(6) The probability of a person catching a certain disease when exposed to it is 0.2 if the person has been inoculated against the disease. This probability rises to 0.9 if the person has not been inoculated. If 70% of the population have been inoculated against the disease, what is the probability that a person who caught the disease when exposed to it had been inoculated against the disease?

4.7   Examples

The following examples illustrate the ideas of this chapter applied to a variety of problems.

4.7.1   *Example*

Two dice are thrown. What is the probability that a 'double' (i.e. both dice showing the same score) is thrown?

We want the probability of six mutually exclusive, joint events, i.e. $(1, 1)$, $(2, 2)$, $(3, 3)$, $(4, 4)$, $(5, 5)$, $(6, 6)$. The throws on the dice may be assumed independent so that, using the product law,

$$P(1 \cap 1) = P(1) \times P(1) = \tfrac{1}{6} \times \tfrac{1}{6} = \tfrac{1}{36}$$

Using the addition law for mutually exclusive events

$$P(\text{double}) = P(1 \cap 1) + P(2 \cap 2) + P(3 \cap 3) + P(4 \cap 4) + P(5 \cap 5) + P(6 \cap 6)$$

$$= \tfrac{1}{36} + \tfrac{1}{36} + \tfrac{1}{36} + \tfrac{1}{36} + \tfrac{1}{36} + \tfrac{1}{36}$$

$$= \tfrac{1}{6}$$

This result can also be found directly from Figure 4.1.

4.7.2 *Example*

When three marksmen take part in a shooting contest their chances of hitting a target are $\tfrac{1}{2}$, $\tfrac{1}{3}$, and $\tfrac{1}{4}$. Calculate the chance that one and only one bullet will hit the target if all men fire simultaneously.   (Northern)

Let

$$E_1 = \{\text{first man hits the target}\}$$
$$E_2 = \{\text{second man hits the target}\}$$
$$E_3 = \{\text{third man hits the target}\}$$

then we have

$$P(E_1) = \tfrac{1}{2} \qquad P(\bar{E}_1) = \tfrac{1}{2}$$
$$P(E_2) = \tfrac{1}{3} \qquad P(\bar{E}_2) = \tfrac{2}{3}$$
$$P(E_3) = \tfrac{1}{4} \qquad P(\bar{E}_3) = \tfrac{3}{4}$$

We require the probabilities of three joint events. Assuming the events are independent, we have, using the product law,

$$P(E_1 \cap \bar{E}_2 \cap \bar{E}_3) = \tfrac{1}{2} \times \tfrac{2}{3} \times \tfrac{3}{4} = \tfrac{1}{4}$$
$$P(\bar{E}_1 \cap E_2 \cap \bar{E}_3) = \tfrac{1}{2} \times \tfrac{1}{3} \times \tfrac{3}{4} = \tfrac{1}{8}$$
$$P(\bar{E}_1 \cap \bar{E}_2 \cap E_3) = \tfrac{1}{2} \times \tfrac{2}{3} \times \tfrac{1}{4} = \tfrac{1}{12}$$

These three joint events are mutually exclusive so the probability that one of them will occur is given by the addition law for mutually exclusive events:

$$P(\text{one and only one bullet strikes target}) = \tfrac{1}{4} + \tfrac{1}{8} + \tfrac{1}{12}$$

$$= \tfrac{11}{24}$$

4.7.3 *Example*

Two teams A and B play a football match against each other. The probabilities for each team of scoring 0, 1, 2, 3 goals are shown in Table 4.2. Calculate the probability of

(a) A winning, (b) a draw, and (c) B winning. (O)

Table 4.2

Number of goals	Probability of scoring A	B
0	0.3	0.2
1	0.3	0.4
2	0.3	0.3
3	0.1	0.1

The possible results of a match are best shown in tabular form as in Figure 4.10, where the probabilities of each joint event have been calculated assuming independence and using the product law. The cells may be thought of as points in a sample space but they no longer represent equiprobable events.

These events are mutually exclusive so that the total probability of A winning can be found by adding the probabilities of each joint event in which A wins. These events are surrounded by the heavy line.

B \ A: number of goals	0	1	2	3
0	0.3 × 0.2 = 0.06	0.3 × 0.2 = 0.06	0.3 × 0.2 = 0.06	0.1 × 0.2 = 0.02
1	0.3 × 0.4 = 0.12	0.3 × 0.4 = 0.12	0.3 × 0.4 = 0.12	0.1 × 0.4 = 0.04
2	0.3 × 0.3 = 0.09	0.3 × 0.3 = 0.09	0.3 × 0.3 = 0.09	0.1 × 0.3 = 0.03
3	0.3 × 0.1 = 0.03	0.3 × 0.1 = 0.03	0.3 × 0.1 = 0.03	0.1 × 0.1 = 0.01

Figure 4.10 Sample space to illustrate Example 4.7.3

(a) $P(A \text{ wins}) = 0.06 + 0.06 + 0.02 + 0.12 + 0.04 + 0.03$
$= 0.33$

(b) $P(\text{draw}) = 0.06 + 0.12 + 0.09 + 0.01$ (values on leading diagonal)
$= 0.28$

(c) $P(B \text{ wins}) = 0.12 + 0.09 + 0.09 + 0.03 + 0.03 + 0.03$
$= 0.39$

The three probabilities calculated above are exhaustive as well as mutually exclusive so as a check we make sure that their sum is 1.

4.7.4 Example

A bag contains three red, four white and five black balls. If three balls are taken what is the probability that they are all the same colour?

We have three possible joint events:

$$P(\text{all white}) = \frac{4}{12} \times \frac{3}{11} \times \frac{2}{10} \text{ (using the product law with conditional probabilities)}$$
$$= \frac{24}{1320}$$

$$P(\text{all red}) = \frac{3}{12} \times \frac{2}{11} \times \frac{1}{10}$$
$$= \frac{6}{1320}$$

$$P(\text{all black}) = \frac{5}{12} \times \frac{4}{11} \times \frac{3}{10}$$
$$= \frac{60}{1320}$$

The total probability is found by adding these probabilities since the events are mutually exclusive:

$$P(\text{all same colour}) = \frac{24}{1320} + \frac{6}{1320} + \frac{60}{1320} = \frac{3}{44}$$

4.7.5 Example

Of the bicycles in a school bicycle shed, 60% belong to boys and the rest to girls. 90% of the bicycles belonging to boys are racers as are 70% of the bicycles belonging to girls. Dynamos are fitted to 5% of the non-racing and 1% of the racing bicycles irrespective of whether the bicycle is owned by a boy or a girl. If a bicycle is chosen at random find the probability that it is (a) a racer with a dynamo belonging to a boy, (b) a racer without a dynamo. A bicycle is chosen at random. If it is not a racer, find the probability that it belongs to a girl.

Figure 4.11 shows the information in the form of a tree diagram.

(a) $P(\text{boy} \cap \text{racer} \cap \text{dynamo}) = P(\text{boy}) \times P(\text{racer}|\text{boy}) \times P(\text{dynamo}|\text{racer})$
$$= 0.6 \times 0.9 \times 0.01 = 0.0054$$

(b) Racing bicycles without dynamos can belong to boys or girls.

$P(\text{girl} \cap \text{racer} \cap \overline{\text{dynamo}}) = P(\text{girl}) \times P(\text{racer}|\text{girl}) \times P(\overline{\text{dynamo}}|\text{racer})$
$$= 0.4 \times 0.7 \times 0.99 = 0.2772$$

Similarly $P(\text{boy} \cap \text{racer} \cap \overline{\text{dynamo}}) = 0.6 \times 0.9 \times 0.99 = 0.5346$

Using the addition law for mutually exclusive events

$$P(\text{racer} \cap \overline{\text{dynamo}}) = 0.2772 + 0.5346 = 0.8118$$

(c) $P(\text{girl}|\overline{\text{racer}}) = \dfrac{P(\text{girl} \cap \overline{\text{racer}})}{P(\overline{\text{racer}})}$ (see equation (4.4.1))

$$P(\overline{\text{racer}}) = P(\text{boy} \cap \overline{\text{racer}}) + P(\text{girl} \cap \overline{\text{racer}})$$
$$= P(\text{boy}) \times P(\overline{\text{racer}} \mid \text{boy}) + P(\text{girl}) \times P(\overline{\text{racer}}|\text{girl})$$
$$= 0.6 \times 0.1 + 0.4 \times 0.3 = 0.06 + 0.12 = 0.18$$

$$P(\text{girl}|\overline{\text{racer}}) = \frac{0.12}{0.18} = \frac{2}{3}$$

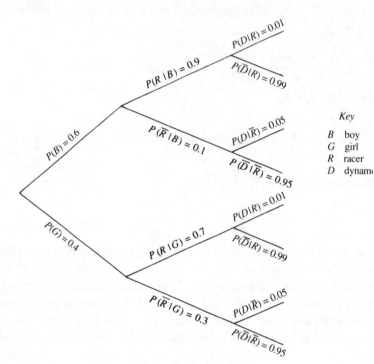

Figure 4.11 Tree diagram to illustrate Example 4.7.5

4.7.6   *Example*

The events *A*, *B* and *C* are such that *A* and *B* are independent and *A* and *C* are mutually exclusive. Given that $P(A)=0.4$, $P(B)=0.2$, $P(C)=0.3$, $P(B \cap C)=0.1$, calculate (a) $P(A \cup B)$, (b) $P(C \mid B)$, (c) $P(B \mid A \cup C)$. Also calculate the probability that one and only one of the events *B*, *C* will occur.   (W)

Figure 4.12 shows a Venn diagram of the sample space. Since *A* and *C* are mutually exclusive, they do not overlap on the Venn diagram.

(a) $P(A \cup B) = P(A) + P(B) - P(A \cap B)$ (equation (4.3.2))

Since *A* and *B* are independent

$P(A \cap B) = P(A)P(B) = 0.4 \times 0.2 = 0.08$ (equation (4.6.1))

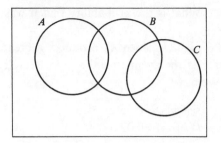

Figure 4.12 Sample space to illustrate Example 4.7.6

and $\qquad P(A \cup B) = 0.4 + 0.2 - 0.08 = 0.52$

(b) $\qquad P(C|B) = \dfrac{P(C \cap B)}{P(B)}$ $\qquad\qquad\qquad$ (equation (4.4.2))

$\qquad\qquad = \dfrac{0.1}{0.2} = 0.5$

(c) $\qquad P(B|A \cup C) = \dfrac{P\{B \cap (A \cup C)\}}{P(A \cup C)}$ $\qquad\qquad$ (from equation (4.4.2))

From Figure 4.12 we see that

$\qquad B \cap (A \cup C) = (B \cap A) \cup (B \cap C)$

Now $P(B \cap A) = 0.08$ as already calculated and $P(B \cap C) = 0.1$ (given) giving

$\qquad P\{B \cap (A \cup C)\} = 0.08 + 0.1 = 0.18$ $\quad$ (using equation (4.3.1), for mutually exclusive events)

Since A and C are mutually exclusive

$\qquad P(A \cup C) = P(A) + P(C)$ $\qquad\qquad\qquad$ (see equation (4.3.1))

$\qquad\qquad\quad = 0.4 + 0.3 = 0.7$

This gives

$\qquad P(B|A \cup C) = \dfrac{0.18}{0.7} = \dfrac{9}{35}$

The probability that one and only one of B and C occurs corresponds to the area on the diagram inside B and C but not inside $B \cap C$. Thus this probability is

$\qquad P(B \cup C) - P(B \cap C)$

$\qquad = P(B) + P(C) - 2(B \cap C)$ $\qquad\qquad\qquad$ (using equation (4.3.2))

$\qquad = 0.2 + 0.3 - 2 \times 0.1$

$\qquad = 0.3$

4.8 Bayes' theorem

A shopkeeper buys a particular kind of light bulb from three manufacturers A_1, A_2 and A_3. She buys 30% of her stock from A_1, 45% from A_2 and 25% from A_3. This means that if she picks a bulb at random $P(A_1) = 0.3$, $P(A_2) = 0.45$ and $P(A_3) = 0.25$. In the past she has found that 2% of A_3's bulbs are faulty whereas only 1% of A_1's and A_2's are. Suppose that she chooses a bulb and finds it is faulty. What is the probability that it was one of A_3's bulbs?

The probability will be greater than $P(A_3)$ ($=0.25$) since A_3 produces a greater proportion of faulty bulbs than A_1 and A_2. If F is the event that the bulb is faulty, then $P(A_3|F)$ is the probability that we require. We have

$$P(A_1)=0.3 \qquad P(A_2)=0.45 \qquad P(A_3)=0.25$$
$$P(F|A_1)=0.01 \qquad P(F|A_2)=0.01 \qquad P(F|A_3)=0.02$$

This information is shown on a tree diagram in Figure 4.13.

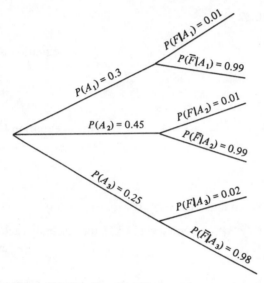

Figure 4.13 Tree diagram to illustrate the example in Section 4.8

Using equations (4.4.1) and (4.4.2)

$$P(F\cap A_3)=P(F|A_3)P(A_3)=P(A_3|F)P(F)$$

Rearranging, the probability we require is

$$P(A_3|F)=\frac{P(F|A_3)P(A_3)}{P(F)} \tag{4.8.1}$$

$P(F)$, the probability that a bulb is faulty (and comes from A_1, A_2 or A_3), is given by the addition law for mutually exclusive events:

$$P(F)=P(F\cap A_1)+P(F\cap A_2)+P(F\cap A_3)$$
$$=P(F|A_1)P(A_1)+P(F|A_2)P(A_2)+P(F|A_3)P(A_3) \qquad \text{(using equation (4.4.2))}$$

Substituting for $P(F)$ in (4.8.1) gives

$$P(A_3|F)=\frac{P(F|A_3)P(A_3)}{P(F|A_1)P(A_1)+P(F|A_2)P(A_2)+P(F|A_3)P(A_3)} \tag{4.8.2}$$

$$= \frac{0.02 \times 0.25}{0.01 \times 0.3 + 0.01 \times 0.45 + 0.02 \times 0.25}$$

$$= 0.4$$

Similarly, if we wish to know the probability that the faulty bulb was supplied by A_1 we have

$$P(A_1|F) = \frac{P(F|A_1)P(A_1)}{P(F|A_1)P(A_1) + P(F|A_2)P(A_2) + P(F|A_3)P(A_3)}$$

$$= \frac{0.01 \times 0.3}{0.01 \times 0.3 + 0.01 \times 0.45 + 0.02 \times 0.25}$$

$$= 0.24$$

And since A_1, A_2 and A_3 are mutually exclusive

$$P(A_2|F) = 1 - 0.4 - 0.24 = 0.36$$

This means that, of the faulty bulbs, 24% come from A_1, 36% from A_2 and 40% from A_3.

Equation (4.8.2) is an example of **Bayes' theorem** which may be stated as follows: if $A_1, A_2, \ldots, A_n$ are n mutually exclusive and exhaustive events in a sample space S and B is another event in S then

$$P(A_k|B) = \frac{P(B|A_k)P(A_k)}{\sum_{i=1}^{n} P(B|A_i)P(A_i)} \tag{4.8.3}$$

for $k = 1, 2, \ldots, n$.

In practice the solution to a particular problem is usually made clearer by drawing a tree diagram rather than using equation (4.8.3), and indeed this approach has already been taken in Examples 4.5.3 and 4.7.5.

Summary

$P(E)$ denotes the probability that event E occurs. $\bar{E}$ or E' is called the **complement** of E and $P(\bar{E})$ denotes the probability that E does not occur.

$$P(\bar{E}) = 1 - P(E)$$

For two events E_1 and E_2:

$P(E_1 \cup E_2)$ denotes the probability that E_1 and/or E_2 occur.

$P(E_1 \cap E_2)$ denotes the probability that both E_1 and E_2 occur.

$P(E_1|E_2)$ denotes the **conditional probability** that E_1 occurs given that E_2 has occurred.

Addition law: $P(E_1 \cup E_2) = P(E_1) + P(E_2) - P(E_1 \cap E_2)$.

Mutually exclusive events are events which cannot both occur. If E_1 and E_2 are mutually exclusive then

$$P(E_1 \cap E_2) = 0, \quad P(E_1|E_2) = 0, \quad P(E_2|E_1) = 0$$

and the addition law becomes

$$P(E_1 \cup E_2) = P(E_1) + P(E_2)$$

Product law: $P(E_1 \cap E_2) = P(E_2) \times P(E_1 | E_2) = P(E_1) \times P(E_2 | E_1)$.

Independent events are events such that the occurrence of one does not affect the probability of the occurrence of the other. If E_1 and E_2 are independent then

$$P(E_1 | E_2) = P(E_1) \quad P(E_2 | E_1) = P(E_2)$$

and the product law becomes

$$P(E_1 \cap E_2) = P(E_1) \times P(E_2)$$

Exhaustive events are a group of events such that they include all possible outcomes. If E_1 and E_2 are exhaustive then $P(E_1 \cup E_2) = 1$.

Projects

(1) *Comparing an experimental probability with its theoretical value*

Toss three dice together 100 times. Count the number of throws in which there are no 6s and use this value to calculate the experimental probability that a throw of three dice will not include a 6. Compare your value with the calculated theoretical value. (Verify that this is 0.58.)

(2) *Estimating the probability that a person is left-handed*

For a sample of 100 people, count the number that are left-handed and hence estimate the probability that a person is left-handed. If possible, it would be interesting to obtain samples from two different populations, for example male and female or two different age groups.

(3) *Advanced Level Statistics Software*

The *Basic probability* section allows the user to define two dice and to choose two events which can result when the dice are thrown. The sample space for the two events is displayed and the probabilities of various compound events and the relationships between these probabilities can be investigated. The probabilities can also be displayed in a tree diagram or a contingency table.

Exercise on Chapter 4

(1) (a) The pages of a book are numbered from 1 to 200. If a page is chosen at random, what is the probability that its number will contain just two digits?

(b) The probability that a January night will be icy is $\frac{1}{4}$. On an icy night the probability that there will be a car accident at a certain dangerous corner is $\frac{1}{25}$. If it is not icy, the probability of an accident is $\frac{1}{100}$. What is the probability that
(i) 13 January will be icy and there will be an accident,
(ii) there will be an accident on 13 January?   (C)

(2) Two events A and B are such that $P(A)=\frac{1}{3}$ and $P(B)=\frac{1}{2}$. If A' denotes the complement of A calculate $P(A'\cap B)$ in each of the cases when
 (a) $P(A\cap B)=\frac{1}{8}$,
 (b) A and B are mutually exclusive,
 (c) A is a subset of B.   (W)

(3) In a certain game a player's turn consists of throwing an unbiased die until he fails to throw a 6 and he is credited with a score equal to the sum of the individual scores thrown during his turn.
 (a) Write down the probabilities that in one turn a player will be credited with a score of (i) 3, (ii) 6, (iii) 9, (iv) 13.
 (b) Calculate the probabilities that in one turn a player will throw exactly (i) one 6, (ii) two 6s.
 (c) Obtain an expression for the probability that in one turn he will throw exactly n 6s.   (L)

(4) An unbiased die F has its faces numbered 1, 2, 3, 4, 5 and 6. Another unbiased die S has its faces numbered 1, 1, 2, 2, 3 and 3. In a game a card is selected at random from a pack of 52 playing cards and if a diamond is obtained die F is thrown; otherwise die S is thrown. Find the probability of scoring 2.   (L)

(5) A girl has three unbiased dice. She starts a game by throwing one of the dice. If she does not throw a 6 the game is over, whereas if she does throw a 6 she then throws the other two dice simultaneously. Calculate the probabilities that in one game she will have thrown
 (a) exactly one 6, (b) exactly two 6s.   (L)

(6) Show that the probability that a point, selected at random inside a circle, is closer to the centre of the circle than to the circumference is $\frac{1}{4}$.
 Points are selected at random inside the circle until a point is closer to the centre than to the circumference. What is the probability that
 (a) exactly three points are selected,
 (b) no more than three points are selected?
 How many points need to be selected so that there is a probability of at least 0.85 that at least one point is closer to the centre than to the circumference?   (C)

(7) A bag contains five different pairs of gloves. Two persons, A and B, take turns to draw a glove from the bag (without replacement), A drawing first. Find the probabilities
 (a) that the first glove drawn by A and the first glove drawn by B do not form a pair,
 (b) that A obtains a pair in his first two draws,
 (c) that B obtains a pair in his first two draws,
 (d) that both A and B obtain a pair in their first two draws,
 (e) that at least one of the persons obtains a pair in his first two draws,

(f)   that neither A nor B obtains a pair in his first two draws,

(g)   that B completes a pair on making his second draw and A on making his third draw.   (JMB)

(8)   (a)   Two people each have a set of seven cards, numbered 1 to 7. Each shows a card drawn at random. Find the probability that the total of the two numbers is (i) even, (ii) odd, (iii) greater than 5.

(b)   A signal consisting of seven dots and/or dashes is to be given. The probability of a dot in any position is $\frac{2}{5}$ and of a dash is $\frac{3}{5}$.
Find the probability that, in a signal, no two consecutive characters are the same.

(c)   A die is loaded so that the chance of throwing a 1 is $\frac{1}{4}x$, the chance of a 2 is $\frac{1}{4}$ and the chance of a 6 is $\frac{1}{4}(1-x)$. The chance of a 3, 4 or 5 is $\frac{1}{6}$.
The die is thrown twice.
Prove that the chance of throwing a total of 7 is
$$\frac{9x-9x^2+10}{72}$$
Find the value of x which will make this chance a maximum, and find this maximum probability.   (SUJB)

(9)   Ruby Welloff, the daughter of a wealthy jeweller, is about to get married. Her father decides that as a wedding present she can select one of two similar boxes. Each box contains three stones. In one box two of the stones are real diamonds, and the other is a worthless imitation; and in the other box one is a real diamond, and the other two are worthless imitations. She has no idea which box is which. If the daughter were to choose randomly between the two boxes, her chance of getting two real diamonds would be $\frac{1}{2}$. Mr Welloff, being a sporting type, allows his daughter to draw one stone from one of the boxes and to examine it to see if it is a real diamond. The daughter decides to take the box that the stone she tested came from if the tested stone is real, and to take the other box otherwise. Now what is the probability that the daughter will get two real diamonds as her wedding present?   (AEB)

(10)   A biased die is such that the probability that any face is shown is proportional to the number shown on that face. Find the probability with which each of the numbers 1, 2, 3, 4, 5, 6 appears. Two independent tosses of this die are made. What is the probability that the sum of the faces is 10?   (AEB)

(11)   Mass-produced glass bricks are inspected for defects. The probability that a brick has air bubbles is 0.002. If a brick has air bubbles the probability that it is also cracked is 0.5 while the probability that a brick free from air bubbles is cracked is 0.005. What is the probability that a brick chosen at random is cracked?
The probability that a brick is discoloured is 0.006. Given that discolouration occurs independently of the other two defects, find the probability that a brick chosen at random has no defects.   (O & C)

(12) (a) The event that Mary goes to a dance is M and the event that Linda goes to the same dance is L. The events L and M are independent and $P(\bar{L}\cap\bar{M})=\frac{1}{4}$, $P(L)+P(M)=\frac{23}{24}$.
Find the probability that both Linda and Mary go to the dance.

(b) A gold urn contains three red balls and four white balls and a silver urn contains five red balls and two white balls. A die is rolled and, if a six shows, one ball is selected at random from the gold urn. Otherwise a ball is selected at random from the silver urn. Find the probability of selecting a red ball.
The ball selected is not replaced and a second ball is selected at random from the same urn. Find the probability that both balls are white. (L)

(13) An experiment is performed with a die and two packs of cards. The die is thrown, and if it shows 1, 2, 3 or 4 a card is drawn at random from the first pack, which contains the usual 52 cards; if the score on the die is 5 or 6 a card is drawn from the second pack which contains only 39 cards, all the clubs having been removed. X denotes the event 'the first pack with 52 cards is used', and Y denotes the event 'the card drawn is a diamond'. Calculate the probabilities
(a) $P(X)$, (b) $P(X\cap Y)$, (c) $P(Y)$, (d) $P(Y|X)$, (e) $P(X|Y)$. (C)

(14) Three men A, B and C agree to meet at the theatre. The man A cannot remember whether they agreed to meet at the Palace or the Queen's and tosses a coin to decide which theatre to go to. The man B also tosses a coin to decide between the Queen's and the Royalty. The man C tosses a coin to decide whether to go to the Palace or not and in this latter case he tosses again to decide between the Queen's and the Royalty. Find the probability that
(a) A and B meet,
(b) B and C meet,
(c) A, B and C all meet,
(d) A, B and C all go to different places,
(e) at least two meet. (C)

(15) The events A and B are such that
$$P(A)=\tfrac{1}{2}$$
$$P(A \text{ or } B \text{ but not both } A \text{ and } B)=\tfrac{1}{3}$$
$$P(B)=\tfrac{1}{4}$$
Calculate $P(A\cap B)$, $P(A'\cap B)$, $P(A|B)$ and $P(B|A')$, where A' is the event 'A does not occur'.
State with reasons whether A and B are (a) independent, (b) mutually exclusive. (C)

(16) Suppose that letters sent by first and second class post have probabilities of being delivered a given number of days after posting according to Table 4.3 (weekends are ignored).

Table 4.3

Days to delivery	1	2	3
First class	0.9	0.1	0
Second class	0.1	0.6	0.3

The secretary of a committee posts a letter to a committee member who replies immediately using the same class of post. What is the probability that four or more days are taken from the secretary posting the letter to receiving the reply if (a) first class, (b) second class post is used?

The secretary sends out four letters and each member replies immediately by the same class of post. Assuming the letters move independently, what is the probability that the secretary receives (c) all the replies within three days using first class post, (d) at least two replies within three days using second class post?   (O)

(17) Define the conditional probability of an event A given that an event B has occurred. A girl uses a home-made metal detector to look for valuable metallic objects on a beach. There is a fault in the machine which causes it to signal the presence of only 95% of the metallic objects over which it passes and to signal the presence of 6% of the non-metallic objects over which it passes. Of the objects over which the machine passes, 20% are metallic.
   (a) Find the probability that a given object over which the machine passes is metallic and machine gives a signal.
   (b) Find the probability of a signal being received by the girl for any given object over which the machine passes.
   (c) Find the probability that the girl has found a metal object when she receives a signal.
   (d) Given that 10% of metallic objects on the beach are valuable, find the proportion of objects, discovered by a signal from the detector, that are valuable. (JMB)

(18) In Camelot it never rains on Friday, Saturday, Sunday or Monday. The probability that it rains on a given Tuesday is $\frac{1}{5}$. For each of the remaining two days, Wednesday and Thursday, the conditional probability that it rains, given that it rained the previous day, is α, and the conditional probability that it rains, given that it did not rain the previous day, is β.
   (a) Show that the (unconditional) probability of rain on a given Wednesday is $\frac{1}{5}(\alpha+4\beta)$, and find the probability of rain on a given Thursday.
   (b) If X is the event that, in a randomly chosen week, it rains on Thursday, Y is the event that it rains on Tuesday, and $\bar{Y}$ is the event that it does not rain on Tuesday, show that
$$P(X|Y)-P(X|\bar{Y})=(\alpha-\beta)^2.$$
   (c) Explain the implications of the case $\alpha=\beta$.   (C)

(19) A certain university examination can be taken after a two-year course (the normal course) or after a one-year course (the fast course); 60% of the students take the normal course. Of those on the normal course 50% are men, whilst of those on the fast course 60% are men. Students who do not pass the examination at the end of the course have to resit six months later; the proportions resitting in the four groups (a) normal course, men, (b) normal course, women, (c) fast course, men, and (d) fast course, women are respectively (a) 40%, (b) 30%, (c) 25% and (d) 12.5%. Calculate
   (i)   the proportion of those candidates taking the examination for the first time who are men,
   (ii) the proportion of women candidates who take the normal course,
   (iii) the proportion of candidates who resit the examination,
   (iv) the proportion of those candidates resitting the examination who are men,
   (v)   the proportion of men who have to resit the examination.   (C)

(20) In a game, which is played by two people, the players extend their hands simultaneously to indicate one of the three objects, 'paper', 'scissors' and 'stone'. 'Paper' beats 'stone', 'stone' beats 'scissors' and 'scissors' beats 'paper'; if the objects are the same the result is a draw. Two players A and B have a contest. At the first turn A indicates 'paper', 'scissors' and 'stone' with probabilities 0.3, 0.4 and 0.3 respectively, while the corresponding probabilities for B are 0.2, 0.3 and 0.5. What is the probability that the first turn results in (a) a win for A, (b) a win for B, (c) a draw?

(21) (a) Five balls numbered 1, 2, 3, 4, 5 are placed in a bag. A and B take it in turns to draw a ball at random from the bag, note its number and replace the ball in the bag. The winner is the first player to draw a ball which has already been drawn. If A draws first find the probability that A wins.
     (b) Four balls numbered 1, 2, 3, 4 are placed in a bag. A and B take it in turns to draw a ball at random from the bag, note its number and replace the ball in the bag. The winner is the player who first draws a ball that he himself has already drawn. If A draws first find the probability that A wins.   (C)

(22) If A_1, A_2 and A_3 are mutually exclusive events whose union is the sample space S of an experiment and B is an arbitrary event of S such that $P(B) \neq 0$, show that

$$P(A_1|B) = \frac{P(A_1)P(B|A_1)}{\sum\limits_{r=1}^{3} P(A_r)P(B|A_r)}$$

and write down the results for $P(A_2|B)$ and $P(A_3|B)$.

   A factory has three machines 1, 2 and 3, producing a particular type of item. One item is drawn at random from the factory's production. Let B denote the event that the chosen item is defective and let A_k denote the event that the item was produced on machine k where $k = 1, 2$ or 3. Suppose that machines 1, 2 and 3 produce respectively 35%, 45% and 20% of the total production of items and that

$$P(B|A_1) = 0.02, \ P(B|A_2) = 0.01, \ P(B|A_3) = 0.03$$

Given that an item chosen at random is defective, find which machine was the most likely to have produced it.   (L)

(23) Three identical bags each contain two balls. The balls are identical apart from their colour. One bag contains two white balls, the second two black balls and the third one black and one white ball. A bag is selected at random and a ball removed from it. If the ball is white what is the probability that the other ball in the bag is also white?

(24) Three events A, B and C are defined in the same sample space. The events A and C are mutually exclusive. The events A and B are independent. Given that $P(A)=\frac{1}{3}$, $P(C)=\frac{1}{5}$, $P(A \cup B)=\frac{2}{3}$, find (a) $P(A \cup C)$, (b) $P(B)$, (c) $P(A \cap B)$.
    Given also that $P(B \cup C)=\frac{3}{5}$, determine whether or not B and C are independent.
    (L, part)

5   Permutations and combinations

5.1   A probability problem

We have used the idea of conditional probability to find the probability that two cards drawn from a pack will both be aces (see Section 4.5). How should our calculation be modified if we wish to find the probability that when five cards are drawn, two of them are aces? We could still use the idea of conditional probability but we are then faced with the problem that there is more than one order in which the cards can be drawn, e.g. $A A \bar{A} \bar{A} \bar{A}$, $\bar{A} A \bar{A} A \bar{A}$ etc. (where A denotes an ace and $\bar{A}$ a card which is not an ace). Before we can study this type of problem further we need to study arrangements or **permutations**.

5.2   Permutations

Suppose four people A, B, C and D are to run in a relay race. In how many different ways can we arrange the order in which they run? The first person can be chosen in 4 ways, the second in 3 ways, the third in 2 ways, and the fourth in 1 way, giving a total of $4 \times 3 \times 2 \times 1 = 24$ ways. If the relay team of four were chosen from ten people, then the first runner could be chosen in 10 ways, the second in 9 ways, the third in 8 ways and the fourth in 7 ways, giving $10 \times 9 \times 8 \times 7 = 5040$ ways of choosing the team, *paying attention to the order in which they run*. This is called a permutation of four objects from ten. In general the number of permutations, ${}^{n}P_{r}$, of r objects from n is given by

$$ {}^{n}P_{r} = n(n-1)\ldots(n-r+1) $$

which can be written more compactly as

$$ {}^{n}P_{r} = \frac{n!}{(n-r)!} \tag{5.2.1} $$

where $n!$ (read as '*n-factorial*') is an abbreviation for

$$ n \times (n-1) \times (n-2) \times \ldots \times 2 \times 1 $$

5.3   Combinations

Frequently we are not concerned with the order in which the objects are chosen but merely which objects are chosen, i.e. a selection or **combination**. To return to the example of relay runners; suppose the number of combinations of four runners which we could make from ten is x. Each of those x selections could be arranged in $4! = 24$ ways, and so

$$ 4! \times \text{number of combinations} = \text{number of permutations} $$

But we already know that the number of permutations is $10 \times 9 \times 8 \times 7$, therefore

$$10 \times 9 \times 8 \times 7 = x \times 4!$$

and

$$x = \frac{10 \times 9 \times 8 \times 7}{4 \times 3 \times 2 \times 1} = 210$$

In general the number of selections or combinations of r objects from n is denoted by $\binom{n}{r}$ or $^n C_r$. Each of these selections can be arranged in $r!$ ways so that

$$r! \times \text{number of combinations} = \text{number of permutations}$$

giving

$$r! \binom{n}{r} = {}^n P_r = \frac{n!}{(n-r)!}$$

Rearranging

$$\binom{n}{r} = \frac{n!}{r! \, (n-r)!} \qquad\qquad (5.3.1)$$

Common sense tells us that $\binom{n}{n}$ must be 1. Since, using equation (5.3.1), we have

$$\binom{n}{n} = \frac{n!}{n! \, 0!} = \frac{1}{0!}$$

we must take $0!$ equal to 1. From this it follows that $\binom{n}{0}$ is also 1 since, using equation (5.3.1),

$$\binom{n}{0} = \frac{n!}{0! \, (n-0)!} = 1$$

5.3.1.   *Example*

A competition consists of selecting three suitable gifts from a list of twenty possible wedding presents. In how many ways can this be done?

$$\text{number of combinations} = \frac{20!}{3!(20-3)!} = \frac{20!}{3! \times 17!}$$

$$= \frac{20 \times 19 \times 18}{1 \times 2 \times 3}$$

$$= 1140$$

5.3.2   Example

How many distinct arrangements can be made of the letters of the word ABRACADABRA?

To start, let us distinguish the like letters by suffixes thus:

$$A_1B_1R_1A_2CA_3DA_4B_2R_2A_5$$

In this form there are 11! possible permutations. However 5! have the As in the same positions and are distinguished only by the suffixes on the As. Removing these reduces the number of permutations by a factor of 5! Repeating this reasoning for the Rs and Bs, the number of distinct arrangements is

$$\frac{11!}{5!\,2!\,2!} = 83\,160$$

5.3.3   Exercise

(1) Calculate the number of different three-card hands which can be dealt from a pack of 52 cards.

(2) The judges in a beauty contest have to arrange ten competitors in order of merit. In how many ways can this be done? Two competitors are to be selected to go on to a further competition. In how many ways can this selection be made?

(3) (a) Evaluate

(i) $^9P_3$, (ii) $^6P_4$, (iii) $\binom{11}{3}$, (iv) $\binom{11}{8}$.

(b) Show that $\binom{n}{r} = \binom{n}{n-r}$.

(4) From a sixth form of 30 boys and 32 girls, two boys and two girls are to be chosen to represent their school. How many possible selections are there?

(5) How many distinct arrangements are there of the letters of the words
(a) DEAR, (b) DEER?

(6) In how many different ways can a committee of four men and four women be seated in a row on a platform if (a) they can sit in any position, (b) no one is seated next to a person of the same sex?

(7) (a) Four boys and two girls sit in a line on stools in front of a coffee-bar. (i) In how many ways can they arrange themselves so that the two girls are together? (ii) In how many ways can they sit if the two girls are not together?

(b) Ten people arrange to travel in two cars, a large saloon car and a mini car. If the saloon car has seats for six and the mini has seats for four, find the number of different ways the party can travel, assuming that the order of seating in each car does not matter and all the people are drivers. (C)

(8) (a) How many integers are there between 1234 and 4321 which contain each of the digits 1, 2, 3 and 4 once and once only?

(b) A teacher can take any or all of six boys with him on an expedition. He decides to take at least three boys. In how many different ways can the party be made up? (C)

(9) (a) Calculate how many different numbers altogether can be formed by taking one, two, three and four digits from the digits 9, 8, 3 and 2, repetitions not being allowed.

(b) Calculate how many of the numbers in part (a) are odd and greater than 800.

(c) If one of the numbers in part (a) is chosen at random, calculate the probability that it will be greater than 300. (L)

(10) (a) How many odd numbers can be formed from the figures 1, 2, 3 and 5 if repetitions are not allowed?

(b) If a diagonal of a polygon is defined to be a line joining any two non-adjacent vertices, how many diagonals are there in a polygon of (i) 5 sides, (ii) 6 sides, (iii) n sides?

(c) (i) Six different books lie on a table, and a girl is told that she can take away as many as she likes but she must not leave empty handed. How many different selections can she make?

(ii) One of these books is a Bible. How many of these selections will include this Bible? (SUJB)

(11) Giving a brief explanation of your method, calculate the number of different ways in which the letters of the word TRIANGLES can be arranged if no two vowels may come together. (C)

5.4 Combinations and probability

Our definition of probability given in equation (4.2.1) was

$$P(E) = \frac{n\{E\}}{n\{S\}}$$

$\{S\}$ was the set of all possible outcomes of a trial and $\{E\}$ was the set of outcomes which resulted in event E. To see how combinations can be used in probability problems look again at the calculation of the probability that two cards drawn from a pack are both aces (which we previously treated using conditional probabilities). In this case the set of all possible outcomes is all the ways in which we can choose two cards from 52, so

$$n\{S\} = \binom{52}{2}$$

The set of outcomes which result in E is all the ways in which two aces can be chosen from the four in the pack, giving

$$n\{E\}=\binom{4}{2}$$

This gives

$$P(\text{two aces})=\frac{n\{E\}}{n\{S\}}$$

$$=\binom{4}{2}\div\binom{52}{2}$$

$$=\frac{4\times3}{1\times2}\div\frac{52\times51}{1\times2}$$

$$=\frac{4\times3}{52\times51}$$

$$=\frac{1}{221}$$

which is, of course, the same result as we obtained before.

We are now in a position to tackle the problem given at the beginning of this chapter: what is the probability that, of five cards drawn from a pack, two are aces?

The two aces can be selected in $\binom{4}{2}$ ways and the remaining three cards in $\binom{48}{3}$ ways giving

$$n\{E\}=\binom{4}{2}\times\binom{48}{3}\quad\text{and}\quad n\{S\}=\binom{52}{5},$$

Therefore

$$P(\text{two aces out of five})=\frac{n\{E\}}{n\{S\}}$$

$$=\binom{4}{2}\binom{48}{3}\div\binom{52}{5}$$

$$=\frac{4\times3}{1\times2}\times\frac{48\times47\times46}{1\times2\times3}\times\frac{5\times4\times3\times2\times1}{52\times51\times50\times49\times48}$$

$$=0.0399$$

5.5 Selecting like objects

The approach used in the previous section can also be applied to the following problem: a bag contains 48 black and 4 white balls. What is the probability that if five balls are drawn from the bag two of them are white?

The fact that the black balls look alike and the white balls look alike does not affect the solution – we could, after all, number the balls if we wished. Thus the calculation in this problem is identical to that in the previous section. (N.B. This example should be contrasted with Example 5.3.2 in which the number of *distinct* arrangements was required.)

5.5.1 *Example*

A bag contains five white, six red and seven blue balls. If three balls are selected at random, what is the probability that they are (a) all red, (b) all different colours?

(a) The total number of ways, $n\{S\}$, in which three balls can be selected out of the eighteen balls in the bag is $\binom{18}{3}$. The number of ways in which three red balls can be drawn is $\binom{6}{3}$ so that

$$P(\text{three red balls}) = \binom{6}{3} \div \binom{18}{3}$$
$$= \frac{6 \times 5 \times 4}{1 \times 2 \times 3} \div \frac{18 \times 17 \times 16}{1 \times 2 \times 3}$$
$$= 0.0245$$

(b) If the balls are all different colours, then one red, one blue and one white must be drawn.

$$\text{number of ways of drawing one white} = \binom{5}{1}$$

$$\text{number of ways of drawing one red} \ \ = \binom{6}{1}$$

$$\text{number of ways of drawing one blue} \ = \binom{7}{1}$$

Therefore

$$P(\text{one red, one white, one blue}) = \binom{5}{1}\binom{6}{1}\binom{7}{1} \div \binom{18}{3}$$
$$= 5 \times 6 \times 7 \div \frac{18 \times 17 \times 16}{1 \times 2 \times 3}$$
$$= 0.257$$

Summary

The number of **permutations** or **arrangements** of r objects chosen from n different objects is given by

$$^nP_r = \frac{n!}{(n-r)!}$$

The number of **combinations** or **selections** of r objects chosen from n different objects is given by

$$\binom{n}{r} = {}^nC_r = \frac{n!}{r!(n-r)!}$$

Exercise on Chapter 5

(1) A box of one dozen eggs contains one that is bad. If three eggs are chosen at random to make an omelette, what is the probability that one of them will be bad?

(2) In a game of bridge the pack of 52 cards is shared equally between four players. What is the probability that a particular player is void in one suit (i.e. has no cards of one suit)?

(3) A bag contains twenty chocolates, fifteen toffees and twelve peppermints. If three sweets are chosen at random what is the probability that they are
   (a) all different,
   (b) all chocolates,
   (c) all the same,
   (d) all toffees or peppermints?

(4) A housewife has some cartons of yoghurt in her refrigerator. Five are 'raspberry', three 'orange', four 'grapefruit' and three 'strawberry'. When her three children come for dinner she picks three cartons at random. Calculate the probability that she picks
   (a) three 'orange' ones,
   (b) first a 'raspberry' one, then a 'strawberry' one, then a 'grapefruit' one,
   (c) one 'raspberry', one 'strawberry' and one 'grapefruit' in any order.   (C)

(5) Prove that the number of different ways in which r objects can be selected from a group of n is
$$\frac{n!}{r!(n-r)!}$$
A class contains 30 children, 18 girls and 12 boys. Four complimentary theatre tickets are distributed at random to the children in the class. What is the probability that
   (a) all four tickets go to girls,
   (b) two boys and two girls receive tickets?   (O)

(6) A pack of 52 cards contains four suits each of thirteen cards. If thirteen cards are taken at random from the pack what is the probability that exactly ten of them are spades?
$$\left(\text{You may take } \binom{52}{13} = 6.35 \times 10^{11}. \right)$$ (O & C)

(7) (a) From an ordinary pack of 52 cards two are dealt face downwards on a table. What is the probability that (i) the first card dealt is a heart, (ii) the second card dealt is a heart, (iii) both cards are hearts, (iv) at least one card is a heart?
   (b) Bag A contains three white counters and two black counters whilst bag B con-

tains two white and three black. One counter is removed from bag *A* and placed in bag *B* without its colour being seen. What is the probability that a counter removed from bag *B* will be white?

(c) A box of 24 eggs is known to contain four old and twenty new. If three eggs are picked at random determine the probability that (i) two are new and the other old, (ii) they are all new.   (SUJB)

(8) A well-shuffled pack of 52 playing cards is dealt out to four players, each receiving thirteen cards. Show that the probability that a particular player receives the four aces is 0.0026.

How many deals are necessary in order that the probability of a particular player receiving all four aces in at least one game exceeds 0.5?   (O)

(9) Sixteen soccer players, from a number of different clubs, form a squad from which the eleven players in the national team are selected.

(a) Find the number of different teams which could be selected from the squad irrespective of the positions in which the men play.

(b) Given that three of the squad are goalkeepers, and a team contains just one goalkeeper, find the number of different ways in which the team can now be selected.

(c) Just four players in the squad, none of whom is a goalkeeper, belong to a Liverpool club. A team is selected at random from the squad of three goalkeepers and thirteen other players. Calculate the probability that all of the four players from the Liverpool club are included in the team.   (L)

(10) Explain what is meant by the conditional probability of an event *A* given event *B*. A standard pack of 52 cards of four suits, each with thirteen denominations, is well-shuffled and dealt out to four players N, S, E and W, each receiving thirteen cards. If N and S have exactly ten cards of a specified suit between them, show that the probability that the three remaining cards of the suit are in one player's hand (either E or W) is 0.22.   (O)

Revision exercise A

(1) The quarterly rainfall in one part of the country over the last few years is given in Table A.1.
  (a) Illustrate this data by a graph.
  (b) On top of this graph, insert another graph showing the four-quarter moving average. *omit*
  (c) In what way(s) is this graph of more use than the first one?
  (d) Is it possible from the evidence shown to calculate estimates for the next two quarters, and, if so, what are they? Give brief reasoning for any answer you give.
  (SUJB)

Table A.1

	Jan.–Mar.	Apr.–June	July–Sept.	Oct.–Dec.
1972	12.4	11.5	15.3	15.1
1973	13.3	11.8	13.5	14.7
1974	12.7	11.3	13.6	16.4
1975	13.2	11.2		

(2) Pearson's formula for the 'skewness' of a distribution is
$$\text{skewness} = \frac{\text{mean} - \text{median}}{\text{standard deviation}}$$
omit

Estimate the skewness for the (grouped) distribution of Table A.2.
State briefly what feature is possessed by the histogram of any distribution which has a positive skewness.
  (C)

Table A.2

Value (centre of interval)	1	2	3	4	5	6	7
Frequency	2	5	8	15	26	33	11

(3) In an agricultural experiment the gains in mass, in kilograms, of 100 pigs during a certain period were recorded as in Table A3.
Construct a histogram and a relative cumulative frequency polygon of these data.

omit

91

Table A.3

Gain in mass (kilograms)	5–9	10–14	15–19	20–24	25–29	30–34
Frequency	2	29	37	16	14	2

Obtain
(a) the median and the semi-interquartile range,
(b) the mean and the standard deviation.
Which of these pairs of statistics do you consider more appropriate in this case, and why?   (AEB)

(4) (a) The independent events A and B occur with probability $\frac{1}{4}$ and $\frac{2}{3}$ respectively. Calculate the probability that
  (i) A and B both occur,
  (ii) A or B or both occur,
  (iii) A occurs and B does not occur.
(b) One pair of opposite faces of a cube is marked with a 1, another pair is marked with a 2 and of the other two faces one is marked with a 3 and the other with a 4. The cube is thrown as a die and is unbiased.
Using a tree diagram, or otherwise, calculate the probability that the sum of the scores is 5 if the die is thrown twice.   (L)

(5) The haemoglobin levels were measured in a sample of 50 people and the results were as in Table A.4, each being correct to one place of decimals.

Table A.4

13.5	15.6	16.3	12.3	13.1	14.2	12.4	11.3	14.0	14.6
13.6	14.8	12.7	10.9	11.0	11.4	15.0	10.1	15.4	11.3
10.7	14.6	13.5	15.1	12.1	12.0	14.2	11.4	15.0	13.3
13.2	9.1	16.9	14.2	15.0	13.6	14.8	11.4	14.8	15.7
13.5	13.5	12.9	13.8	13.7	16.2	11.6	13.8	14.2	10.7

(a) Group the data into eight classes, 9.0–9.9, 10.0–10.9, . . . , 16.0–16.9.
(b) What are the smallest and largest possible measurements which could be included in the class 9.0–9.9?
(c) Draw a cumulative frequency curve of the grouped data and use it to estimate the median value of the sample showing your working.
(d) Find the true median of the sample.   (SUJB)

(6) (a) State what you understand by the following:
   (i) the events A and B are independent,
   (ii) the events C and D are mutually exclusive,
   (iii) the events E, F and G are exhaustive.

   (b) In a certain parliamentary constituency, 30% of the electorate are under 25 years of age. Of those under 25, 45% support the Labour party, 35% support the Conservative party, whilst 20% support various minor parties. The corresponding figures for members of the electorate who are over 25 are 30%, 60% and 10%. Of the younger age group 60% vote, and of the older age group 50% vote, the proportion in each age group being the same for each party. Assuming any selection made to be random, find
   (i) the probability that a member of the electorate who is under 25 votes Conservative,
   (ii) the probability that a member of the electorate votes Conservative,
   (iii) the probability that a member of the electorate votes,
   (iv) the probability that a voter is either Labour or under 25, or both. (JMB)

(7) (a) Two dice are thrown together, and the scores added. What is the probability that (i) the total score exceeds 8, (ii) the total score is 9, or the individual scores differ by 1, or both?

   (b) A bag contains three red balls and four black ones. Three balls are picked out, one at a time and not replaced. What is the probability that there will be two red and one black in the sample?

   (c) A committee of four is to be chosen from six men and five women. One particular man and one particular woman refuse to serve if the other person is on the committee. How many different committees may be formed?   (SUJB)

(8) (a) In a quiz programme, there are five competitors, each of whom makes a random choice out of ten prizes, three of which are booby prizes. No two competitors can have the same prize. What is the probability (i) that none of the booby prizes is selected, (ii) that all three booby prizes are chosen?

   (b) Two poor marksmen, A and B, fight a duel. The probability that A will shoot B at any attempt is $\frac{1}{10}$, and the probability that B will shoot A at any attempt is $\frac{1}{8}$. A shoots first, and then B and A shoot alternately until one or the other is hit, or until A and B have fired six shots each. What is the probability that neither A nor B is shot?   (AEB)

(9) Define the mean, the median and the mode of a frequency distribution. Calculate the median of the frequency distribution given in Table A.5 and explain why you might prefer it to the mean as a measure of central tendency. Represent the distribution by a histogram, assuming the last class extends to £15000.   (O)

Table A.5 *Annual income of 184 employees in a factory*

Annual income (£)	Frequency
0–	9
500–	25
1000–	47
1500–	43
2000–	30
3000–	17
4000–	8
5000–	4
10000–	1
	184

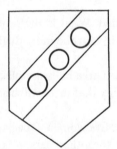

(10)   Three colours are available to Manbury City Football Club in order to colour their new badge, shown here. How many distinct coloured badges can they obtain if no internal boundary shall have the same colour on each side of it?
If one of these coloured badges is drawn at random from those available, what is the probability that the three circles will be coloured the same?   (AEB)

(11)   A tennis match usually consists of either three or five sets, and ends when one side has won a majority of the sets. If the probability of a side winning a set is p, and if the result of each set is independent of any previous results, show that the probability of a match going its full length is $2pq$ in the case of a three-set match and $6p^2q^2$ in the case of a five-set match ($q = 1 - p$).
Show that the first probability is always greater than the second, if $p \neq 0$ or 1.   (O)

(12)   A pack of eight cards consists of the four aces and the four kings from a pack of ordinary playing cards.
(a)   Two cards are dealt at random from this pack of eight cards.
   (i)   Given that at least one of the two cards dealt is an ace, calculate the probability that both cards are aces.

(ii) Given that one of the two cards dealt is the ace of spades, calculate the probability that the other card is an ace.

(b) Suppose now that the eight cards are shuffled and are then dealt one after the other.

   (i) Calculate the probability that the fifth card dealt will be the fourth ace dealt.

   (ii) Calculate the probability that the four aces will be dealt consecutively.

(W)

(13) Two players, A and B, engage in a contest with each other. The contest is won by the first player to win 25 games. No game can be drawn.

When the players have won the same numbers of games, each has a probability $\frac{1}{2}$ of winning the next game.

When A has won fewer games than B he becomes discouraged and has probability $\frac{2}{5}$ of winning the next game.

When B has won fewer games than A he has probability p of winning the next game.

(a) Find the probability that A will win the contest from the position where A has won 22 games and B has won 24 games.

(b) Find, to two significant figures, the value of p if, from the position when A has won 24 games and B has won 20 games, the probability of B winning is 0.25.

(c) Using this value of p calculate, for each player, his probability of winning from the position when each player has won 23 games. (JMB)

(14) Suppose that the values of a random sample taken from some population are $x_1, x_2, \ldots, x_n$. Prove the formula

$$\sum_{i=1}^{n} (x_i - \bar{x})^2 = \sum_{i=1}^{n} x_i^2 - n\bar{x}^2$$

Prior to the start of delicate wage negotiations in a large company, the unions and the management take independent samples of the work force and ask them at what percentage level they believe a settlement should be made. The results are in Table A.6. Assuming that no individual was consulted by both sides, calculate the mean and standard deviation for these 587 workers. (AEB)

Table A.6

Sample	Size	Mean	Standard deviation
'Management'	350	12.4%	2.1%
'Union'	237	10.7%	1.8%

6 Discrete probability distributions

6.1   Introduction

In a packet of ten balloons, three are defective. We can use the results of the previous chapter to find the probabilities that when three balloons, chosen at random, are blown up (a) none, (b) one, (c) two and (d) three of them are defective. We have

(a) $P(\text{none defective}) = \dfrac{\binom{3}{0}\binom{7}{3}}{\binom{10}{3}} = \dfrac{\dfrac{7\times6\times5}{1\times2\times3}}{\dfrac{10\times9\times8}{1\times2\times3}} = 0.292$

(b) $P(\text{one defective}) = \dfrac{\binom{3}{1}\binom{7}{2}}{\binom{10}{3}} = \dfrac{3\times\dfrac{7\times6}{1\times2}}{\dfrac{10\times9\times8}{1\times2\times3}} = 0.525$

(c) $P(\text{two defective}) = \dfrac{\binom{3}{2}\binom{7}{1}}{\binom{10}{3}} = \dfrac{\dfrac{3\times2}{1\times2}\times7}{\dfrac{10\times9\times8}{1\times2\times3}} = 0.175$

(d) $P(\text{three defective}) = \dfrac{\binom{3}{3}\binom{7}{0}}{\binom{10}{3}} = \dfrac{1\times1}{\dfrac{10\times9\times8}{1\times2\times3}} = 0.008$

These results can be summarised in a table which gives the probabilities of different numbers of defective balloons, and which is called a **probability distribution** (see Table 6.1). Since these events are mutually exclusive and exhaustive, the sum of their probabilities must be 1 (assuming that the values have not been rounded off in calculation).

6.1.1   *Exercise*

(1)   A packet of nasturtium seeds contains eight seeds which will give red flowers and ten which will give yellow flowers. If five seeds are planted in a window box, find the probability distribution for the number of plants with yellow flowers.

(2)   What is the probability that a hand of thirteen cards contains
(a) none, (b) one, (c) two, (d) three, (e) four aces?

96

Table 6.1 *Probability distribution for the number of defective balloons*

Number of defective balloons	Probability
0	0.292
1	0.525
2	0.175
3	0.008
	1.000

6.2   Discrete random variables

The 'number of defective balloons' in Section 6.1 is an example of a **discrete random variable**. The 'number of defective balloons' is variable since it can take different numerical values within a given range; it is random because we cannot predict the outcome of counting the number of defective balloons in a particular packet; it is discrete because it can take only certain values in a given range rather than all values in that range. 'The number of yellow flowers in a window box' and 'the number of aces in a hand of thirteen cards' in the questions of Exercise 6.1.1 are other examples of discrete random variables. The term 'variable' is usually used when we are concerned with *probabilities* as we are here. The term 'variate' would be used if we have, say, a consignment of packets of balloons and actually counted the number of balloons in each packet.

A convenient form of notation when discussing discrete random variables is to denote the variable by X and the probability that X takes the value x by $P(X=x)$. For example if X is 'the number of defective balloons' then $P(X=0)$ is 0.292, $P(X=1)=0.525$ etc. Similarly $P(X>1)=P(X=2)+P(X=3)=0.183$. We can also define a **probability function** $p(x)$ such that $p(x)$ is the probability that X takes the value x, i.e. $p(x)=P(X=x)$.

6.3   Expectation

A stall is run at a fête on the following lines: a turn involves taking three balls, without looking, from a bag containg three white and seventeen red balls. (The balls are returned to the bag after each turn.) If you pick all three white balls you win 50p; if your three balls include two white you win 25p; if they include one white you win 5p; otherwise you win nothing. We can make a table showing the probabilities of drawing three, two, one and no white balls and consequently the probability of winning 50p, 25p, 5p and 0p. These probabilities are shown in Table 6.2.

The cost of a turn will need to be set at a value such that the stall makes a profit. In order to do this we need to predict the mean winnings per turn in the long run. This quantity is called the **expectation** or **expected value** of the random variable X and is denoted by $E(X)$. Consider

Table 6.2 *Probability distribution for the amount won in pence, X*

Number of white balls	x	$P(X=x)$
3	50	$\binom{17}{0}\binom{3}{3} \div \binom{20}{3} = \dfrac{1}{1140}$
2	25	$\binom{17}{1}\binom{3}{2} \div \binom{20}{3} = \dfrac{51}{1140}$
1	5	$\binom{17}{2}\binom{3}{1} \div \binom{20}{3} = \dfrac{408}{1140}$
0	0	$\binom{17}{3}\binom{3}{0} \div \binom{20}{3} = \dfrac{680}{1140}$

first a limited number, n, of turns at the stall and suppose that the frequencies of winning 50, 25, 5 and 0 pence are f_1, f_2, f_3, f_4 respectively. Then we have

$$\text{mean winnings} = \frac{f_1 \times 50 + f_2 \times 25 + f_3 \times 5 + f_4 \times 0}{n}$$

$$= \frac{f_1}{n} \times 50 + \frac{f_2}{n} \times 25 + \frac{f_3}{n} \times 5 + \frac{f_4}{n} \times 0$$

Now consider what happens as the number of turns gets larger and larger. The ratios f_i/n tend towards the theoretical probabilities, giving in the limit as n tends to infinity

$$\text{mean winnings} = \frac{1}{1140} \times 50 + \frac{51}{1140} \times 25 + \frac{408}{1140} \times 5 + \frac{680}{1140} \times 0 = 2.95$$

This quantity, 2.95 pence, is the expectation of X. It does not represent the amount won at any one turn but is the mean of the infinite population of all possible turns at the game. As a *population* mean it is also denoted by μ in contrast to $\bar{x}$ which denotes a *sample* mean.

Generalising the result obtained above, the expectation of X is defined by

$$E(X) = \sum_{\text{all } x} xP(X=x) \tag{6.3.1}$$

The notation can be extended to define the expectation of any function of a random variable. For example the expectation of X^2 is given by

$$E(X^2) = \sum_{\text{all } x} x^2 P(X=x)$$

6.4   Expected variance

For the probability distribution in Section 6.3 we can also calculate the expected variance. From equation (3.8.2)

$$\text{variance} = \frac{\sum_{i=1}^{n} f_i(x_i - \bar{x})^2}{\sum_{i=1}^{n} f_i} = \frac{\sum_{i=1}^{n} f_i x_i^2}{\sum_{i=1}^{n} f_i} - \left(\frac{\sum_{i=1}^{n} f_i x_i}{\sum_{i=1}^{n} f_i} \right)^2$$

Replacing $\sum_{i=1}^{n} f_i$ by n,

$$\text{variance} = \sum_{i=1}^{n} \frac{f_i}{n}(x_i - \bar{x})^2 = \sum_{i=1}^{n} \frac{f_i}{n} x_i^2 - \left(\sum_{i=1}^{n} \frac{f_i}{n} x_i \right)^2$$

Using again the ideas developed in Section 6.3 we have f_i/n tending to the corresponding probability as n tends to infinity, and $\bar{x}$ tending to μ. This gives for the variance of the distribution, denoted by var (X) or σ^2,

$$\text{var } (X) = \sum_{\text{all } x} (x - \mu)^2 P(X = x)$$

$$= \sum_{\text{all } x} x^2 P(X = x) - \left\{ \sum_{\text{all } x} x P(X = x) \right\}^2 \qquad (6.4.1)$$

Equation (6.4.1) can be written in expected value notation as

$$\text{var } (X) = E\{(X - \mu)^2\}$$
$$= E(X^2) - \{E(X)\}^2 \qquad (6.4.2)$$

Table 6.3 shows the calculation of the expected value and expected variance for the probability distribution of Table 6.2.

Table 6.3 *Calculation of expected value and expected variance*

x	$P(X=x)$	$xP(X=x)$	$x^2 P(X=x)$
50	$\frac{1}{1140}$	0.0439	2.193
25	$\frac{51}{1140}$	1.1184	27.961
5	$\frac{408}{1140}$	1.7895	8.947
0	$\frac{680}{1140}$	0	0
	1	2.9518	39.101

$$\mu = E(X) = \sum_{\text{all } x} x P(X = x) = 2.9518p$$

$$\text{var } (X) = \sigma^2 = E(X^2) - \{E(X)\}^2$$

$$= \sum_{\text{all } x} x^2 P(X = x) - \left\{ \sum_{\text{all } x} x P(X = x) \right\}^2$$

$$= 39.101 - 2.9518^2$$
$$= 30.39p^2$$
$$\sigma = 5.51p$$

6.4.1   *Exercise*

Find the mean and variance of the random variables in Exercise 6.1.1.

6.5   Median of a discrete probability distribution

Consider first a limited number, n, of measurements of a discrete random variable, X, giving values x_1, x_2 etc. with frequencies f_1, f_2 etc. This is shown in Table 6.4 together with the cumulative frequencies.

Table 6.4 *Cumulative frequency table*

Value of X	Frequency	Cumulative frequency
x_1	f_1	f_1
x_2	f_2	$f_1 + f_2$
x_3	f_3	$f_1 + f_2 + f_3$
etc.	etc.	etc.

The median value, x_M, is such that the cumulative frequency is greater than or equal to $\frac{1}{2}n$, i.e.

$$\sum_{i=1}^{M} f_i \geqslant \tfrac{1}{2}n \tag{6.5.1}$$

and also the total frequency for classes M and above is greater than or equal to $\frac{1}{2}n$, i.e.

$$\sum_{i=M}^{N} f_i \geqslant \tfrac{1}{2}n \tag{6.5.2}$$

where there are N classes. Combining equations (6.5.1) and (6.5.2) gives

$$\sum_{i=1}^{M} f_i \geqslant \tfrac{1}{2}n \leqslant \sum_{i=M}^{N} f_i$$

and dividing by n gives

$$\sum_{i=1}^{M} \frac{f_i}{n} \geqslant \tfrac{1}{2} \leqslant \sum_{i=M}^{N} \frac{f_i}{n}$$

As n tends to infinity the cumulative relative frequencies can be replaced by cumulative probabilities to give the inequality

$$\sum_{i=1}^{M} p(x_i) \geqslant \tfrac{1}{2} \leqslant \sum_{i=M}^{N} p(x_i) \tag{6.5.3}$$

for the median value, x_M, of a discrete random variable. For the example in Table 6.1 taking

X as the number of defective balloons we obtain Table 6.5, showing that the median value of X is 1.

In the event of there being a value of M for which $\sum_{i=1}^{M} p(x_i)$ is *equal* to $\frac{1}{2}$, the inequality (6.5.3) is satisfied by both M and $M+1$. In this case the median is half way between x_M and x_{M+1}.

Table 6.5

k	x_i	$p(x_i)$	$\sum_{i=1}^{k} p(x_i)$	$\sum_{i=k}^{4} p(x_i)$
1	0	0.292	0.292	1.000
2	1	0.525	0.817	0.708
3	2	0.175	0.992	0.183
4	3	0.008	1.000	0.008

6.5.1 *Exercise*

A random variable X has probability function $p(0)=0.1, p(1)=0.3, p(2)=0.4, p(4)=0.2$. Find $E(X)$, var (X) and the median value of X.

6.6 Expected value and variance of a linear function of a random variable X

If we have a random variable X and know the values of $E(X)$ and var (X) then we can also calculate the expected value and variance of any linear function $aX+b$ of X. We have

$$E(aX+b)= \sum_{\text{all } x} (ax+b) P(X=x) \quad \text{(see Section 6.3)}$$

$$= \sum_{\text{all } x} axP(X=x)+ \sum_{\text{all } x} bP(X=x)$$

$$=a \sum_{\text{all } x} xP(X=x)+b \sum_{\text{all } x} P(X=x)$$

$$E(aX+b)=aE(X)+b \tag{6.6.1}$$

$$\text{var}(aX+b)= \sum_{\text{all } x} [(ax+b)-E(aX+b)]^2 P(X=x)$$

$$= \sum_{\text{all } x} [(ax+b)-(aE(X)+b)]^2 P(X=x) \quad \text{(from equation (6.6.1))}$$

$$= \sum_{\text{all } x} [ax-aE(X)]^2 P(X=x)$$

$$= a^2 \sum_{\text{all } x} [(x - E(X))]^2 P(X = x)$$

$$= a^2 \operatorname{var}(X) \qquad \text{(from equation (6.4.2))}$$

$$\operatorname{var}(aX + b) = a^2 \operatorname{var}(X) \qquad\qquad (6.6.2)$$

6.6.1　*Exercise*

A random variable X has $E(X) = 3$ and var $(X) = 4$. Find the expected value and variance of
(a) $-X$, (b) $X + 1$, (c) $2X - 3$.

Summary

For a discrete random variable X we can define a **probability function** $p(x)$ which gives the probability that X takes the value x, a probability denoted by $P(X = x)$.

The **expected value**, **expectation** or **mean** of X is given by

$$\mu = E(X) = \sum_{\text{all } x} x P(X = x)$$

The **variance** of X is given by

$$\sigma^2 = \operatorname{var}(X) = E(X^2) - [E(X)]^2 = \sum_{\text{all } x} x^2 P(X = x) - \left[\sum_{\text{all } x} x P(X = x) \right]^2$$

The **median**, x_M, is the value of X such that

$$\sum_{i=1}^{M} P(X = x_i) \geqslant \tfrac{1}{2} \leqslant \sum_{i=M}^{N} P(X = x_i)$$

If x_M and x_{M+1} both satisfy this inequality then the median lies half way between them.

Project

Comparing an observed frequency distribution with that predicted theoretically

The apparatus required is a box containing beads which are distinguishable only by their colour, e.g. five red and ten white. The box is shaken, a sample of five beads is taken without looking, the number of red beads counted and the sample returned to the box. This is done 100 times and a frequency table for the number of red beads in a sample is made. The observed frequencies can be compared with the predicted theoretical frequencies, which are calculated by multiplying the probabilities by the total frequency, i.e. 100.

Exercise on Chapter 6

(1)　A random variable R can take the values indicated in Table 6.6 with the given probabilities.

(a) Calculate the expected value and variance of R.

(b) Calculate the expected value and variance of R^2.

Table 6.6

r	0	1	2	3	4
$P(r)$	0.4	0.3	0.1	0.1	0.1

(2) A maths teacher pays her child's pocket money in the following way: she rolls a die and gives the child 10p for each spot on the uppermost face of the die. What is the expected value of the child's pocket money?

(3) A man buys eight tickets from a total of 2000 tickets in a raffle where there is just one prize of £50. The price of a ticket is 10p. Given that all the tickets are sold, calculate his expected loss. (L)

(4) A bag contains two red and eight black marbles. A sample of four marbles is to be drawn at random from the bag without replacement.

(a) Show that the probability of obtaining exactly two red marbles in the sample is $\frac{2}{15}$.

(b) Show that the probability of obtaining exactly one red marble in the sample is $\frac{8}{15}$.

(c) Calculate the expected number of red marbles that will be drawn. (L)

(5) Tomorrow I start three days' holiday and I wonder what weather is in store for me. I know that, if it is fine one day, the probability that it will be fine the next day is $\frac{4}{5}$, and if it is wet one day, the probability it is wet the next day is $\frac{3}{5}$. Today it is fine. Draw up the probability distribution for the number of fine days in the next three days. What is the expected number of fine days for my holiday?

Table 6.7

		B	
		Heads	Tails
A	Heads	3	x
	Tails	4	-6

(6) A and B play a game in which each tosses an unbiased coin. Table 6.7 shows the amount in pence that A receives from B for each possible outcome of the game. For example, if both players obtain heads, A receives 3 pence from B while if both

obtain tails A pays B 6 pence. Express A's expectation of gain in one game in terms of x and find the value of x which makes the game fair to both players.

Both players are now given coins which are twice as likely to give heads as tails. How much would A expect to gain in 45 games if x is now -2?   (C)

(7) The probability of a man A winning any game against a man B in a match is $\frac{1}{2}$. The first man to win two games in succession or a total of three games wins the match. Calculate the probability that the match takes exactly
(a) two games, (b) three games, (c) four games, (d) five games.
The winner is given £14 if he wins the match in two or three games and £18 if he wins the match in four or five games. If 100 spectators watch the match, how much should each be charged to cover the expected cost of prizes?   (C)

(8) In a marble game the challenger has two chances to hit her opponent's marble. If she hits it at the first attempt she wins two marbles. If she misses, she can make another attempt and if this is successful she wins one marble. If she misses at both attempts she pays her opponent two marbles. If p is the probability that the challenger hits a marble at a single throw, and p is constant, find the number of marbles she can expect to win in ten turns. What value must p take for this expected value to be zero?

(9) A player throws a die whose faces are numbered 1 to 6 inclusive. If the player obtains a 6 he throws the die a second time, and in this case his score is the sum of 6 and the second number: otherwise his score is the number obtained. The player has no more than two throws.
Let X be the random variable denoting the player's score. Write down the probability distribution of X, and determine the mean of X.   (C)

(10) A game of chance consists of rolling a disc of diameter 2 cm on a horizontal square board. The board is divided into 25 small squares of side 4 cm. A player wins a prize if, when a disc settles, it lies entirely within any one small square. There is a ridge round the outside edge of the board so that the disc always bounces back, cannot fall off and lies entirely within the boundary of the large square.

Prizes are awarded as follows:

centre (the middle square)	50p
inner (the eight squares surrounding the centre)	25p
corner (the four corner squares)	12p
outer (any other small square)	5p

When no skill is involved, the centre of the disc may be assumed to be randomly distributed over the accessible region. Calculate the probability in any one throw of (a) winning a prize of 50p, (b) winning a 12p prize, (c) not winning a prize.
The proprietor wishes to make a profit in the long run, but is anxious to charge as little as possible in order to attract customers. He charges C pence, where C is an integer. Find the lowest value of C which will yield a profit.

A skilful player finds that he can guarantee that a disc will always lie randomly within the boundary of the nine innermost squares. With the cost C of a throw as calculated above, calculate how much profit in the long run he can expect to make on each throw. (JMB)

(11)   An event has probability p of success and $q(=1-p)$ of failure. Independent trials are carried out until at least one success and one failure have occurred. Find the probability that r trials are necessary $(r \geqslant 2)$ and show that this probability equals $(\frac{1}{2})^{r-1}$ when $p=\frac{1}{2}$.
A couple decide that they will continue to have children until either they have both a boy and a girl in the family or they have four children. Assuming that boys and girls are equally likely to be born, what will be the expected size of their completed family?
(O)

(12)   Alan and his younger brother Bill play a game each day. Alan throws three darts at a dartboard and for each dart that scores a bull (which happens with probability p) Bill gives him a penny, while for each dart which misses the bull (which happens with probability $1-p$) Alan gives Bill twopence. By considering all possible outcomes for the three throws, or otherwise, find the distribution of the number of pence (positive or negative) that Bill receives each day. Show that, when $p=\frac{1}{3}$, the mean is 3 and the variance 6. (O)

(13)   In a gambling game between two players, the banker and his opponent, a fair die is thrown repeatedly. If a 6 is thrown in the first three throws the opponent wins that game, otherwise the banker does. If the opponent pays 10p per game and receives 20p each time he wins, show that his expected loss over twenty games is approximately $31\frac{1}{2}$p.
The banker and his opponent agree to a modification of the game so that throwing continues for five throws; the opponent wins as before if a 6 is thrown in the first three throws but if a 6 appears at the fourth or fifth throw the game is a draw and the stake money is added to the prize money for the next game. In the event of successive draws the stake money is carried forward cumulatively. Determine the opponent's expected gain or loss from the first two games, giving your result to two significant figures. (C)

7   The Binomial distribution

7.1   Introduction

On my way to work I have to pass through five sets of traffic lights which operate independently. The probability that I am stopped at a set of traffic lights is $\frac{2}{3}$. What is the probability distribution for the number of times I am stopped at traffic lights?

Let X be the number of times I am stopped and $P(X=x)$ the probability that I am stopped x times. Then to find the probability distribution of X we need to calculate $P(X=0)$, $P(X=1)$, etc. We can calculate $P(X=5)$ using the product law for independent events.

$$P(X=5) = \tfrac{2}{3} \times \tfrac{2}{3} \times \tfrac{2}{3} \times \tfrac{2}{3} \times \tfrac{2}{3} = 0.132$$

The calculation of $P(X=4)$ is more complicated. We know that the probability of not being stopped at a traffic light is $\frac{1}{3}$. Suppose I am stopped at the first four traffic lights and not the last. The probability of this is $(\tfrac{2}{3})^4(\tfrac{1}{3})$. However there are $\binom{5}{4}$ ways in which four out of the five lights can be at red so that

$$P(X=4) = \binom{5}{4}(\tfrac{2}{3})^4(\tfrac{1}{3}) = 0.329$$

Similarly

$$P(X=3) = \binom{5}{3}(\tfrac{2}{3})^3(\tfrac{1}{3})^2 = 0.329$$

$$P(X=2) = \binom{5}{2}(\tfrac{2}{3})^2(\tfrac{1}{3})^3 = 0.165$$

$$P(X=1) = \binom{5}{1}(\tfrac{2}{3})(\tfrac{1}{3})^4 = 0.041$$

$$P(X=0) = (\tfrac{1}{3})^5 = 0.004$$

(As we would expect $P(X=0)+P(X=1)+P(X=2)+P(X=3)+P(X=4)+P(X=5)=1$.)

Similar reasoning can be used to calculate the probability distribution in other situations, e.g. the number of heads obtained when six coins are tossed. Here the probability of obtaining a head at a single toss is $\frac{1}{2}$, and the probability of not obtaining a head is $\frac{1}{2}$; we wish to find the probabilities of no, one, two, three, four, five and six heads in a series of six trials. The probability distribution is given in Table 7.1.

Table 7.1 *Probability distribution for the number of heads obtained when six coins are tossed*

x	$P(X=x)$
0	$\binom{6}{0}(\frac{1}{2})^6 = \frac{1}{64}$
1	$\binom{6}{1}(\frac{1}{2})(\frac{1}{2})^5 = \frac{6}{64}$
2	$\binom{6}{2}(\frac{1}{2})^2(\frac{1}{2})^4 = \frac{15}{64}$
3	$\binom{6}{3}(\frac{1}{2})^3(\frac{1}{2})^3 = \frac{20}{64}$
4	$\binom{6}{4}(\frac{1}{2})^4(\frac{1}{2})^2 = \frac{15}{64}$
5	$\binom{6}{5}(\frac{1}{2})^5(\frac{1}{2}) = \frac{6}{64}$
6	$\binom{6}{6}(\frac{1}{2})^6 = \frac{1}{64}$
	$\overline{1}$

In general, if a single trial can have only two possible mutually exclusive and exhaustive results, either 'success' with probability p or 'failure' with probability $1-p(=q)$, then in a series of n trials, the probability of x successes is given by

$$p(x)=P(X=x)=\binom{n}{x}p^x(1-p)^{n-x}=\binom{n}{x}p^xq^{n-x} \tag{7.1.1}$$

$P(X=x)$ is the term in p^x of the binomial expansion of $(q+p)^n$ and so this distribution is called the **Binomial distribution**. It is applicable in many situations and gives the probability distribution of the discrete random variable X where X is the number of successes in n trials when the following criteria apply:

(i) a single trial has only two possible mutually exclusive and exhaustive results, 'success' and 'failure', with probabilities p and $1-p(=q)$;
(ii) the values of p and q remain constant throughout the trials;
(iii) the result of each trial is independent of previous trials;
(iv) the number of trials, n, is constant.

n and p are the parameters of the distribution, and a convenient short-hand for expressing the fact that X is Binomially distributed with these parameters is to write $X \sim B(n,p)$. For example, $X \sim B(5,0.5)$ means that X is a random variable which is Binomially distributed with $n=5$ and $P=0.5$.

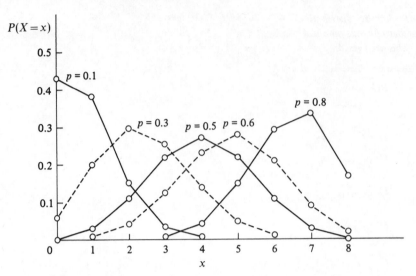

Figure 7.1 The Binomial distribution for various values of p when $n=8$

Figure 7.1 shows frequency polygons for the Binomial distribution for different values of p when $n=8$. Note that the distribution is symmetrical when $p=\frac{1}{2}$, otherwise it is skewed. Figure 7.2 shows the frequency polygon for $n=50$ and $p=0.1$. When n is large, as in this case, the distribution is approximately symmetrical even though $p\neq\frac{1}{2}$. It is important to realise that the situation given in Section 6.3 where three balls were selected from a bag of twenty (three white and seventeen red) *cannot* be treated by the Binomial distribution because, when one ball has been drawn, the probability of drawing a white (or red) ball has changed. The Binomial distribution *can* be applied to 'ball in bag' situations provided that either the sample size is small compared with the population from which the sample is drawn so that the probabilities effectively remain constant, or the balls are taken singly and each one is returned to the bag after its colour has been noted.

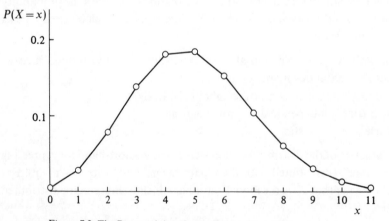

Figure 7.2. The Binomial distribution for $p=0.1$, $n=50$

A convenient method of calculating the probabilities for a Binomial distribution is by means of a **recurrence formula**. This gives $P(X = x + 1)$ in terms of $P(X = x)$. Since

$$P(X = x + 1) = \frac{n!}{(x+1)!(n-[x+1])!} p^{x+1}(1-p)^{n-(x+1)}$$

and

$$P(X = x) = \frac{n!}{x!(n-x)!} p^x (1-p)^{n-x}$$

we have, dividing the first expression by the second,

$$\frac{P(X = x + 1)}{P(X = x)} = \frac{n!}{(x+1)!(n-x-1)!} \times \frac{x!(n-x)!}{n!} \times \frac{p^{x+1}}{p^x} \times \frac{(1-p)^{n-(x+1)}}{(1-p)^{n-x}}$$

$$= \frac{n-x}{x+1} \times \frac{p}{(1-p)}$$

and rearranging

$$P(X = x + 1) = \frac{(n-x)}{(x+1)} \times \frac{p}{(1-p)} \times P(X = x) \qquad (7.1.2)$$

7.1.1 *Exercise*

(1) (a) Discuss whether the following variables will have a Binomial distribution and, if appropriate, give values for the parameters p and n.
  (i)   The number of heads when a fair coin is tossed five times.
  (ii) The number of tosses of a coin needed to get a head.
  (iii) The number of vowels in five-letter words selected at random from a dictionary.
  (iv) The number of odd digits in three-digit random numbers generated by a computer.
  (v)   The number of hearts in a five-card hand dealt from a well-shuffled pack of cards.

   (b) Find the probability distributions for the following.
  (i)   The number of heads when a fair coin is tossed five times.
  (ii) The number of 6s when four dice are rolled.

(2) A regular tetrahedron has one white face and three red faces. The tetrahedron is allowed to fall on a table in such a way that any face has the same chance of resting on the table. It is thrown four times in succession and the number of times a white face rests on the table is noted.
   (a) Find the probability distribution for X where X is the number of times a white face is in contact with the table.

    (b)   State which value of X is most likely to occur.

    (c)   Calculate the expected value of X.

    (d)   Calculate the variance of X.   (L)

(3)   Six children are born in a maternity ward on one day. If the probability of having a girl is 0.48 find the probability distribution for the number of girls. Calculate

    (a)   the most likely number of girls,

    (b)   the probability that the number of boys is the same as the number of girls,

    (c)   the probability that there are more boys than girls.

(4)   Calculate the probability that in a group of seven people

    (a)   none has his or her birthday on a Saturday,

    (b)   two or more have their birthdays on Saturday.

(5)   If there is a probability of 0.2 of failure to get through in any attempt to make a telephone call, calculate the most probable number of failures in ten attempts, and also the probability of three or more failures in ten attempts.   (C)

(6)   A hundred years ago the occupational disease in an industry was such that the workmen had a 20% chance of suffering from it.

    (a)   If six workmen were selected at random what is the probability that two or less of them contracted the disease?

    (b)   How many workmen could have been selected at random before the probability that at least one of them contracted the disease became greater than 0.9?   (C)

(7)   (a)   A fair die is cast; then n fair coins are tossed, where n is the number shown on the die. What is the probability of exactly two heads?

    (b)   A fair die is thrown for as long as necessary for a 6 to turn up. Given that 6 does not turn up at the first throw, what is the probability that more than four throws will be necessary?   (AEB)

(8)   The result of each turn at a fruit machine is independent of the results of previous turns and the probability of winning the jackpot at any one turn is 0.02.

    (a)   Find the probability that in a sequence of ten turns there will be

        (i)   one win of the jackpot,

        (ii)   more than one win of the jackpot.

    (b)   Write down the probability that in a sequence of n turns at the machine the jackpot will not be won. Hence find how many turns are necessary for there to be a probability of at least 0.99 of winning the jackpot at least once.

7.2   An example from industry

All manufacturing processes inevitably produce some defective items. It is usually too costly to check each item and sometimes impossible since a check would destroy the product (e.g. fireworks). Items are usually produced in batches, and a simple form of check is to test a few items from each batch and reject or accept the whole batch on the evidence of this small sample. This is known as a **single sampling scheme**. The sampling scheme can be improved by taking a second sample from a batch if the first sample showed defective item(s). This is known as a **two-stage sampling scheme**.

7.2.1 *Example*

A manufacturer produces light bulbs which are tested in the following way. A batch is accepted in either of the following cases:

(i) a first sample of five shows no faulty bulbs;

(ii) a first sample of five shows one or more faulty bulbs but a second sample of five shows no faulty bulbs.

What is the probability that a batch is accepted if

(a) 2%, (b) 10% of the bulbs in it are faulty?

We assume that the sample size is sufficiently small compared with the batch size to use the Binomial distribution.

(a) With $p=0.02$, $q=0.98$, $n=5$, we have for (i)

$$P(X=0)=(0.98)^5=0.904$$

This is the probability that the batch is accepted at the first test. The probability that it is not accepted at the first test is $1-0.904=0.096$. The probability that there are no defectives in the second sample is $(0.98)^5=0.904$ so that the probability a batch is accepted in case (ii) is $0.096\times0.904=0.087$.

The total probability that the batch is accepted for $p=0.02$ is $0.904+0.087=0.991$.

(b) Repeating the calculation with $p=0.1$, $q=0.9$, the probability that a batch is accepted is $(0.9)^5+(1-0.9^5)0.9^5=0.832$.

To analyse a sampling plan in more detail an **operating characteristic (OC) curve** can be plotted. This gives the probability, $L(p)$, of a batch being accepted for different values of p, the proportion of defectives. If all the items are defective, i.e. $p=1$, then the batch is bound to be rejected and $L(1)=0$. If all the items are perfect, i.e. $p=0$, the batch is bound to be accepted and $L(0)=1$. Figure 7.3 shows the OC curve for the sampling scheme described above for which the reader may verify that:

$$L(p)=2(1-p)^5-(1-p)^{10}$$

In practice the manufacturer and customer have to obtain a balance between two conflicting aims: the manufacturer's desire that he will not reject too many perfect bulbs, and the customer's wish that he is not supplied with too many faulty bulbs.

7.2.2 *Exercise*

(1) Large batches of similar components are delivered to a company. A sample of five articles is taken at random from each batch and tested to destruction. If at least four of the five articles are found to be good, the batch is accepted. Otherwise the batch is rejected.

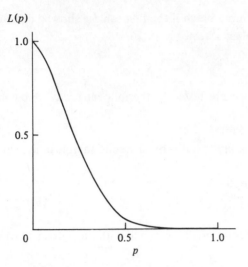

Figure 7.3. Operating characteristic curve for Example 7.2.1

If the fraction defective in the batch is p, show that the probability of accepting the batch is

$$A(p)=(1-p)^4(1+4p)$$

Draw a graph of $A(p)$ against p, for values of p from 0 to 1. From your graph estimate
(a)   the value of p for which $A(p)=0.95$,
(b)   the value of p for which $A(p)=0.05$.   (AEB)

(2)   Articles are turned off a production line in large batches and the probability of any article being faulty is p. An inspection scheme is used for each batch which requires a random sample of ten to be tested. If no faulty article is found the batch is accepted; if two or more are faulty the batch is rejected. If one is faulty a further sample of five is tested and the batch accepted only if none of these is faulty. Show that the probability of accepting a batch is $q^{10}(1+10q^4-10q^5)$ where $q=1-p$ and find the expected number sampled per batch, giving the answer in terms of q.   (SUJB)

(3)   Plastoy Ltd produce large batches of plastic miniature toys (currently submarines) for use as free gifts in cereal packets. A double sampling plan of inspection is adopted as follows. Select eight items from the batch and accept the batch if there are no defectives; reject the batch if there are three or more defectives; otherwise select another sample of eight items. When the second sample is drawn, count the number of defectives in the combined sample of sixteen and accept the batch if the number of defectives is two or less; otherwise reject the batch.
(a)   If the proportion of defectives in a batch is p, find in terms of p the probability that it will be accepted.
(b)   Sketch the operating characteristic (OC) curve. (The values of this curve should be clearly indicated for two values of p other than 0 and 1.)
(c)   If $p=0.2$, calculate the average sample size.   (AEB)

7.3   Mean and variance of a Binomial distribution

Five dice are tossed together N times (where N is a large number) and the number of 3s counted at each throw. What would we expect the mean number of 3s at each throw to be? We can consider the experiment in a different light as $5N$ single throws of a die. Since the probability of getting a 3 when a die is thrown is $\frac{1}{6}$, we would expect to get $5N \times \frac{1}{6}$ 3s altogether. Since these are shared over N throws of five dice, the average number of 3s at each throw of five will be

$$\frac{5N \times \frac{1}{6}}{N} = 5 \times \frac{1}{6}$$

i.e. the value of N is immaterial. This argument can be generalised to give the mean of a Binomial distribution as np:

$$\mu = np \tag{7.3.1}$$

where p is the probability of success at a single trial and n is the number of trials.

Equation (7.3.1) is proved mathematically in Section 7.4. (Another method, using moment generating functions, is given in Section 11.10 and another in question 12 of the Exercise on Chapter 10.)

It is also possible to show mathematically that the variance of a Binomial distribution is npq.

$$\text{variance} = \sigma^2 = npq = np(1-p) \tag{7.3.2}$$

(See Section 7.4.)

7.3.1   *Example*

Calculate the probability distribution for X, the number of 6s obtained when three dice are thrown. Calculate the mean and variance and check that the values obtained agree with the formulae above.

Table 7.2 *Calculation for Example 7.3.1*

x	$P(X=x)$		$xP(X=x)$	$x^2P(X=x)$
0	$\binom{3}{0}(\frac{5}{6})^3$	$=\frac{125}{216}$	0	0
1	$\binom{3}{1}(\frac{1}{6})(\frac{5}{6})^2 = \frac{75}{216}$		$\frac{75}{216}$	$\frac{75}{216}$
2	$\binom{3}{2}(\frac{1}{6})^2(\frac{5}{6}) = \frac{15}{216}$		$\frac{30}{216}$	$\frac{60}{216}$
3	$\binom{3}{3}(\frac{1}{6})^3$	$=\frac{1}{216}$	$\frac{3}{216}$	$\frac{9}{216}$
			$\frac{108}{216}$	$\frac{144}{216}$

$$\mu = E(X) = \sum_{\text{all } x} xP(X=x) = \tfrac{108}{216} = \tfrac{1}{2} \qquad \text{(see equation (6.3.1))}$$

$$E(X^2) = \sum_{\text{all } x} x^2 P(X=x) = \tfrac{144}{216} = \tfrac{2}{3}$$

$$\begin{aligned} \text{variance} &= E(X^2) - [E(X)]^2 \qquad \text{(see equation (6.4.2))} \\ &= \tfrac{2}{3} - (\tfrac{1}{2})^2 \\ &= \tfrac{5}{12} \end{aligned}$$

Using the formulae:

from equation (7.3.1), $\text{mean} = np = 3 \times \tfrac{1}{6} = \tfrac{1}{2}$

from equation (7.3.2), $\text{variance} = npq = 3 \times \tfrac{1}{6} \times \tfrac{5}{6} = \tfrac{5}{12}$

*7.4   Derivation of the mean and variance of a Binomial distribution

Using equation (6.3.1), the mean, μ, is

$$E(X) = \sum_{\text{all } x} xP(X=x)$$

$$= \sum_{x=0}^{n} x \frac{n!}{(n-x)! \, x!} p^x q^{n-x}$$

Writing out the series term by term,

$$\mu = 0 \times q^n + 1 \times npq^{n-1} + 2 \times \frac{n(n-1)}{2 \times 1} p^2 q^{n-2}$$

$$+ 3 \times \frac{n(n-1)(n-2)}{3 \times 2 \times 1} p^3 q^{n-3} + \ldots + n \times p^n$$

$$= npq^{n-1} + n(n-1)p^2 q^{n-2} + \frac{n(n-1)(n-2)}{2 \times 1} p^3 q^{n-3} + \ldots + n \times p^n$$

Taking out the factor np gives

$$\mu = np \left[q^{n-1} + (n-1)pq^{n-2} + \frac{(n-1)(n-2)}{2 \times 1} p^2 q^{n-3} + \ldots + p^{n-1} \right]$$

The square bracket contains the binomial expansion of $(p+q)^{n-1}$ and, since $p+q=1$, this is also 1. Hence

$$\mu = np$$

Using equation (6.4.2), the variance is

$$\sigma^2 = E(X^2) - [E(X)]^2$$

We have already found $E(X)$ so it remains to find $E(X^2)$. This is most easily done using the identity

$$E[X(X-1)] = E(X^2) - E(X)$$

which can be proved as follows:

$$E[X(X-1)] = \sum_{\text{all } x} x(x-1)P(X=x)$$

$$= \sum_{\text{all } x} (x^2-x)P(X=x)$$

$$= \sum_{\text{all } x} x^2 P(X=x) - \sum_{\text{all } x} xP(X=X)$$

$$= E(X^2) - E(X)$$

For the Binomial distribution

$$E[X(X-1)] = \sum_{x=0}^{n} x(x-1)\frac{n!}{(n-x)!\,x!}p^x q^{n-x}$$

Writing out the series term by term, omitting the first two terms since they are both zero,

$$E[X(X-1)] = 2 \times 1 \times \frac{n(n-1)}{2 \times 1}p^2 q^{n-2} + 3 \times 2 \times \frac{n(n-1)(n-2)}{3 \times 2 \times 1}p^3 q^{n-3}$$

$$+ 4 \times 3 \times \frac{n(n-1)(n-2)(n-3)}{4 \times 3 \times 2 \times 1}p^4 q^{n-4} + \ldots + n(n-1)p^n$$

$$= n(n-1)p^2 q^{n-2} + n(n-1)(n-2)p^3 q^{n-3} + \frac{n(n-1)(n-2)(n-3)}{2 \times 1}p^4 q^{n-4}$$

$$+ \ldots + n(n-1)p^n$$

Taking out the factor $n(n-1)p^2$ gives

$$E[X(X-1)] = n(n-1)p^2 \left[q^{n-2} + (n-2)pq^{n-3} + \frac{(n-2)(n-3)}{2 \times 1}p^2 q^{n-4} + \ldots + p^{n-2} \right]$$

Again the sum of the terms in the square bracket is 1, this time because they are the expansion of $(q+p)^{n-2}$. This gives

$$E[X(X-1)] = E(X^2) - E(X) = n(n-1)p^2$$

Rearranging,

$$E(X^2) = n(n-1)p^2 + E(X)$$

Since we have shown $E(X) = np$, we have

$$E(X^2) = n(n-1)p^2 + np$$

and

$$\begin{aligned}
\text{variance} &= E(X^2) - [E(X)]^2 \\
&= n(n-1)p^2 + np - (np)^2 \\
&= np - np^2 \\
&= np(1-p) \\
&= npq
\end{aligned}$$

7.5   Fitting a Binomial distribution to experimental data

Table 7.3 gives the frequency distribution of the number of girls in 100 families, each with four children. We can see how well this data can be modelled by the Binomial distribution by comparing the relative frequencies with the theoretical probabilities for a Binomial distribution with the same mean. The last column of Table 7.3 gives the relative frequencies (which are calculated by dividing the observed frequencies by the total frequency). To calculate the theoretical probabilities we require a value of p, the probability that a child is a girl. This is given by

$$p = \frac{\text{number of girls}}{\text{number of children}} = \frac{\sum_i f_i x_i}{n \sum_i f_i} = \frac{196}{4 \times 100} = 0.49$$

Table 7.3 *Frequency distribution for the number of girls in families with four children*

Number of girls, x_i	Number of families, f_i	$f_i x_i$	Relative frequencies
0	8	0	0.080
1	25	25	0.250
2	37	74	0.370
3	23	69	0.230
4	7	28	0.070
	100	196	1.000

Table 7.4 *Calculation of the theoretical probabilities and expected frequencies for the data in Table 7.3*

Number of girls	Theoretical probabilities		Expected frequencies
0	$100 \times \binom{4}{0}(0.51)^4$	$= 0.068$	6.8
1	$100 \times \binom{4}{1}(0.51)^3 \times (0.49)$	$= 0.260$	26.0
2	$100 \times \binom{4}{2}(0.51)^2 \times (0.49)^2$	$= 0.375$	37.5
3	$100 \times \binom{4}{3}(0.51) \times (0.49)^3$	$= 0.240$	24.0
4	$100 \times \binom{4}{4}(0.49)^4$	$= 0.058$	5.8
		1.001	100.1

The reader may wonder why we cannot assume that $p=\frac{1}{2}$. The reason is that it is well established that more boys are born than girls and so we have to use the data to find a value for p.

Table 7.4 shows the calculation of the theoretical probabilities and also the expected frequencies which are found by multiplying the theoretical probabilities by the total frequency. The totals are not 1 and 100 exactly because the values have been rounded off. It will be seen that there is fairly good agreement between the relative frequencies and the theoretical probabilities. If the variable can indeed be modelled by the Binomial distribution then we would expect these values to get closer together as more samples are taken. Correspondingly there is fairly good agreement between the observed and expected frequencies. Later in the book (Section 16.6) a method will be described for testing how good is the agreement between the observed and expected frequencies.

Summary

The Binomial probability distribution is a suitable model for the discrete random variable X, where X is the number of 'successes' in a series of trials, provided that

(i)   each trial has only two exhaustive and mutually exclusive outcomes, 'success' and 'failure';
(ii) the probability, p, of success is constant;
(iii) the trials are independent;
(iv) n, the number of trials, is constant.

$$P(X=x)=\binom{n}{x}p^x(1-p)^{n-x}$$

$$\text{mean}=\mu=E(X)=np$$
$$\text{variance}=\sigma^2=\text{var}(X)=np(1-p)=npq, \qquad \text{where } q=1-p$$

Recurrence formula

$$P(X=x+1)=\left(\frac{n-x}{x+1}\right)\left(\frac{p}{1-p}\right)P(X=x)$$

Projects

(1)   *Comparing observed frequencies with those predicted by the Binomial distribution*

Toss five dice together a minimum of 100 times counting at each throw:
(a)   the number of 6s;
(b)   the number of 2s and 3s and making a frequency table for each of these two variates.

Compare the observed frequencies in each case with those predicted by the Binomial distribution, taking $n=5$, $p=\frac{1}{6}$ for (a) and $n=5$, $p=\frac{1}{3}$ for (b).

Alternatively a comparison can be made between the theoretical probabilities and the relative frequencies.

If each member of a group of students obtains data then this can be combined to give a larger data set for which a closer agreement between theoretical probabilities and relative frequencies should be found.

(2)   *Advanced Level Statistics Software*

The *Binomial, Poisson, Normal* section illustrates the Binomial distribution graphically and allows up to three graphs to be superimposed. Some suggestions for practical work are:
(a)   investigating the shape of the distribution for different values of n and p;
(b)   comparing the agreement between observed and expected frequencies for experimental data (as in Section 7.5). The parameters can be varied to get the 'best fit';
(c)   simulating random sampling from a Binomial distribution and comparing the observed and expected frequencies.

Exercise on Chapter 7

(1)   The probability that a person chosen at random is left-handed is 0.1. What is the probability that in a group of ten people there is one, and only one, who is left-handed? What is the most likely number of left-handed people in a group of ten?

(2)   (a)   In a certain manufacturing process, it is known that approximately 10% of the items produced are defective. A quality control scheme is set up, by selecting twenty items out of a large batch, and rejecting the whole batch if three or more are defective. Find the probability that the batch is rejected.

(b)   Two boys, John and David, play a game with a die. The die will be thrown four times. David will give John £x if there is an odd number of 6s; otherwise John will give David £1.

If the game is to be a fair one to both John and David, find the value of x.
(SUJB)

(3)   The probability of a success in a single trial is p. Show that the probability of r successes in n independent trials is

$$\frac{n!p^r(1-p)^{n-r}}{r!(n-r)!}$$

One-third of the inhabitants of Monega have blood group P. Find the probability (as a fraction) that at least two people will have blood group P in a random sample of four Monegans. Would your answer be correct for a randomly chosen Monegan family of four people?
State briefly the reasons for your answer.
(O & C)

(4)   Items produced by a certain industrial process are checked by examining samples of ten. It is done 30 times. The data are given in Table 7.5.
Estimate what proportion of defective items there is in the complete consignment, on the basis of the Binomial distribution law.
(SUJB)

Table 7.5

Number defective in sample	0	1	2	3	4	5	6 or more
Number of times in 30 samples	13	11	4	1	1	0	0

(5) In a packet of flower seeds one-third are known to be pink flowering and the remainder are yellow flowering. The seeds are well-mixed and sown in 162 rows with 4 seeds in each row. Assuming that all the seeds germinate,

(a) calculate the expected mean and standard deviation of the number of pink flowering plants per row;

(b) copy and complete Table 7.6.

What is the most likely number of pink flowering plants in a row?   (C)

Table 7.6

Number of pink flowering plants per row	0	1	2	3	4
Expected number of rows					

(6) A shopkeeper found that 5% of the eggs received from a central distributing agency were stale on delivery, and reduced his prices by 5%. A housewife requiring ten fresh eggs was advised to purchase a dozen, the shopkeeper claiming that it was more likely than not that all the eggs in the dozen would be fresh, and furthermore that there was only a one in ten chance of two eggs in the dozen being stale.

Are the shopkeeper's claims valid?

What is the probability that, of the dozen eggs purchased,

(a) one egg is stale,

(b) not more than two eggs are stale?

If each customer accepted the shopkeeper's claims, and increased his or her egg order in the same ratio as the housewife, determine the net percentage change in the shopkeeper's daily receipts from egg sales.   (AEB)

(7) In an experiment a certain number of dice are thrown and the number of 6s obtained is recorded. The dice are all biased and the probability of obtaining a 6 with each individual die is p. In all there were 60 experiments and the results are shown in Table 7.7.

Calculate the mean and the standard deviation of these data.

By comparing these answers with those expected for a Binomial distribution, estimate

(a) the number of dice thrown in each experiment,

(b) the value of p.   (C)

Table 7.7

Number of 6s obtained in an experiment	0	1	2	3	4	More than 4
Frequency	19	26	12	2	1	0

(8) Give a clear and concise definition of the Binomial distribution suitable for readers who understand probability but have never heard of the Binomial distribution.
In some families the probability that a child will have red hair is $\frac{1}{4}$. If one of these families contains five children in all,
(a) find the probability that it will contain at least two children with red hair;
(b) assuming boys and girls are equally probable, find (i) the probability that there is no red-headed boy, (ii) the probability that there is no red-headed girl and (iii) the probability that there is no red-headed child. Hence, or otherwise, find the probability of at least one red-headed boy and at least one red-headed girl.
(O & C)

(9) Define the Binomial distribution, stating the conditions under which it will arise, and find its mean.
A manufacturer of glass marbles produces equal large numbers of red and blue marbles. These are thoroughly mixed together and then packed in packets of six marbles which are random samples from the mixture. Find the probability distribution of the number of red marbles in a packet purchased by a child.
Two boys, Fred and Tom, each buy a packet of marbles. Fred prefers the red ones and Tom prefers the blue ones, so they agree to exchange the marbles as far as possible, in order that at least one of them will have six of the colour he prefers. Find the probabilities that after exchange (a) they will both have the colour they prefer, (b) Fred will have three or more blue ones.
(JMB)

(10) Consider a young man waiting for his young lady who is late. To amuse himself while waiting, he decides to take a walk under the following set of rules. He tosses a fair coin. If the coin falls heads he walks 10 metres north; if the coin falls tails he walks 10 metres south. He repeats this process every 10 metres and thus executes what is called a 'random walk'. What is the probability that after walking 100 metres he will be
(a) back at his starting point,
(b) no more than 10 metres from his starting point,
(c) exactly 20 metres away from his starting point?
(AEB)

(11) A mother has found that 20% of the children who accept invitations to her children's birthday parties do not come. For a particular party she invites twelve children but

has available only ten party hats. What is the probability that there is not a hat for every child who comes to the party?

The mother knows that there is a probability of 0.1 that a child who comes to a party will refuse to wear a hat. If this is taken into account, what is the probability that the number of hats will not be adequate? (O)

(12) Derive the mean and variance of the Binomial distribution.

Mass production of miniature hearing aids is a particularly difficult process and so the quality of these products is monitored carefully. Samples of size six are selected regularly and tested for correct operation. The number of defectives in each sample is recorded. During one particular week 140 samples are taken and the distribution of the number of defectives per sample is given in Table 7.8

Table 7.8

Number of defectives per sample (x)	0	1	2	3	4	5	6
Number of samples with x defectives (f)	27	36	39	22	10	4	2

Find the frequencies of the number of defectives per sample given by a Binomial distribution having the same mean and total as the observed distribution. (AEB)

8   The Poisson distribution

8.1   The problem stated

Table 8.1 shows the frequency of 0, 1, 2, etc. telephone calls arriving at a small telephone exchange in 100 consecutive time intervals of five minutes. (The significance of the last column will become apparent later.)

What kind of distribution would we expect in this situation? We might be tempted to think that the Binomial distribution is applicable since the number of calls is a discrete variable. However, a little further thought reveals certain problems: although we know the number of calls in each time interval, how many 'non-calls' are there? In other words, what number corresponds to the Binomial parameter n and what meaning can we give to p, the probability of a 'success', in this case the occurrence of a telephone call? Leaving aside these problems for the moment, there *is* one statistic which we can calculate and this is the mean number of telephone calls, λ, for a five-minute time interval. From Table 8.1

$$\lambda = \frac{\sum_i f_i x_i}{\sum_i f_i} = \frac{37}{100} = 0.37$$

We can apply the Binomial distribution to this problem if we imagine the five-minute time interval divided into n small time intervals of δt, where n is so large that there can be no more than one telephone call arriving in δt. (This point is discussed further below.) It is now possible to give a meaning to the probability p of a call in time δt, corresponding to the probability of a 'success' in the Binomial distribution:

$$\text{probability of a call in } \delta t = \frac{\text{mean number of calls in five minutes}}{\text{number of } \delta t\text{'s in five minutes}}$$

$$= \frac{\lambda}{n}$$

This means that q, the probability of a 'non-call' or 'failure', is $1 - (\lambda/n)$ and the number of trials is n, the number of δt's in five minutes. Using the Binomial distribution (see equation (7.1.1)), the probability $P(X = x)$ of x calls in five minutes is given by

$$P(X = x) = \binom{n}{x}\left(\frac{\lambda}{n}\right)^x\left(1 - \frac{\lambda}{n}\right)^{n-x} \tag{8.1.1}$$

The value of δt, and consequently n, has still to be specified: the criterion for δt was that it should be so small that not more than one call should arrive in δt. In effect we require $\delta t \to 0$

122

Table 8.1 *Frequency distribution of phone calls arriving at an exchange*

Number of calls, x_i	Number of time intervals, f_i	$f_i x_i$
0	71	0
1	23	23
2	4	8
3	2	6
4 or more	0	0
	100	37

and hence $n \to \infty$, while the mean number of calls, λ, in a five-minute interval remains constant. It can be shown (see Appendix 2) that the limit of equation (8.1.1) is then

$$P(X=x) = \frac{\lambda^x e^{-\lambda}}{x!}$$

Using this expression we can calculate the probability distribution for the number of calls, taking λ equal to the observed mean (i.e. 0.37).

$$P(X=0) = e^{-0.37} = 0.691$$

$$P(X=1) = 0.37 e^{-0.37} = 0.256$$

$$P(X=2) = \frac{0.37^2 e^{-0.37}}{2!} = 0.047$$

$$P(X=3) = \frac{0.37^3 e^{-0.37}}{3!} = 0.006$$

(These values are given to three decimal places.)

$P(X \geqslant 4)$ is found by adding these probabilities and subtracting the total from 1, giving $P(X \geqslant 4) = 0.000$ (to three decimal places). The expected frequencies are found by multiplying these probabilities by the total frequency, i.e. 100. Table 8.2 compares the expected and observed frequencies and it will be seen that reasonable agreement is obtained.

Table 8.2 *Comparison of observed and expected Poisson frequencies for the data in Table 8.1*

Number of calls	Observed frequency	Expected frequency
0	71	69.1
1	23	25.6
2	4	4.7
3	2	0.6
$\geqslant 4$	0	0

8.2   The Poisson distribution

The discrete distribution which we have obtained is called the **Poisson distribution**. It gives the probability of x events occurring in a given interval as

$$p(x) = P(X = x) = \frac{\lambda^x e^{-x}}{x!} \tag{8.2.1}$$

where the mean number of events in the same interval is λ. Besides being applicable to events randomly distributed in time such as telephone calls, it is also applicable to events randomly distributed in space, for example the number of flaws in a given length of rope. For it to be applicable the following conditions must be satisfied:

   (i)   two or more events cannot occur simultaneously;
 (ii)   the events are independent;
(iii)   the mean number of events in a given interval is constant.

   λ is the parameter of the distribution. A convenient short-hand for denoting that the random variable X is Poisson distributed with mean λ is $X \sim Po(\lambda)$.

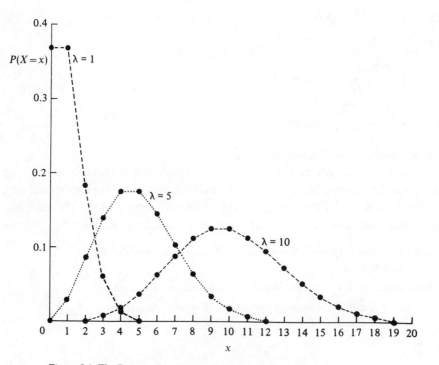

Figure 8.1 The Poisson distribution for various values of λ

   Figure 8.1 shows the Poisson distribution for different values of λ. Note that as λ increases the distribution becomes more symmetrical.

8.2.1   *Example*

The number of cars per minute passing a certain point on a road is Poisson distributed with mean 4. Find
(a) the probability that 4 cars pass in a minute,
(b) the probability that 8 cars pass in two minutes.

(a) The mean number of cars in a minute is 4 so

$$P(X=4)=\frac{4^4e^{-4}}{4!}=0.195$$

(b) The mean number of cars in two minutes is 8 so

$$P(X=8)=\frac{8^8e^{-8}}{8!}=0.140$$

As for the Binomial distribution a recurrence formula can be used to calculate $P(X=x+1)$ from $P(X=x)$ since

$$\frac{P(X=x+1)}{P(X=x)}=\frac{\lambda^{x+1}e^{-\lambda}/(x+1)!}{\lambda^x e^{-\lambda}/x!}$$

which on cancelling and rearranging gives

$$P(X=x+1)=\frac{\lambda}{(x+1)}P(X=x) \qquad\qquad (8.2.2)$$

8.2.2   *Exercise*

(1) The mean number of particles emitted per second by a radioactive source is 3. Calculate the probabilities of 0, 1, 2, 3, 4, 5 and 6 emissions per second. What is the probability that at least one particle is emitted in a second?

(2) The number of demands for taxis to a taxi firm is Poisson distributed with a mean of four demands in 30 minutes. Find the probabilities of
(a) no call in 30 minutes,
(b) one call in 30 minutes,
(c) one call in 1 hour,
(d) two calls in 1 hour.

Table 8.3

Number of vehicles in the period	0	1	2	3	4	5	6	7
Frequency	252	306	235	137	42	24	3	1

(3) The average number of faults in a metre of cloth produced by a particular machine is 0.1. What is the probability that a length of 4 m is free from faults? How long would a piece have to be before the probability that it contains no flaws is less than 0.95?

(4) In checking the proofs of a book for publication it is found that the probability that there are no errors on a page is 0.05. Estimate the mean number of errors per page to the nearest whole number.

   If the book contains 300 pages, estimate the number of pages on which you would expect to find fewer than four errors.   (C)

(5) In a traffic survey a count was made of the number of vehicles passing the survey point in each period of 15 seconds. The survey continued for 1000 such periods, and the results were as in Table 8.3.

   Calculate the mean number of vehicles per period and the theoretical Poisson frequencies with this mean.   (C)

(6) Gnat larvae are distributed at random in pond water so that the number of larvae contained in a random sample of 10 cm^3 of pond water may be regarded as a random variable having a Poisson distribution with mean 0.2. Ten independent random samples, each of 10 cm^3, of pond water, are taken by a zoologist.

   Determine (correct to three significant figures)
   (a) the probability that none of the samples contain larvae,
   (b) the probability that one sample contains a single larva and the remainder contain no larvae,
   (c) the probability that one sample contains two or more larvae and the remainder contain no larvae,
   (d) the expectation of the total number of larvae contained in the ten samples,
   (e) the expectation of the number of samples containing no larvae.   (C)

8.3   The mean and variance of a Poisson distribution

These can be deduced from the mean and variance of the Binomial distribution in the limit when $n \to \infty$, $p \to 0$ but $np = \lambda$ remains constant. For a Binomial distribution $\mu = np$. Therefore for a Poisson distribution

$$\mu = \lambda \tag{8.3.1}$$

   For a Binomial distribution $\sigma^2 = npq$. As $n \to \infty$, $p \to 0$ and $q \to 1$. Writing $np = \lambda$ and $q = 1$, gives

$$\sigma^2 = \lambda \tag{8.3.2}$$

(A rigorous proof of these results is given in Section 8.4.) We thus find an important property of the Poisson distribution which is that its mean is equal to its variance. This gives a simple test of whether or not a distribution is approximately Poissonian.

Table 8.4 extends Table 8.1 and shows the calculation of the mean and variance for the number of calls in a five-minute time interval. In this case the mean is approximately equal to the variance thus indicating that the distribution is approximately Poissonian.

Table 8.4 *Calculation of mean and variance for data in Table 8.1*

Number of calls x_i	Frequency f_i	$f_i x_i$	$f_i x_i^2$
0	71	0	0
1	23	23	23
2	4	8	16
3	2	6	18
$\geqslant 4$	0	0	0
	100	37	57

$$\text{mean} = \frac{\sum_i f_i x_i}{\sum_i f_i} = \frac{37}{100} = 0.37$$

$$\text{variance} = \frac{\sum_i f_i x_i^2}{\sum_i f_i} - \left(\frac{\sum_i f_i x_i}{\sum_i f_i}\right)^2$$

$$= \frac{57}{100} - 0.37^2$$
$$= 0.43$$

8.3.1 *Exercise*

Calculate $P(X=0)$, $P(X=1)$, $P(X=2)$, $P(X=3)$, $P(X=4)$, $P(X=5)$, $P(X\geqslant 6)$ for a Poisson variable with mean 1.2. Using this probability distribution calculate the mean and variance and confirm that they are equal to each other within 0.01. (There is a slight discrepancy since values of $P(X=x)$ for $x\geqslant 6$ have grouped together.)

*8.4 Proof that the mean and variance of a Poisson distribution are λ

We have, for a Poisson distribution,

$$P(X=x) = \frac{\lambda^x e^{-\lambda}}{x!}$$

$$\text{mean} = E(X)$$

$$= \sum_{x=0}^{\infty} x P(X=x)$$

$$= \sum_{x=0}^{\infty} \frac{x \lambda^x e^{-\lambda}}{x!}$$

$$= \frac{0 \times \lambda^0 e^{-\lambda}}{0!} + \frac{1 \times \lambda e^{-\lambda}}{1!} + \frac{2 \times \lambda^2 e^{-\lambda}}{2!} + \frac{3 \times \lambda^3 e^{-\lambda}}{3!} + \cdots + \frac{(x+1)\lambda^{x+1}e^{-\lambda}}{(x+1)!} + \cdots$$

$$= 0 + \lambda e^{-\lambda} + \frac{\lambda^2 e^{-\lambda}}{1!} + \frac{\lambda^3 e^{-\lambda}}{2!} + \cdots + \frac{\lambda^{x+1}e^{-\lambda}}{x!} + \cdots$$

$$= \lambda \left[e^{-\lambda} + \frac{\lambda e^{-\lambda}}{1!} + \frac{\lambda^2 e^{-\lambda}}{2!} + \cdots + \frac{\lambda^x e^{-\lambda}}{x!} + \cdots \right]$$

The terms in the bracket are those of the Poisson distribution. Their sum is therefore 1, since they are the probabilities of mutually exclusive and exhaustive events. Therefore,

$$\text{mean} = \lambda \qquad (8.4.1)$$

Turning to the variance we require $E\{(X-\mu)^2\}$.

$$E\{(X-\mu)^2\} = \sum_{x=0}^{\infty} (x-\lambda)^2 \frac{\lambda^x e^{-\lambda}}{x!}$$

$$= \sum_{x=0}^{\infty} [x(x-1) + x(1-2\lambda) + \lambda^2] \frac{\lambda^x e^{-\lambda}}{x!}$$

(The term in the square bracket has been written in this way so that the first term cancels with the first two terms of $x!$)

$$\text{variance} = E\{(X-\mu)^2\}$$

$$= \sum_{x=0}^{\infty} x(x-1) \frac{\lambda^x e^{-\lambda}}{x!} + (1-2\lambda) \sum_{x=0}^{\infty} \frac{x\lambda^x e^{-\lambda}}{x!} + \lambda^2 \sum_{x=0}^{\infty} \frac{\lambda^x e^{-\lambda}}{x!} \qquad (8.4.2)$$

The second summation is $E(X)$ which we have already found to be λ and the third sum is $\sum_{x=0}^{\infty} P(X=x)$ which is 1. The first two terms of the first sum are both zero, so expanding we have:

$$\sum_{x=0}^{\infty} x(x-1) \frac{\lambda^x e^{-\lambda}}{x!} = \frac{2 \times 1 \times \lambda^2 e^{-\lambda}}{2!} + \frac{3 \times 2\lambda^3 e^{-\lambda}}{3!} + \frac{4 \times 3\lambda^4 e^{-\lambda}}{4!} + \cdots + \frac{(x+2)(x+1)\lambda^{x+2}e^{-\lambda}}{(x+2)!} + \cdots$$

$$= \lambda^2 e^{-\lambda} + \lambda^3 e^{-\lambda} + \frac{\lambda^4 e^{-\lambda}}{2!} + \cdots + \frac{\lambda^{x+2}e^{-\lambda}}{x!} + \cdots$$

$$= \lambda^2 \left[e^{-\lambda} + \lambda e^{-\lambda} + \frac{\lambda^2 e^{-\lambda}}{2!} + \cdots + \frac{\lambda^x e^{-\lambda}}{x!} + \cdots \right]$$

$$= \lambda^2$$

since again the terms in the bracket have the sum 1. Substituting for the three summations in equation (8.4.2) we have

$$\text{variance} = E\{(X-\mu)^2\}$$
$$= \lambda^2 + (1-2\lambda)\lambda + \lambda^2$$
$$= \lambda^2 + \lambda - 2\lambda^2 + \lambda^2$$
$$= \lambda$$

An alternative proof using a moment generating function is given in Section 11.11.

8.5   Applications of the Poisson distribution

The Poisson distribution is used in biological research for counting the number of cells of a particular type in a dilute solution. The well-shaken solution is placed on a slide which is divided into squares and viewed through a microscope. The number of cells in each of the squares is counted, and from the mean, the number of cells per unit volume can be estimated. Agreement of the observed frequencies with a Poisson distribution with the same mean is used to test that the cells are distributed randomly through the solution.

Alternatively, if it is known that the cells are randomly distributed, a quick method is available for estimating the total number of cells present as is shown in the following example.

8.5.1   *Example*

In the situation described above it was found that 22 out of the 500 squares on the slide contained no cells. Estimate the total number of cells on the microscope slide.

The relative frequency for the number of squares containing no cells is $\frac{22}{500}$. Equating this with $P(X=0)$ gives

$$\frac{22}{500}=e^{-\lambda}$$

where λ is the mean number of cells per square. Taking logarithms to the base e

$$-\lambda=\ln\left(\frac{22}{500}\right)=-3.124$$

An estimate of the total number of cells present is given by the mean number of cells per square multiplied by the number of squares, i.e. $3.124 \times 500 = 1562$.

The example above is one in which the events are distributed in space. Examples in which the events are distributed in time are traffic control, radioactive emission and telephone calls arriving at a switchboard.

8.5.2   *Example*

An ambulance station receives on average one emergency call every hour. If there are three ambulances available and the average time for which an ambulance is out on a call is half an hour, what is the probability that the ambulance station cannot cover the emergency calls?

If the ambulance station receives three or less emergency calls in half an hour, then it *can* deal with incoming calls. The mean number of calls in half an hour is $\frac{1}{2}$. The probability that the ambulance station can cope with incoming calls is equal to

$$P(X=0)+P(X=1)+P(X=2)+P(X=3)=e^{-0.5}+0.5e^{-0.5}+\frac{0.5^2}{2!}e^{-0.5}+\frac{0.5^3}{3!}e^{-0.5}$$

$$=0.998$$

The probability that the ambulance station cannot cope is equal to $1 - 0.998 = 0.002$.

(This problem oversimplifies what happens in practice since the mean number of emergency calls in a given time interval will vary during the day.)

8.6   The Poisson distribution as an approximation to the Binomial distribution

8.6.1   *Example*

In a large consignment of apples, 3% are rotten. What is the probability that a carton of 48 apples will contain less than two rotten ones?

The number of rotten apples in a carton follows a Binomial distribution since an apple is either rotten, probability $p = 0.03$, or not rotten, probability $q = 0.97$, and $n(=48)$ is constant. The required probability is

$$P(X = 0) + P(X = 1) = (0.97)^{48} + \binom{48}{1}(0.97)^{47}(0.03)$$

$$= 0.5758$$

Without a calculator this calculation is tedious. It can be simplified using the Poisson distribution. Since this was derived from the Binomial distribution when $n \to \infty$, $p \to 0$, it gives a good approximation to the Binomial distribution for large n and small p. Applying it to the example above we have

$$\lambda = np = 48 \times 0.03 = 1.44$$
$$P(X = 0) + P(X = 1) = e^{-1.44} + 1.44e^{-1.44} = 0.5781$$

which is a reasonable approximation to the value obtained before.

A convenient working rule for using this approximation is that we have $n \geqslant 50$ and $p \leqslant 0.1$.

8.6.2   *Exercise*

(1)   The probability that a brand of light bulb is faulty is 0.01. The light bulbs are packed in boxes of 100. What is the probability that a box chosen at random contains (a) no faulty light bulbs, (b) two faulty light bulbs, (c) at least four faulty light bulbs?

A buyer accepts a consignment of 50 boxes provided that when two boxes are chosen at random they contain at most two faulty light bulbs altogether. What is the probability that a consignment is accepted?

(2)   A large number of screwdrivers from a trial production run is inspected. It is found that the cellulose acetate handles are defective on 1% and that the chrome steel blades are defective on $1\frac{1}{2}\%$ of the screwdrivers, the defects occurring independently.

(a)   What is the probability that a sample of 80 contains no screwdrivers with defective handles?

(b)   What is the probability that a sample of 80 contains more than two defective screwdrivers?

(c) What is the probability that a sample of 80 contains at least one screwdriver with
both a defective handle and a defective blade?   (O & C)

*8.7   Queuing theory

Queues can arise in many situations, for example customers arriving at a shop, telephone
calls arriving at an exchange, cars waiting to be repaired in a garage, etc. We will consider
the situation in which the probability that a person joins the queue in time δt is $\lambda \delta t$ and
the probability that the person at the head of the queue leaves in time δt is $\mu \delta t$. Let $P_0(t)$,
$P_1(t)$, etc. denote the probabilities of there being no, one, etc. customers in the queue at time
t.

Then

$$P_0(t+\delta t) = P_0(t) \times \text{probability of no arrival in } \delta t$$
$$+ P_1(t) \times \text{probability of one departure in } \delta t$$

The probability of a departure in δt is $\mu \delta t$. (δt is assumed to be sufficiently small so that
only one departure is possible.) The probability of an arrival is $\lambda \delta t$ so that the probability
of no arrival is $(1 - \lambda \delta t)$.

Substituting these probabilities:

$$P_0(t+\delta t) = P_0(t)(1 - \lambda \delta t) + P_1(t)\mu \delta t$$

Rearranging

$$\frac{P_0(t+\delta t) - P_0(t)}{\delta t} = \mu P_1(t) - \lambda P_0(t)$$

As $\delta t \to 0$, the left-hand side of this equation becomes, by definition, $\dfrac{dP_0(t)}{dt}$, giving

$$\frac{dP_0(t)}{dt} = \mu P_1(t) - \lambda P_0(t) \tag{8.7.1}$$

Similarly

$$P_x(t+\delta t) = P_x(t) \times \text{probability of no arrivals or departures in } \delta t$$
$$P_{x+1}(t) \times \text{probability of one departure in } \delta t$$
$$+ P_{x-1}(t) \times \text{probability of one arrival in } \delta t$$

This gives

$$P_x(t+\delta t) = P_x(t)(1 - \lambda \delta t)(1 - \mu \delta t) + P_{x+1}(t)\mu \delta t + P_{x-1}(t)\lambda \delta t$$
$$= P_x(t)[1 - \lambda \delta t - \mu \delta t + \lambda \mu (\delta t)^2] + P_{x+1}(t)\mu \delta t + P_{x-1}(t)\lambda \delta t$$

Rearranging

$$\frac{P_x(t+\delta t) - P_x(t)}{\delta t} = -(\lambda + \mu - \lambda \mu \delta t)P(t) + \mu P_{x+1}(t) + \lambda P_{x-1}(t)$$

and as $\delta t \to 0$,

$$\frac{dP_x(t)}{dt} = -(\lambda + \mu)P_x(t) + \mu P_{x+1}(t) + \lambda P_{x-1}(t)$$

It can be shown that, for $\mu > \lambda$, the values of $P_0(t)$, $P_1(t)$, etc. tend to particular values as $t \to \infty$, i.e. a steady state is reached. Then $\dfrac{dP_x(t)}{dt} = 0$ for all values of x and equations (8.7.1) and (8.7.2) become

$$\mu P_1 = \lambda P_0 \tag{8.7.3}$$

and

$$\lambda(P_x - P_{x-1}) = \mu(P_{x+1} - P_x) \tag{8.7.4}$$

(where P_0, P_1, etc. denote the steady state values).

We can use these equations to find P_0, P_1, P_2, etc. since writing equation (8.7.4) for descending values of x we have

$$\lambda(P_x - P_{x-1}) \quad = \mu(P_{x+1} - P_x)$$
$$\lambda(P_{x-1} - P_{x-2}) = \mu(P_x - P_{x-1})$$
$$\vdots \qquad \text{etc.} \qquad \vdots$$
$$\lambda(P_1 - P_0) \quad = \mu(P_2 - P_1)$$
$$\lambda P_0 \qquad \quad = \mu P_1$$

When these equations are added most terms cancel out, giving

$$\lambda P_x = \mu P_{x+1}$$

or

$$\frac{P_{x+1}}{P_x} = \frac{\lambda}{\mu}$$

Thus the successive probabilities form a geometric progression and we have

$$P_1 = \frac{\lambda}{\mu} P_0, \qquad P_2 = \left(\frac{\lambda}{\mu}\right)^2 P_0, \qquad \text{etc.}$$

and in general

$$P_x = \left(\frac{\lambda}{\mu}\right)^x P_0$$

We can find P_0 since we know the sum of all the probabilities must be 1, giving

$$P_0\left(1 + \frac{\lambda}{\mu} + \left(\frac{\lambda}{\mu}\right)^2 + \cdots\right) = 1$$

$$\frac{P_0}{1 - \lambda/\mu} = 1$$

$$P_0 = 1 - \frac{\lambda}{\mu}$$

Therefore

$$P_x = \left(1 - \frac{\lambda}{\mu}\right)\left(\frac{\lambda}{\mu}\right)^x \tag{8.7.5}$$

The average queue length is given by

$$E(X)= \sum_{x=0}^{\infty} x\left(1-\frac{\lambda}{\mu}\right)\left(\frac{\lambda}{\mu}\right)^{x}$$

$$=\frac{\lambda}{\mu}\left(1-\frac{\lambda}{\mu}\right)\sum_{x=0}^{\infty} x\left(\frac{\lambda}{\mu}\right)^{x-1}$$

$$=\frac{\lambda}{\mu}\left(1-\frac{\lambda}{\mu}\right)\left[1+2\left(\frac{\lambda}{\mu}\right)+3\left(\frac{\lambda}{\mu}\right)^{2}+\cdots\right]$$

$$=\frac{\lambda}{\mu}\left(1-\frac{\lambda}{\mu}\right)\frac{1}{(1-\lambda/\mu)^{2}}$$

$$=\frac{\lambda}{\mu-\lambda}$$

If $\lambda>\mu$ no steady state is reached and the queue length will increase indefinitely.

8.7.1 Exercise

(1) Customers arrive at a shop with probability $\lambda\delta t$ (λ constant) of a customer arriving in any small time interval δt and form a queue. The probability that the customer at the head of the queue departs in any small time interval δt is $\mu\delta t$ (μ constant and $\mu>\lambda$). When the queue has reached a steady rate the probability that there are n customers in the queue, including the one being served, is p_n which is independent of t. Show that
$$(\lambda+\mu)p_n=\lambda p_{n-1}+\mu p_{n+1}(n\geqslant 1) \quad \text{and} \quad \lambda p_0=\mu p_1$$
Show that $\mu p_n=\lambda p_{n-1}$ and obtain the values of p_0 and p_1 in terms of λ and μ. Find the probability that the queue contains five or more customers. (C)

(2) A mechanic is responsible for a group of four machines. The probability that a machine in operation breaks down in a small interval of time of length δt is $\lambda\delta t$ (λ constant) and the probability that a machine being serviced is returned to use is $10\lambda\delta t$. The mechanic can work on only one machine at a time.
If p_n is the probability that there are n machines being serviced (including those awaiting servicing) when the system has reached its steady state (i.e. p_n independent of t), prove that $p_1=\frac{2}{5}p_0$.
Obtain equations connecting (a) p_0, p_1, p_2, (b) p_1, p_2, p_3, (c) p_2, p_3, p_4.
Hence obtain the probability that at any instant the mechanic is not working on a machine. (C)

Summary

The Poisson probability distribution is a suitable model for the random variable X, where X is the number of events in a particular interval of time or space, provided that
(i) the events occur independently and at random;
(ii) two or more events cannot occur simultaneously;

(iii)   the mean number of events, λ, in the specified interval is constant.

$$\text{mean} = \lambda \qquad \text{variance} = \lambda$$

The Poisson distribution with mean np can be used as an approximation to the Binomial distribution with parameters n and p provided that n is large and p is small (in practice $n > 50$, $p < 0.1$).

Projects

(1)   *To investigate if the number of cars passing in a given time interval follows a Poisson distribution*

This project should be carried out on a busy road, if it is not to be too lengthy, but not at the time of day when there are traffic jams. Note the number of cars passing in a given time interval for 100 consecutive intervals. The time interval should be chosen so that on average about four cars pass in it. Make a frequency table with the number of cars as the variate. From this calculate the mean and variance. For a Poisson distribution they should be approximately equal.

(2)   *Advanced Level Statistics Software*

The *Binomial, Poisson, Normal* section includes a simulation of a variable which is Poisson distributed. Points are plotted at random on a square mesh and the variable is the number of points in a square of the mesh (see Section 8.5). The relative frequency distribution can be compared graphically with the theoretical distribution with the same mean. Experimental data obtained by the user can also be compared with the corresponding theoretical distribution.

The shape of the Poisson distribution for different values of λ can be investigated and also the extent of the agreement between the Poisson and Binomial distributions when n is large and p is small can be displayed graphically.

The *Queuing* section simulates many situations in which queues form, such as a supermarket checkout, a doctor's surgery or a ticket office. The program allows the user to investigate 'experimentally' the situation described in Section 8.7 and to obtain experimental evidence for the results derived there. More complicated situations involving several queues can also be investigated and various queuing strategies compared.

Exercise on Chapter 8

(1) X is a random variable having a Poisson distribution given by

$$f(x) = \frac{e^{-m} m^x}{x!} \qquad x = 0, 1, 2, \ldots$$

Prove that the mean of X is m and state the variance of X.

The number of telephone calls received per minute at the switchboard of a certain office was logged during the period 10 a.m. to noon on a working day. The results were as in Table 8.5. f is the number of minutes with x calls per minute.

By consideration of the mean and variance of this distribution show that a possible model is a Poisson distribution.

Using the calculated mean and on the assumption of a Poisson distribution calculate

(a)   the probability that two or more calls were received during any one minute,

(b)   the probability that no calls were received during any two consecutive minutes.

(SUJB)

Table 8.5

Calls per minute (x)	0	1	2	3	4	5	6	7	8
f		7	18	27	28	20	11	5	3	1

(2)   (a)   The number of accidents notified in a factory per day over a period of 200 days gave rise to Table 8.6.

   (i)   Calculate the mean number of accidents per day.

   (ii)   Assuming that this situation can be represented by a suitable Poisson distribution, calculate the corresponding frequencies.

(b)   Of items produced by a machine, approximately 3% are defective, and these occur at random. What is the probability that, in a sample of 144 items, there will be at least two which are defective?   (SUJB)

Table 8.6

Number of accidents	0	1	2	3	4	5
Number of days	127	54	14	3	1	1

(3)   National records for the past 100 years were examined to find the number of deaths in each year due to lightning. The most deaths in any year were four which was recorded once. In 35 years, no death was observed and in 38 years only one death. The mean number of deaths per year was 1.00. Draw up a frequency table of the number of deaths per year, and estimate the corresponding expected frequencies for a Poisson distribution having the same mean. Illustrate both frequency distributions graphically. $[1/e = 0.3679.]$ (O)

(4)   The number of emergency admissions each day to a hospital is found to have a Poisson distribution with mean 2.

(a)   Evaluate the probability that on a particular day there will be no emergency admissions.

(b)   At the beginning of one day the hospital has five beds available for emergencies. Calculate the probability that this will be an insufficient number for the day.

(c)   Calculate the probability that there will be exactly three admissions altogether on two consecutive days.   (C)

(5)   (a)   Table 8.7 shows the number of phone calls I received over a period of 150 days.
       (i)   Find the average number of calls per day.
       (ii)   Calculate the frequencies of the comparable Poisson distribution.
     (b)   A firm selling electrical components packs them in boxes of 60. On average, 2% of the components are faulty. What is the chance of getting more than two defective components in a box? (Use the Poisson distribution.)   (SUJB)

Table 8.7

Number of calls	0	1	2	3	4
Number of days	51	54	36	6	3

(6)   A small garage has three cars available for daily hire. The daily demand for these cars may be assumed to have a Poisson distribution with mean 2.
     (a)   Prove that demands for one and two cars on any day are equally probable.
     (b)   Find, as accurately as your tables permit, the probabilities that on a given day exactly no, one, two and three car(s) will be hired.
            Hence, or otherwise, calculate the mean number of cars hired per day.
     (c)   The garage owner charges £6 per day for the hire of a car and his total outgoings per car, irrespective of whether or not it is hired, amount to £1 per day. Calculate, to the nearest penny, the garage owner's expected daily profit from the hiring of these cars.   (W)

(7)   (a)   The number of organic particles suspended in a volume V cm^3 of a certain liquid follows a Poisson distribution with mean $0.1V$.
            Find the probabilities that a sample of 1 cm^3 of the liquid will contain
       (i)   at least one organic particle,
       (ii)   exactly one organic particle.
     (b)   The liquid is sold in vials, each vial containing 10 cm^3 of the liquid. The vials are dispatched for sale in boxes, each box containing 100 vials. Find the probability that a vial will contain at least one organic particle. Hence find the mean and the standard deviation of the number of vials per box of 100 vials that contain at least one organic particle.   (W)

(8)   Specify the conditions under which a Binomial distribution reduces to a Poisson distribution and derive the expression for the Poisson distribution from the expression for the Binomial distribution. Hence derive expressions for the mean and variance of the Poisson distribution.
     A clerk in the ticket issuing office of a suburban railway station noted that the number

of tickets issued for journeys away from London was equal to the number of first-class tickets issued for all journeys, and the number of tickets issued in each category was in the proportion of one in five hundred of all tickets issued.

Determine the probability that, of the 2000 travellers departing from that station between 8 a.m. and 9 a.m.,

(a) exactly three required first-class seats,

(b) more than two travelled away from London.   (AEB)

(9) A new telephone directory is to be published, and before publication takes place the entries have to be checked for misprints, and any necessary corrections made. Previous experience suggests that, on average, 0.1% of the entries will require correction, and that entries requiring correction will be randomly distributed. The directory will contain 240000 entries altogether printed on 800 pages with 300 entries per page. There are two methods of making corrections. For method A the costs are £C per page containing one entry requiring correction and £$3C$ per page containing two or more entries requiring correction. For method B the costs are £$2C$ per page containing one or more entries requiring correction. Calculate the expected costs of correction for each method.   (C)

9 The Normal distribution

9.1 Introduction

Many of the frequency distributions for continuous variables which we have met so far have had a shape similar to Figure 9.1, i.e. they are unimodal and approximately symmetrical. Figure 9.1 shows the (hypothetical) relative frequency density distribution for the height, measured to the nearest 10 cm, of a random sample of 100 men from a large population. The relative frequency density is obtained by dividing the relative frequency by the class width. This means that the area of each bar of the histogram gives the relative frequency for that class and thus the total area of the histogram is 1.

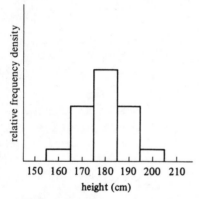

Figure 9.1 Hypothetical relative frequency density distribution for the heights of 100 men measured to the nearest 10 cm

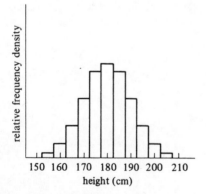

Figure 9.2 Hypothetical relative frequency density distribution for the heights of 200 men measured to the nearest 5 cm

138

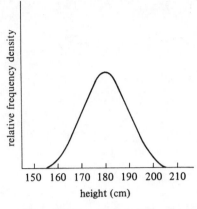

Figure 9.3 Hypothetical relative frequency density distribution for the heights of a large population of men

Suppose we now measure the height more accurately, say to the nearest 5 cm, for a larger sample of 200 from the same population. Then we might get a relative frequency density distribution like Figure 9.2. The area of the histogram is again 1.

If we imagine an idealised situation in which the height is measured more and more accurately for an increasingly large sample, the histogram would approximate to a smooth bell-shaped curve as shown in Figure 9.3. Again the area under the curve is 1. This curve represents the distribution of height in the *population* of men.

A large number of continuous variates have relative frequency distributions which approximate to this shape, e.g. weights, heights, experimental errors in physical sciences, etc.

9.2   The Normal distribution

A mathematical model which describes approximately the shape of many relative frequency distributions, such as the one in Figure 9.3, is the **Normal distribution**. For a continuous random variable X, with mean μ and standard deviation σ, the Normal distribution curve is

$$f(x) = \frac{1}{\sqrt{(2\pi\sigma^2)}} \exp\left\{ -\frac{(x-\mu)^2}{2\sigma^2} \right\} \tag{9.2.1}$$

This curve has the following properties, as shown in Figure 9.4.
 (i) It is symmetrical about $x = \mu$.
 (ii) It has one maximum at $x = \mu$.
(iii) As $x \to \pm\infty$, $f(x) \to 0$.
(iv) The area under the curve is 1.
Thus the Normal distribution may be a suitable model for a variate which is
 (i) continuous,
 (ii) unimodal,
(iii) has a symmetrical frequency distribution,

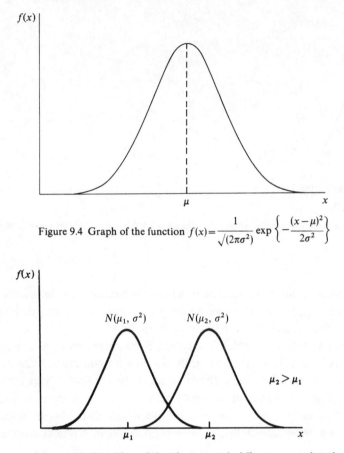

Figure 9.4 Graph of the function $f(x) = \dfrac{1}{\sqrt{(2\pi\sigma^2)}} \exp\left\{ -\dfrac{(x-\mu)^2}{2\sigma^2} \right\}$

Figure 9.5 Two Normal distributions with different means but the same variance

(iv) has class frequencies which fall away rapidly as the variate moves away from the mean.

A convenient way of denoting that X is Normally distributed with mean μ and variance σ^2 is

$$X \sim N(\mu, \sigma^2) \tag{9.2.2}$$

μ and σ are the parameters of the distribution. Their values determine the shape of the distribution. Figure 9.5 shows two Normal distributions with the same variance but different means: altering μ moves the position of the centre of the distribution. Figure 9.6 shows two Normal distributions with the same mean but different variances: the area under each curve is the same and equal to 1 but the curve with the larger variance is more spread out. Although the position and spread of a Normal distribution depend on μ and σ respectively, all Normal distributions share the property that approximately two-thirds of the values lie within 1 standard deviation of the mean, approximately 95% of the values lie within 2 standard deviations of the mean and nearly all the values lie within 3 standard deviations of the mean. In fact if we take *any* multiple of the standard deviation on either side of the mean then the

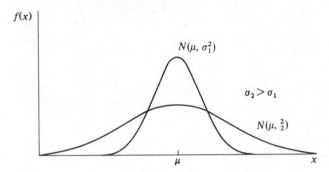

Figure 9.6. Two Normal distributions with the same mean but different variances

same proportion of values is included for *all* Normal distributions. This point is explored mathematically in the next section.

The Normal distribution is sometimes called the **Gaussian distribution** after Gauss (1777–1855) who introduced it in connection with the theory of errors. Since there are many continuous variates which are not even approximately Normally distributed but which are in no way 'abnormal', this name is sometimes preferred. The Normal distribution is one of the most important theoretical distributions for reasons which will emerge in later chapters.

9.2.1   *Exercise*

Show that for the experimental data in Table 1.3 approximately two-thirds of the values lie within 1 standard deviation of the mean, approximately 95% of the values lie within 2 standard deviations of the mean and all the values lie within 3 standard deviations of the mean. The mean and standard deviation of this sample are 12.75 and 3.26 g/l respectively and a cumulative frequency curve is shown in Figure 2.1.

9.3   **Standardisation**

$f(x)$ is a **probability density function**. It does not give the probability that X takes a certain value but that X lies in a certain range: the probability that X lies between x and $x+\delta x$ is $f(x)\,\delta x$. The probability that X lies between x_1 and x_2 is thus given by $\int_{x_1}^{x_2} f(x)\,\mathrm{d}x$ which is shown by the shaded area in Figure 9.7.

If we require the probability that $X < x$, it is given by

$$
\begin{aligned}
F(x) &= P(X < x) \\
&= \int_{-\infty}^{x} f(x)\mathrm{d}x \\
&= \int_{-\infty}^{x} \frac{1}{\sqrt{(2\pi\sigma^2)}} \exp\left\{-\frac{(x-\mu)^2}{2\sigma^2}\right\} \mathrm{d}x
\end{aligned}
\tag{9.3.1}
$$

$F(x)$ is a **cumulative distribution function** (c.d.f.).

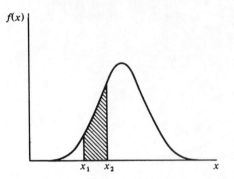

Figure 9.7. A Normal distribution: the shaded area gives the probability that X lies between x_1 and x_2

Unfortunately this integral cannot be performed analytically but must be evaluated numerically. It would be impossible to do this for all values of μ and σ, since they can take an infinite number of values. This problem is overcome by **standardisation**. A **standard deviate** Z is defined such that when $X = x$ the value of Z is given by

$$z = \frac{x - \mu}{\sigma} \tag{9.3.2}$$

which is the number of standard deviations by which x departs from μ. Making a transformation of the integral in equation (9.3.1), using $z = (x - \mu)/\sigma$, $\delta z = \delta x/\sigma$, we have

$$P(Z < z) = F(z)$$

$$= \int_{-\infty}^{z} \frac{1}{\sqrt{(2\pi\sigma^2)}} \left\{ \exp\left(-\frac{z^2}{2}\right) \right\} \sigma \, dz$$

$$= \int_{-\infty}^{z} \frac{1}{\sqrt{(2\pi)}} \left\{ \exp\left(-\frac{z^2}{2}\right) \right\} dz \tag{9.3.3}$$

We now have an integral which does not contain μ or σ. Values of this integral for different values of $z \geqslant 0$ are given in Table A1. Values for $z < 0$ are found by using the symmetrical nature of the curve. The function which appears in the integral:

$$f(z) = \frac{1}{\sqrt{(2\pi)}} \exp\left(-\frac{z^2}{2}\right)$$

is called the standard Normal distribution and is tabulated in Table A2. Since this function is obtained by putting $\mu = 0$, $\sigma = 1$ in equation (9.2.1), $f(z)$ is $N(0, 1)$ and $F(z)$ is its c.d.f.
The following examples illustrate the way in which the table of $F(z)$ is used.

9.4   Examples

9.4.1   *Example*

The weights of a population of women are Normally distributed with mean 60 kg and s.d. 5 kg. What is the probability that the weight of a woman chosen at random is (a) less than 61 kg, (b) less than 65 kg, (c) between 61 kg and 65 kg, (d) greater than 70 kg, (e) less than 57 kg?

We have $\mu = 60$ and $\sigma = 5$. If X is the weight of a woman, then $X = N(60, 5^2)$ and Z, where $z = \frac{1}{5}(x-60)$, is $N(0, 1)$.

(a) $x = 61$, $z = \frac{1}{5}(61-60) = 0.2$.

From Table A1, $P(Z < 0.2) = F(0.2) = 0.5793$.

Therefore the probability that a woman chosen at random weighs less than 61 kg is 0.5793.

(b) $x = 65$, $z = \frac{1}{5}(65-60) = 1$.

From Table A1, $P(Z < 1) = F(1) = 0.8413$.

The probability that a woman chosen at random weighs less than 65 kg is 0.8413.

(c) The probability that the weight of a woman lies between 61 kg and 65 kg is found from the two previous answers by subtraction (see Figure 9.8). So the probability that a woman weighs between 61 kg and 65 kg is $0.8413 - 0.5793 = 0.262$.

(d) $x = 70$, $z = \frac{1}{5}(70-60) = 2$.

From the tables, $P(Z < 2) = F(2) = 0.9772$.

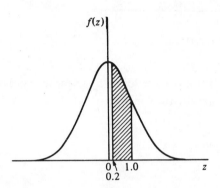

Figure 9.8 Graph to illustrate Example 9.4.1, part (c)

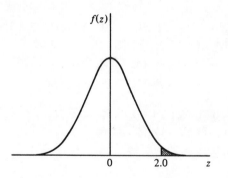

Figure 9.9 Graph to illustrate Example 9.4.1, part (d)

By subtraction (see Figure 9.9), $P(Z > 2) = 1 - 0.9772$. The probability that the woman weighs more than 70 kg is 0.0228.

(e) $x = 57$, $z = \frac{1}{5}(57-60) = -0.6$

Table A1 only gives values of $F(z)$ for $z > 0$. The value for negative values of z is found by subtraction.

By symmetry the shaded area in the left-hand diagram of Figure 9.10 is equal to the unshaded area in the right-hand diagram.

From the tables, $P(Z < +0.6) = F(0.6) = 0.7257$

$$P(Z < -0.6) = P(Z > +0.6) = 1 - 0.7257$$
$$= 0.2743$$

The probability that a woman chosen at random weighs less than 57 kg is 0.2743.

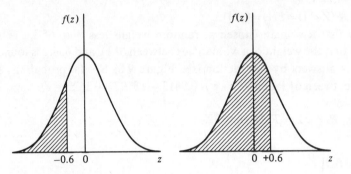

Figure 9.10 Graph to illustrate Example 9.4.1, part (e)

When z is given to 3 decimal places, values of $F(z)$ can be found by linear interpolation in Table A1. For example, if $z = 1.224$, interpolating between $F(1.22) = 0.8888$ and $F(1.23) = 0.8907$ gives

$$F(1.224) = 0.8888 + \tfrac{4}{10} \times 0.0019 = 0.8896 \text{ (to 4 d.p.)}$$

9.4.2   *Exercise*

(1) If $Z \sim N(0, 1)$ find
   (a) $P(Z < 1)$ (b) $P(Z > 2)$ (c) $P(Z < -1.3)$ (d) $P(Z > -0.9)$ (e) $P(Z < 1.96)$
   (f) $P(Z > 0.54)$ (g) $P(Z < -2.92)$ (h) $P(Z > -0.73)$ (i) $P(Z < -1.09)$
   (j) $P(Z > 0.897)$ (k) $P(Z < -2.128)$ (l) $P(Z < 0.543)$ (m) $P(Z > -1.824)$

(2) If $Z \sim N(0, 1)$ find
   (a) $P(1.3 < Z < 2.3)$ (b) $P(-1.2 < Z < 0.9)$ (c) $P(-0.7 < Z < -0.3)$
   (d) $P(-3 < Z < 3)$ (e) $P(-2 < Z < 2)$ (f) $P(-1 < Z < 1)$
   (g) $P(-1.345 < Z < -0.776)$ (h) $P(-0.074 < Z < 2.155)$

(3) For a Normal population with mean 10, standard deviation 5, find the probability that a member chosen at random gives a value of the variate which is
   (a) < 11 (b) > 11 (c) > 5 (d) < 5 (e) between 5 and 11.

(4) IQ scores are $N(100, 225)$. Find the probability that a person chosen at random has an IQ score of
   (a) more than 140   (b) less than 90   (c) between 120 and 130   (d) between 80 and 120.

(5)   The masses (in kg) of bags of sugar produced by a machine are $N(1.13, 0.05^2)$. What is the probability that a bag of sugar weighs less than the nominal mass of 1 kg?

9.4.3   *Example*

A certain brand of light bulbs has a lifetime which is Normally distributed with mean 1500 hours and s.d. 50 hours. What should the guaranteed lifetime of the bulbs be so that only 5% of the bulbs will have to be replaced under guarantee?

Let x_1 hours be the guaranteed lifetime. The information which we have is shown in Figure 9.11. There must be a probability of 0.05 that a bulb chosen at random has a lifetime less than x_1 hours. If z_1 is the value of the standard deviate for the guaranteed lifetime, we have $P(Z<z_1)$ is 0.05. Since z_1 is negative we cannot find it directly from Table A1. Instead we find z_2 such that $F(z_2)=P(Z<z_2)=1-0.05=0.95$. From Table A1, z_2 is 1.645 and by symmetry $z_1=-1.645$. Since

$$z_1 = \frac{x_1 - \mu}{\sigma}$$

we have $-1.645 = \dfrac{x_1 - 1500}{50}$

$x_1 = 1418$ hours

In the previous example the value of $F(z)=0.9500$ does not appear in Table A1, but lies exactly half way between $F(1.64)=0.9495$ and $F(1.65)=0.9505$, giving $z=1.645$ by linear interpolation. Similarly for $F(z)=0.7714$, which lies between $F(0.74)=0.7704$ and $F(0.75)=0.7734$, the value of z is

$$z = 0.740 + \frac{(0.7714 - 0.7704)}{(0.7734 - 0.7704)} \times 0.001$$

$$= 0.743 \text{ (to 3 d.p.)}$$

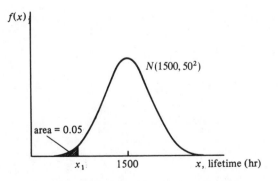

Figure 9.11 Graph to illustrate Example 9.4.3

9.4.4   *Exercise*

(1) Find the value of z such that
  (a) $P(Z<z)=0.6985$ (b) $P(Z>z)=0.5199$ (c) $P(Z<z)=0.1357$
  (d) $P(Z>z)=0.0526$ (e) $P(Z>z)=0.6453$ (f) $P(Z<z)=0.0452$
  (g) $P(Z<z)=0.6955$ (h) $P(Z>z)=0.1768$

(2) If IQ scores are $N(100, 225)$ what IQ is exceeded by (a) 5%, (b) 1% of the population? Find the upper and lower quartiles for IQ scores.

(3) The heights of applicants to the police force are Normally distributed with mean 170 cm and standard deviation 3.8 cm. If 30% of applicants are rejected because they are too small, what is the minimum acceptable height for the police force?

(4) The diameter of washers produced by a machine has a standard deviation of 0.1 mm. What should the mean diameter be if there is to be a probability of only 3% that the diameter exceeds 2.0 mm?

(5) In question (5) of Exercise 9.4.2 to what value must the standard deviation be changed for there to be a probability of 0.1% that a bag weighs less than the nominal mass of 1 kg (assuming that the mean is unchanged)?

9.4.5   *Example*

An athlete finds that in the high jump he can clear a height of 1.68 m once in five attempts and a height of 1.52 m nine times out of ten attempts. Assuming the heights he can clear in various jumps form a Normal distribution, estimate the mean and standard deviation of the distribution.   (AEB)

Figure 9.12 illustrates the information given in this example. Let z_1 be the standard deviate for $x=1.68$. Then
$$F(z_1)=P(Z<z_1)=1-0.2=0.8$$
From Table A1
$$z_1=0.84$$
and also
$$z_1=\frac{1.68-\mu}{\sigma}$$
Therefore
$$0.84=\frac{1.68-\mu}{\sigma}$$
giving
$$0.84\sigma=1.68-\mu \tag{9.4.1}$$

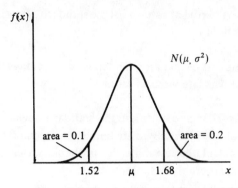

Figure 9.12 Graph to illustrate Example 9.4.5

Similarly if z_2 is the standard deviate for $x = 1.52$, z_2 is negative and so is found from Table A1 as $-z_2'$ where $F(Z < z_2') = 0.9$. This gives

$$z_2' = 1.28$$
$$z_2 = -1.28$$

and also

$$z_2 = \frac{1.52 - \mu}{\sigma}$$

Therefore

$$-1.28 = \frac{1.52 - \mu}{\sigma}$$

$$-1.28\sigma = 1.52 - \mu \qquad (9.4.2)$$

Subtracting equation (9.4.2) from equation (9.4.1)

$$0.84\sigma + 1.28\sigma = 1.68 - 1.52$$
$$2.12\sigma = 0.16$$

giving

$$\sigma = 0.075$$

and

$$\mu = 1.616$$

9.4.6   *Exercise*

(1) The volume (in litres) of liquid in bottles filled by a machine is $N(1.01, 0.01^2)$.
  (a) What is the probability that a bottle contains less than 1 litre?
  (b) To what value must the mean be altered to reduce the probability in (a) to 1% (assuming the standard deviation is unaltered)?

(2) A dart player aiming at a vertical line finds that the perpendicular distance (in cm) of a dart from the line is $N(0, 0.3^2)$ where distances to the right of the line are taken as positive and those to the left as negative. What is the probability that a dart lands more

than 0.5 cm from the line in either direction? To what value must the standard deviation be reduced in order to halve this probability?

(3) A train is due to arrive at Victoria Station at 09.30 daily. On ten successive days the numbers of minutes by which the train was late were as follows.

$$3 \quad 0 \quad 4 \quad -2 \quad -3 \quad 13 \quad 8 \quad -2 \quad 6 \quad 3$$

Show that the mean time of arrival was 09.33 and calculate the standard deviation. On the assumption that times of arrival are Normally distributed with mean 09.33 and the standard deviation you have calculated, estimate the probability that the train will arrive (a) on or before 09.30, (b) more than 8 minutes late.   (C)

(4) The marks of 500 candidates in an examination are Normally distributed with a mean of 45 marks and a standard deviation of 20 marks.
  (a) Given that the pass mark is 41, estimate the number of candidates who passed the examination.
  (b) If 5% of the candidates obtain a distinction by scoring x marks or more, estimate the value of x.
  (c) Estimate the interquartile range of the distribution.   (L)

(5) A sample of 100 apples is taken from a load. The apples have the distribution of sizes shown in Table 9.1.
  Determine the mean and standard deviation of these diameters.
  Assuming that the distribution is approximately Normal with this mean and this standard deviation, find the range of size of apples for packing, if 5% are to be rejected as too small and 5% are to be rejected as too large.   (O & C)

Table 9.1

Diameter to nearest cm	6	7	8	9	10
Frequency	11	21	38	17	13

(6) In an examination 30% of the candidates fail and 10% achieve distinction. Last year the pass mark (out of 200) was 84 and the minimum mark required for a distinction was 154. Assuming that the marks of the candidates were Normally distributed, estimate the mean mark and the standard deviation.   (O & C)

(7) A factory uses machines which produce bars of chocolate whose weights are Normally distributed with mean 110 g and s.d. 8 g. Bars of chocolate which weigh more than 100 g are sold at a profit of 9p per bar. Those which weigh less than 100 g are sold to the employees at the factory at a profit of 1p per bar. Show that the expected profit per 100 bars is about £8.16.

(8) Tests made on two types of electric light bulb show the following: Type A, lifetime distributed Normally with an average life of 1150 hours and a standard deviation of 30 hours.

Type B, long-life bulb, average lifetime of 1900 hours, with standard deviation of 50 hours.

(a) What percentage of bulbs of type A could be expected to have a life of more than 1200 hours?

(b) What percentage of type B would you expect to last longer than 1800 hours?

(c) What lifetime limits would you estimate would contain the central 80% of the production of type A? (SUJB)

(9) Mass-produced electrical resistors have a designed resistance of 500 Ω. The resistances of those produced by machine operator A have a Normal distribution with mean value 501 Ω and standard deviation 3 Ω. The control procedures are designed to reject any whose resistance is below 498 Ω or above 508 Ω.

Find

(a) The proportion of A's production that will be rejected,

(b) the proportion which would be rejected if A adjusted the mean of his production so as to minimise the proportion of rejects,

(c) the value to which A would need to reduce the standard deviation of his production (leaving the mean at 501 Ω) so that the proportion of resistances rejected below 498 Ω would be halved. (C)

(10) The distribution of the length in mm of 717 eggs of cuckoos was found to be as in Table 9.2.

Show that the mean is 22.49 and the standard deviation is 1.00.

In order to simplify recording in the field, it is decided to classify the eggs by length into three groups described as long, medium and short in such a way that one-third of the eggs might be expected to fall in each group. Determine where the divisions on the length scale should be made. (O)

Table 9.2

Length (central value)	19.25	20.25	21.25	22.25	23.25	24.25	25.25	26.25
Frequency	3	22	123	300	201	61	6	1

(11) An extinct species was considered to have an average life of 25 years, with a standard deviation of only 2 years, and to be Normally distributed. Of a family of 50 members of the species, born at the same time, how many would be expected to have lived

(a) between 20 and 26 years,

(b)   less than 22 years?
What would be the age at death of the thirty-fifth member of the family to die?   (AEB)

(12)   A machine produces components in batches of 20000, the lengths of which may be
considered to be Normally distributed.
At the beginning of production, the machine is set to produce the required mean
length of components at 15 mm, and it can then be set to give any one of three standard
deviations: 0.06 mm, 0.075 mm, 0.09 mm.
It costs £850, £550 and £100 respectively to set these deviations.
Any length produced must lie in the range 14.82 mm to 15.18 mm, otherwise it is
classed as defective and costs the company £1.
Which standard deviation should be used, if the decision is to be made purely on the
cost of setting the machine and of the defectives?   (SUJB)

9.5   Fitting a Normal distribution to data

Table 9.3 gives the lifetime of 50 electric light bulbs. The lifetime of an electric light bulb is a
variate which we might expect to be Normally distributed: the observed frequency distribution is unimodal and approximately symmetrical. To see if the distribution is indeed approximately Normal we first calculate the mean and standard deviation of the observed data.
Using these statistics we can then calculate the frequencies which we would expect for a
Normal distribution with the same mean and s.d. Table 9.3 gives the calculation of the
mean and s.d. for the observed data. Alternatively we can compare the relative frequency for
each class with the theoretical probability for a Normal distribution with the same mean and
variance.

Table 9.3 *Lifetimes of 50 light bulbs*

Lifetime (h)	True class limits	Mid-class value x_i	f_i	u_i	$f_i u_i$	$f_i u_i^2$
650–659	649.5–659.5	654.5	1	−4	−4	16
660–669	659.5–669.5	664.5	3	−3	−9	27
670–679	669.5–679.5	674.5	3	−2	−6	12
680–689	679.5–689.5	684.5	7	−1	−7	7
690–699	689.5–699.5	694.5	15	0	0	0
700–709	699.5–709.5	704.5	7	1	7	7
710–719	709.5–719.5	714.5	7	2	14	28
720–729	719.5–729.5	724.5	4	3	12	36
730–739	729.5–739.5	734.5	3	4	12	48
			50		19	181

The values of x have been coded using arbitrary origin $A = 694.5$ and unit $B = 10$.

$$\bar{u} = \frac{\sum\limits_{i=1}^{n} f_i u_i}{\sum\limits_{i=1}^{n} f_i} = \frac{19}{50} = 0.38 \qquad \text{(from equation (2.6.2))}$$

$$\bar{x} = A + B\bar{u} = 694.5 + 10 \times 0.38 \qquad \text{(from equation (2.7.1))}$$
$$= 698.3 \text{ hours}$$

$$s = B \sqrt{\left\{ \frac{\sum\limits_{i=1}^{n} f_i u_i^2}{\sum\limits_{i=1}^{n} f_i} - \left(\frac{\sum\limits_{i=1}^{n} f_i u_i}{\sum\limits_{i=1}^{n} f_i} \right)^2 \right\}} \qquad \text{(from equation (3.9.1))}$$

$$= 10 \sqrt{\left\{ \frac{181}{50} - \left(\frac{19}{50} \right)^2 \right\}}$$
$$= 18.6 \text{ hours}$$

Table 9.4 *Calculation of expected class frequencies for data in Table 9.3*

True class limits	Upper true class limit	z	$F(z)$	Cumulative frequency	Theoretical frequency	Observed frequency
<649.5	649.5	−2.62	0.0044	0.2	0.2	0
649.5–659.5	659.5	−2.09	0.0183	0.9	0.7	1
659.5–669.5	669.5	−1.55	0.0606	3.0	2.1	3
669.5–679.5	679.5	−1.01	0.1562	7.8	4.8	3
679.5–689.5	689.5	−0.47	0.3192	16.0	8.2	7
689.5–699.5	699.5	0.06	0.5239	26.2	10.2	15
699.5–709.5	709.5	0.60	0.7257	36.3	10.1	7
709.5–719.5	719.5	1.14	0.8729	43.6	7.3	7
719.5–729.5	729.5	1.68	0.9535	47.7	4.1	4
729.5–739.5	739.5	2.22	0.9868	49.3	1.6	3
>739.5	∞	∞	1.0000	50.0	0.7	0

Table 9.4 sets out the calculation of the expected class frequencies for an $N(698.3, 18.6^2)$ distribution. The steps are:
  (i) The standard deviates corresponding to the upper class limits are calculated. Note that the classes from $-\infty$ to 649.5 and 739.5 to $+\infty$ are also included since the Normal distribution is defined for $-\infty < x < +\infty$.
 (ii) Table A1 is used to find $F(z)$ for each standard deviate.
(iii) The values of $F(z)$ are converted to theoretical cumulative frequencies by multiplying by the total frequency, in this case 50.

(iv)   The theoretical frequencies in each class have been found from the cumulative frequencies by subtraction. The observed frequencies are given for comparison.

It can be seen that there is reasonable agreement between the observed and theoretical frequencies. In Chapter 16 a method of testing the goodness-of-fit will be described.

9.5.1   *Exercise*

(1)   Calculate the expected frequencies in each class for a Normal distribution with the same mean and s.d. as the data in Exercise 9.4.6, question (5).

(2)   The masses measured on a population of 100 animals were grouped in Table 9.5, after being recorded to the nearest gram.

Table 9.5

Mass (g)	Frequency
$\leqslant 89$	3
90–109	7
110–129	34
130–149	43
150–169	10
170–189	2
$\geqslant 190$	1

Show that the mean is 131.5 and the standard deviation is 20. (Assume the lower and upper classes have the same range as the other classes.)

Find the expected frequencies in each class for a Normal distribution with the same mean and standard deviation.   (O)

9.6   The Normal distribution as an approximation to the Binomial distribution

Figure 7.2 showed that, even when $p \neq \frac{1}{2}$, the Binomial distribution becomes symmetrical for large n. It can be shown mathematically that for large n the Binomial distribution approximates to the Normal distribution. This property can be used to simplify calculation in problems involving the Binomial distribution with large n.

9.6.1   *Example*

What is the probability that if a coin is tossed 100 times it will show 60 or more heads?

Using the Binomial distribution this probability is given by

$$P(X \geqslant 60) = \binom{100}{60}(\tfrac{1}{2})^{60}(\tfrac{1}{2})^{40} + \binom{100}{61}(\tfrac{1}{2})^{61}(\tfrac{1}{2})^{39} + \cdots + (\tfrac{1}{2})^{100}$$

an expression whose calculation is extremely tedious.

The mean and standard deviation of the appropriate Binomial distribution are

$$\text{mean} = np$$
$$= 100 \times \tfrac{1}{2} = 50$$

$$\text{standard deviation} = \sqrt{(npq)}$$
$$= \sqrt{(100 \times \tfrac{1}{2} \times \tfrac{1}{2})} = 5$$

and since n is large this Binomial distribution can be approximated by a Normal distribution with the same mean and variance. Figure 9.13 shows this distribution. Since we are using a continuous distribution as an approximation to a discrete one, the shaded area for $59.5 \leqslant x < 60.5$ gives the probability that the number of heads is 60. Thus the probability that the number of heads is 60 or more is given by the area above 59.5.

$$\text{standard deviate } z = \frac{x - \mu}{\sigma} = \frac{59.5 - 50}{5} = 1.9$$

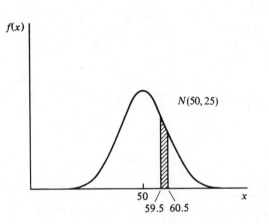

Figure 9.13 Graph to illustrate Example 9.6.1

From Table A1,
$$F(1.9) = P(Z < 1.9) = 0.9713$$
So that
$$P(Z > 1.9) = 0.0287$$
The probability of getting 60 or more heads is 0.0287.

9.7 The Normal distribution as an approximation to the Poisson distribution

Figure 8.1 shows that as the mean λ of a Poisson distribution increases the distribution becomes symmetrical. It can be shown mathematically that for large λ the Poisson distribution approximates to the Normal and this fact can be used to simplify calculation.

9.7.1 Example

A storekeeper knows that on average she supplies 30 fuses in a year. How many fuses should she purchase at the beginning of the year if there is to be a probability of 0.95 that she can meet the demand?

The Poisson distribution can be approximated by a Normal distribution with
$$\text{mean} = \lambda = 30$$
$$\text{variance} = \lambda = 30$$
$$\text{standard deviation} = \sqrt{30} = 5.48$$
as shown in Figure 9.14.

If x_1 is the number of fuses required, the shaded area represents the probability that exactly x_1 fuses are used. (Again we are approximating a discrete distribution by a continuous one.) We require x_1 such that the probability that $X < x_1 + \frac{1}{2}$ is 95%. The corresponding standard deviate is found from Table A1 to be 1.645, giving

$$\frac{x_1 + \frac{1}{2} - 30}{5.48} = 1.645$$
$$x_1 = 38.51$$

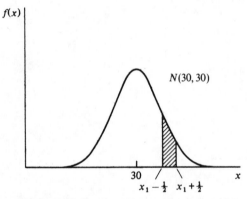

Figure 9.14 Graph to illustrate Example 9.7.1

Or, since x_1 must be a whole number, the storekeeper needs 39 fuses in stock at the beginning of the year.

9.7.2   Exercise

(1) An unbiased coin is tossed 100 times. Write down an expression for the probability of obtaining 54 heads and estimate correct to two significant figures its value using the Normal approximation.   (SUJB)

(2) An urn contains N balls which, apart from colour, are identical; Np balls are red and $N(1-p)$ are white. A random sample of n balls is drawn, with replacement, and R denotes the number of red balls in the sample. Find the following probabilities correct to two significant figures:
 (a) $P(R \geqslant 4)$ if $N = 1000$, $p = 0.1$, $n = 10$;

(b) $P(R \geqslant 4)$ if $N = 1\,000\,000$, $p = 0.003$, $n = 1000$;

(c) $P(R \geqslant 90)$ if $N = 1\,000\,000$, $p = 0.1$, $n = 1000$. (C)

(3) State under what conditions (a) a Binomial distribution may be approximated by a Poisson distribution; (b) a Poisson distribution may be approximated by a Normal distribution.

In a large factory the number of light bulbs that must be replaced each week has a Poisson distribution with mean 20. What is the minimum number of light bulbs that the storekeeper should have in stock at the beginning of each week if he is to be more than 95% certain of having enough bulbs for the replacements needed during the week? (O)

(4) State necessary conditions for an observed quantity to follow the Binomial distribution. Give examples of two quantities you would expect to satisfy these conditions, giving your reasons and the parameters of the distributions.

Jim is cracking nuts which have been chosen at random from a large collection of nuts of which 25% are bad. He cracks 100 nuts.

(a) Write down an expression for the exact probability that he obtains 70 or more good nuts.

(b) Use an approximation to derive a numerical value (correct to two decimal places) for this probability. (O)

Summary

The Normal distribution function is

(i) symmetrical;

(ii) has one maximum at $x = \mu$;

(iii) extends from $-\infty$ to $+\infty$ with $f(x) \to 0$ as $x \to \pm \infty$;

(iv) has an area under the curve equal to 1.

It is a suitable model for continuous variates which are

(i) unimodal;

(ii) symmetrical;

(iii) have frequencies which fall away rapidly as the variate moves away from the mean.

The parameters are the mean, μ, and the standard deviation, σ, denoted by $X \sim N(\mu, \sigma^2)$. The standard deviate, Z, is related to the variable, X, by

$$z = (x - \mu)/\sigma$$

and Z is $N(0, 1)$.

Projects

(1) *Fitting a Normal distribution to experimental data*

Using the data for the first attempt at bisecting a line by eye, obtained in Project 1, Chapter

2 (for which the standard deviation was calculated in Project 1, Chapter 3), find the expected class frequencies for a Normal distribution with the same mean and variance.

(2)   *Advanced Level Statistics Software*

The *Binomial, Poisson, Normal* section allows the user to enter observed frequencies and compare the frequency distribution graphically with a theoretical Normal distribution (see Section 9.5).

The use of the Normal distribution as an approximation to the Binomial can be demonstrated graphically and the closeness of the graphs as n is increased investigated (see Section 9.6). Similarly the agreement between the Normal and Poisson distributions as λ increases can be studied (see Section 9.7).

Exercise on Chapter 9

(1)   Before joining the Egghead Society, every candidate is given an intelligence test which, if applied to the general public, would give a Normal distribution of IQ's with mean 100 and standard deviation 20.

   The candidate is not admitted unless his or her IQ, as given by the test, is at least 130. Estimate the median IQ of the members of the Egghead Society, assuming that their IQ distribution is representative of that of the part of the population having IQ's greater than, or equal to 130.

   What IQ would be expected to be exceeded by one member in ten of the society?

                                                                                      (AEB)

(2)   In Urbania, selection for the Royal Flying Corps (RFC) is by means of an aptitude test based on a week's intensive military training. It is known that the scores of potential recruits on this test follow a Normal distribution with mean 45 and standard deviation 10.

   (a)   What is the probability that a randomly chosen recruit will score between 40 and 60?

   (b)   What percentage of the recruits is expected to score more than 30?

   (c)   In a particular year 100 recruits take the test. Assuming that the pass mark is 50, calculate the probability that less than 35 recruits qualify for the RFC.   (AEB)

(3)   A factory has six machines which intermittently use electric power for 20 minutes in each hour on the average. If the machines are operated independently, show that the probability that four or more will be using power at the same time is about 0.1.

   If the factory had 60 machines, find an approximate number n such that the probability that more than n will be using power at the same time is 0.1.   (O)

(4)   The marks of the large number of candidates taking a particular examination were such that it was reasonable to assume that these marks were Normally distributed.

Half the candidates in the examination scored more than 45 marks and 33% of the candidates scored more than 56 marks.

(a) Using tables as required, determine the mean and variance of the distribution.

(b) The bottom 30% of the candidates failed. Determine the pass mark for the examination.

(c) Find the proportion of the candidates who gained between 50 and 60 marks.

(JMB)

(5) Eggs are classified by weight according to Table 9.6.

100 hens of breed A are found to lay eggs at the rate of 170 per day, the eggs being of mean weight 62 g with standard deviation 6 g. 100 hens of breed B lay 220 eggs per day of mean egg weight 51 g with standard deviation 5 g.

What ratio of hens of breed A to hens of breed B should a farmer keep in order that equal numbers of eggs of class 3 and class 5 should be produced daily? Assume Normal distributions of weight for eggs from each breed of hen.

(O & C)

Table 9.6

Class	2	3	4	5	6
Weight in grams	65–70	60–65	55–60	50–55	45–50

(6) In a large town, one person in 80, on the average, has blood of type X. If 200 blood donors are taken at random, find an approximation to the probability that they include at least five persons having blood of type X.

How many donors must be taken at random in order that the probability of including at least one donor of type X shall be 0.9 or more?

(AEB)

(7) A manufacturer makes electronic components, and the price for which he can sell his products depends on the purity of the materials used in their manufacture. Measured in suitable units, the purity has mean 100 and standard deviation 10, and is Normally distributed. On components with purity in the range 85–115 the manufacturer can make a profit of 20p per item, and on those with purity above 115 he can make a profit of 30p per item. Components with purity in the range 80 to 85 are sold at cost price (£1) and those with purity below 80 are unsaleable, so that the manufacturer incurs a loss of £1 per item. Find his average profit per item.

The manufacturer can raise the mean purity of his components, but only by increasing the cost of manufacture of each item. He decides to raise the mean purity by 2 units, the standard deviation remaining at 10 units, but does *not* change the price of components to *any* range of customers, so that, for example, goods in the 85–115 range are still sold for £1.20, and those in the 80–85 range are still sold for £1. Find, to the nearest

$\frac{1}{10}$p, the increase in the cost per item, if it is found that the manufacturer's average profit per item remains unchanged. (C)

(8) A population of birds consists of equal numbers of males and females. The weights of the males are Normally distributed with mean 15g and s.d. 3 g, while the females' weights are Normal with mean 18 g and s.d. 4.5 g. Draw a graph of the frequency function of the weights of the whole population. Estimate from your graph, or calculate, the probability that a bird drawn at random weighs less than 12 g. (O)

10 Joint distributions

10.1 Bivariate distributions

The distributions which we have considered so far, have depended on only one random variable, but we are frequently interested in specifying two or more random variables for a member of a population. We might, for example, measure the height and weight of an individual. A probability distribution such as this which depends on two random variables is called **bivariate**. Table 10.1 gives the joint probability distribution for two discrete random variables: X, the size of a family, and Y, the number of bedrooms which they use. (The values given are hypothetical.) We denote the probability that X takes the value x and Y the value y by $P(X = x, Y = y)$. For example, the probability that a family chosen at random has 2 members and 3 bedrooms is denoted by $P(X = 2, Y = 3)$ and from Table 10.1 this probability is 0.08. Note that the grand total of the probabilities must be 1.

Table 10.2 reproduces Table 10.1 but with the row and column totals given. The row

Table 10.1 *Bivariate probability distribution for family size and number of bedrooms*

		\(x\)				
		1	2	3	4	5
	1	0.04	0.03	0.01	0.01	0.01
	2	0.04	0.09	0.09	0.07	0.05
y	3	0.03	0.08	0.13	0.12	0.11
	4	0.01	0.01	0.02	0.02	0.03

Table 10.2 *Marginal probability distribution for Table 10.1*

		\(x\)					
		1	2	3	4	5	
	1	0.04	0.03	0.01	0.01	0.01	0.10
	2	0.04	0.09	0.09	0.07	0.05	0.34
y	3	0.03	0.08	0.13	0.12	0.11	0.47
	4	0.01	0.01	0.02	0.02	0.03	0.09
		0.12	0.21	0.25	0.22	0.20	

159

totals form what is known as the **marginal distribution of** Y. This gives the probability of obtaining a particular value of Y irrespective of the value of X. For example, $P(Y=1)$ is the probability that $Y=1$ and from the table this probability is 0.10. Similarly the column totals form the **marginal distribution of** X from which, for example, $P(X=2)$ is 0.21.

If X and Y are independent we have from equation (4.6.1) that

$$P(X=x, Y=y)=P(X=x)P(Y=y)$$

In this case X and Y are not independent since, for example,

$$P(X=1, Y=2)=0.04$$

but

$$P(X=1)P(Y=2)=0.12 \times 0.34 = 0.0408$$

10.1.1 *Exercise*

Two discrete variables X and Y have the bivariate probability distribution given in Table 10.3.
(a)   What is $P(X=2, Y=1)$?
(b)   Find the value of c.
(c)   Find the marginal distributions of X and Y.
(d)   Are X and Y independent?

Table 10.3

		x		
		0	1	2
	0	c	0.05	0.1
y	1	0.1	0.15	0.15
	2	0.15	0.1	0.1

10.2   Mean of the sum of two random variables

In a game two six-sided dice are thrown. Each die has one side numbered 6, two sides numbered 3, and three sides numbered 1. The scores on the two dice form a bivariate distribution. Since the variables are independent we can calculate the joint probabilities using $P(X=x, Y=y)=P(X=x)P(Y=y)$, and these are given in Table 10.4.

The mean scores for each die are the same and are given by

$$E(X)=E(Y)=\sum_{\text{all } x} xP(X=x)=\sum_{\text{all } y} yP(Y=y)$$
$$=1 \times \tfrac{1}{2}+3 \times \tfrac{1}{3}+6 \times \tfrac{1}{6}$$
$$=2\tfrac{1}{2}$$

In the game the total score, $X + Y$, is found by adding the scores on the two dice. The probability distribution of this total, $P(X+Y=x+y)$, can be found using the probabilities in Table 10.4 and is shown in Table 10.5. The mean of the total score is given by

$$E(X+Y)= \sum_{\text{all } (x+y)} (x+y)P(X+Y=x+y) \qquad (10.2.1)$$
$$= 2 \times \tfrac{1}{4}+4 \times \tfrac{1}{3}+6 \times \tfrac{1}{9}+7 \times \tfrac{1}{6}+9 \times \tfrac{1}{9}+12 \times \tfrac{1}{36}$$
$$= 5$$

Table 10.4 *Bivariate probability distribution for two dice*

		x 1	3	6	$P(Y=y)$
y	1	$\tfrac{1}{2} \times \tfrac{1}{2}=\tfrac{1}{4}$	$\tfrac{1}{3} \times \tfrac{1}{2}=\tfrac{1}{6}$	$\tfrac{1}{6} \times \tfrac{1}{2}=\tfrac{1}{12}$	$\tfrac{1}{2}$
	3	$\tfrac{1}{2} \times \tfrac{1}{3}=\tfrac{1}{6}$	$\tfrac{1}{3} \times \tfrac{1}{3}=\tfrac{1}{9}$	$\tfrac{1}{6} \times \tfrac{1}{3}=\tfrac{1}{18}$	$\tfrac{1}{3}$
	6	$\tfrac{1}{2} \times \tfrac{1}{6}=\tfrac{1}{12}$	$\tfrac{1}{3} \times \tfrac{1}{6}=\tfrac{1}{18}$	$\tfrac{1}{6} \times \tfrac{1}{6}=\tfrac{1}{36}$	$\tfrac{1}{6}$
$P(X=x)$		$\tfrac{1}{2}$	$\tfrac{1}{3}$	$\tfrac{1}{6}$	1

Table 10.5 *Probability distribution for the sum of the scores on two dice*

$x+y$	$P(X+Y=x+y)$
2	$P(1, 1)=\tfrac{1}{4}$
4	$P(1, 3)+P(3, 1)=\tfrac{1}{6}+\tfrac{1}{6}=\tfrac{1}{3}$
6	$P(3, 3)=\tfrac{1}{9}$
7	$P(6, 1)+P(1, 6)=\tfrac{1}{12}+\tfrac{1}{12}=\tfrac{1}{6}$
9	$P(3, 6)+P(6, 3)=\tfrac{1}{18}+\tfrac{1}{18}=\tfrac{1}{9}$
12	$P(6, 6)=\tfrac{1}{36}$

We find that the mean for the sum of the scores is equal to the sum of the individual means for the two dice, a result which might have been expected intuitively. It is, in fact, a general result which can be proved as follows. Equation (10.2.1) can be written

$$E(X+Y)= \sum_{\text{all } x} \sum_{\text{all } y} (x+y)P(X=x, Y=y)$$

since the values of $(x+y)$ come from all possible pairs of x and y.

$$E(X+Y)= \sum_{\text{all } x} \sum_{\text{all } y} (x+y)P(X=x, Y=y)$$

$$= \sum_{\text{all } x} \sum_{\text{all } y} xP(X=x, Y=y)+ \sum_{\text{all } x} \sum_{\text{all } y} yP(X=x, Y=y)$$

$$= \sum_{\text{all } x} x \sum_{\text{all } y} P(X=x, Y=y) + \sum_{\text{all } y} y \sum_{\text{all } x} P(X=x, Y=y)$$

$$= \sum_{\text{all } x} xP(X=x) + \sum_{\text{all } y} yP(Y=y)$$

(where we have used the definition of marginal probability).

Therefore
$$E(X+Y)=E(X)+E(Y) \tag{10.2.2}$$
This result is true for any two random variables whether or not they are independent.

10.2.1   *Exercise*

(1)   The random variables X and Y are independent and have probability distributions as shown in Table 10.6.

Find the probability distribution of $Z=X+Y$ and hence verify that $E(X+Y)=E(X)+E(Y)$. (L)

Table 10.6

a	1	2	b	1	2
$P(X=a)$	0.4	0.6	$P(Y=b)$	0.7	0.3

(2)   Verify that, although the variables X and Y in Exercise 10.1.1 are not independent, $E(X)+E(Y)=E(X+Y)$.

10.3   Mean of the product of two independent random variables

We can prove a result similar to that of the previous section in this case. We have

$$E(XY)= \sum_{\text{all } x} \sum_{\text{all } y} xyP(X=x, Y=y)$$

$$= \sum_{\text{all } x} \sum_{\text{all } y} xyP(X=x)P(Y=y) \quad \text{(for *independent* variables)}$$

$$= \sum_{\text{all } x} xP(X=x) \sum_{\text{all } y} yP(Y=y)$$

which, using equation (6.3.1), gives
$$E(XY)=E(X)E(Y) \tag{10.3.1}$$
The mean of the product of two *independent* random variables is the product of their means.

10.3.1 *Exercise*

For the independent random variables X and Y, whose probability distributions are given in Exercise 10.2.1, question (1), find the probability distribution of XY and verify that $E(XY) = E(X)E(Y)$.

10.4 Variance of the sum of two independent random variables

We can investigate the relationship between the variance of the sum of two independent random variables and the variance of each variable taken separately using the example in Section 10.2.

$$\text{var}(X) = E(X^2) - \{E(X)\}^2 \qquad \text{(see equation (6.4.2))}$$
$$= \sum_{\text{all } x} x^2 P(X=x) - \{E(X)\}^2$$
$$= 1^2 \times \tfrac{1}{2} + 3^2 \times \tfrac{1}{3} + 6^2 \times \tfrac{1}{6} - (2\tfrac{1}{2})^2$$
$$= 3.25$$

and var(Y) is also 3.25. Also

$$\text{var}(X+Y) = E\{(X+Y)^2\} - \{E(X+Y)\}^2$$
$$= \sum_{\text{all } x+y} (x+y)^2 P(X+Y=x+y) - \{E(X+Y)\}^2$$
$$= 2^2 \times \tfrac{1}{4} + 4^2 \times \tfrac{1}{3} + 6^2 \times \tfrac{1}{9} + 7^2 \times \tfrac{1}{6} + 9^2 \times \tfrac{1}{9} + 12^2 \times \tfrac{1}{36} - 5^2$$
$$= 6.5$$

We find var$(X+Y) =$ var $(X)+$var (Y).

This can be shown generally as follows. Let $E(X) = \mu_X$ and $E(Y) = \mu_Y$, then $E(X+Y) = \mu_X + \mu_Y$ and

$$\text{var } (X+Y) = E[\{(X+Y) - (\mu_X + \mu_Y)\}^2]$$
$$= E[\{(X-\mu_X) + (Y-\mu_Y)\}^2]$$
$$= E[(X-\mu_X)^2 + (Y-\mu_Y)^2 + 2(X-\mu_X)(Y-\mu_Y)]$$

Therefore

$$\text{var } (X+Y) = E[(X-\mu_X)^2] + E[(Y-\mu_Y)^2] + 2E[(X-\mu_X)(Y-\mu_Y)] \qquad (10.4.1)$$

(since from equation (10.2.2) the expectation of the sum of random variables is equal to the sum of their expectations). The first two terms are the variances of X and Y respectively. $E[(X-\mu_X)(Y-\mu_Y)]$ is called the **covariance** of X and Y, cov(X, Y). It can be rewritten as follows

$$\text{cov}(X, Y) = E[(X-\mu_X)(Y-\mu_Y)]$$
$$= E[XY - \mu_X Y - \mu_Y X + \mu_X \mu_Y]$$
$$= E(XY) - \mu_X E(Y) - \mu_Y E(X) + \mu_X \mu_Y$$
$$= E(XY) - \mu_X \mu_Y - \mu_Y \mu_X + \mu_X \mu_Y$$
$$\text{cov}(X, Y) = E(XY) - \mu_X \mu_Y \qquad (10.4.2)$$

If X and Y are independent, then, using equation (10.3.1), $E(XY)=E(X)E(Y)=\mu_X\mu_Y$ and $\mathrm{cov}(X,\ Y)=0$. Equation (10.4.1) then becomes

$$\mathrm{var}(X+Y)=\mathrm{var}(X)+\mathrm{var}(Y) \tag{10.4.3}$$

It is left as an exercise for the reader to show that if X and Y are random variables and a and b are constants then

$$E(aX+bY)=aE(X)+bE(Y) \tag{10.4.4}$$

and further if X and Y are independent

$$\mathrm{var}(aX+bY)=a^2\ \mathrm{var}(X)+b^2\ \mathrm{var}(Y) \tag{10.4.5}$$

Two particularly important results which follow from this are found by putting $a=1, b=-1$,

$$E(X-Y)=E(X)-E(Y) \tag{10.4.6}$$
$$\mathrm{var}(X-Y)=\mathrm{var}(X)+\mathrm{var}(Y) \tag{10.4.7}$$

Note that the mean of the difference equals the difference of the means but that the variance of the difference is the *sum* of the variances.

The results of equations (10.2.2) and (10.4.3) can be generalised for more than two variables to give

$$E(X\pm Y\pm Z\pm\ \ldots)=E(X)\pm E(Y)\pm E(Z)+\ \ldots \tag{10.4.8}$$
$$\mathrm{var}(X\pm Y\pm Z\pm\ \ldots)=\mathrm{var}(X)+\mathrm{var}(Y)+\mathrm{var}(Z)+\ \ldots \tag{10.4.9}$$

This additive property of variance is one reason why variance, or s.d., is preferred as a measure of dispersion.

10.4.1 *Example*

X and Y are two independent random variables such that $E(X)=2$, $\mathrm{var}(X)=3$, $E(Y)=4$ and $\mathrm{var}(Y)=5$.
(a) Find the expected value and variance of $3X+4Y+6$.
(b) If X_1 and X_2 are two independent observations of X, find the expected value and variance of X_1 and X_2.

(a) From equations (10.4.4) and (10.4.8)

$$E(3X+4Y+6)=3E(X)+4E(Y)+E(6)$$
$$=3\times2+4\times4+6 \quad \text{(since the expected value of the constant, 6, must be 6)}$$
$$=28$$

From equation (10.4.5) and (10.4.9)

$$\mathrm{var}(3X+4Y+6)=3^2\mathrm{var}(X)+4^2\mathrm{var}(Y)+\mathrm{var}(6)$$
$$=9\times3+16\times5 \quad \text{(since the variance of a constant is zero)}$$
$$=107$$

(b) $E(X_1 - X_2) = E(X_1) - E(X_2)$
           $= 2 - 2 = 0$

since X_1 and X_2 are both independent observations of X. Similarly

$\text{var}(X_1 - X_2) = \text{var}(X_1) + \text{var}(X_2)$ (see equation (10.4.7))
           $= 3 + 3 = 6$

10.4.2 *Exercise*

(1) The two random variables X and Y have the joint probability distribution given in Table 10.7.
   (a) Show that X and Y are not independent.
   (b) Find the covariance of X and Y.

   Table 10.7

		x	
		1	2
y	1	0.1	0.3
	2	0.4	0.2

(2) The joint probability distribution of two discrete random variables X and Y is displayed in Table 10.8, the entries in the body of the table being $P(X = x, Y = y)$.
   (a) Find $E(X)$ and $E(Y)$.
   (b) Determine the distribution of $Z = 2X - Y$ and verify that $E(Z) = 2E(X) - E(Y)$.
   (c) Let (X_1, Y_1) and (X_2, Y_2) denote two independent observations of (X, Y). By using the distribution of Z or otherwise, find the probability that $2(X_1 - X_2) = Y_1 - Y_2$.   (W)

   Table 10.8

			x	
		0	1	2
	0	0.1	0.1	0
y	1	0.1	0.2	0.1
	2	0.1	0.2	0.1

(3) Table 10.9 gives the joint probability distribution of two discrete random variables X and Y. Thus for example,
$$P(X = 0, Y = 1) = \alpha \quad \text{and} \quad P(X = 1, Y = 3) = \beta$$
You are given that $0 < \alpha < 1$ and $0 < \beta < 1$.

Table 10.9

		x		
		0	1	2
y	1	α	β	α
	2	β	0	β
	3	α	β	α

(a) Show that $\alpha+\beta=\frac{1}{4}$.
(b) Find the numerical values of $E(X)$ and $E(Y)$ and show that $E(XY)=E(X)E(Y)$.
(c) Determine whether or not X and Y are independent.
(d) Find the variance of $Z=X+Y$ in terms of α.   (W)

(4) Find the covariance of the joint probability distribution in question (2).

(5) If X and Y are two independent random variables, with means μ_X and μ_Y and variances σ_X^2 and σ_Y^2 respectively, find the covariance of
(a) X and $X+Y$, (b) $X+Y$ and $X-Y$.

(6) X and Y are two independent random variables such that

$$E(X)=1 \qquad E(Y)=2 \qquad \text{var}(X)=3 \qquad \text{var}(Y)=4$$

Find the expected value and variance of (a) $X+Y$, (b) $2X-3Y$, (c) $X+2Y-4$.

(7) X_1 and X_2 are two independent observations of the random variable X which has $E(X)=3$ and var$(X)=1$. Find the expected value and the variance of $(X_1+X_2)/2$, i.e. the mean of X_1 and X_2. What would the expected value and variance be for the mean of n observations?

*10.5   **The distribution of the sum of two randomly distributed independent Poisson variables**

Suppose we have two randomly distributed Poisson variables, X_1 with mean a_1 and X_2 with mean a_2. If they are independent then using the results of this chapter their sum has mean and variance given by

$$E(X_1+X_2)=E(X_1)+E(X_2)=a_1+a_2$$
$$\text{var}(X_1+X_2)=\text{var}(X_1)+\text{var}(X_2)=a_1+a_2$$

Since the sum of X_1 and X_2 has its mean and variance equal, this suggests that it is also Poisson distributed. We can show that this is indeed so as follows. Since X_1 and X_2 are independent the probability that $X_1=x_1$ and $X_2=x_2$ is given by the product of the probabilities for the events taken separately:

Thus $P(X_1=x_1, X_2=x_2)=\dfrac{a_1^{x_1}\exp(-a_1)}{x_1!}\times\dfrac{a_2^{x_2}\exp(-a_2)}{x_2!}$

Letting the sum of x_1+x_2 be n, we can replace x_2 by $n-x_1$ giving

$$P(X_1=x_1, X_2=n-x_1)=\frac{a_1^{x_1}\exp(-a_1)}{x_1!}\times\frac{a_2^{n-x_1}\exp(-a_2)}{(n-x_1)!}$$

$$=\exp[-(a_1+a_2)]\frac{a_1^{x_1}a_2^{n-x_1}}{x_1!(n-x_1)!}$$

This gives the probability that $X_1=x_1$ and $X_1+X_2=n$. However, we require the probability that $X_1+X_2=n$ irrespective of the value of x_1, and x_1 can take any value from 0 to n. The total probability that $X_1+X_2=n$ is given by

$$P(x_1+x_2=n)=\exp[-(a_1+a_2)]\sum_{x_1=0}^{n}\frac{a_1^{x_1}a_2^{n-x_1}}{x_1!(n-x_1)!}$$

$$=\frac{\exp[-(a_1+a_2)]}{n!}\sum_{x_1=0}^{n}\frac{n!}{x_1!(n-x_1)!}a_1^{x_1}a_2^{n-x_1}$$

$$=\frac{\exp[-(a_1+a_2)]}{n!}\sum_{x_1=0}^{n}\binom{n}{x_1}a_1^{x_1}a_2^{n-x_1}$$

The term in the summation is the (x_1+1)th term in the expansion of $(a_1+a_2)^n$, giving

$$P(x_1+x_2=n)=\frac{\exp[-(a_1+a_2)](a_1+a_2)^n}{n!}$$

This is a Poisson probability distribution with mean (a_1+a_2).

10.5.1   *Exercise*

(1) Telephone calls reach a secretary independently and at random, internal ones at a mean rate of two in any five-minute period, and external ones at a mean rate of one in any five-minute period. Calculate the probability that there will be more than two calls in any period of two minutes. (O & C)

(2) The numbers of emissions per minute from two sources of radioactivity are independent random variables X_1 and X_2 having Poisson distributions with means 4 and 6 respectively.
   (a) Calculate the probability that in any minute the total number of emissions from the two sources is equal to 2.
   (b) Write down an expression for the probability that in any minute the value of X_1 is exactly twice the value of X_2.
   (c) Determine the mean and variance of $Z=3X_1-2X_2$. (L)

10.6   Continuous variables

The results in this chapter, which have been proved for discrete variables, are also applicable to continuous variables. The proofs are similar but with the summations replaced by the integrals:

$$\mu = E(X) = \int xf(x)\,dx \tag{10.6.1}$$

$$\sigma^2 = \mathrm{var}(X) = E\{(X-\mu)^2\} = \int (x-\mu)^2 f(x)\,dx \tag{10.6.2}$$

where $f(x)$ is the probability density function of the variable X.

10.6.1   *Example*

A person's journey to work consists of three stages where the means and standard deviations for the times taken are given in Table 10.10.

Table 10.10

	Time taken (min)	
	Mean	s.d.
Walk to bus stop	5	1.4
Waiting at bus stop	10	5
Journey on bus	35	7

What is the mean and s.d. for the total duration of the journey?

      Let X be the time taken to walk to the bus stop,

        Y be the time spent waiting at the bus stop,

        Z be the time spent on the bus.

From equation (10.4.8)

$$E(X+Y+Z) = E(X) + E(Y) + E(Z)$$
$$= 5 + 10 + 35 = 50$$

From equation (10.4.9)

$$\mathrm{var}(X+Y+Z) = \mathrm{var}(X) + \mathrm{var}(Y) + \mathrm{var}(Z)$$
$$= 1.4^2 + 5^2 + 7^2$$
$$= 75.96$$
$$\sqrt{[\mathrm{var}(X+Y+Z)]} = 8.72$$

The mean and s.d. for the total duration of the journey are 50 minutes and 8.72 minutes respectively.

10.7   Linear combinations of independent Normal variables

Besides the additive property of the mean and variance which was used in the previous section, a linear combination of two or more independent Normal variables has the important property that it is also Normal.

10.7.1 *Example*

A bus is due at a bus-stop at 11.10 a.m. Its actual time of arrival, Y, is Normally distributed with a mean of 11.14 a.m. and standard deviation of 4 minutes. A regular passenger arrives at the bus-stop at a time, X, which is Normally distributed with a mean of 11.09 a.m. and a standard deviation of 2 minutes.

(a) What is the probability that the passenger arrives after 11.10 a.m.?
(b) What is the probability that the bus arrives before 11.10 a.m.?
(c) What is the probability that the passenger misses the bus?
(d) What is the probability that the passenger catches the bus every day in a working week of 5 days?

(a) Measuring time in minutes from 11 a.m. we have $\mu_X = 9$ min, $\sigma_X = 2$ min,

$$z = \frac{10-9}{2} = 0.5$$

From Table A1

$$P(Z < 0.5) = F(0.5) = 0.6915$$
$$P(Z > 0.5) = 1 - 0.6915 = 0.3085$$

The probability that the passenger arrives after 11.10 a.m. is 0.3085.

(b) We have $\mu_Y = 14$ min, $\sigma_Y = 4$ min,

$$z = \frac{10-14}{4} = -1$$
$$P(Z < -1) = P(Z > +1)$$

From Table A1

$$P(Z < 1) = 0.8413$$

Therefore the probability that the bus arrives before 11.10 a.m. is $1 - 0.8413 = 0.1587$.

(c) The probability that the passenger misses the bus is *not* given by the product of the probabilities calculated in parts (a) and (b). We have also to include for example the probability that $X > 11$ and $Y < 11$ and so on. Instead we consider the distribution of $Y - X$. This will have

$$\text{mean} = E(Y-X) = E(Y) - E(X) = 14 - 9 = 5 \text{ min}$$
$$\text{var}(Y-X) = \text{var}(Y) + \text{var}(X)$$
$$= 4^2 + 2^2$$
$$= 20$$
$$\text{s.d. of } (Y-X) = \sqrt{20} = 4.472$$

The passenger will miss the bus if $y - x < 0$. The probability of this is given by the shaded area in Figure 10.1.

$$z = \frac{0-5}{4.472} = -1.118$$

$$P(Z < -1.118) = P(Z > +1.118)$$
$$= 1 - F(1.118)$$
$$= 1 - 0.8682 \quad \text{(using interpolation in Table A1)}$$
$$= 0.1318$$

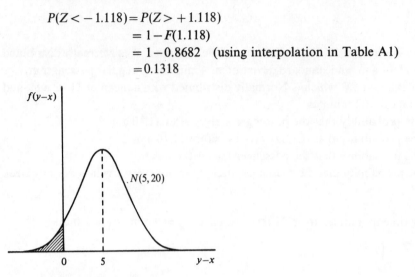

Figure 10.1 Graph to illustrate Example 10.7.1, part (c)

(d)   The probability that the passenger catches the bus on any one day is $1 - 0.1318 = 0.8682$ (from (c)). Therefore the probability that she catches it each day for 5 days is given by $(0.8682)^5 = 0.493$.

10.7.2   *Exercise*

(1)   The weight of luggage that aircraft passengers take with them is distributed with mean 20 kg and standard deviation 5 kg. A certain type of aircraft carries 100 passengers. What is the probability that the total weight of the passengers' luggage exceeds 2150 kg?   (O)

(2)   The independent random variables X_1, X_2, X_3 have means μ_1, μ_2, μ_3 and variances $\sigma_1^2, \sigma_2^2, \sigma_3^2$ respectively. State the mean and variance of the random variable $Y = a_1 X_1 + a_2 X_2 + a_3 X_3$ where a_1, a_2 and a_3 are constants.

Norman Longlegs is a well-known international athlete. His best event is the 'hop–step–jump'. In this event, as the name suggests, an athlete takes a long run up to a starting board whereupon he hops, then steps and finally jumps. His recorded distance is from the starting board to his final position. Norman has observed that the three sections of his leap all follow independent Normal distributions. The hop has a mean of 4 m and standard deviation 0.6 m; the step has a mean of 2 m and standard deviation 0.5 m; the jump has a mean of 3 m and standard deviation 0.5 m.

The world record for this event is a distance of 10.5 m. What is the probability that Norman will break this record on any given attempt?

In the European championships Norman is allowed three attempts. Assuming these attempts are independent, what is the probability that he breaks the world record at these championships?

(You should assume that all leaps are fair and count.)   (AEB)

(3) The mass, at harvest, of the fruit of a particular tree has been found to have a Normal distribution. Records show that of 200 fruits harvested, 20 were below 125 g in mass and 40 above 155 g. What is your estimate of the mean and standard deviation of the distribution?

Fruits from another tree have masses that are Normally distributed with mean 133 g and standard deviation 10 g. Four fruits chosen at random, are made up into packets. What percentage of packets will be less than 500 g in mass? (O)

(4) The diameters of axles supplied by a factory have a mean value of 19.92 mm and a standard deviation of 0.05 mm. The inside diameters of bearings supplied by another factory have a mean of 20.04 mm and a standard deviation of 0.03 mm. What is the mean and standard deviation of the random variable defined to be the diameter of a bearing less the diameter of an axle?

Assuming that both dimensions are Normally distributed, what percentage of axles and bearings taken at random will not fit? (O & C)

(5) A doctor working in a clinic finds that the consulting times of his patients are independently Normally distributed with mean 5 minutes and standard deviation 1.5 minutes. He sees his patients consecutively with no gaps between them, starting at 10 a.m. At what time should the tenth patient arrange to meet a taxi so as to be 99% certain that he will not keep it waiting? If the doctor sees 22 patients in all, what is the probability that he will finish before noon? (O)

(6) Show that the variance of the difference of two independent variables is equal to the sum of their variances.

A runs a mile race against B. A's times over a mile are Normally distributed with mean 250 seconds and standard deviation 4 seconds, while B's are also Normal with mean 246 seconds and standard deviation 3 seconds. Find the probabilities that
(a) B wins the race,
(b) both runners run the mile in under 4 minutes,
(c) at least one runner does the mile in under 4 minutes.
What further assumptions have you made in obtaining your answers? (O)

Summary

If X and Y are two random variables then

$$E(aX+bY)=aE(X)+bE(Y)$$

If X and Y are also *independent* then

$$E(XY)=E(X)E(Y)$$

and

$$\text{var}(aX+bY)=a^2\text{var}(X)+b^2\text{var}(Y)$$

(The above results can be extended for more than two variables.)

The covariance of X and Y is defined by

$$\text{cov}(X, Y) = E[(X - \mu_X)(Y - \mu_Y)] = E(XY) - E(X)E(Y)$$

and is zero for independent variables.

The sum of two independent Poisson variables is also Poisson distributed.

A linear combination of Normally distributed variables is also Normally distributed.

Project

The joint distribution of shoe size and collar size

For as many male subjects as possible obtain pairs of measurements of shoe size and collar size. Classify the results in a two-way table with shoe size as one variate and collar size as the other. Make a corresponding table of relative frequencies, including the marginal distributions. Investigate whether or not the two variates are independent.

A similar investigation can be made for female subjects using shoe size and dress size as the two variates.

Exercise on Chapter 10

(1) The random variable X is the number of black marbles obtained when three marbles are selected at random, one at a time *with* replacement, from a bag containing three red and seven black marbles. The random variable Y is the number of black marbles obtained when two marbles are selected at random, one at a time *without* replacement, from a second bag containing six red and four black marbles. Copy and complete Table 10.11 which gives the probability distributions of X and Y.
(a) Find $E(X)$ and $E(Y)$.
(b) If $Z = XY$, find $E(Z)$.   (L)

Table 10.11

a	0	1	2	3	b	0	1	2
$P(X = a)$					$P(Y = b)$			

(2) The mass of a biscuit is a Normal variable with mean 50 g and standard deviation 4 g. A packet contains 20 biscuits. The mass of the packing material is a Normal variable with mean 100 g and standard deviation 3 g. Find the probability that the total mass of the packet
(a) exceeds 1074 g,
(b) is less than 1120 g,
(c) lies between 1074 g and 1120 g.   (C)

(3) On a piece-work operation a company pays a bonus to any employee who processes in excess of 300 kg of raw material in a day. The daily amounts processed by two employees A and B are independent and Normally distributed, the mean and standard deviation of the amounts processed by A being 291 kg and 9 kg respectively, and of the amounts processed by B being 282 kg and 12 kg respectively.
Calculate, to two significant figures in each case,
(a) the proportion of days on which both A and B will earn the bonus,
(b) the probability that the combined daily amount processed by A and B will exceed 600 kg,
(c) the proportion of days on which the amount processed by B will exceed that processed by A.   (W)

(4) A die is thrown once and X denotes the score obtained. Calculate $E(X)$ and show that $\text{var}(X) = \frac{35}{12}$.
The die is thrown twice, and X_1 and X_2 denote the scores obtained. Tabulate the probability distribution of $Y = |X_1 - X_2|$ and find $E(Y)$.
The random variable Z is defined by $Z = X_1 - X_2$. State with reasons (but without necessarily evaluating the quantities concerned) whether or not
(a) $E(Z^2) = E(Y^2)$, (b) $\text{var}(Z) = \text{var}(Y)$.   (C)

(5) An employer has to interview twenty candidates for a job. Her experience has been that she may treat the length of an interview as Normally distributed with mean ten minutes and standard deviation three minutes. She begins to interview at 9 a.m. At what time should she ask for coffee to be brought to her if she is to be 99% certain that she will have seen 50% of the candidates by then?
What is the probability that she will finish the interviews by 1 p.m. if she takes fifteen minutes over coffee?   (O)

(6) At a wayside garage the number of vehicles arriving from the north in one minute has a Poisson distribution with mean λ while the number arriving from the south in the same period has a Poisson distribution with mean μ. Assuming these distributions are independent, show that the total number of vehicles arriving in one minute has a Poisson distribution with mean $\lambda + \mu$.
If $\lambda = 1.0$ and $\mu = 1.8$ find the probability that in a one-minute period
(a) no vehicles arrive,
(b) more than two vehicles arrive.
(c) If exactly three vehicles arrive in a one-minute period, find the probability that they all come from the same direction.   (O & C)

(7) In a certain population, the heights of men are Normally distributed with mean 172 cm and standard deviation 10 cm, and the heights of women are Normally distributed with mean 165 cm and standard deviation 8 cm. Calculate the probability that
(a) a man chosen at random is taller than 180 cm,

(b) a man and a woman chosen at random are both taller than 180 cm,

(c) of a man and a woman chosen at random neither is taller than 180 cm,

(d) a man chosen at random is taller than a woman chosen at random.   (C)

(8) The time of arrival of a bus at a bus stop varies in a Normal distribution with a mean of 09.00 a.m. and a standard deviation of 2 minutes. Independently a second bus departs from this stop at a time which varies in a Normal distribution with a mean of 09.01 a.m. (i.e. one minute past 09.00 a.m.) and a standard deviation of 1 minute. Find the probability that

(a) the first bus arrives before the second bus leaves,

(b) this happens on five given consecutive days.   (O & C)

(9) The mass of a certain article, made on each of two machines, is a Normal variable, the production of the first machine having mean 11.3 g and standard deviation 1.2 g and that of the second machine having mean 11.9 g and standard deviation 1.1 g. The first machine produces 40% of the combined production.

The articles are used in pairs selected at random from the combined production; a pair is rejected if the masses of the two articles differ by more than 2.7 g. Determine the proportion of pairs that are rejected.   (C)

(10) X and Y are independent random variables with means and variances μ_X, σ_X^2 and μ_Y, σ_Y^2 respectively, and you may assume that for any such independent variables $E(XY) = E(X)E(Y)$.

Find expressions for

(a) the expectation of the area of a square of side X,

(b) the expectation and variance of the area of a rectangle of sides X and Y,

(c) the expectation of the volume of a cuboid with a square base of side X and with height Y.   (C)

(11) An unbiased cubical die has its faces marked with the figures 1, 1, 1, 1, 2, 2. Write down the probability that a series of throws begins with r 1s followed by exactly t 2s. Find the marginal distributions of r and t. Find also the mean value of r. Investigate whether r and t are independent.   (C)

(12) (a) A random variable, X, is $B(1, p)$. Write down the probability distribution of X and show, from first principles, that the mean and variance of X are p and $p(1-p)$ respectively.

(b) A random variable, $Y = X_1 + X_2 + \ldots + X_n$, where $X_1, X_2, \ldots$ are independent and each is $B(1, p)$. Y is $B(n, p)$ since it is the number of successes in a series of n independent trials where the probability of success at a single trial is p. Use the result obtained in (a) to show that the mean and variance of Y are np and $np(1-p)$ respectively.

Revision exercise B

(1) $X_1, X_2, X_3, \ldots, X_n$ are n independent Normal random variables. What is the distribution of $X_1 + X_2 + \ldots + X_n$?

The time which a patient spends in consultation with the doctor at a surgery is Normally distributed with mean 10.5 minutes and standard deviation 2.5 minutes. The patients' appointments are spaced at 10 minute intervals. On one particular morning the doctor has 15 patients to see, starting at 9 a.m.

(a) What is the probability that every patient spends more than the allotted time of 10 minutes with the doctor?

(b) Assuming that the patients always arrive early, so that the doctor is never kept waiting, calculate the probability that the surgery finishes by 11:30 a.m.

(c) A patient with an appointment at 10:00 a.m. has been offered a lift home by a friend. At what time should she ask her friend to collect her if there is to be a probability of at least 0.99 that she does not keep the friend waiting?

(2) Based on statistical evidence, a life insurance company uses Table B.1 for the calculation of premiums. The table shows, per thousand of population, the number of persons expected to survive to a particular age.

Use the table to estimate the following probabilities.

(a) That a person born now will die in the next ten years.

(b) That a person born now will survive to age 60.

(c) That a person born now will die between the ages of 30 and 40.

(d) That a person aged 40 will die in the next ten years.

The probability that a person aged 60 will die within the next ten years is 0.3. The company has a life policy for people aged 60 such that if the person aged 60 dies within the next ten years his family gets £5000. Survivors get nothing.

Calculate the single premium that the company should charge so as to break even in the long run. (Ignore any interest on premiums and any administrative costs.)

Twenty people take out this policy. The company charges each person a single premium of £1800. Find the probability that the company will make a loss.

Assume that the data in the table were based on the ages of all the people in the UK who died in 1976. State, with reasons, whether the use of a table constructed in this way

Table B.1

Age	0	10	20	30	40	50	60	70	80	90	100
Number of survivors	1000	980	966	949	920	874	770	539	260	40	0

is likely to lead the insurance company to overestimate or to underestimate the premiums it should charge.   (JMB)

(3) The life in days, x, of an insect is such that $\log_{10}x$ is Normally distributed with mean 2 and standard deviation 0.2. What is the probability that an insect will have a life of

(a) more than 200 days,

(b) between 50 and 150 days inclusive?

Two insects have lifetimes of t_1 and t_2, and ρ is the ratio t_1/t_2. What will be the distribution of $\log_{10}\rho$ if their lifetimes are independent?   (O)

(4) The following data give the litter sizes of 100 litters of pigs. Arrange the data in a frequency distribution and illustrate the data graphically. Also calculate the mean litter size and the standard deviation.

6	4	12	8	11	7	9	10	6	7
5	7	14	5	8	7	4	11	9	10
7	8	11	6	3	6	8	9	12	6
10	16	5	9	5	12	8	8	6	10
6	13	7	6	4	9	11	7	5	6
9	7	5	12	7	9	7	6	8	7
8	7	6	8	7	8	5	10	9	4
13	5	4	7	8	9	7	7	6	11
10	6	6	7	5	11	9	8	10	13
7	11	10	6	12	4	8	6	9	5

                                                                                  (O)

(5) A random variable x is distributed according to the Poisson distribution with parameter λ. Write down the probability that $x=r$ $(r=0, 1, 2, \ldots)$, and also give the mean and variance of the distribution. What happens to the distribution when λ becomes large?

A storekeeper notices that the weekly demand for a piece of equipment is Poisson distributed with mean 25. About how many items of this equipment should she have in stock at the beginning of the week to be 95% certain that she will be able to meet the demand during the week?   (O)

(6) A driver uses a light van with a maximum permitted load of 315 kg to transport crates of oranges. These crates, when full, have weights which are Normally distributed with mean 30 kg and standard deviation 1.5 kg. Ten crates, chosen at random, are loaded into the van. State the form of the distribution of the total load and find its mean and variance. Hence find the probability that the van will be overloaded.

Find the probability that eleven randomly chosen crates will not overload the van. Some of the crates are damaged and some oranges have fallen out. The driver weighs a particular undamaged crate and makes each of three damaged crates up to that weight.

He loads these four together with six other undamaged crates into the van. Find the probability that the van will be overloaded.   (JMB)

(7) The lifetimes of electric light bulbs of brands A and B are independent and Normally distributed. For brand A bulbs the mean and the standard deviation of the lifetimes are 1010 hours and 5 hours, respectively, while for brand B bulbs the corresponding values are 1020 and 10 hours, respectively.

    (a) Calculate the probability that a brand A bulb will have a lifetime in excess of 1020 hours.

    (b) Calculate the probability that a brand A bulb will have a longer lifetime than a brand B bulb.

    (c) A box contains 8 bulbs of brand A and 2 bulbs of brand B. If one bulb is drawn at random from the box, calculate the probability that its lifetime will exceed 1020 hours.   (W)

(8) A student sits a multiple-choice test. On any given question, the student either knows the answer, in which case she answers it correctly, or she does not know the answer, in which case she guesses hoping to guess the right answer. Assuming that p is the probability that the student knows the answer, and that for each question five possible answers are printed, what is the probability that the student answers correctly?

The examiner is now confronted with this problem: having observed that the student got the correct answer, what is the probability that she knew the answer?

Can you help?

Sketch a graph of the probability the student answers correctly against the probability that the student knows the answer.

How does a multiple-choice test compare with a conventional test in the same subject area?   (AEB)

(9) The following are three of the classical problems in probability.

    (a) Compare the probability of a total of 9 with the probability of a total of 10 when three fair dice are tossed once.

                                (Galileo and Duke of Tuscany)

    (b) Compare the probability of at least one 6 in four tosses of a fair die with the probability of at least one double-6 in 24 tosses of two fair dice.

                                       (Chevalier de Méré).

    (c) Compare the probability of at least one 6 when six dice are rolled with the probability of at least two 6s when twelve dice are rolled.

                                          (Pepys to Newton)

Solve each of these problems.   (AEB)

(10) When an experienced kingfisher tries to catch a fish the probability that he is success-ful is $\frac{1}{3}$. Find the probability that
(a) he catches exactly two fish in five attempts,
(b) he catches at least two fish in five attempts.
A less-experienced kingfisher is only successful, on the average, in one attempt out of ten. Using a suitable approximation, calculate the probability that he catches more fish in 200 attempts than the experienced kingfisher catches in 20 attempts.   (C)

(11) The makers of a certain brand of breakfast cereal give away one picture card with each packet of cereal. There are six picture cards in a set and it may be presumed that a packet is equally likely to contain any one of the six cards.
(a) A family buys k packets of cereal. Determine the probability of the k cards obtained being all different from one another for the cases $k=4$ and $k=7$.
(b) A family buys three packets of cereal. Find the mean and variance of the number of different picture cards that they obtain.
(c) Two families each purchase three cereal packets. Both families find that they have three different picture cards. Determine the probability that all six picture cards are different.   (C)

(12) In a very large population of snails one-quarter have bright markings and the re-mainder dull markings. The probability of a snail with bright markings being eaten by birds during a season is $\frac{2}{3}$ while the corresponding probability for a snail with dull markings is $\frac{1}{9}$.
(a) Six snails are chosen at random at the beginning of the season. What is the probability that (i) all of them are bright, (ii) four or more of them are bright?
(b) A snail is chosen at random at the beginning of the season. What is the prob-ability it will be eaten during the season?
(c) A snail with bright markings has a mass of 20 g and one with dull markings a mass of 30 g. There are N snails at the beginning of the season. Assuming that there is no mortality except that resulting from consumption by birds, what is the expected total mass of the snails at the end of the season?   (O)

(13) Of the cars produced by a factory, it is known that the probability that any one car develops a fault in the first three months of use is 0.1.
(a) Calculate the probability that at least two cars from a random sample of ten cars develop a fault during the first three months of use.
(b) Later, when considering a much larger sample of 1000 cars, a statistician assumes that the distribution of cars which develop a fault approximates to a Normal distribution. Estimate the probability that between 100 and 115 cars inclusive develop a fault during the first three months of use.   (L)

(14) In a certain field, each puffball which is growing in one year gives rise to a number, X, of new puffballs in the following year. None of the original puffballs is present in the

following year. The probability distribution of the random variable X is as follows:
$$P(X=0)=P(X=2)=0.3, \quad P(X=1)=0.4$$
Find the probability distribution of Y, the number of puffballs resulting from there being two puffballs in the previous year, and show that the variance of Y is 1.2.
Hence, or otherwise, determine the probability distribution of the number, Z, of puffballs present in year 3, given that there was a single puffball present in year 1. Find also the mean and variance of Z. (C)

(15) In an experiment there are two bags, H and K, which contain marbles. In H there are three red and seven black marbles and in K there are six red and four black marbles. An unbiased die is rolled and, if a score of at least 5 is obtained, a marble is selected at random from H; otherwise a marble is selected at random from K.
If event A is 'A red marble is selected' and event B is 'A score of 5 or 6 is obtained on the die', calculate
(a) $P(B)$, (b) $P(A)$, (c) $P(A \cap B)$, (d) $P(A \mid B)$, (e) $P(\bar{A} \cap B)$, where $\bar{A}$ is the event 'not A'.
If the experiment is carried out 500 times, find the expected number of times that a red marble is selected. (L)

(16) (a) Every year very small numbers of American wading birds lose their way on migration between North and South America and arrive in Great Britain instead, so that in September the proportion of American waders amongst the waders in Great Britain is about one in ten thousand.
At Dunsmere (a bird reserve in Great Britain) one September, there are twenty thousand waders, which may be regarded as a random sample of the waders present in Great Britain. Determine the probability that there are
(i) no American waders present at Dunsmere,
(ii) more than two American waders present at Dunsmere.
(b) Three-quarters of all the sightings in Great Britain of American waders are made in the autumn. Suppose that next year there will be ten sightings of American waders at Dunsmere. Assuming that all sightings are independent of one another, determine the probability that exactly seven of these ten sightings will be made in the autumn. (C)

(17) (a) A man throws two fair dice and receives a number of pence equal to the product of the numbers of spots shown by the uppermost faces of the dice. What is his expectation at each throw of the dice?
(b) An electric circuit contains twenty components, each of which has a probability 0.01 of being defective. Calculate the probability that none of the components is defective.
(c) A bag contains three red counters, four white counters and five blue counters. Two counters are drawn at random. Find the probability that they are of different colours. (AEB)

(18) Define the conditional probability of an event A given that an event B has occurred. A commuter, who always travels by car, has a choice of three routes from her office to her home. If she travels by route A there is only a 10% chance of being home by 6 p.m., but it is a more pleasant route than the other two. If she travels by route B there is a 60% chance that she will be home by 6 p.m. If she travels by route C there is a 40% chance that she will be home by 6 p.m. She chooses routes A, B, C with probabilities of $\frac{1}{6}, \frac{1}{3}, \frac{1}{2}$ respectively.

  (a) Find the probability that, on a day taken at random, she chooses route C and gets home by 6 p.m.

  (b) One day an unexpected visitor calls at her home at 6 p.m. Find the probability that the commuter has arrived home by then.

  (c) Given that she has arrived home by 6 p.m. find the probability that she travelled by route C.

  (d) On a particular day, route C was closed for roadworks and all traffic using that route was diverted via route A. This increased traffic reduced the chance of her being home by 6 p.m. along that route to 5%, traffic along route B being unaffected by the roadworks. Given that the commuter was not aware of the roadworks when she left the office and that she arrived home before 6 p.m., find the probability that she travelled by route B.   (JMB)

(19) At a certain university in Cambford students attending a first course in statistics are asked by the lecturer, Professor Thomas Bayes, to complete ten example sheets during the course. At the end of the course each student sits an examination as a result of which he or she either passes or fails. Assuming that
  (i) the number, N, of example sheets completed by any student has a Binomial distribution given by

$$P(N=n) = \binom{10}{n}(\tfrac{2}{3})^n(\tfrac{1}{3})^{10-n} \qquad n = 0, 1, \ldots, 10$$

  and
  (ii) the probability of a student passing the examination given that he or she completed n sheets during the course, is $n/10$,

  (a) what is the (unconditional) probability that a student passes the examination,

  (b) what is the probability that a student selected at random from the examination pass list had in fact completed four example sheets or less?   (AEB)

(20) (a) The probability that Catherine beats Sarah in a game of snooker is $\frac{2}{3}$. If they play six games, calculate the probability that Catherine will win at least three of them.

  (b) Twenty unbiased coins are tossed and the number of heads counted. This experiment is repeated 1000 times. Use the Normal distribution as an approximation to the Binomial distribution to calculate the number of times eight or more heads are to be expected.   (C)

(21) A cubical die is biased in such a way that the probability of scoring n ($n=1$ to 6) is proportional to n. Determine the mean value and variance of the score obtained in a single throw.

What would be the mean and variance if the score showing were doubled? (O & C)

(22) (a) The random variable X has a Poisson distribution and is such that $P(X=2)=3P(X=4)$. Find, correct to three decimal places, the values of (i) $P(X=0)$, (ii) $P(X\leqslant4)$.

(b) The number of characters that are mistyped by a copytypist in any assignment has a Poisson distribution, the average number of mistyped characters per page being 0.8. In an assignment of 80 pages calculate, to three decimal places,

(i) the probability that the first page will contain exactly two mistyped characters,

(ii) the probability that the first mistyped character will appear on the third page,

(iii) an approximate value for the probability that the total number of mistyped characters in the 80 pages will be at most 50. (W)

(23) The independent random variables X and Y have Normal distributions with means μ_1, μ_2 and variances σ_1^2, σ_2^2 respectively.

State the distribution of the random variable $X-Y$.

Two detergents, A and B, are each packed in cartons with a nominal weight of 840 g. It is observed that, of the cartons of A, 50% contain less than 860 g and 24.2% contain more than 874 g. Of the cartons containing B, 6.3% contain less than 824.75 g and 83.4% contain less than 887.25 g. Assuming that the weights have Normal distributions, calculate the means and standard deviations of these distributions.

Find the probability that a carton of detergent A weighs less than 840 g.

A carton of detergent A and a carton of detergent B are picked at random. What is the probability that the carton containing detergent B is heavier than the carton containing detergent A?

A housewife buys five packets of detergent A. Find the probability that the lightest packet weighs more than 840 g. (JMB)

(24) A telephone was monitored for a period of time in which 80 calls were made. The duration, in minutes, of each telephone call was recorded and Table B.2 was obtained. The interval -3.75, for example, signifies over 2.5 minutes and up to and including 3.75 minutes.

Construct a cumulative frequency table and draw a cumulative frequency curve for these figures. Use your curve to estimate

Table B.2

Length of call in minutes	0–1.25	–2.5	–3.75	–5.0	–6.25	–7.5	–8.75	–10.0	–15.0	over 15
Frequency	0	4	9	15	21	20	8	2	1	0

(a) the median length of telephone call,
(b) the 20th percentile,
(c) the number of calls which lasted between 6 and 9 minutes.   (C)

(25) (a) State under what circumstances the Binomial distribution will arise. Explain how, and under what conditions, a Normal distribution can be used as an approximation to a Binomial distribution.
A machine produces articles of which on average 10% are defective. Use a suitable Normal approximation to calculate the probability that, in a random sample of 400 articles, more than 52 will prove to be defective.
(b) A telephone exchange receives calls at random at an average rate of 25 calls every fifteen minutes. Use the Normal approximation to the Poisson distribution to calculate the probability that less than 30 calls, but not less than 15 calls, are received in a fifteen-minute period.   (JMB)

(26) If a pure-bred white rabbit and a pure-bred black rabbit are mated the resulting first generation is black. If, however, this first generation is interbred, genetic theory predicts that the second generation will contain both white rabbits (with probability $\frac{1}{4}$) and black rabbits (with probability $\frac{3}{4}$).
(a) Calculate the probability that a second generation litter of 8 rabbits contains 2 white and 6 black rabbits.
(b) Calculate the probability that out of 400 such second generation rabbits
(i) 320 or more are black, (ii) exactly 300 are black.

(27) A fair coin and two dice, one red and one green, are thrown simultaneously. If the coin falls heads the 'score' X is the sum of the scores on both dice, but if it falls tails. the 'score' X is the score on the red die alone. Draw up a table showing the probability $P(X=r)$ that X takes the value r for $r=1, 2, \ldots, 12$.
Show that
$$P(5 \leqslant X \leqslant 7) = \frac{27}{72}$$
Calculate the mean of X.   (C)

11 Other theoretical distributions

11.1 Modelling variates

The three models for variates which have already been discussed are the Binomial and Poisson distributions for discrete variates and the Normal distribution for continuous variates. Although these are among the most important theoretical distributions, there are variates which cannot be modelled by them. This chapter first takes another look at discrete probability distributions, in particular the Uniform and Geometrical distributions. Models for continuous variables are then discussed, in particular the Uniform and Exponential distributions. Finally moment generating functions, bivariate distributions of continuous variables and distributions of related variables are described.

11.2 Discrete Uniform (or Rectangular) distribution

This is the theoretical distribution which we would expect, for example, for the score when a die is thrown. It is shown in Figure 11.1. Each probability is $\frac{1}{6}$ since their sum must be 1.

Figure 11.2 shows a generalised Uniform distribution in which X can take n values 1, 2, 3, . . ., n, and $P(X=x)$ is uniformly equal to $\frac{1}{n}$, since the sum of the probabilities must be 1. We have

$$\text{mean} = E(X) = \sum_{\text{all } x} xP(X=x) \qquad \text{(see equation (6.3.1))}$$

$$= \sum_{x=1}^{n} x \times \frac{1}{n}$$

$$= \frac{1}{n} \sum_{x=1}^{n} x$$

The sum is the sum of the first n natural numbers, giving

$$E(X) = \frac{1}{n} \times \tfrac{1}{2}n(n+1)$$

Therefore

$$\text{mean} = E(X) = \tfrac{1}{2}(n+1) \qquad\qquad\qquad (11.2.1)$$

which we would expect from considerations of symmetry.

To calculate the variance we need $E(X^2)$.

$$E(X^2) = \sum_{\text{all } x} x^2 P(X=x)$$

183

$$= \sum_{x=1}^{n} x^2 \times \frac{1}{n}$$

$$= \frac{1}{n} \sum_{x=1}^{n} x^2$$

The sum is that of the squares of the first n natural numbers, giving

$$E(X^2) = \frac{1}{n} \times \tfrac{1}{6}n(n+1)(2n+1)$$

$$= \tfrac{1}{6}(n+1)(2n+1)$$

$$\text{variance} = E(X^2) - [E(X)]^2 \qquad \text{(see equation (6.4.2))}$$
$$= \tfrac{1}{6}(n+1)(2n+1) - \tfrac{1}{4}(n+1)^2$$
$$= \tfrac{1}{12}(n+1)[2(2n+1) - 3(n+1)]$$
$$= \tfrac{1}{12}(n+1)(n-1)$$
$$= \tfrac{1}{12}(n^2 - 1)$$

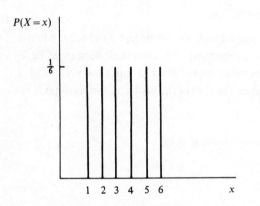

Figure 11.1 Probability distribution for the score when a die is thrown

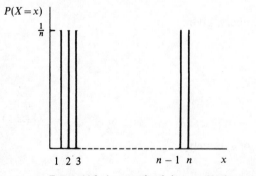

Figure 11.2 A generalised discrete Uniform distribution

We can also calculate a function which gives the probability that X is less than or equal to a particular value of X, say x_0. This function, $F(x_0)$, is called the **cumulative distribution function** (or **distribution function**), and is calculated from

$$F(x_0) = P(X \leqslant x_0) = \sum_{X \leqslant x_0} P(X = x) \tag{11.2.2}$$

For the Uniform distribution we have

$$F(x_0) = \sum_{X \leqslant x_0} \frac{1}{n} = \frac{x_0}{n} \qquad \text{for } x_0 = 1, 2, \ldots, n$$

A median can also be calculated for this discrete random variable. In Section 6.5 it was shown that the median value x_M satisfies the inequality

$$\sum_{i=1}^{M} p(x_i) \geqslant \tfrac{1}{2} \leqslant \sum_{i=M}^{n} p(x_i)$$

which can also be written

$$P(X \leqslant x_M) \geqslant \tfrac{1}{2} \leqslant P(X \geqslant x_M)$$

For the throw on a die, where $n = 6$, two values of x_M, 3 and 4, satisfy these inequalities and so the median is half way between them, i.e. 3.5. This would be expected from considerations of symmetry.

11.3　The Geometric distribution

This is a distribution which arises when we have a series of independent trials (such as those considered in connection with the Binomial distribution) where each trial can have only two possible mutually exclusive and exhaustive outcomes with constant probabilities. The variable, however, is not the number of successful trials but the number of trials required to achieve a success. Thus the number of trials is not constant but is itself the variable. Suppose we throw a die until a 6 is obtained and define the random variable X as the number of throws required to get a 6. Then, since the probability of a 6 is $\tfrac{1}{6}$, we have

$$P(X = 1) = \tfrac{1}{6}$$
$$P(X = 2) = (\tfrac{5}{6}) \times (\tfrac{1}{6}) = \tfrac{5}{36}$$
$$P(X = 3) = (\tfrac{5}{6})^2 \times (\tfrac{1}{6}) = \tfrac{25}{216}$$

and so on.

The probability function, $p(x)$, is

$$p(x) = P(X = x) = (\tfrac{5}{6})^{x-1} (\tfrac{1}{6})$$

and in general, when the probability of success is p, we have

$$p(x) = P(X = x) = (1 - p)^{x-1} p \qquad (x > 0) \tag{11.3.1}$$

The mean of the geometric distribution is given by

$$E(X) = \sum_{\text{all } x} x(1-p)^{x-1}p$$

$$= 1p + 2(1-p)p + 3(1-p)^2p + \ldots$$
$$= p[1 + 2(1-p) + 3(1-p)^2 + \ldots] \tag{11.3.2}$$

The reader may verify that the expansion of

$$(1-x)^{-2} = 1 + 2x + 3x^2 \ldots$$

so the summation in the bracket of equation (11.3.2) is $[1-(1-p)]^{-2} = p^{-2}$, giving

$$E(X) = p \times p^{-2} = 1/p \tag{11.3.3}$$

The cumulative distribution function, $F(x_0)$ can be found as follows. Since $X \leqslant x_0$ and $X > x_0$ are mutually exclusive and exhaustive events we have

$$F(x_0) = P(X \leqslant x_0) = 1 - P(X > x_0)$$

Now $P(X > x_0)$ is the probability that there is no success in the first x_0 trials giving

$$F(x_0) = 1 - (1-p)^{x_0}$$

11.4   Example

A discrete distribution is defined by
$$P(X = r) = \lambda r \qquad (r = 1, 2, \ldots, n)$$
Find the value of λ and the mean of the distribution. Show that the variance is $\frac{1}{18}(n-1)(n+2)$.
What is the median value when $n = 12$?   (O)

The sum of the probabilities over all r must be 1, giving

$$\sum_{r=1}^{n} P(X = r) = \sum_{1}^{n} \lambda r = 1$$

Therefore

$$\lambda \sum_{1}^{n} r = \frac{1}{2}\lambda n(n+1) = 1$$

giving

$$\lambda = \frac{2}{n(n+1)} \quad \text{and} \quad P(X = r) = \frac{2r}{n(n+1)}$$

$$\text{mean} = \sum_{r=1}^{n} rP(X = r)$$

$$= \sum_{r=1}^{n} r \frac{2r}{n(n+1)}$$

$$= \frac{2}{n(n+1)} \sum_{r=1}^{n} r^2$$

$$= \frac{2}{n(n+1)} \times \frac{1}{6}n(n+1)(2n+1)$$

$$= \frac{1}{3}(2n+1)$$

For the variance we need to evaluate $\sum\limits_{r=1}^{n} r^2 P(X=r)$.

$$\sum_{r=1}^{n} r^2 P(X=r) = \sum_{r=1}^{n} r^2 \frac{2r}{n(n+1)}$$

$$= \frac{2}{n(n+1)} \sum_{r=1}^{n} r^3$$

$$= \frac{2}{n(n+1)} \times \tfrac{1}{4} n^2 (n+1)^2$$

$$= \tfrac{1}{2} n(n+1)$$

$$\text{variance} = \sum_{r=1}^{n} r^2 P(X=r) - \left[\sum_{r=1}^{n} r P(X=r)\right]^2$$

$$= \tfrac{1}{2} n(n+1) - \tfrac{1}{9}(2n+1)^2$$

which after some manipulation gives

$$\text{variance} = \tfrac{1}{18}(n-1)(n+2)$$

When $n=12$, $\lambda = \tfrac{1}{78}$. If x_M is the median then

$$P(X \leqslant x_M) \geqslant \tfrac{1}{2} \leqslant P(X \geqslant x_M)$$

This gives

$$\sum_{r=1}^{k} \tfrac{1}{78} r \geqslant \tfrac{1}{2} \leqslant \sum_{r=k}^{12} \tfrac{1}{78} r$$

$$\tfrac{1}{78} \times \tfrac{1}{2} k(1+k) \geqslant \tfrac{1}{2} \leqslant \tfrac{1}{78} \times \tfrac{1}{2}(12-k+1)(k+12) \qquad [\text{using sum of an A.P.} = \tfrac{1}{2} n(a+l)]$$

$$k(1+k) \geqslant 78 \leqslant (13-k)(k+12)$$

giving, by inspection, the solution $k=9$.

11.4.1 *Exercise*

(1) Find the mean and variance for the following random variables
   (a) the score when a fair die is thrown,
   (b) the result of picking a digit at random from the digits 0 to 9.

(2) I decide to make a telephone call from a call-box one evening and to keep trying different call-boxes until I find one which is empty. If the probability that a call-box is empty is constant and equal to $\tfrac{4}{5}$, what is the probability that I have to try (a) three call-boxes, (b) more than three call-boxes?
   What is the expected value for the number of call-boxes tried and the most likely number of call-boxes tried?

(3) When a marksman shoots at a target the probability that he will hit it is $\tfrac{9}{10}$. Assuming that this probability is constant and that the trials are independent, calculate the mean number of shots needed to hit the target.
   If the marksman has already had s shots and failed to hit the target, show that the probability that he will fail to hit the target in the next t shots is independent of the value

of s, i.e. $P(X>s+t\,|\,X>s)=P(X>t)$, where X is the number of shots needed to hit the target. Comment on this result.

(4) The discrete variable X has only integer values and takes the value x with probability $P(x)$. Define the mean of X and the variance of X.
Given that $P(x)=k\,|\,3-x\,|$, where k is a constant, for $x=1,2,3,\ldots,6$, and $P(x)=0$ for all other x, determine the value of k.
Calculate
(a) the mean of X,
(b) the standard deviation of X,
(c) the mean of X^2. (C)

(5) The number of times that a certain item of electronic equipment operates before having to be discarded is a random variable X with distribution

$$f(x)=P(X=x)=\begin{cases} k(\tfrac{1}{3})^x & x=0,1,2,\ldots \\ 0 & \text{otherwise} \end{cases}$$

(a) Show that $k=\tfrac{2}{3}$.
(b) What is the probability that the number of times that the equipment will operate before having to be discarded is
(i) greater than 5,
(ii) an even number (regarding 0 as even)?
(c) For integers $m(\geqslant 0)$ and $n(\geqslant 0)$,
(i) find $P(X\geqslant n)$,
(ii) show that $P(X\geqslant (m+n)\,|\,X\geqslant m)=P(X\geqslant n)$ and comment upon this result. (AEB)

(6) Each of a set of n identical fair dice has faces numbered 1 to 6. Obtain the probability that, when every die is rolled once, all the scores are less than or equal to 5.
Obtain the probability P_r that the highest score in a single throw of all n dice has value r for $r=1,2,\ldots,6$.
Determine the mean of r and show that for $n=3$ its value is $4\tfrac{23}{24}$. (C)

(7) Fergus Lightfingers, an educated thief, has broken into a house and has come upon a large safe. Lying upon the table is a bunch of k similar keys, only one of which will open the safe. He considers two possible strategies:
(a) randomly select keys, one at a time *without replacement*, until successful;
(b) randomly select keys, one at a time *with replacement*, until successful.
Let N, a random variable, be the number of keys including the successful one tried by Fergus in order to open the safe. Derive the probability distribution of N for both strategies. Calculate the expected value of N in each case.
Use your statistical judgement in order to select the strategy that Fergus should use.

$$\left(\text{You may assume that } \sum_{n=1}^{\infty} nx^{n-1}=1/(1-x)^2 \text{ for } |x|<1.\right)$$ (AEB)

(8) An examination consists of two successive parts, of which the first must be passed before the second is attempted. Candidates may sit each part twice, and it may be assumed that any candidate who fails at his first sitting takes the opportunity of a resit. If the probability of passing the first part at any given sitting is p_1 and the probability of passing the second part at any given sitting is p_2 and all sittings are independent, write down the probability distribution of the total number of attempts and show that its mean is $(2-p_1)[1+p_1(2-p_2)]$. (You should include candidates who ultimately fail as well as those who ultimately pass.) If $p_1=p_2=p$, find the value of p for which the expected number of attempts is maximised and show that the maximum expected number of attempts is $(34+14\sqrt{7})/27$. (O)

(9) Player A is about to serve in a game of badminton against B. If A wins this rally, she will score 1 point and can serve again. This continues until A loses a rally, when neither player scores, but B gains the right to serve. The game then continues in the same way but with B serving, and so on. The outcome of each rally depends only on which player serves and is otherwise independent of all previous rallies.

The probability that either player wins a rally in which she has served is $p(\neq 0, 1)$ while the probability that the non-server wins is $q(=1-p)$. Find the probability that A wins exactly r rallies before losing the right to serve. Find also the average number of points she will have gained before losing the right to serve.

The probability that A, serving first, scores the first point is f. By considering the result of the first rally, or otherwise, show that

$$f=\frac{1}{1+q}$$

(O & C)

11.5 Continuous distributions

In Section 9.1 the idea of modelling a continuous variate by a continuous curve was introduced and the reader who has not already looked at this section will find it helpful to do so now. Figures 9.1 and 9.2 show the relative frequency density histogram for different sizes of class interval. In each case the area of a block gives the probability that a randomly chosen value will fall in that class and the total area of the histogram is 1. As the class interval is decreased and the sample size increased the histogram becomes smoothed out as shown in Figure 9.3. The shape of this smooth curve depends on the way the variable is distributed in the population. The particular variable discussed in Chapter 9 had a bell-shaped Normal distribution but the same ideas could be extended to any continuous variate; whatever the shape of the histogram, it would become smoothed out with decreasing class width and increasing sample size to give a smooth curve, with an area underneath the curve of 1. Figure 11.3 shows a possible distribution. The shaded area represents the probability that X takes a value between x_1 and x_2. In some cases it is possible to describe the shape of the curve with a mathematical function, $f(x)$, called the **probability density function**. We will look first at two such probability density functions which can be used to model relatively commonly occurring variables and then at further examples based on other mathematical models.

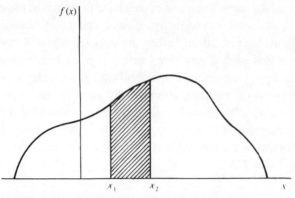

Figure 11.3 A generalised continuous probability density function

11.6   Continuous Uniform distribution

Suppose each pupil in a class measured the length of his or her pencil to the nearest cm. A recorded length of 20 cm would indicate that the true length, l, of the pencil lay in the range $19.5 \leqslant l < 20.5$. The difference between the true length and the recorded length is called a 'rounding off error'. The probability distribution we should expect for the rounding off errors is shown in Figure 11.4, since all values of the rounding off error are equally likely. It is known as a **continuous Uniform distribution**. A general form is shown in Figure 11.5. X is a random variable, Uniformly distributed between a and b. Since the area under the probability density function curve must be 1, the probability density function $f(x)$ is $\dfrac{1}{b-a}$ for $a \leqslant x \leqslant b$ and zero elsewhere.

For a continuous random variable X, equation (6.3.1)

$$E(X) = \sum_{\text{all } x} x P(X = x)$$

becomes

$$\mu = E(X) = \int x f(x)\, dx \tag{11.6.1}$$

where $P(X = x)$ has been replaced by $f(x)dx$ and summation by integration. Similarly, equation (6.4.2)

$$\text{variance} = \sum_{\text{all } x} x^2 P(X = x) - \left[\sum_{\text{all } x} x P(X = x) \right]^2$$

becomes

$$\text{variance} = \sigma^2 = \int x^2 f(x)\, dx - \left[\int x f(x)\, dx \right]^2 \tag{11.6.2}$$

Applying these formulae to the Uniform distribution shown in Figure 11.5 we have

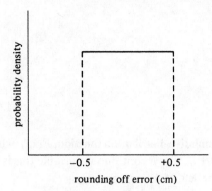

Figure 11.4 Probability distribution for the rounding off error when a length is measured to the nearest cm

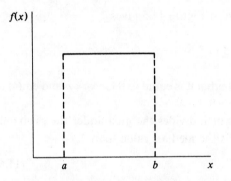

Figure 11.5 A generalised continuous Uniform distribution

$$\text{mean} = E(X) = \int xf(x)\,dx$$

$$= \int_a^b \frac{x}{b-a}\,dx$$

$$= \left[\frac{x^2}{2(b-a)} \right]_a^b$$

$$\text{mean} = E(X) = \tfrac{1}{2}(a+b) \tag{11.6.3}$$

which we should expect from considerations of symmetry.

$$\text{variance} = \int x^2 f(x)\,dx - \left[\int xf(x)\,dx \right]^2$$

$$= \int_a^b \frac{x^2}{b-a}\,dx - \left(\frac{a+b}{2} \right)^2$$

$$= \left[\frac{x^3}{3(b-a)} \right]_a^b - \frac{(a+b)^2}{4}$$

$$= \frac{b^3 - a^3}{3(b-a)} - \frac{(a^2 + 2ab + b^2)}{4}$$

$$= \tfrac{1}{3}(b^2 + ab + a^2) - \tfrac{1}{4}(a^2 + 2ab + b^2)$$

which, with some manipulation, gives

$$\text{variance} = \tfrac{1}{12}(a-b)^2 \tag{11.6.4}$$

As for discrete variables, we can calculate a **cumulative distribution function**, $F(x_0)$, which gives the probability that X is less than or equal to x_0. For a continuous variable this is the area under the probability density function to the left of $X = x_0$, so

$$F(x_0) = \int_{-\infty}^{x_0} f(x)\mathrm{d}x \tag{11.6.5}$$

which for the continuous uniform distribution in Figure 11.5 gives

$$F(x_0) = \int_a^{x_0} \frac{1}{b-a}\mathrm{d}x = \frac{x_0 - a}{b-a} \qquad \text{for } a \leqslant x_0 \leqslant b$$

To define $F(x_0)$ completely we also need to state that it is equal to 0 for $x_0 < a$ and equal to 1 for $x_0 > b$.

The median value of X is that value of X which divides the area under the probability density function into two equal halves; if x_M is the median value then

$$F(x_M) = \tfrac{1}{2} \tag{11.6.6}$$

Obviously for the Uniform distribution x_M will be $\tfrac{1}{2}(a+b)$ from considerations of symmetry.

11.6.1 *Exercise*

(1) Buses arrive punctually at the local bus-stop every fifteen minutes. If I leave my house and walk to the bus-stop without bothering to see whether a bus is due what are the mean and variance of the time which I have to wait for a bus?

(2) A continuous random variable X has a Rectangular distribution over the interval 0 to h. Find the variance of X.
The measured length L of the stems of daffodils removed from an experimental plot may be regarded as the sum of the true length l and an independent error e introduced by rounding off the measurement to the nearest unit. The variance of the true lengths of the stems is 2.5 cm^2. Find the variance of L if measurement is made to the nearest cm.
Also recommend to what accuracy the measurement should be made in order that the rounding off error shall increase the variance of the measured length by less than 1%, compared with the variance of the true length.   (O)

11.7   The Exponential distribution

This is a continuous distribution which can be derived from the Poisson distribution. Consider the situation in which telephone calls arrive randomly at an exchange, i.e. the number of phone calls in a given interval has a Poisson distribution. If the length of time between one phone call and another is measured, these times form a continuous distribution which has a probability density function which can be obtained as follows. Let the average number of calls in unit time be λ. Then, if time t has elapsed since a particular call, the probability that no further call has arrived is given by $P(X=0)=e^{-\lambda t}$ (from the Poisson distribution with mean λt, see Chapter 8). The probability that one call arrives in the next Δt is given by $P(X=1)=\lambda\Delta te^{-\lambda\Delta t}$ (from the Poisson distribution with mean $\lambda\Delta t$). Using the multiplication law for independent events (equation (4.6.2)): P(time elapsing between calls is between t and $t+\Delta t)=P$(no calls arrive in $t)\times P$(1 call arrives in Δt)

$$= P(X=0)\times P(X=1)$$
$$= e^{-\lambda t}\times\lambda\Delta te^{-\lambda\Delta t}$$

If Δt is small, $e^{-\lambda\Delta t}$ can be written as a series:

$$e^{-\lambda\Delta t}=1-\lambda\Delta t+\frac{(\lambda\Delta t)^2}{2!}+\cdots$$

giving

$$P(X=0)\times P(X=1)=e^{-\lambda t}\times\lambda\Delta t\left(1-\lambda\Delta t+\frac{(\lambda\Delta t)^2}{2!}+\cdots\right)$$

Ignoring terms in $(\lambda\Delta t)^2$ and higher powers,

$$P(X=0)\times P(X=1)=e^{-\lambda t}\lambda\Delta t \tag{11.7.1}$$

If $f(t)$ is the probability density function (p.d.f.) for the time elapsing between calls, then

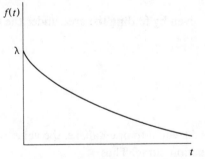

Figure 11.6 The Exponential distribution, $f(t)=\lambda e^{-\lambda t}$

$f(t)\Delta t$ is the probability that the time elapsing between calls is between t and $(t+\Delta t)$. Comparing this with equation (11.7.1) gives

$$f(t)=\lambda e^{-\lambda t} \tag{11.7.2}$$

This distribution is shown in Figure 11.6. The distribution with p.d.f. $f(t)=\lambda e^{-\lambda t}(t\geqslant0)$ and

$f(t)=0$ $(t<0)$, where $\lambda>0$, is known as the **Exponential distribution**.

The mean of the Exponential distribution is, using equation (11.6.1),

$$\text{mean} = \int tf(t)\,dt$$

$$= \int_0^\infty \lambda t e^{-\lambda t}\,dt$$

$$= [-t e^{-\lambda t}]_0^\infty - \int_0^\infty (-e^{-\lambda t})\,dt \qquad \text{(using integration by parts)}$$

$$= (0-0) - \left[\frac{1}{\lambda}e^{-\lambda t}\right]_0^\infty$$

$$\text{mean} = \frac{1}{\lambda} \qquad\qquad\qquad (11.7.3)$$

and using equation (11.6.2)

$$\text{variance} = \int t^2 f(t)dt - \left[\int tf(t)dt\right]^2$$

$$= \int_0^\infty t^2 \lambda e^{-\lambda t}\,dt - \frac{1}{\lambda^2}$$

$$= [-t^2 e^{-\lambda t}]_0^\infty + \int_0^\infty 2t(e^{-\lambda t})\,dt - \frac{1}{\lambda^2} \qquad \text{(using integration by parts)}$$

$$= \frac{2}{\lambda^2} - \frac{1}{\lambda^2} \qquad \text{(using the result for the integral involved in calculating the mean)}$$

$$\text{variance} = \frac{1}{\lambda^2} \qquad\qquad\qquad (11.7.4)$$

$$\text{standard deviation} = \frac{1}{\lambda} \qquad\qquad\qquad (11.7.5)$$

Thus the mean and s.d. are equal.

The cumulative distribution function (c.d.f.) is given by finding the area under the p.d.f. up to a particular value of t, say t_0.

$$F(t_0) = \int_0^{t_0} \lambda e^{-\lambda t}\,dt$$

$$= 1 - e^{-\lambda t_0}$$

The median t_M is the value of t which makes the c.d.f. equal to one-half, i.e. the value which bisects the area under the probability density function curve. Thus

$$F(t_M) = 1 - e^{-\lambda t_M} = 0.5$$

giving

$$e^{-\lambda t_M} = 0.5$$

Taking reciprocals and then logs to the base e

$$t_M = \frac{\ln 2}{\lambda} \qquad\qquad\qquad (11.7.6)$$

The Exponential distribution can also be applied to the failure time of components *provided that* the probability of failure does not depend on the length of time for which the component has been used.

11.7.1 *Example*

In a certain type of yarn the average number of flaws per metre is 0.01. What is the probability that the distance between consecutive flaws is more than 100 m?

Assuming that the flaws occur at random, the distance X m between consecutive flaws will be Exponentially distributed with probability distribution function
$$f(x)=\lambda e^{-\lambda x}=0.01 e^{-0.01x}$$
as shown in Figure 11.6.

The probability that the distance between consecutive flaws is more than 100 m is given by the shaded area and is

$$P(X>100)=\int_{100}^{\infty} 0.01 e^{-0.01x}\,dx$$
$$=\left[-e^{-0.01x}\right]_{100}^{\infty}$$
$$=e^{-1}$$
$$=0.37$$

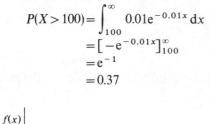

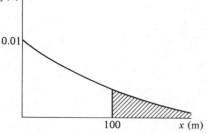

Figure 11.7 Graph to illustrate Example 11.7.1

11.7.2 *Exercise*

(1) The random variable X has the probability density function
$$f(x)=ae^{-ax} \quad (0<x<\infty)$$
Show that the cumulative distribution function of X is $F(x)=1-e^{-ax}$.
The above distribution, with parameters $a=0.8$, is proposed as a model for the length of life, in years, of a species of bird. Find the expected frequencies, of a total of 50 birds, that would fall in the class intervals (years) 0–, 1–, 2–, 3–, 4–, 5 and over. (O)

(2) A batch of high-power light bulbs is such that the probability that any bulb fails before x hours, when kept on continuously, is
$$F(x)=1-e^{-x/10} \quad (x\geqslant 0)$$

Find

(a) the median time to failure,

(b) the density function of the distribution of the time to failure,

(c) the mean and variance of the distribution,

(d) the probability that a bulb will fail between five and ten hours.   (O)

(3) For the light bulbs in question (2) calculate the probability that a light bulb will last more than 10 hours given that it has already lasted 5 hours.

Show that the probability that the bulb will last another t hours given that it has already lasted s hours is independent of the value of s. Comment on this result.

11.8   Worked examples using other theoretical distributions

11.8.1   *Example*

A continuous random variable has

$$f(x)=3x^2 \qquad 0 \leqslant x \leqslant 1$$
$$f(x)=0 \qquad \text{elsewhere}$$

Find (a) the mean, (b) the variance, (c) the cumulative distribution function, (d) the median, (e) $P(0.25 < X < 0.75)$.

Figure 11.8 shows the probability density function.

(a) $E(X) = \mu = \int xf(x)dx$

$$= \int_0^1 x \cdot 3x^2 dx$$

$$= [\tfrac{3}{4}x^4]_0^1 = \tfrac{3}{4}$$

(b) Variance $= \sigma^2 = \int x^2 f(x)dx - \mu^2$

$$= \int_0^1 x^2 \cdot 3x^2 dx - (\tfrac{3}{4})^2$$

$$= [\tfrac{3}{5}x^5]_0^1 - (\tfrac{3}{4})^2 = \tfrac{3}{80}$$

(c) When $x_0 < 0$, $F(x_0) = 0$.

When $0 \leqslant x_0 \leqslant 1$, $F(x_0) = \int_0^{x_0} f(x)dx$

$$= \int_0^{x_0} 3x^2 dx$$

$$= [x^3]_0^{x_0} = x_0^3$$

When $x_0 > 1,$ $F(x_0) = 1$

(d) The median, x_M, is given by
$$F(x_M) = \tfrac{1}{2}$$
$$x_M^3 = \tfrac{1}{2}$$
$$x_M = 0.794 \text{ (to 3 d.p.)}$$

(e) The required probability is represented by the shaded area in Figure 11.8.

$$P(0.25 < X < 0.75) = P(X < 0.75) - P(X < 0.25)$$
$$= F(0.75) - F(0.25)$$
$$= 0.75^3 - 0.25^3$$
$$= 0.406\,25$$

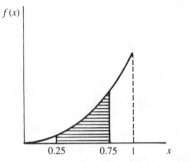

Figure 11.8 Graph to illustrate Example 11.8.1

11.8.2 *Example*

Petrol is delivered to a garage every Monday morning. At this garage the weekly demand for petrol, in thousands of units, is a continuous random variable X distributed with a probability density function of the form
$$f(x) = \begin{cases} ax^2(b-x) & 0 \leqslant x \leqslant 1 \\ 0 & \text{otherwise} \end{cases}$$

(a) Given that the mean weekly demand is 600 units, determine the values of a and b.
(b) If the storage tanks at this garage are filled to their total capacity of 900 units every Monday morning, what is the probability that in any given week the garage will be unable to meet the demand for petrol?
(c) What is the mode of X?   (AEB)

(a) Since the area under the density function curve is 1,

$$\int f(x)\,dx = \int_0^1 ax^2(b-x)\,dx = 1$$

giving
$$\int_0^1 (ax^2 b - ax^3)\,dx = 1$$
$$[\tfrac{1}{3}ax^3 b - \tfrac{1}{4}ax^4]_0^1 = 1$$
$$\tfrac{1}{3}ab - \tfrac{1}{4}a = 1$$
$$4ab - 3a = 12 \qquad\qquad (11.8.1)$$

Also we are given the mean $= 600 = 0.6$ thousand.

$$\text{mean} = \int xf(x)\,dx = \int_0^1 ax^3(b-x)\,dx = 0.6$$
$$[\tfrac{1}{4}ax^4 b - \tfrac{1}{5}ax^5]_0^1 = 0.6$$
$$\tfrac{1}{4}ab - \tfrac{1}{5}a = 0.6$$
$$5ab - 4a = 12 \qquad\qquad (11.8.2)$$

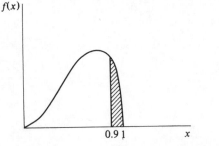

Figure 11.9 Graph to illustrate Example 11.8.2

Solving equations (11.8.1) and (11.8.2) simultaneously gives

$$a = 12, \qquad b = 1$$

(b) The density function $f(x) = 12x^2(1-x)$ is shown schematically in Figure 11.9.

The garage will be unable to meet the demand if the demand exceeds 0.9 thousand gallons. This probability is given by the shaded area in Figure 11.9.

$$\text{probability} = \int_{0.9}^1 12x^2(1-x)\,dx$$
$$= \left[\frac{12x^3}{3} - \frac{12x^4}{4}\right]_{0.9}^1$$
$$= [4x^3 - 3x^4]_{0.9}^1$$
$$= [4-3] - [4 \times 0.9^3 - 3 \times 0.9^4]$$
$$= 0.0523$$

(c) The mode of X occurs where there is a (local) maximum, that is when $f'(x) = 0$. We have

$$f(x) = 12x^2(1-x) = 12x^2 - 12x^3$$

Differentiating gives

$$f'(x) = 24x - 36x^2 = 12x(2 - 3x)$$

$f'(x)=0$ when $x=0$ or $x=\frac{2}{3}$. The former value refers to the minimum at the origin and the mode is thus $\frac{2}{3}$.

11.8.3 Example

It is proposed to model the annual salaries £X paid to people in a particular occupation using the distribution function

$$F(x)=1-kx^{-2.5} \quad \text{for } x \geqslant x_b$$

where £x_b is the lowest salary paid.
(a) Find k in terms of x_b and sketch the resulting density function.
(b) Determine the modal salary.
(c) Given that $x_b=1800$, find the mean salary.
(d) Determine the median salary for this occupation.
(e) Find the proportion of the workforce which earns less than the mean salary.
(f) State, with reasons, which of the mean, median or mode you would regard as the most appropriate measure of the 'average' salary for this occupation. (JMB)

(a) $F(x)$ gives the probability that X lies below a certain value. Since x_b is the minimum salary, $F(x_b)$ must be zero giving

$$F(x_b)=1-kx_b^{-2.5}=0$$
$$k=x_b^{2.5}$$

The probability density function is found by differentiating $F(x)$ (since $F(x)$ is obtained from $f(x)$ by integration).

$$f(x)=\frac{\mathrm{d}F(x)}{\mathrm{d}x}$$
$$=\frac{\mathrm{d}}{\mathrm{d}x}(1-x_b^{2.5}x^{-2.5})$$
$$=2.5x_b^{2.5}x^{-3.5} \qquad (x_b \leqslant x)$$

It is shown in Figure 11.10.

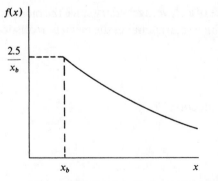

Figure 11.10 Graph to illustrate Example 11.8.3

(b) The modal salary can be seen from Figure 11.10 to be x_b.

(c) The mean salary is given by

$$\text{mean} = \int xf(x)\,dx$$

$$= \int_{x_b}^{\infty} x \times 2.5x_b^{2.5}x^{-3.5}dx$$

$$= \int_{x_0}^{\infty} 2.5x_b^{2.5}x^{-2.5}dx$$

$$= \left[-2.5x_b^{2.5} \times \frac{x^{-1.5}}{1.5} \right]_{x_b}^{\infty}$$

$$= 2.5x_b^{2.5}\frac{x_b^{-1.5}}{1.5} \quad = \frac{2.5}{1.5}x_b$$

If $x_b = £1800$

$$\text{mean} = \frac{2.5}{1.5} \times 1800 = £3000$$

(d)   The median salary is such that it bisects the area under the density curve and is thus the value for which the cumulative distribution function is 0.5. If x_M is the median salary

$$F(x_M) = 1 - x_b^{2.5}x_M^{-2.5} = 0.5$$
$$x_M^{2.5} = 2x_b^{2.5}$$
$$x_M = 2^{2/5}x_b$$

Substituting $x_b = £1800$ gives

$$x_M = £2375$$

(e)   The proportion of the work force which earns less than the mean salary of £3000 is given by the distribution function for $x = 3000$

$$F(3000) = 1 - 1800^{2.5} \times 3000^{-2.5}$$
$$= 1 - 0.6^{2.5}$$
$$= 0.721$$

(f)   The median is the most appropriate measure of an 'average' salary since the mode is the lowest salary which is not typical and the 'tail' of high salaries makes the mean unrealistically high as a measure of average salary.

11.8.4   *Example*

A continuous random variable has probability function, $f(x)$,

$$f(x) = 0 \qquad x < 0$$
$$f(x) = x \qquad 0 \leqslant x < 1$$
$$f(x) = \tfrac{1}{2} \qquad 1 < x \leqslant 2$$
$$f(x) = 0 \qquad x > 2$$

(a) Sketch $f(x)$ and show that it satisfies the conditions to be a probability density function.

(b) Find the cumulative distribution function $F(x)$.

(c) Calculate the mean and variance of X.

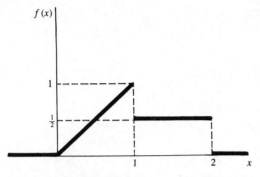

Figure 11.11 Probability density function for Example 11.8.4

(a) Figure 11.11 shows $f(x)$. It can be seen that $f(x)$ is never negative. Also the area under the curve is easily seen to be 1.

(b) For $x_0 < 0,$ $\qquad F(x_0) = 0$

For $0 \leqslant x_0 < 1,$ $\qquad F(x_0) = \int_0^{x_0} x\,dx = \tfrac{1}{2}x_0^2$

At $x_0 = 1,$ $\qquad F(x_0) = \tfrac{1}{2}$

For $1 < x_0 \leqslant 2,$ $\qquad F(x_0) = \tfrac{1}{2} + \int_1^{x_0} \tfrac{1}{2}dx = \tfrac{1}{2} + [\tfrac{1}{2}x]_1^{x_0} = \tfrac{1}{2}x_0$

At $x_0 = 2$, $F(x_0) = 1$ and is also equal to 1 for all values of x_0 greater than 2.

(c) The mean of X is given by

$$E(X) = \int_{\text{all } x} xf(x)dx$$

$$= \int_0^1 x \cdot x\,dx + \int_1^2 x \cdot \tfrac{1}{2}dx$$

$$= [\tfrac{1}{3}x^3]_0^1 + [\tfrac{1}{4}x^2]_1^2 = \tfrac{13}{12}$$

To find the variance we first calculate

$$\int_{\text{all } x} x^2 f(x)dx = \int_0^1 x^2 \cdot x\,dx + \int_1^2 x^2 \cdot \tfrac{1}{2}dx$$

$$= [\tfrac{1}{4}x^4]_0^1 + [\tfrac{1}{6}x^3]_1^2 = \tfrac{17}{12}$$

and $\quad \operatorname{var}(X) = \tfrac{17}{12} - (\tfrac{13}{12})^2$
$$= 0.243 \text{ (to 3 decimal places)}$$

11.8.5 *Exercise*

(1) The continuous random variable X has probability density function

$$f(x) = kx^3 \qquad 0 \leqslant x \leqslant 1$$
$$f(x) = 0 \qquad \text{elsewhere}$$

Find
(a) the value of k,
(b) the cumulative distribution function,
(c) the median of X,
(d) the expected value and variance of X,
(e) the probability that X is greater than the mean value of X.

(2) The continuous random variable X has probability density function

$$f(x) = kx(1 - x) \qquad 0 \leqslant x \leqslant 1$$
$$f(x) = 0 \qquad \text{elsewhere}$$

Find
(a) the value of k,
(b) the mode of X,
(c) the cumulative distribution function,
(d) the mean and variance of X.

(3) A continuous variable X is distributed at random between two values, $x = 0$ and $x = 2$, and has a probability density function of $ax^2 + bx$. The mean is 1.25.
(a) Show that $b = \frac{3}{4}$, and find the value of a.
(b) Find the variance of X.
(c) Verify that the median value of X is approximately 1.3.
(d) Find the mode.   (SUJB)

(4) A random variable X takes values x such that $0 \leqslant x \leqslant b$ and its probability density function $\phi(x)$ is given by
$$\phi(x) = x \text{ when } 0 \leqslant X \leqslant \tfrac{1}{2}$$
$$\phi(x) = \tfrac{1}{2} \text{ when } \tfrac{1}{2} \leqslant X \leqslant b$$
$$\phi(x) = 0 \text{ otherwise}$$
(a) Sketch the graph of $\phi(x)$.
(b) Show that $b = 2\frac{1}{4}$.
(c) Find the probability that X takes a value between $\frac{1}{4}$ and $\frac{1}{2}$.
(d) Find the expected value of X.   (L)

(5) Define the probability density function and the distribution function of a continuous random variable. Explain graphically, or otherwise, the relation between these two functions.

A student cycles to school each day. He is supposed to be at school by 8.50 a.m. but aims at getting there by 8.45 a.m. Over a full year his arrival times are noted and recorded. The student never arrives earlier than 8.35 a.m. and never later than 8.55 a.m. An examination of these data suggests that an appropriate model for the distribution of his arrival times is given by the probability density function $f(t)$ shown in Figure 11.12, where the student arrives t minutes after 8.45 a.m.

State the value of $f(t)$ when $t=0$.

Find, for a day chosen at random,

(a) the probability that he arrives by 8.42 a.m.;

(b) the probability, in terms of t, that the student arrives before the time given by t, where $-10 < t < 0$;

(c) the probability, in terms of t, that he arrives before the time given by t, where $0 < t < 10$.

Hence specify fully the distribution function $F(t)$.

Sketch the graph of $F(t)$. (JMB)

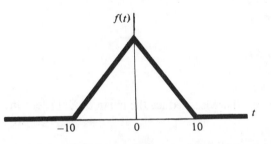

Figure 11.12 Graph to illustrate Exercise 11.8.4, question (5)

(6) X is a continuous random variable with probability density function given by
$$f(x) = \begin{cases} ke^{-2x} & (x \geqslant 0) \\ 0 & (x < 0) \end{cases}$$

(a) Prove that $k=2$.

(b) Calculate $E(X)$ and $\text{var}(X)$.

(c) The median of a continuous distribution is defined to be the number m such that $P(X \geqslant m) = \frac{1}{2}$. Prove (do not merely verify) that in this case $m = \frac{1}{2} \ln 2$.

(7) (a) A continuous variable x is distributed at random between the values 2 and 3 and has a probability density function of $6/x^2$. Find the median value of x.

(b) A continuous random variable X takes values between 0 and 1, with a probability density function of $Ax(1-x)^3$.
Find the value of A, and the mean and standard deviation of X. (SUJB)

(8) The continuous variable X has probability density function $f(x)$ where
$$f(x)=0 \qquad (x<-1 \text{ and } x>2)$$
$$f(x)=ax^2+bx+c \qquad (-1\leqslant x\leqslant +2, a, b, c \text{ constant})$$
Given that $f(-1)=0$ and the mean of X is $\frac{5}{4}$, find the values of a, b, c. The value x_1 of X is such that $P(X\leqslant x_1)=\frac{1}{8}$. Show that $x_1=\frac{1}{2}$. (C)

(9) The distribution of a random variable x, where $0\leqslant x\leqslant 1$, has probability density function kx^θ where k and θ are constants $(\theta>-1)$. Find k in terms of θ, and evaluate the mean and variance of x.
If $\theta=1$, show that the median of the distribution is $1/\sqrt{2}$ and the interquartile range is $(\sqrt{3}-1)/2$. (O)

(10) A random variable X has (cumulative) distribution function
$$F(x)=\begin{cases} 0 & (x\leqslant 0) \\ \frac{1}{4}x^2 & (0\leqslant x\leqslant 1) \\ \alpha x+\beta & (1\leqslant x\leqslant 2) \\ \frac{1}{4}(5-x)(x-1) & (2\leqslant x\leqslant 3) \\ 1 & (3\leqslant x) \end{cases}$$
Find
(a) the values of the constants α and β,
(b) the probability that $1.5\leqslant X\leqslant 2.5$,
(c) the probability density function $f(x)$.
Sketch the graph of $f(x)$, and hence, or otherwise, deduce the mean of X. Determine also the variance of X. (C)

(11) A random variable X has probability density function $f(x)$ given by
$$f(x)=kx(1-x) \qquad (0\leqslant x\leqslant 1)$$
$$=0 \qquad \text{otherwise}$$
Show that the mean and variance of X are 0.5 and 0.05 respectively.
Find the probability that an observation chosen at random from this distribution is more than two standard deviations from the mean. (O)

(12) The continuous random variable X has probability density function $f(x)$ defined by
$$f(x)=\begin{cases} \dfrac{c}{x^4} & (x<-1) \\ c(2-x^2) & (-1\leqslant x\leqslant 1) \\ \dfrac{c}{x^4} & (x>1) \end{cases}$$
(a) Show that $c=\frac{1}{4}$.
(b) Sketch the graph of $f(x)$.
(c) Determine the cumulative distribution function $F(x)$.
(d) Determine the expected value of X and the variance of X. (C)

*11.9   Moment generating functions

The examples in this chapter have shown how the mean and standard deviation can be calculated for theoretical probability distributions using the appropriate summations for discrete variables and integrals for continuous variables. As mentioned in Chapters 7 and 8 the calculation can sometimes be simplified by using a mathematical device called the **moment generating function**. For a discrete variable X, the moment generating function $M(t)$ is defined by

$$M(t) = \sum_{\text{all } x} p(x)e^{xt} \tag{11.9.1}$$

Assuming that e^{xt} can be expanded as a series, equation (11.9.1) becomes

$$M(t) = \sum_{\text{all } x} p(x)\left(1 + xt + \frac{(xt)^2}{2!} + \frac{(xt)^3}{3!} + \cdots\right)$$

Differentiating with respect to t,

$$\frac{dM(t)}{dt} = \sum_{\text{all } x} p(x)\left(x + x^2 t + \frac{x^3 t^2}{2!} + \cdots\right) \tag{11.9.2}$$

and putting $t = 0$

$$\left(\frac{dM(t)}{dt}\right)_{t=0} = \sum_{\text{all } x} xp(x) \tag{11.9.3}$$

The right-hand side of this equation is the expected value (or mean) of X.
   Differentiating again, from equation (11.9.2),

$$\frac{d^2 M(t)}{dt^2} = \sum_{\text{all } x} p(x)(x^2 + x^3 t + \cdots)$$

and putting $t = 0$ again

$$\left(\frac{d^2 M(t)}{dt^2}\right)_{t=0} = \sum_{\text{all } x} x^2 p(x) \tag{11.9.4}$$

The variance of X is given by

$$\text{variance }(X) = \sum_{\text{all } x} x^2 p(x) - \left[\sum_{\text{all } x} xp(x)\right]^2$$

$$= \left\{\frac{d^2 M(t)}{dt^2}\right\}_{t=0} - \left[\left\{\frac{dM(t)}{dt}\right\}_{t=0}\right]^2 \tag{11.9.5}$$

The power of the moment generating function to calculate means and variances is best illustrated by an example.

*11.10   Calculation of the mean and variance of the Binomial distribution

The Binomial probability distribution is defined by

$$p(x) = \binom{n}{x} p^x (1-p)^{n-x} \qquad \text{for } x = 0, 1, \ldots, n$$

This gives

$$M(t) = \sum_{x=0}^{n} \binom{n}{x} e^{xt} p^x (1-p)^{n-x}$$

Rearranging,

$$M(t) = \sum_{x=0}^{n} \binom{n}{x} (pe^t)^x (1-p)^{n-x}$$

which is also a binomial expansion, giving

$$M(t) = [pe^t + (1-p)]^n$$

Differentiating with respect to t,

$$\frac{dM(t)}{dt} = pe^t n [pe^t + (1-p)]^{n-1}$$

and

$$\left\{ \frac{dM(t)}{dt} \right\}_{t=0} = np \tag{11.10.1}$$

Differentiating again with respect to t,

$$\frac{d^2 M(t)}{dt^2} = pe^t n(n-1) pe^t [pe^t + (1-p)]^{n-2} + pe^t n [pe^t + (1-p)]^{n-1}$$

Thus

$$\left\{ \frac{d^2 M(t)}{dt^2} \right\}_{t=0} = p^2 n(n-1) + np \tag{11.10.2}$$

From equation (11.9.3),

$$\text{mean} = np$$

From equation (11.9.5),

$$\begin{aligned}
\text{variance} &= \left\{ \frac{d^2 M}{dt^2} \right\}_{t=0} - \left[\left\{ \frac{dM}{dt} \right\}_{t=0} \right]^2 \\
&= p^2 n(n-1) + np - (np)^2 \\
&= n^2 p^2 - p^2 n + np - n^2 p^2 \\
&= np(1-p) \\
&= npq \qquad (\text{since } p + q = 1)
\end{aligned}$$

*11.11   Mean and variance of a Poisson distribution

The Poisson distribution is defined by

$$p(x) = \frac{\lambda^x e^{-\lambda}}{x!} \qquad \text{for } x = 0, 1, 2, \ldots$$

This gives

$$M(t) = \sum_{x=0}^{\infty} \left(\frac{e^{xt} \lambda^x e^{-\lambda}}{x!} \right)$$

Taking $e^{-\lambda}$ outside the summation since it is constant,

$$M(t) = e^{-\lambda} \sum_{x=0}^{\infty} \frac{(\lambda e^t)^x}{x!}$$

Rearranging by putting $e^{\lambda e^t}$ outside the summation and cancelling it by putting $e^{-\lambda e^t}$ inside

$$M(t) = e^{-\lambda} e^{\lambda e^t} \sum_{r=0}^{\infty} \frac{e^{-\lambda e^t}(\lambda e^t)^x}{x!}$$

The effect of this is to make the terms in the expansion those of a Poisson distribution, mean λe^t. Their sum is 1, giving

$$M(t) = e^{-\lambda} e^{\lambda e^t}$$

$$\frac{\mathrm{d}M(t)}{\mathrm{d}t} = \lambda e^t e^{-\lambda} e^{\lambda e^t} \tag{11.11.1}$$

$$\frac{\mathrm{d}^2 M(t)}{\mathrm{d}t^2} = \lambda e^t e^{-\lambda} e^{\lambda e^t} + \lambda e^t e^{-\lambda} \lambda e^t e^{\lambda e^t} \tag{11.11.2}$$

From (11.11.1),

$$\left\{ \frac{\mathrm{d}M(t)}{\mathrm{d}t} \right\}_{t=0} = E(R) = \lambda$$

From (11.11.2),

$$\left\{ \frac{\mathrm{d}^2 M(t)}{\mathrm{d}t^2} \right\}_{t=0} = E(R^2) = \lambda + \lambda^2$$

Thus,

$$\text{mean} = E(R) = \lambda$$
$$\text{variance} = E(R^2) - [E(R)]^2$$
$$= (\lambda + \lambda^2) - \lambda^2$$
$$= \lambda$$

*11.12   Moment generating functions for continuous variables

For a continuous variable X with probability density function $f(x)$, the moment generating function $M(t)$ is defined by

$$M(t) = \int f(x) e^{xt} \, \mathrm{d}x \tag{11.12.1}$$

As for a discrete variable,

$$E(X) = \left\{ \frac{\mathrm{d}M(t)}{\mathrm{d}t} \right\}_{t=0} \tag{11.12.2}$$

$$E(X^2) = \left\{ \frac{\mathrm{d}^2 M(t)}{\mathrm{d}t^2} \right\}_{t=0} \tag{11.12.3}$$

11.12.1 *Example*

Find the moment generating function of the Uniform distribution $f(x)=1$ $(0 \leqslant x \leqslant 1)$, $f(x)=0$ elsewhere (see Section 11.6). Use it to find the mean and variance of the distribution.

$$M(t) = \int f(x)e^{xt} \, dx$$

$$= \int_0^1 1 \times e^{xt} \, dx$$

$$= \left[\frac{e^{xt}}{t} \right]_0^1$$

$$= \frac{1}{t}(e^t - 1)$$

Expanding e^t as a series (to avoid the problems caused by the t in the denominator when t is put equal to 0) gives

$$M(t) = \frac{1}{t}\left(1 + t + \frac{t^2}{2!} + \frac{t^3}{3!} + \frac{t^4}{4!} + \cdots - 1 \right)$$

$$= 1 + \frac{t}{2} + \frac{t^2}{6} + \frac{t^3}{24} + \cdots$$

$$\frac{dM(t)}{dt} = \frac{1}{2} + \frac{t}{3} + \frac{t^2}{8} + \cdots$$

$$\frac{d^2M(t)}{dt^2} = \frac{1}{3} + \frac{t}{4} + \cdots$$

Where $t = 0$

$$\text{mean} = \left\{ \frac{dM(t)}{dt} \right\}_{t=0} = \frac{1}{2}$$

$$\left\{ \frac{d^2M(t)}{dt^2} \right\}_{t=0} = \frac{1}{3}$$

$$\text{variance} = \left\{ \frac{d^2M(t)}{dt^2} \right\}_{t=0} - \left[\left\{ \frac{dM(t)}{dt} \right\}_{t=0} \right]^2$$

$$= \frac{1}{3} - \frac{1}{4}$$

$$= \frac{1}{12}$$

11.12.2 *Exercise*

(1) A random variable X has the probability density function $f(x)$ given by

$$f(x) = ce^{-2x} \qquad 0 < x < \infty$$
$$= 0 \qquad \text{otherwise}$$

Find the moment generating function of X and hence, or otherwise, show that the mean is $\frac{1}{2}$ and the variance $\frac{1}{4}$.

Show also that the median of the distribution is $\frac{1}{2} \ln 2$ and the interquartile range is $\frac{1}{2} \ln 3$.

(O)

(2) A discrete random variable is such that $P(X=r)=p_r$ where $r=0, 1, 2, \ldots$. The probability generating function $P(t)$ is defined by $P(t)=\sum\limits_{r=0}^{\infty} P_r t^r$.

Show that the moment generating function $M(t)$ of x about the origin is given by $M(t)=P(e^t)$.

The discrete Rectangular distribution is defined by $P(x=r)=1/n(r=0, 1, 2, \ldots, n-1)$. Show that the moment generating function $M(t)$ of x about the origin is given by

$$M(t)=\frac{(e^{nt}-1)}{n(e^t-1)}$$ (O)

(3) Show that the moment generating function for the random variable X which is Geometrically distributed with parameter p is $M(t)=p/(e^{-t}+p-1)$ and hence that $E(X)=1/p$ and $\text{var}(X)=(1-p)/p^2$.

(4) The probability generating function for the random variable R is
$$G(t)=p_0+p_1 t+p_2 t^2 + \cdots$$
Find $G(1)$ and show that the mean and variance of R are $G'(1)$ and $G''(1)+G'(1)-[G'(1)]^2$ respectively.

If $q_r=P(R>r)$ for all r, show that

$$(1-t)\sum_{r=0}^{\infty} q_r t^r=1-G(t)$$

If the random variable M is defined to be $\min(r_1, r_2, \ldots, r_k)$, where $r_1, r_2, \ldots, r_k$ are k independent values of R, prove that
$$P(M=r)=(q_r-1)^k-(q_r)^k.$$
If $P(R=r)=\alpha\theta^r$, where α and θ are constants such that $0<\theta<1$, find α and q_r in terms of θ and show that

$$G(t)=\frac{1-\theta}{1-\theta t}$$

Give as simple an expression as you can for the probability generating function for M, where R is as given; find the mean value and the variance of M. (O & C)

*11.13 Probability distributions of related variables

Consider the following problem. Cubic boxes are made so that the length of an edge, X, has a Uniform probability distribution with $9.5 \leqslant x \leqslant 10.5$ cm. What will be the probability distribution of the volume Y? The probability that X lies between x and $x+\delta x$ is δx. Let the probability density function of Y be $g(y)$. If, when X lies between x and $x+\delta x$, Y lies between y and $y+\delta y$, then

$$g(y)\delta y=\delta x \quad \text{(since } f(x)=1)$$ (11.13.1)
Since $y=x^3$, Y lies between 9.5^3 and 10.5^3.
We have
$$y^{1/3}=x$$
Differentiating,
$$\tfrac{1}{3}y^{-2/3}\delta y=\delta x$$

Substituting this value of δx in (11.13.1) gives

$$g(y)\delta y = \tfrac{1}{3}y^{-2/3}\delta y$$

and so

$$g(y) = \tfrac{1}{3}y^{-2/3} \qquad (9.5^3 \leqslant y \leqslant 10.5^3)$$

This distribution is shown in Figure 11.13.

This argument can be generalised for any random variable Y, which is functionally related to another random variable, X, by $y = h(x)$ where X is Uniformly distributed over an interval l. Then the probability that X lies between x and $x + \delta x$ is $\delta x/l$. If the probability distribution of Y is $g(y)$, then

$$g(y)\delta y = \frac{\delta x}{l}$$

or, in the limit as $\delta x \to 0$,

$$g(y) = \frac{1}{l}\frac{\mathrm{d}x}{\mathrm{d}y} \qquad (11.13.2)$$

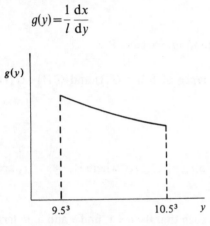

Figure 11.13 Graph to illustrate Section 11.13

If for the function $y = h(x)$ there is an inverse function $x = h^{-1}(y)$, then

$$\frac{\mathrm{d}x}{\mathrm{d}y} = \frac{\mathrm{d}}{\mathrm{d}y}[h^{-1}(y)]$$

Substituting in (11.11.2)

$$g(y) = \frac{1}{l}\frac{\mathrm{d}}{\mathrm{d}y}\{h^{-1}(y)\} \qquad (11.13.3)$$

(Equation (11.13.3) will only apply if there is a one-to-one correspondence between x and y, so that $h^{-1}(y)$ is defined uniquely for all x.)

11.13.1 *Example*

Given that $y = \ln x$ and X is a random variable Uniformly distributed in the interval 1 to 10, find the mean value of Y.

We have

$$\bar{y} = \int yg(y)\,\mathrm{d}y \qquad (11.13.4)$$

In this case, since the probability distribution of y is not required explicitly, the expression for $\bar{y}$ can be transformed into an integral in x. From (11.13.2)

$$g(y) = \frac{1}{9} \frac{dx}{dy}$$

Substituting for $g(y)$ and y in (11.13.4),

$$\bar{y} = \int \ln x \times \frac{1}{9} \times \frac{dx}{dy} \times dy$$

$$= \frac{1}{9} \int_1^{10} \ln x \, dx$$

$$= \frac{1}{9} [x \ln x]_1^{10} - \frac{1}{9} \int_1^{10} x \times \frac{1}{x} dx \qquad \text{(using integration by parts)}$$

$$= \frac{1}{9} \times 10 \ln 10 - \frac{1}{9} \times 9$$

$$= \frac{10}{9} \ln 10 - 1$$

$$= 1.56$$

If X is not Uniformly distributed but has density function $f(x)$, then equation (11.13.1) becomes

$$g(y)\delta y = f(x)\delta x \qquad\qquad\qquad (11.13.5)$$

11.13.2 *Example*

The random variable X has the density function $f(x) = x^2 (0 \leqslant x \leqslant 1)$. If the variable Y is the area of a circle, radius X, find the mean value of Y and its density function.

Let the density function of Y be $g(Y)$. Then

$$\text{mean} = E(Y)$$

$$= \int y g(y) \, dy$$

$$= \int y f(x) \, dx \qquad \text{(from equation (11.13.4))}$$

$$= \int_0^1 \pi x^2 \times x^2 \, dx \qquad \text{(since } y = \pi x^2)$$

$$= [\tfrac{1}{5}\pi x^5]_0^1 = \tfrac{1}{5}\pi$$

From equation (11.13.5),

$$g(y) \frac{dy}{dx} = f(x)$$

Substituting,

$$g(y) \times 2\pi x = x^2$$

$$g(y) = \frac{x}{2\pi}$$

and since $\pi x^2 = y$,

$$x = \sqrt{\left(\frac{y}{\pi}\right)} \qquad \text{(taking only the positive root since we are dealing with lengths)}$$

giving

$$g(y) = \frac{1}{2\pi}\sqrt{\left(\frac{y}{\pi}\right)}$$

11.13.3 *Exercise*

(1)   The total surface area, A, of a right circular cone is given by the formula $A = \pi r^2 + \pi r l$. The slant height l is a constant $2a$ and the base radius r is Uniformly distributed in the interval $(0, a)$. Given that $A = \pi Y$,
   (a)   find the mean of Y and hence the mean of A,
   (b)   find the median of A,
   (c)   show that the probability density function $f(y)$ of Y is

$$\frac{1}{2a\sqrt{(a^2 + y)}} \qquad\qquad\qquad \text{(C)}$$

(2)   Write down the probability density function and the cumulative distribution function of a random variable which is Uniformly distributed over the interval $[a, b]$.
   A person drives to work, a distance of 12 miles. The time she takes, in minutes, to cover the journey is Uniformly distributed over the interval $[20, 30]$. Let V denote the car's average speed in miles per hour on such a journey.
   Find an expression for $P(V \leqslant v)$, where v is an arbitrary value between 24 and 36.
   Hence, or otherwise, find
   (a)   the probability density function of V,
   (b)   the probability that on such a journey the car's average speed will be in excess of 30 m.p.h.,
   (c)   the median average speed for the journey (that is, the average speed which is exceeded with probability $\frac{1}{2}$). (W)

(3) A is a fixed point on a circle of centre O and radius r, and P is a point chosen at random on the circle, so that the angle at O in the triangle AOP is Uniformly distributed between 0 and π.
   Show that the probability density function of the length X of the chord AP is

$$\frac{2}{\pi\sqrt{(4r^2 - x^2)}}$$

for x between 0 and $2r$, and zero outside this range. (x represents an actual value taken by the random variable X.)
   Calculate the probability that the chord is longer than the radius. Find also the median value of X.
   Q is a fixed point on the circle and $AQ = k$. Find in terms of k and r the probability that $AP < AQ$. (JMB)

(4) The line $y+2x=k$ crosses the coordinate axes Ox and Oy at P and Q respectively. Given that the area of triangle OPQ is A, show that $A=\frac{1}{4}k^2$.

A random variable takes values k such that $0\leqslant k\leqslant 5$ and is Rectangularly distributed in this interval.

(a) Show that the expected value of A is $\frac{25}{12}$.

(b) Calculate the variance of A. (L)

(5) The operational lifetime in hundreds of hours of a battery-operated calculator may be regarded as a continuous random variable having probability density function

$$f(x)=cx(10-x) \qquad 5\leqslant x\leqslant 10$$
$$f(x)=0 \qquad\qquad \text{otherwise}$$

(a) Find the value of c and of the expected operational lifetime of such a calculator.

(b) The purchase price of such a calculator is £20 and its running cost (for batteries) amounts to 20 pence per hundred hours operation. Thus, the overall average cost in pence per hundred hours operation of a calculator whose operational lifetime is X hundred hours is given by $Y=20+(2000/X)$.

(i) Evaluate $E(Y)$, the expected overall average cost per hundred hours.

(ii) Find the probability that the overall average cost per hundred hours will exceed £2.70. (W)

(6) The maximum length to which a string of natural length a metres can be stretched before it snaps is $a(1+X^2)$ metres, where X is a continuous random variable whose probability density function is

$$f(x)=4x \qquad 0.25\leqslant x\leqslant 0.75$$
$$f(x)=0 \qquad \text{otherwise}$$

(a) Calculate the probability that a string can be stretched to $1\frac{1}{2}$ times its natural length without snapping.

(b) Find the value of $E(X^2)$ and hence find μ, the mean maximum stretched length of strings of natural length 1 metre.

(c) Find the probability density function of $Y=1+X^2$, the maximum stretched length of a string of natural length 1 metre, and use it to verify the value of μ you obtained in (b). (W)

*11.14 Continuous bivariate distributions

Discrete bivariate distributions were discussed in Section 10.1. The ideas developed there can be extended to continuous distributions. The joint probability density function $f(x, y)$ of two random variables X and Y is such that $f(x, y)\delta x\delta y$ gives the probability that

$$x<X<x+\delta x \qquad \text{and} \qquad y<Y<y+\delta y$$

$f(x, y)$ can be visualised as a surface in three dimensions. $f(x, y)\delta x\delta y$ is the volume of a pillar below the surface with a base of $\delta x\delta y$ and height $f(x,y)$, as shown in Figure 11.14. $f(x,y)$ must have the property that

$$\iint f(x, y)\,\mathrm{d}x\mathrm{d}y=1 \qquad\qquad (11.14.1)$$

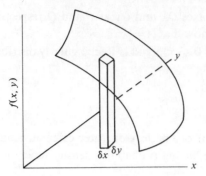

Figure 11.14 The probability density function for a continuous bivariate distribution

since this integral represents the sum of the probabilities of all possible pairs of values of X and Y.

As before the probability density function of one variable, without regard to the value of the other random variable, is called the **marginal probability density function**. For a discrete variable

$$P(X=x)= \sum_{\text{all } y} P(X=x, Y=y)$$

This is the sum of the probabilities where X takes a particular value x_i but Y can take all possible values. For a continuous variable the marginal density functions are defined by

$$f_X(x)= \int_{-\infty}^{+\infty} f(x, y)\,dy \tag{11.14.2}$$

$$f_Y(y)= \int_{-\infty}^{+\infty} f(x, y)\,dx \tag{11.14.3}$$

If X and Y are independent then, for discrete variables, we found $P(X=x, Y=y)=P(X=x)P(Y=y)$ for all x and y. The corresponding formula for continuous distributions is

$$f(x, y)=f_X(x)f_Y(y) \tag{11.14.4}$$

for all x and y.

In Section 10.4 the **covariance** of X and Y was defined as

$$\text{cov}(X, Y)= E(XY)-\mu_X\mu_Y \qquad \text{(see equation (10.4.2))}$$

where μ_X and μ_Y are the means of X and Y respectively. For continuous variables

$$\mu_X= \iint xf(x, y)\,dx\,dy \tag{11.14.5}$$

$$\mu_Y= \iint yf(x, y)\,dx\,dy \tag{11.14.6}$$

$$E(XY)= \iint xyf(x, y)\,dx\,dy \tag{11.14.7}$$

giving

$$\text{cov}(X, Y)= \iint xyf(x, y)\,dx\,dy - \iint xf(x, y)\,dx\,dy \iint yf(x, y)\,dx\,dy \tag{11.14.8}$$

11.14.1 *Example*

The joint probability density function of X and Y is $f(x, y) = k(1 - x - y)$ over the region for which $x + y \leqslant 1$, $1 \geqslant y \geqslant 0$ and $1 \geqslant x \geqslant 0$, and zero elsewhere. Find
(a) the marginal probability density function of X,
(b) the value of k,
(c) the probability density function of Y when $X = \frac{1}{2}$ and hence the mean value of Y when $X = \frac{1}{2}$,
(d) the covariance of X and Y.

The density function is a plane surface as indicated in Figure 11.15.
(a) Using equation (11.14.2),

$$f_X(x) = \int f(x, y)\, dy$$

$$= \int_0^{1-x} k(1 - x - y)\, dy$$

The upper limit is $1 - x$ since, for a given y,

$$x + y \leqslant 1 \Rightarrow y \leqslant 1 - x$$

and the lower limit 0 since this is the minimum value of y for all x. Thus

$$f_X(x) = [k\{(1 - x)y - \tfrac{1}{2}y^2\}]_0^{1-x}$$
$$= \tfrac{1}{2}k(1 - x)^2$$

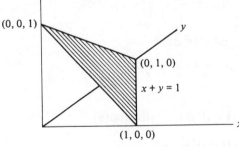

Figure 11.15 Graph to illustrate Example 11.14.1

(b) k can be found using the fact that $\int f_X(x)\, dx = 1$ since the sum of the marginal probabilities must be 1.

$$1 = \int f_X(x)\, dx = \int_0^1 \tfrac{1}{2}k(1 - x)^2\, dx$$
$$= \tfrac{1}{2}k[-\tfrac{1}{3}(1 - x)^3]_0^1$$
$$= \tfrac{1}{6}k$$
$$k = 6$$

(c)   Let $f(y \mid x)$ be the conditional density function of Y for a given x.
When $X = \frac{1}{2}$,
$$f(y \mid x) = k'(1 - \tfrac{1}{2} - y) = k'(\tfrac{1}{2} - y)$$

k' must take a value such that $\int f(y \mid x)\, dy = 1$.

When $X = \frac{1}{2}$, the maximum value of Y is also $\frac{1}{2}$ since $x + y \leq 1$. Thus
$$1 = \int f(y \mid x)\, dy = \int_0^{1/2} k'(\tfrac{1}{2} - y)\, dy$$
$$= k'[\tfrac{1}{2}y - \tfrac{1}{2}y^2]_0^{1/2}$$
$$= \tfrac{1}{8}k'$$
$$k' = 8$$

The mean value of Y when $X = \frac{1}{2}$ is given by
$$\text{mean} = \int y f(y \mid x)\, dy$$
$$= \int_0^{1/2} y \times 8(\tfrac{1}{2} - y)\, dy$$
$$= 8[\tfrac{1}{4}y^2 - \tfrac{1}{3}y^3]_0^{1/2}$$
$$= \tfrac{1}{6}$$

(d) $\text{cov}(X, Y) = \iint xy f(x, y)\, dx\, dy - \iint x f(x, y)\, dx\, dy \iint y f(x, y)\, dx\, dy$
$$= \iint 6xy(1 - x - y)\, dx\, dy - \iint 6x(1 - x - y)\, dx\, dy \iint 6y(1 - x - y)\, dx\, dy$$

Evaluating the integrals separately (and in each integrating first with respect to x),
$$\int_0^1 \int_0^{1-y} 6xy(1 - x - y)\, dx\, dy = \int_0^1 6y[\tfrac{1}{2}x^2 - \tfrac{1}{3}x^3 - \tfrac{1}{2}x^2 y]_0^{1-y}\, dy$$
$$= \int_0^1 y(1 - y)^3\, dy$$
$$= [\tfrac{1}{2}y^2 - \tfrac{3}{3}y^3 + \tfrac{3}{4}y^4 - \tfrac{1}{5}y^5]_0^1$$
$$= \tfrac{1}{20}$$

$$\int_0^1 \int_0^{1-y} 6x(1 - x - y)\, dx\, dy = \int_0^1 (1 - y)^3\, dy \qquad \text{(see above)}$$
$$= [-\tfrac{1}{4}(1 - y)^4]_0^1$$
$$= \tfrac{1}{4}$$

By symmetry
$$\iint 6y(1 - x - y)\, dx\, dy = \tfrac{1}{4}$$

Thus
$$\text{cov}(X, Y) = \tfrac{1}{20} - (\tfrac{1}{4} \times \tfrac{1}{4})$$
$$= -\tfrac{1}{80}$$

Distributions in which the marginal distributions of X and Y are both Normal are called **bivariate Normal distributions**. They are discussed further in Sections 17.3 and 18.9.

11.14.2 *Exercise*

(1) The variable x is uniformly distributed in $(-1, 1)$; two independent observations of x are taken giving values x_1 and x_2. Show how the joint distribution of x_1, x_2 can be represented on a suitable diagram. Obtain and sketch the distribution function of $X = x_2 - x_1$. Hence or otherwise show that $\mathrm{var}(X) = \frac{2}{3}$. \hfill (C)

(2) The variable x has frequency function $f(x)$ and mean zero. Write down the joint frequency function of two independent observations x_1 and x_2.
Define the expectations of any function $g(x_1, x_2)$ of x_1 and x_2 and hence obtain the mean of $X = a_1 x_1 + a_2 x_2$ where a_1, a_2 are constants. By considering $E(X^2)$ find the variance of X. Hence prove that

$$\mathrm{var}\left(\frac{x_1 + x_2}{2}\right) = \frac{\mathrm{var}(x)}{2}$$ \hfill (C)

(3) The joint distribution of x and y is Uniform over the triangle with vertices $(0, 2)$, $(0, -2)$ and $(a, 0)$, where a is a positive constant. The mean of x is 1. Find the value of a and show that the conditional distribution of y given x is

$$f(y\,|\,x) = \frac{3}{4(3-x)}$$

Find the covariance of x and y and explain whether or not x and y are independent. \hfill (C)

(4) The joint distribution of X and Y is Uniform over the square with vertices $(1, 0)$, $(0, 1)$, $(-1, 0)$ and $(0, -1)$.
If the probability that the values of X and Y satisfy the inequalities $-a \leqslant x+y \leqslant a$ and $-a \leqslant y-x \leqslant a$ is $\frac{1}{2}$, find the value of a.
Write down the joint probability density function of X and Y and obtain the marginal probability density function of X. Find the mean and variance of X.
If $U = 3X + 2$ and $V = 2Y + 1$, obtain
(a) the mean of U,
(b) the variance of U,
(c) the covariance of U and V. \hfill (C)

(5) The continuous variable X has probability density function $f(x) = \theta e^{-\theta x}$ where θ is some positive constant and $x \geqslant 0$. In order to estimate θ, a sample of n values x_1, $x_2, \ldots, x_n$ is drawn from this population. Write down the joint probability density function P of this sample. By considering P as a function of θ, find the value $\hat{\theta}$ of θ which maximises P. \hfill (C)

Summary

Discrete Uniform distribution

$P(X=x)=1/n$ for $x=1, 2, \ldots, n$

$E(X)=\frac{1}{2}(n+1)$

$\text{var}(X)=\frac{1}{12}(n^2-1)$

Geometric distribution

$P(X=x)=(1-p)^{x-1}p$ for $x>0$

$E(X)=1/p$

Continuous distributions

The **probability density function**, $f(x)$, of a continuous random variable X, is such that

(i) $P(x<X<x+\delta x)=f(x)\delta x$

(ii) $f(x)\geqslant 0$

(iii) $\displaystyle\int_{\text{all}\,x} f(x)\mathrm{d}x=1$

The **cumulative distribution function**, $F(x_0)$ is such that

(i) $F(x_0)=P(X<x_0)=\displaystyle\int_{-\infty}^{x_0} f(x)\mathrm{d}x$

(ii) $F'(x)=f(x)$

Mean $=E(X)=\displaystyle\int_{\text{all}\,x} xf(x)\mathrm{d}x$

Variance $=\text{var}(X)=\displaystyle\int_{\text{all}\,x} x^2f(x)\mathrm{d}x-\left[\int_{\text{all}\,x} xf(x)\mathrm{d}x\right]^2$

The **median**, x_M, is given by $F(x_M)=\frac{1}{2}$

The **mode** is that value of x for which $f(x)$ is a maximum.

Continuous Uniform distribution

$f(x)=1/(b-a)$ for $a\leqslant x\leqslant b$

$E(X)=\frac{1}{2}(a+b)$

$\text{var}(X)=\frac{1}{12}(a-b)^2$

Exponential distribution

$f(x)=\lambda e^{-\lambda x}$ $x\geqslant 0$

$E(X)=1/\lambda$

$\text{var}(X)=1/\lambda^2$

Projects

The *Probability density functions* section of *Advanced Level Statistics Software* demonstrates the idea of these functions visually by areas under graphs and corresponding digital readings. The analogy between $\sum_{\text{all}x} P(X=x)=1$ for discrete X and $\int_{\text{all}x} f(x)\mathrm{d}x=1$ for continuous X is apparent in the program and encourages insight into the use of integration methods for the calculation of probabilities, means and variances.

The documentation also suggests several practical problems which can be tackled (using the program) by choosing the appropriate probability density function as a mathematical model.

Exercise on Chapter 11

(1) A continuous random variable X has probability density function $f(x)$ given by $f(x)=0$ for $x<0$ and $x>3$ and between $x=0$ and $x=3$ its form is as shown in Figure 11.16.
  (a) Find the value of A.
  (b) Express $f(x)$ algebraically and obtain the mean and variance of X.
  (c) Find the median value of X.
  A sample X_1, X_2 and X_3 is obtained. What is the probability that at least one is greater than the median value?   (SUJB)

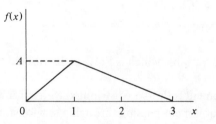

Figure 11.16 Graph to illustrate question (1)

(2) A continuous random variable X has probability density function $f(x)$ defined by
$$f(x)=\begin{cases}12(x^2-x^3) & 0\leqslant x\leqslant 1 \\ 0 & \text{otherwise}\end{cases}$$
Find the mean and standard deviation of X; find also its mean deviation about the mean.   (O & C)

(3) The continuous random variable X has probability density function given by
$$f(x)=\begin{cases}k(1+x^2) & \text{for } -1\leqslant x\leqslant 1 \\ 0 & \text{otherwise}\end{cases}$$
where k is a constant. Find the value of k, and determine $E(X)$ and $\text{var}(X)$.
A is the event $X>\frac{1}{2}$; B is the event $X>\frac{3}{4}$. Find
  (a) $P(B)$,
  (b) $P(B\mid A)$.   (C)

(4) The continuous random variable X is distributed with probability density function

$$f(x) = cx^3(1 - x^2) \qquad 0 < x < 1$$
$$f(x) = 0 \qquad\qquad \text{otherwise}$$

Find
   (a) the value of the constant c,
   (b) the value of $E(X^2)$,
   (c) the cumulative distribution function of X,
   (d) the probability density function of $Y = 1 - X^2$, and hence verify that $E(Y) = 1 - E(X^2)$.   (W)

(5) (a) The continuous variable X is distributed over the interval $(0, a)$ with probability density function $f(x)$ and distribution function $F(x)$. Show that the region of the x–y plane bounded by the lines $x = 0$ and $y = 1$ and the arc of $y = F(x)$ from the origin to $(a, 1)$ has an area equal to the mean of X.
   (b) The continuous variable Z has distribution function $F(z)$ as shown in Table 11.1. Estimate the median and the 30th and 70th percentiles of Z. By using the result of part (a), or otherwise, estimate also the mean of Z.   (C)

Table 11.1

	5	6	7	8	9	10	11
$F(z)$	0	0.02	0.11	0.24	0.61	0.97	1

(6) Write down the probability that a random variable which is Poisson distributed with parameter λ takes the value $r (r = 0, 1, 2, \dots)$.
   The number of defects, r in a piece of equipment is Poisson distributed with parameter λ. The values of r for each such piece of equipment passing through a service station are recorded, but, naturally, items for which $r = 0$ are not observed, and the resulting observed distribution is a Poisson distribution for which all values $r = 0$ are missing. Find the theoretical probabilities that $r = 1, 2, 3, \dots$ for such a distribution, and show that its mean is $\lambda/(1 - e^{-\lambda})$.   (O)

(7) Show that, if a frequency distribution has a mode at $x = M$, the cumulative distribution has a point of inflexion at $x = M$. Is it possible for the gradient at the point of inflexion to be zero?
   Sketch cumulative frequency distributions for (a) a bimodal distribution, (b) the Normal distribution, (c) a U-shaped distribution.   (O)

(8) A variable X has a probability density function given by

$$\begin{aligned} &0 \quad \text{for } x < \alpha \\ &f(x) \quad \text{for } \alpha \leqslant x \leqslant \beta \\ &0 \quad \text{for } x > \beta \end{aligned}$$

(x represents an actual value taken by the random variable X.)

Give two conditions that must be satisfied by the function $f(x)$.

In the case where $\alpha=0$, $\beta=1$ and $f(x)=kx(x-1)^2$, determine the value of k. Show that there is no suitable value for k when $\alpha=-1$ and $\beta=1$.

Calculate the mean and variance of X for the distribution for which k has been determined. Find the value of X for which the probability density function is a maximum and sketch the probability density function.   (JMB)

(9) The random variable X has a Normal distribution. Its probability density function is

$$f(x)=\frac{1}{\sigma\sqrt{(2\pi)}}\exp\left\{-\frac{(x-\mu)^2}{2\sigma^2}\right\}\qquad -\infty<x<\infty$$

where $\sigma>0$ and $-\infty<\mu<\infty$.

Verify that the mean and variance of X are μ and σ respectively. (You may assume that

$$\frac{1}{\sqrt{(2\pi)}}\int_{-\infty}^{+\infty}\exp\left(-\frac{t^2}{2}\right)dt=1.)$$

(10) A circle has centre O and radius a. Two points P and Q are taken at random on the circumference. The triangle OPQ has area A.

Obtain and sketch the distribution function of A. Show that the median of A is $a^2/(2\sqrt{2})$ and find the mean of A.   (C)

(11) The random variables X_1 and X_2 are independent, and Z is defined to be the greater of X_1 and X_2. Explain why

$$P(Z\leqslant z)=P(X_1\leqslant z)\times P(X_2\leqslant z)$$

Hence, or otherwise, find the cumulative distribution function $F(z)$ of Z, given that X_1 and X_2 both have a Rectangular distribution taking values between 0 and a.

Find the probability density function of Z and find also the expected value of Z.   (C)

(12) Whenever a large group of people is exposed to an infectious disease, the number of cases is a random variable having a Poisson distribution with unknown mean μ. However, if there are no cases, the presence of the disease passes unnoticed. Show that the probability that an observed outbreak of the disease has r cases is

$$\frac{\mu^r}{(e^\mu-1)r!}\qquad\text{where }r=1,2,\ldots$$

The numbers of cases observed in five outbreaks were 3, 2, 6, 3 and 1. Show that the likelihood (i.e. probability) of these observations is L, where

$$\ln L=15\ln\mu-5\ln(e^\mu-1)+K$$

with K independent of μ.

Find an equation for the maximum likelihood estimate of μ in the form $e^{-\mu}=A+B\mu$ where A and B are constants. By plotting a graph of $e^{-\mu}$ and drawing a suitable straight line on this graph, find an approximate value for the maximum likelihood estimate of μ.   (O & C)

(13) A fair coin is tossed repeatedly and it is decided to stop tossing as soon as three heads have been obtained. Show that the probability, p_n, that exactly n tosses are necessary is given by

$$p_n = (n-1)(n-2)2^{-n-1}$$

Hence show that $\sum_{n=1}^{\infty} (n-2)(n-3)2^{-n} = 2.$ (O)

12   Sampling

12.1   The need for sampling

In many cases it is not possible to obtain information about all members of a population, for the following reasons:
(1)   The collecting of the information may destroy the sample, e.g. testing fireworks or electric fuses.
(2)   The population may be infinite, e.g. the measurements of a physical constant such as g using a particular apparatus.
(3)   It may be impracticable to make a measurement for every member of the population, e.g. measuring the length of ants of a particular species.
(4)   Even if a measurement could be made for each member of a population, considerations of time and expense usually dictate otherwise.

12.2   Random sampling

In order for a sample to be representative of the whole population each member of the population must have an equal chance of being chosen. A sample chosen in this way is called a **random sample**.

The simplest method of selecting a random sample is by using a table of **random numbers** (see Table A3). Such tables are now normally compiled electronically but could be made using any device which gives the digits 0 to 9 with equal probability. Such a device is shown if Figure 12.1. It is a prism whose cross-section is a decagon and whose faces are labelled 0 to 9.

Suppose we wish to select two days at random from the month of August using a random number table. Each day is allocated a number 01, 02, 03, etc., up to 31. Note that each day must have the same number of digits in its number so that each number has an equal probability of being chosen. Any starting position can be chosen in Table A3. Suppose we obtain the pairs of digits: (46), (51), 06, (59), (60), 16. The numbers shown in brackets do not correspond to any members of our population and are rejected. Pairs of digits are taken until we have sufficient to give a sample of the required size. In this case the random sample will consist of August 6th and August 16th.

To reduce the amount of numbers which has to be rejected, we can allocate more than one number to each member of the population, on a cyclic basis, thus:
> August 1st   01, 32, 64
> August 2nd   02, 33, 65 etc.

Each member of the population must have the same number of numbers allocated to it. Using this method the first two random numbers we obtained before, i.e. 46 and 51, correspond to August 15th and August 20th.

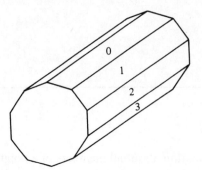

Figure 12.1 A device for generating random numbers

12.3   Periodic sampling

This is a method of sampling where every nth member of the population is chosen. It is quicker and easier than using random numbers and might be appropriate for, say, selecting names from an electoral register. In some situations it is not suitable, since, for example, choosing every tenth item produced by a machine might coincide with a periodicity of the machine.

12.4   Stratified random sampling

As its name implies, this method involves dividing the population into strata. A random sample is then selected from each stratum. The size of each sample is in proportion to the size of the stratum from which it is taken. The advantage of stratified random sampling is that the accuracy of the mean is greater than for an unstratified sample of the same size. Sometimes, however, the differences between the strata may be so great that calculation of a mean for the whole population may seem inappropriate.

12.5   Drawing a random sample from a discrete distribution

Random numbers can be used to simulate the drawing of a sample from a given distribution. Suppose we wish to choose a random sample of five from a Binomial distribution for which $p = \frac{1}{3}$, $n = 3$.

The possible values of the random variable and the corresponding probabilities are given in Table 12.1. We can use random numbers to draw a sample if we assign numbers so that the probability of selecting $x = 0$ is $\frac{8}{27}$ etc. These are shown in the third column of Table 12.1, using a cyclic method as before to use as many digits as possible. From the table of random numbers we obtain the pairs of digits

(94), 68, 81, (97), (98), 25, 39, 68

and the corresponding values of r are

1, 3, 2, 1, 1

Other discrete distributions can be treated in a similar way. Table 12.2 shows the method for a Poisson distribution with $\lambda = 0.3$. In this case the probabilities have to be rounded off, here (arbitrarily) to four decimal places, and so the values of the variable $\geqslant 5$ have been

Table 12.1 *Choosing a random sample from a Binomial distribution*

x	$P(X=x)$	Random digits
0	$(\frac{2}{3})^3=\frac{8}{27}$	01–08, 28–35, 55–62
1	$3(\frac{2}{3})^2(\frac{1}{3})=\frac{12}{27}$	09–20, 36–47, 63–74
2	$3(\frac{2}{3})(\frac{1}{3})^2=\frac{6}{27}$	21–26, 48–53, 75–80
3	$(\frac{1}{3})^3=\frac{1}{27}$	27 54 81

Table 12.2 *Drawing a random sample from a Poisson distribution*

x	$P(X=x)$	Cumulative probability	Random numbers
0	0.7408	0.7408	0000–7407
1	0.2222	0.9630	7408–9629
2	0.0333	0.9963	9630–9962
3	0.0033	0.9996	9963–9995
4	0.0003	0.9999	9996–9998
$\geqslant 5$	0.0001	1.0000	9999

grouped together. The random numbers start from 0000 so that they all have four digits. If from the table of random numbers we obtain, for example, the four digit number 7452, the corresponding value of the variable is 1.

12.6   Drawing a random sample from a continuous distribution

Suppose we wish to simulate drawing a random sample from a Normal distribution. In this case the variate is continuous and so can be selected with varying degrees of accuracy. The probability of getting a value of the standard deviate below a certain value is found from Table A1. For example the probability of a standard deviate z where $z<0.65$ is 0.7422 and this probability could be represented by assigning it the random numbers 0000 to 7421. Similarly, the probability that $z<0.64$ is 0.7389 and could be represented by the random numbers 0000–7388. Then the probability $0.64\leqslant z<0.65$ would be represented by the random numbers 7389 to 7421. This suggests that to select a random sample from a Normal distribution we can first select four-figure random numbers and then convert them to $F(z)$, the area under the standardised Normal probability distribution, by putting a decimal point in front. From Table A1 the corresponding value of z is found and hence x, the value of the variable. This is indeed the method used apart from an important proviso. The four-figure random numbers are 0000 to 9999 and if we take the corresponding values of $F(z)$ as 0.0000 to 0.9999, the values of z will not be symmetrically distributed about their mean, 0. To avoid this we add 0.00005 to each $F(z)$ giving a range of 0.00005 to 0.99995 which is symmetrical about the mean value of $F(z)$, i.e. 0.5, and gives values of z symmetrical about 0.

12.6.1   *Example*

Select a random sample of four values of the variable from a Normal distribution mean 10, s.d. 2. (The measurements should be correct to 1 decimal place.)

The method is set out in Table 12.3.

Four 4-digit random numbers are taken from Table A3. They are converted to values of $F(z)$ by adding a decimal point and 0.00005. From Table A1 the range in which Z lies is found and the values of z are converted to values of x using

$$z = (x - \mu)/\sigma$$

with $\mu = 10$, $\sigma = 2$. (If necessary the range of Z can be reduced by using interpolation in Table A1.) Correct to one decimal place the four randomly chosen values of X are 6.6, 12.8, 14.3 and 11.1.

Table 12.3 *Drawing a random sample from a Normal distribution*

Random numbers	$F(z)$	Range of Z	Range of X
0452	0.04525	$-1.70 < z < -1.69$	$6.60 < x < 6.62$
9197	0.91975	$1.40 < z < 1.41$	$12.80 < x < 12.82$
9847	0.98475	$2.16 < z < 2.17$	$14.32 < x < 14.34$
7116	0.71165	$0.55 < z < 0.56$	$11.10 < x < 11.12$

A similar method can be used for other continuous distributions. Random numbers are taken and converted to a value of the cumulative distribution function in the same way as they were for the Normal distribution. Then the corresponding value of the variable is found using the c.d.f. For example, a continuous Uniform distribution over the range 1 to 3 has probability density function

$$f(x) = \tfrac{1}{2} \quad 1 \leqslant x \leqslant 3$$

and cumulative distribution function

$$F(x) = \tfrac{1}{2}(x - 1)$$

Using the random number 6432 gives 0.643 25 for the value of $F(x)$ so that

$$0.643\,25 = \tfrac{1}{2}(x - 1)$$

giving

$$x = 2.2865$$

12.7   A biological example

A botanist wishes to investigate the flora in a field which measures 20 m square and proposes to do so by selecting at random five areas, each one metre square and studying these areas in detail. To select the areas the field is divided into a grid of 1 metre squares, as shown in Figure 12.2. Each square is defined by a pair of two-figure numbers, e.g. the square in the top left-hand corner is 0000. As before numbers can be allocated on a cyclic basis so that,

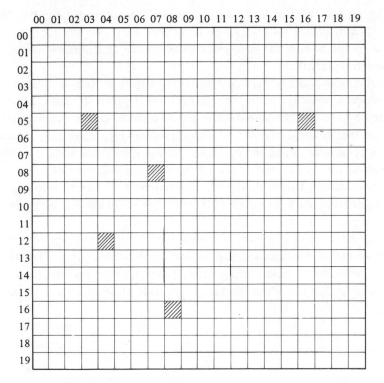

Figure 12.2. Diagram to illustrate Section 12.7

for example, 22, 42, 62, 82 all correspond to 02. Using the random number table gives five sets of four digits:

> 67 28, 96 25, 68 36, 24 72, 03 85

The corresponding squares are

> 07 08, 16 05, 08 16, 04 12, 03 05

They are shown shaded in Figure 12.2.

12.8   Practical sampling

In discussing and comparing sampling schemes the following criteria should be borne in mind:

(i)   the randomness of the sample,

(ii) time,

(iii) cost,

(iv) convenience to the person being questioned.

Consider, for example, some of the ways in which a survey might be made in a small town to find out whether parents of children under five consider the nursery school facilities satisfactory. A truly random sample is one in which all of the parents have an equal chance of being chosen. This could be achieved by selecting names from the electoral register using random numbers and interviewing those chosen. This has the disadvantages that (i) the time and expense involved in travelling to peoples' homes would be considerable, especially since more than one visit would be required if they were out, and (ii) a large number of those chosen would not have children under five and further names would have to be chosen to replace them.

The latter disadvantage could be overcome by selecting the sample from a list of parents with children under five, possibly obtainable from the local Health Authority. The sampling could be stratified by dividing the parents into groups according to which district of the town they live in so that different income (and possibly ethnic) groups are fairly represented.

An attractive way of overcoming the first disadvantage mentioned above, i.e. the time and expense involved in travelling, would seem to be offered by selecting names at random from the telephone directory. This method is not satisfactory since (i) many people, generally those less well off, do not have a phone, and (ii) people are suspicious of being phoned by strangers.

One of the simplest ways of obtaining a sample would be to stop people with small children in the town centre. This method is quick and cheap but has the disadvantage that the sample is not necessarily random. In practice, however, a compromise may have to be made between obtaining a random sample and considerations of time, cost and convenience.

Project

Estimation of the total length of road in an area covered by an Ordnance Survey sheet

Ordnance Survey sheets are already divided into squares. Use the method described in Section 12.7 to select twenty squares from a 1:50000 map and for each square estimate the length of road (include only coloured roads as many of those left white are only farm tracks). From the mean length of road per square estimate the total length of road on the map.

Exercise on Chapter 12

(1) A random sample of 200 adults from a particular residential section of a city is required. Explain clearly and concisely what is meant by *random sample* in this context and suggest a method for obtaining such a sample.
One suggested method was firstly to select 200 households at random and secondly to select one adult at random from each household. Explain briefly why this method will not produce a random sample.   (C)

(2) Explain how you would conduct a survey of customers at a supermarket on a particular day to determine (a) the mean length of time spent in the supermarket, (b) the mean amount of money spent.
Copies of the receipts given to all the customers will be available but any additional information cannot be obtained from more than 10% of the customers.   (O)

(3)   The following is a sequence of 50 random digits.

    28566   86259   00958   67172   09612
    87941   86435   70383   10287   06202

Use these to select the following random samples, explaining in detail your method:

(a)   an observation from a Binomial distribution with $p=\frac{1}{4}$, $n=10$;

(b)   two observations from a Poisson distribution with mean 0.1;

(c)   two letters of the alphabet, chosen without replacement;

(d)   a point in a circle of radius 1 inch.   (O)

(4)   A crude model of a large city is given by a circle of radius 5 cm representing high density of population, inside a concentric circle of radius 10 cm. This map is divided into square sampling units of 0.2 cm side. Draw this representation on graph paper and use the table of random numbers in question (3) to select a sample of eight units from the inner circle and two units from the outer ring. Pay careful attention to the problems of definition, and describe in detail your method of selection, marking your final sample on the map.

The number of overcrowded families in each unit was counted. If the eight inner units gave values of 10, 16, 8, 11, 12, 10, 7, 14 and the outer units gave values of 5 and 9, obtain an estimate for the total number of overcrowded families in the city.   (O)

(5)   The methods that follow are suggested as ways of generating equiprobable random digits. In each case, find the frequency distribution of the digits generated and state, with your reasons, whether you consider that the method is satisfactory for its declared purpose.

(a)   Throw two fair dice. Record the sum of the scores when the sum is 2–9; record the sum 10 as 0, and the sum 11 as 1; reject 12.

(b)   Toss a fair penny four times. Record a head as 0 and a tail as 1 so that the result of a trial is four digits in order $abcd$, e.g. 0110. Interpret $abcd$ as the number $a \times 2^3 + b \times 2^2 + c \times 2 + d$ (e.g. 0110→6); record the number if it is 0–9, reject it if it is greater than 9.   (O)

(6)   A manufacturer of a new soap powder wishes to predict the likely volume of sales in a town. Four schemes, as below, are proposed for selecting people for a questionnaire. Discuss the merits of each and choose one, explaining why you think it is the best.

(a)   Take every 20th name on the electoral register of the town.

(b)   Choose people entering a supermarket, ensuring that the numbers in each sex, age and social class category are proportional to the number in the population.

(c)   Select houses at random from a town plan and interview one person from each.

(d)   Choose at random one name from each page of the telephone directory and ring them up.   (O)

(7)   Discuss the purpose of stratification in carrying out a sample survey.

In a survey of the Health Service in a town (see Table 12.4), patients were asked if they had consulted their doctor in the last year. The sample was stratified by age and

Table 12.4

Stratum	Population size	Sample size	Number in sample visiting doctor
Male children	1500	10	6
Male adults	5000	50	10
Female children	2000	10	6
Female adults	6000	50	20

sex and was drawn at random within each stratum. Estimate the percentage of the population of the town who had consulted their doctor in the last year.   (O)

(8) Use the sequence of random digits
      56 16 88 87 60 32 15 69 26 72 39 27
to select an observation at random from each of the following distributions. Explain clearly the method you use for each distribution.
(a) Binomial distribution with $p=\frac{1}{2}$, $n=4$.
(b) Poisson distribution with mean 0.2.
(c) Normal distribution with mean 5, variance 4 (correct to 1 d.p.).   (O)

(9) What is meant by the term 'random sample'?
The government decides to hold a referendum to determine whether the 'British people' are for or against a new compulsory retirement age of 50 for all workers. Unfortunately, however, the Exchequer does not have sufficient funds available to conduct a referendum. A helpful statistician suggests that a sample will provide equivalent information at a greatly reduced cost. Alternative ways of choosing the sample are proposed, as listed below.
(a) Insert a full page advertisement in *The Times* newspaper, asking readers to return a coupon to the Central Statistical Office indicating their preference.
(b) Take three cities, say London, Manchester and Glasgow, and ask every rate-payer in each city.
(c) Include a compulsory question on the subject as part of the standard passport application form, during August 1984 only.
(d) Take the telephone directories for each area in Great Britain and telephone the 1st, 101st, 201st, ..., etc. private subscriber listed in each directory.
Comment on the appropriateness of each proposal. How would *you* choose a suitable sample?   (AEB)

(10) A sample of twenty is to be selected from your school to take an intelligence test and so find their IQ. Describe in detail how you would select the sample and use it to estimate the mean IQ for the school. You should bear in mind the age (and possibly sex) structure of your school, as well as any other relevant points.   (O)

(11) What is meant by a 'random sample'? Give an example of a method of non-random sampling which might be used in practice in place of random sampling, stating briefly its advantages and disadvantages.

The following is a sequence of random digits:

43401   33545   55105   43850   57493
64406   74935   53926   27709   87668

Use them in order to select the following random samples, explaining in detail your method:

(a)   two hours from the 24 in a day, chosen without replacement,

(b)   a point in a triangle with sides of length 10, 10, $10\sqrt{2}$ cm.   (O)

13 Sampling distributions

13.1 Estimators

The main purpose of taking a sample is to obtain information about the parameters of the population from which the sample is drawn. For example, the mean of a sample gives us an **estimate** of the mean of the population.

If we took another sample from the population and calculated *its* mean we should be most unlikely to obtain the same value as we did for the first sample. In fact, if we continued taking samples and calculating their means, these means would have a frequency distribution of their own. If we consider all possible values that the mean can take when all possible random samples (of a given size) are drawn from the population then we can form the probability distribution of the sample mean. The random variable defined by this probability distribution, in this case the sample mean, is called an **estimator**. The probability distribution of an estimator is called its **sampling distribution**.

In this chapter we look at sampling distributions, in particular that of the mean, and the properties which an estimator needs to give a 'good' estimate of a population parameter.

13.2 An unbiased estimate of the mean

One of the first requirements of an estimator is that it should be **unbiased**. This means that the expected value of the sampling distribution of the estimator should be equal to the parameter which is being estimated. It seems intuitively obvious that the variable, $\bar{X}$, the mean of a sample, should give an unbiased estimate of μ, the population mean. For a sample size n, $\bar{X}$ is calculated from n independent observations of X, which we will call $X_1, X_2, \ldots, X_n$. We can show that $\bar{X}$ is an unbiased estimate of μ as follows:

$$\bar{X} = (X_1 + X_2 + \cdots + X_n)/n$$
$$E(\bar{X}) = E\{(X_1 + X_2 + \cdots + X_n)/n\}$$

$$= E\left\{\frac{X_1}{n} + \frac{X_2}{n} + \cdots + \frac{X_n}{n}\right\}$$

$$= \left\{\frac{E(X_1)}{n} + \frac{E(X_2)}{n} + \cdots + \frac{E(X_n)}{n}\right\} \qquad \text{(from equation (10.4.4))}$$

$$= \frac{\mu}{n} + \frac{\mu}{n} + \cdots + \frac{\mu}{n} \qquad \text{(from the definition of expected value, Section 6.3)}$$

therefore

$$E(\bar{X}) = \mu \qquad\qquad\qquad (13.2.1)$$

232

13.3   The sampling distribution of the mean

We know that each sample will give a different estimate of the population mean. In order to find out how close an estimate will be to the population parameter we need to study the sampling distribution of the mean in more detail and to find out how it is related to the population distribution. We will start by considering a particular numerical example.

Consider a large population which consists of equal numbers of the digits 1, 2 and 3. The mean of the population is given by

$$\mu = \sum_{\text{all } x} xP(X=x) \qquad (\text{see Section 6.3})$$
$$= \tfrac{1}{3} \times 1 + \tfrac{1}{3} \times 2 + \tfrac{1}{3} \times 3$$
$$= 2$$

and its variance by

$$\sigma^2 = \sum_{\text{all } x} x^2 P(X=x) - \left[\sum_{\text{all } x} xP(X=x) \right]^2 \qquad (\text{see Section 6.4})$$
$$= \tfrac{1}{3} \times 1^2 + \tfrac{1}{3} \times 2^2 + \tfrac{1}{3} \times 3^2 - 2^2$$
$$= \tfrac{14}{3} - 4 = \tfrac{2}{3}$$

If we take samples, size two, from the population, the possible pairs of values are (1, 1), (1, 2), (2, 1), (2, 2), (2, 3), (3, 2), (3, 3), (1, 3), (3, 1). (Since the population is large we need not concern ourselves with whether or not sampling is with replacement but the theory of this chapter is concerned only with sampling *with* replacement.)

Figure 13.1 gives the sample space for the means of the samples. The sample means $\bar{x}$ with their corresponding probabilities are given in Table 13.1 together with the calculation of

$$\sum_{\text{all } \bar{x}} \bar{x}P(\bar{X}=\bar{x}) \quad \text{and} \quad \sum_{\text{all } \bar{x}} \bar{x}^2 P(\bar{X}=\bar{x})$$

We have

$$\text{mean of sampling distribution} = \sum_{\text{all } \bar{x}} \bar{x}P(\bar{X}=\bar{x}) = 2$$

which, as we expected, is the mean of the original or parent population.

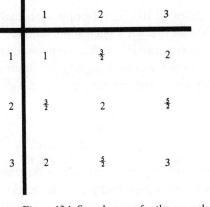

Figure 13.1. Sample space for the example in Section 13.3

Table 13.1

$\bar{x}$	$P(\bar{X}=\bar{x})$	$\bar{x}P(\bar{X}=\bar{x})$	$\bar{x}^2P(\bar{X}=\bar{x})$
1	$\frac{1}{9}$	$\frac{1}{9}$	$\frac{1}{9}$
$\frac{3}{2}$	$\frac{2}{9}$	$\frac{1}{3}$	$\frac{1}{2}$
2	$\frac{3}{9}$	$\frac{2}{3}$	$\frac{4}{3}$
$\frac{5}{2}$	$\frac{2}{9}$	$\frac{5}{9}$	$\frac{25}{18}$
3	$\frac{1}{9}$	$\frac{1}{3}$	1
		2	$\frac{13}{3}$

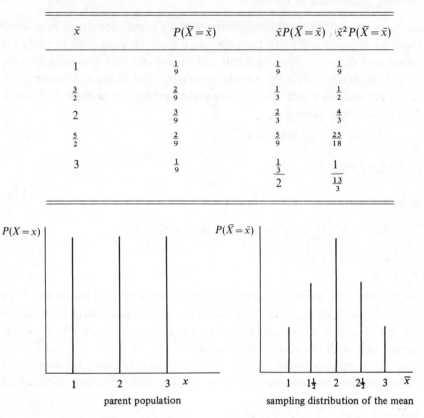

parent population   sampling distribution of the mean

Figure 13.2 Probability distributions for the parent population and the means of the samples for the example in Section 13.3.

$$\text{variance of sampling distribution} = \sum_{\text{all } \bar{x}} \bar{x}^2 P(\bar{X}=\bar{x}) - \left[\sum_{\text{all } \bar{x}} \bar{x}P(\bar{X}=\bar{x})\right]^2$$
$$= \frac{13}{3} - 2^2$$
$$= \frac{1}{3}$$

Figure 13.2 illustrates the probability distributions of the parent population and the sampling distribution of the mean. The diagram shows that the values of the sample mean cluster more closely about the mean than the values of the variable in the parent population. This is reflected in the values for the variance: the variance of the sampling distribution of the mean is half that of the parent population. This is a particular example of a theorem which is as follows:

13.3.1   Theorem

If all possible random samples, size n, are drawn (with replacement) from a population, mean μ and s.d. σ, then the means of the samples have a probability distribution known as the sampling distribution of the mean, with mean μ and s.d. $\sigma/\sqrt{n}$. The standard deviation of the sampling distribution of the mean is known as the **standard error (s.e.) of the mean**.

Proof of Theorem 13.3.1

We have already shown in Section 13.2 that $E(\bar{X}) = \mu$ and $E(\bar{X})$ is the mean of the sampling distribution of the mean.

The variance of the sampling distribution is $\mathrm{var}(\bar{X})$. We have

$$
\begin{aligned}
\mathrm{var}(\bar{X}) &= \mathrm{var}\left\{\sum_{i=1}^{n} \frac{X_i}{n}\right\} \\
&= \frac{1}{n^2}\,\mathrm{var}\left\{\sum_{i=1}^{n} X_i\right\} \quad \text{(from equation (10.4.5))} \\
&= \frac{1}{n^2}\{\mathrm{var}(X_1) + \mathrm{var}(X_2) + \cdots + \mathrm{var}(X_n)\} \quad \text{(from equation (10.4.9))} \\
&= \frac{1}{n^2} \times n\sigma^2 \\
&= \frac{\sigma^2}{n}
\end{aligned}
\tag{13.3.1}
$$

Thus the s.d. of the sampling distribution of the mean is $\sigma/\sqrt{n}$.

If the sampling is *without replacement* and the population size is N then equation (13.3.1) becomes

$$
\mathrm{var}(\bar{X}) = \frac{\sigma^2}{n}\left(\frac{N-n}{N-1}\right)
$$

It can be seen that if n is very much smaller than N then this formula gives approximately the same result as equation (13.3.1). In this book it is assumed that the sample size is always much less than the population size so that even if sampling is without replacement (the more usual situation), equation (13.3.1) may still be used.

Whether the sampling is with or without replacement $\mathrm{var}(\bar{X})$ decreases as the sample size increases. This confirms what we would expect intuitively: the larger the sample size, the closer the sample mean is likely to be to the population mean.

13.3.2   *Exercise*

(1)   A large population consists of equal numbers of the digits 1 and 3. Find the mean and variance of this population.

Find the probability distribution of the mean of samples size three taken from this population and verify that its mean is equal to the population mean and its variance is equal to one-third of the population variance.

(2)   The discrete random variable J has the distribution given in Table 13.2.
(a)   Find the mean μ and variance σ^2 of the distribution. Random samples size two are taken from the distribution. By considering all possible samples, obtain the probability distribution of the mean of such samples. Verify that this distribution has mean μ and variance $\frac{1}{2}\sigma^2$.
(b)   What would be the mean and variance of the distribution of the mean of random samples of size three from the original distribution?

Table 13.2

j	-2	-1	0	1	2
$P(J=j)$	0.1	0.2	0.4	0.2	0.1

13.4   An unbiased estimator of variance

Just as the sample mean varies from sample to sample, so does the sample variance. The form of the sampling distribution of the variance is considered in Section 19.1: here we are concerned with using a sample to obtain an unbiased estimate of population variance, σ^2. We might expect the random variable $\sum_{i=1}^{n} \dfrac{(X_i-\mu)^2}{n}$ to be an unbiased estimator of σ^2 and this can be proved as follows by finding its expected value:

$$E\left[\sum_{i=1}^{n}\frac{(X_i-\mu)^2}{n}\right]=E\left[\frac{(X_1-\mu)^2}{n}+\frac{(X_2-\mu)^2}{n}+\cdots+\frac{(X_n-\mu)^2}{n}\right]$$

$$=E\left[\frac{(X_1-\mu)^2}{n}\right]+E\left[\frac{(X_2-\mu)^2}{n}\right]+\cdots+E\left[\frac{(X_n-\mu)^2}{n}\right]$$

(using equation (10.2.2))

$$=\frac{1}{n}E[(X_1-\mu)^2]+\frac{1}{n}E[(X_2-\mu)^2]+\cdots+\frac{1}{n}E[(X_n-\mu)^2]$$

(using equation (10.4.4))

$$=\frac{1}{n}\sigma^2+\frac{1}{n}\sigma^2+\cdots+\frac{1}{n}\sigma^2$$

$$=\sigma^2$$

Unfortunately we are not usually in the position of requiring an *estimate* of σ when we *know* μ. In most cases we have only an estimate of μ, i.e. $\bar{x}$. Using $\bar{x}$ we can calculate the s.d., s, of the sample, from the formula

$$s^2=\sum_{i=1}^{n}\frac{(x_i-\bar{x})^2}{n}$$

However, we cannot use $s^2=\sum_{i=1}^{n}\dfrac{(x_i-\bar{x})^2}{n}$ to give an unbiased estimate of variance, since the sum of the squares of the deviations of the x_i's from $\bar{x}$ is less than the sum of the squares of the deviations from μ and consequently s^2 underestimates σ^2.

We *can* find an unbiased estimator of σ^2 as follows:

$$\sigma^2=E\left\{\sum_{i=1}^{n}\frac{(X_i-\mu)^2}{n}\right\}$$

$$=E\left\{\sum_{i=1}^{n}\frac{[(X_i-\bar{X})-(\mu-\bar{X})]^2}{n}\right\}$$

$$=E\left\{\sum_{i=1}^{n}\frac{[(X_i-\bar{X})^2-2(X_i-\bar{X})(\mu-\bar{X})+(\mu-\bar{X})^2}{n}\right\}$$

$$= E\left\{ \sum_{i=1}^{n} \frac{(X_i - \bar{X})^2}{n} - 2(\mu - \bar{X}) \sum_{i=1}^{n} \frac{(X_i - \bar{X})}{n} + n \times \frac{(\mu - \bar{X})^2}{n} \right\}$$

The second term is zero since

$$\sum_{i=1}^{n} (X_i - \bar{X}) = \sum_{i=1}^{n} X_i - \sum_{i=1}^{n} \bar{X}$$

$$= n\bar{X} - n\bar{X} = 0$$

so we have

$$\sigma^2 = E\left\{ \sum_{i=1}^{n} \frac{(X_i - \bar{X})^2}{n} \right\} + E\{(\mu - \bar{X})^2\} \tag{13.4.1}$$

The first term is $E(S^2)$ where S^2 is the random variable $\sum_{i=1}^{n} \frac{(X_i - \bar{X})^2}{n}$. The second term,

$E\{(\mu - \bar{X})^2\}$ or $E\{(\bar{X} - \mu)\}^2$, is $\text{var}(\bar{X})$ which was shown in the proof of Theorem 13.3.1 to be

$\frac{\sigma^2}{n}$. Thus

$$\sigma^2 = E(S^2) + \frac{\sigma^2}{n}$$

Rearranging,

$$\sigma^2 = \frac{n}{n-1} E(S^2)$$

$$= E\left\{ \frac{n}{n-1} S^2 \right\} \tag{13.4.2}$$

Substituting for S,

$$\sigma^2 = E\left\{ \left(\frac{n}{n-1} \right) \left(\sum_{i=1}^{n} \frac{(X_i - \bar{X})^2}{n} \right) \right\}$$

$$\sigma^2 = E\left\{ \sum_{i=1}^{n} \frac{(X_i - \bar{X})^2}{n-1} \right\} \tag{13.4.3}$$

Equation (13.4.3) gives us an unbiased estimator of variance, which we shall denote by $\hat{S}^2$, where

$$\hat{S}^2 = \sum_{i=1}^{n} \frac{(X_i - \bar{X})^2}{n-1} \tag{13.4.4}$$

and $\hat{S}$ and S are related by

$$\hat{S} = \sqrt{\left(\frac{n}{n-1} \right)} S \tag{13.4.5}$$

The term $n-1$ in the denominator of equation (13.4.4) is referred to as the number of **degrees of freedom** and is given the symbol v. The reason for this name is as follows. If we knew μ then the variance could be calculated from n *independent* deviations, using $\sum_{i=1}^{n} \frac{(x_i - \mu)^2}{n}$. If instead we measure the deviations from $\bar{x}$, then we have only $n-1$ independent deviations, as when $(n-1)$ deviations are given the last deviation can be deduced using the fact that $\sum_{i=1}^{n} (x_i - \bar{x}) = 0$. One degree of freedom has been 'lost' since only $n-1$ of the deviations can be varied independently.

Equation (13.4.5) shows that, for large n, there is only a small error in taking S^2 rather than $\hat{S}^2$ as an estimator of σ^2.

13.4.1 *Example*

Five measurements of the volume of acid required in a titration are 25.1, 25.2, 25.2, 25.0, 25.5 cm³. Use these results to obtain estimates for the mean and s.d. of the volume of acid required.

First we need to calculate $\bar{x}$ and s as shown in Table 13.3 and the calculations that follow.

Table 13.3

x_i	f_i	u_i	$f_i u_i$	$f_i u_i^2$
25.0	1	0	0	0
25.1	1	1	1	1
25.2	2	2	4	8
25.5	1	5	5	25
	$\overline{5}$		$\overline{10}$	$\overline{34}$

Using $A = 25.0$, $B = 0.1$,

$$\bar{x} = A + B \frac{\sum_{i=1}^{n} f_i u_i}{\sum_{i=1}^{n} f_i}$$

$$= 25 + 0.1 \times \tfrac{10}{5} = 25.2$$

$$s^2 = B^2 \left\{ \frac{\sum_{i=1}^{n} f_i u_i^2}{\sum_{i=1}^{n} f_i} - \left(\frac{\sum_{i=1}^{n} f_i u_i}{\sum_{i=1}^{n} f_i} \right)^2 \right\}$$

$$= 0.1^2 \{ \tfrac{34}{5} - (\tfrac{10}{5})^2 \} = 0.0280$$

The unbiased estimate of μ is $\bar{x} = 25.2$ cm.

The unbiased estimate of σ^2 is

$$\hat{s}^2 = \frac{n}{n-1} s^2 = \tfrac{5}{4} \times 0.0280 = 0.0350$$

So

$$\hat{s} = 0.187 \text{ cm}^3$$

*13.5   Relative efficiency and consistency

If we have two estimators which both give an unbiased estimate of a population parameter, we would prefer to use the one for which the sampling distribution is more closely clustered about the true value of the parameter, i.e. the sampling distribution with the smaller variance. This is the more **efficient** estimator. The ratio of the variances of the two sampling distributions gives a measure of **relative efficiency** on a scale between 0 and 1. For example, both the mean and the median give unbiased estimates of the mean of a Normal distribution. However, it can be shown that for large samples, the sampling distribution of the median is Normal with standard error $1.25\sigma/\sqrt{n}$, and so the median is a less efficient estimator than the mean, which has a standard error of $\sigma/\sqrt{n}$.

A good estimator of variance should also be **consistent**. This means that the larger n the closer the statistic is likely to be to the parameter it estimates. If G is an estimator of γ then this is achieved by having

$$E(G) \to \gamma \tag{13.5.1}$$
$$\text{var}(G) \to 0 \tag{13.5.2}$$

as $n \to \infty$.

We have already shown that $\bar{X}$ as an estimator of μ satisfies the first of these criteria irrespective of the value of n, and it satisfies the second since $\text{var}(\bar{X}) = \sigma^2/n$ (see equation (13.3.1)).

13.5.1   *Example*

A discrete random variable X can take values 0, 1 and 2 only, with respective probabilities $\tfrac{1}{2}\theta$, $1-\theta$ and $\tfrac{1}{2}\theta$, where θ is an unknown number between 0 and 1. Let X_1 and X_2 denote two randomly observed values of X. List the possible values of $\{X_1, X_2\}$ that may arise and calculate the probability of each possibility; verify that your probabilities sum to unity. By calculating the value of $(X_1 - X_2)^2$ for each possible $\{X_1, X_2\}$ determine the sampling distribution of $(X_1 - X_2)^2$. Hence show that $Y = \tfrac{1}{2}(X_1 - X_2)^2$ is an unbiased estimator of θ and express its sampling variance in terms of θ.

Since θ is the probability that X will not take the value 1, another possible estimator of θ is the proportion of sample values not equal to 1; for a sample of two observations this estimator is given by $Z = \tfrac{1}{2}N$, where N is the number of observations (0, 1 and 2) not equal to 1. State, giving your reasons, which of Y and Z you would prefer as the estimator of θ. (W)

Table 13.4 sets out the possible values $\{x_1, x_2\}$ together with their probabilities. The reader should check that the sum of these probabilities is 1. The third column gives the value of $(x_1 - x_2)^2$ for each $\{x_1, x_2\}$. Table 13.5 gives the sampling distribution of $(X_1 - X_2)^2$. The fourth and fifth columns of this table give $yP(Y=y)$ and $y^2P(Y=y)$ which are required for

Table 13.4

$\{x_1, x_2\}$	$P(x_1, x_2)$	$(x_1 - x_2)^2$
0, 0	$\frac{1}{4}\theta^2$	0
0, 1	$\frac{1}{2}\theta(1-\theta)$	1
0, 2	$\frac{1}{4}\theta^2$	4
1, 0	$\frac{1}{2}\theta(1-\theta)$	1
1, 1	$(1-\theta)^2$	0
1, 2	$\frac{1}{2}\theta(1-\theta)$	1
2, 0	$\frac{1}{4}\theta^2$	4
2, 1	$\frac{1}{2}\theta(1-\theta)$	1
2, 2	$\frac{1}{4}\theta^2$	0

Table 13.5

$(x_1 - x_2)^2$	y	$P(Y=y)$	$yP(Y=y)$	$y^2P(Y=y)$
0	0	$\frac{1}{2}\theta^2 + (1-\theta)^2$	0	0
1	$\frac{1}{2}$	$2\theta(1-\theta)$	$\theta(1-\theta)$	$\frac{1}{2}\theta(1-\theta)$
4	2	$\frac{1}{2}\theta^2$	θ^2	$2\theta^2$
			θ	$\frac{3}{2}\theta^2 + \frac{1}{2}\theta$

calculating the mean and variance of the sampling distribution of Y [where $Y = \frac{1}{2}(X_1 - X_2)^2$]. We find $E(Y) = \sum_{\text{all } x} yP(Y=) = \theta$, showing that Y is an unbiased estimator of θ. The sampling variance of Y is given by

$$\Sigma y^2 P(Y=y) - [\Sigma y P(Y=y)]^2 = \tfrac{3}{2}\theta^2 + \tfrac{1}{2}\theta - \theta^2$$

$$= \tfrac{1}{2}\theta^2 + \tfrac{1}{2}\theta$$

$$= \tfrac{1}{2}\theta(\theta + 1)$$

N, the number of observations in a sample of two which are not equal to 1, is Binomially distributed with $n=2$, $p=\theta$, $q=1-\theta$. Thus the mean and variance of the sampling distribution of N are

mean $= np = 2\theta$

variance $= npq = 2\theta(1-\theta)$

Since $Z = \frac{1}{2}N$, the mean and variance of its sampling distribution are

mean $= \frac{1}{2} \times 2\theta = \theta$ \hfill (see equation (10.4.4))

variance $= (\frac{1}{2})^2 \times 2\theta(1-\theta) = \frac{1}{2}\theta(1-\theta)$ \hfill (see equation (10.4.5))

Since the sampling distribution of Z has the smaller variance, Z is the preferred estimator.

13.5.2 *Exercise*

(1) Each trial of a random experiment has probability p $(0 < p < 1)$ of yielding a success. In n_1 independent trials of the experiment the number of successes obtained was r_1. Write down an unbiased estimate, $\hat{p}_1$, of p and find its standard error in terms of n_1 and p.

In a further n_2 independent trials of the same experiment the number of successes obtained was r_2. Let $\hat{p}_2$ denote the unbiased estimate of p from these n_2 trials. Verify that $\frac{1}{2}(\hat{p}_1 + \hat{p}_2)$ is an unbiased estimate of p, and find its standard error in terms of n_1, n_2 and p.

Determine the range of values of the ratio n_1/n_2 for which the estimate $\frac{1}{2}(\hat{p}_1 + \hat{p}_2)$ is to be preferred to each of $\hat{p}_1$ and $\hat{p}_2$. (W)

(2) Explain the terms (a) unbiased estimator, (b) consistent estimator, and indicate how possession of these properties helps to ensure a 'good' estimator.

Let $X_1, X_2, \ldots, X_n$ be a random sample from some population with distribution $f(x)$ and let

$$S^2 = \frac{\sum\limits_{i=1}^{n} (X_i - \bar{X})^2}{n-1} \qquad \text{for } n > 1$$

Show that S^2 is an unbiased and a consistent estimator for σ^2, the population variance. (AEB)

(3) Explain what is meant by the sampling distribution of an estimator.

Explain what you understand by (a) an unbiased estimator, (b) a consistent estimator, (c) the relative efficiency of two estimators of the same parameter.

In order to estimate the mean μ of a population, random observations x_1, x_2, x_3 are taken of a random variable X which has variance σ^2. Find the relative efficiency of the two estimators $\hat{\mu}_1$ and $\hat{\mu}_2$ where

$$\hat{\mu}_1 = \frac{x_1 + x_2 + x_3}{3}, \qquad \hat{\mu}_2 = \frac{x_1 + 2x_2}{3} \qquad \text{(JMB)}$$

(4) A random sample of n_1 observations is made from a population with unknown mean μ and variance σ^2. For this sample the mean $\bar{x}_1$ and variance s_1^2 are calculated. A second sample, size n_2, has mean $\bar{x}_2$ and variance s_2^2. Show that an unbiased estimate of the population mean μ is given by

$$\frac{n_1 \bar{x}_1 + n_2 \bar{x}_2}{n_1 + n_2}$$

and an unbiased estimate of the population variance σ^2 is given by

$$\frac{n_1 s_1^2 + n_2 s_2^2}{n_1 + n_2 - 2}$$

(5) To estimate the mean of a population, two observations x_1 and x_2 are made of the random variable X, which has mean μ and variance σ^2. Show that $\hat{\mu} = kx_1 + (1-k)x_2$ is an unbiased estimator of μ and find the value of k for which this estimator is most efficient.

13.6   The central limit theorem

If a sample, size n, is taken from a Normal population, the sampling distribution of the mean is also Normal. Even if the original population is not Normal, it can be shown that, as n increases, the sampling distribution of the mean approaches a Normal distribution. This result is called the **central limit theorem** and is of fundamental importance. It is usually assumed that for values of $n \geqslant 30$ the sampling distribution of the mean is Normal.

13.6.1   *Example*

What is the probability that the mean of 100 digits taken from a random number table is greater than 5.0?

Random numbers form a discrete Uniform distribution. By symmetry
mean $= 4.5$

In Section 11.2 the variance for a Uniform distribution where the variable takes the values 1, 2, 3, ..., n was shown to be $\frac{1}{12}(n^2 - 1)$. The numbers 0, 1, 2, ..., 9 will have the same

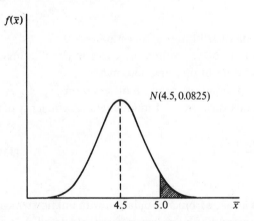

Figure 13.3 Graph to illustrate Example 13.6.1

variance as 1, 2, 3, ..., 10, since a change of origin does not alter the variance. Thus
$$\text{variance of random numbers} = \frac{1}{12}(10^2 - 1)$$
$$= 8.25$$
Using equation (13.3.1), the variance of the sampling distribution of the mean of 100 random digits is
$$\frac{\sigma^2}{n} = \frac{8.25}{100} = 0.0825$$

and the mean of the sampling distribution of the mean is 4.5. The central limit theorem tells us that the sampling distribution of the mean is Normal as shown in Figure 13.3. The s.d. of this distribution is $\sqrt{0.0825} = 0.287$. The probability that the mean of 100 numbers is greater than 5 is given by the shaded area.

$$z = \frac{5.0 - 4.5}{0.287} = 1.74$$

$$\begin{aligned} \text{required probability} &= P(Z > 1.74) \\ &= 1 - P(Z < 1.74) \\ &= 1 - 0.9591 \\ &= 0.0409 \end{aligned}$$

13.6.2 *Exercise*

(1) The body length of a certain species of insect is Normally distributed with mean 3.1 mm, s.d. 0.2 mm.
   (a) What is the probability that an insect chosen at random has a body length greater than 3.12 mm?
   (b) What is the probability that the mean body length of a sample of (i) 9 insects, and (ii) 100 insects is greater than 3.12 mm?

(2) Explain what is meant by the standard error of the mean.
   For each of the following large populations (a)–(c), three possible standard deviations (i)–(iii) are given. In each case, select the standard deviation you believe to be the most reasonable and use it to obtain a range of values within which the mean of a sample of 100 values is likely to lie with 95% probability.
   (a) The weights in kg of adult males. Mean is 66 kg, s.d:
       (i) 1, (ii) 8, (iii) 16.
   (b) The salaries of typists. Mean is £795, s.d:
       (i) 110, (ii) 425, (iii) 1410.
   (c) The number of matches in a box of nominal contents 50. Mean is 51.6, s.d:
       (i) 0.6, (ii) 5.3, (iii) 20.2.   (O)

(3) In a certain examination with a very large entry, the percentage marks obtained by the male candidates were found to follow a Normal distribution with a mean of 54 and a standard deviation of 16. Let $\bar{X}$ denote the mean of the percentage marks scored by a random sample of four male candidates. What is the sampling distribution of $\bar{X}$? Calculate the probability that $\bar{X}$ will exceed 70 and the value c such that there is a probability of 0.95 that $\bar{X}$ will be within c marks of the mean mark of 54.
   In the same examination the percentage marks obtained by the female candidates were found to follow a Normal distribution with a mean of 59 and a standard deviation of 20. Let $\bar{Y}$ denote the mean of the percentage marks scored by a random sample of five female candidates. What is the sampling distribution of $\bar{Y} - \bar{X}$? Calculate the probability that the value of $\bar{Y}$ will be greater than the value of $\bar{X}$.   (W)

13.7   An unbiased estimator of population proportion

If the probability that a member of a population possesses an attribute is p then we know from Section 7.1 that X, the number of members of sample size n which possess this attribute, is Binomially distributed, $B(n, p)$. We might expect $P_S = X/n$, the proportion in the sample which shows the attribute, to be an unbiased estimator of p and this can be shown as follows:

$$
\begin{aligned}
E(P_S) &= E(X/n) \\
&= E(X)/n \\
&= np/n \qquad \text{(see Section 7.4)} \\
&= p
\end{aligned}
\tag{13.7.1}
$$

We can also find the variance of the sampling distribution of P_S since

$$
\begin{aligned}
\text{var}(P_S) &= \text{var}(X/n) \\
&= \text{var}(X)/n^2 \\
&= np(1-p)/n^2 \qquad \text{(see Section 7.4)} \\
&= p(1-p)/n
\end{aligned}
\tag{13.7.2}
$$

When n is large the sampling distribution of X tends to a Normal distribution. Thus the sampling distribution of P_S also tends to a Normal distribution with mean p/n and variance $p(1-p)/n$. The standard deviation of this sampling distribution, $\sqrt{\{p(1-p)/n\}}$, is called the **standard error of a proportion**.

Summary

Unbiased estimate of population mean, μ, $\bar{x} = \sum_{i=1}^{n} x_i/n$

Unbiased estimate of popular variance, σ^2, $\hat{s}^2 = ns^2/(n-1)$

$$
= \sum_{i=1}^{n} (x_i - \bar{x})^2/(n-1)
$$

Unbiased estimate of population proportion, p, $p_S = x/n$

The **sampling distribution of the mean** has mean μ and variance σ^2/n, where μ and σ^2 are the population mean and variance respectively. When n is large this sampling distribution approximates to a Normal distribution; this result is known as the **central limit theorem**.

The **sampling distribution of the sample proportion** has mean p and variance $p(1-p)/n$, where p is the population proportion. When n is large this sampling distribution approximates to a Normal distribution.

Projects

(1)   *The sampling distribution of the mean*

Using the table of random numbers, Table A3, as the population, take 200 samples of ten digits each. Calculate the mean of each sample and present the results in a frequency table with classes 1.4–2.0, 2.1–2.7, 2.8–3.4, 3.5–4.1, 4.2–4.8 etc. (These classes have been chosen because they are symmetrically distributed about the expected mean.) Illustrate by a frequency polygon.

   Calculate:

(i)   the mean and variance for the original population, i.e. a discrete Rectangular distribution for which $P(r) = \frac{1}{10}$ for $r = 0, 1, 2, \ldots, 9$;

(ii)   the mean and variance for the frequency table of the sample means.

   Verify that (a) the mean of the means of the samples is approximately equal to the mean of the original population, (b) the variance of the distribution of the means is approximately equal to one-tenth of the variance of the original population (since in this case $n = 10$). (The agreement is only approximate since not all of the possible samples are considered.)

   The population from which the samples were drawn has mean 4.5, variance $\frac{99}{12}$ (see Section 11.2) so that, using the central limit theorem, we expect the sampling distribution of the mean to be approximately Normal with mean 4.5, variance $\dfrac{99}{12 \times 10} = 0.825$. Using these parameters calculate the expected frequencies for classes 1.4–2.0, 2.1–2.7, etc., for the means of 200 samples. Compare with the observed frequencies by drawing a frequency polygon using the same axes as before.

(2)   *Advanced Level Statistics Software*

The section *Sampling distributions and confidence intervals* contains two programs which can be used to demonstrate the ideas of this chapter.

(a)   *Sampling distribution of the mean*

This program extends the work described in project (1). It allows random sampling from a number of standard populations and also from populations defined by the user. The sampling distribution of the mean is displayed as a histogram together with its mean and variance. The change in shape of the histogram as the sample size increases provides support for the central limit theorem and the relationship between the population mean and variance and the mean and variance of the sampling distribution of the mean can be verified 'experimentally'.

(b)   *Estimating the variance of a population*

The program *Estimators of variance* provides 'experimental evidence' for the results derived mathematically in Section 13.4. It allows the comparison of three estimators of variance, s^2,

$\hat{s}^2$ and $\sum_{i} (x_i - \mu)^2/n$, by simulating the taking of random samples from a given population. The results show that the first estimator is biased while the latter two are not.

Exercise on Chapter 13

(1) The number of days that each of five employees (A, B, C, D, E) in an office was absent from work during a year is shown in Table 13.6.

Table 13.6

Employee	A	B	C	D	E
Number of days absent	10	6	0	4	0

(a) Calculate the mean μ and the variance σ^2 of the numbers of days these employees were absent from work.

(b) Three of these employees are selected at random without replacement. Let $\bar{X}$ denote the mean number of days absent for the chosen three employees.
   (i)   Determine the sampling distribution of $\bar{X}$ and display it in a table.
   (ii) Determine whether or not $\bar{X}$ is an unbiased estimator of μ.
   (iii) Find the variance of $\bar{X}$ and verify that it is equal to one-half of the variance of the sample mean if the three employees are chosen with replacement.

(W)

(2) A random sample x_1, x_2 is drawn from a distribution with mean μ and standard deviation σ. State the mean and standard deviation of the distribution of (a) $x_1 + x_2$, (b) $x_1 - x_2$, (c) $\bar{x}$.

A student's performance is equally good in two subjects. The marks she might be expected to score in each subject may be treated as independent observations drawn from a Normal distribution with mean 45 and standard deviation 5. Two procedures might be used to decide whether to give the student an overall pass. One is to demand that she pass separately in each subject, the pass mark being 40; the other is to require that her mean mark in the two subjects exceeds 40. Find the probability that the student will obtain an overall pass by each of these procedures. (O)

(3) The random variables $X_1, X_2, \ldots, X_n$ are independent and each has a Normal distribution with mean μ and variance 1. The random variable $\bar{X}$ is defined to be $(X_1 + X_2 + \cdots + X_n)/n$. Determine, in terms of n, the value v which is such that, when $\mu = 0$, the probability of $\bar{X}$ exceeding v is 0.05.

For this value of v it is desired that the probability of $\bar{X}$ being less than v when $\mu = 0.2$ should be at most 0.10. Calculate the smallest possible value of n which satisfies this requirement. (C)

(4) (a) If $X_1, X_2, \ldots, X_n$ is a random sample from the distribution
$$f(x) = \begin{cases} xe^{-x/\theta}/\theta^2 & x \geqslant 0 \\ 0 & \text{otherwise} \end{cases} \quad \theta > 0$$
show that $T = \sum_{i=1}^{n} X_i/2n$ is an unbiased and consistent estimator of θ.

(b) Suppose $X_1, X_2, \ldots, X_n$ is a random sample from a Normal distribution with mean μ and variance 1. What is the distribution of the sample mean $\bar{X}$?
Calculate the sample size required to ensure that the probability of $\bar{X}$ being within 0.2 of μ is at least 0.95. (AEB)

(5) Explain what is meant by the sampling distribution of the mean, and discuss briefly the properties of the distribution.
By considering all possible outcomes, find the sampling distribution of the total score obtained when two unbiased dice are thrown. Find the mean and variance of the distribution.
If $2n$ dice are thrown, and n is large, what distribution is a close approximation to that of the total score? (O)

(6) A cricketer, at any stage of any innings, has a constant probability k of being out without adding to his score. If his batting average, on completed innings only, is A, show that $\dfrac{1}{A+1}$ gives an estimate of k.
Find the median of the theoretical distribution of the batsman's completed scores if $k = \frac{1}{10}$. (AEB)

(7) Explain what is meant by the expectation of a random variable.
A random sample is drawn from a large population in which a proportion p have a certain rare disease. Sampling continues until a predetermined number a of the sample are found to have the disease, and at this stage the sample size is r. Find the probability distribution of r, and show that $(a-1)/(r-1)$ is an unbiased estimate of p, i.e. that
$$E\{(a-1)/(r-1)\} = p$$
(O)

14 Confidence limits

14.1 Introduction: confidence limits of the mean (σ known)

In the previous chapter we discussed estimators of population parameters and their sampling distributions. We found, for example, that the mean of a sample gave an unbiased estimate of the population mean. Such an estimate, which is in the form of a single value, is sometimes called a **point estimate**. This is to distinguish it from an alternative form of giving an estimate called an **interval estimate**. An interval estimate gives a range of values which has a certain probability of containing the population parameter. This chapter describes the way in which some interval estimates are calculated from the appropriate sampling distributions.

We will start by calculating an interval estimate for the population mean, μ, in the situation where the population standard deviation, σ, is known but μ is not. *If n is large*, the central limit theorem tells us that the sampling distribution of $\bar{X}$ will be Normal, as shown in Figure 14.1, with mean μ and s.d. $\sigma/\sqrt{n}$. We can use this distribution to find a range of values within which $\bar{X}$ will lie with a certain probability. Suppose we wish to calculate a range of values for $\bar{X}$ so that $\bar{X}$ lies within this range with 95% probability. Let $\bar{x}_u$ and $\bar{x}_l$ be the upper and lower values of this range. They are shown in Figure 14.1 placed symmetrically on either side of μ. The shaded area is 0.95, so that the area above $\bar{x}_u$ is 0.025 and below it 0.975. Using Table A1, the standard deviates corresponding to $\bar{x}_l$ and $\bar{x}_u$ are -1.96 and 1.96 respectively, so that

$$1.96 = \frac{\bar{x}_u - \mu}{\sigma/\sqrt{n}} \quad \text{giving } \bar{x}_u = \mu + \frac{1.96\sigma}{\sqrt{n}}$$

and

$$-1.96 = \frac{\bar{x}_l - \mu}{\sigma/\sqrt{n}} \quad \text{giving } \bar{x}_l = \mu - \frac{1.96\sigma}{\sqrt{n}}$$

Thus there is a 95% probability that $\bar{X}$ lies in the range

$$\mu - \frac{1.96\sigma}{\sqrt{n}} < \bar{X} < \mu + \frac{1.96\sigma}{\sqrt{n}}$$

This inequality can be rearranged to give an interval which includes μ with a probability of 95%:

$$\bar{X} - \frac{1.96\sigma}{\sqrt{n}} < \mu < \bar{X} + \frac{1.96\sigma}{\sqrt{n}}$$

In this expression $\bar{X}$ is a random variable. If, for a particular sample, $\bar{X}$ takes the value $\bar{x}$, we can calculate an interval:

$$\bar{x} - \frac{1.96\sigma}{\sqrt{n}} < \mu < \bar{x} + \frac{1.96\sigma}{\sqrt{n}} \tag{14.1.1}$$

This interval is called the **95% confidence interval of the mean** and its end-points are called the **95% confidence limits of the mean.** μ is fixed, and so for a particular sample the interval calculated in (14.1.1) either does or does not include μ and we do not know which is the case. What we *do* know is that if we calculate confidence intervals by this method then there is a probability of 95% that the interval *does* include μ.

Other confidence limits are sometimes used, e.g. 99%, and can be found by using the appropriate value of the standard deviate. The 99% confidence limits are

$$\bar{x} - \frac{2.58\sigma}{\sqrt{n}} < \mu < \bar{x} + \frac{2.58\sigma}{\sqrt{n}} \qquad\qquad (14.1.2)$$

Notice that the confidence interval must *increase* if we are to become *more* confident that it contains μ. Equations (14.1.1) and (14.1.2) can also be used for a small sample from a Normal population, since in this case the sampling distribution is Normal.

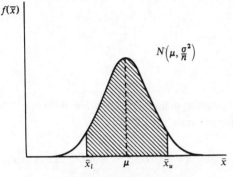

Figure 14.1 Graph to illustrate Section 14.1

14.1.1 *Example*

The standard deviation for a method of measuring the concentration of nitrate ions in water is known to be 0.05 ppm. If 100 measurements give a mean of 1.13 ppm, calculate the 95% confidence limits for the true mean.

Using $\bar{x} = 1.13$, $n = 100$ and $\sigma = 0.05$,

$$1.13 - \frac{1.96 \times 0.05}{\sqrt{100}} < \mu < 1.13 + \frac{1.96 \times 0.05}{\sqrt{100}} \qquad \text{(from equation (14.1.1))}$$
$$1.12 < \mu < 1.14$$

14.1.2 *Exercise*

(1) A machine produces washers whose diameter is known to be Normally distributed with a s.d. of 0.04 mm. In order to find the mean diameter of the washers produced, a random sample of nine washers is taken whose mean diameter is found to be 3.14 mm.
Calculate (a) 95%, (b) 98% confidence limits for the mean diameter of washers produced by the machine.

(2) The masses of sweets produced by a machine are known to have a standard deviation of
0.5 g. A sample of 50 sweets has a mean mass of 15.21 g. Calculate a 99% confidence
interval for the mean mass of sweets produced by the machine. Why is it not necessary to
assume that the masses are Normally distributed in this calculation?

14.2   Confidence limits for a large sample (σ unknown)

In practice it is unusual to know σ^2 but not μ. However, we can obtain an unbiased estimate
$\hat{s}^2$ of σ^2 from the sample. This estimate varies from sample to sample but for *large* samples
the variation is so small compared with $\hat{s}^2$ itself that we can replace σ^2 by $\hat{s}^2$ in equation
(14.1.1). This gives for the 95% confidence limits of the mean

$$\bar{x} - \frac{1.96\hat{s}}{\sqrt{n}} < \mu < \bar{x} + \frac{1.96\hat{s}}{\sqrt{n}} \qquad (14.2.1)$$

Since $\hat{s} = s\sqrt{n}/\sqrt{(n-1)}$ (see equation (13.4.5)), this expression can also be written as

$$\bar{x} - \frac{1.96s}{\sqrt{(n-1)}} < \mu < \bar{x} + \frac{1.96s}{\sqrt{(n-1)}} \qquad (14.2.2)$$

14.2.1   *Example*

Fifty measurements of the acceleration due to gravity, g, had a mean value of 9.8 m s^{-2} and a
s.d. of 0.75 m s^{-2}. What are the 95% confidence limits for g?

Using equation (14.2.2) with $\bar{x} = 9.8$, $s = 0.75$ and $n = 50$, the 95% confidence limits of the
mean are

$$9.8 - \frac{1.96 \times 0.75}{\sqrt{49}} < \mu < 9.8 + \frac{1.96 \times 0.75}{\sqrt{49}}$$
$$9.6 < \mu < 10.0$$

14.2.2   *Example*

In the previous example how many measurements would be necessary to reduce the 95%
confidence limits to $9.7 < \mu < 9.9$?

We have
$$\frac{1.96s}{\sqrt{(n-1)}} = 0.1$$
Rearranging
$$n - 1 = (1.96 \times 0.75/0.1)^2$$
$$n = 217$$

14.2.3   *Exercise*

(1) Fifty children were selected at random from the pupils at a school and each was asked
how many hours a week he or she spent in watching television. The mean of the sample

was 17.2 hours and the standard deviation was 5.3 hours. Calculate the (a) 95%, (b) 98% confidence interval for the mean number of hours spent a week in watching television for the population consisting of all the children in the school.

(2) Fifty boxes of matches were selected at random from a large carton of such boxes. The numbers of matches in each of the 50 boxes were counted and the mean and standard deviation of these numbers were found to be 48 and 0.5 respectively. Between what limits would you expect the mean for all of the boxes in the carton to lie with 0.95 probability? (C)

(3) On 1 January 100 new Eternity light bulbs were installed in a certain building, together with a device which records how long each light bulb is in use. By 1 March all 100 bulbs had failed, and the recorded lifetimes, t (in hours of use since 1 January) are summarised in Table 14.1.
Obtain values for the sample mean and the sample standard deviation for this set of data. (Assume measurements are to the nearest second.)
Assuming that the bulbs constituted a random sample of Eternity light bulbs, obtain a symmetric 99% confidence interval for the mean lifetime of Eternity light bulbs. (C)

Table 14.1

Time	Frequency
$0 < t \leqslant 50$	31
$50 < t \leqslant 100$	24
$100 < t \leqslant 150$	20
$150 < t \leqslant 200$	13
$200 < t \leqslant 300$	11
$300 < t \leqslant 500$	1
	100

Table 14.2

Diameter (mm)	11.1	11.2	11.3	11.4	11.5	11.6	11.7
f		1	6	24	33	22	12	2

(4) The random variable X takes values x_i with associated frequencies f_i ($i = 1, 2, \ldots, n$) and the mean of these values is $\bar{x}$. $N = \sum_{i=1}^{n} f_i$. If c is a constant prove the formula

$$\frac{1}{N} \sum_{i=1}^{n} f_i(x_i - \bar{x})^2 = \frac{1}{N} \sum_{i=1}^{n} f_i(x_i - c)^2 - (\bar{x} - c)^2$$

The diameters of the heads of 100 rivets from a factory production line were measured correct to the nearest 0.1 mm and the results were as in Table 14.2.

Using an assumed mean of 11.4, calculate the sample mean and standard deviation of the diameters.

Determine 95% confidence limits for the population mean diameter, stating any assumptions that you make.   (SUJB)

14.3   Confidence limits for a small sample from a Normal population (σ unknown)

If small samples, size n, are drawn from a Normal population, their means are Normally distributed with mean μ and s.d. $\sigma/\sqrt{n}$. However we can no longer use the confidence limits derived for large samples because this derivation rested on the fact that $(\bar{x}-\mu)/(\sigma/\sqrt{n})$ was Normally distributed. For large samples, even when we did not know σ, we could assume that $(\bar{x}-\mu)/(\hat{s}/\sqrt{n})$ was still approximately Normal. This is no longer true for small samples because the variation of $\hat{s}$ from sample to sample is too large to be ignored. The statistic $(\bar{x}-\mu)/(\hat{s}/\sqrt{n})$ is called 't' and its distribution is called the **Student t-distribution** (after the statistician W. S. Gossett who published papers on it under the pen-name 'Student'). Its form depends on the 'degrees of freedom' v, mentioned in connection with the estimation of σ (see Section 13.4) and, as in that case, we have $v=n-1$. For large n, the t-distribution approximates to the Normal distribution, a property which was used in Section 14.2. As n decreases the distribution remains bell-shaped but becomes more spread out as shown in Figure 14.2. This spread reflects the uncertainty introduced because of the variation in $\hat{s}$. To denote the dependence of t on the degrees of freedom we write

$$t_{n-1}=\frac{\bar{x}-\mu}{\hat{s}/\sqrt{n}} \tag{14.3.1}$$

Since

$$\hat{s}=\sqrt{\left(\frac{n}{n-1}\right)}s$$

we can also write

$$t_{n-1}=\frac{\bar{x}-\mu}{s/\sqrt{(n-1)}} \tag{14.3.2}$$

Because n can take any value, tables for the t-distribution are not given in the form of cumulative probability values. Instead they are given in the form shown in Table A4. This table gives what are called the **percentage points** of the t-distribution for different values of n.

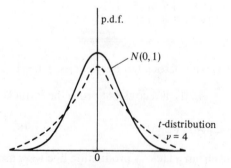

Figure 14.2 Graph comparing the standard Normal distribution and the t-distribution with $v=4$.

The percentage points give a value of t outside which t lies with a certain probability. For example, if $n=8$ ($\Rightarrow v=7$) then, using Table A4, 5% of the values of t lie outside the range -2.36 to $+2.36$ and consequently 95% of the values lie within this range. In general if we require the $\alpha\%$ confidence limits for $n-1$ degrees of freedom, the appropriate value of t will lie in the row for $v=n-1$ and the column for $(100-\alpha)\%$. We can denote this value by $t_{n-1,(100-\alpha)\%}$. Equation (14.2.2) for the 95% confidence limits becomes

$$\bar{x}-t_{n-1,5\%}\times\frac{s}{\sqrt{(n-1)}} < \mu < \bar{x}+t_{n-1,5\%}\times\frac{s}{\sqrt{(n-1)}} \qquad (14.3.3)$$

and in general the $\alpha\%$ confidence limits will be

$$\bar{x}-t_{n-1,(100-\alpha)\%}\times\frac{s}{\sqrt{(n-1)}} < \mu < \bar{x}+t_{n-1,(100-\alpha)\%}\times\frac{s}{\sqrt{(n-1)}} \qquad (14.3.4)$$

The last line of the t-table, $v=\infty$, gives the percentage points of the Normal distribution.

14.3.1   Example

Ten measurements of the zero error on an ammeter yield the results 0.13, -0.09, 0.06, 0.15, -0.02, $+0.03$, $+0.01$, -0.02, -0.07, $+0.05$ A. Calculate the 95% confidence limits of the mean zero error. (Assume the errors are Normally distributed.)

$$\bar{x}=\tfrac{1}{10}(0.13-0.09+0.06+0.15-0.02+0.03+0.01-0.02-0.07+0.05)$$
$$=\frac{0.23}{10}$$
$$=+0.023$$
$$s^2=\tfrac{1}{10}(0.13^2+0.09^2+0.06^2+0.15^2+0.02^2+0.03^2+0.01^2+0.02^2+0.07^2+0.05^2)$$
$$-\left(\frac{0.23}{10}\right)^2$$
$$s=0.0742$$

We have $n=10$, $v=9$. From Table A4, $t_{9,5\%}=2.26$. Using equation (14.3.3), the 95% confidence limits of the mean are

$$0.023-\frac{2.26\times0.0742}{\sqrt{9}} < \mu < 0.023+\frac{2.26\times0.0742}{\sqrt{9}}$$
$$-0.033 < \mu < 0.079$$

14.3.2   Exercise

(1)   The diameters of 25 steel rods are measured and found to have a mean of 0.980 cm and a standard deviation of 0.015 cm. Find 99% confidence limits for the population mean.   (O & C)

(2)   The masses, in grams, of thirteen ball bearings taken at random from a batch are
21.4, 23.1, 25.9, 24.7, 23.4, 24.5, 25.0, 22.5, 26.9, 26.4, 25.8, 23.2, 21.9.
Calculate a 95% confidence interval for the mean mass of the population, supposed Normal, from which these masses were drawn.   (AEB)

(3)   A random sample of six eggs taken from a day's production of a poultry farm had the following masses, measured in grams: 51.2, 52.6, 53.1, 53.2, 53.2, 54.7. Making a suitable assumption, which should be stated, find 95% confidence limits for the mean mass of the eggs produced that day.   (C)

(4)   Twelve cotton threads are taken at random from a large batch, and the breaking strengths are found to be 7.41, 7.01, 8.34, 8.29, 8.08, 6.60, 6.59, 7.39, 4.72, 8.65, 8.51 and 8.01 mN respectively. Assuming the breaking strengths of the threads form a Normal distribution, find 95% confidence limits for the mean breaking strength of threads in the batch.   (AEB)

14.4   Confidence interval of a proportion from a large sample

In Section 13.7 we saw that the sampling distribution of P_S, the proportion of a sample possessing a given attribute, was Normal with mean p/n and variance $p(1-p)/n$, where p is the proportion of the population possessing the attribute and n is the sample size. We can develop an argument similar to that of Section 14.1 to give an equation corresponding to equation (14.1.1) for the 95% confidence interval for p:

$$p_S - 1.96\sqrt{[p(1-p)/n]} < p < p_S + 1.96\sqrt{[p(1-p)/n]}$$

Since we do not know the value of p in order to estimate the standard error of the proportion, $\sqrt{[p(1-p)/n]}$, we must replace p by p_S in this term to give as the approximate 95% confidence interval of a proportion

$$p_S - 1.96\sqrt{[p_S(1-p_S)]} < p < p_S + 1.96\sqrt{[p_S(1-p_S)]} \qquad (14.4.1)$$

14.4.1   *Example*

An opinion poll is taken as to how an electorate will vote in a forthcoming referendum. Out of a random sample of 100, 40 say 'yes' and 60 say 'no'. What is the 95% confidence interval for the proportion of the population who will vote 'yes'?

We have $n = 100$ and $p_S = \frac{40}{100} = 0.4$. Substituting these values in equation (14.4.1) gives the 95% confidence interval of the population proportion voting 'yes' as

$$0.4 - 1.96\sqrt{\left(\frac{0.4 \times 0.6}{100}\right)} < p < 0.4 + 1.96\sqrt{\left(\frac{0.4 \times 0.6}{100}\right)}$$

$$0.3 < p < 0.5$$

It should be noted that, provided the sample is sufficiently small compared with the population for p to be regarded as constant, the accuracy with which we can estimate a proportion depends only on the absolute size of the sample and not on its size relative to the whole population.

14.4.2 *Example*

How large should the sample have been in the previous example to reduce the confidence interval to 1%?

The confidence limits required are 0.4 ± 0.005 giving

$$1.96 \sqrt{\left(\frac{0.4 \times 0.6}{n}\right)} = 0.005$$

$$n = 36\,880$$

14.4.3 *Exercise*

(1)   Out of a random sample of 50 children from a school, 24 were found to have been vaccinated against whooping-cough. Calculate the 95% confidence limits for the proportion of children at the school who have been vaccinated against whooping-cough.

(2)   At a school of 1200 pupils it is found that a random sample of 40 pupils contains five who are left-handed. Find the 95% confidence limits for
      (a)   the proportion of pupils in the school who are left-handed,
      (b)   the number of pupils in the school who are left-handed.

(3)   In a sample of 400 shops taken in 1972, it was discovered that 136 of them sold carpets at below the list prices which had been recommended by manufacturers.
      (a)   Estimate the percentage of all carpet-selling shops selling below list price.
      (b)   Calculate the 95% confidence limits for this estimate, and explain briefly what these mean.
      (c)   What size sample would have to be taken in order to estimate the percentage to within $\pm 2\%$?   (SUJB)

(4)   Table 14.3 shows the number of cases of and deaths from diptheria at the City of Toronto Hospital in the years 1900–10 under antitoxin and ordinary treatments. Obtain an estimate (with an estimate of the standard error) of the probability that a patient treated with antitoxin died.

Table 14.3

Treatment	Cases	Deaths
Antitoxin	228	37
Ordinary	337	28

Give an approximate 95% symmetric confidence interval for this probability. It was required to estimate this probability with a standard error of 0.01. Estimate, to the nearest 100, the number of patients that should have been treated.

Give an approximate 95% symmetric confidence interval for the probability that a patient treated with the ordinary treatment died.

Comment on the relative effectiveness of the antitoxin treatment and the ordinary treatment, stating, in coming to your conclusions, any assumption you have made about the allocation of patients to the different treatments.   (JMB)

Summary

Confidence interval of the mean

(a) σ known, large samples from any population and small samples from Normal populations:

$$\bar{x} - z\sigma/\sqrt{n} < \mu < \bar{x} + z\sigma/\sqrt{n}$$

where z takes the values shown in Table 14.4.

Table 14.4

Confidence interval	95%	98%	99%
z	1.96	2.33	2.58

(b) σ not known, large samples from any population:

$$\bar{x} - zs/\sqrt{(n-1)} < \mu < \bar{x} + zs/\sqrt{(n-1)}$$

with values of z as in Table 14.4.

(c) σ not known, small samples from a Normal population:

$$\bar{x} - t_{n-1,(100-\alpha)\%} \times \frac{s}{\sqrt{(n-1)}} < \mu < \bar{x} + t_{n-1,(100-\alpha)\%} \times \frac{s}{\sqrt{(n-1)}}$$

with values of t obtained from Table A4.

Confidence interval of a proportion

$$p_S - z\sqrt{[p_S(1-p_S)]} < p < p_S + z\sqrt{[p_S(1-p_S)]}$$

with values of z as in Table 14.4.

Projects

(1)   *Confidence limits of a proportion*

For the data obtained in Project (2), Chapter 4, find 95% confidence limits for the proportion of left-handed people in the population from which the sample was drawn.

(2)   *Advanced Level Statistical Software*

The section *Sampling distributions and confidence intervals* contains two programs under the heading *Confidence intervals* which can be used to illustrate the ideas of this chapter.

(a) *Theory.* This shows graphically and interactively the method described in Section 14.1 for deducing a confidence interval for the population mean from the sampling distribution of the mean. Different sample sizes can be used and different confidence intervals found.

(b) *Demonstration.* This simulation demonstrates the meaning of 'degree of confidence' by displaying graphically the confidence intervals calculated from a large number of random samples taken from a population of known mean. The user can see the proportion of confidence intervals which include the population mean. Different levels of confidence can be chosen and the user can choose whether the population standard deviation is known or not.

Exercise on Chapter 14

(1) (a) When an object is weighed on a chemical balance the readings obtained are subject to random errors which are known to be independent and Normally distributed with mean zero and standard deviation 1 mg. A certain object is to be weighed nine times on such a balance and the mean of the nine readings is to be calculated. Find the probability that the mean of the nine readings will be within 0.5 mg of the true weight of the object.

(b) Another weighing device is undergoing tests to determine its accuracy. A certain object of known true weight 50 mg was weighed ten times on this device and the readings in mg were

$$49, 51, 49, 52, 49, 50, 52, 51, 49, 48$$

(i) Calculate an unbiased estimate of the variance of the errors in readings using this device.

(ii) Calculate 95% confidence limits for the mean error in readings using this device.   (W)

(2) Discuss briefly the relative merits of estimating an unknown parameter by means of either a single value or a confidence interval.

(a) Crates of bananas are packed in the West Indies with a nominal net mass of 55 kilograms. However, on their arrival in Liverpool, this has usually decreased due to ripening and shrinkage. A large batch of such crates has just arrived aboard SS *Gauss*. A random sample of twelve crates is selected and their net masses are recorded in kilograms as listed below.

56.4, 52.1, 49.5, 56.4, 48.1, 54.5, 47.8, 58.0, 48.4, 53.9, 46.7, 56.0

Assuming that this sample came from an underlying Normal population with variance 16, calculate a 95% confidence interval for the mean mass of the population.

(b) The drained masses, in kilograms, of ten catering size tins of peaches taken at random from a batch are

2.57, 2.05, 1.65, 2.62, 2.44, 1.48, 2.31, 1.58, 2.60, 1.85

Assuming that this sample came from an underlying Normal population, calculate a 95% confidence interval for the mean of the population.   (AEB)

(3) (a) In order to calculate a confidence interval for the mean mass of packets of butter produced by a machine, a random sample of ten packets is taken. These have masses (measured in kg) of $x_1, x_2, \ldots, x_{10}$ such that

$$\sum_{i=1}^{10} x_i = 2.57 \qquad \sum_{i=1}^{10} x_i^2 = 0.6610$$

Calculate 95% confidence limits for the mean.

(b) If it is known that the standard deviation of the mass of a packet of butter is 0.008 kg, what is the least number of packets that would need to be sampled in order to give a 95% confidence interval for the mean mass whose width is less than 0.002 kg?

(4) A random sample of 600 was chosen from the adults living in a town in order to investigate the number x of days of work lost through illness. Before taking the sample it was decided that certain categories of people would be excluded from the analysis of the number of working days lost although they would not be excluded from the sample. In the sample 180 were found to be from these categories. For the remaining 420 members of the sample $\Sigma x = 1260$ and $\Sigma x^2 = 46000$.

(a) Estimate the mean number of days lost through illness, for the restricted population, and give a 95% confidence interval for the mean.

(b) Estimate the percentage of people in the town who fall into the excluded categories, and give a 99% confidence interval for this percentage.

(c) Give two examples, with reasons, of people who might fall into the excluded categories.   (O)

(5) (a) A random sample of n observations from a population distribution had the values $x_1, x_2, \ldots, x_n$, whose mean is $\bar{x}$. Show that for any value of c,

$$\sum_{i=1}^{n} (x_i - c)^2 \equiv \sum_{i=1}^{n} (x_i - \bar{x})^2 + n(c - \bar{x})^2$$

Hence find the value of c for which $\sum_{i=1}^{n} (x_i - c)^2$ is a minimum.

(b) A random sample of 12 values from a Normal distribution, whose mean μ and variance σ^2 are unknown, were such that

$$\sum_{i=1}^{12} x_i = 5472 \qquad \sum_{i=1}^{12} (x_i - 450)^2 = 1620$$

   (i) Calculate unbiased estimates of μ and σ^2.
   (ii) Determine a 95% confidence interval for μ.
   (iii) Given that $(451, 463)$ was a 95% confidence interval for μ based on *another* random sample of 12 values from the same Normal distribution, deduce the corresponding unbiased estimates of μ and σ^2 from this sample.   (W)

(6) A random sample of 500 fish is taken from a lake, marked, and returned to the lake. After a suitable interval a second sample of 500 is taken and 25 of these are found to be marked. By considering the number of marked fish in the second sample, estimate the number of fish in the lake and, by considering a confidence interval for the proportion of marked fish in the lake, obtain a 95% confidence interval for the number of fish.   (O)

(7) (a) A school dental service wishes to estimate the average number of teeth with fillings of the 600 pupils at a secondary school. Explain how you would select a sample of pupils for a dentist to inspect.
   (b) A survey of 3000 randomly chosen households in England revealed that 250 had moved during the previous year. Estimate 95% confidence limits for the percentage of households moving during the year considered.   (O)

(8) An estimate is required of the proportion of a large number of consumers who are likely to purchase a particular brand of butter. Determine the smallest sample size that should be taken in each of the following situations:
   (a) The population proportion is known to be in the range from 0.1 and 0.2 and it is required that there should be a probability of at least 0.99 that the difference between the sample proportion and the population proportion is less than 0.02.
   (b) Nothing is known about the value of the population proportion and it is required that there should be a probability of at least 0.95 that the difference between the sample proportion and the population proportion is less than 0.03.   (L)

(9) When s independent sets of n Binomial trials produce $r_1, r_2, \ldots, r_s$ successes the formula $\hat{p} = \Sigma r_i / sn$ is used to find an estimate $\hat{p}$ of p, the probability of success in a single trial. Obtain the variance of $\hat{p}$ and show that approximate 95% confidence limits for p are given by the roots of the equation
$$sn(sn + 3.84)p^2 - 2(\Sigma r_i + 1.92)snp + (\Sigma r_i)^2 = 0$$
if 1.96^2 is taken as 3.84.

In one set of observations $n=10$, $s=5$ and r_i takes the values 1, 2, 1, 3 and 1. Determine whether $p=0.1$ lies within the confidence limits given by the equation.   (C)

(10) The continuous variable X has probability density function

$$f(x)=2(a+3-x)/9 \qquad \text{for} \quad a \leqslant x \leqslant a+3$$

$$f(x)=0 \qquad \text{elsewhere}$$

In this a is an unknown constant. In a single observation X is found to be 5. Find an unbiased estimate for a and limits within which a lies with 95% confidence.

A sample of 50 values of X is found to have a mean of 5.1. Find an unbiased estimate for a based on this sample and limits within which a will lie with approximately 95% confidence.   (C)

15   Significance testing

15.1   Setting up a hypothesis

A person claims that she can tell whether the tea or the milk is put into a cup of tea first. To test her claim we ask her to perform a series of trials. In each trial she tastes two cups of tea which are identical in every respect except that one has the tea put in first and the other the milk put in first. The two cups are presented in a random order and she has to identify the cup with the milk put in first. If she is correct seven times out of eight, ought we to accept her claim?

We may feel that if she is right more than a certain number of times, we should accept her claim; otherwise we should reject it. To decide what should be our boundary line we need to set up a mathematical model. If we are sceptical of her claim and think she is guessing we would expect the probability of success at a single trial to be $\frac{1}{2}$. Consequently the probability of X successes in eight trials would be Binomially distribute with $p = \frac{1}{2}$, $n = 8$. Using this hypothesis we can calculate the probability of getting the observed result, i.e. not more than one failure. Such a hypothesis is called a **null hypothesis**. We should also set up an **alternative hypothesis** which states, as its name implies, an alternative to the null hypothesis. In this case it will be that the taster is not guessing, i.e. $p > \frac{1}{2}$. We do not need to specify an exact value of the parameter for the alternative hypothesis since it is not used to calculate probabilities.

Denoting the null hypothesis by H_0 and the alternative hypothesis by H_1 we write

> Model: Binomial
>
> H_0: $p = \frac{1}{2}$
>
> H_1: $p > \frac{1}{2}$

Using the null hypothesis we can calculate the probability of making no more than one mistake by calculating the probability of seven or more correct guesses. The Binomial distribution gives this probability as

$$P(X \geqslant 7) = P(X = 7) + P(X = 8)$$
$$= \binom{8}{7}(\tfrac{1}{2})^7(\tfrac{1}{2}) + (\tfrac{1}{2})^8$$
$$= 0.035$$

This means that if the taster is guessing there is a probability of only 0.035 that she will be correct seven or more times out of eight, and so such a result is unlikely. To decide whether to accept or reject the null hypothesis we have to be more precise about what we mean by 'unlikely'. The usual convention is that events with a probability of 0.05 or less are 'unlikely'. Using this convention the above result is unlikely to arise *by chance* if the null hypothesis is true and so we reject the null hypothesis.

If the taster had been correct only six times out of eight, the required probability is the

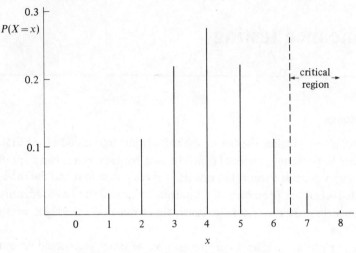

Figure 15.1. Diagram showing the critical region for the example in Section 15.1

probability that the taster makes no more than two mistakes, and, assuming the null hypothesis is true, this probability is

$$P(X \geqslant 6) = \binom{8}{6}(\tfrac{1}{2})^6(\tfrac{1}{2})^2 + \binom{8}{7}(\tfrac{1}{2})^7(\tfrac{1}{2}) + (\tfrac{1}{2})^8$$
$$= 0.145$$

Using our convention, this would not be deemed unlikely and H_0 is retained. Thus the possible outcomes of the experiment can be divided into two sets: $X < 7$ and $X \geqslant 7$ according to whether or not H_0 is retained. Those values of the variate for which H_0 is rejected form the **critical region**. This is shown diagramatically in Figure 15.1. A result which falls in the critical region is said to be **significant**. Further, if, on the null hypothesis, the probability of falling in the critical region is $\leqslant 0.05$ or 5%, then the result is said to be 'significant at the 5% level', and 5% is called the **significance level** of the test. Other levels of significance are sometimes used, notably 1% and 0.1%.

The significance test described above is called a **one-sided** or **one-tailed** test because the alternative hypothesis specifies that the change in p, if any, occurs in one direction only, i.e. an increase in this case, and so the critical region falls in one 'tail' of the distribution. The following example uses a **two-sided** or **two-tailed** test.

15.1.1   *Example*

A coin is tested for bias by tossing it twelve times and counting the number of heads. If the result is two heads, is there evidence, at the 2% significance level, that the coin is biased? What is the critical region for this test?

Again we start by assuming that the coin is not biased, i.e. $p = \tfrac{1}{2}$. Before we start the test we have no idea in which direction, if any, the coin is biased and so the alternative hypothesis specifies a change of p in either direction. We have:

Model: Binomial
H_0: $p = \frac{1}{2}$
H_1: $p \neq \frac{1}{2}$

If the null hypothesis is true then the number of heads, X, is Binomially distributed, $B(12, \frac{1}{2})$. In this case either a high or a low number of heads could lead us to reject the null hypothesis and so we require

$$P(X \leqslant 2 \text{ or } X \geqslant 10) = 2 \times P(X \leqslant 2) \qquad \text{(since the distribution is symmetrical)}$$
$$= 2 \times \{(\tfrac{1}{2})^{12} + (\tbinom{12}{1})(\tfrac{1}{2})(\tfrac{1}{2})^{11} + (\tbinom{12}{2})(\tfrac{1}{2})^2(\tfrac{1}{2})^{10}\}$$
$$= 0.0386 = 3.86\% > 2\%$$

The probability of the observed (or a more extreme) result is greater than 2% and so the result is not significant at the 2% level. The null hypothesis is retained: there is no evidence at this significance level that the coin is biased.

The critical region gives those values of X for which the null hypothesis will be rejected. Table 15.1 shows the probability distribution for $B(12, \frac{1}{2})$.

Table 15.1 *Probability distribution for X where X is $B(12, \frac{1}{2})$*

x	$P(X=x)$
0	0.000 24
1	0.002 93
2	0.016 11
3	0.053 71
4	0.120 85
5	0.193 36
6	0.225 59
7	0.193 36
8	0.120 85
9	0.053 71
10	0.016 11
11	0.002 93
12	0.000 24

From this table we can see that

$$P(X \leqslant 1) + P(X \geqslant 11) = 0.006\,34 = 0.6\% < 2\%$$
$$P(X \leqslant 2) + P(X \geqslant 10) = 0.038\,56 = 3.9\% > 2\%$$

and so the critical region, which is shared between the two tails of the distribution, is $X \leqslant 1$ and $X \geqslant 11$.

It is most important to realise that we can rarely prove or disprove a null hypothesis. For example, when we perform a test at the $\alpha\%$ significance level there is a probability of $\alpha\%$ that the result falls in the critical region when the null hypothesis is true. This means that there is a probability of $\alpha\%$ that a true null hypothesis will be rejected. In Example 15.1.1 this means that there is a 2% risk of saying the coin is biased when it is not. If the test had been performed at the 5% significance level the observed result would have been significant and the null hypothesis rejected but in this case the risk of rejecting a true null hypothesis has risen to 5%. The risk of errors involved in significance testing is discussed further in Section 15.12.

15.1.2   *Exercise*

(1)   The tea-tasting experiment is modified so that at each trial the taster is offered four cups of tea. One of these is 'milk-first' and the others are 'tea-first'. Again the cups are presented in a random order. She has to identify the milk-first cup. She makes the correct identification three times out of ten. Test at the 5% level her claim that she can identify the milk-first tea correctly, stating clearly your null and alternative hypotheses. How many times would she have to be correct before you would accept her claim, using the same level of significance?

(2)   In a multiple choice test a student has to choose between three answers for each question in a test consisting of ten questions. If he gets six questions right test, at the 5% level, the null hypothesis that he is guessing.

(3)   The national average pass rate for an exam is 70%. A teacher finds that six out of her twelve pupils pass. Is there evidence that this group did significantly worse than average?

(4)   It is suspected that a die is biased towards a 6. This is tested by throwing the die eight times. The result is three 6s. Is there evidence at the 2% significance level that the die is biased towards a 6?

15.2   **Significance tests on the mean of a Normal distribution (σ known)**

We often wish to test whether a sample is drawn from a population of specified mean, μ. We will start by considering the situation in which the population is Normally distributed with known standard deviation σ.

15.2.1   *Example*

A machine should be set to produce bags of sugar whose weights are Normally distributed with $\mu = 1000$ g, $\sigma = 5$ g. To check the setting, a sample of nine bags is taken and the mean weight is found to be 1003 g. Is the machine correctly set? (Assume σ cannot change.)

We must choose a null hypothesis that assumes the mean given for the machine is correct, so that we can calculate the probability of observing a sample whose mean is 1003 g. We take

Model: Normal
H_0: $\mu = 1000$ g, $\sigma = 5$ g

Since we are interested in differences either way from $\mu = 1000$ g, this is a two-tailed test and
$$H_1: \quad \mu \neq 1000 \text{ g}$$

According to H_0, the sampling distribution for the mean, $\bar{X}$, of a sample of nine bags is Normally distributed with $\mu = 1000$ g, s.d. $= \sigma/\sqrt{n} = 5/\sqrt{9} = 1.67$ g.

For the observed sample mean, 1003, we have:

$$z = (1003 - 1000)/1.67 = 1.80$$

Since we are carrying out a two-sided test we require

$$\begin{aligned}
P(z < 1.80) + P(z > 1.80) &= 2 \times P(z > 1.80) \quad \text{(since the distribution is symmetrical)}\\
&= 2 \times [1 - P(z < 1.80)]\\
&= 2 \times (1 - 0.9641)\\
&= 2 \times 0.0359\\
&= 0.0718 = 7.18\%
\end{aligned}$$

If we adopt a 5% significance level for our test then this result is not significant: there is no evidence that machine setting is incorrect.

A quicker method of arriving at the same result is to work with the critical region for the statistic z rather than to calculate an exact value for the probability, as was done above. Figure 15.2 shows the standard Normal distribution with the critical region for a test at the 5% significance level. Since the test is two-sided the critical region is divided equally between the two tails of the distribution. If a result falls in the critical region then the null hypothesis is rejected. For a two-sided test, this happens when $|z| \geqslant 1.96$. In the calculation above we found that $z = 1.80$: this result does not fall in the critical region and so there is no reason to reject the null hypothesis.

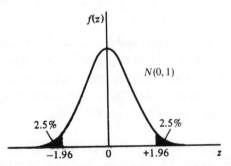

Figure 15.2 Graph showing the critical region for example 15.2.1

Suppose the previous example had been altered so that the question asked had been 'Is the machine set too high?' We now need to carry out a one-tail test for which we have:
Model: Normal
$$H_0: \quad \mu = 1000 \text{ g}, \sigma = 5 \text{ g}$$
$$H_1: \quad \mu > 1000 \text{ g}$$

The critical region is shown in Figure 15.3 and is given by $z \geqslant 1.64$. The previous calculation gave $z = 1.80$. This value is significant at the 5% level. We reject the null hypothesis and accept the alternative hypothesis: the machine is set too high.

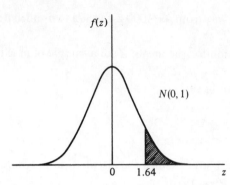

Figure 15.3 Graph showing the critical region for a one-tail test

The critical values of z can be conveniently found from the last row, $v = \infty$, of Table A4. For a two-tail test at the $\alpha\%$ level the critical value is given in the $\alpha\%$ column; for a one-tail test in the $2\alpha\%$ column.

In practice we would not carry out a one- and a two-tail test on the same set of results. The null and alternative hypotheses are defined *before* the data are collected and the choice between a one- and a two-tailed test depends on prior knowledge. For example, if we wished to see whether a catalyst increased the rate of a reaction then we know before we start that we are looking for an increase. If the actual results showed a decrease then there would be no need to carry out the test.

The method given in this section is applicable even if the population from which the sample is drawn is not Normal *provided that the sample is large*. This is a consequence of the central limit theorem.

15.2.2   *Exercise*

(1)   A machine is designed to produce rope with a breaking strain of 1000 N. The breaking strain is known to be Normally distributed with s.d. 21 N. A new material is introduced into the rope which it is hoped will increase the breaking strain. A random sample of nine pieces of rope had a mean breaking strain of 1012 N. Is there evidence at the 5% significance level that the mean breaking strain has increased?

(2)   A machine filling bottles of orange squash is adjusted to deliver 0.725 litre with a standard deviation of 0.010 litre. A sample of 50 bottles is checked and the mean quantity is found to be 0.721. Determine whether this should be taken to be significantly different from 0.725 at the 5% level.
In a later check the manufacturer decides on a more stringent test, using the 2% level. If he now takes a sample of 40 bottles and the mean turns out to be 0.722, is this mean significantly different from 0.725?   (C)

(3)   A factory produces washers of mean thickness 3 mm with a standard deviation of 0.2 mm. Each day, as a routine check, the thickness of a random sample of 100 washers is measured and the mean calculated and recorded. Every 30 days, these means are

assembled into a frequency table. What would you expect the mean and standard deviation of this table to be?

On one day, the mean of the sample of 100 washers is 3.036 mm. Is this significantly different from the expected value?   (O)

(4) Explain the difference between a one-tail and a two-tail significance test.

A test of mental ability has been constructed such that, for adults in Great Britain, the test score is Normally distributed with mean 100 and standard deviation 15. A doctor wishes to test whether sufferers from a particular disease differ from the general population in their performance on this test. He chooses a random sample of ten from his patients. Their scores on the test are

119, 131, 95, 107, 125, 90, 123, 89, 103, 103.

What would you conclude?   (O)

(5) The mean number of letters per word in a dictionary of the English language is 6.8 and the standard deviation of the number of letters per word is 2.5.

Work out the mean number of letters per word for the words in question 3 and test whether it appears to come from this dictionary population. Is this a valid test of the hypothesis that the question is worded in typical English?   (O)

(6) Bill has used a particular type of razor for shaving for a long time. The length of time (in seconds) that he takes to shave is Normally distributed with mean 240 and s.d. 20. He changes to a new razor and finds that his shaving times on nine consecutive days are 210, 220, 230, 220, 250, 230, 260, 210, 240. Assuming that the s.d. of his shaving time has not changed, test whether his mean shaving time has changed with the new razor.

(7) The mass of packs of unwrapped chocolates is Normally distributed with mean 508 g and s.d. 4 g. I am told that a pack of chocolates weighs 520 g but I am not told whether the chocolates are unwrapped or not. Carry out a significance test to show that there is evidence that the chocolates are wrapped.

15.3   Significance tests (σ unknown): large samples

If σ is unknown but the sample is *large*, then the test statistic z can still be used, with σ replaced by $\hat{s}$ (as in Section 14.2). This gives

$$z = \frac{\bar{x} - \mu}{\hat{s}/\sqrt{n}} = \frac{\bar{x} - \mu}{s/\sqrt{(n-1)}}$$

15.3.1   *Example*

One hundred measurements of a variate gave $\sum_{i=1}^{100} x_i = 151$, $\sum_{i=1}^{100} x_i^2 = 390$. Could these measurements have come from a population, mean 1.5?

$$\text{sample mean, } \bar{x} = \left(\sum_{i=1}^{n} x_i \right) \Big/ n = 151/100 = 1.51$$

$$\text{sample s.d., } s = \sqrt{\left\{ \frac{\sum\limits_{i=1}^{n} x_i^2}{n} - \left(\frac{\sum\limits_{i=1}^{n} x_i}{n} \right)^2 \right\}}$$

$$= \sqrt{\left\{ \tfrac{390}{100} - \left(\tfrac{151}{100} \right)^2 \right\}}$$

$$= 1.27$$

$$H_0: \mu = 1.5$$

$$H_1: \mu \neq 1.5$$

$$z = \frac{\bar{x} - \mu}{s/\sqrt{(n-1)}} = \frac{1.51 - 1.5}{1.27/\sqrt{99}} = 0.078$$

This value of z is not significant at the 5% level since the critical region is $|z| \geqslant 1.96$. H_0 is retained: the measurements could have come from a population mean 1.5.

15.3.2   *Exercise*

(1) A random sample of the men marrying in a town had the age distribution given in Table 15.2.

Table 15.2

Age	Under 18	18–24	25–31	32–38	39–45	46–52	Over 52	Total
Coded value		0	1	2	3	4		
Frequency	0	101	62	25	10	2	0	200

By using the suggested coding, or otherwise, estimate the mean and variance of the population from which the sample is drawn. (Quote your results to two decimal places.)

The mean age of men at marriage in the large country in which the town is situated is 25.90 years. Test whether the men in the town differ significantly from the men in the whole country in the age at which they marry. (State your null hypothesis and the significance level you use.)   (O)

(2) The times taken by a salesman to travel between two shops on 50 occasions averaged 64 minutes with a s.d. of 6.3 minutes. He claims that this provides evidence that the journey takes longer since he changed to a smaller car, as before he averaged 60 minutes. Do you agree with the salesman?

(3) Explain briefly what is meant by a significance level of $\alpha\%$.

A student was asked to mark, by eye, the centre of a line drawn on a sheet of paper. She repeated this 50 times, using a new test sheet each time. The signed deviations from the centre, d, were measured in millimetres and the quantities $\Sigma d = -60.0$, $\Sigma d^2 = 197.44$ calculated. Is there evidence that the student does not locate the mean position of her bisection marks on the centre of the line?   (O)

(4) A pilot wishes to check whether the average depth of a section of river mouth is still 6.1 fathoms as his chart suggests. He takes 30 soundings at random points and finds that the mean depth is 5.8 fathoms with a s.d. of 1.1 fathoms. Test at the 5% significance level whether the mean depth has changed.

(5) A machine which fills orange squash bottles should be set to deliver 725 ml. A sample of 50 bottles is checked and the mean quantity is found to be 721 ml and the sample s.d. is 13 ml. Does this differ significantly from 725 ml at the 1% level?

(6) A new surgical technique has been developed in an attempt to reduce the time that patients have to spend in hospital after a particular operation. In the past the mean time spent in hospital was 5.3 days. For the first 40 patients on whom the new technique was used the mean time spent in hospital was 5.0 days and the sample s.d. was 0.4 days. Is there evidence that the new technique has decreased the time spent in hospital?

15.4   Significance tests (σ unknown): small samples

For *small* samples the statistic

$$t_{n-1} = \frac{\bar{x} - \mu}{\hat{s}/\sqrt{n}} = \frac{\bar{x} - \mu}{s/\sqrt{(n-1)}}$$

must be used. It should only be used if the population from which the sample is drawn is Normal.

15.4.1   *Example*

A manufacturer claims that his light bulbs have an average lifetime of 1500 hours. A purchaser decides to check this claim and finds that for six bulbs the lifetimes are 1472, 1486, 1401, 1350, 1610, 1590 hours. Does this evidence support the manufacturer's claim?

We have to assume the lifetimes of the light bulbs are Normally distributed. Then we have

     Model: Normal

         H_0: $\mu = 1500$ h

         H_1: $\mu \neq 1500$ h

     Two-tail test

Using Table A4 the critical region is $|t_5| \geqslant 2.57$ for a test at the 5% significance level.

     The reader should check that for the observed lifetimes

$$\bar{x} = 1484.8 \text{ h}, \quad s = 93.2 \text{ h}$$

$$t_{n-1} = \frac{\bar{x} - \mu}{s/\sqrt{(n-1)}}$$

$$t_5 = \frac{1484.8 - 1500}{93.2/\sqrt{5}} = -0.36$$

This result is not significant at the 5% level. The null hypothesis is retained and the manufacturer's claim is vindicated.

15.4.2 *Exercise*

(1) Packets of breakfast cereal claim that the minimum net weight of the contents is 450 g. The weights of the contents of seven packets are:

$$445, \; 453, \; 447, \; 451, \; 440, \; 460, \; 449$$

Is there any evidence at the 5% significance level that the packets are underweight?

(2) The lives of six candles are found to be 8.1, 8.7, 9.2, 7.8, 8.4, 9.4 hours. Estimate the population mean and show that the estimate of the population variance is 0.388. The manufacturer claims that the average life is $9\frac{1}{2}$ hours. Making a suitable assumption concerning the nature of the distribution of the life of a candle, carry out a statistical test of the manufacturer's claim. Give full details of your test.   (C)

(3) A student titrates 10 ml of 0.1 M acid against 0.1 M alkali five times and obtains the following results for the volume of alkali:

$$9.88, \; 10.18, \; 10.23, \; 10.39, \; 10.25 \, \text{ml}$$

Is there any evidence that these results show a bias from the expected value of 10 ml?

(4) Eight volunteers tested a food which the manufacturer claimed would help people to slim. At the end of the test they had lost $1, 2, 0, 1, -2, 0, 3, 3$ kg respectively. Assuming that these losses are a random sample from a Normal distribution, carry out a t-test to determine whether the mean loss differs significantly from zero, and comment on the manufacturer's claim.   (C)

*15.5   Difference between two means for large samples

Suppose we take large samples from two populations as indicated below:

	Population 1	*Population 2*
	mean $= \mu_1$	mean $= \mu_2$
	s.d. $= \sigma_1$	s.d. $= \sigma_2$
	sample size $= n_1$	sample size $= n_2$
	sample mean $= \bar{x}_1$	sample mean $= \bar{x}_2$
	sample s.d. $= s_1$	sample s.d. $= s_2$

$\bar{X}_1$ will be Normally distributed (since n_1 is large) with mean μ_1 and s.d. $\sigma_1/\sqrt{n_1}$, and $\bar{X}_2$ will be Normally distributed with mean μ_2 and s.d. $\sigma_2/\sqrt{n_2}$. The difference between the means, $\bar{X}_1 - \bar{X}_2$, will also be Normally distributed with mean $\mu_1 - \mu_2$ and s.d. $\sqrt{\{(\sigma_1^2/n_1) + (\sigma_2^2/n_2)\}}$ (see Section 10.4). We frequently wish to test whether two samples come from populations with the same mean in which case $\mu_1 - \mu_2 = 0$.

15.5.1 Example

A firm employs 300 women and 100 men. The mean number of days absent last year for the women was 5.3 with a s.d. of 2.2 and for the men the corresponding figures were 6.2 and 2.9. Is the difference between the means significant?

Model: Normal

H_0: $\mu_1 = \mu_2$ therefore $\mu_1 - \mu_2 = 0$

H_1: $\mu_1 \neq \mu_2$

Two-tail test

The test statistic is

$$z = \frac{(\bar{x}_1 - \bar{x}_2) - (\mu_1 - \mu_2)}{\sqrt{\left\{\dfrac{\sigma_1^2}{n_1} + \dfrac{\sigma_2^2}{n_2}\right\}}}$$

$$= \frac{\bar{x}_1 - \bar{x}_2}{\sqrt{\left\{\dfrac{\sigma_1^2}{n_1} + \dfrac{\sigma_2^2}{n_2}\right\}}}$$

since from H_0, $\mu_1 - \mu_2 = 0$.

If σ_1 and σ_2 are not known, then, because the samples are large, σ_1 and σ_2 can be replaced by $\hat{s}_1$ and $\hat{s}_2$. Since $\hat{s} = \sqrt{(n/(n-1))}s$ this gives

$$z = \frac{\bar{x}_1 - \bar{x}_2}{\sqrt{\{s_1^2/(n_1-1) + s_2^2/(n_2-1)\}}}$$

$$= \frac{5.3 - 6.2}{\sqrt{\{2.2^2/299 + 2.9^2/99\}}}$$

$$= -2.83$$

The critical region for z is $|z| \geqslant 1.96$ so that z is significant at the 5% (two-tail) level and we reject the null hypothesis. There is a significant difference between the mean absences of men and women.

The theory for small samples is beyond the scope of this book.

15.5.2 Exercise

(1) It is found that over a certain period at one telephone exchange 200 subscribers taken at random made a total of 13 248 calls. During the same time, a random sample of 300 subscribers at another exchange made a total of 20 922 calls. The standard deviation of the number of calls made by a subscriber at either exchange in the period is 8.

Is there any evidence of a difference between the subscribers at the two exchanges in their average frequency of calls?

Find 95% confidence limits for the mean number of calls made in the period per subscriber at each exchange. (AEB)

(2) Samples of leaves were collected from two oak trees A and B. The number of galls was counted on each leaf and the mean and standard deviation of the number of galls per leaf was calculated with the results given in Table 15.3.

Table 15.3

Tree	A	B
Sample size	60	80
Mean	11.4	10.7
s.d.	2.6	3.1

Assuming Normal distributions, do the data provide evidence at the 5% significance level of different population means for the two trees? (SUJB)

(3) In an investigation into the effectiveness of a particular course in speed reading a group of 500 students was split into two groups, A and B, of sizes 300 and 200 respectively, thought to have been chosen at random.

Those in group A were given no special instruction; those in group B were given a course in speed reading. Each student was asked to read the same passage and the time taken was measured. The results were

Group A: mean time 78.4 s, variance 14 s^2

Group B: mean time 77.4 s, variance 15 s^2

Carry out a significance test to see if there is evidence that the course has improved reading speed. State carefully your null hypothesis, alternative hypothesis and final conclusion.

You learn later that, of the original 500 students, 200 students had decided for themselves that they wanted to take the course in speed reading and that these students became group B. Discuss briefly how this might affect your previous conclusion. (JMB)

(4) Using the data in question (9) of the Exercise on Chapter 2, test whether boys wash their hair more frequently than girls.

(5) Using the data in Section 2.1, test whether the number of letters per word for the child's book is significantly lower than the value for *Gulliver's Travels*.

*15.6 Testing if two samples come from the same population

In this case we wish to test whether $\bar{x}_1 - \bar{x}_2$ differs significantly from zero as in the previous example. However, since our null hypothesis is now that the two samples are from the *same* population, we have $\sigma_1 = \sigma_2 = \sigma$ (say) and the s.d. of $\bar{x}_1 - \bar{x}_2$ is therefore $\sigma\sqrt{\{1/n_1 + 1/n_2\}}$. If we know σ we can use the test statistic

$$z = \frac{\bar{x}_1 - \bar{x}_2}{\sigma\sqrt{\left\{\dfrac{1}{n_1} + \dfrac{1}{n_2}\right\}}} \tag{15.6.1}$$

More usually σ is not known. We need to make an unbiased estimate $\hat{s}$ of it from both the samples and use the test statistic t. It can be shown that, if s_1 and s_2 are the standard deviations of the two samples, the most efficient unbiased estimate of the s.d. of the population is given by

$$\hat{s} = \sqrt{\left\{\frac{n_1 s_1^2 + n_2 s_2^2}{n_1 + n_2 - 2}\right\}} \tag{15.6.2}$$

The denominator represents the number of degrees of freedom of this estimate so that the test statistic

$$t_{n_1 + n_2 - 2} = \frac{\bar{x}_1 - \bar{x}_2}{\sqrt{\left\{\left(\dfrac{n_1 s_1^2 + n_2 s_2^2}{n_1 + n_2 - 2}\right)\left(\dfrac{1}{n_1} + \dfrac{1}{n_2}\right)\right\}}} \tag{15.6.3}$$

can be used provided that the populations are Normal and/or the samples are large.

15.6.1 *Example*

A market gardener decides to test a new pesticide, which the manufacturer claims increases the yield, by applying it to one of his two orchards. The treated orchard contains twenty trees and the mean and s.d. of the yield per tree are 98 kg and 10 kg respectively. The untreated orchard contains fifteen trees and the corresponding values are 94 kg and 8 kg. Test whether these results are consistent with the yields being drawn from the same population.

> Model: Normal
> H_0: $\mu_1 = \mu_2$, $\sigma_1 = \sigma_2 = \sigma$
> H_1: samples from different populations
> $\bar{x}_1 = 98$ kg, $\bar{x}_2 = 94$ kg
> $s_1 = 10$ kg, $s_2 = 8$ kg
> $n_1 = 20$, $n_2 = 15$

The unbiased estimate of variance using equation (15.6.2) is

$$\hat{s} = \sqrt{\left\{\frac{n_1 s_1^2 + n_2 s_2^2}{n_1 + n_2 - 2}\right\}} = \sqrt{\left\{\frac{20 \times 10^2 + 15 \times 8^2}{20 + 15 - 2}\right\}} = 9.47 \text{ kg}$$

Using equation (15.6.3),

$$t_{33} = \frac{98-94}{9.47\sqrt{\{\frac{1}{20}+\frac{1}{15}\}}} = 1.24$$

This is not significant at the 5% level (two-tail) and H_0 is retained. The results are consistent with the samples being drawn from the same population.

Strictly speaking, before such a test is made, a test should first be made on the variances of the samples to see whether a pooled estimate of variance is justified (see Section 19.4). If there is a significant difference between the variances, then the analysis described is no longer valid.

15.6.2   *Exercise*

(1) In a butter-packing plant the quantity of butter packed in a day using a certain type of machine is a Normal variable with a standard deviation of 39 kg. Two packers *A* and *B* average 1518 kg and 1499 kg per day respectively over a 26-day month. Is the performance of the two operatives significantly different?
A third packer *C* averages 1480 kg per day for her first 26-day month. Is this a significantly worse performance than *B*'s?
(For each test you should state clearly your null and alternative hypotheses.)   (C)

Table 15.4

Source	Lengths in mm							
Britain	12.3	12.7	13.1	10.8	11.3	11.8	12.4	13.2
N. Africa	10.6	9.8	11.5	10.0	11.1			

(2) The lengths of the femur in samples of *Mus homunculus* from two sources (Britain and North Africa) are given in Table 15.4.
The mean length of the femur is known to be characteristic of each breed of *Mus homunculus*. Test whether the data are consistent with the assumption that *Mus homunculus* in Britain and North Africa are of the same breed.   (C)

(3) In an experiment 22 mice were divided into two groups, one of which was given a special diet. After an interval the gains in weight of the mice were measured, with the results given in Table 15.5.
The variance of weight increases may be assumed to be the same for both populations of which these groups are samples, those being fed a special diet and those being ordinarily fed. Calculate an estimate of this common variance from the combined results of both groups, and discuss whether the difference in the observed weight increases is significant.   (C)

Table 15.5

	Number	Mean gain	Variance
Special diet	10	20.6	4.51
Control group	12	8.2	3.17

15.7 Paired tests

15.7.1 *Example*

Table 15.6 gives the times taken (in minutes) by eight typists to type the same number of words using two different typewriters. Do the data indicate any difference in speeds for the two typewriters?

Table 15.6

Typist	A	B	C	D	E	F	G	H
X, time using typewriter 1	6.3	4.5	7.1	8.4	3.7	3.9	4.7	5.2
Y, time using typewriter 2	5.1	4.4	6.2	7.3	4.5	4.0	3.6	5.1

In this case it would be incorrect to calculate the means for typewriter 1 and typewriter 2 as in Section 15.6 since the variations between the typists could swamp any difference due to the machines. Instead we compute the difference, D, for each typist, since if there is no difference between the machines then we would expect the mean difference, $\bar{D}$, to be zero. Provided the original populations are Normal, $\bar{D}$ will also be approximately Normally distributed.

Table 15.7 shows the calculation of the mean $\bar{d}$, and the s.d., s_d, of the sample. (Note that $\text{var}(D) \neq \text{var}(X) + \text{var}(Y)$ since the values of X and Y used to calculate each d_i are not independent. In fact $\text{var}(D) < \text{var}(X) + \text{var}(Y)$.)

$$\bar{d} = \frac{3.6}{8} = 0.45 \text{ min.}$$

$$s_d = \sqrt{\left\{ \frac{5.34}{8} - \left(\frac{3.6}{8} \right)^2 \right\}}$$

$$= 0.68 \text{ min.}$$

If μ_D is the mean of the population from which D is drawn we have:

Model: Normal·

H_0: $\mu_D = 0$

H_1: $\mu_D \neq 0$

Two-tail test

Using t as the test statistic, since the s.d. s_d is estimated from the sample, we have

Table 15.7 *Calculation for paired t-test*

Typist	$d_i = x_i - y_i$	d_i^2
A	1.2	1.44
B	0.1	0.01
C	0.9	0.81
D	1.1	1.21
E	−0.8	0.64
F	−0.1	0.01
G	1.1	1.21
H	0.1	0.01
	3.6	5.34

$$t_{n-1} = \frac{0 - \bar{d}}{s_d / \sqrt{(n-1)}}$$

$$= \frac{-0.45}{0.68 / \sqrt{7}} = -1.75$$

This value of t is not significant at the 5% (two-tail) level and H_0 is retained. The data do not indicate a difference in speed for the two typewriters.

15.8   The sign test

This test is sometimes used instead of the paired t-test. Consider again the data in example 15.7.1 (see Table 15.8). A plus sign in the last row indicates that typewriter 1 was faster and a minus sign that typewriter 2 was faster. If we adopt the null hypothesis that there is no difference between the two typewriters we would expect an equal number of plus and minus signs. In fact we have two minus signs out of eight. The number of minus signs will be Binomially distributed with, on our null hypothesis, $p = \frac{1}{2}$, $n = 8$. The test is two-tailed since we are only concerned with whether the typewriters differ in speed.

Model: Binomial

H_0: $p = \frac{1}{2}$

H_1: $p \neq \frac{1}{2}$

Two-tail test

The probability of observing two or less minus signs is

Table 15.8

Typist	A	B	C	D	E	F	G	H
Time using typewriter 1	6.3	4.5	7.1	8.4	3.7	3.9	4.7	5.2
Time using typewriter 2	5.1	4.4	6.2	7.3	4.5	4.0	3.6	5.1
	+	+	+	+	−	−	+	+

$$(\tfrac{1}{2})^8 + \binom{8}{1}(\tfrac{1}{2})^7(\tfrac{1}{2}) + \binom{8}{2}(\tfrac{1}{2})^6(\tfrac{1}{2})^2 = 0.145$$

Thus the probability of observing $\leqslant 2$ or $\geqslant 6$ minus signs is 0.29 and the observed number of minus signs is not significant at the 5% level. H_0 is retained (as it was when the paired t-test was performed). The sign test can be used whether or not the populations are Normal.

The sign test is an example of a **non-parametric test**. Non-parametric tests make no assumptions about the distribution from which the sample is drawn. In particular they do not assume that the population distribution is Normal as many of the tests described in this chapter do.

15.8.1 *Exercise*

(1) Ten marksmen shot at targets with two types of rifle. Their scores out of 100 were as in Table 15.9.
Apply the sign test to the hypothesis that the rifles are equally good. Also use the t-test for paired values to test the same hypothesis. What assumption is made in applying this test, but not in applying the sign test? (AEB)

Table 15.9

Marksman	A	B	C	D	E	F	G	H	I	J
Rifle type I	93	99	90	87	85	94	88	91	96	79
Rifle type II	89	93	86	92	78	90	91	87	92	86

(2) During negotiations between the union and management of a large firm two alternative offers are put to the union side:
(i) old rates plus 20% increase across the board,
(ii) new rates based on a production bonus scheme.
The union statistician, Percy Glum, considers these offers and calculates the pay that 25 typical employees would receive from each offer. These are summarised in Table 15.10.

Table 15.10

Employee	1	2	3	4	5	6	7	8	9	10	11	12	13
Old rates plus 20% (£)	56	43	59	62	38	49	53	37	71	53	47	39	37
New rates (£)	67	58	58	75	47	51	52	49	75	59	56	41	42

Employee	14	15	16	17	18	19	20	21	22	23	24	25
Old rates plus 20% (£)	68	27	68	75	42	53	61	56	58	35	46	37
New rates (£)	65	31	72	84	45	54	65	61	57	39	49	39

By use of the sign test, or otherwise, determine whether the new rates will lead, on average, to an increase of more than the 20% on the old rates.   (AEB)

15.9   Significance of a proportion (large samples)

In this section we return to the situation considered at the beginning of the chapter where we have a variable which is Binomially distributed, the difference being that we will consider large samples so that the Normal approximation can be used.

15.9.1   *Example*

On a national basis the success rate for people taking their driving test for the first time is 40%. A driving instructor claims that his record is superior because, of the 50 pupils of his who took the test for the first time last year, 25 passed. Is his claim justified?

We have

> Model: Binomial approximated by Normal
> H_0: $p = 0.4$
> H_1: $p > 0.4$
> One-tail test

On the null hypothesis the number of people, X, who pass first time in a sample of 50, is a variable which is Binomially distributed with

$$\mu = np = 50 \times 0.4 = 20$$
$$\sigma = \sqrt{(npq)} = \sqrt{(50 \times 0.4 \times 0.6)} = \sqrt{12}$$

Since n is large, X is approximately Normally distributed with mean 20, s.d. 3.46 (see Section 9.6). The number in the sample who pass first time is 25. Since the variance of the population is known we can use the test statistic z. As we have a *single* measurement of the variable X,

$$z = \frac{x - \mu}{\sigma}$$
$$= \frac{25 - 20}{\sqrt{12}} = 1.44$$

This value of z is not significant at the 5% level (one-tail). H_0 is retained and the instructor's claim is not justified.

Strictly speaking a continuity correction of $\pm \frac{1}{2}$ should be applied. In this case this would lead to a value of $z = (24.5 - 20)/\sqrt{12} = 1.30$. However, this correction is frequently omitted.

The solution to this problem can also be given in terms of proportions since the sampling distribution of the proportion in the sample, P_S, is $N[p, p(1-p)/n]$. We have

$$z = \frac{p_S - p}{\sqrt{\left[\dfrac{p(1-p)}{n} \right]}}$$

$$= -\frac{0.5 - 0.4}{\sqrt{\left[\dfrac{0.4 \times 0.6}{50}\right]}}$$

$$= 1.44$$

which, of course, gives the same result as before. In this case the continuity correction, if applied, is $\pm\frac{1}{2}n$.

15.9.2 *Exercise*

(1) After a survey a market research company asserted that 75% of TV viewers watched a certain programme. Another company interviewed 75 viewers and found that 51 watched the programme and 24 did not. Does this provide evidence at the 5% level of significance that the first company's figure of 75% was incorrect?   (SUJB)

(2) In a multiple choice examination paper, a candidate has to select which of four possible answers to a question is the correct one. On a paper with 100 questions he gets 34 correct answers. Explain carefully, with supporting calculations, whether you regard this result as contradicting the supposition that his answers are obtained entirely by guesswork.

(3) Explain what is meant by a standard error.
A certain method of scaling examination marks is supposed to fix the quartiles at 25 and 75. Out of 1000 candidates, 541 have marks between these limits. Is this evidence that the method has failed?   (O)

(4) You are engaged as an expert witness for the prosecution in a court case in which a gaming club is accused of running an unfair roulette wheel. The evidence is that out of 3700 trial spins, zero (on which the club wins) turned up 140 times. There are 37 possible scores on a trial spin, labelled 0 to 36, and these should have equal probability. Test whether there is evidence that the wheel is biased. Explain briefly what this test of significance means, bearing in mind you have to convince a non-mathematical jury.   (O)

(5) If births are equally likely on any day of the week then the proportion of babies born at the weekend should be $\frac{2}{7}$. Out of a random sample of 100 children it was found that 23 were born at the weekend. Does this provide evidence that the proportion of babies born at the weekend differs from $\frac{2}{7}$?

* 15.10   Difference between two proportions (large samples)

15.10.1 *Example*

In a random sample of 500 people from a certain town there are 270 men, of whom 160 are smokers, and 230 women, of whom 110 are smokers. Is there evidence that the men of the town are more likely to smoke than the women?

If p_1 is the probability that a man from the town smokes and p_2 is the corresponding probability for women, then

$H_0: p_1 = p_2 = p$ (say)

$H_1: p_1 > p_2$

One-tail test

The numbers of men and women who smoke are each Binomially distributed but since the number in the sample is large, the Binomial distribution can be approximated by the Normal distribution. Our best estimate of p is found by combining all the data:

$$\hat{p} = \frac{\text{number who smoke}}{\text{number in sample}} = \frac{160 + 110}{500} = 0.54$$

According to H_0, the observed proportion of men who smoke, P_1, has s.d. $\sqrt{(pq/n_1)}$, where n_1 is the number of men in the sample (see Section 14.4). Similarly for women, the observed proportion, P_2, has s.d. $\sqrt{(pq/n_2)}$ where n_2 is the number of women in the sample. Thus $P_1 - P_2$ has s.d. σ_{1-2} given by

$$\sigma_{1-2} = \sqrt{\left\{ pq \left(\frac{1}{n_1} + \frac{1}{n_2} \right) \right\}}$$

Using our estimate of p, $\hat{p} = 0.54$, this gives for an estimate $\hat{s}_{1-2}$ of σ_{1-2}

$$\hat{s}_{1-2} = \sqrt{\left\{ 0.54 \times 0.46 \left[\frac{1}{270} + \frac{1}{230} \right] \right\}} = 0.0447$$

According to H_0 the mean value of $P_1 - P_2$ is 0. The observed value is

$$\frac{160}{270} - \frac{110}{230} = 0.114$$

Using the test statistic z since n is large,

$$z = \frac{0.114 - 0}{0.0447} = 2.55$$

This value is significant at the 5% level (one-tail). H_0 is rejected and there is evidence that men are more likely to smoke than women. (Another method of treating this problem is the subject of Chapter 16.)

15.10.2 *Exercise*

(1) A television rental organisation supplies its service mechanics with small vans for use when visiting customers. In 1975, the London branch used vans of type A and 15 out of a total of 60 spent at least one day off the road being repaired. The Edinburgh branch used vans of type B in the same year and the corresponding figures were 20 out of a total of 40. Is there a significant difference between the two proportions?

A manager of the organisation wishes to use these figures to compare the reliability of the vans of the two types to help him decide whether the organisation should use one type of van rather than the other in both cities. Comment on (a) what may be inferred about relative reliability from the significance test, (b) what extra information, if any, would be useful when comparing reliability.   (O)

(2) Test whether the proportion of patients who die when they receive antitoxin treatment is significantly different from the proportion who die when they receive ordinary treatment for the data given in Exercise 14.4.3, question (4).

15.11   Significance tests using the Poisson distribution

The ideas developed in this chapter can also be applied when the Poisson distribution is a suitable model for the population from which the sample is drawn.

15.11.1 *Example*

Over a number of years the average number of breakdowns of an office photocopier has been six per month. A new photocopier is installed and the number of breakdowns in the first month is reduced to one. Is this evidence that the new photocopier is more reliable than the old one? Encouraged by this result the office decides to keep the photocopier and the total number of breakdowns for the first year is 50. Does this confirm the idea that the new photocopier is more reliable?

Assuming that breakdowns are events which are randomly distributed in time, we have

$$\text{Model:} \quad \text{Poisson}$$
$$H_0: \quad \lambda = 6$$
$$H_1: \quad \lambda < 6$$

$$P(X \leqslant 1) = e^{-6} + 6 \times e^{-6}$$
$$= 0.0174 = 1.74\% < 5\%$$

The result is significant at the 5% level and there is evidence that the new photocopier is more reliable than the old.

Again adopting the null hypothesis that the new machine has the same reliability as the old one, the mean number of breakdowns per year will be Poisson distributed with mean $= 12 \times 6 = 72$. Since this is large, the number of breakdowns per year will be approximately Normally distributed with mean and variance both equal to 72. We have

$$\text{Model:} \quad \text{Poisson approximated by Normal}$$
$$H_0: \quad \lambda = 72$$
$$H_1: \quad \lambda < 72$$

We calculate the test statistic

$$z = (50 - 72)/\sqrt{72} = -2.59 < -1.64$$

This result is also significant at the 5% level and suggests that the new photocopier is more reliable than the old one. (Strictly speaking a continuity correction should be applied.)

15.11.2 *Exercise*

(1)   The average number of flaws per 100 metre length of a yarn produced by a machine has been found to be seven. A new machine is installed and the first 100 metre length has three flaws. Does this provide evidence that the new machine is better than the old?

(2)   In an intensive survey of duneland it was found that the average number of plants of a

particular species was 26 per square metre. After a hard winter the number of these plants found growing in a randomly chosen area of one square metre was 15. Is there evidence that the hard winter has tended to kill off this species of plant?

*15.12   Type I and Type II errors

When we test a null hypothesis by applying a significance test to a sample we can never be *certain* that our conclusion is correct. All we know is that our decision is probably correct. For example if we reject a null hypothesis it is because we obtained a value of the test statistic in the critical region and this event is unlikely if the null hypothesis is true. We can make two types of error:

Type I: the null hypothesis is rejected when it is in fact true.
Type II: the null hypothesis is retained when it is in fact false.

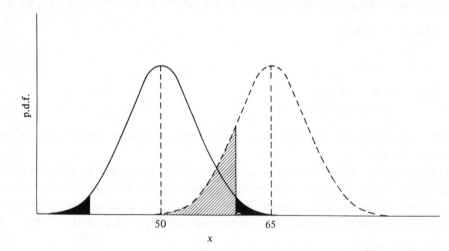

Figure 15.4 Diagram showing the probabilities of making Type I and Type II errors for the example in Section 15.12

The probability of making a Type I error is easily calculated since it is the probability that the test statistic lies in the critical region and is thus equal to the significance level of the test.

The probability of a Type II error cannot be calculated unless we specify a particular value of the parameter for the alternative hypothesis. Suppose we are sampling from a Normal distribution with known standard deviation, σ, equal to 5 and wish to test $H_0 : \mu = 50$ against $H_1 : \mu = 65$ by taking a single measurement. The solid curve in Figure 15.4 shows the distribution of a single measurement, X, if the null hypothesis is true and the broken curve shows the distribution if the alternative hypothesis is true. At the 5% level of significance the probability of making a Type I error is given by the solid black area corresponding to $|z| > 1.96$. The upper critical value of X, i.e. the value of X above which H_0 is rejected, is given by

$$z = (x - \mu)/\sigma$$
$$1.96 = (x - 50)/5$$
$$x = 59.8$$

We can now calculate the probability of a type II error which is given by the hatched area. We have

$$z = (59.8 - 65)/5$$
$$= 1.04$$
$$P(Z < -1.04) = P(Z > 1.04)$$
$$= 1 - P(Z < 1.04)$$
$$= 1 - 0.8508$$
$$= 0.1492$$
$$= 15\%$$

We can reduce the first error by using a lower significance level, e.g. 1%. This will move the upper critical value of X to the right in Figure 15.4 which unfortunately increases the probability of a Type II error. Similarly reducing the Type II error will increase the Type I error. If, however, we are prepared to take a larger sample and use its mean to calculate the test statistic then both errors can be reduced because the standard deviation of the sampling distributions is reduced. If, for example, we take samples size four then the standard error of the mean is $5/\sqrt{4} = 2.5$. If the upper critical value of $\bar{X}$ is kept as 59.8 we have

$$P(\text{Type I error}) = P[Z > (59.8 - 50)/2.5]$$
$$= P(Z > 3.92)$$
$$= 0.005\%$$
$$P(\text{Type II error}) = P[Z < (59.8 - 65)/2.5]$$
$$= (Z < -2.08)$$
$$= 1.9\%$$

In an experiment the critical value and the sample size can be chosen to give acceptable values for both types of error. An example is given in question (3) of the next exercise.

15.12.1 *Example*

A box is known to contain either (H_0) ten white counters and ninety black counters or (H_1) fifty white counters and fifty black counters. In order to test hypothesis H_0 against hypothesis H_1, four counters are drawn at random from the box without replacement. If all four counters are black H_0 is accepted. Otherwise it is rejected. Find the size of the Type I and Type II errors for this test.   (AEB)

Type I error

H_0 is rejected when it is in fact true. H_0 is rejected if less than four black counters are obtained. The probability of this event is most easily calculated by finding the probability that all four counters are black.

$$P(\text{four black}) = \tfrac{90}{100} \times \tfrac{89}{99} \times \tfrac{88}{98} \times \tfrac{87}{97} = 0.652$$

Therefore the probability of a Type I error is $1 - 0.652 = 0.348$.

Type II error

H_0 is retained when it is false and H_1 is true. If H_1 is true the probability of selecting four black counters is

$$\tfrac{50}{100} \times \tfrac{49}{99} \times \tfrac{48}{98} \times \tfrac{47}{97} = 0.059$$

This is the probability of a Type II error.

If the probability of a Type II error occurring for a specific alternative hypothesis is β, then $1 - \beta$ gives the probability that we reject a false null hypothesis, i.e. we make the correct decision. This probability is known as the **power** of a test. In the previous example, with the specified alternative hypothesis, the power was $1 - 0.059 = 0.941$.

15.12.2 *Exercise*

(1) You are provided with a coin which may be biased. In order to test this you are allowed to toss it twelve times and count the number, r, of heads to decide. If the coin is really fair you wish to have at least a 95% chance of saying so. For what value of r should you decide the coin is fair?
     If you adopt your procedure with a coin which is actually biased two to one in favour of heads, what is the probability that you decide the coin is biased?   (O)

(2) A sample of twenty items is taken from what is believed to be a Normal population with mean 24 and standard deviation 5. Obtain the range of values within which the mean of the sample must lie in order that the sample may be accepted as coming from the population if the significance level of the test is 5%. What is the probability that we shall reject the conclusion that the sample comes from this population when it in fact does so?
     Assuming that the standard deviation is correct but the mean of the population is in fact 25, what is the probability that we shall accept the original hypothesis when it is untrue in this particular way?   (C)

(3) A machine produces nails whose lengths are Normally distributed with mean μ cm and standard deviation 0.1 cm. When the machine is working correctly $\mu = 3.0$, but occasionally the machine goes wrong, in which case $\mu = 3.05$, the standard deviation remaining 0.1 cm. In order to decide whether the machine is working correctly, the lengths of the nails in a sample of n nails are measured, and the sample mean $\bar{x}$ is found. If the value of $\bar{x}$ exceeds a predetermined value v then it is concluded that the machine has gone wrong; otherwise the machine is presumed to be working correctly. It is required that there should be a probability of no more than 5% of presuming that the machine has gone wrong when in fact it is working correctly, and that there should also be a probability of no more than 10% of presuming the machine to be working

correctly when it has gone wrong. Determine appropriate values of n and v, if n is to be as small as possible.   (C)

(4)   State what you understand by the critical region and the power of a test.

    (a)   A trial has two possible outcomes: success and failure. To test the null hypothesis that the probability, p, of a success is 0.25, an experiment consisting of ten independent trials is performed. If six or more successes are observed the null hypothesis is rejected. Find the significance level of the test.

        If p is actually 0.5, find the power of the test.

    (b)   The life of a particular type of projector bulb has a mean value of 50 hours and standard deviation of 10 hours. It is thought that a different design of bulb will have a longer life, but it is expected that the standard deviation will not change. A random sample of 25 bulbs of the new type is obtained. The sample mean $\bar{x}$, which may be assumed to be Normally distributed, is to be used to test for an increase in mean life. If the significance level of the test is 1%, find the critical region for the sample mean.

        Find the power of the test when the mean life for the improved bulb is (i) 56 hours, (ii) 52 hours.   (JMB)

15.13   Control charts

In industrial processes it is important to check that the process is under control. For example, if a machine is meant to produce packets of sugar with a particular mean weight μ, the process can be tested by taking a sample of n bags and finding their mean weight $\bar{x}$. We know that $\bar{x}$ will vary from sample to sample but (assuming the weights are Normally distributed) we expect 95% of the values of $\bar{x}$ to lie within $\pm 1.96\sigma/\sqrt{n}$ of μ and 99.8% of the values of $\bar{x}$ to lie within $\pm 3.09\sigma/\sqrt{n}$ of μ. The population s.d. σ can be estimated from past data. The object of a control chart is to provide information about the process over a period of time, in a visual form. Figure 15.5 shows a control chart for the process described above. For each sample the mean is plotted and, if the process is under control, these means will be Normally distributed about the target value μ. There are also two pairs of horizontal lines on the chart: the **warning lines** at $\mu + 2\sigma/\sqrt{n}$ and $\mu - 2\sigma/\sqrt{n}$, within which approximately 95% of the values should lie, and the **action lines** at $\mu + 3\sigma/\sqrt{n}$ and $\mu - 3\sigma/\sqrt{n}$, within which approximately 99.8% of the values should lie. (2 and 3 are used rather than 1.96 and 3.09 to simplify the arithmetic.) The value of n is usually made quite small, i.e. 4 or 5. In Figure 15.5 it will be seen that the mean for sample 7 lies between the upper warning and action lines. Since this happens for about 1 in 40 samples there is no cause for alarm. Should the next sample mean be in the same region, however, it suggests that the mean weight delivered by the machine may have changed and the process should be checked. Similarly, if a sample mean falls outside either of the action lines, an event which should occur only 1 in 500 times, the process should be checked. It will be seen that basically a control chart displays a series of significance tests.

    A control chart can also be made to test the variability of a process. An increase in variability may mean that tolerance limits are no longer met or that the machine is about to

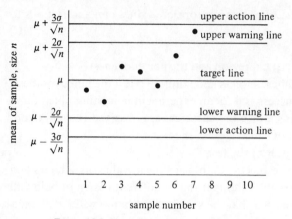

Figure 15.5 Control chart for the mean of a sample

break down. Since the calculation of the s.d. for each sample would be tedious, the range R is used. Normally, only upper action and warning limits are required. There are tables which give these, and the target value of R, for different values of n and σ.

A control chart can also be used when an attribute, such as the number of defectives in a sample, is under test. Suppose we know that, when a process is under control, a proportion p of the items is defective (and this proportion is acceptable). Then the number of defective items, X, in a sample will be Binomially distributed with $P(X=x)=\binom{n}{x}p^x(1-p)^{n-x}$. In this case we are usually concerned lest p become too large so we require only an upper action limit A chosen so that

$$P(X \geqslant A)= \sum_{x \geqslant A}^{n} P(X=x) \leqslant \tfrac{1}{1000}$$

and an upper warning limit W chosen so that

$$P(X \geqslant W)= \sum_{x \geqslant W}^{n} P(X=x) \leqslant \tfrac{1}{40}$$

Usually p will be small and n will be large so that the Binomial probabilities can be approximated by Poisson ones, which are more easily calculated. Suppose we have a process which,

Table 15.10

x	$P(X=x)$	$P(X \geqslant x)$
0	0.6065	1.0000
1	0.3033	0.3935
2	0.0758	0.0902
3	0.0126	0.0144
4	0.0016	0.0018
5	0.0002	0.0002

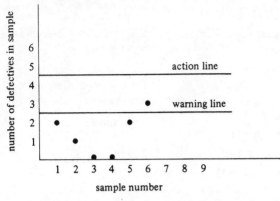

Figure 15.6 A typical control chart for the number of defectives in a sample

when under control, gives 1% of items defective and we take samples size 50. The mean number of defective items per sample should be $0.01 \times 50 = 0.5$. Table 15.10 gives, for this value of λ, the Poisson probability and the probability that $X \geqslant x$, for increasing values of x. When there are 3 defectives we are over the warning limit and when there are 5 defectives we are over the action limit. Figure 15.6 shows a suitable control chart with the warning line between 2 and 3 defectives and the action line between 4 and 5 defectives.

15.13.1 *Exercise*

(a) In an industrial manufacturing process, when production is under control, one unit in fifty is defective. A sample of 100 units is taken at random every half-hour. Sketch a control chart for the number of defectives found in a sample, showing the 1 in 40 and 1 in 1000 lines.

(b) Something goes wrong with the process, so that one unit in twenty is defective. Calculate the probability that the number in a random sample of 100 will go outside (i) the 1 in 40 line, (ii) the 1 in 1000 line.

(c) What is the probability that the process will continue out of control for two hours without any sample exceeding the 1 in 1000 limit?   (AEB)

Summary

Test of	Test statistic	Valid if
Mean; σ known	$z = \dfrac{\bar{x} - \mu}{\sigma/\sqrt{n}}$	Normal population and/or large sample
Mean; σ unknown	$z = \dfrac{\bar{x} - \mu}{\hat{s}/\sqrt{n}} = \dfrac{\bar{x} - \mu}{s/\sqrt{(n-1)}}$	large sample
Mean; σ unknown	$t_{n-1} = \dfrac{\bar{x} - \mu}{\hat{s}/\sqrt{n}} = \dfrac{\bar{x} - \mu}{s/\sqrt{(n-1)}}$	Normal population
Equal population means; σ_1, σ_2 known	$z = \dfrac{\bar{x}_1 - \bar{x}_2}{\sqrt{\left\{ \dfrac{\sigma_1^2}{n_1} + \dfrac{\sigma_2^2}{n_2} \right\}}}$	Normal populations and/or large samples
Equal population means; σ_1, σ_2 unknown	$z = \dfrac{\bar{x}_1 - \bar{x}_2}{\sqrt{\left\{ \dfrac{s_1^2}{n_1 - 1} + \dfrac{s_2^2}{n_2 - 1} \right\}}}$	large samples
Same population; σ known	$z = \dfrac{\bar{x}_1 - \bar{x}_2}{\sigma\sqrt{\left\{ \dfrac{1}{n_1} + \dfrac{1}{n_2} \right\}}}$	Normal population and/or large samples
Same population; σ unknown	$z = \dfrac{\bar{x}_1 - \bar{x}_2}{\hat{s}\sqrt{\left\{ \dfrac{1}{n_1} + \dfrac{1}{n_2} \right\}}}$	large samples
Same population; σ unknown	$t_{n_1 + n_2 - 2} = \dfrac{\bar{x}_1 - \bar{x}_2}{\hat{s}\sqrt{\left\{ \dfrac{1}{n_1} + \dfrac{1}{n_2} \right\}}}$ where $\hat{s}^2 = \dfrac{n_1 s_1^2 + n_2 s_2^2}{n_1 + n_2 - 2}$	Normal population
Proportion	$z = \dfrac{p_s - p}{\sqrt{[p(1-p)/n]}}$	large sample
Equal proportions	$z = (p_1 - p_2) \bigg/ \sqrt{\left[\hat{p}(1-\hat{p})\left(\dfrac{1}{n_1} + \dfrac{1}{n_2} \right) \right]}$ where $\hat{p} = \dfrac{n_1 p_1 + n_2 p_2}{n_1 + n_2}$	large samples
Mean of Poisson distribution	$z = \dfrac{x - \lambda}{\sqrt{\lambda}}$	large sample

Projects

(1)   *Significance test on data for bisecting a line by eye*

For the data obtained in Project 1, Chapter 2, test whether the mean of the measured lengths for the first attempt at bisecting a line by eye differs significantly from zero. Repeat for the second attempt.

(2)   *Testing whether a coin is biased*

Toss a coin 100 times, counting the number of heads. Test whether the proportion of heads differs significantly from $\frac{1}{2}$.

(3)   *Significance test on the difference between two proportions*

If data were obtained in Project 2, Chapter 4, for the proportion of left-handed people in samples from two different populations, test whether these proportions differ significantly.

(4)   *Advanced Level Statistics Software*

The section *Theory of hypothesis testing* provides the teacher with a set of interactive demonstrations to stimulate class discussion and investigation of the topics covered in this chapter. The basic ideas are illustrated by concentrating on two simple models.

(a)   *Coin throwing*

This illustrates Section 15.1. The user can choose different values of n and p and investigate the critical region for different significance levels and different alternative hypotheses. The relationship between Type I errors and significance level is also demonstrated by means of a simulation.

(b)   *Normal distribution*

This program seeks to put the student in the role of experimenter and to give a feeling for the strengths and weaknesses of statistical tests. Random samples can be taken from a population of unknown mean and used to carry out significance tests on a null hypothesis about the population mean. The program allows an interactive investigation of significance levels and Type I and Type II errors.

Exercise on Chapter 15

(1)   The mean of a random sample of n observations, $x_1, x_2, \ldots, x_n$, from a Normal distribution is $\bar{x}$. It is proposed to test the null hypothesis that the population mean is μ_0, against some alternative hypothesis. State how your decision as to whether to use the t-distribution for such a test would be influenced by (i) the value of n, (ii) whether the population standard deviation is known to you.

You are given that $\bar{x}=12.9$, $n=10$, $\sum_{i=1}^{n} x_i^2 = 1683$.

(a) Test the null hypothesis that the population mean is 12 against the alternative hypothesis that the mean is not 12.

(b) Determine a two-sided, symmetric, 95% confidence interval for the mean and explain carefully what this confidence interval means. (JMB)

(2) Over a period of years the average number of road deaths during the New Year Festival period in Ruritania has been 27. This year there were 35, a rise of approximately 30% and the country's press was full of gloomy comment on declining driving standards. Make suitable calculations to demonstrate that the probability of there being at least the observed number of road deaths is about $7\frac{1}{2}\%$.
Write an account of your argument and conclusions as if addressing an intelligent reader but one having no knowledge of statistics or probability theory. (C)

(3) What are the conditions under which a variable might be distributed according to the Binomial distribution?
An investigator suspects that there might be an unnecessary rounding off of weights recorded by a spring balance. In a spot check, he finds that, out of ten recorded weights, six end in the digits 0 or 5. How strong is the evidence that his suspicions are justified? (O)

(4) Explain the meaning of the term 'confidence interval'.
The expressions $\Sigma(x_i-\bar{x})^2/n$ and $\Sigma(x_i-\bar{x})^2/(n-1)$ are both used in connection with variance for a set of observations $x_1, x_2, \ldots, x_n$. Explain the circumstances in which each is used and hence distinguish between them.
For such a set of 81 independent observations from a Normal distribution, $\Sigma x_i = -36$ and $\Sigma x_i^2 = 736$. Construct a 95% confidence interval for the mean of their probability distribution, and use it to test whether this mean is likely to be zero.
Explain, either by carrying out the appropriate calculations, or otherwise, how you would conduct this test without using a confidence interval. (O)

(5) Explain how Student's t-distribution may be used to test the hypothesis that a random sample of n observations is derived from a population whose mean is μ_0, assuming the population to be Normal.

Table 15.11

Pupil	A	B	C	D	E	F	G	H	I	J
Mark before tape-slides	3	15	14	18	10	3	5	8	9	11
Mark after tape-slides	4	18	14	16	12	6	5	9	10	15

Ten pupils took a test in geography before and after a series of tape-slide sequences on that subject. Their marks (out of 20) were as in Table 15.11.

Test, at the 5% level of significance, the hypothesis that the pupils' performance is not affected by the series of tape-slide sequences.

State the assumptions made in applying the test.   (AEB)

(6) Explain what is meant by a 95% confidence interval for a population mean.

A factory manufacturing ammeters tests them for zero errors in their calibration. From past routine tests, it is known that the standard deviation of these errors is 0.3. A batch of nine ammeters, taken from one worker's production, has zero errors of 1.0, −0.1, −0.3, 1.6, 0.5, 0.4, 0.5, 0.2, −0.2. Test whether there is evidence of a bias in the ammeters produced by this worker and establish a 95% confidence interval for the mean zero of his ammeters.   (O)

(7) Two alternative hypotheses concerning the probability density function of a random variable are

$$H_0: f(x) = 2x \qquad 0 < x < 1$$
$$\qquad = 0 \qquad \text{otherwise}$$
$$H_1: f(x) = 2(1-x) \quad 0 < x < 1$$
$$\qquad = 0 \qquad \text{otherwise}$$

Give a sketch of the probability density function for each case.

The following test procedure is decided upon. A single observation of X is made and if X exceeds a particular value c, where $0 < c < 1$, then H_0 is accepted, otherwise H_1 is accepted. Find the value of c if the probability of accepting H_1 given that H_0 is true is $\frac{1}{9}$. With this value of c, find the probability of accepting H_0 given that H_1 is true.   (C)

(8) A blindfold subject was given a sample of butter and one of margarine and asked to state which was butter. This was repeated to give six tests in all, the samples being presented in a random order on each occasion. The subject correctly identified the butter five times out of six. Find the probability of five or six correct identifications by a subject who is not able to distinguish between butter and margarine. State, with reasons, whether the subject's performance would lead you to believe that she could identify the butter.

The experiment was carried out simultaneously with a total of 24 subjects. The total number of correct identifications was 83 out of a total of 144 trials. Test if the group as a whole could identify the butter significantly better than might be expected.   (O)

(9) Explain what is meant by the sampling distribution of the mean. What shape would you expect this to have for large samples?

A machine is designed to produce rods 2 cm long with a standard deviation of 0.02 cm. The lengths may be taken as Normally distributed. The machine is moved to a new position in the factory, and, in order to check whether the setting for the mean length has altered, the lengths of the first nine rods produced are measured. The standard deviation may be considered to be unchanged. If these lengths, in cm, are as given below, test whether the setting has been altered or not.

2.04, 1.97, 1.99, 2.03, 2.04, 2.10, 2.01, 1.98, 2.07   (O)

(10)   An engineer wishes to compare the results obtained by two methods of measuring the breaking strains of a certain type of wire rope. Describe carefully the design of an experiment for this purpose which would require a two-sample t-test for its analysis. In such an experiment the measurements of breaking strain (x) obtained from six observations using the first method gave $\Sigma x = 492$, $\Sigma x^2 = 43\,850$, whilst eight observations using the second method gave $\Sigma x = 608$, $\Sigma x^2 = 50\,766$. Test if the measurements came from the same population.   (C)

(11)   In the course of a survey concerning the proportion of left-handed children the figures in Table 15.12 were obtained from two schools.
Show that an approximate 95% confidence interval for the population proportion, p, of left-handed children derived from the data from school 1 is $0.25 < p < 0.32$, and calculate a corresponding interval for school 2.

Table 15.12

	Number of children	Proportion left-handed
School 1	620	0.284
School 2	475	0.341

Explain briefly what is wrong with the following argument: 'Since these two confidence intervals overlap, we cannot reject, at the 5% significance level, the hypothesis that the populations from which the children in the two schools are samples each have the same proportion of left-handed children.'
Calculate the overall proportion of left-handed children in both schools, and show that the observed difference in proportions is significant at the 5% level.   (C)

(12)   Experimental data concerning a variable X, which measures the reliability of a certain electronic component, are as follows: $\Sigma x = 1164.2$, $\Sigma x^2 = 13911.6$, $n = 100$. Calculate the sample mean and standard deviation from these figures. Explain whether, on the evidence of this sample, you would reject the hypothesis that the mean value of X is 12.
Figures collected over a long period have established that the mean and standard deviation of X are 12 and 2 respectively. After a change in the manufacturing process it is expected that the mean will have been *increased*, but it may be assumed that the standard deviation remains equal to 2. A sample of n values of X is taken, with sample mean m: if m is greater than some critical value it will be accepted that the mean has

in fact increased, but if m is less than the critical value the increase is not established. State carefully appropriate null and alternative hypotheses for this situation, and find, in terms of n, the critical value for a 1% significance level. (C)

(13) (a) In one county in England, a random sample of 225 twelve year old boys and 250 twelve year old girls was given an arithmetic test. The average mark for the boys was 57 with a standard deviation of 12, whilst the average for the girls was 60 with a standard deviation of 15.
Assuming that the distributions are Normal, does this provide evidence at the 2% level that twelve year old girls are superior to twelve year old boys at arithmetic?

(b) An IQ test which had been standardised giving a mean of 100 and a standard deviation of 12 was given to a random sample of 50 children in one area. The average mark obtained was 105.
Does this provide evidence, at the 5% level, that children from this area are generally more intelligent? (SUJB)

(14) Describe what is meant by a random sample of observations of a random variable. A battery manufacturer claims that his batteries have a mean life of 8 hours when used in a particular model of calculating machine. Describe how you would use a significance test to examine this claim on the basis of a large random sample of observed lifetimes. You should explain clearly the hypotheses you would consider, the choice of significance level, and the details of the test. State what is meant by concluding that the null hypothesis is rejected at the 5% significance level.
A random sample of 121 batteries has a mean life of 7.56 hours and, for this sample, $s^2 = 5.30$ hours^2. Test whether these data would lead to rejection of the manufacturer's claim, at the 5% significance level. (JMB)

(15) A chemical is delivered in batches to a factory for use in a production process. It is important that the percentage of manganese in the chemical should not decrease significantly in successive batches. The first batch delivered is to act as a control. Ten determinations of percentage manganese are made, with results as follows:
Control batch (% manganese) 3.3, 3.7, 3.5, 4.1, 3.4, 3.5, 4.0, 3.8, 3.2, 3.7.
Show that the control mean is 3.62, and estimate the standard deviation.
The results of the ten determinations for a later batch are:
Batch X (% manganese) 3.2, 3.6, 3.1, 3.4, 3.0, 3.4, 2.8, 3.1, 3.3, 3.6.
Determine whether the mean of this batch is significantly smaller than 3.62. Use a 5% level of significance, and justify any assumptions you make. (AEB)

Revision exercise C

(1) A multiple choice test consists of 40 questions, each with five possible answers of which one only is correct. A lazy student answers the test by rolling a die. Explain carefully how the lazy student could make a random choice of answers in this way and estimate using a Normal approximation the probability that he will get
   (a) less than 7 correct answers,
   (b) more than 5 but less than 11 correct answers,
   (c) exactly 10 correct answers. (L)

(2) The score, S, gained by an expert rifleman with a single shot, is a random variable with the following probability distribution:

$$P(S=8)=0.01, \quad P(S=9)=0.29, \quad P(S=10)=0.70.$$

   (a) Use a Normal approximation to determine the probability that the rifleman obtains six or more scores of 8 in a series of 900 independent shots.
   (b) Find the expectation and variance of S.
   (c) Use a Normal approximation to determine the probability that the rifleman scores less than 96 with ten independent shots. (C)

(3) Table C.1 gives the retail price index of fruit and vegetables for the end of March, June, September and December from March 1974 to March 1977.
   Plot a graph of these retail price indices against time.
   Calculate and tabulate quarterly moving averages and plot these moving averages on the same graph. Draw a straight line showing the general trend of the values of these moving averages. Read from this line the general trend values for the end of March, June, September and December of 1976.

Table C.1

Month	1974	1975	1976	1977
		Year		
March	100	118	135	146
June	112	124	141	
September	99	108	122	
December	116	130	145	

The 'relative deviation' is defined as the retail price index divided by the general trend value at a particular time. Calculate the four relative deviations for 1976 and find their arithmetic mean.   (L)

(4) (a) Two cards are drawn at random, without replacement, from an ordinary pack of 52 cards. Find the probability that they are
   (i)   of the same suit,
   (ii) of the same value (both aces, both kings, etc.),
   (iii) either of the same suit or the same value.

(b) Two cards are drawn at random, one from each of two ordinary packs. Find the probability that they are
   (i)   of the same suit,
   (ii) of the same value,
   (iii) either of the same suit, the same value, or both.

(c) Three fair cubical dice are thrown. Find the probability that the sum of the numbers of spots on the upper faces is a perfect square.   (AEB)

(5) The discrete rectangular distribution is defined by
$$P(x=r)=1/n \qquad (r=0, 1, 2, \ldots, n-1).$$
Find the mean of the distribution and show that the variance is $\frac{1}{12}(n^2-1)$.
Find the mean and variance of the continuous Rectangular distribution over the interval 0 to 1.   (O)

(6) During his career the scores of a professional cricketer had a mean of 28 runs per innings and a standard deviation of 6.3 runs.
Calculate the standard deviation of the means of samples of 30 innings.
If a random sample of 30 innings were selected, between what limits would you expect the mean of this sample to lie with a probability of 0.95?
Over the final two years his mean scores were 29.6 and 24.5 for 49 and 36 innings respectively. Calculate whether or not these are likely to be due to random variation.
(C)

(7) Give three major characteristics of a Poisson distribution.
The annual number of trees struck by lightning, on a large estate, had the distribution given in Table C.2 over a hundred years.
Calculate the mean and variance of the data.
Without performing a significance test state, with reasons, whether the data support the hypothesis that the annual loss of trees has a Poisson distribution. On the assumption that the hypothesis is true, give a 95% confidence interval for the population mean.   (O)

Table C.2

Number of trees struck	0	1	2	3	4	>4
Number of years	34	38	20	6	2	0

(8)   Two gauges are used to test the thickness of manufactured metal sheets.
Over a long period it is found that 1.25% of the sheets will pass through the smaller
gauge of 1.4 mm while 95.4% will pass through the larger gauge of 1.6 mm.
Assuming that the distribution of sheet thickness is Normal, find its mean and
standard deviation.
At the next stage of manufacture two sheets are clamped together to make a thick
plate. Find the mean and the standard deviation of the thickness of these plates.
If a plate will pass through a gauge of 3.2 mm but not through one of 2.8 mm, find
the probability that both the sheets of which it is composed will pass through the
1.6 mm gauge but not through the 1.4 mm gauge.   (O & C)

(9)   A manufacturer of model railways produces units of rolling stock which can be
classified as (i) motorised or not, (ii) goods or passenger and (iii) British Rail or pre-
war companies. 10% of the units are motorised. Of the motorised units 60% are
passenger and of the unmotorised units 70% are goods. Of the motorised passenger
units 50% are BR as are 40% of the unmotorised passenger units. Of the motorised
goods units 30% are in the pre-war company colours as are 60% of the unmotorised
goods units.
Calculate the proportions of
(a)   units that are unmotorised BR,
(b)   units that are motorised or BR or both,
(c)   BR units that are goods units,
(d)   pre-war company motorised units that are passenger units.   (C)

(10) A random variable X has probability density function $f(x)$ given by
$$f(x) = k(1 - x^2) \quad 0 \leqslant x \leqslant 1$$
$$= 0 \qquad\qquad \text{otherwise}$$
Show that the mean, μ, and variance, σ^2, of X are $\frac{3}{8}$ and $\frac{19}{320}$ respectively. Hence show
that the probability of a randomly chosen observation from this distribution lying
outside the range $\mu - 2\sigma$ to $\mu + 2\sigma$ is about 0.03.   (O)

(11) The masses of loaves from a certain bakery are Normally distributed with mean 500 g
and standard deviation 20 g.
(a)   Determine what percentage of the output would fall below 475 g and what
percentage would be above 530 g.
(b)   The bakery produces 1000 loaves daily at a cost of 8p per loaf and can sell all
those above 475 g at 20 p each but it is not allowed to sell the rest. Calculate the
expected daily profit.
(c)   A sample of 25 loaves yielded a mean mass of 490 g. Does this provide evidence
of a reduced population mean? Use the 5% level of significance and state whether
the test is one-tailed or two.   (SUJB)

(12) All the inhabitants of an estate are cared for by one doctor. The doctor has a card for each house on which he records the names of adults and children together with age, sex, etc. Explain how you would choose a random sample of children on the estate. A random sample of 80, which is one-tenth of the total number of children, is chosen and it is found that 60 of them have been vaccinated against a particular disease. Estimate the number of children on the estate who have been vaccinated and give a 95% confidence interval for this total.   (O)

(13) The sex of twenty babies born in a maternity hospital is to be recorded. Assume that the probability of any baby being a boy is 0.5.
      (a) Write down an expression for the probability that exactly ten of the babies will be boys and find this probability.
      (b) Find the probability that there will be more boys than girls.
      In fact, observations at the hospital over a long period of time have established that 51% of babies born are boys.
      (c) Show that, based on this information, the probability of the event considered in (a) above is reduced by less than 0.5%.
      A statistics student wishes to carry out a significance test relating to the probability of a baby being a boy. Her null hypothesis is that this probability is 0.5. She decides to record the sex of twenty babies born at the hospital and reject her null hypothesis if there are more than 13 boys. Find the significance level of this test.
      Given that the probability of a baby being a boy is actually 0.51, use the Normal approximation to the Binomial distribution to find the power of her test.   (JMB)

(14) Using only the numbers 8, 7, 5, 1 without repetition, calculate
      (a) the number of different four-digit numbers which can be formed,
      (b) the number of odd numbers exceeding 700 which can be formed,
      (c) the probability that, if a number is chosen at random from all the one, two, three and four digit numbers which can be formed from the given numbers, it will exceed 800.   (L)

(15) Table C.3 shows the durations of 40 telephone calls from an office via the office switchboard.
      Obtain an estimate of the mean and standard deviation of the data.
      Estimate the median, and lower and upper quartiles.   (O & C)

Table C.3

Duration in minutes	$\leqslant 1$	1–2	2–3	3–5	5–10	$\geqslant 10$
Number of calls	6	10	15	5	4	0

(16) X_1 and X_2 are independent random variables with means μ_1 and μ_2 and variances σ_1^2 and σ_2^2 respectively. Give the mean and variance of $X_1 - X_2$.

A random sample of size n_1 from the first of the above distributions has mean $\bar{X}_1$. Give the mean and variance of the distribution of $\bar{X}_1$.

An independent random sample of size n_2 taken from the second distribution has mean $\bar{X}_2$. Use the results you have stated to deduce the mean and variance of the distribution of $\bar{X}_1 - \bar{X}_2$.

What additional deduction can you make about the distributions of $\bar{X}_1$ and $\bar{X}_2$ if the original distributions are Normal?

A production line is set to produce articles of mass 454 g. The mean mass of a random sample of twelve from the line is found to be 451.5 g. Assuming that the mass is Normally distributed with variance 25 g^2, test whether the line is producing articles significantly under the nominal mass. (O)

(17) Explain what are meant by the quartiles of a frequency distribution, and verify that, for a Normal distribution with zero mean and unit variance, the quartiles are ± 0.67.

An attainment test is standardised to provide a Normally distributed score with mean 100 and standard deviation 16. In a sample of 1000 scores, 540 are found to lie within the range 89 to 111. Do you regard this as evidence that the population from which the sample is drawn may be unusual? (O)

(18) The number 8888 is obtained from a table of random digits. Use it to select an observation at random from each of the following distributions. Your method should be clearly indicated by your written working.
(a) Rectangular distribution with range 1 to 3 (correct to 4 d.p.).
(b) Binomial distribution with parameters 5, $\frac{2}{3}$.
(c) Poisson distribution with mean 2.
(d) Normal distribution with mean 10, variance 25 (correct to 1 d.p.). (O)

(19) A batch of 20 items is inspected as follows. A random sample of five items is drawn from the batch without replacement and the number of defective items in the sample is counted. If this number is two or more the batch is rejected; if there is no defective item in the sample the batch is accepted; if there is exactly one defective item in the sample, then a further random sample of five items is drawn without replacement from the remaining 15 items in the batch. If this second sample includes at least one defective item then the batch is rejected; otherwise the batch is accepted.

Suppose that a batch to be inspected consists of exactly two defective items and 18 non-defective items.
(a) Calculate the probabilities that
(i)   the batch will be accepted on the basis of the first sample,
(ii) a second sample will be taken and the batch will then be accepted,
(iii) the batch will be rejected.
(b) Find the expected number of items that will have to be sampled to reach a decision on the batch. (W)

(20) Define the median of (a) a discrete theoretical distribution, (b) a continuous theoretical distribution, (c) an un-grouped sample. (Explain the symbols that you introduce.)

Give two examples (one discrete and one continuous) of variables that might be observed in practice for which the median is a better measure of central tendency than the mean. Make a sketch of the frequency distribution of each variable, and mark in the approximate location of the median and the mean.   (O)

(21) State, with reasons, which of the distributions – Binomial, Rectangular, Normal or Poisson – provides the best model for each of the following variates. In each case estimate the value(s) of the parameter(s) of the distribution chosen.

(a) The number of red blood cells in a cubic centimetre of solution which is taken from a well-mixed dilute solution of blood. Five successive samples gave the cell-counts: 5, 2, 7, 6, 2.

(b) The rounding error made in measuring the length of metal rods to the nearest 5 mm. This error is the difference between the true length and the length recorded after rounding to the nearest 5 mm; assume there is no other source of error.

(c) The number of left-handed pupils sitting at a table for lunch at a large school. Each table has six pupils and a count at five tables, chosen at random one day, gave the numbers of left-handed pupils as 0, 0, 1, 1, 0.

(d) The masses of packs of 50 screws. Five packs chosen at random had masses of 262, 259, 261, 257, 261 g.   (O)

(22) If x is distributed according to a Poisson distribution with mean λ, write down the probability that x equals r.

How is this probability modified if the values $x=0$ are unobservable? Prove that the mean is now $\lambda/(1-e^{-\lambda})$, and find the variance.   (O)

(23) In a certain geographical region, the heights of girls and boys in the age range sixteen to eighteen years can be regarded as having Normal distributions as follows.

Girls: mean 162.5 cm, standard deviation 4.0 cm

Boys: mean 173.5 cm, standard deviation 4.8 cm

Find the probability that (a) a girl, (b) a boy is taller than 170.5 cm.

A school sixth form in the area contains 64 girls and 36 boys in this age range. Regarding the girls and boys as random samples from the given Normal populations, determine how many students in the sixth form would be expected to be taller than 170.5 cm.

Mean values of samples of size 64 and 36, drawn from the given Normal populations of heights of girls and boys respectively, are denoted by $\bar{x}_G$ and $\bar{x}_B$ respectively.

State or calculate the means and variances of the sampling distributions of means $\bar{x}_G$ and $\bar{x}_B$ and of the sampling distribution of differences $\bar{x}_B - \bar{x}_G$. Deduce the probability that in the sixth form referred to above the mean height of the boys will be at least 12 cm more than that of the girls.

State briefly, giving a reason, whether or not it would be acceptable to regard the populations of heights of girls and boys aged sixteen to eighteen in this area as combining to form a single population of heights with a Normal distribution.   (JMB)

(24) Exquay City Council is considering building a vast new sports complex for its 500 000 residents. As part of a feasibility study you (as their helpful statistician) are asked to undertake a sample survey of the local population and ascertain their views on all aspects of this venture. Give details of the methods you would use paying particular attention to the method of enquiry, design of the survey, sampling procedures, choice of sample size, sources of secondary statistics and the analysis and interpretation of results.   (AEB)

(25) The variable X is uniformly distributed over the interval $a \leqslant x \leqslant a+b$, where a and b are unknown constants.
A sample of three independent observations (x_1, x_2, x_3) is taken, where $x_1 < x_2 < x_3$.
Show that the probability density function of x_1 is

$$\frac{3}{b^3}(a+b-x_1)^2.$$

Find the value of $E(x_1)$.
By considering the values of $E(x_1)$ and $E(x_3)$, obtain unbiased estimates of a and b when $x_1 = 7$ and $x_3 = 11$.   (C)

(26) Explain what is meant by the sampling distribution of a statistic.
Given that a random sample of n observations is drawn from a Normal distribution having mean μ and variance σ^2, specify the sampling distribution of the sample mean. State what you know about the sampling distribution of the sample median and describe an experiment, which would demonstrate the difference between this sampling distribution and that of the sample mean.
Explain what is meant by the relative efficiency of two unbiased estimators. The sample mean and the sample median of a large sample of size n from a Normal distribution are to be used to estimate the population mean. State which estimator you would expect to be more efficient and give your reason.
Both the sample mean and the sample median may be assumed to be unbiased and consistent estimators of the population mean when the sample is drawn from a Normal population. Explain what is meant, in this context, by consistent and unbiased. State, with reasons, which of these properties may not apply to these estimators if the population is not Normal.   (JMB)

(27) Distinguish between situations requiring a two-sample t-test and a paired-sample t-test. What distributional assumptions are made in each case?
The weights of dressed poultry from two factories are to be compared. Sample weights (in suitable units) from the two factories are given in Table C.4.
Use the appropriate t-test to determine whether the mean weights of dressed poultry from the two factories differ significantly assuming the s.d. for each factory is the same.   (C)

Table C.4

Factory A	6.0	6.2	6.8	6.3	7.1	6.5
Factory B	5.6	6.0	5.9	6.7	6.4	6.0

(28) Define the Poisson distribution. State its mean and variance. State under what circumstances the Normal distribution can be used as an approximation to the Poisson distribution.

Readings, on a counter, of the number of particles emitted from a radioactive source in a time T seconds have a Poisson distribution with mean $250\,T$. A ten-second count is made. Find the probabilities of readings of (a) more than 2600, (b) 2400 or more. A reading of 2000 is obtained, but the time T is not known. By considering a symmetrical two-sided 95% confidence interval, derive a quadratic equation whose roots are 95% confidence limits for T.   (JMB)

(29) The quadratic equation $ax^2 + bx + c = 0$ has real roots if and only if $b^2 \geqslant 4ac$. Find the probability that the equation has real roots when $a = 1$, b is Uniformly distributed in $(0, 1)$ and c is independently Uniformly distributed in $(-1, 1)$.

(You may find it helpful to use a diagram in which (b, c) are cartesian coordinates of a point.)

Show that, when $b = 1$, a is Uniformly distributed in $(0, 1)$ and c is independently Uniformly distributed in $(-1, 1)$, the probability that the roots are real is approximately $\frac{4}{5}$.   (C)

(30) The variable x is distributed Normally with unknown mean μ and known variance σ^2; independent observations $x_1, x_2, \ldots, x_n$ are taken. Write down the joint probability density function P of this sample.

Regarding P as a function of μ, find, by considering $\ln P$ or otherwise, the value $\hat{\mu}$ of μ which maximises P. If $\hat{\mu}$ is used as an estimate of μ determine whether it is a biased estimate.

In a sample of ten observations the value of Σx was 74; the value of σ was known to be 2. Obtain 95% confidence limits for μ and explain clearly the meaning of the term 'confidence limits'.

$$\left[\text{If } x \text{ is } \mathcal{N}(\mu, \sigma^2) \quad \text{then} \quad f(x) = \frac{1}{\sigma\sqrt{2\pi}} \exp\left\{ \frac{-(x-\mu)^2}{2\sigma^2} \right\} \right]$$ (C)

(31) The moment generating function (m.g.f.) of a continuous variable t is defined as $M_t(\theta) = E(e^{t\theta})$. Expanded as a power series in θ, it is written

$$M_t(\theta) = 1 + \mu_1'\theta + \mu_2'\frac{\theta^2}{2!} + \mu_3'\frac{\theta^3}{3!} + \cdots$$

Prove that
$$E(t) = \mu_1'$$

$$\text{var}(t) = \mu'_2 - (\mu'_1)^2$$

The variable t measures the interval between successive events in a Poisson process, i.e. a process in which the probability of an event in any interval δt is $\lambda \delta t$, independent of the probability for any other interval. Obtain the frequency function of t.

Hence obtain the m.g.f. of t, $M_t(\theta)$, taking $\theta < \lambda$. Show that the mean of t is $1/\lambda$ and find its variance. (C)

(32) The chance that a new member joins a commune in any interval of time δt is $\lambda \delta t$ and the chance that any member of the commune leaves in δt is $\mu \delta t$. When the commune has been in existence for a long time the probability that there are n members is p_n, which is independent of time. Prove that
$$(\lambda + n\mu)p_n = \lambda p_{n-1} + \mu(n+1)p_{n+1} \qquad (n \geqslant 1)$$
and obtain the equation connecting p_0 and p_1.

Show that
$$p_n = e^{-\lambda/\mu}(\lambda/\mu)^n/n! \qquad (n = 0, 1, 2, \dots)$$
If λ is much larger than μ obtain an approximate lower limit below which there is only a 5% chance that the number of members in the commune will fall. (C)

(33) A suspension contains a proportion p_1 of cells which take up the stain eosin; these cells are dead and the remainder are living. A proportion p_2 of the living cells are damaged. Write down the probability that a sample of n cells contains r cells which are living and damaged.

Show that the probability that a sample of n cells contains r cells which are living and damaged and also s cells which are living and undamaged is
$$n!p_1^{n-r-s}p_2^r q_1^{r+s}q_2^s/r!s!(n-r-s)!$$
where $q_1 = 1 - p_1$, $q_2 = 1 - p_2$.

Obtain the covariance of r and s. (C)

16 The χ^2-test. Goodness of fit

16.1 An experiment

Table 16.1 shows the results of an experiment in which four coins were thrown 160 times. The results are divided into classes according to the number of heads obtained each time. For comparison the theoretical frequencies predicted by the Binomial distribution have been calculated, assuming that the coins are unbiased and using the parameters $p=\frac{1}{2}$, $n=4$. These frequencies are usually called the **expected frequencies**.

As we would expect there is not exact agreement between the observed and expected frequency for each class, since the frequency for each class is a random variable which varies from sample to sample. Our problem is to test whether the observed frequencies differ significantly from those calculated using the null hypothesis that the distribution is Binomial with $p=\frac{1}{2}$, $n=4$. Let O_i denote the observed and E_i the expected frequency in the ith class. As a first step we might calculate the discrepancy between the two values and sum over the classes, as shown in the third column of Table 16.2. This, of course, produces the result zero. We can avoid this by squaring the discrepancies, as shown in the fourth column of Table 16.2. To add the values in this column as it stands would mean that the difference between 10 and 15 would be given the same weight as the difference between 35 and 40 although the percentage difference in the first case is much greater. It can be shown (using mathematics beyond the scope of this book) that the appropriate statistic to use is

Table 16.1 *Frequency distribution of the number of heads when four coins are tossed*

Number of heads	Observed frequency	Expected frequency
0	15	$160 \times \binom{4}{0}(\frac{1}{2})^4 = 10$
1	46	$160 \times \binom{4}{1}(\frac{1}{2})^3(\frac{1}{2}) = 40$
2	54	$160 \times \binom{4}{2}(\frac{1}{2})^2(\frac{1}{2})^2 = 60$
3	35	$160 \times \binom{4}{3}(\frac{1}{2})(\frac{1}{2})^3 = 40$
4	10	$160 \times \binom{4}{4}(\frac{1}{2})^4 = 10$
	160	160

Table 16.2 *Calculation of X^2 for data in Table 16.1*

O_i	E_i	$O_i - E_i$	$(O_i - E_i)^2$	$(O_i - E_i)^2/E_i$
15	10	+5	25	2.5
46	40	+6	36	0.9
54	60	−6	36	0.6
35	40	−5	25	0.625
10	10	0	0	0
		0		4.625

$\displaystyle\sum_{i=1}^{n} \left\{ \frac{(O_i - E_i)^2}{E_i} \right\}$ whose calculation is shown in the last column of Table 16.2. We shall call this statistic X^2. The square emphasises that it is always a positive quantity.

16.2 Degrees of freedom

If the experiment described in Section 16.1 was repeated with the same coins, different values of O_i and consequently of X^2 would have been obtained. In other words, X^2 has a sampling distribution. This sampling distribution is approximately the same as a theoretical distribution known as the χ^2 **(or chi-squared) distribution** ('chi' is pronounced as the 'ki' in 'kite'). (χ^2 is often used to denote X^2 as well as the sampling distribution of X^2.) It can be shown that the form of the χ^2-distribution depends on the 'degrees of freedom' (and consequently it is often written χ_v^2). We have already met the term 'degrees of freedom' in Section 13.4. In the present instance v is the number of expected frequencies which can be varied independently. In the example in Table 16.2 there are five expected frequencies but, since the total frequency is fixed at 160, when four frequencies are given, the fifth is known, and so we have $v = 4$. The fact that the total frequency must equal 160 is known as a **constraint**. In general, v is given by

$$\text{degrees of freedom} = \text{number of classes} - \text{number of constraints} \qquad (16.2.1)$$

Figure 16.1 shows the form of the χ^2-distribution for some different values of v.

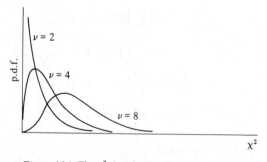

Figure 16.1 The χ^2-distribution for various values of v

16.3   Significance testing using the χ^2-distribution

As the discrepancy between the observed and expected frequencies increases so does the value of X^2. To decide if a value of X^2 calculated using a given null hypothesis is significant we use Table A6. This gives the percentage points of the χ^2-distribution for different values of v. It is a one-tail table and gives the probability that χ_v^2 exceeds a certain value. This probability is given by the shaded area in Figure 16.2. For example, the probability is 5% that $\chi_3^2 > 7.81$, 99.5% that $\chi_{14}^2 > 4.07$, etc. Using this table we are in a position to calculate if the value of $X^2 = 4.625$ calculated in Table 16.2 is significant. The critical region is $\chi_4^2 > 9.49$ at the 5% significance level, so the value of X^2 obtained is not significant and we retain the null hypothesis that the distribution of throws is Binomial with $p = \frac{1}{2}$, $n = 4$.

Although in a χ^2-test we normally test if X^2 exceeds the critical value, very *low* values of X^2 should be regarded with suspicion since they also have a low probability. For example there is only a 5% probability that $\chi_4^2 < 0.711$. Such a low value of X^2 is almost too good to be true and may indicate that the sample is not random, or the data are fictitious.

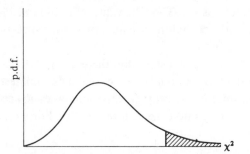

Figure 16.2 Schematic diagram showing the critical region for a χ^2-test

16.4   Conditions in which the χ^2-test is applicable

The χ^2-test should only be used when the sampling distribution of X^2 approximates closely to a χ^2-distribution. The conditions for this are
 (i)   the total frequency is not less than 50,
 (ii) the expected class frequencies are not less than 5.
If the second condition is not met, it can be complied with by combining one or more classes.

The agreement between the X^2 and χ^2 distributions can be improved when $v = 1$ by making an adjustment known as **Yates' correction**, which involves reducing each value of $|O_i - E_i|$ by $\frac{1}{2}$.

16.4.1   *Example*

On a national basis the success rate for people taking their driving test for the first time is 40%. A driving instructor's records show that for the 50 pupils of his who took the test for the first time last year, 25 passed. Does his success rate differ from the national success rate?

Table 16.3

	O_i	E_i	$O_i - E_i$	$\|O_i - E_i\| - \frac{1}{2}$	$\{\|O_i - E_i\| - \frac{1}{2}\}^2 / E_i$
Pass	25	20	+5	$4\frac{1}{2}$	1.0125
Fail	25	30	−5	$4\frac{1}{2}$	0.675
			0		$X^2 = 1.6875$

We take the null hypothesis that the instructor's results do not differ from the national success rates, that is

$$H_0 : p = 0.4$$
$$H_1 : p \neq 0.4$$

This gives Table 16.3 for the observed and expected frequencies. Notice that to use all the information we include the frequencies for pass and fail. In this case $v = 1$, since we have two classes and one restriction (that the total frequency is 50). Since $v = 1$, Yates' correction has been applied. The critical region at the 5% level is $\chi_1^2 > 3.84$. The value of X^2 obtained is not significant at the 5% level and there is no evidence that the driving instructor's success rate differs from the national rate.

A problem similar to this was solved in Section 15.9 using z but there the question asked was 'Is the instructor's success rate *better* than the national one?' so that a one-tail test was used. The χ^2-test is basically a two-tail test since X^2 is always positive and takes no account of the sign of the difference between the observed and expected frequencies. For a one-tail test the z-method is preferable.

16.4.2   *Exercise*

(1)   The following table purports to be a sample of 100 random digits. Test whether the frequencies of the digits differ significantly from expectation.

11584   42689   08394   57019   33922   22413   21138   83541   53216   74935
51186   49197   30157   28543   51328   49788   31489   18971   28719   97121   (O)

(2)   Two fair dice are thrown 432 times. Find the expected frequencies of scores of 2, 3, 4, . . . , 12.

Two players A and B are each given two dice and told to throw them 432 times, recording the results.

The frequencies reported are given in Table 16.4.

Table 16.4

Scores	2	3	4	5	6	7	8	9	10	11	12
A's frequency	18	33	28	54	62	65	66	42	30	27	7
B's frequency	14	22	34	51	58	73	63	45	38	25	9

Is there any evidence that either pair of dice is biased?

What can be said about B's alleged results?   (AEB)

16.5   Testing a distribution for Normality

In Section 9.5 a Normal distribution was fitted to data. We are now in a position to test how good the fit is. Although the Normal distribution is continuous, the data were divided into classes. We can use the observed and expected frequencies in each class to calculate X^2 and test the null hypothesis that the observed values come from a Normal distribution with a specified mean and s.d. Table 16.5 gives the observed and expected frequencies taken from Table 9.4.

The first four and the last three classes have been combined so that all E_i are $\geqslant 5$. The table shows the calculation of X^2. In this example there are six classes and three constraints: the total frequency is 50, the mean (698.3) and the s.d. (18.6) are calculated from the data. So we have

$$v = 6 - 3 = 3$$

The critical region is $\chi_3^2 > 7.81$. Thus the value of X^2 is not significant and the null hypothesis is retained. If the values for the mean and s.d. had been given rather than calculated from the data, then there would have been only one constraint.

Table 16.5 *Calculation of X^2 for data in Table 9.4*

Class	O_i		E_i		$O_i - E_i$	$(O_i - E_i)^2/E_i$
< 649.5	0		0.2			
649.5–659.5	1	7	0.7	7.8	−0.8	0.082
659.5–669.5	3		2.1			
669.5–679.5	3		4.8			
679.5–689.5	7		8.2		−1.2	0.176
689.5–699.5	15		10.2		4.8	2.259
699.5–709.5	7		10.1		−3.1	0.951
709.5–719.5	7		7.3		−0.3	0.012
719.5–729.5	4		4.1			
729.5–739.5	3	7	1.6	6.4	0.6	0.056
> 739.5	0		0.7			
					0	$X^2 = 3.536$

16.6   Testing the fit of a Binomial distribution

The example given in Section 16.1 was one in which a distribution was tested to see if it was Binomial with a given value of p. In Section 7.5 a Binomial distribution was fitted to data and p was not given but calculated from the observed frequencies. The observed and expected frequencies obtained are reproduced in Table 16.6. We wish to test the null hypothesis that the observed frequencies are Binomially distributed with $p = 0.49$, $n = 4$.

Table 16.6 *Calculation of X^2 for data in Table 7.3*

Number of girls	O_i	E_i	$O_i - E_i$	$(O_i - E_i)^2/E_i$
0	8	6.8	1.2	0.212
1	25	26.0	−1.0	0.038
2	37	37.5	−0.5	0.007
3	23	24.0	−1.0	0.042
4	7	5.8	+1.2	0.248
	100	100.1	−0.1	$X^2 = 0.547$

In this case, besides the constraint that the total frequency is 100, there is the added constraint that p was calculated from the data so that

$v = 5 - 2 = 3$

The critical region is $\chi^2 > 7.81$. Thus X^2 is not significant at the 5% level, the null hypothesis is retained and the observed distribution conforms to a Binomial distribution with $p = 0.49$, $n = 4$.

16.7 Testing the fit of a Poisson distribution

In Section 8.1 a Poisson distribution was fitted to data: the observed and expected frequencies are reproduced in Table 16.7. We wish to test the null hypothesis that the data are Poisson distributed with a mean equal to the mean of the data, which was found to be 0.37. The calculation of X^2 is shown in Table 16.7. There are two constraints; first, that the total frequency is 100 and, second, that the mean is calculated from the data. There are three classes since the last three have been combined, giving

$v = 3 - 2 = 1$

Since $v = 1$, Yates' correction has been applied.

The critical region is $\chi^2 > 3.84$. Thus X^2 is not significant at the 5% level and we retain the null hypothesis that the data are Poisson distributed with a mean of 0.37.

If a value for the mean had been given rather than calculated from the data, then there would have been only one constraint.

Table 16.7 *Calculation of X^2 for the data in Table 8.2*

Number of calls	O_i	E_i	$O_i - E_i$	$|O_i - E_i| - \frac{1}{2}$	$\{|O_i - E_i| - \frac{1}{2}\}^2/E_i$
0	71	69.1	+1.9	1.4	0.028
1	23	25.6	−2.6	2.1	0.172
2	4 ⎫	4.7 ⎫			
3	2 ⎬6	0.6 ⎬5.3	+0.7	0.2	0.008
⩾4	0 ⎭	0.0 ⎭			
			0		$X^2 = 0.208$

16.7.1 *Exercise*

(1) Two dice were thrown 216 times, and the number of 6s at each throw were counted. The results were as in Table 16.8.

Test the hypothesis that the distribution is Binomial with the parameter $p=\frac{1}{6}$.

Explain how the test would be modified if the hypothesis to be tested is that the distribution is Binomial with the parameter p unknown. (Do not carry out the test.)   (O)

Table 16.8

Number of 6s	0	1	2	Total
Frequency	130	76	10	216

(2) A man kept count of the number of letters he received each day over a period of 78 days (excluding Sundays). The frequencies of the number of letters per day and of the Poisson distribution with the same mean (0.88) and total frequency are given in Table 16.9.

Do the observations show a significant departure from a Poisson distribution? (O)

Table 16.9

Letters per day	Number of days	Poisson frequencies
0	33	32.4
1	26	28.4
2	14	12.6
3 or more	5	4.6

(3) For a period of six months 100 similar hamsters were give a new type of feedstuff. The gains in mass are recorded in Table 16.10.

Table 16.10

Gain in mass (g) x	Observed frequency f
$-\infty < x \leqslant -10$	3
$-10 < x \leqslant -5$	6
$-5 < x \leqslant 0$	9
$0 < x \leqslant 5$	15
$5 < x \leqslant 10$	24
$10 < x \leqslant 15$	16
$15 < x \leqslant 20$	14
$20 < x \leqslant 25$	8
$25 < x \leqslant 30$	3
$30 < x < \infty$	2

It is thought that these data follow a Normal distribution, with mean 10 and variance 100. Use the χ^2-distribution at the 5% level of significance to test this hypothesis. Describe briefly how you would modify this test if the mean and variance were unknown.   (AEB)

Table 16.11

x	0	1	2	3	4	5	6	7	8 or more
f	3	7	12	10	8	5	3	2	0

(4) A group of students are required to carry out an experiment in which the results are expected to have a Poisson distribution. Their results for 50 replications of the experiment are as in Table 16.11.

Estimating the mean of the Poisson distribution by the mean of these observations, obtain the appropriate estimated frequencies and test how well these data fit the expected form.

State what you might suspect about the students' results.   (C)

16.8   Contingency tables

Sometimes we wish to test if two attributes of a population are associated, i.e. if they occur together. A common example is whether inoculation is associated with the prevention of disease. In this case one attribute is whether or not a person is inoculated and the other attribute is whether or not they are attacked by the disease. Table 16.12 gives the (fictitious) results for a random sample of 100, where the total frequency has been divided into rows and columns according to attribute. This is known as a **contingency table.** On the null hypothesis that inoculation has no effect in preventing the disease, the marginal totals can be used to calculate the expected frequencies as follows. First we have

$$P \text{ (inoculated)} = \tfrac{70}{100}, \qquad P \text{ (attacked)} = \tfrac{35}{100}$$
$$P \text{ (not inoculated)} = \tfrac{30}{100}, \qquad P \text{ (not attacked)} = \tfrac{65}{100}$$

Since according to our null hypothesis the events attacked and not attacked are independent of the events inoculated and not inoculated we have, using the product law (see Section 4.6),

$$P \text{ (inoculated and attacked)} = \frac{70}{100} \times \frac{35}{100}$$

Table 16.12 *Contingency table for inoculation and disease*

	Attacked	Not attacked	
Inoculated	20	50	70
Not inoculated	15	15	30
	35	65	100

Table 16.13 *Calculation of expected frequencies for Table 16.12*

	Attacked	Not attacked	
Inoculated	$\dfrac{70 \times 35}{100} = 24.5$	$\dfrac{70 \times 65}{100} = 45.5$	70
Not inoculated	$\dfrac{30 \times 35}{100} = 10.5$	$\dfrac{30 \times 65}{100} = 19.5$	30
	35	65	100

Table 16.14 *Calculation of X^2 for data in Table 16.12*

O_i	E_i	$O_i - E_i$	$\|O_i - E_i\| - \frac{1}{2}$	$\{\|O_i - E_i\| - \frac{1}{2}\}^2/E_i$
20	24.5	−4.5	4	0.65
50	45.5	+4.5	4	0.35
15	10.5	+4.5	4	1.52
15	19.5	−4.5	4	0.82
		0		$X^2 = 3.34$

$$P \text{ (inoculated and not attacked)} = \frac{70}{100} \times \frac{65}{100}$$

$$P \text{ (not inoculated and attacked)} = \frac{30}{100} \times \frac{35}{100}$$

$$P \text{ (not inoculated and not attacked)} = \frac{30}{100} \times \frac{65}{100}$$

The expected frequencies are found by multiplying these probabilities by 100, and are shown in Table 16.13. Notice that the row and column totals are the same as before. It can be seen that the expected frequencies could be calculated more directly using the rule

$$\text{expected frequency} = \frac{\text{row total} \times \text{column total}}{\text{grand total}}$$

We are now in a position to calculate X^2. How many degrees of freedom will χ^2 have? The answer is $v = 1$ since in the calculation of the expected frequencies, when one frequency was found, the other frequencies could be found by subtraction from the marginal totals. Table 16.14 shows the calculation of X^2 using Yates' correction. This value of X^2 is not significant at the 5% level. The null hypothesis is retained and there is no evidence that the inoculation is effective against the disease.

16.9   Larger contingency tables

Table 16.15 shows a random sample of houses classified by region and type. Does the type of housing vary between regions? Taking as our null hypothesis that the type of housing and the region are independent, the expected frequencies are calculated in Table 16.16.

Table 16.15 *Contingency table for housing and region.* (Source: *The General House-hold Survey, 1973*, OPCS, HMSO, 1976)

	Detached	Semi-detached	Terraced	
North	95	297	242	634
West Midlands	175	417	362	954
South East	703	994	861	2558
	973	1708	1465	4146

Table 16.16 *Expected frequencies for data in Table 16.15*

	Detached	Semi-detached	Terraced	
North	$\dfrac{973 \times 634}{4146} = 149*$	$\dfrac{1708 \times 634}{4146} = 261*$	$\dfrac{1465 \times 634}{4146} = 224$	634
West Midlands	$\dfrac{973 \times 954}{4146} = 224*$	$\dfrac{1708 \times 954}{4146} = 393*$	$\dfrac{1465 \times 954}{4146} = 337$	954
South East	$\dfrac{973 \times 2558}{4146} = 600$	$\dfrac{1708 \times 2558}{4146} = 1054$	$\dfrac{1465 \times 2558}{4146} = 904$	2558
	973	1708	1465	4146

Table 16.17 *Calculation of X^2 for data in Table 16.15*

O_i	E_i	$O_i - E_i$	$(O_i - E_i)^2 / E_i$
95	149	-54	19.6
297	261	36	5.0
242	224	18	1.4
175	224	-49	10.7
417	393	24	1.5
362	337	25	1.9
703	600	103	17.7
994	1054	-60	3.4
861	904	-43	2.0
		0	$X^2 = 63.2$

There are four degrees of freedom, since, when the frequencies marked with an asterisk have been calculated, the other expected frequencies can be found by subtracting from the marginal totals. The calculation of X^2 is given in Table 16.17. The critical region is $\chi_4^2 > 9.49$ so the value of X^2 is significant at the 5% level: in fact it is significant at the 0.1% level. The

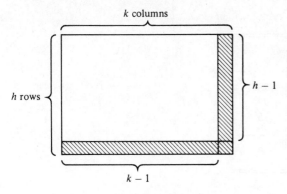

Figure 16.3. Diagram to illustrate the degrees of freedom of an $h \times k$ contingency table

null hypothesis is rejected and the result indicates that there is a strong association between type of housing and region.

A table with h rows and k columns is called an $h \times k$ contingency table. Its degrees of freedom are $(k-1)(h-1)$, since, as indicated in Figure 16.3, the frequencies in the last row and column can be calculated by subtraction of the other frequencies from the marginal totals.

16.9.1 *Exercise*

(1) Explain why the X^2 statistic calculated from a 2×2 contingency table only has one degree of freedom.
     Out of 100 rats fed with diet A, 65 showed signs of vitamin deficiency, while out of 100 rats fed with diet B, only 53 suffered from vitamin deficiency. Do the proportions of vitamin-deficient rats on the two diets differ significantly?   (O)

(2) Table 16.18 summarises the incidence of cerebral tumours in 141 neurosurgical patients.
     Find the expected frequencies on the hypothesis that there is no association between the type and site of a tumour. Use the χ^2-distribution to test this hypothesis.   (AEB)

Table 16.18

Site of tumour	Type of tumour		
	Benign	Malignant	Others
Frontal lobes	23	9	6
Temporal lobes	21	4	3
Elsewhere	34	24	17

Table 16.19

	A	B	C	
Credit	10	5	13	28
Pass	31	38	28	97
Fail	29	20	26	75
	70	63	67	200

(3) Oral tests are conducted by three examiners separately. The numbers of candidates in the categories credit, pass, fail are as shown in Table 16.19.

Use a χ^2-test to examine the hypothesis that the examiners do not differ in their standards of awards.

State the assumptions made.   (AEB)

16.10   Relationship between χ^2 and Normal distributions

If $X_1, X_2, \ldots, X_n$ are *independent* $N(0, 1)$ distributions, then $\sum_{i=1}^{n} X_i^2$ is said to be a χ^2 random variable with n degrees of freedom. In particular if X is $N(0, 1)$ then X^2 is a χ^2 random variable with one degree of freedom. In Section 16.2 we stated that the statistic $X^2 = \sum_{i=1}^{n} (O_i - E_i)^2 / E_i$ has a sampling distribution which is χ^2. We will now prove that this is true for the particular case in which there are two classes. Let the probability of being in the first class be p and the probability of being in the second class be q where $p + q = 1$. If the observed frequencies are n_1 and n_2, the total frequency is $n = n_1 + n_2$. The expected frequencies will be np and $n(1 - p)$. This information is summarised in Table 16.20.

Then

$$X^2 = \sum_i \frac{(O_i - E_i)^2}{E_i}$$

$$= \frac{(n_1 - np)^2}{np} + \frac{(n_2 - nq)^2}{nq}$$

$$= \frac{(n_1 - np)^2}{np} + \frac{(n_2 - (n - np))^2}{nq} \quad \text{(since } nq = n(1 - p))$$

$$= \frac{(n_1 - np)^2}{np} + \frac{(np - n_1)^2}{nq} \quad \text{(since } n_1 + n_2 = n)$$

$$= \frac{(np - n_1)^2}{npq} (p + q)$$

$$= \frac{(np - n_1)^2}{npq} \quad \text{(since } p + q = 1)$$

Table 16.20 *Observed and expected frequencies for two classes*

	Observed frequency	Expected frequency
Class 1	n_1	np
Class 2	n_2	nq

n_1 is Binomially distributed since we have n trials and a probability p that the result of a trial is in class 1. If n is large then the distribution of n_1 can be approximated by a Normal distribution with mean np and s.d. $\sqrt{(npq)}$ Thus $(np-n_1)\sqrt{(npq)}$ is a standardised Normal deviate z and $X^2 = z^2$. From the definition given at the beginning of this section $\chi_1^2 = z^2$. Thus in this case $X^2 = \chi_1^2$. This is consistent with the rule for calculating the degrees of freedom since in this case there are two classes and one constraint: $n_1 + n_2 = n$.

Summary

Chi-squared (χ^2) test for frequencies, test statistic X^2 where

$$X^2 = \sum_i \frac{(O_i - E_i)^2}{E_i}$$

If $v = 1$, use **Yates' correction**:

$$X^2 = \sum_i \frac{(|O_i - E_i| - 0.5)^2}{E_i}$$

X^2 has a χ_v^2 distribution with v degrees of freedom:

Type of test	Conditions	v
Binomial fit, n classes	(a) p known	(a) $n-1$
	(b) p unknown	(b) $n-2$
Poisson fit, n classes	(a) λ known	(a) $n-1$
	(b) λ unknown	(b) $n-2$
Normality, n classes	(a) μ, σ known	(a) $n-1$
	(b) μ, σ unknown	(b) $n-3$
Contingency table, $h \times k$		$(h-1)(k-1)$

Projects

(1)   *Testing whether there is an association between eye-colour and the wearing of spectacles*

For as large a sample as possible classify each person in a 2×2 contingency table as indicated below:

	Wears spectacles	Does not wear spectacles
Blue or blue/grey eyes		
Non-blue eyes		

To make classification simple 'wears spectacles' should include those who own spectacles or contact lenses, even if they do not wear them all the time. It is probably better to ask the subject his or her eye-colour to avoid bias by the person collecting the data. Use χ^2 to test for association between eye-colour and the wearing of spectacles.

(2)   *Testing the fit of theoretical distributions to observed data using the χ^2-test*

(a)   Binomial distribution using the data for project (1), Chapter 7.
(b)   Poisson distribution using the data for project (1), Chapter 8.
(c)   Normal distribution using the data for project (1), Chapter 9.

(3)   *Advanced Level Statistics Software*

The section *Chi-squared test* contains a number of programs which can be used to illustrate the ideas of this chapter.

(*a*)   *Proportions*

This includes a simulation which puts the user in the role of experimenter. Four populations are given in each of which a number of attributes occur in different proportions. The user selects one population to define a null hypothesis. The computer then selects a sample from one of the populations chosen at random and the user can carry out a significance test to decide whether the null hypothesis was correct or not.

(b)   *Goodness-of-fit*

This program can be used for testing the goodness of fit of data to standard distributions or to distributions with given expected frequencies or for contingency tables. It allows a given set of data to be tested quickly and easily against a variety of null hypotheses about the population.

(c)   *Demonstration*

This is a simulation for random sampling which shows how the chi-squared distribution is constructed for two degrees of freedom and how this can be generalised for higher degrees of freedom. The effect of a constraint on the number of degrees of freedom is also shown.

Exercise on Chapter 16

(1) In a large town, the number of road accidents reported daily over 300 working days gave the results in Table 16.21.

Table 16.21

Number of accidents reported in a day (x)	0	1	2	3	4	5	6	7	8
Number of days (f)	17	43	69	68	50	28	13	8	4

Compare these frequencies with those of a Poisson distribution having the same mean and total frequency.

Comment on the agreement.   (AEB)

(2) (a) A large haulage company employs drivers to work a 'round-the-clock' system The drivers' union is concerned that some periods are more dangerous than others. The management contests this, claiming that no one period is more dangerous than any other. The following data on the incidence of traffic accidents by time of day, for this group over the previous two years is presented (Table 16.22).

Are these results consistent with the management's claim?

Table 16.22

Time of day (24 hr clock)	00.01–04.00	04.01–08.00	08.01–12.00	12.01–16.00	16.01–20.00	20.01–24.00	Total
Number of accidents	14	16	24	22	24	20	120

(b) The same company wishes to examine whether there is an association between accident proneness and colourblindness. The results for a group of 80 drivers (with a minimum of five years' employment) are as in Table 16.23.

Table 16.23

		Colourblind	
		No	Yes
Accidents during last five years	None	22	5
	One or more	38	15

Is there any evidence of an association between colourblindness and accident proneness?   (AEB)

(3) Explain how to calculate the degrees of freedom for the χ^2-statistic in
(a) a goodness-of-fit test,
(b) a test of no association of the two factors in an $h \times k$ contingency table.
An ecologist collected organisms of a particular species from three beaches and counted the number of females in each sample (the remainder were males).

Beach	1	2	3
Number of females	44	86	110
Total number in sample	100	200	200

Test if the proportion of females differed significantly between the beaches.
Find the percentage of females at each beach and comment on the results.   (O)

(4) In routine tests of seeds of a certain flower, batches of hundreds are allowed to germinate and the colour of the resulting blooms is noted. 25% are expected to be red. It is suspected that a certain laboratory assistant may have been recording data carelessly. In eight successive batches, he returns the numbers of red blooms (out of 100 in each case) as 18, 20, 26, 21, 37, 16, 30, 32. Does this evidence support the suspicion?   (O)

(5) Table 16.24 gives the distribution for the number of heavy rainstorms reported by 330 weather stations in the United States of America over a one-year period.
(a) Find the expected frequencies of rainstorms given by the Poisson distribution having the same mean and total as the observed distribution.
(b) Use the χ^2-distribution to test the adequacy of the Poisson distribution as a model for these data.   (AEB)

Table 16.24

Number of rainstorms (x)	0	1	2	3	4	5	More than 5
Number of stations (f) reporting x rainstorms	102	114	74	28	10	2	0

(6) A doctor made a comparison of ointment A and ointment B for the cure of a skin disease. She chose at random which ointment to use for each patient and assessed the result after two weeks. Of the 95 patients receiving ointment A, 85 were cured, while of the 105 patients receiving ointment B, 78 were cured. Is there evidence that one ointment is better than the other?
Suppose ointment A had been used by doctor C on her patients and ointment B had been used by doctor D on his patients and the same numbers of patients and cures resulted. Would this affect your interpretation of the data?   (O)

(7) Given that a random variable which has a χ^2-distribution with n degrees of freedom can be represented as the sum of the squares of n independent standardised Normal variables, show that the sum of two independent χ^2 variables is itself a χ^2 variable and explain, with justification, how the degrees of freedom of the three variables are related. In making a scientific measurement a technician has to estimate the position of a

Table 16.25

Final digit	0	1	2	3	4	5	6	7	8	9
Frequency	11	27	16	23	13	31	14	18	24	23

needle between two successive divisions of a scale in order to obtain the final digit of his reading. Table 16.25 shows the final digit recorded in 200 such measurements. State what frequencies you would have expected, and justify your choice. Test whether the data are consistent with your expectation, and comment as fully as possible on the result of your analysis. (O)

(8) Test whether the data of Exercise 9.5.1, question (2), follow a Normal distribution whose mean and s.d. are equal to the values calculated from the data.

(9) A chain store offers rain hats for sale in three colours: red, blue and green. A sales manager wonders if the colour preference of customers differs in London and a county town. In the London store 48 hats were sold in a week and of these 19 were red, 14 blue and 15 green. In the county town branch 32 hats were sold and of these 6 were red, 16 blue and 10 green. Is there evidence of differential colour preference between London and the county town?
Are any colours significantly preferred to the others? (O)

(10) Use the χ^2-distribution to test the adequacy of the Binomial distribution as a model for the data in question (12) of the exercise on Chapter 7.

17 Correlation

17.1 Scatter diagrams

In Chapter 16 we developed a theory to test whether two *attributes* of a population are associated with each other: the theory of this chapter is concerned with the relationship between two *variates* for a population. Table 17.1 gives the marks, X and Y, obtained by a group of students in each of two mathematics examinations.

As we would expect, each student tends to obtain similar marks in both papers. This is illustrated graphically in Figure 17.1. Such a graph is known as a **scatter diagram**. Each

Table 17.1

Student	X, mark in paper 1	Y, mark in paper 2
A	42	31
B	84	83
C	50	42
D	42	60
E	33	28
F	50	63
G	69	59
H	81	92
I	50	73
J	35	40

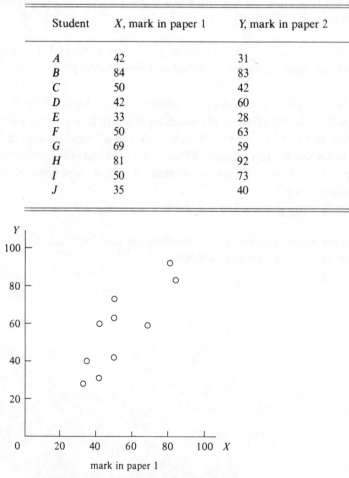

Figure 17.1. Scatter diagram for the data in Table 17.1

320

point represents the values of the two variates under consideration for a particular member of the sample. In a case such as this, where high X values are associated with high Y values and low X values with low Y values, we say there is **direct correlation**.

The data shown in Table 17.2 are shown on a scatter diagram in Figure 17.2. In this case there is **inverse correlation**.

The data in Table 17.3 gives the scores obtained on each of two dice when they were thrown together 15 times, and the corresponding scatter diagram is shown in Figure 17.3. In this case there is no obvious correlation.

Table 17.2 *Number of working horses and number of tractors in England and Wales (in ten thousands)* (Data from *A Century of Agricultural Statistics*, HMSO)

Year	Number of horses	Number of tractors
1938	67	6
1942	49	10
1946	44	18
1948	38	23
1950	29	30
1952	21	33
1954	15	39
1956	11	43

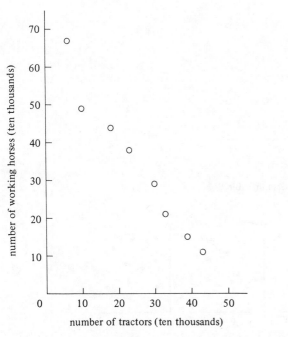

Figure 17.2. Scatter diagram for the data in Table 17.2

Table 17.3

Score on first die	Score on second die
2	5
4	2
5	4
5	1
3	4
6	3
4	2
5	3
3	5
6	1
5	4
6	6
2	3
3	2
1	2

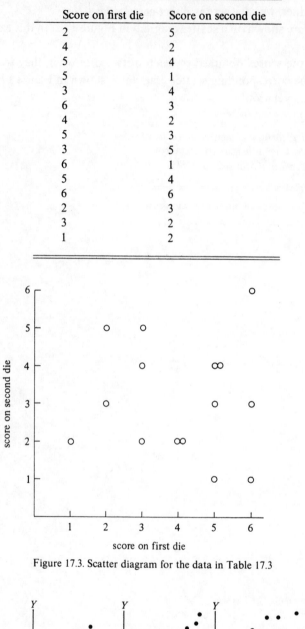

Figure 17.3. Scatter diagram for the data in Table 17.3

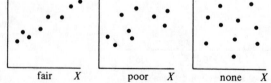

Figure 17.4. Diagrams to illustrate different degrees of correlation

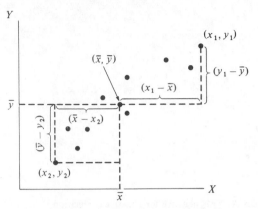

Figure 17.5. Diagram showing why cov(X, Y) is positive for positive correlation

17.2   Measurement of correlation

The scatter diagrams in Figure 17.4 show a difference in the degree of correlation which can be readily appreciated by eye. How can we measure the degree of correlation quantitatively? In Section 10.4 we met an expression $E(X - \mu_X)(Y - \mu_Y)$ which is termed the covariance, cov(X, Y), of two random variables X and Y, and it was proved there that cov(X, Y) is zero if X and Y are independent. If X and Y are not independent cov(X, Y) differs from zero. This can be seen by reference to Figure 17.5. For the point (x_1, y_1), $x_1 - \bar{x}$ and $y_1 - \bar{y}$ are both positive and therefore their product is positive also. For the point (x_2, y_2), $(x_2 - \bar{x})$ and $(y_2 - \bar{y})$ are both negative so that their product is positive. In fact for the majority of points $(x_i - \bar{x})(y_i - \bar{y})$ is positive leading to a positive estimate for cov(X, Y). Similarly for an inverse correlation such as that shown in Figure 17.6 the product $(x_i - \bar{x})(y_i - \bar{y})$ is generally negative and the estimated value of cov(X, Y) is also negative. Only in cases where there is no correlation will cov(X, Y) be zero since then positive and negative values of $(x_i - \bar{x})(y_i - \bar{y})$ are equally likely.

It can be shown that the unbiased estimate of cov(X, Y) is

$$\frac{1}{n-1} \sum_{i=1}^{n} (x_i - \bar{x})(y_i - \bar{y})$$

This depends not only on the degree of correlation but also on the spread of values of X and of Y. To form a basis of comparison the covariance must be standardised so that it does not depend on the scales on the X and Y axes. This can be done by making $x_i - \bar{x}$ into a standardised deviate by dividing by $\hat{s}_x$, the unbiased estimate of σ_x, and correspondingly for Y. This gives as an expression for the degree of correlation

$$\frac{1}{n-1} \sum_{i=1}^{n} \frac{(x_i - \bar{x})}{\hat{s}_x} \times \frac{(y_i - \bar{y})}{\hat{s}_y}$$

This statistic is called r and is known as the (product moment) **correlation coefficient**.

Substituting

$$\hat{s}_x = \sqrt{\left\{ \frac{1}{n-1} \sum_{i=1}^{n} (x_i - \bar{x})^2 \right\}} \quad \text{and} \quad \hat{s}_y = \sqrt{\left\{ \frac{1}{n-1} \sum_{i=1}^{n} (y_i - \bar{y})^2 \right\}},$$

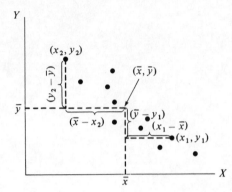

Figure 17.6. Diagram showing why cov(X, Y) is negative for negative correlation.

this becomes

$$r = \frac{\sum\limits_{i=1}^{n} (x_i - \bar{x})(y_i - \bar{y})}{\sqrt{\left[\sum\limits_{i=1}^{n} (x_i - \bar{x})^2 \sum\limits_{i=1}^{n} (y_i - \bar{y})^2\right]}} \qquad (17.2.1)$$

To simplify calculation this formula can be rewritten using the following relationships (see equation (3.7.1)):

$$\sum_{i=1}^{n} (x_i - \bar{x})^2 = \sum_{i=1}^{n} x_i^2 - \left(\sum_{i=1}^{n} x_i\right)^2 \bigg/ n$$

$$\sum_{i=1}^{n} (y_i - \bar{y})^2 = \sum_{i=1}^{n} y_i^2 - \left(\sum_{i=1}^{n} y_i\right)^2 \bigg/ n$$

$\sum\limits_{i=1}^{n} (x_i - \bar{x})(y_i - \bar{y})$ can also be rewritten in an alternative form, since

$$\sum_{i=1}^{n} (x_i - \bar{x})(y_i - \bar{y}) = \sum_{i=1}^{n} x_i y_i - \sum_{i=1}^{n} \bar{x} y_i - \sum_{i=1}^{n} \bar{y} x_i + \sum_{i=1}^{n} \bar{x}\bar{y}$$

$$= \sum_{i=1}^{n} x_i y_i - \bar{x} \sum_{i=1}^{n} y_i - \bar{y} \sum_{i=1}^{n} x_i + n\bar{x}\bar{y}$$

$$= \sum_{i=1}^{n} x_i y_i - n\bar{x}\bar{y} - n\bar{x}\bar{y} + n\bar{x}\bar{y}$$

$$= \sum_{i=1}^{n} x_i y_i - n\bar{x}\bar{y}$$

$$= \sum_{i=1}^{n} x_i y_i - \left(\sum_{i=1}^{n} x_i \sum_{i=1}^{n} y_i\right) \bigg/ n$$

Using these alternative forms, equation (17.2.1) becomes

$$r = \frac{n \sum\limits_{i=1}^{n} x_i y_i - \sum\limits_{i=1}^{n} x_i \sum\limits_{i=1}^{n} y_i}{\sqrt{\left[\left\{n \sum\limits_{i=1}^{n} x_i^2 - \left(\sum\limits_{i=1}^{n} x_i\right)^2\right\}\left\{n \sum\limits_{i=1}^{n} y_i^2 - \left(\sum\limits_{i=1}^{n} y_i\right)^2\right\}\right]}} \qquad (17.2.2)$$

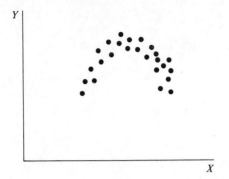

Figure 17.7. Scatter diagram showing correlation which is non-linear

Table 17.4 *Life expectancy and number of people per physician.* (Data from *Planet Earth*, published by the *Sunday Times*)

Country	Life expectancy (years)	People per physician (thousands)
Burma	47	9.6
Canada	72	0.7
China	50	3.4
Haiti	44	13.4
Malaysia	57	4.7
Madagascar	41	10.0
United Kingdom	71	0.9
Pakistan	47	6.1
Turkey	55	2.3
Venezuala	64	1.2
Zambia	43	16.1

It can be shown that r can only take values between $+1$ and -1. For exact direct linear correlation, i.e. when the points on the scatter diagram lie exactly on a straight line of positive slope, $r = +1$; for exact inverse linear correlation, $r = -1$. If there is no correlation r is zero. It is important to remember that r only measures *linear* correlation. For the scatter diagram shown in Figure 17.7 r would be close to zero: there is obviously correlation between X and Y but the relationship is not linear. Conversely for the data shown in Table 17.4 and illustrated in Figure 17.8 r takes the value -0.83 even though the relationship is evidently not linear. In fact we should not expect a linear relationship since, however few physicians there are, the life expectancy can never be negative!

(Other pitfalls in interpreting r are discussed below in Section 17.4.)

17.2.1 *Example*

Calculate r for the data in Table 17.1.

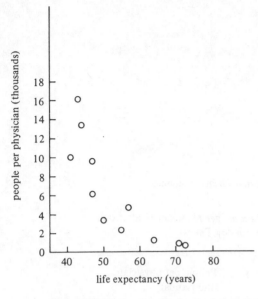

Figure 17.8. Scatter diagram for the data in Table 17.4

Denoting the marks in paper 1 and paper 2 by X and Y respectively, the calculation is shown in Table 17.5. Substitution in (17.2.2) gives

$$r = \frac{10 \times 33541 - 536 \times 571}{\sqrt{[(10 \times 31720 - 536^2)(10 \times 36841 - 571^2)]}}$$
$$= 0.825$$

This rather tedious calculation can sometimes be simplified by using coded values. If we use coded values u_i and v_i for x_i and y_i such that

$$x_i = A + Bu_i \Rightarrow \bar{x} = A + B\bar{u}$$
$$y_i = C + Dv_i \Rightarrow \bar{y} = C + D\bar{v}$$

Table 17.5 *Calculation of r for data in Table 17.1*

x_i	y_i	x_i^2	y_i^2	$x_i y_i$
42	31	1764	961	1302
84	83	7056	6889	6972
50	42	2500	1764	2100
42	60	1764	3600	2520
33	28	1089	784	924
50	63	2500	3969	3150
69	59	4761	3481	4071
81	92	6561	8464	7452
50	73	2500	5329	3650
35	40	1225	1600	1400
$\Sigma x_i = 536$	$\Sigma y_i = 571$	$\Sigma x_i^2 = 31\,720$	$\Sigma y_i^2 = 36\,841$	$\Sigma x_i y_i = 33\,541$

(see Section 2.7), then from equation (17.2.1)

$$r = \frac{\sum_{i=1}^{n}(x_i - \bar{x})(y_i - \bar{y})}{\sqrt{\left[\sum_{i=1}^{n}(x_i - \bar{x})^2 \sum_{i=1}^{n}(y_i - \bar{y})^2\right]}}$$

$$= \frac{\sum_{i=1}^{n}(Bu_i - B\bar{u})(Dv_i - D\bar{v})}{\sqrt{\left[\sum_{i=1}^{n}(Bu_i - B\bar{u})^2 \sum_{i=1}^{n}(Dv_i - D\bar{v})^2\right]}}$$

$$= \frac{\sum_{i=1}^{n}(u_i - \bar{u})(v_i - \bar{v})}{\sqrt{\left[\sum_{i=1}^{n}(u_i - \bar{u})^2 \sum_{i=1}^{n}(v_i - \bar{v})^2\right]}}$$

which using the identity proved above (see equation (17.2.2)) becomes

$$r = \frac{n\sum_{i=1}^{n}u_i v_i - \sum_{i=1}^{n}u_i \sum_{i=1}^{n}v_i}{\sqrt{\left[\left\{n\sum_{i=1}^{n}u_i^2 - \left(\sum_{i=1}^{n}u_i\right)^2\right\}\left\{n\sum_{i=1}^{n}v_i^2 - \left(\sum_{i=1}^{n}v_i\right)^2\right\}\right]}} \qquad (17.2.3)$$

Modern calculators simplify the computation of r, many of them being able to calculate it directly when the values of X and Y are fed in. However, it is wise to draw a scatter diagram first to see whether or not the calculation of r is appropriate. (When r is calculated the values of x_i^2, y_i^2 and $x_i y_i$ should not be rounded off too much as this may result in a value of $|r|$ greater than one!)

17.2.4 Exercise

(1) Calculate the correlation coefficient for the data in (a) Table 17.2, (b) Table 17.3.

(2) The following experiment was performed at the Muchmore Crops Institute. Carnations were grown on standard plots inside and outside glasshouses. For each plot the amount of a certain vital, but toxic, chemical was measured together with the average number of blooms per plant.
The results were as in Tables 17.6 and 17.7.
Calculate the product moment correlation coefficient for each set of data.   (AEB)

Table 17.6 *Glasshouse crop*

Amount of chemical in standard plot x (micrograms)	3	4	6	7	8	10	12	15	16
Average number of blooms per plant y for this plot	3.2	2.9	3.7	2.2	1.8	2.3	1.7	0.8	0.3

(You are given that $\Sigma v = 18.9$. $\Sigma v^2 = 49.33$: other sums should be calculated.)

Table 17.7 *Outdoor crop*

Amount of chemical in standard plot x (micrograms)	3	5	6	10	11	12	14	15
Average number of blooms per plant y for this plot	4.0	4.2	3.6	2.3	2.5	1.9	1.3	1.1

(You are given that $\Sigma y = 20.9$, $\Sigma y^2 = 64.65$; other sums should be calculated.)

(3) (a) Pupils transferring from primary to secondary education are given two verbal reasoning tests. The scores of twelve pupils (quoted relative to the mean score for each test) are in Table 17.8.

Show that the product moment correlation coefficient of the test scores is approximately 0.871.

Table 17.8

Pupil	A	B	C	D	E	F	G	H	J	K	L	M
Test 1	−15	−14	−10	−5	−4	−1	2	5	10	13	17	20
Test 2	−10	−7	−4	−6	−1	6	−2	5	9	0	10	12

(b) Corresponding values of the variables X and Y are given in Table 17.9. These values give a product moment correlation coefficient of 0.845.

Table 17.9

X	−15	−14	−10	−5	−1	4	10	17	20
Y	−10	−7	0	5	8	10	11	10	9

Compare and contrast, without further calculation, the relationship between the test scores in (a) and the relationship between X and Y. (C)

17.3   Sampling distribution of r; Fisher's transformation

r is calculated from a sample and gives an estimate of the parameter ρ of the population from which the sample is drawn. Returning to the derivation of equation (17.2.1) in Section 17.2 we see that

$$E(r) = \rho = \frac{\text{cov}(X, Y)}{\sigma_X \sigma_Y}$$

The sampling distribution of r depends both on n and ρ. It is symmetrical for $\rho=0$ but otherwise is considerably skewed. Significance tests and confidence limits for r are most easily dealt with by making a transformation defined by

$$z'=\tfrac{1}{2}\ln\left(\frac{1+r}{1-r}\right),\qquad \zeta=\tfrac{1}{2}\ln\left(\frac{1+\rho}{1-\rho}\right) \tag{17.3.1}$$

This transformation is due to Fisher, who showed that the sampling distribution of z' is approximately Normal with mean ζ and variance $1/(n-3)$, whatever the value of ρ, for a random sample from a bivariate Normal population. (Bivariate Normal populations are discussed in Section 18.9.) Table A5 gives the values of z' corresponding to different values of r. z' should not be confused with z, the standard Normal deviate.

17.3.1 *Example*

Does the value of $r=0.825$, obtained in Example 17.2.1 for ten pairs of values, differ significantly from zero?

$H_0: \rho=0, \zeta=0$

$H_1: \rho\neq0, \zeta\neq0$

On the null hypothesis, z' is Normally distributed with mean 0, s.d. $=1/\sqrt{(10-3)}=1/\sqrt{7}$. The observed value of r is 0.825 and from Table A5 the corresponding value of z' is 1.172.

The standardised deviate is $\dfrac{1.172}{1/\sqrt{7}}=3.1$. The critical region at the 5% level is |standardised deviate| > 1.96. Thus the value of r obtained is significantly different from zero at the 5% level.

17.3.2 *Example*

Calculate the 95% confidence limits for the value of r obtained in Example 17.2.1.

The 95% confidence limits for z' are

$z'\pm1.96\times$ s.d. of ζ

$$=1\cdot172\pm1.96\times\frac{1}{\sqrt{7}}\qquad\text{(using the values calculated in Example 17.3.1)}$$

$$=1.172\pm0.741$$

$$=0.431 \text{ to } 1.913$$

Using Table A5 the corresponding range for r is 0.41 to 0.957.

17.3.3 *Example*

Test whether the values obtained for the correlation coefficient for two samples in Exercise 17.2.2, question (3), are significantly different.

For the first sample, $r_1=0.871$, $n_1=12$.

For the second sample, $r_2=0.845$, $n_2=9$.

$H_0: \rho_1=\rho_2\Rightarrow\zeta_1=\zeta_2$

$H_1: \rho_1\neq\rho_2$

On the null hypothesis $z'_1 - z'_2$ is Normally distributed with mean zero and

$$\text{variance} = \frac{1}{n_1 - 3} + \frac{1}{n_2 - 3} \qquad \text{(see Sections 10.6 and 10.7)}$$

$$= \frac{1}{12 - 3} + \frac{1}{9 - 3}$$

$$= \tfrac{5}{18}$$

If $\left.\begin{array}{l} r_1 = 0.871, \quad z'_1 = 1.337 \\ r_2 = 0.845, \quad z'_2 = 1.238 \end{array}\right\}$ from Table A5

giving $z'_1 - z'_2 = 1.337 - 1.238 = 0.099$

The standardised deviate for $z'_1 - z'_2$ is $\dfrac{0.099}{\sqrt{(5/18)}} = 0.188$

This value is not significant at the 5% level and we retain the null hypothesis that the samples have the same correlation coefficient.

Another method of testing if r differs significantly from 0 is to use the fact that, if the population correlation coefficient ρ is 0 then the statistic $\left| \dfrac{r\sqrt{(n-2)}}{\sqrt{(1-r^2)}} \right|$ has a t-distribution with $n-2$ degrees of freedom. (Again the population from which the sample is drawn must be a bivariate Normal one.) This gives another method of doing Example 17.3.1, in which we tested if $r = 0.825$, for ten pairs of values, differed significantly from 0. We have

$$\left| \frac{r\sqrt{(n-2)}}{\sqrt{(1-r^2)}} \right| = \frac{0.825\sqrt{(10-2)}}{\sqrt{(1-0.825^2)}} = 4.13$$

The critical region for a two-tail test at the 5% level is $|t_8| > 2.31$ so that the correlation coefficient of 0.825 is significantly different from 0.

17.3.4 *Exercise*

(1) Ten athletes have best performances at the high jump and long jump as in Table 17.10. Calculate the coefficient of correlation between x and y.

Use Fisher's transformation to find 98% confidence limits for the correlation coefficient between best performance at the high jump and the long jump in the (supposed) bivariate Normal distribution from which the pairs (x, y) are drawn.   (AEB)

(2) Test using Fisher's transformation and a 5% level of significance the hypothesis that the samples in Exercise 17.2.2, question (2), have the same correlation coefficient.

(3) The bivariate frequency distribution of t (age in years) and n (number of eggs laid) is shown for a sample of 100 birds of a particular species in Table 17.11.

Table 17.10

Athlete	A	B	C	D	E	F	G	H	I	J
High jump x m	1.8	2.1	1.9	2.0	1.8	1.8	1.6	1.8	1.9	2.3
Long jump y m	6.7	7.6	6.3	6.8	5.9	7.9	5.5	5.6	6.5	7.2

Table 17.11

		Age in years (t)				
		1	2	3	4	5
Number of	1	11	4	0	0	0
eggs (n)	2	1	16	8	1	0
	3	0	2	18	6	1
	4	0	0	2	13	5
	5	0	0	0	4	8

(a) Calculate the product moment correlation coefficient for these data.

(b) Assuming the above data comprise a random sample for a population with a bivariate Normal distribution, use Fisher's transformation $z' = \tanh^{-1} r$ to find 95% confidence limits for the true population correlation coefficient ρ.

17.4 Some fallacies in the interpretation of r

(i) Correlation should not be confused with causation. Figures for the years 1955–65 show high correlation between the number of television licences and the number of road accidents in this country but no one would suppose that one of these factors *causes* the other. Such a spurious relationship can result when each of the two variables depends on a third variable, in this case the 'standard of living', which produces a simultaneous change in both of them. It is particularly common if the variables are measured over a period of time.

(ii) Even if it appears that there is a causal relationship between two variables, the correlation coefficient does not help us to establish which variable depends on which.

(iii) As already mentioned a non-significant value of r only implies an absence of *linear* correlation.

(iv) A linear relationship established over a particular range of values of X and Y should not be assumed to hold outside that range by extrapolation. For example, there is a strong direct correlation between the age and weight of a baby, but to extend this linear relationship would imply that older children and adults continued to grow at this same rate!

17.5 Spearman's rank correlation coefficient, r_S

A manufacturer of margarine has been experimenting with different recipes and wishes to test public reaction to them. Table 17.12 shows how two tasters rank eight varieties in order of preference. Hardly surprisingly the testers do not show the same order of preference but the manufacturer would like to know whether there is any degree of correlation between their rankings.

In this case we do not have two continuous variates which are Normally distributed but

Table 17.12

Variety	Rankings by Taster 1	Taster 2
A	5	7
B	4	3
C	2	1
D	1	2
E	6	6
F	7	8
G	3	4
H	8	5

two discrete variates in the form of the rankings. Using these rankings we can calculate the correlation coefficient using formula (17.2.2). However, since the values of X (and Y) are the first n integers, this formula can be considerably simplified. If there are n ranks then

$$\sum_{i=1}^{n} x_i = \sum_{i=1}^{n} y_i = \sum_{i=1}^{n} i = \tfrac{1}{2}n(n+1)$$

$$\sum_{i=1}^{n} x_i^2 = \sum_{i=1}^{n} y_i^2 = \sum_{i=1}^{n} i^2 = \tfrac{1}{6}n(n+1)(2n+1)$$

Using these expressions the denominator of formula (17.2.2) becomes

$$n \times \tfrac{1}{6}n(n+1)(2n+1) - [\tfrac{1}{2}n(n+1)]^2$$
$$= \tfrac{1}{12}n^2(n^2-1) \qquad \text{(after some manipulation)}$$

The numerator of (17.2.2) can also be simplified by letting d_i be the difference between ranks for the ith item. Then

$$d_i = x_i - y_i$$

$$\sum_{i=1}^{n} d_i^2 = \sum_{i=1}^{n} (x_i - y_i)^2 = \sum_{i=1}^{n} x_i^2 - 2 \sum_{i=1}^{n} x_i y_i + \sum_{i=1}^{n} y_i^2$$

Rearranging,

$$\sum_{i=1}^{n} x_i y_i = \frac{1}{2}\left[\sum_{i=1}^{n} x_i^2 + \sum_{i=1}^{n} y_i^2 - \sum_{i=1}^{n} d_i^2 \right]$$

$$= \frac{1}{2}\left[2 \times \tfrac{1}{6}n(n+1)(2n+1) - \sum_{i=1}^{n} d_i^2 \right]$$

Using this expression for $\sum_{i=1}^{n} x_i y_i$ and substituting for $\sum_{i=1}^{n} x_i$ and $\sum_{i=1}^{n} y_i$ as before, the numerator of equation (17.2.2) becomes

$$\tfrac{1}{2}n\left[2 \times \tfrac{1}{6}n(n+1)(2n+1) - \sum_{i=1}^{n} d_i^2 \right] - \{\tfrac{1}{2}n(n+1)\}^2$$

$$= \tfrac{1}{12}n^2(n^2-1) - \tfrac{1}{2}n \sum_{i=1}^{n} d_i^2$$

Combining the expressions obtained for the numerator and denominator we obtain for the

rank correlation coefficient, r_S,

$$r_S = 1 - \frac{6 \sum\limits_{i=1}^{n} d_i^2}{n(n^2 - 1)} \qquad\qquad (17.5.1)$$

This correlation coefficient is due to Spearman (1904) and is usually called after him. Obviously when the rankings are identical the d_i's are all zero and $r_S = 1$.

17.5.1   *Example*

Calculate the Spearman rank correlation coefficient for the data in Table 17.12 (reproduced in Table 17.13).

Table 17.13

Variety	Taster 1, x_i	Taster 2, y_i	d_i	d_i^2
A	5	7	-2	4
B	4	3	$+1$	1
C	2	1	$+1$	1
D	1	2	-1	1
E	6	6	0	0
F	7	8	-1	1
G	3	4	-1	1
H	8	5	$+3$	9
			0	18

$$r_S = 1 - \frac{6 \times 18}{8(8^2 - 1)} = 0.79 \quad \text{(using equation (17.5.1))}$$

As for r, r_S can vary between -1 and $+1$. The critical values of r_S at the 5% level, taking the null hypothesis that there is no correlation, are given in Table 17.14. As the number of

Table 17.14 (Adapted from Neave, *Elementary Statistical Tables*, 1981)

Number of ranks	Critical value of $|r_S|$
5	1.00
6	0.89
7	0.79
8	0.74
9	0.70
10	0.65
20	0.45
25	0.40
50	0.28

ranks increases the critical values appropriate for r can be used. Using this table the value of $r_S = 0.79$ obtained in the preceding example is significant at the 5% level since the critical region is $|r_S| > 0.74$ indicating there is a degree of correlation between the rankings of the two tasters.

In the example given here the variate measured by the tasters, i.e. how much they liked the margarine, was qualitative and the correlation could *only* be measured by computing r_S. Rank correlation is also used for quantitative variables when *neither* of them is Normally distributed. One problem that may arise in this case is that two or more values may be equal. What ranking value should they be given? Consider the following arranged in increasing order:

4.3, 5.1, 5.1, 6.3, 7.5, 8.6, 8.6, 8.6

The second and third values are 'tied' and are both given an average ranking of $2\frac{1}{2}$. Similarly the 6th, 7th and 8th values are given the average ranking of 7. The complete sequence of rankings is therefore: 1, $2\frac{1}{2}$, $2\frac{1}{2}$, 4, 5, 7, 7, 7. Note that the sequence has the same total as 1, 2, 3, 4, 5, 6, 7, 8.

17.5.2   *Example*

Two judges of an international skating competition award the marks given in Table 17.15. Calculate the Spearman rank correlation coefficient.

Do the judges agree on the order in which they place the candidates?

Table 17.15

	GB	France	USSR	Competitor W. Germany	E. Germany	USA	Canada
Judge A	5.8	5.5	5.9	4.9	5.9	5.6	5.0
Judge B	5.5	5.4	5.8	5.3	5.7	5.7	5.7

Judge A's marks, placed in descending order, are

Mark	5.9	5.9	5.8	5.6	5.5	5.0	4.9
Rank	$1\frac{1}{2}$	$1\frac{1}{2}$	3	4	5	6	7

with the rankings below.

For Judge B, the marks and their ranks are

Mark	5.8	5.7	5.7	5.7	5.5	5.4	5.3
Rank	1	3	3	3	5	6	7

The calculation of r_S is shown in Table 17.16.

Our null hypothesis is that there is no correlation between the judges' rankings. Using Table 17.14 the critical region for $n = 7$ is $|r_S| > 0.79$. The value obtained is not significant at the 5% level. We retain H_0: there is no evidence that the judges agree on the order in

Table 17.16

Competitor	Judge A's rank	Judge B's rank	d_i	d_i^2
GB	3	5	-2	4
France	5	6	-1	1
USSR	$1\frac{1}{2}$	1	$\frac{1}{2}$	$\frac{1}{4}$
W. Germany	7	7	0	0
E. Germany	$1\frac{1}{2}$	3	$-1\frac{1}{2}$	$2\frac{1}{4}$
USA	4	3	$+1$	1
Canada	6	3	$+3$	9
			0	$17\frac{1}{2}$

Using equation (17.5.1),
$$r_S = 1 - \frac{6 \times 17\frac{1}{2}}{7(7^2-1)} = 0.6875$$

which they place the competitors. (Strictly speaking, the formula for r_S should be modified for tied ranks since its derivation used the fact that the ranks were the first n natural numbers. However, the correction involved is small.)

17.5.3 *Exercise*

(1) The organisers of a flower competition intend to base their order of merit on the opinions of judge X and judge Y. The marks given by the two judges are set out in Table 17.17.
(a) Carry out a rank correlation test to determine whether the two judges' opinions are consistent.
(b) Determine an order of merit of the competitors. (L)

(2) In a village flower show the six competitors in the finals had their entries assessed by three judges. The placings were as in Table 17.18.
Calculate a rank correlation coefficient between (a) the first and second judges' placings, and (b) the first and third judges' placings. Comment on your results. (C)

Table 17.17

Competitor	A	B	C	D	E	F	G	H	I	J
Judge X marks (max. 100)	48	50	55	51	51	47	48	46	52	50
Judge Y marks (max. 100)	18	19	29	22	26	14	22	11	24	17

Table 17.18

Competitor	P	Q	R	S	T	U
1st Judge	3	5	6	1	4	2
2nd judge	4	3	5	2	6	1
3rd judge	2	6	4	1	3	5

Table 17.19

x	29	81	60	88	91	91	86	99	73	42
y	74	86	63	74	70	63	41	81	29	56

Table 17.20

Competitor	A	B	C	D	E	F	G	H	I	J
Judge X	4	9	2	5=	3	10	5=	7	8	1
Judge Y	6	10	2	8	1	9	7	4	5	3

(3) Explain briefly how a scatter diagram can show whether there is direct or indirect correlation between two quantities. Give one example each of data where (a) direct, (b) indirect correlation might be expected.

Table 17.19 shows some values of a variable x and the corresponding values of a second variable y. Calculate a coefficient of rank correlation between x and y and comment briefly on the result you obtain.   (L)

(4) (a) X and Y were judges at a beauty contest in which there were ten competitors. Their rankings are shown in Table 17.20

Calculate a coefficient of rank correlation between these two sets of ranks and comment briefly on your result.

(b) Illustrate by means of two scatter diagrams rank correlation coefficients of 0 and -1 between two variables X and Y.   (C)

17.6   Kendall's rank correlation coefficient, τ

A second rank correlation coefficient may be obtained as follows. Consider the data in Table 17.21 which shows the ranks of ten students (A to J) in two different aptitude tests: one for mathematics and one for English.

If the students came in exactly the same order in both tests then any pair of students that we chose would appear in the same order in both lists. The basis of the calculation of Kendall's τ

Table 17.21

	A	B	C	D	E	F	G	H	I	J
Maths	7	1	4	8	10	5	3	2	6	9
English	10	2	1	5	8	4	7	6	3	9

Table 17.22

	B	H	G	C	F	I	A	D	J	E
Maths	1	2	3	4	5	6	7	8	9	10
English	2	6	7	1	4	3	10	5	9	8

is to allot a score of $+1$ to a pair of objects in the same order for both lists and a score of -1 for a pair of objects not in the same order. For example, in Table 17.21, B comes above D in both lists so that the pair (B, D) gives a score of $+1$; B is above C in the first list and below it in the second so that the pair (B, C) gives a score of -1. The pairs are most easily compared by rearranging the lists so that the first has its rankings in the correct order. Doing this gives Table 17.22. Looking at the pairs for the English test which include rank 2 we have $(2,6)$, $(2,7), (2, 1), (2,4), (2,3), (2,10), (2,5), (2,9), (2,8)$. The corresponding students are in the same order in both lists except for the pair underlined giving a score of $8 - 1 = 7$. The pairs for the English test which include 6 are $(6, 7), (6, 1), (6, 4), (6, 3), (6, 10), (6, 5), (6, 9), (6, 8)$ (where $(6, 2)$ is excluded because we have already considered it). The score for these pairs is $4 - 4 = 0$. Repeating for all possible pairs gives a total score of $+17$ (check this). The total number of pairs is $\binom{10}{2} = 45$. Thus the maximum possible score is 45, obtained when both rankings are the same, and the minimum possible score is -45, obtained when one ranking is the exact reverse of the other. **Kendall's rank correlation coefficient,** τ, is defined by:

$$\tau = \frac{\text{score}}{\text{maximum possible score}}$$

$$= \frac{17}{45} = 0.38$$

In general, if S is the score obtained in a ranking of n objects, for which the maximum possible score is $\binom{n}{2} = \frac{1}{2}n(n - 1)$, we have

$$\tau = \frac{S}{\frac{1}{2}n(n - 1)} \tag{17.6.1}$$

The largest value of τ is $+1$ when both rankings are the same and the smallest value is -1 when one ranking is the exact reverse of the other.

The method described above can be set out compactly as shown in Table 17.23.

Total score = number of larger ranks to right − number of smaller ranks to right
$$= 31 - 14 = 17$$

Table 17.23 *Calculation of Kendall's* τ

Second ranking	2	6	7	1	4	3	10	5	9	8	Total
Number of larger ranks to right	8	4	3	6	4	4	0	2	0	0	31
Number of smaller ranks to right	1	4	4	0	1	0	3	0	1	0	14

Table 17.24 *Critical values of* τ (Adapted from Neave, *Elementary Statistical Tables*, 1981)

Number of ranks	Critical value of $|\tau|$
5	1.00
6	0.87
7	0.71
8	0.64
9	0.56
10	0.51
20	0.33

(Remember that to use this method the lists must be rearranged so that the first is in correct ranking order.)

To perform a significance test using Kendall's τ we take as our null hypothesis that there is no correlation between the two rankings. Table 17.24 gives the critical values (using a significance level of 5%) which $|\tau|$ must exceed if we are to reject this null hypothesis.

We see from this table that the value of τ which we obtained, 0.38, is not significant at the 5% level since it does not exceed the critical value of 0.51: we keep our null hypothesis that there is no correlation between the two rankings.

17.6.1   *Example*

Calculate τ for the data on the international skating competition given in Example 17.5.2.

The competitors placed in order as given by judge A with the corresponding ranks given by judge B are shown in Table 17.25.

Table 17.25

	USSR E. Germany	GB	USA	France	Canada	W. Germany
Judge A	$1\frac{1}{2}$	3	4	5	6	7
Judge B	$\begin{cases} 1 \\ 3 \end{cases}$	5	3	6	3	7

Table 17.26

Second ranking	Number of larger ranks to right	Number of smaller ranks to right
1	5	0
3	3	0
5	2	2
3	2	0
6	1	1
3	1	0
7	0	0
	$\overline{14}$	$\overline{3}$

With tied ranks the method of counting the ranks to the right which are smaller or larger has to be modified as follows.

(i) Since USSR and E. Germany are equally ranked by judge A, the ranks allotted by judge B could be placed either in the order 1, 3 or in the order 3, 1. For this reason they are given one above the other in the last line of the table.

(ii) Equal ranks to the right score 0, since this is mid-way between $+1$ and -1.

Using these modifications the calculation of τ is given in Table 17.26.

$$S = 14 - 3 = 11$$

$$\tau = \frac{S}{\frac{1}{2}n(n-1)}$$

$$= \frac{11}{\frac{1}{2} \times 7 \times 6}$$

$$= 0.52$$

This value of τ is not significant at the 5% level and there is no evidence that the judges agree in their rankings.

17.6.2 *Exercise*

Calculate Kendall's τ for each question in Exercise 17.5.3.

Summary

The **product moment correlation coefficient, r,** is calculated from

$$r = \frac{\sum\limits_{i=1}^{n} (x_i - \bar{x})(y_i - \bar{y})}{\sqrt{\left[\sum\limits_{i=1}^{n} (x_i - \bar{x})^2 \sum\limits_{i=1}^{n} (y_i - \bar{y})^2 \right]}}$$

$$= \frac{n \sum_{i=1}^{n} x_i y_i - \sum_{i=1}^{n} x_i \sum_{i=1}^{n} y_i}{\sqrt{\left[\left\{ n \sum_{i=1}^{n} x_i^2 - \left(\sum_{i=1}^{n} x_i \right)^2 \right\} \left\{ n \sum_{i=1}^{n} y_i^2 - \left(\sum_{i=1}^{n} y_i \right)^2 \right\} \right]}}$$

Fisher's transformation defines z' where

$$z' = \tfrac{1}{2} \ln \left(\frac{1+r}{1-r} \right)$$

Spearman's rank correlation coefficient, r_S, is defined by

$$r_S = 1 - \frac{6 \sum_{i=1}^{n} d_i^2}{n(n^2 - 1)}$$

Kendall's rank correlation coefficient, τ, is calculated from

$$\tau = \frac{\text{score}}{\tfrac{1}{2} n(n-1)}$$

Projects

(1)   *Correlation between height and foot length*

Obtain pairs of measurements for ten to twenty people of the same sex. They could either be adults or a group of children of approximately the same age. (Foot length is most easily measured by placing the subject's heel against a vertical wall.) Calculate the correlation coefficient and test if it differs significantly from zero.

(2)   *Correlation between two examination marks*

For a group of five to ten people, rank each person according to his or her examination mark in each of two subjects. Calculate the Spearman rank correlation coefficient and test if it differs significantly from zero. Repeat for Kendall's rank correlation coefficient.

(3)   *Advanced Level Statistics Software*

The section *Correlation* contains three programs which illustrate the ideas of this chapter.

(a)   *Investigation of the product moment correlation coefficient, r*

This allows the user to move the points around on a scatter diagram in order to get a 'feel' for the relationship between the distribution of the points and the value of *r*.

(b)   *Investigation of Spearman's rank correlation coefficient, r_S*

This demonstrates the calculation of r_S and allows the user to see the effect of altering one of the sets of rankings.

(c)   *Analysis of data*

This allows users to enter their own data and to test for significant correlation against a null hypothesis of no correlation.

Exercise on Chapter 17

(1)   In an experiment the values of two variables, X and Y, are measured. Ten such experiments were performed with the following results for (X, Y):

(6, 13), (12, 2), (9, 12), (5, 15), (2, 17), (12, 5), (8, 10), (3, 13), (11, 12), (7, 11).

Illustrate these data by means of a scatter diagram and comment briefly on the type of correlation that this shows.

Calculate a coefficient of rank correlation between the ten values of X and Y.   (C)

(2)   In each of the following sections, which purport to be extracts from reports, the second sentence is an inference from the statement made in the first sentence. State whether the inferences are valid or invalid, and give the reasons for your decisions.

(a)   The amount of fertiliser applied was varied from plot to plot and the correlation coefficient between the yield of corn from a plot and the amount of fertiliser applied was found to be 0.02. This shows that there was no relation between yield and amount of fertiliser applied.

(b)   Inspection of the police reports of car accidents in the town during 1975 revealed that, when the number of accidents involving drivers of a particular age was correlated with that age, the correlation coefficient was -0.72. We conclude that older drivers are less likely to have an accident than younger drivers.

(c)   The correlation coefficient between the sugar content s of the peas and the length of time t they have been in the greengrocer's shop was negative. It follows that s decreases with increasing t.

(d)   The correlation coefficient of percentage of children over sixteen at school and the Gross National Product, over the years for which we have records, is 0.91, which is a high correlation. It is obvious that if many more children can be persuaded to stay on at school after sixteen then the Gross National Product will increase substantially.   (O)

(3)   (a)   Explain the use of (i) the product moment correlation coefficient, (ii) the coefficient of correlation by ranks.

Give two examples of the appropriate application of each.

(b)   At the final judging of a 'Cow of the Year Show', two judges gave the descending orders of merit of ten cows as $EAHJBIFCGD$ and $EHJAFICBDG$. Find the rank correlation coefficient between these two orders. Discuss the significance of the result.   (AEB)

(4)   Define the product moment correlation coefficient and explain how you would interpret values of 0 and 1.

Guess the value of the correlation coefficient between the variables in the following situations and interpret your estimate.

(a) The height of water and the volume of road traffic at London Bridge, if high tide is at 7 a.m. The interval between successive high tides is about 12 hours.

(b) The marks in paper I and total marks in a two-paper examination.

(5) Explain clearly what is meant by the statistical term 'correlation'.

Vegboost Industries, a small chemical firm specialising in garden fertilisers, set up an experiment to study the relationship between a new fertiliser compound and the yield from tomato plants. Eight similar plants were selected and treated regularly throughout their life with x grams of fertiliser diluted in a standard volume of water. The yield y, in kilograms, of good tomatoes was measured for each plant. Table 17.27 summarises the results.

(a) Calculate the product moment correlation coefficient for these data.

(b) Calculate Spearman's rank correlation coefficient for these data.

(c) Is there any evidence of a relationship between these variables? Justify your answer. (No formal test is required.)   (AEB)

Table 17.27

Plant	A	B	C	D	E	F	G	H
Amount of fertiliser x (g)	1.2	1.8	3.1	4.9	5.7	7.1	8.6	9.8
Yield y (kg)	4.5	5.9	7.0	7.8	7.2	6.8	4.5	2.7

(6) Pierre Catalyst, a scientist of some repute, has produced the following data.

$$(x_1, y_1), (x_2, y_2), \ldots, (x_n, y_n)$$

He requests your statistical help. He asks you to calculate a measure of correlation and suggests the product moment correlation coefficient, a formula for which is

$$r = \frac{\sum_{i=1}^{n} x_i y_i - n\bar{x}\bar{y}}{\sqrt{\left[\left(\sum_{i=1}^{n} x_i^2 - n\bar{x}^2\right)\left(\sum_{i=1}^{n} y_i^2 - n\bar{y}^2\right)\right]}}$$

However, in view of the type of data, you decide to substitute for the x's and y's their corresponding ranks, giving

$$(r_{x_1}, r_{y_1}), (r_{x_2}, r_{y_2}), \ldots, (r_{x_n}, r_{y_n})$$

By substituting these ranked data into the above formula, show how the formula may be modified for use with ranked data, and hence deduce Spearman's coefficient of rank correlation,

$$r_S = 1 - \frac{6 \sum_{i=1}^{n} d_i^2}{n(n^2 - 1)}$$

where d_i is the difference in the ranks of x_i and y_i, and you may assume in your derivation that there are no tied ranks.

Pierre's data are as follows:

(19, 12), (52, 33), (33, 21), (57, 32), (49, 28), (45, 22), (39, 22), (25, 19).

Calculate r_S for these data. (AEB)

(7) Explain how you would calculate the product moment correlation coefficient from a sample of n pairs of values x_i, y_i ($i = 1, 2, \ldots, n$).

The number of eggs laid, x, by a certain species of bird is either 1 or 2, and this is related to the age of the bird, y, which is also 1 or 2. The frequencies of the four possible combinations of values x, y are recorded for a total of n birds, as shown in Table 17.28. Show that the product moment correlation coefficient between x and y is $(ad - bc)/\{(a+b)(c+d)(a+c)(b+d)\}^{1/2}$. (O)

Table 17.28

		Number of eggs laid (x)		Total
		1	2	
Age y	1	a	b	$a+b$
(years)	2	c	d	$c+d$
	Total	$a+c$	$b+d$	n

(8) What is meant by the statistical terms 'independent' and 'uncorrelated', and how are they related?

At the University of Batsula, students for the degree in chemical engineering take two examinations. They have a part I examination at the end of the second year of their studies, and a part II examination at the end of the third year. Degree classification

Table 17.29

		Part I marks					
		40–49	50–59	60–69	70–79	80–89	90–99
	40–49	3	5	4	0	0	0
	50–59	3	6	6	2	0	0
Part II marks	60–69	0	5	9	5	2	0
	70–79	0	0	5	10	8	1
	80–89	0	0	0	5	6	5
	90–99	0	0	0	2	4	4

depends upon an average of these marks. Table 17.29 gives the part I and part II marks for a particular set of 100 students.

Use the coding method to calculate the product moment correlation coefficient for these data. (Assumed means of 64.5 for part I marks and 74.5 for part II marks should be used.)   (AEB)

18 Linear regression

18.1 Analysing the results of an experiment

Figure 18.1 illustrates the apparatus used in a simple experiment which many people will have performed for themselves. When weights are added to the scale pan, the spring stretches. Table 18.1 shows the results obtained when different loads were applied in a random order, and the corresponding scatter diagram is shown in Figure 18.2. In this experiment the values of Y, the length of the spring in cm, were measured for preselected values of X, the load in newtons, and for this reason X is called the **independent variable** and Y the **dependent variable**.

Figure 18.2 suggests that there is a linear relationship between X and Y: how should we draw a straight line to represent this relationship? Drawing a line by eye is obviously not satisfactory, since the result will be subjective, but as a method it can lead us to a mathematical method. Figure 18.3 shows schematically the points on a scatter diagram and a possible straight line which relates them. In this experiment the values of X are extremely accurately known. The measurement of the length of the spring is less accurate. If the experiment were repeated (using the same loads) the values of Y for a given value of X would show random variation. It is this variation which we may reasonably assume causes the points on the scatter diagram to deviate from a straight line. For example, in Figure 18.3 (x_1, y_1) deviates by e_1 and (x_2, y_2) by e_2 (in the opposite direction) from the straight line which has been drawn. We can represent the relationship between any pair of values (x_i, y_i) by

$$y_i = \alpha + \beta x_i + e_i \qquad (18.1.1)$$

where $\alpha + \beta x_i$ represents the linear relationship between y_i and x_i and e_i is a random error. β is called the **coefficient of regression of Y on X.** We shall assume that the e_i's are independent of x_i and Normally distributed with mean 0 and s.d. $\sigma_{y|x}$. Figure 18.4 shows the

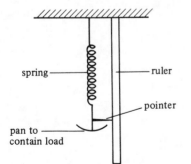

Figure 18.1. Apparatus for measuring how the length of a spring varies with the load applied

345

Table 18.1 *Results for extension of a spring*

x_i, load (in newtons)	y_i, length of spring (cm)
0.1	10.7
0.2	11.3
0.3	12.0
0.4	12.4
0.5	13.0
0.6	13.7
0.7	14.5
0.8	15.1
0.9	15.6
1.0	16.0

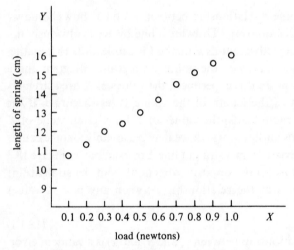

Figure 18.2. Scatter diagram for the data in Table 18.1

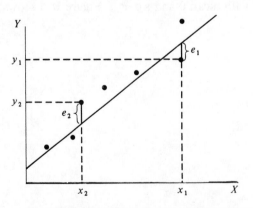

Figure 18.3. Schematic diagram showing the deviation of the measurements from a possible straight line relating X and Y

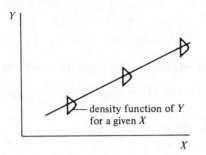

Figure 18.4. Diagram showing the distribution of repeated values of Y for a given value of X

distribution of repeated measurements of y_i for each x_i and the appropriate line relating x_i and y_i, which passes through the mean values of the y_i distributions.

18.2   The method of least squares

The parameters α and β are estimated by the **method of least squares,** so called because estimates, $\hat{a}$ and $\hat{b}$, of α and β respectively are chosen so as to minimise $\sum\limits_{i=1}^{n} e_i^2$. ($n$ is the number of points on the scatter diagram.) The squares of the deviates are used for the same reasons as the squares of the deviations are used in the calculation of standard deviation (see Section 3.6).

Rearranging equation (18.1.1)

$$e_i = y_i - \alpha - \beta x_i$$

$$\sum_{i=1}^{n} e_i^2 = \sum_{i=1}^{n} (y_i - \alpha - \beta x_i)^2$$

This expression can be varied by varying α and β. $\hat{a}$ and $\hat{b}$, the estimates of α and β, are chosen so that it is minimised. The appropriate values of $\hat{a}$ and $\hat{b}$ are found by putting the partial derivatives of $\sum\limits_{i=1}^{n} (y_i - \hat{a} - \hat{b} x_i)^2$ with respect to $\hat{a}$ and to $\hat{b}$ equal to zero:

$$\frac{\partial}{\partial \hat{a}} \sum_{i=1}^{n} (y_i - \hat{a} - \hat{b} x_i)^2 = \sum_{i=1}^{n} -2(y_i - \hat{a} - \hat{b} x_i) = 0$$

$$\frac{\partial}{\partial \hat{b}} \sum_{i=1}^{n} (y_i - \hat{a} - \hat{b} x_i)^2 = \sum_{i=1}^{n} -2x_i(y_i - \hat{a} - \hat{b} x_i) = 0$$

This gives two simultaneous equations in $\hat{a}$ and $\hat{b}$. These equations can be rewritten as follows:

$$\sum_{i=1}^{n} -2(y_i - \hat{a} - \hat{b} x_i) = 0$$

gives

$$\sum_{i=1}^{n} y_i - n\hat{a} - \hat{b} \sum_{i=1}^{n} x_i = 0 \tag{18.2.1}$$

and

$$\sum_{i=1}^{n} -2x_i(y_i - \hat{a} - \hat{b} x_i) = 0$$

gives

$$\sum_{i=1}^{n} x_i y_i - \hat{a} \sum_{i=1}^{n} x_i - \hat{b} \sum_{i=1}^{n} x_i^2 = 0 \qquad (18.2.2)$$

(18.2.1) and (18.2.2) are known as the **normal equations**. They can be solved simultaneously. Subtracting (18.2.2) multiplied by n from (18.2.1) multiplied by $\sum_{i=1}^{n} x_i$ gives:

$$\sum_{i=1}^{n} x_i \sum_{i=1}^{n} y_i - \hat{b} \left(\sum_{i=1}^{n} x_i \right)^2 - n \sum_{i=1}^{n} x_i y_i + n\hat{b} \sum_{i=1}^{n} x_i^2 = 0$$

Rearranging,

$$\hat{b} = \frac{n \sum_{i=1}^{n} x_i y_i - \sum_{i=1}^{n} x_i \sum_{i=1}^{n} y_i}{n \sum_{i=1}^{n} x_i^2 - \left(\sum_{i=1}^{n} x_i \right)^2} \qquad (18.2.3)$$

From (18.2.1) $\hat{a}$, the estimated value of α, is given by

$$\hat{a} = \left(\sum_{i=1}^{n} y_i - \hat{b} \sum_{i=1}^{n} x_i \right) \Big/ n$$

giving

$$\hat{a} = \bar{y} - \hat{b}\bar{x} \qquad (18.2.4)$$

The relationship between x and y is given by

$$y = \hat{a} + \hat{b}x \qquad (18.2.5)$$

and this is known as the **regression line of Y on X.** An alternative form is given by substituting the expression (18.2.4) for $\hat{a}$ in equation (18.2.5):

$$y = \bar{y} - \hat{b}\bar{x} + \hat{b}x$$

giving

$$y - \bar{y} = \hat{b}(x - \bar{x}) \qquad (18.2.6)$$

From (18.2.6) we can see that the regression line passes through $(\bar{x}, \bar{y})$, a fact which is useful when drawing it on a scatter diagram.

Table 18.2

x_i	y_i	$x_i y_i$	x_i^2
0.1	10.7	1.07	0.01
0.2	11.3	2.26	0.04
0.3	12.0	3.60	0.09
0.4	12.4	4.96	0.16
0.5	13.0	6.50	0.25
0.6	13.7	8.22	0.36
0.7	14.5	10.15	0.49
0.8	15.1	12.08	0.64
0.9	15.6	14.04	0.81
1.0	16.0	16.00	1.00
5.5	134.3	78.88	3.85

18.2.1 Example

Calculate the regression line of Y on X for the data given in Table 18.1 (reproduced in Table 18.2), and use it to predict the length for a load of 0.65 N.

$$n = 10$$

$$\bar{x} = \frac{\sum_{i=1}^{n} x_i}{n} = \frac{5.5}{10} = 0.55$$

$$\bar{y} = \frac{\sum_{i=1}^{n} y_i}{n} = \frac{134.3}{10} = 13.43$$

$$\hat{b} = \frac{n \sum_{i=1}^{n} x_i y_i - \sum_{i=1}^{n} x_i \sum_{i=1}^{n} y_i}{n \sum_{i=1}^{n} x_i^2 - \left(\sum_{i=1}^{n} x_i\right)^2}$$

$$= \frac{10 \times 78.88 - 5.5 \times 134.3}{10 \times 3.85 - 5.5^2}$$

$$= 6.08$$

The regression line of Y on X is

$$y - \bar{y} = \hat{b}(x - \bar{x})$$
$$y - 13.43 = 6.08(x - 0.55)$$
$$y = 6.08x + 10.1$$

To predict the length for a load of 0.65 N we substitute this value of x into the equation of the regression line

$$y = 6.08 \times 0.65 + 10.1$$
$$= 14.1 \text{ cm}$$

18.3 Coded values

The calculation in the previous section can be greatly simplified using coded values as in Section 17.2. With $x_i = A + Bu_i$, $y_i = C + Dv_i$

$$\hat{b} = \frac{D}{B} \left\{ \frac{n \sum_{i=1}^{n} u_i v_i - \sum_{i=1}^{n} u_i \sum_{i=1}^{n} v_i}{n \sum_{i=1}^{n} u_i^2 - \left(\sum_{i=1}^{n} u_i\right)^2} \right\} \tag{18.3.1}$$

(Calculation may often be further simplified by choosing a value of A which makes $\sum_{i=1}^{n} u_i = 0$.)

18.3.1 Example

Calculate the regression line of Y on X for the data in Table 18.1 using coded values.

Table 18.3

x_i	y_i	u_i	v_i	u_iv_i	u_i^2
0.1	10.7	−5	−2.3	11.5	25
0.2	11.3	−4	−1.7	6.8	16
0.3	12.0	−3	−1.0	3.0	9
0.4	12.4	−2	−0.6	1.2	4
0.5	13.0	−1	0	0	1
0.6	13.7	0	0.7	0	0
0.7	14.5	1	1.5	1.5	1
0.8	15.1	2	2.1	4.2	4
0.9	15.6	3	2.6	7.8	9
1.0	16.0	4	3.0	12.0	16
		−5	4.3	48.0	85

Taking $A=0.6$, $C=13.0$, $B=0.1$, $D=1$ we have Table 18.3. Using equation (18.3.1)

$$\hat{b}=\frac{1}{0.1}\times\frac{10\times48.0-(-5)\times4.3}{10\times85-(-5)^2}$$

$$=6.08$$

$$\bar{x}=A+B\bar{u} \qquad\qquad \text{(see equation (2.7.1))}$$

$$=0.6+0.1\times\left(\frac{-5}{10}\right)$$

$$=0.55$$

$$\bar{y}=C+D\bar{v} \qquad\qquad \text{(see equation (2.7.1))}$$

$$=13+1\times\frac{4.3}{10}$$

$$=13.43$$

and, of course, the regression line is, as before,

$$y=6.08x+10.1$$

18.3.2   Exercise

(1)   A scientist, working in an agricultural research station, believes there is a relationship between the hardness of the shells of eggs laid by chickens and the amount of a certain food supplement put into the diet of the chickens. He selects ten chickens of the same breed and collects the data of Table 18.4.

(Hardness is measured on a 0–10 scale, 10 being the hardest. There are no units attached.)

(a)   Calculate the equation of the regression line of y on x.

(b)   Calculate the product moment correlation coefficient.

(c)   Do you believe that this linear model will continue to be appropriate no matter how large or small x becomes?

Justify your reply.   (AEB)

Table 18.4

Chicken	A	B	C	D	E	F	G	H	I	J
Amount of food supplement x(g)	7.0	9.8	11.6	17.5	7.6	8.2	12.4	17.5	9.5	19.5
Hardness of shells y	1.2	2.1	3.4	6.1	1.3	1.7	3.4	6.2	2.1	7.1

Table 18.5

Year (x)	1963	1964	1965	1966	1967	1968	1969	1970	1971	1972
Consumption (y) (millions of gallons)	32.5	37.1	35.5	37.7	41.5	46.4	44.8	45.8	53.9	62.0

(2) The figures in Table 18.5 give the wine consumption in the United Kingdom in millions of gallons (y) for the years 1963 to 1972 (x).

Draw a scatter diagram to show these data.

Determine the least squares estimate of the regression line of y on x, showing all your working. Draw this line on your scatter diagram and use it to estimate the consumption for 1973.

Comment on the appropriateness of a 'linear' regression model in this case, given also that the actual wine consumption in 1973 was 78.3 million gallons. (JMB)

(3) The body and heart masses of fourteen ten-month-old male mice are given in Table 18.6.
   (a) Draw a scatter diagram of these data.
   (b) Calculate the equation of the regression line of y on x and draw this line on the scatter diagram.
   (c) Calculate the product moment coefficient of correlation. (AEB)

(4) A regression line, $y = a + bx$, is to be fitted to a set of data points (x, y). The data are coded to $X = (x - c_1)/d_1$, $Y = (y - c_2)/d_2$, and in terms of these the regression line is $Y = A + BX$. Find a and b in terms of A and B and the coding constants.

In such a problem the values of the independent variable are equally spaced. Explain, with reference to the appropriate least squares equations, how this simplifies the fitting of the line.

Table 18.6

Body mass (x) (grams)	27	30	37	38	32	36	32	32	38	42	36	44	33	38
Heart mass (y) (milligrams)	118	136	156	150	140	155	157	114	144	159	149	170	131	160

Table 18.7

Age (weeks)	11	12	13	14	15	16
Mass (g)	357	382	404	423	440	451

Table 18.7 shows the mass of a certain animal at weekly intervals.

State whether it would be more appropriate to fit a regression line of age on mass or mass on age to these data, and justify your choice. What value does the line of your choice give for the mass at 17 weeks?

Comment on the validity of your estimate. (You are advised to plot a rough graph.)

(O)

*18.4   Estimating a value for $\sigma^2{}_{y|x}$

For a value of x_i the value of Y predicted by the regression line is given by
$$y_i' = \hat{a} + \hat{b}x_i$$
The difference between y_i and y_i', known as a **residual**, gives the value of e_i for that point. Each value of $y_i' - y_i$ gives a value of e_i from a distribution which is $\mathcal{N}(0, \sigma^2_{y|x})$. The unbiased estimate $\hat{s}_{y|x}$ of $\sigma_{y|x}$ is given by

$$\hat{s}_{y|x} = \sqrt{\left(\frac{\sum\limits_{i=1}^{n} (y_i' - y_i)^2}{n-2}\right)} \tag{18.4.1}$$

The divisor is $(n-2)$ since two degrees of freedom are lost because there are two constraints: the values of $\hat{a}$ and $\hat{b}$ are calculated from the values of X and Y.

18.4.1   *Example*

Obtain an estimate of $\sigma^2_{y|x}$ for the data in Table 18.1.

In Section 18.2 the regression line of Y on X was calculated as $y = 6.08x + 10.1$. Using this equation, the predicted values for Y are given in Table 18.8.

From equation (18.4.1)

$$\hat{s}_{y|x} = \sqrt{\left(\frac{\sum\limits_{i=1}^{n} (y_i' - y_i)^2}{n-2}\right)}$$

$$= \frac{0.117\,84}{8}$$

$$= 0.121$$

Table 18.8

x_i	y_i	y_i'	$(y_i'-y_i)^2$
0.1	10.7	10.708	0.000 06
0.2	11.3	11.316	0.000 26
0.3	12.0	11.924	0.005 78
0.4	12.4	12.532	0.017 42
0.5	13.0	13.140	0.019 60
0.6	13.7	13.748	0.002 30
0.7	14.5	14.356	0.020 74
0.8	15.1	14.964	0.018 50
0.9	15.6	15.572	0.000 78
1.0	16.0	16.180	0.032 40
			0.117 84

*18.5   Confidence limits for β

How accurate is the estimate, $\hat{b}$, which we have made of β? This section will show how the confidence limits for β can be found in terms of $\sigma_{y|x}$, the s.d. of the random errors, e_i. To recapitulate, we assume the e_i's are randomly distributed with a Normal distribution mean 0, s.d. $\sigma_{y|x}$. Thus, by definition,

$$E(e_i)=0 \tag{18.5.1}$$

$$\text{var}(e_i)=\sigma_{y|x}^2 \tag{18.5.2}$$

We will now calculate the expected value and variance of $\hat{b}$ in terms of the e_i's.
From equation (18.2.3)

$$\hat{b}=\frac{n\sum_{i=1}^{n} x_i y_i - \sum_{i=1}^{n} x_i \sum_{i=1}^{n} y_i}{n\sum_{i=1}^{n} x_i^2 - \left(\sum_{i=1}^{n} x_i\right)^2}$$

Substituting $y_i=\beta x_i+\alpha+e_i$ (equation (18.1.1)) the numerator becomes

$$n\sum_{i=1}^{n} x_i(\beta x_i+\alpha+e_i)-\sum_{i=1}^{n} x_i \sum_{i=1}^{n} (\beta x_i+\alpha+e_i)$$

$$=n\beta\sum_{i=1}^{n} x_i^2+n\alpha\sum_{i=1}^{n} x_i+n\sum_{i=1}^{n} x_i e_i-\beta\left(\sum_{i=1}^{n} x_i\right)^2-n\alpha\sum_{i=1}^{n} x_i-\sum_{i=1}^{n} x_i\sum_{i=1}^{n} e_i$$

$$=\beta\left[n\sum_{i=1}^{n} x_i^2-\left(\sum_{i=1}^{n} x_i\right)^2\right]+n\sum_{i=1}^{n} x_i e_i-n\sum_{i=1}^{n} \bar{x}e_i \quad \left(\text{using } \sum_{i=1}^{n} x_i=n\bar{x}\right)$$

$$=\beta\left[n\sum_{i=1}^{n} x_i^2-\left(\sum_{i=1}^{n} x_i\right)^2\right]+n\sum_{i=1}^{n} (x_i-\bar{x})e_i$$

Dividing by the denominator $n\sum_{i=1}^{n} x_i^2-\left(\sum_{i=1}^{n} x_i\right)^2$ in the expression for $\hat{b}$, we have

$$\hat{b} = \beta + \frac{n \sum\limits_{i=1}^{n}(x_i - \bar{x})e_i}{n \sum\limits_{i=1}^{n} x_i^2 - \left(\sum\limits_{i=1}^{n} x_i\right)^2}$$

$$= \beta + \frac{n \sum\limits_{i=1}^{n}(x_i - \bar{x})e_i}{n \sum\limits_{i=1}^{n}(x_i - \bar{x})^2} \qquad \text{(using equation (3.7.1))}$$

$$= \beta + \frac{\sum\limits_{i=1}^{n}(x_i - \bar{x})e_i}{\sum\limits_{i=1}^{n}(x_i - \bar{x})^2}$$

In calculating the expected value and variance of $\hat{b}$, the term in x_i is constant for each e_i since the values of x_i are predetermined.

This gives

$$E(\hat{b}) = E\left[\beta + \frac{\sum\limits_{i=1}^{n}(x_i - \bar{x})e_i}{\sum\limits_{i=1}^{n}(x_i - \bar{x})^2}\right]$$

$$= \beta + \frac{\sum\limits_{i=1}^{n}(x_i - \bar{x})E(e_i)}{\sum\limits_{i=1}^{n}(x_i - \bar{x})^2}$$

$$= \beta \qquad \text{(since } E(e_i) = 0 \text{ from equation (18.5.1))}$$

Thus $\hat{b}$ gives an unbiased estimate of β. Also

$$\text{var}(\hat{b}) = \text{var}\left[\frac{\sum\limits_{i=1}^{n}(x_i - \bar{x})e_i}{\sum\limits_{i=1}^{n}(x_i - \bar{x})^2}\right]$$

since β is constant.

Using the relationship $\text{var}(cy) = c^2 \text{var}(y)$ where c is a constant (see equation (10.4.5))

$$\text{var}(\hat{b}) = \frac{\sum\limits_{i=1}^{n}(x_i - \bar{x})^2 \, \text{var}(e_i)}{\left[\sum\limits_{i=1}^{n}(x_i - \bar{x})^2\right]^2}$$

$$= \frac{\sum\limits_{i=1}^{n}(x_i - \bar{x})^2 \sigma_{y|x}^2}{\left[\sum\limits_{i=1}^{n}(x_i - \bar{x})^2\right]^2} \qquad \text{(using equation (18.5.2))}$$

$$\text{var}(\hat{b}) = \frac{\sigma_{y|x}^2}{\sum\limits_{i=1}^{n}(x_i - \bar{x})^2} \qquad (18.5.5)$$

Assuming the sampling distribution of $\hat{b}$ is Normal, the 95% confidence limits of β are given by

$$\beta = \hat{b} \pm \frac{1.96\sigma_{y|x}}{\sqrt{\left\{\sum_{i=1}^{n}(x_i - \bar{x})^2\right\}}} \qquad (18.5.6)$$

If $\sigma_{y|x}$ is estimated from the sample as $\hat{s}_{y|x}$ then the 95% confidence limits of β are

$$\beta = \hat{b} \pm \frac{t_{n-2,5\%}\hat{s}_{y|x}}{\sqrt{\left\{\sum_{i=1}^{n}(x_i - \bar{x})^2\right\}}} \qquad (18.5.7)$$

where the t-distribution is used because the variance is estimated from the sample with $n-2$ degrees of freedom.

18.5.1 *Example*

Calculate the 95% confidence limits for the estimate of β for the data in Table 18.1.

In equation (18.5.5) we cannot substitute $\sigma_{y|x}$ but only the estimate of it, $\hat{s}_{y|x}$, which we found in Section 18.4 to be 0.121.

$\sum_{i=1}^{n}(x_i - \bar{x})^2$ can be found most simply using the identity

$$\sum_{i=1}^{n}(x_i - \bar{x})^2 = \sum_{i=1}^{n}x_i^2 - \left(\sum_{i=1}^{n}x_i\right)^2 \Big/ n$$

$$= 3.85 - \frac{5.5^2}{10} \qquad \text{(using the values obtained in Example 18.2.1)}$$

$$= 0.825$$

which gives our estimate of the variance of $\hat{b}$ as

$$\sqrt{[\text{var}(\hat{b})]} = \frac{\hat{s}_{y|x}}{\sqrt{\left\{\sum_{i=1}^{n}x_i^2 - \left(\sum_{i=1}^{n}x_i\right)^2 \Big/ n\right\}}} = \frac{0.121}{\sqrt{0.825}}$$

$$= 0.133$$

The 95% confidence limits of β are, from equation (18.5.7),

$$\beta = \hat{b} \pm t_{n-2,5\%}\sqrt{[\text{var}(\hat{b})]}$$
$$= 6.08 \pm 2.31 \times 0.133$$
$$= 6.08 \pm 0.31$$

*18.6   Confidence limits for α

From equation (18.2.4)

$$\hat{a} = \bar{y} - \hat{b}\bar{x}$$

$$= \frac{1}{n}\sum_{i=1}^{n}y_i - \hat{b}\bar{x}$$

Thus

$$E(\hat{a}) = \frac{1}{n} \sum_{i=1}^{n} E(y_i) - E(\hat{b}\bar{x})$$

Since

$$y_i = \alpha + \beta x_i + e_i$$
$$E(y_i) = \alpha + \beta x_i + E(e_i)$$
$$\qquad = \alpha + \beta x_i$$

giving

$$E(\hat{a}) = \frac{1}{n} \sum_{i=1}^{n} (\alpha + \beta x_i) - \bar{x} E(\hat{b})$$
$$\qquad = \alpha + \beta\bar{x} - \bar{x}\beta$$
$$\qquad = \alpha$$

showing that $\hat{a}$ is an unbiased estimate of α. Also

$$\mathrm{var}(\hat{a}) = \mathrm{var}\left\{ \sum_{i=1}^{n} y_i/n - \hat{b}\bar{x} \right\}$$

It can be shown that the covariance of $\bar{y}$ and $\hat{b}$ is zero so that

$$\mathrm{var}(\hat{a}) = \mathrm{var}\left(\frac{\sum\limits_{i=1}^{n} y_i}{n} \right) + \mathrm{var}(\hat{b}\bar{x})$$

$$\qquad = \frac{1}{n^2} \sum_{i=1}^{n} \mathrm{var}(y_i) + \bar{x}^2 \,\mathrm{var}(\hat{b}) \qquad\qquad \text{(see equation (10.4.5))}$$

Since $y_i = \alpha + \beta x_i + e_i$,
$$\mathrm{var}(y_i) = \mathrm{var}(e_i) = \sigma_{y|x}^2$$

and equation (18.5.5) gives a value for $\mathrm{var}(\hat{b})$. Substituting, we have

$$\mathrm{var}(\hat{a}) = \frac{1}{n^2} \times n\sigma_{y|x}^2 + \frac{\bar{x}^2 \sigma_{y|x}^2}{\sum\limits_{i=1}^{n} (x_i - \bar{x})^2}$$

$$\mathrm{var}(\hat{a}) = \sigma_{y|x}^2 \left[\frac{1}{n} + \frac{\bar{x}^2}{\sum\limits_{i=1}^{n} (x_i - \bar{x})^2} \right] \qquad\qquad (18.6.1)$$

18.6.1   *Example*

Find the s.d. and 95% confidence limits for α for the data in Table 18.1.

We do not have an exact value for $\sigma_{y|x}$ but only its estimate, found in Section 18.4 to be 0.121. The summation $\sum\limits_{i=1}^{n} (x_i - \bar{x})^2$ was found in Example 18.5.1 to be 0.825 and $\bar{x} = 0.55$. Substituting these values in equation (18.6.1) gives

$$\mathrm{var}(\hat{a}) = 0.121^2 \left[\frac{1}{10} + \frac{0.55^2}{0.825} \right]$$
$$\sqrt{[\mathrm{var}(\hat{a})]} = 0.0827$$

The 95% confidence limits of α are

$$\alpha = \hat{a} \pm t_{n-2,5\%} \sqrt{[\text{var}(\hat{a})]}$$

where the t-distribution is used because var($\hat{a}$) is estimated from the sample. Substituting

$$\alpha = 10.1 \pm 2.31 \times 0.0827$$
$$= 10.1 \pm 0.2$$

*18.7   Confidence limits of predicted values

In Example 18.2.1 the regression line was used to predict the true value of Y, y_0, for a value of X, x_0. To do this we can use equation (18.2.6):

$$y_0 - \bar{y} = \hat{b}(x_0 - \bar{x})$$

which gives

$$y_0 = \hat{b}(x_0 - \bar{x}) + \bar{y}$$

Since the covariance of $\bar{y}$ and $\hat{b}$ is zero, using equation (10.4.5) gives

$$\text{var}(y_0) = (x_0 - \bar{x})^2 \, \text{var}(\hat{b}) + \text{var}(\bar{y})$$

From equation (18.5.5)

$$\text{var}(\hat{b}) = \sigma_{y|x}^2 \Big/ \sum_{i=1}^{n} (x_i - \bar{x})^2$$

and

$$\text{var}(\bar{y}) = \sigma_{y|x}^2 / n \qquad\qquad\qquad \text{(see Theorem 13.3.1)}$$

giving

$$\text{var}(y_0) = \sigma_{y|x}^2 \left[\frac{1}{n} + \frac{(x_0 - \bar{x})^2}{\sum_{i=1}^{n} (x_i - \bar{x})^2} \right] \qquad\qquad (18.7.1)$$

Returning to the example in Section 18.2, the regression line of Y on X was

$$y = 6.08x + 10.1$$

When $x = 0.65$, $y = 6.08 \times 0.65 + 10.1 = 14.10$.

In Example 18.4.1 we found $\hat{s}_{y|x} = 0.121$ and in Example 18.5.1 $\sum_{i=1}^{n} (x_i - \bar{x})^2 = 0.825$. Using equation (18.7.1) gives our estimate of the variance of y_0 as

$$\text{var}(y_0) = 0.121^2 \left[\frac{1}{10} + \frac{(0.65 - 0.55)^2}{0.825} \right]$$
$$\text{s.d.} \, (y_0) = 0.0405$$

and the 95% confidence limits of y_0 are

$$y_0 = 14.10 \pm 2.31 \times 0.0405$$
$$= 14.10 \pm 0.09$$

where, as before t_{n-2} has been used since the s.d. was estimated from the sample.

Study of equation (18.7.1) shows that the confidence limits for y_0 will have the smallest range when $x_0 = \bar{x}$, and the range increases towards the ends of the regression line.

18.7.1   *Example*

It is known that the true response Y in a certain chemical experiment is a linear function of the operating temperature X. However, the experimental determinations of Y are subject

Table 18.9

Temperature (X)	30	40	50
Observed responses (Y)	14	10	7
	12	11	6

to random errors, so that when an experiment is performed at temperature x_i the observed response y_i is such that

$$y_i = \alpha + \beta x_i + e_i$$

where $\alpha + \beta x_i$ is the true response and e_i is the error. Table 18.9 gives the observed responses in six experiments, two at each of three temperatures.

Use the data to obtain the least squares estimate of the linear relationship connecting X and Y. (You are given that $\sum_i x_i y_i = 2270$.)

The errors, e_i, are independent and Normally distributed with zero mean and unit standard deviation.

Calculate 90% confidence limits for

(a)   the value of α, (b) the value of β,

(c)   the true value of Y, when X is 50.   (W)

Using the six pairs of values in the table we have

$$\sum_i x_i y_i = 2270, \qquad \sum_i x_i^2 = 10\,000,$$

$$\sum_i x_i = 240, \qquad \sum_i y_i = 60$$

From equation (18.2.3),

$$\hat{b} = \frac{n \sum_{i=1}^{n} x_i y_i - \sum_{i=1}^{n} x_i \sum_{i=1}^{n} y_i}{n \sum_{i=1}^{n} x_i^2 - \left(\sum_{i=1}^{n} x_i \right)^2}$$

$$= \frac{6 \times 2270 - 240 \times 60}{6 \times 10\,000 - 240^2}$$

$$= -0.325$$

From equation (18.2.4),

$$\hat{a} = \bar{y} - \hat{b}\bar{x}$$

$$= \tfrac{60}{6} - (-0.325)\tfrac{240}{6}$$

$$= 23$$

From equation (18.5.5),

$$\mathrm{var}(\hat{b}) = \sigma_{y|x}^2 \bigg/ \sum_{i=1}^{n} (x_i - \bar{x})^2$$

$$= \sigma_{y|x}^2 \bigg/ \left\{ \sum_{i=1}^{n} x_i^2 - \left(\sum_{i=1}^{n} x_i \right)^2 \bigg/ n \right\}$$

We are given $\sigma_{y|x}=1$ so

$$\text{var}(\hat{b})=1^2\Big/\left(10\,000-\frac{240^2}{6}\right)=\frac{1}{400}$$

s.d. $(\hat{b})=0.05$

From equation (18.6.1),

$$\text{var}(\hat{a})=\sigma_{y|x}^2\left[\frac{1}{n}+\frac{\bar{x}^2}{\sum\limits_{i=1}^{n}(x_i-\bar{x})^2}\right]$$

$$=1^2\left[\frac{1}{6}+\frac{40^2}{400}\right]$$

s.d. $(\hat{a})=2.04$

(a) Using the value of $\hat{a}$ and its variance obtained above, the 90% confidence limits of α are

$$\alpha=23\pm1.64\times2.04=23\pm3.35$$

(where z is used since $\sigma_{y|x}$ is known).

(b) Using the value of $\hat{b}$ and its variance obtained above, the 90% confidence limits of β are

$$\beta=-0.325\pm1.64\times0.05=-0.325\pm0.082$$

(c) Using the regression line of Y on X, the value of Y, y_0, when $x_0=50$ is given by

$$y_0=\hat{b}x_0+\hat{a}=-0.325\times50+23=6.75$$

From equation (18.7.1) the variance of this predicted value is given by

$$\text{var}(y_0)=\sigma_{y|x}^2\left[\frac{1}{n}+\frac{(x_0-\bar{x})^2}{\sum\limits_{i=1}^{n}(x_i-\bar{x})^2}\right]$$

$$=1^2\left[\frac{1}{6}+\frac{(50-40)^2}{400}\right]$$

$$\sqrt{[\text{var}(y_0)]}=0.645$$

The 90% confidence limits of the predicted value are

$$y_0=6.75\pm1.64\times0.645$$
$$=6.8\pm1.1$$

18.7.2 *Exercise*

(1) Two variables x and y of interest in an experiment are known to be linearly related, but the coefficients in this relationship are not known. A series of 15 experiments was conducted in which three determinations of y were made for each of five values of x. The x-values are accurate but the determinations of the y-values are subject to independent random errors that are Normally distributed with mean zero and standard deviation 1.25. The observed values in the series of experiments are shown in Table 18.10.

The following quantities were calculated from the table.

$$\sum x=45,\qquad \sum y=180,\qquad \sum x^2=165,\qquad \sum xy=420.$$

(a) Calculate the equation of the least squares estimate of the linear relationship between x and y.

(b) Estimate the true value of y when $x=4$. Determine the standard error of this

Table 18.10

x	1	2	3	4	5
	19	17	12	9	3
y	18	16	11	10	3
	21	17	13	7	4

estimate. Explain why this estimate of y when $x=4$ is preferable to that obtained from averaging the three observed values of y when $x=4$.

(c) Calculate a 90% confidence interval for the true value of y when $x=4$.   (W)

(2) In an experiment to find the Young modulus for a brass wire the eleven pairs of values of x (suspended mass in kg) and y (length of wire in mm -7000 mm) given in Table 18.11 are obtained. The equation connecting x and y is assumed to take the form $y=c+kx$. Obtain the least squares estimate values for c and k and 95% confidence limits for k.
$$(\Sigma x^2 = 57.25, \ \Sigma y^2 = 7.22, \ \Sigma xy = 10.0)$$ (C)

(3) The size (z) of an organism was measured at different times (x) giving the data shown in the first two rows of Table 18.12. The third row of the table gives the values of $y=\log_{10}z$ to two decimal places. Without carrying out any nontrivial calculations show that the assumption of a linear relationship between y and x is more realistic than between z and x.
The following quantities were calculated from the data:
$$\sum x = 25, \qquad \sum x^2 = 165, \qquad \sum y = 3.6, \qquad \sum xy = 23.28.$$
Suppose that $y=\alpha+\beta x$ and that for given values of x the observed values of y are subject to independent errors which are Normally distributed with mean zero and standard deviation 0.02.

(a) Calculate the least squares estimates of α and β.

(b) Obtain 95% confidence limits for the value of y when $x=10$. Hence find 95% confidence limits for the size of the organism at time $x=10$.   (W)

Table 18.11

x	1	1.5	2	2.5	3	3.5	3	2.5	2	1.5	1
y	-1.1	-0.6	0	0.4	0.9	1.5	1.0	0.6	0.1	-0.5	-0.9

Table 18.12

Time (x)	1	3	5	7	9
Size (z)	1.48	3.02	5.37	9.55	17.38
$y=\log_{10}z$	0.17	0.48	0.73	0.98	1.24

(4) In an investigation of the effect of duration of training (x) on performance time (y) for a certain repetitive job, the following observations were obtained from 26 trainees:

$$\sum x = 104, \qquad \sum y = 208, \qquad \sum (x - \bar{x})^2 = 56.$$

$$\sum (x - \bar{x})(y - \bar{y}) = -56, \qquad \sum (y - \bar{y})^2 = 62.$$

Plot the linear relationship of y to x which best fits the observations.

Calculate 95% confidence limits for the value predicted for y from this relationship when $x = 6$. Sketch the form of these confidence limits for varying values of x.

Calculate the value predicted for y when $x = 12$: what does this value suggest to you concerning the form of the relationship between y and x?   (C)

(5) Repeat Example 18.7.1 (a) and (b) using an estimate of $\sigma_{y|x}$ obtained from the data.

18.8   Regression line of X on Y

If the values of Y were predetermined and the values of X subject to experimental error then the appropriate regression line to find would be the **regression line of X on Y**. In this case,

$$x_i = \alpha' + \beta' y_i + e_i'$$

where the e_i''s are independent of y_i and Normally distributed with mean 0 and s.d. $\sigma_{x|y}$. β' is the **coefficient of regression of X on Y**. The regression line is found by minimising the sum of the squares of the deviations in the x-direction, shown in Figure 18.5, giving

$$\hat{b}' = \text{est}(\beta') = \frac{n \sum_{i=1}^{n} x_i y_i - \sum_{i=1}^{n} x_i \sum_{i=1}^{n} y_i}{n \sum_{i=1}^{n} y_i^2 - \left(\sum_{i=1}^{n} y_i \right)^2} \qquad (18.8.1)$$

$$\hat{a}' = \text{est}(\alpha') = \bar{x} - \hat{b}' \bar{y} \qquad (18.8.2)$$

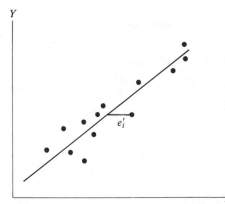

Figure 18.5 Scatter diagram showing the deviation of each x_i from the regression line of X on Y

18.9 Two regression lines

The situation described in Section 18.1 where only one variable, Y, is subject to random variation usually only occurs in scientific experimentation. In other fields this is not always so. Consider, for example, the relationship between the height, Y, of an adult and the length of his or her foot, X. Figure 18.6 shows the type of scatter diagram we might obtain for a random sample from a population. Here we have two variables, X and Y, which are obviously correlated but neither can be treated as an independent variable in the sense used in Section 18.1. X and Y are **jointly Normally distributed**. This means that for any given value of X the values of Y are Normally distributed. If we calculate the mean value of y_i for each x_i, these means fall approximately on a straight line, the regression line of Y on X, as shown by the open circles in Figure 18.7. Similarly for any given value of Y, the values of X are Normally distributed: the mean values of x_i for each y_i, shown by the solid circles in Figure 18.7, fall approximately on a straight line, the regression line of X on Y. These lines do not coincide unless there is perfect correlation between X and Y. In the most extreme case where there is no correlation at all, the best prediction of Y for any value of X will be $\bar{y}$ and the best prediction of X for any value of Y will be $\bar{x}$. The regression lines will then be as shown in Figure 18.8.

Figure 18.6. Scatter diagram for a sample from a joint Normal distribution

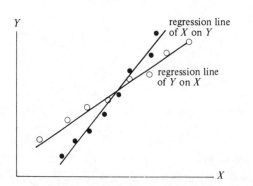

Figure 18.7. Graph showing the regression lines of Y on X and of X on Y

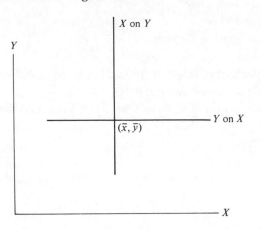

Figure 18.8. The two regression lines for variables which are not correlated

Each regression line can be found using the method of least squares (see Sections 18.2 and 18.8). The product of the gradients $\hat{b}$ and $\hat{b}'$ is related to the correlation coefficient since

$$\hat{b}\hat{b}' = \frac{n\sum_{i=1}^{n}x_iy_i - \sum_{i=1}^{n}x_i\sum_{i=1}^{n}y_i}{n\sum_{i=1}^{n}x_i^2 - \left(\sum_{i=1}^{n}x_i\right)^2} \times \frac{n\sum_{i=1}^{n}x_iy_i - \sum_{i=1}^{n}x_i\sum_{i=1}^{n}y_i}{n\sum_{i=1}^{n}y_i^2 - \left(\sum_{i=1}^{n}y_i\right)^2} \qquad \text{(from equations (18.2.3) and (18.8.1))}$$

$$= r^2 \qquad \text{(from equation (17.2.2))} \tag{18.9.1}$$

The lines cross at $(\bar{x}, \bar{y})$ since both lines go through this point.

18.9.1 Example

Table 18.13 gives the height and the foot length for nine women. Calculate both regression lines and use the appropriate line to predict

Table 18.13 *Height and foot length for nine women (Y, height in cm; X, right foot length in cm)*

y_i	x_i	v_i	u_i	v_i^2	u_i^2	u_iv_i
166	25.0	+6	−1.0	36	1	−6
154	22.0	−6	−4.0	36	16	+24
172	26.0	+12	0	144	0	0
174	26.0	+14	0	196	0	0
158	22.0	−2	−4.0	4	16	8
167	23.0	+7	−3.0	49	9	−21
160	22.5	0	−3.5	0	12.25	0
168	24.0	+8	−2.0	64	4	−16
175	24.5	+15	−1.5	225	2.25	−22.5
		54	−19.0	754	60.5	−33.5

(a) the foot length for a woman height 170 cm,
(b) the height of a woman whose foot length is 23.5 cm.

v_i is the coded value of y_i using an arbitrary origin of 160 and u_i is the coded value of x_i using an arbitrary origin of 26.0. In both cases the unit is 1.

To calculate both regression lines we require $\sum_i u_i, \sum_i v_i, \sum_i u_i^2, \sum_i v_i^2, \sum_i u_i v_i$ and these are calculated in Table 18.13.

Regression line of Y on X: $y = \hat{b}x + \hat{a}$

$$\hat{b} = \frac{n \sum_{i=1}^{n} u_i v_i - \sum_{i=1}^{n} u_i \sum_{i=1}^{n} v_i}{n \sum_{i=1}^{n} u_i^2 - \left(\sum_{i=1}^{n} u_i\right)^2}$$ (equation (18.3.1))

$$= \frac{9 \times (-33.5) - 54 \times (-19.0)}{9 \times 60.5 - (-19.0)^2} = 3.948$$

$$\bar{x} = 26 + \bar{u} = 26 + \frac{(-19)}{9} = 23.89$$

$$\bar{y} = 160 + \bar{v} = 160 + \frac{54}{9} = 166$$

$$\hat{a} = \bar{y} - \hat{b}\bar{x} = 166 - 3.948 \times 23.89$$ (equation (18.2.4))

$$= 71.68$$

The regression line of Y on X is
$$y = 3.95x + 71.7$$

Regression line of X on Y: $x = \hat{b}'y + \hat{a}'$

$$\hat{b}' = \frac{n \sum_{i=1}^{n} u_i v_i - \sum_{i=1}^{n} u_i \sum_{i=1}^{n} v_i}{n \sum_{i=1}^{n} v_i^2 - \left(\sum_{i=1}^{n} v_i\right)^2}$$ (from equation (18.8.1) using coded values)

$$= \frac{9 \times (-33.5) - 54(-19)}{9 \times 754 - 54^2} = 0.1872$$

$$\hat{a}' = \bar{x} - \hat{b}'\bar{y}$$ (equation (18.8.2))

$$= 23.89 - 0.1872 \times 166$$

$$= -7.185$$

The regression line of X on Y is
$$x = 0.187y - 7.19$$

These regression lines are shown in Figure 18.9.

(a) In predicting the average foot length for women whose height is 170 cm we are treating the height, Y, as the independent variable and X as the dependent variable. The appropriate regression line to use is that of X on Y. Substituting $y = 170$ cm gives
$$x = 0.187 \times 170 - 7.19 = 24.6 \text{ cm}$$

(b) In predicting the average height of women whose foot length is 23.5 cm, the appropriate regression line to use is that of Y on X since Y is now the dependent variable. Substituting $x = 23.5$ cm gives
$$y = 3.95 \times 23.5 + 71.7 = 164.5 \text{ cm}$$

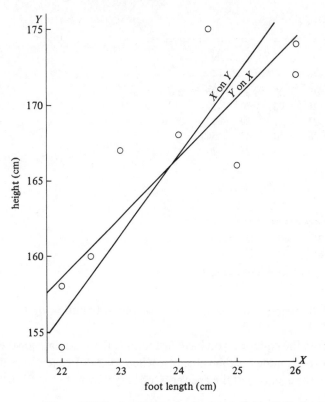

Figure 18.9. Scatter diagram for the data in Table 18.13, showing the two regression lines

The correlation coefficient between height and foot length is given by

$$r = \sqrt{(\hat{b}\hat{b}')} = \sqrt{(3.95 \times 0.187)}$$
$$= 0.86$$

Only when two variables are measured for a sample chosen *at random* do both regression lines, Y on X and X on Y, have meaning. If the values of Y are measured for certain predetermined values of X, only the regression line of Y on X has meaning; if values of X are measured for predetermined values of Y, only the regression line of X on Y has meaning.

18.9.2 *Exercise*

(1) A sample of twenty marriages was chosen from those taking place in England and Wales. The age of the husband y and of the wife x for each marriage are given in Table 18.14. You are given that

$$\sum x = 497, \qquad \sum y = 578$$

Plot a scatter diagram of the data. The slope of the regression line of y on x is 0.79 and of x on y is 0.67. Plot these lines on the diagram. Use your diagram to predict the age of the wife of a husband aged 35.

Calculate the correlation coefficient of x and y from the slopes of the regression lines.

(O)

Table 18.14

x	y	x	y	x	y	x	y
22	23	21	32	23	25	21	25
16	26	19	21	26	29	29	28
25	27	28	23	21	29	23	20
17	26	25	28	20	43	54	58
27	29	25	25	26	28	29	33

Table 18.15

x	25	30	35	40	45	50
y	78	70	65	58	48	42

(2) Calculate the equation of the regression line of y on x for the distribution of Table 18.15.
Is it possible to calculate from the equation you have just found (a) an estimate for the value of x when $y = 54$, (b) an estimate for the value of y when $x = 37$? In each case, if the answer is 'yes', calculate the estimate. If the answer is 'no', say why not.   (SUJB)

(3) The striped ground cricket (*Nemobius fasciatus fasciatus*) is known to change the rate of its chirping as the temperature changes. Table 18.16 shows the rate of chirping (y = chirps per second) and the corresponding temperature ($x = {}^\circ$C) for fifteen such crickets.
Exhibit these data graphically.
Calculate the least squares regression line of y on x showing all your working. Draw the line on your diagram.
Estimate the number of chirps per second from a cricket when the temperature is 30°C.
It is hoped to use the frequency of chirping to determine the temperature. Give reasons why the line you have just drawn is not suitable for this purpose.   (JMB)

(4) Ten boys compete in throwing a cricket ball, and Table 18.17 shows the height of each boy (x cm) to the nearest cm and the distance (y m) to which he can throw the ball.

Table 18.16

x	20.8	21.0	22.0	24.0	24.6	26.5	27.0	27.0	27.8	28.1	28.5	28.6	29.0	31.5	34.0
y	15.4	14.7	16.0	15.5	14.4	15.0	16.0	17.1	17.1	17.2	16.2	17.0	18.4	20.0	19.8

Table 18.17

Boy	A	B	C	D	E	F	G	H	I	J
x	122	124	133	138	144	156	158	161	164	168
y	41	38	52	56	29	54	59	61	63	67

Find the equations of the regression lines of y on x, and of x on y. No diagram is needed. Calculate also the coefficient of correlation.

Estimate the distance to which a cricket ball can be thrown by a boy 150 cm in height.

(AEB)

Summary

Regression line of Y on X, $y = \alpha + \beta x$

Model: $y_i = \alpha + \beta x_i + e_i$ where e_i is $N(0, \sigma^2_{y|x})$

$\hat{b}$ (least square estimate of β) $= \dfrac{n \sum\limits_{i=1}^{n} x_i y_i - \sum\limits_{i=1}^{n} x_i \sum\limits_{i=1}^{n} y_i}{n \sum\limits_{i=1}^{n} x_i^2 - \left(\sum\limits_{i=1}^{n} x_i \right)^2}$

$\hat{a}$ (least squares estimate of a) $= \bar{y} - \hat{b}\bar{x}$

$\hat{s}_{y|x}$ (unbiased estimate of $\sigma_{y|x}$) $= \sqrt{ \left\{ \dfrac{\sum\limits_{i=1}^{n} (y_i' - y_i)^2}{n-2} \right\} }$

where $y_i' - y_i$ (the residuals) $= \hat{a} + \hat{b}x_i - y_i$

Regression line of X on Y, $x = \alpha' + \beta' y$

$\hat{b}'$ (least squares estimate of β') $= \dfrac{n \sum\limits_{i=1}^{n} x_i y_i - \sum\limits_{i=1}^{n} x_i \sum\limits_{i=1}^{n} y_i}{n \sum\limits_{i=1}^{n} y_i^2 - \left(\sum\limits_{i=1}^{n} y_i \right)^2}$

$\hat{a}'$ (least square estimate of α') $= \bar{x} - \hat{b}'\bar{y}$

$\hat{b}\hat{b}' = r^2$

Projects

(1)   *Relationship between foot length and height*

For the data of Chapter 17, Project (1), calculate (a) the regression line for predicting height from foot length, and (b) the regression line for predicting foot length from height.

(2)   *Advanced Level Statistics Software*

The section on *Regression* contains a number of programs related to the work of this chapter:
(a)   The two different regression models (described in Sections 18.1 and 18.9) are illustrated by simulations involving a large amount of data.
(b)   The method of least squares is demonstrated in an interactive fashion. The regression line is shown together with the residuals and the line can be moved until the sum of the squares of the residuals is minimised.
(c)   Users can input their own data. This is displayed graphically, together with one or both regression lines and the values of the slope(s) and intercept(s) and their associated standard deviations.

Exercise on Chapter 18

(1)   Define the regression line of a variable y on x.
A white and a red six-sided die are tossed and the total score y observed. If x is the score obtained with the red die, find the equation of the lines of regression of y on x and of x on y. Comment on your results.   (O)

(2)   The state of Tempora demands that every household in the country shall have a reliable clock. Inspectors are being introduced throughout the country to implement the policy. The Chief Inspector has the data of Table 18.18 on the population size of towns, where Inspection Units have been set up, and the number of man-hours spent on inspection.
(a)   Calculate the regression line for predicting the number of man-hours from the population size (note that the mean value of each variate is a whole number).
(b)   Predict the manpower required (in man-hours) for a new Inspection Unit to be installed in a town with a population of 17000.   (O)

Table 18.18

Population (thousands)	3	4	5	9	13	15	18	20	21	22
Man-hours (thousands)	8	11	13	18	24	26	31	32	34	33

(3)   The results in Table 18.19 show the yield y, in grams, from a chemical experiment corresponding to an input of x grams of a certain substance to the process.

Table 18.19

Input x (g)	5.6	6.3	8.5	4.2	7.4	5.1	9.6	4.8	6.9	5.9
Yield y (g)	82	78	86	65	91	80	95	72	89	74

It is decided to fit a model of the form
$$y = a + b \log_{10} x$$
(a)   Verify that this is a reasonable course to take *either* by plotting y against x on log paper *or* by plotting y against $\log_{10} x$ on ordinary graph paper.
(b)   Calculate the equation of the regression line of y on $\log_{10} x$.
(c)   Draw this line on your graph.   (AEB)

(4)   A survey of the pocket money received by children in a primary school was made by choosing at random four children of each of the ages 5, 7, 9 and 11 years. The amounts of pocket money received are given in Table 18.20.
Plot these data on a scatter diagram. Plot also the mean pocket money for each age. Find the regression equation for predicting pocket money from age, and draw it on your diagram.   (O)

Table 18.20

Age (years)	Pocket money (p)
5	2, 8, 10, 12
7	9, 13, 14, 16
9	9, 14, 16, 21
11	18, 19, 23, 36

(5)   The data in Table 18.21 give the number of beds and the weekly running costs per patient of ten hospitals. Calculate a linear regression equation and use it to find which hospital appears to be the most expensive and which the cheapest.
Note that the means of each variable are whole numbers.   (O)

(6)   Explain briefly how the principle of least squares is used to find a regression line based on a sample of size n. Illustrate on a rough sketch the distances whose squares are minimised taking care to distinguish the dependent and independent variates.
Table 18.22 shows the yields (y) obtained in an agricultural experiment in tonnes per hectare after using x tonnes of fertiliser per hectare.
(a)   Find the means of x and y.
(b)   Plot the measurements and their means on a graph of yield (y) against fertiliser (x).
(c)   Calculate the regression line of y on x in the form $y = a + bx$.

Table 18.21

Hospital	Number of beds	Cost per patient (£)
A	800	40
B	300	47
C	220	52
D	750	38
E	600	43
F	190	53
G	1100	39
H	400	44
I	240	50
J	400	44

Table 18.22

Fertiliser (x)	0	0.2	0.4	0.6
Yield (y)	1.26	1.47	1.87	2.00

(d) Draw the regression line you have calculated on the graph.

(e) Estimate the total yield in tonnes from a 2.2 hectare field if 0.5 tonne of fertiliser is used altogether.   (O & C)

(7) Table 18.23 gives the values, for twenty families, of family size (x) and monthly expenditure (£) on rent (y). Calculate the linear regression equation of y on x, and use it to estimate the mean expenditure of families of size 4. Would you prefer to use this estimate or the mean of the data for $x=4$?

(O)

Table 18.23

x	y	x	y	x	y	x	y	x	y
1	6	2	5	3	10	4	9	5	10
1	6	2	7	3	10	4	11	5	15
1	8	2	7	3	14	4	13	5	18
1	8	2	9	3	18	4	19	5	21

(8) In an experiment a man is asked to read letters in a weak light. The light intensity (x) and the percentage of correct readings of letters (y) were measured and n pairs (x_i, y_i)

obtained. Since the point $(0, 0)$ must lie on the line relating y to x, the equation of the line of best fit is of the form $y = bx$. Obtain an expression for b by minimising the residual sum of squares,

$$\sum_{i=1}^{n} (y_i - bx_i)^2$$

Evaluate b for the data in Table 18.24 for which $\Sigma y = 364$, $\Sigma xy = 1844$, $\Sigma y^2 = 24\,500$. With this value for b evaluate the residual sum of squares. Plot the data, the line $y = bx$ and the point $(\bar{x}, \bar{y})$ on a suitable diagram. (C)

Table 18.24

x	0	1	2	3	4	5	6	7
y	0	10	28	31	57	69	71	98

(9) Find the 95% confidence limits for the values of $\hat{a}$ and $\hat{b}$ calculated in question (6). Find also the 95% confidence limits for the value of y estimated in (6) (e).

19 Sampling distribution of $\hat{S}^2$, F-test, analysis of variance

The sampling distribution of $\hat{S}^2$ for a Normal population

In Chapter 13 we discussed sampling distributions, in particular the sampling distribution of the mean. The unbiased estimate of variance calculated from a sample also has a sampling distribution since different samples from the same population will give different estimates of the variance of that population. The sampling distribution of the unbiased estimator of variance, $\hat{S}^2$, is related to the χ^2-distribution. From equation (13.4.4) we have

$$\hat{S}^2 = \frac{\sum\limits_{i=1}^{n} (X_i - \bar{X})^2}{n-1}$$

Rearranging and dividing both sides of the equation by σ^2 gives

$$(n-1)\frac{\hat{S}^2}{\sigma^2} = \frac{\sum\limits_{i=1}^{n} (X_i - \bar{X})^2}{\sigma^2}$$

$$= \sum\limits_{i=1}^{n} \left(\frac{X_i - \bar{X}}{\sigma}\right)^2$$

On the right-hand side we have the summation of terms of the type $((X_i - \bar{X})/\sigma)^2$. But $(X_i - \bar{X})/\sigma$ is $N(0, 1)$ and so $(n-1)\hat{S}^2/\sigma^2$ is the sum of the squares of independent standardised Normal deviates and therefore has a χ^2-distribution (see Section 16.10). It has $n-1$ degrees of freedom, rather than n, because $\bar{X}$ is used and not μ. Using this distribution, confidence limits for σ^2 can be found and significance tests performed in a way analogous to that for the mean.

*19.2 **Confidence limits for σ^2**

19.2.1 *Example*

The following lengths were measured for a random sample of ten rods from a large box.

10.1 cm, 9.9 cm, 9.5 cm, 10.3 cm, 9.8 cm, 9.9 cm, 10.1 cm, 10.0 cm, 10.5 cm, 10.2 cm

Find the 95% confidence limits for the s.d. of the length of the rods in the box.

We first calculate $\hat{s}^2$ (see Table 19.1).

    A, arbitrary origin = 10.0

    B, unit = 0.1

Table 19.1

x_i	f_i	u_i	f_iu_i	$f_iu_i^2$
9.5	1	-5	-5	25
9.8	1	-2	-2	4
9.9	2	-1	-2	2
10.0	1	0	0	0
10.1	2	1	2	2
10.2	1	2	2	4
10.3	1	3	3	9
10.5	1	5	5	25
	$\overline{10}$		$\overline{3}$	$\overline{71}$

$$\hat{s}^2 = B^2\left[\frac{\sum\limits_{i=1}^{n} f_iu_i^2}{\sum\limits_{i=1}^{n} f_i} - \left(\frac{\sum\limits_{i=1}^{n} f_iu_i}{\sum\limits_{i=1}^{n} f_i}\right)^2\right]\left(\frac{n}{n-1}\right) \qquad \text{(using equations (3.9.1) and (13.4.5))}$$

$$= 0.1^2\left[\tfrac{71}{10} - (\tfrac{3}{10})^2\right] \times \tfrac{10}{9}$$

$$= 0.078$$

$$\hat{s} = 0.28$$

There are nine degrees of freedom so $(n-1)\hat{S}^2/\sigma^2$ has a χ_9^2-distribution. Thus the 95% confidence limits of $(n-1)\hat{s}^2/\sigma^2$ are

$$\chi_{(9,97.5\%)}^2 < (n-1)\hat{s}^2/\sigma^2 < \chi_{(9,2.5\%)}^2$$

Substituting and obtaining the appropriate values of χ^2 from Table A6,

$$2.7 < \frac{9 \times 0.078}{\sigma^2} < 19.02$$

Rearranging

$$\frac{9 \times 0.078}{2.7} > \sigma^2 > \frac{9 \times 0.078}{19.02}$$

$$0.26 > \sigma^2 > 0.0369$$

$$0.51 > \sigma > 0.19$$

In general, $\alpha\%$ confidence limits of σ^2 are given by

$$\chi_{n-1,(100+\alpha)/2}^2 < (n-1)\hat{s}^2/\sigma^2 < \chi_{n-1,(100-\alpha)/2}^2$$

or, rearranging,

$$\frac{(n-1)\hat{s}^2}{\chi_{n-1,(100-\alpha)/2}^2} < \sigma^2 < \frac{(n-1)\hat{s}^2}{\chi_{n-1,(100+\alpha)/2}^2} \qquad (19.2.1)$$

19.2.2 Exercise

Find the 95% confidence limits for the population s.d. which was estimated in Example 13.4.1.

*19.3   Significance test for $\hat{s}^2$

19.3.1   Example

A machine is designed to produce rods with a mean length of 10.0 cm and a s.d. of 0.2 cm. A sample of twenty rods has a s.d. of 0.3 cm. Does this indicate that the machine has become more variable?

$$H_0 : \sigma = 0.2 \qquad H_1 : \sigma > 0.2 \qquad \text{One-tail test}$$

We have $s = 0.3$

therefore $\hat{s} = 0.3\sqrt{\frac{20}{19}}$

$$(n-1)\frac{\hat{s}^2}{\sigma^2} = \frac{19 \times 0.3^2}{0.2^2} \times \frac{20}{19} = 45$$

Now $(n-1)\hat{S}^2/\sigma^2$ has a χ^2_{19}-distribution. Since this is a one-tail test, $\chi^2_{19,5\%} = 30.14$ is the critical value. Thus $(n-1)\hat{s}^2/\sigma^2$ is significant at the 5% level and the null hypothesis is rejected: the machine has become more variable.

*19.4   The F-test

In Example 15.6.1 we assumed that the two samples came from the same population, and combined them to obtain an estimate of the s.d. of that population. The F-test is designed to test the hypothesis that the variances calculated from two samples are estimates of the same population variance. It is valid when the samples are independent and the populations from which they are drawn are Normal.

Suppose we have a sample of n_1 with s.d. s_1 and unbiased estimate of variance, $\hat{s}_1^2$, and a second sample of n_2 with s.d. s_2 and unbiased estimate of variance, $\hat{s}_2^2$. If $\hat{s}_1^2$ and $\hat{s}_2^2$ are both estimates of the same population variance we expect the ratio $\hat{s}_1^2/\hat{s}_2^2$ to be close to one. This ratio is called F and its sampling distribution depends on the degrees of freedom of both $\hat{s}_1$ and $\hat{s}_2$, i.e. on $v_1 = n_1 - 1$ and $v_2 = n_2 - 1$. The 5% and $2\frac{1}{2}\%$ points of the **F-distribution** are given in Tables A7 and A8. These tables give only the upper percentage points of the F-distribution since F is calculated so that it is greater than one. For a one-tail test we have $H_0: \sigma^2 = \sigma_1^2 = \sigma_2^2$ and $H_1: \sigma_1^2 > \sigma_2^2$, and for an $\alpha\%$ level of significance, the critical value of F is taken from the $\alpha\%$ table; for example, for $v_1 = 6$, $v_2 = 4$, 5% significance level, the critical value of F is 6.16. For a two-tail test we have $H_0: \sigma^2 = \sigma_1^2 = \sigma_2^2$ and $H_1: \sigma_1^2 \neq \sigma_2^2$, and for an $\alpha\%$ level of significance, the critical value of F is taken from the $\frac{1}{2}\alpha\%$ table; for example, for $v_1 = 6$, $v_2 = 4$, 5% significance level, F is 9.20.

19.4.1   Example

Test whether the assumption made in Example 15.6.1, that both samples came from populations with the same variance, was valid.

We have

$$H_0: \sigma^2 = \sigma_1^2 = \sigma_2^2 \quad H_1: \sigma_1^2 \neq \sigma_2^2$$
$$n_1 = 20 \qquad n_2 = 15$$
$$s_1 = 10 \qquad s_2 = 8$$

giving

$$\hat{s}_1 = 10\sqrt{\tfrac{20}{19}} \qquad \hat{s}_2 = 8\sqrt{\tfrac{15}{14}}$$
$$F_{19,14} = \hat{s}_1^2/\hat{s}_2^2 = 10^2 \times \tfrac{20}{19}/8^2 \times \tfrac{15}{14} = 1.54$$

From the $2\tfrac{1}{2}\%$ table, with $v_1 = 19$, $v_2 = 14$, the critical value of F is about 2.9. Thus $\hat{s}_1^2/\hat{s}_2^2$ is not significant at the 5% level. We retain the null hypothesis: the assumption made was valid.

19.4.2   Exercise

(1)   Under the direction of an agricultural research foundation in Holland a study of the length of tulip stems was undertaken. In this particular experiment two varieties of tulip were selected and a random sample was taken from each. Stem lengths were measured in centimetres. The results were as in Table 19.2.

Assuming that both samples came from underlying Normal populations, test, at the 5% level of significance, the hypothesis, that there is no difference in the variability of the two samples. What further tests might be completed on these data?   (AEB)

Table 19.2

Variety 1	35.8	34.5	37.1	37.5	32.5	34.0	33.0
(Keizerskroon)	39.0	37.7	38.4	36.6	35.4	36.7	
Variety 2	34.3	38.8	38.5	36.4	31.9	30.0	36.9
(Schoonoord)	40.0	36.6	33.1	36.1	35.0		

(2)   An explorer measured the lengths of the feet of ten adult males of tribe A with the following results: 9.4, 10.8, 10.9, 9.0, 10.0, 11.1, 10.5, 9.5, 9.7, 9.8 inches.

He also measured the lengths of the feet of twelve men of tribe B, obtaining: 8.4, 8.8, 10.0, 10.3, 9.3, 8.4, 9.0, 8.5, 8.5, 9.1, 8.3, 8.6 inches.

Is there evidence of a real difference between the distributions of lengths of feet in the two tribes?   (AEB)

*19.5   One-way analysis of variance

Table 19.3 shows the results obtained when each of three experimentalists measured a variate four times.

There are two possible reasons for the different mean values obtained by A, B and C.

Firstly, there is the random variation in any measurement which leads to a different result each time the measurement is made. Secondly, there may be a true difference between the measurements made by A, B and C; that is their measurements are random samples from different populations. How can we test whether or not the samples are drawn from the same or different populations? We will generalise the problem to consider h samples each

Table 19.3 *Results obtained when each of three people measure a variate four times* (mean of all values $= 13$)

Person A	14	15	13	14	Mean for $A = 14$
Person B	13	12	16	11	Mean for $B = 13$
Person C	10	11	14	13	Mean for $C = 12$

Table 19.4 *Generalisation of Table 19.3*

x_{11}	x_{12}	$\cdots$	x_{1j}	$\cdots$	x_{1n}	$\bar{x}_1$
x_{21}	x_{22}	$\cdots$	x_{2j}	$\cdots$	x_{2n}	$\bar{x}_2$
$\vdots$	$\vdots$		$\vdots$		$\vdots$	$\vdots$
x_{i1}	x_{i2}	$\cdots$	x_{ij}	$\cdots$	x_{in}	$\bar{x}_i$	means of samples
$\vdots$	$\vdots$		$\vdots$		$\vdots$	$\vdots$
x_{h1}	x_{h2}	$\cdots$	x_{hj}	$\cdots$	x_{hn}	$\bar{x}_h$
					$\bar{x}$	mean of all values

with n members as shown in Table 19.4 where x_{ij} is the jth measurement of the ith sample. The means of the samples are $\bar{x}_1, \bar{x}_2, \ldots, \bar{x}_h$ and the mean of all the values grouped together is $\bar{x}$. If the samples all come from the same population we have

$$H_0: \mu_1 = \mu_2 = \cdots = \mu_h \qquad \sigma_1^2 = \sigma_2^2 = \cdots = \sigma_h^2$$

Estimates of variance can be made in various ways:

(i)   Within-class variation

For each sample a variance can be calculated. This involves the calculation for each sample of $\sum_{j=1}^{n} (x_{ij} - \bar{x}_i)^2$ and we have

$$E\left[\sum_{j=1}^{n} (X_{ij} - \bar{X}_i)^2\right] = (n-1)\sigma^2 \qquad \text{(from equation (13.4.3))}$$

Summing over all h samples we have

$$E\left[\sum_{i=1}^{h} \sum_{j=1}^{n} (X_{ij} - \bar{X}_i)^2\right] = h(n-1)\sigma^2$$

This gives a 'within-sample' estimate of variance of

$$\sum_{i=1}^{h} \sum_{j=1}^{n} \frac{(x_{ij} - \bar{x}_i)^2}{h(n-1)}$$

with $h(n-1)$ degrees of freedom.

For the data in Table 19.3 we have

$$\text{Person } A \qquad \sum_{j=1}^{4} (x_{1j} - \bar{x}_1)^2 = (14-14)^2 + (15-14)^2 + (13-14)^2 + (14-14)^2 = 2$$

Person B $\qquad \sum_{j=1}^{4} (x_{2j} - \bar{x}_2)^2 = (13-13)^2 + (12-13)^2 + (16-13)^2 + (11-13)^2 = 14$

Person C $\qquad \sum_{j=1}^{4} (x_{3j} - \bar{x}_3)^2 = (10-12)^2 + (11-12)^2 + (14-12)^2 + (13-12)^2 = 10$

and so

$$\sum_i \sum_j (x_{ij} - \bar{x}_i)^2 = 2 + 14 + 10 = 26$$

and the estimate of σ^2 is

$$\frac{26}{3(4-1)} = 2.9$$

with 9 degrees of freedom. Notice that this estimate does not depend on the mean for any individual: had, for example, all of A's measurements been increased by say, 5, this estimate of the variance would be unaltered. However, had the variability of A, B and C's measurements increased, so would this estimate of that variance.

(ii) Between-class variation

This is estimated by calculating the variance of the means. The theoretical variance of the mean of a sample size n is σ^2/n (see Theorem 13.3.1) so that, using equation (13.4.3),

$$E\left[\frac{\sum_{i=1}^{h}(\bar{X}_i - \bar{X})^2}{h-1}\right] = \frac{\sigma^2}{n}$$

Rearranging,

$$E\left[n \sum_{i=1}^{h}(\bar{X}_i - \bar{X})^2\right] = (h-1)\sigma^2$$

giving a 'between-sample' estimate of variance of

$$\frac{n}{h-1} \sum_{i=1}^{h} (\bar{x}_i - \bar{x})^2$$

with $h-1$ degrees of freedom.

For the data in Table 19.3:

$$n \sum_{i=1}^{h} (\bar{x}_i - \bar{x})^2 = 4[(14-13)^2 + (13-13)^2 + (12-13)^2] = 8$$

and the estimate of variance is

$$\frac{8}{3-1} = 4$$

with 2 degrees of freedom.

This estimate does not depend on the 'within-sample' variability because it is calculated using the means of the samples. However, if one of these means is altered so is this estimate of variance. In particular, as the difference between the means increases so does the 'between-class' estimate of variance.

In this particular example the 'between-class' estimate of variance, 4, is greater than the 'within-class' estimate, 2.9. To test whether it is significantly greater we use the F-test:

$$F_{2,9} = \frac{4}{2.9} = 1.4$$

The critical value of $F_{2,9}$ for a 5% one-tail test is 4.26. The value obtained is not significant at the 5% level: there is no evidence of difference between the means of the measurements made by different laboratory assistants.

There is a third way in which the variance could be calculated, where the data are treated as one large sample. This estimate of variance involves the calculation of $\sum_{i=1}^{h} \sum_{j=1}^{n} (x_{ij} - \bar{x})^2$ which measures the 'total variation'. Using equation (13.4.3)

$$E\left[\sum_{i=1}^{h} \sum_{j=1}^{n} (X_{ij} - \bar{X})^2 \right] = (nh - 1)\sigma^2$$

The reader may verify that for the data in Table 19.3 $\sum_{i=1}^{h} \sum_{j=1}^{n} (x_{ij} - \bar{x})^2 = 34$. This value is the sum of the 'within-class' sum of squares, 26, and the 'between- class' sum of squares, 8, a general result which may be proved as follows.

Using the identity

$$x_{ij} - \bar{x} = (x_{ij} - \bar{x}_i) + (\bar{x}_i - \bar{x})$$

we have on squaring and summing over i and j

$$\sum_{i=1}^{h} \sum_{j=1}^{n} (x_{ij} - \bar{x})^2 = \sum_{i=1}^{h} \sum_{j=1}^{n} (x_{ij} - \bar{x}_i)^2 + \sum_{i=1}^{h} \sum_{j=1}^{n} (\bar{x}_i - \bar{x})^2 + 2 \sum_{i=1}^{h} \sum_{j=1}^{n} (x_{ij} - \bar{x}_i)(\bar{x}_i - \bar{x})$$

Now

$$\sum_{j=1}^{n} (x_{ij} - \bar{x}_i) = 0 \qquad \text{for each } i$$

and

$$\sum_{i=1}^{h} \sum_{j=1}^{n} (\bar{x}_i - \bar{x})^2 = n \sum_{i=1}^{h} (\bar{x}_i - \bar{x})^2$$

giving

$$\sum_{i=1}^{h} \sum_{j=1}^{n} (x_{ij} - \bar{x})^2 = \sum_{i=1}^{h} \sum_{j=1}^{n} (x_{ij} - \bar{x}_i)^2 + n \sum_{i=1}^{h} (\bar{x}_i - \bar{x})^2 \qquad (19.5.1)$$

The results obtained are summarised in Table 19.5 where we note the important result that values in the last row are the sums of the values in the first two rows both for the 'sums of squares' and the degrees of freedom. Although the total variation is not of use in analysing

Table 19.5 *Summary of one-way analysis of variance*

Source of variation	Sum of squares	Degrees of freedom	Estimate of variance
Between samples	$n\sum_{i=1}^{h} (\bar{x}_i - \bar{x})^2$	$h-1$	$n \sum_{i=1}^{h} \dfrac{(\bar{x}_i - \bar{x})^2}{(h-1)}$
Within samples	$\sum_{i=1}^{h} \sum_{j=1}^{n} (x_{ij} - \bar{x}_i)^2$	$h(n-1)$	$\sum_{i=1}^{h} \sum_{j=1}^{n} \dfrac{(x_{ij} - \bar{x}_i)^2}{h(n-1)}$
Total	$\sum_{i=1}^{h} \sum_{j=1}^{n} (x_{ij} - \bar{x})^2$	$hn - 1$	

the results, because it depends both on 'within-class' and 'between-class' variation, it can be used to simplify calculation as we will see in the next section.

*19.6   Aids to calculation

Just as in the calculation of variance, there are identities which can be used to simplify the calculation of the sums of squares. The total sum of squares may be calculated using the identity

$$\sum_{i=1}^{h}\sum_{j=1}^{n}(x_{ij}-\bar{x})^2 = \sum_{i=1}^{h}\sum_{j=1}^{n}x_{ij}^2 - \frac{T^2}{N} \qquad \text{(see Section 3.7) (19.6.1)}$$

where T, the grand total, is given by

$$T = \sum_{i=1}^{h}\sum_{j=1}^{n}x_{ij}$$

and $N=nh$, the total number of measurements. The 'within-sample' sum of squares is given by

$$\sum_{i=1}^{h}\sum_{j=1}^{n}(x_{ij}-\bar{x}_i)^2 = \sum_{i=1}^{h}\left(\sum_{j=1}^{n}x_{ij}^2 - \frac{T_i^2}{n}\right)$$

$$= \sum_{i=1}^{h}\sum_{j=1}^{n}x_{ij}^2 - \sum_{i=1}^{h}\frac{T_i^2}{n} \qquad (19.6.2)$$

where T_i is the total of the ith class. With these two sums of squares calculated, the 'between-sample' sum of squares can be found by subtraction.

19.6.1   *Example*

The yields of tomato plants grown using different types of fertiliser are given in Table 19.6. Is there evidence that the fertilisers produce different yields?

Our null hypothesis is that samples are drawn from the same population. The calculation can be simplified by subtracting a constant from all values and by using a unit. (Since we finally take a *ratio* of variances the unit will not alter the value of F obtained). Taking 4 from each value in the table and using a unit of 0.1 gives Table 19.7.
Now $n=5$, $h=3$, $N=15$

$$\sum_{i=1}^{h}\sum_{j=1}^{n}x_{ij}^2 = 447$$

Table 19.6

	Yield (kg)				
Fertiliser X	3.5	4.0	3.8	4.1	4.4
Fertiliser Y	4.7	5.0	4.5	5.3	4.6
Fertiliser Z	3.6	3.9	4.2	4.1	4.0

Table 19.7

						T_i	T_i^2
Fertiliser X	-5	0	-2	$+1$	$+4$	-2	4
Fertiliser Y	$+7$	$+10$	$+5$	$+13$	$+6$	41	1681
Fertiliser Z	-4	-1	$+2$	$+1$	$+0$	-2	4
						$T=37$	$\sum\limits_i T_i^2 = 1689$

Table 19.8

Source of variation	Sum of squares	d.f.	Estimate of σ^2	F
Between samples	246.5	2	$246.5 \div 2 = 123$	$F_{2,12} = \frac{123}{9.1}$
Within samples	109.2	12	$109.2 \div 12 = 9.1$	$= 13.5$
Total	355.7	14		

From equation (19.6.1),

$$\sum_{i=1}^{h} \sum_{j=1}^{n} (x_{ij} - \bar{x})^2 = 447 - \frac{37^2}{15} = 355.7$$

From equation (19.6.2),

$$\sum_{i=1}^{h} \sum_{j=1}^{n} (x_{ij} - \bar{x}_i)^2 = 447 - \frac{1689}{5} = 109.2$$

and by subtraction

$$n \sum_{i=1}^{h} (\bar{x}_i - \bar{x})^2 = 355.7 - 109.2 = 246.5$$

Table 19.8 summarises these calculations.

The critical value of $F_{2,12}$ for a 5% one-tail test is 3.89. The value obtained is significant at the 5% level. The null hypothesis is rejected and there is evidence that the fertilisers produce different mean yields.

The assumptions made when the F-test is carried out in a one-way analysis of variance are:

(i) each sample comes from a Normal population,

(ii) the samples come from populations with equal variance even if the means of the populations differ.

The second assumption is made in the null hypothesis and is the basis for the calculation of a pooled 'within-sample' estimate of variance.

19.6.2   Exercise

(1) Three samples, each consisting of six blocks of wood, are taken: a different drying technique is used on each sample and the percentages of water remaining are measured.

Table 19.9

Technique	x	Σx	Σx^2
1	1.0, 1.1, 1.4, 1.2, 1.5, 1.3	7.5	9.55
2	0.8, 0.6, 1.0, 1.1, 0.9, 1.3	5.7	5.71
3	0.6, 0.4, 0.8, 0.9, 0.5, 0.6	3.8	2.58

The amounts (x) by which these percentages exceed the optimum percentage are given in Table 19.9.

State the assumptions you would need to make in order to carry out an analysis of variance on these data. What does this analysis test? Carry out the overall analysis of variance and also compare technique 1 with technique 2.   (C)

Table 19.10

	x	Σx	$(\Sigma x)^2$	Σx^2
98 °C	5.3, 5.5, 5.9, 6.5	23.2	538.24	135.40
94 °C	5.0, 5.5, 6.0, 6.3,	22.8	519.84	130.94
90 °C	4.2, 4.8, 5.0, 5.6	19.6	384.16	97.04
86 °C	5.5, 4.1, 4.6, 4.2	18.4	338.56	85.86
82 °C	3.9, 5.0, 5.3, 4.8	19.0	361.00	91.34

(2) In dyeing cloth the temperature of the dying vat may affect the amount by which the cloth shrinks during the process. Table 19.10 shows the observations of the percentage shrinkage (x) from twenty pieces of cloth dyed at five different temperatures.

State the assumptions about x which should be satisfied if an F-test is to be used.

(a) Perform an F-test to determine whether the mean shrinkage for different temperatures differs significantly.

(b) It has been suggested that there is a difference in the shrinkage of cloth according to whether the temperature of the vat is above or below 92° C. Investigate whether the data support this theory.   (C)

19.7   Two-way analysis of variance

Suppose that the experimentalists who had obtained the results in Table 19.3 had performed each of their measurements using a different method as indicated in Table 19.11.

There are now three possible sources of variation:

(i)   random variation,
(ii) variation between methods,
(iii) variation between people.

Table 19.11 *Measurements by different people using different methods*

	Method I	Method II	Method III	Method IV	
Person A	14	15	13	14	Mean for $A = 14$
Person B	13	12	16	11	Mean for $B = 13$
Person C	10	11	14	13	Mean for $C = 12$

Mean for I $= 12\frac{1}{3}$, mean for II $= 12\frac{2}{3}$, mean for III $= 14\frac{1}{3}$, mean for IV $= 12\frac{2}{3}$

Table 19.12 *Generalisation of Table 19.11*

x_{11}	x_{12}	$\cdots$	x_{1j}	$\cdots$	x_{1k}	$\bar{x}_{1\cdot}$
x_{21}	x_{22}	$\cdots$	x_{2j}	$\cdots$	x_{2k}	$\bar{x}_{2\cdot}$
$\vdots$	$\vdots$		$\vdots$		$\vdots$	
x_{i1}	x_{i2}	$\cdots$	x_{ij}	$\cdots$	x_{ik}	$\bar{x}_{i\cdot}$
$\vdots$	$\vdots$		$\vdots$		$\vdots$	
x_{h1}	x_{h2}	$\cdots$	x_{hj}	$\cdots$	x_{hk}	$\bar{x}_{h\cdot}$
$\bar{x}_{\cdot 1}$	$\bar{x}_{\cdot 2}$	$\cdots$	$\bar{x}_{\cdot j}$	$\cdots$	$\bar{x}_{\cdot k}$	$\bar{x}$

As in one-way analysis of variance the total variation measured by $\sum_i \sum_j (x_{ij} - \bar{x})^2$ can be split up, this time into three parts corresponding to the three possible sources of variation. Let the data be classified into h rows and k columns as shown in Table 19.12. $\bar{x}_{i\cdot}$ is the mean of the ith row, $\bar{x}_{\cdot j}$ is the mean of the jth column and $\bar{x}$ is the overall mean. On the null hypothesis that all the measurements come from the same population, variance σ^2, the $\bar{x}_{i\cdot}$'s have variance σ^2/k and

$$E\left[\sum_{i=1}^{h} (\bar{X}_{i\cdot} - \bar{X})^2 \right] = (h-1)\sigma^2/k$$

as before. The $\bar{x}_{\cdot j}$'s have variance σ^2/h and

$$E\left[\sum_{j=1}^{k} (\bar{X}_{\cdot j} - \bar{X})^2 \right] = (k-1)\sigma^2/h$$

Table 19.13 *Summary of two-way analysis of variance*

Source of variation	Sum of squares	Degrees of freedom
Between rows	$k \sum_i (\bar{x}_{i\cdot} - \bar{x})^2$	$h-1$
Between columns	$h \sum_j (\bar{x}_{\cdot j} - \bar{x})^2$	$k-1$
Residual	by subtraction	by subtraction
Total	$\sum_i \sum_j (x_{ij} - \bar{x})^2$	$hk-1$

As before the total variation is $\sum_{i=1}^{h} \sum_{j=1}^{k} (x_{ij} - \bar{x})^2$. The **residual variation** which measures the random variation of the measurements can be found by subtraction, as can its degrees of freedom. These results are summarised in Table 19.13. An F-test can be performed either to test for variation between rows by comparing the 'between-rows' and 'residual' estimates of variance or to test for variation between columns by comparing the 'between-columns' and 'residual' estimates of variance. The test assumes that the row and column effects, if any, are additive.

19.7.1 *Example*

Perform a two-way analysis of variance for the data in Table 19.11.

As in Section 19.6, the calculation can be simplified by subtracting a constant from all values. Subtracting 13 from all values in Table 19.11 gives Table 19.14. (Again a unit can be used if convenient.) The sums of squares can be calculated using the following identities (see Section 3.7).

$$\sum_{i=1}^{h} \sum_{j=1}^{k} (x_{ij} - \bar{x})^2 = \sum_{i=1}^{h} \sum_{j=1}^{k} x_{ij}^2 - N\bar{x}^2 \quad \text{(where } N = hk)$$

$$= \sum_{i=1}^{h} \sum_{j=1}^{k} x_{ij}^2 - T^2/N \quad \left(\text{where } T = \sum_{i=1}^{h} \sum_{j=1}^{k} x_{ij} \right) \tag{19.7.1}$$

$$k \sum_{i=1}^{h} (\bar{x}_{i.} - \bar{x})^2 = k \sum_{i=1}^{h} \bar{x}_{i.}^2 - kh\bar{x}^2$$

$$= \frac{1}{k} \sum_{i=1}^{h} T_{i.}^2 - \frac{T^2}{N} \tag{19.7.2}$$

(since $\bar{x}_{i.} = T_{i.}/k$ and $\bar{x} = T/N$).
Similarly

$$h \sum_{j=1}^{k} (\bar{x}_{.j} - \bar{x})^2 = \frac{1}{h} \sum_{j=1}^{k} T_{.j}^2 - \frac{T^2}{N} \tag{19.7.3}$$

From Table 19.14, $\sum_{i=1}^{h} \sum_{j=1}^{k} x_{ij}^2 = 34$, $T = 0$, $N = 12$, $h = 3$, $k = 4$, $\sum_{i=1}^{h} T_{i.}^2 = 32$ and $\sum_{j=1}^{k} T_{.j}^2 = 22$.

Table 19.14

	Method I	Method II	Method III	Method IV	Row totals $T_{i.}$
Person A	$+1$	$+2$	0	$+1$	4
Person B	0	-1	$+3$	-2	0
Person C	-3	-2	1	0	-4
Columns total $T_{.j}$	-2	-1	$+4$	-1	$0 =$ grand total T

Using the identities above

$$\sum_i \sum_j (x_{ij} - \bar{x})^2 = 34 - 0/12 = 34$$

$$k \sum_i (\bar{x}_{i\cdot} - \bar{x})^2 = \tfrac{1}{4} \times 32 - 0/12 = 8$$

$$h \sum_j (\bar{x}_{\cdot j} - \bar{x})^2 = \tfrac{1}{3} \times 22 - 0/12 = 7\tfrac{1}{3}$$

Putting the numerical values in Table 19.13 we have Table 19.15, where the residual values have been found by subtraction.

Table 19.15

Source of variation	Sum of squares	Degrees of freedom	Estimate of σ^2
Between people	8	2	$8 \div 2 = 4$
Between methods	$7\tfrac{1}{3}$	3	$7\tfrac{1}{3} \div 3 = 2.44$
Residual	$18\tfrac{2}{3}$	6	$18\tfrac{2}{3} \div 6 = 3.11$
Total	34	11	

Comparing the 'between-people' and 'residual' estimates of variance we have $F_{2,6} = 4/3.11 = 1.29$. The critical value of $F_{2,6}$ for a 5% one-tail test is 5.14. The observed value of F is not significant at the 5% level and there is no evidence of differences between people.

Comparing 'between-methods' and 'residual' estimates of variance we see that the former is the smaller so that there is no evidence of difference between methods.

This chapter gives only an introduction to analysis of variance. For a more-advanced treatment which shows the full power of the method, see *Statistical Methods* by G. Snedecor and W. Cochran.

19.7.2   *Exercise*

(1) Four diets were compared on premature babies with three types of respiratory disease. Table 19.16 gives the increase in mass, in kilograms, for these babies.

Table 19.16

Respiratory disease	Diets 1	2	3	4
A	3.2	3.9	2.7	2.0
B	2.3	3.0	3.9	4.5
C	2.7	3.4	5.7	6.3

Carry out an analysis of variance and test for differences between diets and between diseases. (AEB)

(2) Four kinds of metal finishes a, b, c, d, for outside use, are tested in three different towns A, B, C, by leaving a panel of each kind exposed to the weather for one year. The panels are examined at the end of the year and given a merit score out of 100 for their condition. The results are given in Table 19.17.
Carry out an analysis of variance and test for differences between towns and between finishes.
State your conclusions. (AEB)

Table 19.17

| Metal finish | Town | | |
	A	B	C
a	70	86	66
b	61	72	59
c	29	48	22
d	48	68	46

Summary

$\alpha\%$ confidence interval for variance

$$\frac{(n-1)\hat{s}^2}{\chi^2_{n-1,(100-\alpha)/2}} < \sigma^2 < \frac{(n-1)\hat{s}^2}{\chi^2_{n-1,(100+\alpha)/2}}$$

The F-test for comparing two variances

$$F = \frac{\hat{s}_1^2}{\hat{s}_2^2} \qquad \text{where } \hat{s}_1 > \hat{s}_2$$

One-way analysis of variance

Source of variation	Sum of squares	Degrees of freedom
Between samples	$n\sum_{i=1}^{h} (\bar{x}_i - \bar{x})^2$	$h-1$
Within samples	$\sum_{i=1}^{h}\sum_{j=1}^{n} (x_{ij} - \bar{x}_i)^2$	$h(n-1)$
Total	$\sum_{i=1}^{h}\sum_{j=1}^{n} (x_{ij} - \bar{x})^2$	$hn-1$

Two-way analysis of variance

Source of variation	Sum of squares	Degrees of freedom
Between rows	$k \sum_{i} (\bar{x}_{i \cdot} - \bar{x})^2$	$h - 1$
Between columns	$h \sum_{j} (\bar{x}_{\cdot j} - \bar{x})^2$	$k - 1$
Residual	by subtraction	by subtraction
Total	$\sum_{i} \sum_{j} (x_{ij} - \bar{x})^2$	$hk - 1$

Projects

(1)   *Testing whether two variances differ significantly*

For each project on Chapter 3, find unbiased estimates of the variance for the two populations from which the samples were drawn. Test whether they differ significantly.

(2)   *Advanced Level Statistics Software*

The section on *Sampling distributions and confidence intervals* includes a simulation of the sampling distribution of variance for random samples taken from a Normal distribution of known variance. This can be compared with the chi-squared distribution.

Exercise on Chapter 19

(1)   Three brands of petrol were compared on five makes of car. Table 19.18 gives the kilometres travelled in each case, on a standard amount of petrol under similar conditions.

Table 19.18

Petrol brand	Make of car				
	A	B	C	D	E
1	31.0	33.5	28.0	40.1	34.1
2	29.5	31.4	25.0	30.2	XXX
3	22.7	32.1	26.4	29.8	30.1

Unfortunately the observation intended for 'petrol 2' and 'car E' was found to be grossly in error due to a faulty instrument. No problems were encountered with any of the other observations, but for technical reasons an observation for 'petrol 2' and 'car E' could not be duplicated.

(a) Estimate this missing observation by the arithmetic mean of the other two observations for 'car E'.

(b) Now, assuming that this estimate is the actual observation for that cell, carry out the standard analysis of variance and test, at the 5% level of significance, for differences between makes of car and between brands of petrol.

(c) Comment critically on the above estimation procedure and subsequent analysis.

(AEB)

(2) A contractor wishing to purchase a large quantity of galvanised sheeting obtained quotations and samples from four manufacturers. He measured the thickness of the zinc coating on six pieces of sheeting from each manufacturer, obtaining the following mean thicknesses (measured on a conventional scale):

Manufacturer	A	B	C	D
Mean thickness	17	18	22	19

The individual thicknesses were analysed in the appropriate analysis of variance, giving residual mean square 2.5.

Perform an F-test to determine whether the mean thickness differed significantly between the four manufacturers.

(C)

(3) In an examination in mathematics, twenty students at Greyfriars School had a mean mark of 52, and the sum of squares of deviations from this mark was 1312.

At Dotheboys Hall, seventeen boys sat for the same examination, obtaining a mean mark of 36, and the sum of squares of deviations from this mean was 1401. Use the F-test to test the hypothesis that the two samples are drawn from populations having the same variance.

Use a two-sample t-test to find whether there is a significant difference in mathematical ability between the two schools.

Calculate 95% confidence limits for the mean mark of the population, supposed Normal, from which the marks of the twenty students at Greyfriars were drawn.

(AEB)

Table 19.19

Lengths of cuckoos' eggs from hedge-sparrow nests (mm)	22.0, 23.9, 20.9, 23.8, 25.0, 24.0, 21.7, 22.8, 23.1, 23.5, 23.0
Lengths of cuckoos' eggs from reed-warbler nests (mm)	23.2, 22.0, 22.2, 21.2, 21.6, 21.9, 22.9, 22.8.

(4) Table 19.19 gives the lengths, in millimetres, of cuckoos' eggs. The eggs for the first sample were taken from the nests of hedge-sparrows and the eggs for the second sample were taken from the nests of reed-warblers.

Use the F-test at the 5% level of significance to test the hypothesis that the two samples were drawn from populations having the same variance.

Use a two-sample t-test at the 5% level of significance to find whether cuckoos' eggs from hedge-sparrows nests are significantly larger than cuckoos' eggs from reed-warbler nests.

(AEB)

Revision exercise D

---

(1) Derive the mean and variance of the Binomial distribution.

It is found at a restaurant that, on the average, one in eight of the parties who book tables fail to appear. The restaurant has 48 tables and on one evening had accepted bookings for 52 tables. What is the probability that all the parties who appear can be accommodated? (AEB)

(2) A failure time, X, has density function $\lambda e^{-\lambda x}$ for $x \geqslant 0$, $\lambda > 0$. Find
  (a) the distribution function,
  (b) the mean and variance,
  (c) the median,
  (d) the time below which it is 95% certain that there will be no failure. (O)

(3) (a) The set of all possible (equally likely) outcomes of an experiment is denoted by A. The events R, S and T are subsets of A. The probability of the event R can be expressed as

$$Pr(R) = \frac{n(R)}{n(A)}$$

where $n(X) =$ number of elements in set X.

Express similarly (i.e. as the ratio of the numbers of elements in two sets) the probabilities that
  (i) R and S both occur,
  (ii) either R and/or S occurs but T does not occur,
  (iii) R occurs, given that T occurs.

(b) The probability that an electric pump will fail during a given time interval (measured in hundreds of hours after being started) is given in Table D.1.

Table D.1

Time (hundreds of hours)	0–1	1–2	2–3	3–4	4–5	5–6	6–7
Probability	0.05	0.10	0.25	0.30	0.17	0.09	0.04

   (i) After it has run for 300 hours without failing, show that the probability it will run for at least 200 hours longer is 0.217 and estimate the average duration of trouble-free running still remaining after the first 300 hours. The cooling water for a machine is supplied by three of these pumps.

When one pump breaks down the machine can continue to run with only
two pumps, but when a second pump fails the machine must be stopped.

(ii) Find the probability that this machine will run for more than 300 hours.

(iii) Find the probability that this machine stops between 300 and 400 hours
after starting.   (O & C)

(4) A girl visits a record shop on Saturday mornings. The number of records she buys
at a visit may be regarded as having a Poisson distribution with mean 1.1. State why
neither the Binomial distribution nor the continuous Uniform distribution is likely
to provide a satisfactory model.

At the beginning of a year the girl wonders how much shelf space she will need for her
new records. On the assumption that she makes 50 visits to the record shop in the
year, for how many records should she provide space if she is to be 95% certain that
it will be adequate for the records she buys?   (O)

(5) The probability of a bomber plane completing one mission during a period of the
Second World War was 0.9. How many missions could be flown *before* the probability
of completing them all became less than one-half?

A flight of five such planes was sent on a mission. Calculate the probability that the
number that completed the mission was

(a) exactly two,

(b) at most two.   (C)

(6) In the Growmore Market Centre plants are inspected for the presence of the deadly
red angus bug. The number of bugs per leaf is known to follow a Poisson distribution
with mean one. What is the probability that any one leaf on a given plant will have
been attacked (at least one bug is found on it)?

A random sample of twelve plants is taken. For each plant ten leaves are selected at
random and inspected for these bugs. If more than eight leaves on any particular plant
have been attacked then the plant is destroyed. What is the probability that exactly
two of these twelve plants are destroyed?   (AEB)

(7) The number of births in a certain town over a period of ten years was as in Table D.2.
Calculate the five-yearly moving averages and plot a graph to display these and the
original data. What do you think is the trend?   (SUJB)

Table D.2

Year	1	2	3	4	5	6	7	8	9	10
Births	610	420	645	490	595	390	630	510	495	350

(8) Table D.3 gives the heights of 100 men. Verify that the mean is 70.32 in and the standard deviation is 2.74 in. Draw a cumulative frequency diagram of the distribution and use it to estimate the median and the two quartiles. (You should assume the lower and upper classes have a width of 2 in.)

Table D.3

Height in in.	Frequency
less than 66	4
66–67	11
68–69	23
70–71	30
72–73	19
74–75	10
76 or more	3

(O)

(9) A large transport undertaking runs three types of vehicles: vans, tippers and flat trucks. Of the total, 30% are vans and 50% are tippers. Of the vans, 20% are new (i.e. have been purchased within the last year), as are 30% of the tippers and 25% of the flat trucks.

The vehicles are either diesel or petrol engined. Two-thirds of the new vans and five-sixths of the old vans are petrol-engined. Two-thirds of the new tippers and five-sevenths of the old tippers are diesel-engined.

Overall, 15% of the vehicles are new diesels and 39% of the vehicles are old diesels. Find

(a) the proportion of vehicles that are new petrol-engined flat trucks,

(b) the proportion of vehicles that are old and petrol-engined,

(c) the proportion of petrol-engined vehicles that are vans,

(d) the proportion of new vehicles that are petrol-engined.   (C)

(10) Prove that the number of different ways in which r objects can be selected from a group of n is

$$\frac{n!}{r!(n-r)!}$$

A hand of five cards is selected without replacement from a well-shuffled pack of 52 cards consisting of four suits each of thirteen denominations. Find the probability that the five cards are of five different denominations and show that it is approximately 0.5.   (O)

(11) Explain the term 'degrees of freedom' and explain why the divisor $(n-1)$ is used in estimating the variance from a sample of n observations.

Table D.4 gives the numbers of electors in two samples who say they will vote Conservative or Labour. Draw up a similar table giving the expected numbers on the hypothesis that the samples are drawn from the same population. How many degrees of freedom has this table?

Table D.4 *Voting intentions of electors in two samples*

	Sample A	Sample B
Vote Conservative	144	206
Vote Labour	56	94

Test the null hypothesis that the samples are drawn from the same population. (O)

(12) The following table purports to be a series of 100 random digits. Draw up a frequency table of the occurrence of each digit and test whether the mean of this distribution differs significantly from the mean of the theoretical distribution you would expect if the digits are random. Explain carefully your argument at each step and in particular your use of theoretical distributions.

16165 98638 01030 29071 72618 71114 61056 81894 10249 14283
35411 07893 27591 95984 12957 35230 86339 02829 44463 08770

(O)

(13) (a) The marks in Table D.5 were awarded by two judges at a music competition. Calculate a coefficient of rank correlation.

Table D.5

	Judge 1	Judge 2
Child 1	10	9
Child 2	5	6
Child 3	8	10
Child 4	7	5
Child 5	9	8

Table D.6

Child	1	2	3	4	5	6	7	8
Arithmetic mark (x)	45	33	27	23	18	14	8	0
English mark (y)	31	33	18	20	19	9	13	1

(b) Determine, by calculation, the equation of the regression line of x on y based on the information in Table D.6 about eight children.

(SUJB)

(14) In a workshop there are four workers and five machines, producing similar articles. The production per shift was observed, every worker using each of the five machines for a whole shift. The results were as in Table D.7.

Table D.7

Worker	Machine				
	I	II	III	IV	V
A	17	41	22	62	32
B	34	31	26	64	35
C	34	50	26	66	39
D	22	47	13	57	32

Carry out an analysis of variance and test for differences between workers and between machines.

(There is no need to test differences between individual pairs.)   (AEB)

(15) Two independent random variables, X_1 and X_2, have Poisson distributions with means λ_1 and λ_2 respectively. Write down the probability that $(X_1, X_2)=(x_1, x_2)$ where x_1 and x_2 are given non-negative integers, and hence write down the probability that $(X_1, X_2)=(x_1, n-x_1)$ where x_1 and n are given integers, $0 \leqslant x_1 \leqslant n$. By allowing x_1 to vary appropriately (but keeping n fixed) find the probability that $X_1+X_2=n$, and hence deduce that X_1+X_2 has a Poisson distribution. What is the mean of this distribution?   (O)

(16) A research worker has a liquid containing yeast cells in suspension. He puts a drop of this liquid on a slide marked with a grid consisting of 48 equal squares which form a 6×8 rectangle. The slide is viewed through a microscope. The number of yeast cells in each square is shown below.

```
4  1  3  5  2  3  1  3
1  2  1  3  1  1  0  2
2  3  0  2  0  1  0  4
5  0  0  3  1  2  2  6
1  0  2  0  0  2  0  2
2  3  4  1  4  2  2  7
```

The total number of yeast cells in the 48 squares is 96. From previous experience the research worker believes that the number of yeast cells in each square follows a Poisson distribution with mean 2.

(a) Construct a frequency distribution table for the number of yeast cells in a square.

(b) Suggest why a Poisson distribution may be expected to be a suitable model.

(c) Use a standard statistical test to examine whether or not these data conform to a Poisson distribution with mean 2.

(d) The research worker suspects that there is a tendency for the yeast cells to be located away from the centre. Construct the frequency distribution table for the number of yeast cells in the 24 outer squares of the rectangle. Examine whether there is sufficient evidence to support the research worker's suspicion.   (JMB)

(17) (a) State, with reasons, which, if any, of the standard distributions might serve as suitable models for the following situations, giving in each case a sketch of a possible histogram or probability density function.

   (i)   The number of road accidents which occur at a particular junction during one week.

   (ii) The time people spend waiting for a bus on a route where buses run every x minutes but no timetable is published and there are always sufficient empty seats for the waiting passengers.

   (iii) The number of questions answered correctly by a student who guesses the answers to each of the n questions in a multiple choice test, each equation having four possible responses of which one alone is correct.

   (b) (i) If, in (a)(iii) above, $n = 10$ find the probability that the student obtains exactly three correct answers.

   (ii) Given that the pass mark is 5, find the probability that the student passes the test.   (JMB)

(18) Discuss the fallacies (if any) in the following statements.

   (a) As the confidence level increases from 95% to 99% the interval for the sample mean gets smaller, because we are more certain of including the right value.

   (b) Standard measure is the standard deviation expressed as a percentage of the mean.

   (c) The regression coefficient always lies between -1 and $+1$.

   (d) The deviation from zero, being less than two standard errors, was significant at the 5% level, showing conclusively that the null hypothesis of a zero mean is correct.   (O)

(19) From n pairs of values, (x_i, y_i), $i = 1, 2, \ldots, n$, the following quantities are calculated.

$$n = 20, \sum x_i = 400, \sum y_i = 220, \sum x_i^2 = 8800, \sum x_i y_i = 4300, \sum y_i^2 = 2620$$

Find the linear regression equations of y on x and x on y.

Which would be the more useful if

   (a) x is the age in years and y is the reaction time in milliseconds of twenty people,

   (b) x is the cost (£000) and y the floor space (in 100 m^2) of twenty buildings? (O)

(20)   A farmer has an orchard containing large numbers of two varieties (A and B) of apple trees. One year the farmer selected at random one tree of each variety, and kept a careful count of the fates of all the apples from these two trees. Some apples fell from the trees before picking time; some were eaten by insects; some eaten apples fell and some apples remained uneaten and on the trees until picking time. The farmer's results are given in Table D.8.

Table D.8

	Variety A			Variety B	
	Fallen	On tree		Fallen	On tree
Eaten	150	50	Eaten	90	50
Uneaten	40	160	Uneaten	20	240

You may assume, when answering the questions below, that the fate of an individual apple was independent of the fate of all other apples.

(a)   Before any apple had fallen or been eaten, the farmer selected at random a variety A apple and stated that it would not fall before picking time. Estimate the probability that he was correct.

(b)   At picking time the farmer accidentally trod on a fallen apple. Assuming that this apple was equally likely to have been any one of the fallen apples, estimate the probability that it was of variety A.

(c)   Give an approximate symmetric 95% confidence interval for p_A, the proportion of variety A apples remaining on the tree and uneaten until picking time.

(d)   The proportion of variety B apples remaining on the tree and uneaten until picking time is p_B. Determine whether there is evidence at the 0.1% significance level of a difference between p_A and p_B.   (C)

(21)   Explain briefly what is meant by the following terms when used in an acceptance sampling situation:

(a)   a single sampling plan,

(b)   a double sampling plan,

(c)   the operating characteristic curve.

Large batches of electrical components are produced for use in computer manufacture. A double sampling plan of inspection is adopted as follows. Select twelve items from the batch and accept the batch if there are no defectives, reject the batch if there are three or more defectives, otherwise select another sample of twelve items. When the second sample is drawn count the number of defectives in the combined sample of 24 and accept the batch if the number of defectives is two or less, otherwise reject the batch.

If the proportion of defectives in a batch is p find, in terms of p, the probability it will be accepted. Calculate the risk of rejecting a batch for which $p=\frac{1}{12}$. Comment on this result.   (AEB)

(22) A manufacturer wishes to estimate the proportion of cars fitted with radios in a small town and the surrounding district. The following schemes for choosing a sample are suggested. State the criteria you would use for assessing these schemes, and discuss the relative merits of the schemes. Suggest improvements if any occur to you, and state the scheme you would prefer.

(a) Choose at random 200 names from the telephone directory. Ring the corresponding numbers and ask about the cars belonging to the household.

(b) Take every nth name from the electoral register, choosing n so that the total sample size is 200. Visit the homes of the people chosen and ask about the household's cars.

(c) Stop cars as they enter the High Street on a weekday morning and check whether or not they have radios. Inspect 200.   (O)

(23) A random sample of n pairs is drawn from a bivariate Normal population having a correlation coefficient ρ_1. The sample correlation coefficient, r_1, of these data is calculated. Show how Fisher's transformation

$$z'_1 = \tanh^{-1} r_1 = 1.1513 \log_{10} \left[\frac{1+r_1}{1-r_1} \right]$$

may be used to test the hypothesis that $\rho_1 = \theta \neq 0$.

Suppose that a second independent sample of n_2 pairs is drawn from a bivariate Normal population having a correlation coefficient ρ_2. The sample correlation coefficient r_2 of these data is calculated. Show how Fisher's transformation may be adapted to test the hypothesis $\rho_1 = \rho_2$.

If $n_1 = 28$ and $n_2 = 35$ with $r_1 = 0.5$ and $r_2 = 0.3$, test, at the 5% level, the hypothesis that these samples were drawn from populations having the same correlation coefficient.   (AEB)

(24) (a) A non-negative integer R takes the value r with probability given by $P(R=r) = k(n-r)$ for $0 \leqslant r \leqslant n$ and $P(R=r)=0$ for $r>n$ where n is a fixed positive integer and k is a constant. Find the value of k in terms of n. Find also the mean and variance of R.

(b) The probability density function for values x of a continuous variate X is given by $f(x)=k(n-x)$ for $0 \leqslant x \leqslant n$ and $f(x)=0$ elsewhere, where k is a constant. Find k in terms of n. Find also the mean and variance of X.

If b is such that $P(X>b)=0.05$ show that $(1-b/n)^2=0.05$ and hence find b when $n=10$.   (O & C)

(25) Explain the terms (a) consistent estimator, (b) unbiased estimator. A random sample of eight, drawn from a Normal distribution, is found to be 112, 156, 406, 216, 447,

141, 315, 451. Calculate the unbiased estimate of the population variance, 95% confidence limits for the population mean and 95% confidence limits for the population variance.   (AEB)

(26) Show that, if the regression line of y on x is derived from seven pairs of values $(x_1, y_1), (x_2, y_2), \ldots, (x_7, y_7)$, where $x_i = a + id$, the estimated slope of the line may be written

$$\sum_{i=1}^{7} \frac{(i-4)y_i}{28d}$$

Hence, or otherwise, find the regression line of height on age from the data in Table D.9.

(O)

Table D.9

Age (years)	5	6	7	8	9	10	11
Height (cm)	99	105	111	117	123	128	133

(27) Explain the fallacy in each of the following arguments, and give the correct conclusions.

(a) Y is a Normal random variable with mean 0, variance 25. The probability that $Y \leqslant 5$ is obtained from the table of the Normal integral with $x = (5 + \frac{1}{2})/5$, so we conclude that this probability is 0.8643.

(b) X_1 and X_2 are independent random variables with means μ_1 and μ_2, variances σ_1^2 and σ_2^2 respectively. Hence $X_1 - X_2$ has mean $\mu_1 - \mu_2$, variance $\sigma_1^2 + \sigma_2^2$, and $(X_1 - X_2) + X_2$ has mean $(\mu_1 - \mu_2) + \mu_2 = \mu_1$ variance $(\sigma_1^2 + \sigma_2^2) + \sigma_2^2 = \sigma_1^2 + 2\sigma_2^2$. But $(X_1 - X_2) + X_2 = X_1$, so we conclude that X_1 has mean μ_1 variance $\sigma_1^2 + 2\sigma_2^2$.

(c) Two independent observations, 26 and 45, arise from Normal distributions of unknown (possibly the same) means and the same variance, 25. Hence the mean of the first distribution must lie between 16 and 36 and that of the second between 35 and 55. These ranges overlap, so we conclude that with 95% certainty the two distributions are the same.   (O)

(28) In a simulation problem, it is necessary to generate values of a random variable which is Normally distributed with mean 0 and variance 1. One way proposed is to add ten random digits together, the digits 0 to 9 being generated with equal probability, and standardise the total appropriately. Do you think this method would be satisfactory? Give your reasons for your answer, and explain how the total would be standardised. Use a table of random digits to generate five such values of this proposed standardised Normal deviate.   (O)

(29) A man, Mr Knowall, claims to be able to recognise a well-known brand, A, of whisky blindfold. On nine occasions he is given two glasses in random order, one containing

brand A and the other containing brand X. On eight occasions he names the brands correctly. Would you consider his claim justified?

The same experiment is repeated the following day, and this time he names the brand correctly in seven out of nine trials. How does this affect your opinion of his claim?

(AEB)

(30) Discuss the fallacies in the following statements:
  (a) The length of wing varied from a minimum of 8.5 cm to a maximum of 21.6 cm. The mean for all seventeen birds was 13.6 cm and the standard deviation was 0.49 cm. The standard error of the mean is thus $\sigma/\sqrt{(n-1)}$ or 0.12 cm and so we can be 95% certain that the true sample mean lies between 13.4 cm and 13.8 cm.
  (b) Since accident statistics show that the probability that a person will be involved in a road accident in a year is 0.02, the probability that he will be involved in two accidents in the same year is 0.0004. (O)

(31) A random variable x has for its distribution function
$$F(x) = \tanh^2 x \qquad (x \geqslant 0)$$
$$= 0 \qquad\qquad (x < 0)$$
that is to say, the probability that a value taken at random from the distribution is less than any number X is $F(X)$.

By differentiating $F(x)$ with respect to x, find the frequency (probability density) function $f(x)$ of x. Differentiate
$$\tanh x - x \operatorname{sech}^2 x$$
with respect to x and hence find the mean of x.

Calculate the median, quartiles and semi-interquartile range of x. (AEB)

(32) (a) State the essential features of random sampling.
Distinguish between sampling with replacement and sampling without replacement.

State precisely how you would draw a random sample without replacement in each of the following cases, explaining carefully how you would deal with any practical difficulties.
   (i) A sample of size 5 from a carton containing 24 jars of jam.
   (ii) A sample of size 30 from a sixth form college with 200 students.
   (iii) A sample of size 30 from the voters who live in a village of population 1000.
  (b) In an opinion poll taken in a large constituency, 1600 voters indicated their voting preference as follows:
Conservative 840; Labour 760.
   (i) Estimate the proportion of voters that will vote Conservative.
   (ii) Based on this estimate, calculate the 95% symmetric confidence interval for the proportion of people that will vote Conservative.
   (iii) Estimate the size of sample required to ensure that the 95% symmetric confidence interval for the proportion of people that will vote Conservative has range 0.02. (JMB)

(33) Define the arithmetic mean, the median and the standard deviation of a probability
distribution.
Evaluate the mean and standard deviation for each of the following distributions:
(a)   a Binomial distribution in which $n=5$ and $p=\frac{1}{5}$;
(b)   a Poisson distribution with parameter 2;
(c)   a Normal distribution for which the probability of a negative value of the
random variable is 0.3085 and the mode is 2;
(d)   a Rectangular distribution over the range 0 to 2.   (O)

(34) What is meant by the sampling distribution of a statistic? If random samples of size n
are drawn from an unspecified distribution with mean μ and variance σ^2, what is the
sampling distribution of the sample mean as n tends to infinity?
The distribution of breaking loads for certain fibres has mean 20 units and standard
deviation 2 units. A rope is assumed to be made up of 64 independent fibres, and to
have a breaking load which is the sum of the breaking loads of all the fibres in it.
Find the probability that such a rope will support a weight of 1300 units. The manufacturers wish to quote a breaking load for such ropes that will be satisfied by 99% of
the ropes. Determine what breaking load should be quoted.   (AEB)

(35) The results of measurements of the freezing point ($^\circ$C) of a test solution by a class of
first-year students were as follows:
$$-0.03, 0.00, -0.02, -0.19, 0.04, 0.06, 0.31, -0.05, -0.02, 0.13$$
A class of second-year students produced the following results:
$$0.98, 0.71, 0.06, -0.22, -0.84, 0.20, -0.12, 0.68, -0.50, -0.66, 0.37$$
The theoretical value is known to be $-0.13\,^\circ$C.
Examine these results and state your conclusions.   (AEB)

(36) Comment critically on the following statements.
(a)   It is a sad reflection on the difficulties facing modern educational establishments
that no fewer than 47% of children are below average intelligence.
(b)   The majority of housewives tested could not tell the difference between butter
and margarine.
(c)   The number of matches in a box is Normally distributed with mean 50 and s.d. 2.
(d)   A correlation coefficient of $+1$ means that there is an approximate relationship
between two variables.   (O)

(37) A medical investigator states that half the elderly people given anaesthetics for opera-
tions suffer from complications. On examining his records, it is found that 36 such
people out of a random sample of 100 in fact have complications. Is this evidence that
his statement is justified? Explain very carefully each step of your argument and
point out why you have used the particular theoretical distributions you have in
your answer.
What is a 95% confidence interval for the proportion of elderly people suffering
from such complications?   (AEB)

(38)   A loom is used to produce cloth. Occasionally, at random, the machine falters and
       a flaw appears across the cloth. In the past it has been found that the distance between
       flaws in the cloth follows an Exponential distribution with mean 1 metre. State
       briefly why an Exponential distribution would be expected to serve as a reasonable
       model in this situation.
       The 100 distances between successive flaws on a given day are shown in Table D.10.
       (a) Plot these data as a histogram. On the same diagram draw an appropriately
            scaled graph of the density function of the Exponential distribution with mean 1.
       (b) Calculate the corresponding expected frequencies for an Exponential distribu-
            tion with mean 1 and test whether this model gives a reasonable fit to the data.
            (Two significant figure accuracy for expected frequencies is accepted.)   (JMB)

Table D.10

Distance between flaws	Frequency
0 to 0.5 m	44
0.5 to 1.0 m	20
1.0 to 2.0 m	22
2.0 to 3.0 m	10
More than 3 m	4

(39)   Discuss and criticise the following extract from a report.
           'The heights, h, and weights, w, of 100 adult men were measured. The heights had
       a mean of 1.80 metres and a standard deviation of 0.68 metre. A χ^2 goodness-of-fit
       test, based in 99 degrees of freedom, showed that the distribution was Normal.
       The mean weight was 80 kg. The correlation coefficient between the values of
       h and w was 1.02, and, as this is not significantly different from 1, there is a very
       strong relationship between h and w. The regression equation of w on h is
       $w = 76.4 + 2.0h$. This cannot be correct, however, since for a new-born baby of
       height 0.3 metre, it gives a weight of 77.0 kg, which is absurd.'   (O)

(40)   If $\bar{x}$ is the arithmetic mean of the n numbers $x_1, x_2, \ldots, x_n$, prove that
       $$\sum (x - \bar{x})^2 = \sum x^2 - n\bar{x}^2$$
       Independent random samples are taken as follows:
       20 from a population having mean 2 and standard deviation 1,
       30 from a population having mean 5 and standard deviation 2, and
       40 from a population having mean 4 and standard deviation 3.
       Find the expectations of the mean and variance of the whole 90, regarded as one
       sample.   (AEB)

(41)   In a model of the game of billiards, the probability of player A scoring a point is p and missing a shot is $q = 1 - p$. Player A continues playing until he misses, when the turn passes to his opponent. The number of points he accumulates is the length of his turn, and this can be zero. Show that the probability that player A has scored exactly k points after r turns have been completed is

$$\binom{r+k-1}{k} q^r p^k$$

Hence show that the expected number of points he scores after r turns is rp/q.   (O)

(42)   A man, when deciding where to spend his holiday, compared the number of rainy days in August at two resorts A and B. For the years for which he had records, he found that resort A had more rainy days than resort B in 50 years and the reverse was the case in 31 years. He ignored the years in which the number of rainy days was the same. Test if the percentage of years in which A had more rainy days than B differs significantly from 50%.

Describe an alternative method of measuring the amount of rain in August at each resort, and describe briefly how you would make a test of the relative amount of rain at the resorts using your measure.   (O)

(43)   Explain clearly the following terms used in hypothesis testing:
(a)   null and alternative hypotheses,
(b)   Type I and Type II errors,
(c)   significance level,
(d)   power of a test.
A coin is tossed ten times and eight heads and two tails result. Test, at the 5% level of significance, the hypothesis that this coin is unbiased.   (AEB)

(44)   For each of the stages of a three-stage rocket, the extra velocity imparted in the stage is a Normal variable. For the first stage, in which the initial velocity is zero, the extra velocity has mean 3.15 km s^{-1} and standard deviation 0.03 km s^{-1}; for the second stage, the extra velocity has mean 3.96 km s^{-1} and standard deviation 0.04 km s^{-1}. For the third stage there is a probability of 0.95 that the extra velocity exceeds 4.9478 km s^{-1} and a probability of 0.05 that it exceeds 5.1122 km s^{-1}. Find, to three significant figures the mean and standard deviation of the extra velocity for the third stage.
Find the probabilities that
(a)   the velocity exceeds 3.10 km s^{-1} at the end of the first stage,
(b)   the velocity has not reached 7.00 km s^{-1} at the end of the second stage,
(c)   the velocity has not reached 12.30 km s^{-1} at the end of the third stage.   (C)

(45)   The joint probability density function of X and Y is
$$\phi(x, y) = k(1 - x^2 - y^2)$$
over the region for which $x^2 + y^2 \leqslant 1$ and $y \geqslant 0$. Find the marginal probability density function of X and the value of the constant k.

Write down the probability density function of Y for a given value of X and obtain the mean value of Y when $X = x_0$.

(46) The figures below give the percentage extension under a given load of two indepen-dent random samples of yarn, the first before washing, the second after six washings.

        Unwashed yarn   12.3, 13.7, 10.4, 11.4, 14.9, 12.6

        Washed yarn   15.7, 10.3, 12.6, 14.5, 12.6, 13.8, 11.9

Assuming that both samples came from Normal distributions, test whether there is a significant difference between the two samples,

(a) as regards variability,

(b) as regards the mean percentage extension.   (AEB)

(47) The range, R km, is given in terms of the angle of elevation of the gun, α, by the formula $R = 16 \sin 2\alpha$.

The angle α varies uniformly over the interval $(\frac{2}{9}\pi, \frac{5}{18}\pi)$. Find the interval within which R lies and state the values of α corresponding to the extreme values of R. Obtain the distribution function $F(r)$ of R and calculate the median value of the range.

Sketch the distribution function, indicating the position of the median on your sketch.

                                                             (C)

(48) Of 1000 schoolboys examined, 180 were found to have flat feet and 92 were short-sighted. Of these 26 had both short-sight and flat feet. Test the hypothesis that short-sight and flat feet are independent.

Calculate 95% confidence limits for the fraction having flat feet in the population from which the sample was drawn.

What can be said about the proposition that at least one boy in five of the population has flat feet?   (AEB)

(49) Twelve people of different ages were given a memory test with the following results:

Age (years)	x	70	68	62	53	50	46	35	28	25	22	20	18
Test score	y	48	50	60	55	62	74	69	78	82	80	93	90

Plot these points on a scatter diagram and calculate the regression line of y on x. Arrange these scores according to rank (age 70 to 18 ranking from 1 to 12 and scores 48 to 93 ranking from 12 to 1) and calculate a rank order correlation coefficient. Make a brief coment on the result.   (C)

(50) From your experience as statistician in the Mental Health Unit of a large hospital you know that the number of cases of depressive illness referred per month by general practitioners is a Poisson variable with mean 3. In May 1973 you notice that the total number of such cases referred by the practitioners in the preceding four months is 2.

Analyse this result as you consider appropriate and write a paragraph reporting and explaining your conclusion to the Director of the Unit, who has had little statistical training.   (C)

Appendices

Appendix 1 Σ-notation

Σ-notation is used to write the sum of a series in a conveniently condensed form. For example the sum of the first n integers can be written as $\sum\limits_{r=1}^{n} r$ which is read as 'the sum of terms like r where r takes integral values from 1 to n'. Thus

$$\sum_{r=1}^{5} r^2 = 1^2 + 2^2 + 3^2 + 4^2 + 5^2 = 55$$

$$\sum_{r=1}^{3} (2r+1) = (2 \times 1 + 1) + (2 \times 2 + 1) + (2 \times 3 + 1) = 15$$

Exercise 1

(1) Evaluate the following:

(a) $\sum\limits_{r=1}^{3} 2r^3$ (b) $\sum\limits_{r=1}^{4} (3+4r)$ (c) $\sum\limits_{r=1}^{10} (r^2 + 3r + 1)$

(2) Write the following in Σ-notation:
  (a) $3 \times 1^2 + 3 \times 2^2 + 3 \times 3^2 + \cdots + 3 \times 10^2$
  (b) $(8 \times 1 + 1) + (8 \times 2 + 1) + (8 \times 3 + 1) + \cdots + (8 \times 7 + 1)$
  (c) $2 \times 1^5 + 2 \times 2^5 + \cdots + 2 \times n^5$
  (d) $2^1 + 2^2 + 2^3 + \cdots + 2^n$

If x takes a series of n values $x_1, x_2, x_3, \ldots, x_n$ their sum can be written as follows:

$$x_1 + x_2 + x_3 + \cdots + x_n = \sum_{i=1}^{n} x_i$$

Similarly

$$x_1^2 + x_2^2 + x_3^2 + \cdots + x_n^2 = \sum_{i=1}^{n} x_i^2$$

If we have another variable, y, which takes n values $y_1, y_2, y_3, \ldots, y_n$, then

$$x_1 y_1 + x_2 y_2 + \cdots + x_n y_n = \sum_{i=1}^{n} x_i y_i$$

Exercise 2

If $x_1 = 1$, $x_2 = 3$, $x_3 = 4$, $x_4 = 5$ and $y_1 = 7$, $y_2 = 12$, $y_3 = 14$, $y_4 = 20$, evaluate

(a) $\sum\limits_{i=1}^{4} x_i$ (b) $\sum\limits_{i=1}^{4} y_i$ (c) $\sum\limits_{i=1}^{4} x_i^2$ (d) $\sum\limits_{i=1}^{4} x_i y_i$ (e) $\sum\limits_{i=1}^{4} 2x_i y_i^2$

402

Theorem 1

$$\sum_{i=1}^{n} kx_i = k \sum_{i=1}^{n} x_i \qquad \text{where } k \text{ is a constant.}$$

Proof

$$\sum_{i=1}^{n} kx_i = kx_1 + kx_2 + \cdots + kx_n$$

$$= k(x_1 + x_2 + \cdots + x_n)$$

$$= k \sum_{i=1}^{n} x_i$$

Theorem 2

$$\sum_{i=1}^{n} (a + x_i) = na + \sum_{i=1}^{n} x_i \qquad \text{where } a \text{ is a constant.}$$

Proof

$$\sum_{i=1}^{n} (a + x_i) = (a + x_1) + (a + x_2) + \cdots + (a + x_n)$$

$$= na + (x_1 + x_2 + \cdots + x_n)$$

$$= na + \sum_{i=1}^{n} x_i$$

Theorem 3

$$\sum_{i=1}^{n} (x_i + y_i) = \sum_{i=1}^{n} x_i + \sum_{i=1}^{n} y_i$$

Proof

$$\sum_{i=1}^{n} (x_i + y_i) = (x_1 + y_1) + (x_2 + y_2) + \cdots + (x_n + y_n)$$

$$= (x_1 + x_2 + \cdots + x_n) + (y_1 + y_2 + \cdots + y_n)$$

$$= \sum_{i=1}^{n} x_i + \sum_{i=1}^{n} y_i$$

Example

If $\sum_{i=1}^{6} x_i = 21$, $\sum_{i=1}^{6} y_i = 40$, $\sum_{i=1}^{6} x_i^2 = 91$, $\sum_{i=1}^{6} y_i^2 = 300$ and $\sum_{i=1}^{6} x_i y_i = 164$,

evaluate (a) $\sum_{i=1}^{6} (x_i^2 + 7)$, (b) $\sum_{i=1}^{6} (x_i + y_i)^2$.

(a) $\displaystyle\sum_{i=1}^{6} (x_i^2 + 7) = \sum_{i=1}^{6} x_i^2 + 6 \times 7$

$\qquad\qquad\quad = 91 + 42$

$\qquad\qquad\quad = 133$

(b) $\displaystyle\sum_{i=1}^{6} (x_i + y_i)^2 = \sum_{i=1}^{6} (x_i^2 + 2x_i y_i + y_i^2)$

$\qquad\qquad\qquad = \displaystyle\sum_{i=1}^{6} x_i^2 + 2\sum_{i=1}^{6} x_i y_i + \sum_{i=1}^{6} y_i^2$

$\qquad\qquad\qquad = 91 + 2 \times 164 + 300$

$\qquad\qquad\qquad = 719$

Exercise 3

Using the values of $\displaystyle\sum_{i=1}^{6} x_i, \sum_{i=1}^{6} y_i, \sum_{i=1}^{6} x_i y_i, \sum_{i=1}^{6} x_i^2, \sum_{i=1}^{6} y_i^2$ given above, evaluate

(a) $\displaystyle\sum_{i=1}^{6} (x_i + 3)$ (b) $\displaystyle\sum_{i=1}^{6} (x_i^2 + y_i^2)$ (c) $\displaystyle\sum_{i=1}^{6} 3y_i$ (d) $\displaystyle\sum_{i=1}^{6} (x_i + 2)(y_i + 1)$ (e) $\displaystyle\sum_{i=1}^{6} (x_i + 7)^2$

Appendix 2   Theorems

Theorem 1

$$\lim_{n \to \infty} \binom{n}{x}\left(\frac{a}{n}\right)^x = \frac{a^x}{x!}$$

Proof

$$\binom{n}{x}\left(\frac{a}{n}\right)^x = \frac{n(n-1)(n-2)\ldots(n-x+1)}{x!} \times \frac{a^x}{n^x}$$

$$= \frac{n(n-1)(n-2)\ldots(n-x+1)}{n^x} \times \frac{a^x}{x!}$$

$$= 1\left(1 - \frac{1}{n}\right)\left(1 - \frac{2}{n}\right)\cdots\left(1 - \frac{[x-1]}{n}\right) \times \frac{a^x}{x!}$$

As $n \to \infty$, terms like $\left(1 - \dfrac{\{x-1\}}{n}\right) \to 1$

so that

$$\lim_{n \to \infty} \binom{n}{x}\left(\frac{a}{n}\right)^x = \frac{a^x}{x!}$$

Theorem 2

$$\lim_{n\to\infty}\left(1+\frac{x}{n}\right)^n = e^x$$

Proof

$$\left(1+\frac{x}{n}\right)^n = 1+n\left(\frac{x}{n}\right)+\frac{n(n-1)}{2!}\left(\frac{x}{n}\right)^2+\cdots+\frac{n(n-1)(n-r+1)}{r!}\left(\frac{x}{n}\right)^r+\cdots$$

$$= 1+x+1\left(1-\frac{1}{n}\right)\frac{x^2}{2!}+\cdots+1\left(1-\frac{1}{n}\right)\times\cdots\times\left(1-\frac{[r-1]}{n}\right)\frac{x^r}{r!}+\cdots$$

As $n\to\infty$, terms like $1-\frac{[r-1]}{n}\to1$

So that

$$\lim_{n\to\infty}\left(1+\frac{x}{n}\right)^n = 1+x+\frac{x^2}{2!}+\cdots+\frac{x^r}{r!}+\cdots$$

$$= e^x$$

Theorem 3

$$\lim_{n\to\infty}\binom{n}{x}\left(\frac{a}{n}\right)^x\left(1-\frac{a}{n}\right)^{n-x} = \frac{a^x}{x!}e^{-a}$$

Proof

$$\lim_{n\to\infty}\binom{n}{x}\left(\frac{a}{n}\right)^x\left(1-\frac{a}{n}\right)^{n-x} = \lim_{n\to\infty}\binom{n}{x}\left(\frac{a}{n}\right)^x\left(1-\frac{a}{n}\right)^{+n}\left(1-\frac{a}{n}\right)^{-x}$$

From Theorem 1, the limit of the first two terms is $\frac{a^x}{x!}$.

From Theorem 2, putting $x=-a$, the limit of the third term is e^{-a} and

$$\lim_{n\to\infty}\left(1-\frac{a}{n}\right)^{-x} = 1 \quad\text{since } \frac{a}{n}\to0 \text{ and }\left(1-\frac{a}{n}\right)\to1.$$

Combining these results

$$\lim_{n\to\infty}\binom{n}{x}\left(\frac{a}{n}\right)^x\left(1-\frac{a}{n}\right)^{n-x} = \frac{a^x}{x!}e^{-a}$$

Glossary of notation

α – intercept of regression line

$\hat{a}$ – least squares estimate of α

β – slope of regression line

$\hat{b}$ – least squares estimate of β

$B(n, p)$ – Binomial distribution with n trials, probability of 'success' p

$\text{cov}(X, Y)$ – covariance of X and Y

E – an event in sample space

$E(X)$ – expected value of the random variable X

$f(x)$ – probability density function (p.d.f.) of variable X

$F(x)$ – cumulative distribution function (c.d.f.) of variable X

H_0 – null hypothesis

H_1 – alternative hypothesis

λ – mean of a Poisson distribution

μ – mean of a variable

M – median of a sample

ν – degrees of freedom

n – parameter of a Binomial distribution or number of members of a sample

^nP_r – the number of permutations of r objects taken from n

$\binom{n}{r}$ – the number of combinations of r objects taken from n

$N(\mu, \sigma^2)$ – Normal distribution, mean μ, variance σ^2

$P(E)$ – probability that the event E occurs at a single trial

$P(\bar{E})$ – probability that the event E does not occur at a single trial

$P(E_1 \cup E_2)$ – probability that event E_1 and/or event E_2 occurs

$P(E_1 \cap E_2)$ – probability that events E_1 and E_2 both occur

$P(E_1 \mid E_2)$ – probability that event E_1 occurs given that E_2 has occurred

$P(X = x)$ – probability that a discrete random variable, X, takes the value x

$P(X = x_1, Y = y_1)$ – joint probability that $X = x_1$, $Y = y_1$

$Po(\lambda)$ – Poisson distribution with mean λ

p – probability of a 'success'

q – probability of a 'failure'

Q_1 – lower quartile

Q_3 – upper quartile

ρ – correlation coefficient

r – estimate of ρ

r_S – Spearman's rank correlation coefficient

σ – standard deviation (s.d.) of a variable

σ^2 – variance of a variable

s – standard deviation of a sample

$\hat{s}$ – unbiased estimate of σ

S – sample space

t_{n-1} – the statistic $\dfrac{\bar{x}-\mu}{\hat{s}/\sqrt{n}}$

τ – Kendall's rank correlation coefficient

$\mathrm{var}(X)$ – variance of the random variable X

$\bar{x}$ – mean of a sample

X – a random variable

X^2 – statistic which estimates χ^2

z – standard Normal deviate

Selected bibliography

The following books are not textbooks but give general background reading:
Facts from Figures, M. J. Moroney (Penguin). A classic introduction to Statistics.
Statistics in Action, Peter Sprent (Penguin). An introduction to the practical applications of Statistics.
Lady Luck, Warren Weaver (Penguin). An introduction to probability theory based on games of chance.
Statistics – A New Approach, W. Allen Wallis and Harry V. Roberts (Methuen). This book contains a large number of examples of the practical application of Statistics.

Further information on selected topics can be found in the following books. Those marked with an asterisk are more advanced and are included particularly for teachers.

(1) **Time series**
   Facts from Figures (*op. cit.*), Chapter 17.
   An Introduction to the Theory of Statistics, G. U. Yule and M. G. Kendall (Griffin), Chapter 26.
(2) **Queuing theory**
   Queuing Theory, J. A. Panico (Prentice-Hall).
(3) **Practical sampling**
   Use and Abuse of Statistics, W. J. Reichmann (Penguin), Chapters 17–19.
   Sampling Methods for Censuses and Surveys (4th edition) F. Yates (Griffin), Chapters 1–4.
(4) **Control charts and OC curves**
   Facts from Figures (*op. cit.*), Chapters 10–12.
   Statistics for Technology, C. Chatfield (Chapman and Hall), Chapter 12. (This book also describes other applications of Statistics to industrial processes.)
(5) **Rank correlation**
   Rank Correlation Methods, M. G. Kendall (Griffin).
(6) **Analysis of variance**
   Statistics for Technology (*op. cit.*), Chapters 10 and 11.
   Statistical Methods (6th edition), G. W. Snedecor and W. G. Cochran (Iowa State University Press), Chapters 10 and 11.

Answers

Chapter 1

Exercise on Chapter 1

(1) discrete (a), (c), (f); continuous (b), (d), (e), (g).
(2) (a) 19.95–20.45, 20.45–20.95, 20.95–21.45, 21.45–21.95; 20.2, 20.7, 21.2, 21.7 (mm)
     (b) 19.995–20.495, 20.495–20.995, 20.995–21.495, 21.495–21.995; 20.245, 20.745, 21.245, 21.745 (mm)
     (c) 1–2, 2–3, 3–4, 4–5, 5–6; 1.5, 2.5, 3.5, 4.5, 5.5 (yr)
     (d) 57.5–58.5, 58.5–59.5, 59.5–60.5, 60.5–61.5, 61.5–62.5, 62.5–63.5; 58, 59, 60, 61, 62, 63 (kg)
     (e) 139.5–149.5, 149.5–159.5, 159.5–169.5, 169.5–179.5; 144.5, 154.5, 164.5, 174.5 (cm)
     (f) 139.95–149.95, 149.95–159.95, 159.95–169.95, 169.95–179.95; 144.95, 154.95, 164.95, 174.95 (cm)
(3) 119.5–129.5, 129.5–139.5, 139.5–149.5, 149.5–159.5, 159.5–169.5, 169.5–179.5; 124.5, 134.5, 144.5, 154.5, 164.5, 174.5 (cm); relative frequencies: 0.035, 0.211, 0.298, 0.316, 0.123, 0.018

Chapter 2

2.4.1

(1) 2   (2) 24.5 yr   (3) £2209   (4) 63 years (using linear interpolation)

2.6.1
(1) 28.7 yr   (2) 9.75 yr

2.7.1

(1) 2.13   (2) 10.22 h   (3) 24.4

2.13.1

(1) four-quarterly moving averages 187.25, 188, 189.5, 190.5, 191.25, 193, 193.5, 194.75, 196; estimate 183 (£1000)
(2) £82, £85, £87.5, £89.5, £91.5, £94.5, £96, £97.5, £101; estimate £10/year
(3) 73.8, 75.8, 77.8, 76.4, 74.0, 72.8, 72.2, 71.8 (thousands)
(4) 6 bi-monthly 4.4, 4.5, 4.7, 5.1, 5.0, 5.2, 5.2, 5.3, 5.4 (h)

Exercise on Chapter 2

(1) 4.47; 4; 1, 2, 4; median   (2) 147.8 cm   (3) (b) P 65.9, Q 71.3
(4) (b) 4.475, 4.525, 4.500, 4.458, 4.450, 4.550, 4.525, 4.242, 4.117, 3.958, 3.942, 3.950, 3.892, 3.867, 3.883, 3.767, 3.742, 3.650, 4.025, 3.975, 3.958, 3.992, 3.917, 3.933, 4.017 (h)
(5) (a) £62   (b) £74   (c) 72% (taking upper true class limits as £35.995, £39.995 etc.) True class limits: £0–£34.995; £35.995–£39.995, etc. Corresponding frequencies: 0.1, 0.2, 0.4, 0.6, 0.7, 0.7, 1.3, 0.9, 0.8, 0.4. Mean = 68
(6) Moving averages: 3105.75, 3125.75, 3158.50, 3193.75, 3235.00, 3268.50, 3281.50, 3298.25

(7)   62.53, 66.68
(8)   20.39
(9)   Girls: 2.56, 3, 2 and 3; Boys: 3.58, 3, 3
(10)   182

Chapter 3

3.4.1

(1)   91; 37, 148 (g)
(2)   69% (taking measurements to nearest mm)
(3)   6.5; 4, 9
(4)   (a) 96.5 min   (b) 4.5 min   (c) 64 (taking measurements to nearest second)
(5)   for A, median 131 h, semi-interquartile range 237 h; corresponding values for B are 126 h, 90 h

3.6.2

(a) 3, 1.414   (b) 57, 1.414   (c) 30, 14.14   (d) 57, 34.79

3.8.2

2.219

3.9.2

(1)   26.67, 21.82   (2) 9, 2, 2.523   (a) 10, 10   (b) 6, 2.43   (3) 5.25, 0.8732   (4) 2.39
(5)   (a) A 33, 19.4; B 23, 16.9; B more consistent   (b) 1.94, 1.69 (mm)
(6)   (a) 24, 05   (b) 26 s
(7)   7.09, 4.39
(8)   31.6 s, 1.46 s   (a) 0.527 min, 0.0243 min   (b) 30.6 s, 1.46 s

3.10.2

61.72, 7.79

Exercise on Chapter 3

(1)   (a) 100.7, 14.51   (b) 73
(2)   depends on class intervals chosen; for ungrouped data, s.d. = 11.6 m
(3)   (a) 65.5 kg   (b) 6.12 kg; s.d. increases
(4)   1.32, 1.08, 1.04; 1.30 (kg)
(5)   (b) 46 600   (c) 46 500; 20 000 (km)
(6)   (a) $\mu + c, \sigma$ (b) $k\mu, k\sigma$; $a = \frac{5}{6}$, $b = 22$
(7)   12.08 yr, 1.83 yr
(8)   31.375 s, 7.738 s, 32 s, 11 s, 68%
(9) $\frac{2}{3}$, 26, 54, 10, 74

Chapter 4

4.2.1

(1)   (a) $\frac{1}{2}$ (b) $\frac{1}{2}$ (c) $\frac{1}{13}$ (d) $\frac{1}{4}$ (e) $\frac{1}{3}$ (2) (a) $\frac{2}{3}$ (b) $\sqrt{3}/2$ (c) $\frac{3}{4}$

4.2.4

(1) (a) $\frac{1}{6}$ (b) $\frac{1}{6}$ (c) $\frac{5}{12}$
(2) (a) $\frac{1}{4}$ (b) $\frac{5}{8}$ (c) $\frac{7}{16}$
(3) $\frac{3}{8}$
(4) $\frac{4}{9}, \frac{1}{3}$

4.3.3

(1) (a) (i) yes (ii) no (b)(i) no (ii) no (c)(i) no (ii) no (d)(i) yes (ii) yes
(2) yes, since $P(C \cup D) = P(C) + P(D)$ (a) 0.9 (b) 0.7
(3) (a) $\frac{2}{5}$ (b) $\frac{3}{10}$ (c) $\frac{3}{5}$ (d) $\frac{1}{10}$
(5) (a) 0.5 (b) 0.1 (c) 0.3 (d) 0.2

4.4.3

(1) (a) $\frac{3}{4}$ (b) $\frac{1}{2}$ (c) $\frac{1}{2}$
(2) (a) $\frac{4}{17}$ (b) $\frac{13}{51}$
(3) $\frac{14}{45}$
(4) (a) $\frac{62}{131}$ (b) $\frac{69}{131}$ (c) $\frac{42}{131}$ (d) $\frac{43}{131}$ (e) $\frac{29}{69}$ (f) $\frac{23}{42}$ (g) $\frac{22}{62}$ (h) $\frac{39}{62}$ (i) $\frac{48}{69}$

4.6.4

(1) (a)(i) $\frac{1}{6}$ (ii) $\frac{1}{2}$ (iii) $\frac{2}{3}$ (b)(i) yes, $P(A \cap B) = P(A) \times P(B)$ (ii) no, $P(A \cup B) \neq P(A) + P(B)$
(2) $\frac{17}{32}$
(3) (a) 0.000 005 (b) 0.999 995
(4) (a) 0.686 (b) 0.938 (c) 0.731
(5) (a)(i) 0.3, 0.3 (ii) $\frac{3}{7}$, 0.3 (b) $\frac{3}{11}$
(6) 0.341

Exercise on Chapter 4

(1) (a) $\frac{9}{20}$ (b)(i) $\frac{1}{100}$ (ii) $\frac{7}{400}$ (2)(a) $\frac{3}{8}$ (b) $\frac{1}{2}$ (c) $\frac{1}{6}$
(3) (a)(i) $\frac{1}{6}$ (ii) 0 (iii) $\frac{1}{36}$ (iv) $\frac{1}{216}$ (b)(i) $\frac{5}{36}$ (ii) $\frac{5}{216}$ (c) $\frac{5}{6}(\frac{1}{6})^n$
(4) $\frac{7}{24}$
(5) (a) $\frac{25}{216}$ (b) $\frac{10}{216}$
(6) (a) $\frac{9}{64}$ (b) $\frac{37}{64}$; 7
(7) (a) $\frac{8}{9}$ (b) $\frac{1}{9}$ (c) $\frac{1}{9}$ (d) $\frac{1}{63}$ (e) $\frac{13}{63}$ (f) $\frac{50}{63}$ (g) $\frac{1}{63}$
(8) (a)(i) $\frac{25}{49}$ (ii) $\frac{24}{49}$ (iii) $\frac{39}{49}$ (b) $(\frac{6}{25})^3$ (c) $\frac{1}{2}, \frac{49}{288}$
(9) $\frac{2}{3}$
(10) $P(j) = j/21, j = 1, \ldots, 6$; 0.166
(11) 0.005 99; 0.987
(12) (a) $\frac{5}{24}$ (b) $\frac{2}{3}, \frac{11}{126}$
(13) (a) $\frac{2}{3}$ (b) $\frac{1}{6}$ (c) $\frac{5}{18}$ (d) $\frac{1}{4}$ (e) $\frac{3}{5}$
(14) (a) $\frac{1}{4}$ (b) $\frac{1}{4}$ (c) $\frac{1}{16}$ (d) $\frac{1}{4}$ (e) $\frac{3}{4}$
(15) $\frac{5}{24}, \frac{1}{24}, \frac{5}{6}, \frac{1}{12}$; (a) not independent since $P(A)P(B) \neq P(A \cap B)$ (b) not mutually exclusive since $P(A \cap B) \neq 0$
(16) (a) 0.01 (b) 0.87 (c) 0.96 (d) 0.085
(17) (a) 0.19 (b) 0.238 (c) 0.798 (d) 0.0798
(18) (a) $\beta + \frac{1}{5}(\alpha - \beta)(\alpha + 4\beta)$
(19) (i) 0.54 (ii) $\frac{15}{23}$ (iii) 0.29 (iv) $\frac{18}{29}$ (v) $\frac{1}{3}$
(20) (a) 0.32 (b) 0.35 (c) 0.33
(21) (a) $\frac{296}{625}$ (b) $\frac{661}{1024}$
(22) machine 1 (probability = 0.4)
(23) $\frac{2}{3}$
(24) (a) $\frac{8}{15}$ (b) $\frac{1}{2}$ (c) $\frac{1}{6}$; independent

Chapter 5

5.3.3

(1) 22 100   (2) 3.6288 × 10⁶, 45
(3) (a)(i) 504 (ii) 360 (iii) 165 (iv) 165
(4) 215 760
(5) (a) 24   (b) 12
(6) (a) 40 320   (b) 1152
(7) (a)(i) 240 (ii) 480   (b) 210
(8) (a) 22   (b) 42
(9) (a) 64   (b) 18   (c) $\frac{21}{32}$
(10) (a) 48   (b)(i) 5 (ii) 9 (iii) $\frac{1}{2}n(n-3)$ (c)(i) 63 (ii) 32
(11) 151 200

Exercise on Chapter 5

(1) $\frac{1}{4}$
(2) $4 \times \binom{39}{13} \div \binom{52}{13} = 0.051$
(3) (a) 0.222   (b) 0.0703   (c) 0.112   (d) 0.180
(4) (a) $\frac{1}{455}$ (b) $\frac{2}{91}$ (c) $\frac{12}{91}$
(5) (a) 0.112   (b) 0.368
(6) 4.1×10^{-6}
(7) (a)(i) $\frac{1}{4}$ (ii) $\frac{1}{4}$ (iii) $\frac{1}{17}$ (iv) $\frac{15}{34}$ (b) $\frac{13}{30}$ (c)(i) 0.375 (ii) 0.563
(8) 263
(9) (a) 4368   (b) 858   (c) 0.294

Revision exercise A

(1) (b) 13.575, 13.8, 13.875, 13.425, 13.325, 13.175, 13.05, 13.075, 13.5, 13.625, 13.6   (d) general trend is neither up nor down so take predicted value as average of three previous years
(2) mean 5.01, s.d. 1.418, median 5.269; skewness −0.18; tail on right-hand side
(3) (a) 17.1 kg, 4.1 kg   (b) 17.85 kg, 5.57 kg;   (a) because of positive skew
(4) (a)(i) $\frac{1}{6}$ (ii) $\frac{3}{4}$ (iii) $\frac{1}{12}$ (b) $\frac{2}{9}$
(5) (a) frequencies: 1, 4, 7, 6, 12, 10, 7, 3   (b) 8.95–9.95   (c) 13.5   (d) 13.55
(6) (b)(i) 0.21 (ii) 0.273 (iii) 0.53 (iv) 0.538
(7) (a)(i) $\frac{5}{18}$ (ii) $\frac{1}{3}$ (b) $\frac{12}{35}$ (c) 294
(8) (a)(i) $\frac{1}{12}$ (ii) $\frac{1}{12}$ (b) 0.239
(9) £1627 (taking incomes to nearest £)
(10) 96, $\frac{1}{4}$
(12) (a)(i) $\frac{3}{11}$ (ii) $\frac{3}{7}$ (b)(i) $\frac{2}{35}$ (ii) $\frac{1}{14}$
(13) (a) $\frac{2}{25}$ (b) 0.84   (c) A wins 0.39, B wins 0.61
(14) 11.71, 2.17

Chapter 6

6.1.1

(1) $P(0)=0.0065, P(1)=0.0816, P(2)=0.2941, P(3)=0.3922, P(4)=0.1961, P(5)=0.0294$
(2) (a) 0.3038   (b) 0.4388   (c) 0.2135   (d) 0.0412   (e) 0.0026

6.4.1

(1) 2.78, 0.944   (2) 1.000, 0.706

6.5.1

1.9, 1.49, 2

6.6.1

(a) $-3, 4$ (b) 4, 4   (c) 3, 16

Exercise on Chapter 6

(1) (a) 1.2, 1.76   (b) 3.2, 25.4
(2) 35p
(3) 60p
(4) (c) $\frac{4}{5}$
(5) 2.208
(6) $\frac{1}{4}(x+1)$, $x=-1$; 50p
(7) (a) $\frac{1}{2}$ (b) $\frac{1}{4}$ (c) $\frac{1}{8}$ (d) $\frac{1}{8}$; 15p
(8) $10(7p-2-3p^2)$, $p=\frac{1}{3}$
(9) $E(X)=4\frac{1}{12}$
(10) (a) $\frac{1}{81}$ (b) $\frac{4}{81}$ (c) $\frac{56}{81}$; $C=5p$, profit 5p
(11) 2.75
(12) $P(-3)=p^3$, $P(0)=3p^2(1-p)$, $P(3)=3p(1-p)^2$, $P(6)=(1-p)^3$
(13) 2.4p

Chapter 7

7.1.1

(1) (a)(i) yes, fixed number (5) of independent trials, $p=\frac{1}{2}$ (ii) no, number of trials not
fixed   (iii) no, trials not independent   (iv) yes, fixed number (3) of effectively independent
trials, $p=\frac{1}{2}$ (v) no, p is not constant

(b)(i)

x (number of heads)	0	1	2	3	4	5
$P(X=x)$	$\frac{1}{32}$	$\frac{5}{32}$	$\frac{10}{32}$	$\frac{10}{32}$	$\frac{5}{32}$	$\frac{1}{32}$

(ii)

x	0	1	2	3	4
$P(X=x)$	$\frac{625}{1296}$	$\frac{500}{1296}$	$\frac{150}{1296}$	$\frac{20}{1296}$	$\frac{1}{1296}$

(2) (a)

x	0	1	2	3	4
$P(x)$	$\frac{81}{256}$	$\frac{108}{256}$	$\frac{54}{256}$	$\frac{12}{256}$	$\frac{1}{256}$

(b) 1   (c) 1   (d) $\frac{3}{4}$

(3)

r (number of girls)	0	1	2	3	4	5	6
$P(r)$	0.020	0.109	0.253	0.311	0.215	0.079	0.012

   (a) 3   (b) 0.311   (c) 0.382
(4)   (a) 0.34   (b) 0.264
(5)   2; 0.3222
(6)   (a) 0.901   (b) 11
(7)   (a) 0.258   (b) 0.579
(8)   (a)(i) 0.167 (ii) 0.0162   (b) $(0.98)^n$, 228

7.2.2

(1)   (a) 0.08   (b) 0.66
(2) $10 + 50q^9 - 50q^{10}$
(3)   (a)$(1-p)^8[1+4p(1-p)^6(2+21p)]$ (c) 13.03

Exercise on Chapter 7

(1) $P(1)=0.387$; 1
(2)   (a) 0.323   (b) £1.49
(3) $\frac{11}{27}$; no, since trials not independent.
(4)   0.087
(5)   (a) $1\frac{1}{3}$, $2\sqrt{2/3}$ (b) 32, 64, 48, 16, 2; 1
(6)   prob. all fresh $=0.54$, first claim valid; prob. two stale $=0.099$, second claim valid
          (a) 0.341   (b) 0.98; 14%
(7)   mean 1, s.d. 0.89   (a) 5   (b) 0.2
(8)   (a) $\frac{47}{128}$ (b)(i) $(\frac{7}{8})^5$ (ii) $(\frac{7}{8})^5$ (iii) $(\frac{3}{4})^5$; 0.2115
(9)   Probability distribution is Binomial with $p=\frac{1}{2}$, $n=6$ (a) 0.226   (b) 0.0730
(10)   (a) 0.246   (b) 0.246   (c) 0.410
(11)   0.275; 0.11
(12)   16.5, 42.4, 45.4, 25.9, 8.3, 1.4, 0.1

Chapter 8

8.2.2

(1)   0.0498, 0.1494, 0.2240, 0.2240, 0.1680, 0.1008, 0.0504, 0.9502
(2)   (a) 0.0183   (b) 0.0733   (c) 0.002 68   (d) 0.010 73
(3)   prob. 4 m faultless $=0.67$; 0.513 m
(4)   mean 3 errors; 194 pages
(5)   mean 1.5; 223.1, 334.7, 251.0, 125.5, 47.1, 14.1, 3.5, 1.0
(6)   (a) 0.135   (b) 0.271   (c) 0.0290   (d) 2   (e) 8.19

8.6.2

(1)   (a) 0.368   (b) 0.184   (c) 0.0190; 0.677
(2)   (a) 0.449   (b) 0.32   (c) 0.0119

8.7.1

(1) $p_n = \left(\dfrac{\mu - \lambda}{\mu}\right)\left(\dfrac{\lambda}{\mu}\right)^n; \left(\dfrac{\lambda}{\mu}\right)^5$

(2) (a) $4p_0 + 10p_2 - 13p_1 = 0$ (b) $3p_1 + 10p_3 - 12p_2 = 0$ (c) $2p_2 + 10p_4 - 11p_3 = 0$, 0.647

Exercise on Chapter 8

(1) mean 2.917, variance 2.860 (a) 0.788 (b) 0.002 93
(2) (a)(i) 0.5 (ii) 121.3, 60.7, 15.2, 2.5, 0.32, 0.03 (b) 0.929
(3)

Observed	35	38	20	6	1
Expected	36.8	36.8	18.4	6.1	1.9

(4) (a) 0.135 (b) 0.017 (c) 0.195
(5) (a)(i) 1.04 (ii) 53.0, 55.1, 28.7, 9.9, 2.6 (b) 0.121
(6) (a) $2e^{-2}$ (b) 0.1353, 0.2707, 0.2707, 0.3233; 1.782 (c) £7.69
(7) (a)(i) 0.0952 (ii) 0.0905 (b) 0.632; 63.2, 4.82
(8) (a) 0.195 (b) 0.762
(9) method A £266C, method B £415C

Chapter 9

9.4.2

(1) (a) 0.8413 (b) 0.0228 (c) 0.0968 (d) 0.8159 (e) 0.9750 (f) 0.2946 (g) 0.001 75
    (h) 0.7673 (i) 0.1379 (j) 0.1849 (k) 0.0167 (l) 0.7064 (m) 0.9659
(2) (a) 0.0861 (b) 0.7008 (c) 0.1401 (d) 0.9973 (e) 0.9545 (f) 0.6826 (g) 0.1296
    (h) 0.5139
(3) (a) 0.5793 (b) 0.4207 (c) 0.8413 (d) 0.1587 (e) 0.4206
(4) (a) 0.003 83 (b) 0.2525 (c) 0.0684 (d) 0.8176
(5) 0.004 66

9.4.4

(1) (a) 0.52 (b) −0.05 (c) −1.10 (d) 1.62 (e) −0.373 (f) −1.693 (g) 0.511 (h) 0.928
(2) (a) 124.7 (b) 135.0; 110.1, 89.9
(3) 168 cm
(4) 1.8119 mm
(5) 0.0421 kg

9.4.6

(1) (a) 0.1587 (b) 1.023 litres
(2) 0.0956, 0.253 cm
(3) s.d. 4.8 min (a) 0.27 (b) 0.15
(4) (a) 290 (b) 78 (c) 27
(5) 8 cm, 1.158 cm; 6.10–9.90 cm
(6) $\mu = 104$, $\sigma = 38.8$
(8) (a) 4.75% (b) 97.7% (c) 1112–1188 hours
(9) (a) 0.169 (b) 0.096 (c) 2.13 Ω
(10) 22.92, 22.06 mm
(11) (a) 34.3 (b) 3.3; 26.05 yr
(12) second setting; costs are £904, £878, £1012

9.5.1

(1)

Class	<5.5	5.5–6.5	6.5–7.5	7.5–8.5	8.5–9.5	9.5–10.5	>10.5
Frequency	1.5	8.3	23.5	33.4	23.5	8.3	1.5

(2)   1.8, 11.8, 32.2, 35.6, 15.5, 2.7, 0.2

9.7.2

(1) $\binom{100}{54}(\tfrac{1}{2})^{100}$; 0.0579

(2)   (a) 0.013 (b) 0.35 (c) 0.87

(3)   27

(4)   (a) $P(\geqslant 70) = \sum_{70}^{100} \binom{100}{r}(\tfrac{3}{4})^{r}(\tfrac{1}{4})^{100-r}$ (b) 0.90

Exercise on Chapter 9

(1)   137: 149 4

(2)   (a) 0.6247   (b) 93.32%   (c) 0.785

(3) $n = 24$

(4)   (a) 45, 625   (b) 31.6   (c) 14.4%

(5)   194: 100

(6)   0.102; 184

(7)   17.1p; 1.6p

(8)   0.125

Chapter 10

10.1.1

(a)   0.15   (b) 0.1   (c) $P(X=0)=0.35$, $P(X=1)=0.3$, $P(X=2)=0.35$, $P(Y=0)=0.25$,
$P(Y=1)=0.4$, $P(Y=2)=0.35$ (d) no

10.2.1

(1)

z	2	3	4
$P(z)$	0.28	0.54	0.18

$E(X)=1.6$, $E(Y)=1.3$, $E(X+Y)=2.9$

(2) $E(X)=1.0$, $E(Y)=1.1$, $E(X+Y)=2.1$

10.3.1

XY	1	2	4
$P(XY)$	0.28	0.54	0.18

$E(X)=1.6$, $E(Y)=1.3$, $E(XY)=2.08$

10.4.2

(1) (b) -0.1

(2) (a) $E(X)=0.9$, $E(Y)=1.2$

(b)

z	-2	-1	0	1	2	3
$P(z)$	0.1	0.1	0.3	0.2	0.2	0.1

$E(z)=0.6$

(c) 0.2

(3) (b) $E(X)=1$, $E(Y)=2$ (c) no, $\text{cov}(X, Y)=0$ is a necessary but not sufficient condition for independence (d) $4\alpha+1$

(4) 0.12

(5) (a) σ_X^2 (b) $\sigma_X^2-\sigma_Y^2$

(6) (a) 3, 7 (b) -4, 48 (c) 1, 19

(7) $3, \frac{1}{2}; 3, \frac{1}{n}$

10.5.1

(1) 0.121

(2) (a) 2.27×10^{-3} (b) $\sum_{n=0}^{\infty} \dfrac{96^n e^{-10}}{n!(2n)!}$ (c) 0, 60

10.7.2

(1) 0.0014

(2) $\sum_1^3 a_i\mu_i, \sum_1^3 a_i^2\sigma_i^2$; 0.0526; 0.1496

(3) 143.1 g, 14.15 g; 5.5%

(4) 0.12 mm, 0.0583; 1.97%

(5) 11.01 a.m.; 92.2%

(6) (a) 0.788 (b) 1.4×10^{-4} (c) 0.0289; assume distributions Normal

Exercise on Chapter 10

(1) $P(X=a) \frac{27}{1000}, \frac{189}{1000}, \frac{441}{1000}, \frac{343}{1000}$; $P(Y=b) \frac{5}{15}, \frac{8}{15}, \frac{2}{15}$
(a) $E(X)=2\frac{1}{5}$, $E(Y)=\frac{4}{5}$ (b) $1\frac{19}{25}$

(2) (a) 0.924 (b) 0.864 (c) 0.789

(3) (a) 1.06% (b) 0.0359 (c) 27.4%

(4) $E(X)=3.5$; $E(Y)=\frac{35}{18}$ (a) true (b) false

(5) 11.02 a.m.; 0.97

(6) (a) 0.0608 (b) 0.531 (c) 0.069

(7) (a) 0.212 (b) 0.006 38 (c) 0.764 (d) 0.709

(8) (a) 0.673 (b) 0.138

(9) 0.104

(10) (a) $\mu_X^2+\sigma_X^2$ (b) $\mu_X\mu_Y$, $\mu_X^2\sigma_Y^2+\mu_Y^2\sigma_X^2+\sigma_X^2\sigma_Y^2$ (c) $\mu_Y(\mu_X^2+\sigma_X^2)$

(11) $P(R=r, T=t)=2^{r+1}/3^{r+t+1}$, $P(R=r)=2^r/3^{r+1}$, $P(T=t)=2/3^t$; $E(R)=2$; yes

Revision exercise B

(1) (a) 0.000 278   (b) 0.219   (c) 10.29 a.m.

(2) (a) 0.02 (b) 0.77 (c) 0.029 (d) 0.05

£1500; 0.23; overestimate since life expectancy increases with improving health standards

(3) (a) 0.066   (b) 0.745; $N(0, 0.08)$

(4) 7.88, 2.55

(5) 33

(6) $N(300, 22.50)$, 8×10^{-4}; 0.0013; 0.017

(7) (a) 0.0228   (b) 0.186   (c) 0.118

(8) $(1+4p)/5$; $5p/(1+4p)$; multiple-choice gives higher marks

(9) (a) 0.1157, 0.125   (b) 0.5177, 0.4914   (c) 0.6651, 0.6187

(10) (a) $\frac{80}{243}$ (b) $\frac{131}{243}$; 0.9975

(11) (a) $\frac{5}{18}$, 0   (b) $2\frac{19}{36}$, $\frac{395}{1296}$ (c) $\frac{1}{20}$

(12) (a)(i) $1/4^6$ (ii) $154/4^6$ (b) $\frac{1}{4}$ (c) $21\frac{2}{3}N$ g

(13) (a) 0.264   (b) 0.468

(14)

y	0	1	2	3	4
$P(y)$	0.09	0.24	0.34	0.24	0.09

z	0	1	2	3	4
$P(z)$	0.447	0.232	0.222	0.072	0.027

mean $= 1$, variance $= 1.2$

(15) (a) $\frac{1}{3}$ (b) $\frac{1}{2}$ (c) $\frac{1}{10}$ (d) $\frac{3}{10}$ (e) $\frac{7}{10}$; 250

(16) (a)(i) 0.135 (ii) 0.323   (b) 0.250

(17) (a) 12.25p   (b) 0.82   (c) $\frac{47}{66}$

(18) (a) 0.2   (b) 0.417   (c) 0.48   (d) 0.86

(19) (a) $\frac{2}{3}$ (b) 0.042 42

(20) (a) 0.9   (b) 868

(21) $4\frac{1}{3}$, $2\frac{2}{9}$; $8\frac{2}{3}$, $8\frac{8}{9}$

(22) (a)(i) 0.135 (ii) 0.947   (b)(i) 0.144 (ii) 0.111 (iii) 0.0458

(23) $N(\mu_1 - \mu_2, \sigma_1^2 + \sigma_2^2)$; A 860, 20; B 863, 25; 0.1587; 0.537; 0.421

(24) (a) 5.7 min   (b) 4 min   (c) 34 (taking upper true class limits as 1.25, 2.5 etc.)

(25) (a) 0.0189   (b) 0.798

(26) (a) 0.311   (b)(i) 0.012 (ii) 0.046

(27)

r	1	2	3	4	5	6	7	8	9	10	11	12
$P(X=r)$	$\frac{6}{72}$	$\frac{7}{72}$	$\frac{8}{72}$	$\frac{9}{72}$	$\frac{10}{72}$	$\frac{11}{72}$	$\frac{6}{72}$	$\frac{5}{72}$	$\frac{4}{72}$	$\frac{3}{72}$	$\frac{2}{72}$	$\frac{1}{72}$

mean $= 5.25$

Chapter 11

11.4.1

(1) (a) 3.5, $\frac{35}{12}$ (b) 4.5, 8.25

(2) (a) $\frac{4}{125}$ (b) $\frac{1}{125}$; 1.25, 1

(3) $\frac{10}{9}$; the probability of succeeding does not depend on how many failures there have already been

(4) $k = \frac{1}{9}$ (a) 4   (b) 2   (c) 20

(5) (b)(i) $(\frac{1}{3})^6$ (ii) $\frac{3}{4}$ (c)(i) $(\frac{1}{3})^n$ (ii) the probability of a component lasting for n more times or more does not depend on the number of times it has already been used

(6) $(\frac{5}{6})^n$; $(\frac{1}{6})^n$, $(\frac{r}{6})^n - (\frac{r-1}{6})^n$ for $r = 2, 3, \ldots, 6$; $1 - \sum\limits_{r=1}^{6} (\frac{r}{6})^n$

(7) (a) $P(N = n) = 1/k$, $n = 1, 2, \ldots, k$; $E(N) = \frac{1}{2}(k + 1)$
     (b) $P(N = n) = (k - 1)^{n-1}/k^n$, $n = 1, 2, \ldots, k$; $E(N) = k$;
     method (a) is preferable

(8) $P(2) = p_1 p_2 + (1 - p_1)^2$, $P(3) = p_1 p_2(1 - p_1) + p_1(1 - p_2)$, $P(4) = p_1(1 - p_1)(1 - p_2)$; $p = (4 - \sqrt{7})/3$

(9) $p^r q$; p/q

11.6.1

(1) 7.5 min, 18.75 min^2

(2) $\frac{1}{12}h^2$; 2.58 cm^2; to nearest 0.5 cm

11.7.2

(1) 27.5, 12.4, 5.6, 2.5, 1.1, 0.9

(2) (a) $10 \ln 2 = 6.93$ hr   (b) $\frac{1}{10}e^{-x/10}$ (c) 10 hr, 100 hr^2 (d) 0.24

(3) 0.6065; the probability of a bulb failing does not depend on how long it has been used.

11.8.5

(1) (a) 4   (b) $F(x_0) = 0$, $x_0 < 1$; $F(x_0) = x_0^4$, $0 \leqslant x_0 \leqslant 1$; $F(x_0) = 1$, $x_0 > 1$ (c) 0.841   (d) 0.8, 0.026   (e) 0.590

(2) (a) 6   (b) 0.5   (c) $F(x_0) = 0$, $x_0 < 0$; $F(x_0) = 3x_0^2 - 2x_0^3$, $0 \leqslant x_0 \leqslant 1$; $F(x_0) = 1$, $x_0 > 1$ (d) 0.5, 0.05

(3) (a) $-\frac{3}{16}$ (b) $\frac{19}{80}$ (d) 2

(4) (c) $\frac{3}{32}$ (d) $1\frac{47}{192} = 1.24$

(5) $\frac{1}{10}$ (a) 0.245   (b) $\frac{1}{200}(10 + t)^2$ (c) $1 - \frac{1}{200}(10 - t)^2$

(6) (b) $\frac{1}{2}$, $\frac{1}{4}$

(7) (a) $2\frac{2}{5}$ (b) 20, $\frac{1}{3}$, $\sqrt{\frac{2}{63}}$

(8) $a = \frac{1}{9}$, $b = \frac{2}{9}$, $c = \frac{1}{9}$

(9) $k = (\theta + 1)$, mean $= (\theta + 1)/(\theta + 2)$, variance $= (\theta + 1)/\{(\theta + 3)(\theta + 2)^2\}$

(10) (a) $\alpha = \frac{1}{2}$, $\beta = -\frac{1}{4}$ (b) $\frac{7}{16}$

(c)
$$f(x) = \begin{cases} 0 & (x \leqslant 0) \\ \frac{1}{2}x & (0 \leqslant x \leqslant 1) \\ \frac{1}{2} & (1 \leqslant x \leqslant 2) \\ -\frac{1}{2}x + 1\frac{1}{2} & (2 \leqslant x \leqslant 3) \\ 0 & (3 \leqslant x) \end{cases}$$
mean $= 1\frac{1}{2}$, variance $= \frac{5}{12}$

(11) 0.016

(12) (c)
$$F(x_0) = \begin{cases} -\dfrac{1}{12x_0^3} & (x_0 < -1) \\ \frac{1}{2} + \frac{1}{2}x_0 - \frac{1}{12}x_0^3 & (-1 \leqslant x_0 \leqslant 1) \\ 1 - \dfrac{1}{12x_0^3} & (1 < x_0) \end{cases}$$
(d) $E(X) = 0$, $\text{var}(X) = \frac{11}{15}$

11.12.2

(1) $M(t) = c/(2-t)$ where $c = 2$

(4) $\alpha = (1-\theta)$, $q_r = \theta^{r+1}$ (where R takes values 0, 1, 2, etc.)

$$\text{p.g.f.} = \frac{\theta^{-k}-1}{1-t\theta^k}, \quad \text{mean} = \frac{1}{1-\theta^k} \quad \text{variance} = \frac{\theta^k}{(1-\theta^k)^2}$$

11.13.3

(1) (a) $\frac{4}{3}a^2$, $\frac{4}{3}\pi a^2$ (b) $\frac{5}{4}\pi a^2$

(2) $f(x) = 1/(b-a)$; $F(x_0) = (x_0-a)/(b-a)$; $P(V \leqslant v) = 3 - (72/v)$
    (a) $f(v) = 72/v^2$ (b) 0.4   (c) 28.8 m.p.h.

(3) $\frac{2}{3}$; $r\sqrt{2}$; $\dfrac{2}{\pi}\sin^{-1}\dfrac{k}{2r}$

(4) (b) $\frac{125}{36}$

(5) (a) $c = \frac{3}{250}$, 687.5 h   (b)(i) 320p (ii) 0.792

(6) (a) $\frac{1}{8}$ (b) $\frac{5}{16}$, $\frac{21}{16}$ (c) $g(y) = 2$ ($\frac{17}{16} \leqslant y \leqslant \frac{25}{16}$); $g(y) = 0$ elsewhere

11.14.2

(1) $F(x_0) = 0$ ($x_0 \leqslant -2$), $F(x_0) = \frac{1}{8}(2+x_0)^2$ ($-2 \leqslant x_0 \leqslant 0$), $F(x_0) = 1 - \frac{1}{8}(2-x_0)^2$ ($0 \leqslant x_0 \leqslant 2$),
    $F(x_0) = 1$ ($2 \leqslant x_0$)

(2) $f(x_1, x_2) = f(x_1)f(x_2)$;

$$E[g(x_1, x_2)] = \iint g(x_1, x_2)f(x_1)f(x_2)\,dx_1\,dx_2;$$

$E(X) = 0$; $\text{var}(X) = a_1^2\,\text{var}(x_1) + a_2^2\,\text{var}(x_2) = (a_1^2 + a_2^2)\,\text{var}\,x$

(3) $a = 3$; $\text{cov}(X, Y) = 0$; not independent

(4) $a = 1/\sqrt{2}$; $f(x, y) = \frac{1}{2}$; $f_X(x) = 1-x$ ($0 \leqslant x \leqslant 1$), $f_X(x) = 1+x$ ($-1 \leqslant x \leqslant 0$); $E(X) = 0$, $\text{var}(X) = \frac{1}{6}$
    (a) 2   (b) $1\frac{1}{2}$ (c) 0

(5) $\hat{\theta} = n\Big/\sum_i x_i$, $E(X) = 1/\theta$

Exercise on Chapter 11

(1) (a) $\frac{2}{3}$ (b) $f(x) = \frac{2}{3}x$ ($0 \leqslant x \leqslant 1$), $f(x) = -\frac{1}{3}x + 1$ ($1 \leqslant x \leqslant 3$), $f(x) = 0$ otherwise; mean $= \frac{4}{3}$,
    variance $= \frac{7}{18}$ (c) 1.268; $\frac{7}{8}$

(2) 3/5, 1/5; 0.167

(3) 3/8, 0, 2/5;   (a) $\frac{85}{512}$ (b) $\frac{85}{152}$

(4) (a) 12   (b) $\frac{1}{2}$ (c) $F(x_0) = 0$, $x < 0$; $F(x_0) = 3x_0^4 - 2x_0^6$, $0 \leqslant x_0 \leqslant 1$; $F(x_0) = 1$, $x_0 > 1$
    (d) $g(y) = 6y(1-y)$

(5) (b) 8.7; 8.1, 9.2; 8.5

(6) $P(r) = \dfrac{\lambda^r e^{-\lambda}}{r!(1-e^{-\lambda})}$

(7) no

(8) $\displaystyle\int_\alpha^\beta f(x)\,dx = 1$ and $f(x) \geqslant 0$ for $\alpha \leqslant x \leqslant \beta$; $k = 12$; $\frac{2}{5}$, $\frac{1}{25}$; $x = \frac{1}{3}$

(10) $F(A) = 0$ ($A \leqslant 0$), $F(A) = \dfrac{2}{\pi}\sin^{-1}\left(\dfrac{2A}{a^2}\right)\left(0 \leqslant A \leqslant \dfrac{a^2}{2}\right)$, $F(A) = 1$ $\left(\dfrac{a^2}{2} \leqslant A\right)$; mean $\dfrac{a^2}{\pi}$

(11) $F(z) = 0$ ($z \leqslant 0$), $F(z) = z^2/a^2$ ($0 \leqslant z \leqslant a$), $F(z) = 1$ ($z \geqslant a$); $f(z) = 0$ ($z \leqslant 0$ and $z \geqslant a$), $f(z) = 2z/a^2$
    ($0 \leqslant z \leqslant a$); $E(Z) = \frac{2}{3}a$

(12) $A = 1$, $B = -\frac{1}{3}$; $\mu = 2.82$

Chapter 12

Exercise on Chapter 12

(4) 63 000

(5) (a)

r	0	1	2	3	4	5	6	7	8	9	
$F(r)$	3	2	1	2	3	4	5	6	5	4	not satisfactory

(b)

r	0	1	2	3	4	5	6	7	8	9	
$F(r)$	1	1	1	1	1	1	1	1	1	1	satisfactory

(6) (a) time consuming   (b) satisfactory   (c) not random   (d) not random

(7) 37.9%

(9) none gives a random sample

Chapter 13

13.3.2

(1) 2, 1

$\bar{x}$	1	$\frac{5}{3}$	$\frac{7}{3}$	3
$P(\bar{X}=\bar{x})$	$\frac{1}{8}$	$\frac{3}{8}$	$\frac{3}{8}$	$\frac{1}{8}$

(2) (a) $\mu=0$, $\sigma^2=1.2$

13.5.2

(1) $\dfrac{r_1}{n_1}$, $\sqrt{\left\{\dfrac{p(1-p)}{n_1}\right\}}$; $\dfrac{1}{2}\left[p(1-p)\left(\dfrac{1}{n_1}+\dfrac{1}{n_2}\right)\right]^{1/2}$; $\dfrac{1}{3}<\dfrac{n_1}{n_2}<3$

(3) $\hat{\mu}_1$ is more efficient; var($\hat{\mu}_1$): var($\hat{\mu}_2$)=3:5

(5) $k=0.5$

13.6.2

(1) (a) 0.4602   (b)(i) 0.3821 (ii) 0.1587

(2) (a)(ii) (64.4 − 67.6) kg   (b)(i) £773 − £817   (c)(i) 51.48 − 51.72

(3) $N(54, 64)$, 0.0228, $c=16$; $N(5, 144)$, 0.662

Exercise on Chapter 13

(1) (a) 4, 14.4

(b) (i)

$\bar{X}$	$6\frac{2}{3}$	$5\frac{1}{3}$	$4\frac{2}{3}$	$3\frac{1}{2}$	2	$1\frac{1}{3}$
$P(\bar{X})$	0.1	0.2	0.2	0.3	0.1	0.1

(iii) 2.4

(2) (a) 2μ, $\sigma\sqrt{2}$ (b) 0, $\sigma\sqrt{2}$ (c) μ, $\sigma/\sqrt{2}$; 0.71, 0.92

(3) $v=1.645/\sqrt{n}$, $n\geqslant215$

(4) (a) $E(X)=2\theta$, var(X)$=\theta^2/n$ (b) $N(\mu, 1/n)$; $n\geqslant97$

(5) 7, 5.83; $N(7n, 5.83n)$
(6) 6

(7) $P(R=r)=\binom{r-1}{a-1}p^a(1-p)^{r-a}$ $(r \geqslant a)$

Chapter 14

14.1.2

(1) (a) (3.114–3.166) mm   (b) (3.109–3.171) mm
(2) (15.03–15.39) g; because of the central limit theorem

14.2.3

(1) (a) (15.72–18.68) h   (b) (15.44–18.96) h
(2) 47.86–48.14
(3) 105.5 h, 78.1 h; (84.7–125.3) h
(4) 11.41 mm, 0.120 mm; (11.39–11.43) mm

14.3.2

(1) (0.9714–0.9886) cm
(2) (23.1–25.3) g
(3) population Normal; (51.81–54.19) g
(4) (6.754–8.182) mN

14.4.3

(1) 0.34–0.62
(2) (a) 0.023–0.227   (b) 27–273
(3) (a) 34%   (b) 29.4%–38.6%   (c) 2155
(4) 0.162, s.e. = 0.024; 0.114–0.210; 1400; 0.054–0.112;
     Assuming patients are allocated to the different treatments at random, antitoxin treatment seems less effective. The next two chapters give methods of testing this.

Exercise on Chapter 14

(1) (a) 0.866   (b)(i) 2.00 mg (ii) −1.01 to 1.01 mg
(2) (a) (50.0–54.6) kg   (b) (1.80–2.44) kg
(3) (a) (0.252–0.262) kg   (b) 246
(4) (a) 2.04–3.96   (b) 25.2%–34.8%   (c) retired, unemployed
(5) (a) $c = \bar{x}$ (b)(i) 456, 108 (ii) 449.4–462.6 (iii) 457, 89
(6) 10 000, 7240–16 200
(7) (b) (7.3–9.3)%
(8) (a) 26 500   (b) 1068
(9) yes
(10) 4, 2.47–4.96; 4.1, 3.90–4.10

Chapter 15

15.1.2

(1) $H_0 : p = \frac{1}{4}$, $H_1 : p > \frac{1}{4}$, probability of three of more correct identifications = 0.47, retain H_0; six or more times

(2) $P(X \geqslant 6) = 0.0766$ if X is $B(10, \frac{1}{3})$; not sig. at 5% level
(3) $P(X \leqslant 6) = 0.1178$ if X is $B(12, 0.7)$; not sig. at 5% level
(4) $P(X \geqslant 3) = 0.1348$ if X is $B(8, \frac{1}{6})$; not sig. at 5% level

15.2.2

(1) $z = 1.71$; sig. at 5% level (1-tail)
(2) $z = 2.83$, sig. at 5% level (2-tail); $z = 1.90$, not sig. at 2% level (2-tail)
(3) 3 mm, 0.02 mm; $z = 1.8$, not sig. at 5% level (2-tail)
(4) $z = 1.79$, not sig. at 5% level (2-tail)
(5) $\bar{x} = 4.6$, $z = 7.7$, sig. at 5% level (2-tail); no, since in written English certain short words, e.g. 'a', 'and', occur frequently.
(6) $z = -1.50$; not sig. at 5% level (2-tail)
(7) $z = +3$; sig. at 5% level (1-tail)

15.3.2

(1) 26.75 yr, 42.22 yr^2; $z = 1.85$, not sig. at 5% level (2-tail)
(2) $z = 4.44$, sig. at 1% level (1-tail)
(3) $z = 5.3$, sig. at 5% level (2-tail)
(4) $z = -1.47$, not sig. at 5% level (2-tail)
(5) $z = -2.2$, not sig. at 1% level (2-tail)
(6) $z = -4.68$, sig. at 1% level (1-tail)

15.4.2

(1) $t_6 = -0.298$; not sig. at 10% level (1-tail)
(2) 8.6; assume Normal, $t_5 = 3.54$, sig. at 5% level (2-tail)
(3) $t_4 = 2.21$, not sig. at 5% level (2-tail)
(4) $t_7 = 1.67$, not sig. at 5% level (2-tail)

15.5.2

(1) $z = 4.8$, sig. at 5% level (2-tail); 65.13–67.35, 68.83–70.65
(2) $z = 1.44$, not sig. at 5% level (2-tail)
(3) $z = 2.86$, sig. at 5% level (1-tail); better-motivated students more likely to improve, i.e. samples not random
(4) $z = 4.6$, sig. at 1% level (1-tail)
(5) $z = -2.15$, sig. at 5% level (1-tail)

15.6.2

(1) $z = 1.76$, not sig. at 5% level (2-tail); $z = 1.76$, sig. at 5% level (1-tail)
(2) $t_{11} = 3.47$, sig. at 5% level (2-tail)
(3) 4.157, $t_{20} = 14.2$, sig. at 5% level (2-tail)

15.8.1

(1) $P(\leqslant 3-$ or $\geqslant 7-) = 0.34$, not sig. at 5% level (2-tail); $t_9 = 1.16$, not sig. at 5% level (2-tail); Normality
(2) $P(\geqslant 21 +) = 0.0005$, sig. at 5% level (1-tail); yes; $t_{24} = 5.17$, sig. at 5% level (1-tail)

15.9.2

(1) no, $z = 1.40$, not sig. at 5% level (2-tail)
(2) yes, $z = 2.08$, sig. at 5% level (1-tail)
(3) yes, $z = 2.59$, sig. at 5% level (2-tail)
(4) yes, $z = 4.06$, sig. at 5% level (1-tail)

15.10.2

(1) yes, $z = 2.57$, sig. at 5% level (2-tail)
(2) yes, $z = 2.89$, sig. at 5% level (2-tail)

15.11.2

(1) $P(X \leqslant 3) = 0.082$ if X is $Po(7)$; not sig. at 5% level (1-tail)
(2) $z = -2.16$; sig. at 5% level (1-tail)

15.12.2

(1) $r = 3$ to 9; 0.182
(2) 21.81–26.19; 0.05; 0.855
(3) $n = 35, v = 3.028$
(4) (a) 2%, 0.377 (b) $\bar{x} > 54.66$ (i) 0.749 (ii) 0.0918

15.13.1

(a) 1 in 40 line between 5 and 6 defectives, 1 in 1000 line between 8 and 9 defectives
(b) (i) 0.384 (ii) 0.0681 (iii) 0.754

Exercise on Chapter 15

(1) (a) $t_9 = 1.96$, not sig. at 5% level (2-tail) (b) 12.9 ± 1.04
(3) $P(\geqslant 6) = 0.0064$, suspicion justified
(4) -1.10–0.21, includes zero therefore mean is likely to be zero
(5) $t_9 = 2.33$, sig. at 5% level (2-tail); assume both populations are Normal
(6) yes, $z = 4$, sig. at 5% level (2-tail); 0.2–0.6
(7) $a = \frac{1}{3}; \frac{4}{9}$
(8) $P(5$ or $6) = 0.109$; not sig. at 5% level; yes, $z = 1.83$, sig. at 5% level (1-tail)
(9) Normal; $z = 4$, sig. at 5% level (2-tail)
(10) yes, $t_{12} = 0.429$, not sig. at 5% level (2-tail)
(11) $0.30 < p < 0.38$; 0.309; $z = 3.03$
(12) 11.642, 1.892; no, $z \simeq t_{99} = 1.88$, not sig. at 5% level (2-tail); $12 + 4.66/\sqrt{n}$
(13) (a) yes, $z = 2.4$, sig. at 5% level (1-tail)
      (b) yes, $z = 2.95$, sig. at 5% level (1-tail)
(14) yes, $z \simeq t_{120} = 2.1$, sig. at 5% level (2-tail)
(15) 3.62, 0.29; $t_9 = 4.5$, sig. at 5% level (1-tail)

Revision exercise C

(1) (a) 0.277   (b) 0.682   (c) 0.118
(2) (a) 0.879   (b) 9.69, 0.2339   (c) 0.28
(3) 106.75, 111.25, 114.25, 116.5, 120.0, 124.25, 128.5, 132.0, 135.75, 138.5, 130.0, 133.5, 137.0, 140.5;
      1.04, 1.06, 0.89, 1.03; 1.0
(4) (a)(i) $\frac{4}{17}$ (ii) $\frac{1}{17}$ (iii) $\frac{5}{17}$ (b)(i) $\frac{1}{4}$ (ii) $\frac{1}{13}$ (iii) $\frac{4}{13}$ (c) $\frac{17}{108}$
(5) $\frac{1}{2}(n-1); \frac{1}{2}, \frac{1}{12}$
(6) 1.15; 25.8–30.2; yes, $z = 1.78$, not sig. at 5% level (2-tail); no, $z = 3.33$, sig. at 5% level (2-tail)
(7) 1.04, 0.96; yes, mean $\simeq$ variance; 0.84–1.24
(8) $\mu = 1.51$ mm, $\sigma = 0.051$ mm; 3.028, 0.0721; 0.90
(9) (a) 0.36   (b) 0.46   (c) 0.670   (d) 0.714
(11) (a) 10.6%, 6.7%   (b) £98.90   (c) yes, $z = 2.5$, sig. at 5% level (1-tail)

(12) 524–676

(13) (a) $\binom{20}{10} 0.5^{20} = 0.176$ (c) 0.411 (using Normal approx.); 6%, 0.07

(14) (a) 24 (b) 28 (c) $\frac{15}{32}$

(15) 2.64, 1.9; 2.3; 1.4, 2.9 (min)

(16) $\mu_1 - \mu_2$, $\sigma_1^2 + \sigma_2^2$; μ_1, σ_1^2/n_1; $\mu_1 - \mu_2$, $(\sigma_1^2/n_1) + (\sigma_2^2/n_2)$; both Normal; yes, $z = 1.7$, sig. at 5% level (1-tail)

(17) yes, $z = 2.0$, sig. at 5% level (2-tail)

(19) (a)(i) $\frac{21}{38}$ (ii) $\frac{5}{19}$ (iii) $\frac{7}{38}$ (b) 6.97

(21) (a) Poisson, $\lambda = 4.4$ (b) Uniform over -2.5 to $+2.5\,\text{mm}$ (c) Binomial, $p = \frac{1}{15}$, $n = 6$
      (d) Normal, $N(260, 4)$

(22) $P(r) = \dfrac{e^{-\lambda}\lambda^r}{r!(1 - e^{-\lambda})}$; variance $= \dfrac{[\lambda(1 - e^{-\lambda}) - \lambda^2 e^{-\lambda}]}{(1 - e^{-\lambda})^2}$

(23) (a) 0.0228 (b) 0.734; 28; $\bar{x}_G$ 162.5 cm, 0.25 cm^2; $\bar{x}_B$ 173.5 cm, 0.64 cm^2; $\bar{x}_B - x_G$ 11.0 cm,
      0.89 cm^2; 0.145; no, will be bimodal

(25) $a + \frac{1}{4}b$; $a = 5$, $b = 8$

(27) no, $t_{10} = 1.66$, not sig. at 5% level (2-tail)

(28) (a) 0.0222 (b) 0.9778; $6250T^2 - 100\,096T + 4\,000\,000 = 0$

(29) $\frac{13}{24}$

(30) $\bar{x}$, unbiased; 6.16–8.64

(31) $\lambda e^{-t\lambda}$; $\lambda/(\lambda - \theta)$; $1/\lambda^2$

(32) $\lambda p_0 = \mu p_1$; $(\lambda/\mu) - 1.645(\lambda/\mu)^{1/2}$

(33) $\dfrac{n!}{r!(n-r)!}\, p_2^r q_1^r (1 - p_2 q_1)^{n-r}$; $-np_2 q_1^2 q_2$

Chapter 16

Yates' correction has been applied and classes combined if expected frequencies are less than 5.

16.4.2

(1) yes, $X^2 = 20.2$, 9 d.f., sig. at 5% level
(2) 12, 24, 36, 48, 60, 72, 60, 48, 36, 24, 12;
     for A, $X^2 = 14.5$, for B, $X^2 = 2.12$, both 10 d.f.; B's results are too good to be true

16.7.1

(1) reject H_0, $X^2 = 9.6$, 2 d.f., sig. at 5% level
(2) no, $X^2 = 0.23$, 1 d.f., not sig. at 5% level
(3) Retain H_0, $X^2 = 3.2$, 7 d.f., not sig. at 5% level.
(4) 3; 2.5, 7.5, 11.2, 11.2, 8.4, 5.0, 2.5, 1.1, 0.6; $X^2 = 0.28$, 3 d.f.; too good to be true

16.9.1

(1) no, $X^2 = 2.8$, 1 d.f., not sig. at 5% level
(2)

21.0	10.0	7.0
15.5	7.4	5.2
41.5	19.7	13.8

no evidence of association; $X^2 = 7.9$, 4 d.f., not sig. at 5% level

(3) $X^2 = 6,7$, 4 d.f., not sig. at 5% level, examiners do not differ in standards

Exercise on Chapter 16

(1) $\bar{x} = 2.97$, $X^2 = 1.2$, 6 d.f.; too good to be true
(2) (a) yes, $X^2 = 4.25$, 5 d.f., not sig. at 5% level
     (b) no, $X^2 = 0.47$, 1 d.f., not sig. at 5% level
(3) yes, $X^2 = 6.56$, 2 d.f., sig. at 5% level; beach 3 differs from the other two; percentages are 44%, 43%, 55%
(4) yes, $X^2 = 20.8$, 8 d.f., sig. at 5% level
(5) (a) 99.4, 119.3, 71.6, 28.6, 8.6, 2.1, 0.4 (b) $X^2 = 0.45$, 3 d.f., not sig. at 5% level; Poisson model adequate
(6) yes, $X^2 = 6.7$, 1 d.f., sig. at 5% level; yes
(7) $X^2 = 19.5$, 9 d.f., sig. at 5% level
(8) $X^2 = 3.4$, 1 d.f., not sig. at 5% level; follows Normal distribution
(9) no, $X^2 = 4.9$, 2 d.f., not sig. at 5% level; no, $X^2 = 0.6$, 2 d.f., not sig. at 5% level
(10) $X^2 = 13.1$, 3 d.f., sig. at 5%; Binomial distribution is not an adequate model

Chapter 17

17.2.4

(1) (a) −0.98 (b) −0.03
(2) −0.91, −0.98

17.3.4

(1) 0.58; (−0.22)−0.91
(2) yes, $z = 1.3$, not sig. at 5% level (2-tail)
(3) (a) 0.88 (b) 0.83−0.92

17.5.3

(1) (a) $r_S = 0.88$, sig. at 5% level, judges are consistent (b) *C, I, E, D, B, G, J, A, F, H*
(2) (a) $r_S = 0.66$ (b) $r_S = 0.54$; neither value sig. at 5% level, no agreement in ranking
(3) $r_S = 0.28$, not sig. at 5% level, no evidence of correlation.
(4) (a) $r_S = 0.75$, sig. at 5% level, evidence that judges agree

17.6.2

(1) $\tau = 0.73$, sig. at 5% level, judges are consistent
(2) (a) $\tau = 0.47$ (b) $\tau = 0.47$; neither value sig. at 5% level, no evidence of agreement in ranking
(3) $\tau = 0.178$, not sig. at 5% level, no evidence of correlation
(4) $\tau = 0.53$, sig. at 5% level, evidence that judges agree

Exercise on Chapter 17

(1) $r_S = -0.86$, $\tau = -0.71$; both values sig. at 5% level, evidence of inverse correlation
(2) (a) invalid – plots may differ (b) invalid – number of drivers may vary with age
     (c) valid (d) invalid – confuses correlation and causation
(3) (b) $r_S = 0.87$, $\tau = 0.69$; both values sig. at 5% level, evidence that judges agree
(5) (a) −0.37 (b) −0.27 (c) no evidence of a linear relationship but a quadratic relationship might exist

(6) $r_S = 0.97$
(8) $r = 0.78$

Chapter 18

18.3.2

(1) (a) $y = 0.486x - 2.397$ (b) 0.997 (c) no, the line predicts hardnesses greater than 10 and less than 0
(2) $y = 2.79x - 5451$; 53.7×10^6 gallons
(3) (b) $y = 2.75x + 48.35$ (c) 0.79
(4) mass on age; $y = 18.9x + 154$; 476 g; not valid, since relationship not linear

18.7.2

(1) (a) $\hat{y} = -4x + 24$ (b) 8, 0.395 (mean of three observed values of Y when $x = 4$ is 8.67 with s.e. $= 0.722$) (c) 7.4–8.6
(2) $k = 0.9948$, $c = -1.998$; 0.92–1.07 mm
(3) (a) $\hat{a} = 0.06$, $\hat{b} = 0.132$ (b) 1.344–1.416; 22.1–26.1
(4) $y = -x + 12$; 5.67–6.33; 0, not linear
(5) (a) 18.8–27.2 (b) (-0.428)–(-0.222)

18.9.2

(1) 29 yr; 0.73
(2) $y = -1.45x + 114$ (a) no (b) 60.4
(3) $y = 0.383x + 6.43$; 17.9
(4) $y = 0.527x - 25.4$; $x = 1.008y + 94.4$; 0.73; 53.7 m

Exercise on Chapter 18

(1) $y = x + 3.5$; $x = 0.5y$
(2) (a) $y = 1.33x + 5.68$ (b) 28 300
(3) (b) $y = 22.6 + 73.6 \log_{10}x$
(4) $y = 2.5x - 5$
(5) $y = -0.0157x + 52.88$ (where $y = $ cost, $x = $ number of beds); D most expensive, G cheapest
(6) (a) $\bar{x} = 0.3$, $\bar{y} = 1.65$ (c) $y = 1.31x + 1.257$ (e) 3.42
(7) $y = 2.4x + 4$; 13.6, use mean as relationship probably not linear
(8) $b = 13.17$; 212
(9) $\hat{s}_{y|x} = 0.078$; $\hat{b} = 0.56 - 2.06$; $\hat{a} = 0.98 - 1.54$; 3.03–3.81 tonnes

Chapter 19

19.2.2

0.11–0.54

19.4.2

(1) $F_{12,13} = 2.08$, not sig. at 5% level (2-tail), no difference in variability; can test if means differ using pooled estimate of variance

(2) no difference in variability, $F_{9,11}=1.21$, not sig. at 5% level (2-tail) difference in means, $t_{20}=3.9$, sig. at 5% level (2-tail)

19.6.2

(1) means differ significantly, $F_{2,15}=13.3$; no difference in variability between 1 and 2, $F_{5,5}=1.7$, not sig. at 5% level; means of 1 and 2 differ, $t_{10}=2.39$, sig. at 5% level (2-tail)
(2) (a) $F_{4,15}=3.7$, mean shrinkages for different temperatures differ significantly   (b) calculation of t_6 for pairs of temperatures gives no sig. difference if both in pair are above 92°C or both below: data support theory

19.7.2

(1) no difference between diseases or diets, $F_{2,6}=1.65$, $F_{3,6}=0.93$
(2) both finishes and towns differ significantly, $F_{3,6}=103$, $F_{2,6}=52$

Exercise on Chapter 19

(1) (a) 32.1   (b) $F_{4,8}=4.4$, $F_{2,8}=5.4$; both makes of car and brands of petrol differ significantly   (c) not valid
(2) $F_{3,20}=11.2$, mean thickness differs significantly
(3) $F_{16,19}=1.27$, variances do not differ significantly; $t_{35}=5.5$, means do differ significantly (2-tail test); 48.1–55.9
(4) $F_{10,7}=2.9$, variances do not differ significantly; $t_{17}=1.8$, sig. at 5% level (1-tail)

Revision exercise D

(1) 0.8962
(2) (a) $1-e^{-\lambda x}$ (b) λ^{-1}, λ^{-2} (c) $\frac{1}{\lambda}\ln 2$ (d) $\frac{1}{\lambda}\ln\left(\frac{20}{19}\right)$
(3) (a) (i) $\dfrac{n(R\cap S)}{n(A)}$ (ii) $\dfrac{n(R\cup S\cap T')}{n(A)}$ (iii) $\dfrac{n(R\cap T)}{n(T)}$ (b) (i) 128 h (ii) 0.648 (iii) 0.432
(4) 67
(5) 6   (a) 0.0081   (b) 0.00856
(6) 0.632; 0.156
(7) 552, 508, 550, 523, 524, 475; downward
(8) 70.3 in.; 68.3 in.; 72.2 in.
(9) (a) 0.02   (b) 0.35   (c) 52.2%   (d) 42.3%
(10) $\dbinom{13}{5}\times 4^5 \bigg/ \dbinom{52}{5}$
(11)

140	210
60	90

$X^2=0.49$, 1 d.f. (Yates' correction applied), not sig. at 5% level, retain H_0
(12) 4.26; does not differ significantly from 4.5; $z=0.84$
(13) (a) $r_S=0.6$, $\tau=0.4$ (b) $x=1.23y-1.17$

(14) no evidence of difference between workers, $F_{3,12}=2.73$; evidence of difference between machines, $F_{4,12}=38.4$

(15) $\lambda_1+\lambda_2$

(16) (a)

Number of cells	0	1	2	3	4	5	6	7
Number of squares	10	10	13	7	4	2	1	1

(c) do conform to a Poisson distribution, mean 2; $X^2=2.98$, 4 d.f.

(d)

Number of cells	0	1	2	3	4	5	6	7
Number of squares	0	5	7	4	4	2	1	1

mean $=2.92$; Test H_0: mean $=2$. $z=3.2$, mean is significantly greater than 2. Research worker's suspicion is confirmed. (Another possibility is to test if the proportion of cells in the outer squares is significantly greater than 0.5.)

(17) (a)(i) Poisson (ii) Uniform (iii) Binomial   (b) (i) 0.25 (ii) 0.078

(19) $y=13.5-0.125x$, $x=25.5-0.5y$ (a) y on x (b) x on y

(20) (a) $\frac{21}{40}$ (b) $\frac{19}{30}$ (c) 0.352–0.448   (d) $z=4$, sig. at 0.1% level (2-tail)

(21) $(1-p)^{12}[1+12p(1-p)^{11}+210p^2(1-p)^{10}]$; 0.2978

(22) (a) not random   (b) expensive   (c) inconvenient to public

(23) $z=0.90$, no sig. difference at 5% level (2-tail)

(24) (a) $\dfrac{2}{n(n+1)}$, $\dfrac{n-1}{3}$, $\dfrac{n^2+n-2}{18}$

(25) 20 178, 162.0–399.0, 8822–83 580

(26) $y=5.71x+70.9$

(27) (a) correction for discrete variable applied incorrectly
(b) X_1 and X_1-X_2 are not independent
(c) should consider distribution of difference between two observations

(28) yes, $(T-4.5)/9.1$

(29) yes, $P(8 \text{ or } 9 \text{ correct})=0.02$; no change, $P(15, 16, 17 \text{ or } 18 \text{ correct})=0.004$

(30) (a) range and s.d. inconsistent; s.e. of mean is $s/\sqrt{(n-1)}$; confidence limits are for *population mean*
(b) accidents to the same person are not independent events

(31) $2 \operatorname{sech}^2 x \tanh x$; 1; $\frac{1}{2} \ln \left(\dfrac{\sqrt{2}+1}{\sqrt{2}-1}\right)$; $\frac{1}{2} \ln 3$, $\frac{1}{2} \ln \left(\dfrac{2+\sqrt{3}}{2-\sqrt{3}}\right)$; 0.38

(32) (b) (i) 0.525 (ii) 0.501–0.549 (iii) 9580

(33) (a) 1, 0.89   (b) 2, 1.4   (c) 2, 4   (d) 1, 0.58

(34) $N(\mu, \sigma^2/n)$; 0.1056; 1243

(35) Second-year students' measurements are more variable, $F_{10,9}=20$; mean of first-year students' measurements differs significantly from $-0.13°C$, $t_9=3.7$; mean of second-year students' measurements does not differ significantly from $-0.13°C$, $t_{10}=1.06$

(36) (a) Presumably 'average' means 'mean'. We would expect about half the children to be below average intelligence. If 'average' means 'median' then exactly half are below average intelligence!
(b) What does 'majority' mean? How were the tests made?
(c) The number of matches cannot be Normally distributed since it is a discrete variable. It cannot even be approximately Normally distributed with such a small s.d.
(d) A correlation of $+1$ means there is an *exact* mathematical relationship between the two variables.

(37) no, $z=2.8$, sig. at 5% level (2-tail); 0.27–0.45

(38) (b) 39, 24, 23, 8.6, 5.0; reasonable fit, $X^2=1.78$, 4 d.f.

(39) s.d. is unreasonably large; χ^2-test should have many fewer d.f.; r cannot be greater than 1; cannot expect to use regression line outside range in which measurements were made

(40) $\frac{35}{9}$, 6.76

(42) $X^2 = 4.0$, 1 d.f. (Yates' correction applied) or $z = 2.1$; both sig. at 5% level (2-tail)

(43) $P(\geqslant 8$ or $\leqslant 2$ heads$) = 0.11$, coin is unbiased.

(44) 5.03, 0.050   (a) 0.952   (b) 0.0139   (c) 0.988

(45) $\frac{2}{3}k(1-x^2)^{3/2}$, $4/\pi$, $\frac{3}{8}\sqrt{(1-x_0^2)}$

(46) (a) $F_{6,5} = 1.23$, not sig. at 5% level (2-tail)

   (b) $t_{11} = 0.54$, not sig. at 5% level (2-tail)

(47) $R = 16 \sin(4\pi/9)$ when $\alpha = 2\pi/9$ and $5\pi/18$, $R = 16$ when $\alpha = \pi/4$;

$$F(r) = \frac{18}{\pi}\left(\sin^{-1}\frac{r}{16} - \frac{4\pi}{9}\right); \ 15.94 \text{ km.}$$

(48) $X^2 = 6.4$, 1 d.f. (Yates' correction applied), short-sight and flat feet are not independent; 0.156–0.204; $z = 1.58$, observed proportion does not differ significantly from 0.2

(49) $y = -0.751x + 101$; $r_s = -0.97$, $\tau = -0.88$; strong inverse correlation.

(50) probability of only 0.000 52 of observing such a low number of cases if mean is unchanged

Appendix 1

Exercise 1

(1)   (a) 72   (b) 52   (c) 560

(2)   (a) $\displaystyle\sum_{r=1}^{10} 3r^2$ (b) $\displaystyle\sum_{r=1}^{7} (8r+1)$ (c) $\displaystyle\sum_{r=1}^{n} 2r^5$ (d) $\displaystyle\sum_{r=1}^{n} 2^r$

Exercise 2

(a) 13   (b) 53   (c) 51   (d) 199   (e) 6530

Exercise 3

(a) 39   (b) 391   (c) 120   (d) 277   (e) 679

Tables

431

Table A1 Normal distribution function

z	F(z)	z	F(z)	z	F(z)	z	F(z)	z	F(z)
0.00	0.5000 $_{40}$	0.50	0.6915 $_{35}$	1.00	0.8413 $_{25}$	1.50	0.9332 $_{13}$	2.00	0.97725 $_{53}$
.01	.5040 $_{40}$	.51	.6950 $_{35}$	.01	.8438 $_{23}$	.51	.9345 $_{12}$	.01	.97778 $_{53}$
.02	.5080 $_{40}$	.52	.6985 $_{34}$	.02	.8461 $_{24}$	.52	.9357 $_{13}$	.02	.97831 $_{51}$
.03	.5120 $_{40}$	.53	.7019 $_{35}$	.03	.8485 $_{23}$	.53	.9370 $_{12}$	.03	.97882 $_{50}$
.04	.5160 $_{39}$	.54	.7054 $_{34}$	.04	.8508 $_{23}$	.54	.9382 $_{12}$	.04	.97932 $_{50}$
0.05	0.5199 $_{40}$	0.55	0.7088 $_{35}$	1.05	0.8531 $_{23}$	1.55	0.9394 $_{12}$	2.05	0.97982 $_{48}$
.06	.5239 $_{40}$	.56	.7123 $_{34}$	.06	.8554 $_{23}$	.56	.9406 $_{12}$	.06	.98030 $_{47}$
.07	.5279 $_{40}$	.57	.7157 $_{33}$	.07	.8577 $_{22}$	.57	.9418 $_{11}$	.07	.98077 $_{47}$
.08	.5319 $_{40}$	.58	.7190 $_{34}$	.08	.8599 $_{22}$	.58	.9429 $_{12}$	.08	.98124 $_{45}$
.09	.5359 $_{39}$	.59	.7224 $_{33}$	.09	.8621 $_{22}$	.59	.9441 $_{11}$	.09	.98169 $_{45}$
0.10	0.5398 $_{40}$	0.60	0.7257 $_{34}$	1.10	0.8643 $_{22}$	1.60	0.9452 $_{11}$	2.10	0.98214 $_{43}$
.11	.5438 $_{40}$	.61	.7291 $_{33}$	.11	.8665 $_{21}$	.61	.9463 $_{11}$	.11	.98257 $_{43}$
.12	.5478 $_{39}$	.62	.7324 $_{33}$	.12	.8686 $_{22}$	.62	.9474 $_{10}$	.12	.98300 $_{41}$
.13	.5517 $_{40}$	.63	.7357 $_{32}$	.13	.8708 $_{21}$	.63	.9484 $_{11}$	.13	.98341 $_{41}$
.14	.5557 $_{39}$	.64	.7389 $_{33}$	.14	.8729 $_{20}$	.64	.9495 $_{10}$	.14	.98382 $_{40}$
0.15	0.5596 $_{40}$	0.65	0.7422 $_{32}$	1.15	0.8749 $_{21}$	1.65	0.9505 $_{10}$	2.15	0.98422 $_{39}$
.16	.5636 $_{39}$	.66	.7454 $_{32}$	.16	.8770 $_{20}$	.66	.9515 $_{10}$	.16	.98461 $_{39}$
.17	.5675 $_{39}$	.67	.7486 $_{31}$	.17	.8790 $_{20}$	.67	.9525 $_{10}$	.17	.98500 $_{37}$
.18	.5714 $_{39}$	.68	.7517 $_{32}$	.18	.8810 $_{20}$	.68	.9535 $_{10}$	.18	.98537 $_{37}$
.19	.5753 $_{40}$	.69	.7549 $_{31}$	.19	.8830 $_{19}$	.69	.9545 $_{9}$	.19	.98574 $_{36}$
0.20	0.5793 $_{39}$	0.70	0.7580 $_{31}$	1.20	0.8849 $_{20}$	1.70	0.9554 $_{10}$	2.20	0.98610 $_{35}$
.21	.5832 $_{39}$	.71	.7611 $_{31}$	.21	.8869 $_{19}$	.71	.9564 $_{9}$	.21	.98645 $_{34}$
.22	.5871 $_{39}$	.72	.7642 $_{31}$	.22	.8888 $_{19}$	.72	.9573 $_{9}$	.22	.98679 $_{34}$
.23	.5910 $_{38}$	.73	.7673 $_{31}$	.23	.8907 $_{18}$	.73	.9582 $_{9}$	.23	.98713 $_{32}$
.24	.5948 $_{39}$	.74	.7704 $_{30}$	.24	.8925 $_{19}$	.74	.9591 $_{8}$	.24	.98745 $_{33}$
0.25	0.5987 $_{39}$	0.75	0.7734 $_{30}$	1.25	0.8944 $_{18}$	1.75	0.9599 $_{9}$	2.25	0.98778 $_{31}$
.26	.6026 $_{38}$	.76	.7764 $_{30}$	.26	.8962 $_{18}$	.76	.9608 $_{8}$	.26	.98809 $_{31}$
.27	.6064 $_{39}$	.77	.7794 $_{29}$	.27	.8980 $_{17}$	.77	.9616 $_{8}$	.27	.98840 $_{30}$
.28	.6103 $_{38}$	.78	.7823 $_{29}$	.28	.8997 $_{18}$	.78	.9625 $_{8}$	.28	.98870 $_{29}$
.29	.6141 $_{38}$	.79	.7852 $_{29}$	.29	.9015 $_{17}$	.79	.9633 $_{8}$	.29	.98899 $_{29}$
0.30	0.6179 $_{38}$	0.80	0.7881 $_{29}$	1.30	0.9032 $_{17}$	1.80	0.9641 $_{8}$	2.30	0.98928 $_{28}$
.31	.6217 $_{38}$	.81	.7910 $_{29}$	.31	.9049 $_{17}$	.81	.9649 $_{7}$	.31	.98956 $_{27}$
.32	.6255 $_{38}$	.82	.7939 $_{28}$	.32	.9066 $_{16}$	.82	.9656 $_{8}$	.32	.98983 $_{27}$
.33	.6293 $_{38}$	.83	.7967 $_{28}$	.33	.9082 $_{17}$	.83	.9664 $_{7}$	.33	.99010 $_{26}$
.34	.6331 $_{37}$	.84	.7995 $_{28}$	.34	.9099 $_{16}$	.84	.9671 $_{7}$	.34	.99036 $_{25}$
0.35	0.6368 $_{38}$	0.85	0.8023 $_{28}$	1.35	0.9115 $_{16}$	1.85	0.9678 $_{8}$	2.35	0.99061 $_{25}$
.36	.6406 $_{37}$	.86	.8051 $_{27}$	.36	.9131 $_{16}$	.86	.9686 $_{7}$	.36	.99086 $_{25}$
.37	.6443 $_{37}$	.87	.8078 $_{28}$	.37	.9147 $_{15}$	.87	.9693 $_{6}$	.37	.99111 $_{23}$
.38	.6480 $_{37}$	.88	.8106 $_{27}$	.38	.9162 $_{15}$	.88	.9699 $_{7}$	.38	.99134 $_{24}$
.39	.6517 $_{37}$	.89	.8133 $_{26}$	.39	.9177 $_{15}$	.89	.9706 $_{7}$	.39	.99158 $_{22}$
0.40	0.6554 $_{37}$	0.90	0.8159 $_{27}$	1.40	0.9192 $_{15}$	1.90	0.9713 $_{6}$	2.40	0.99180 $_{22}$
.41	.6591 $_{37}$	.91	.8186 $_{26}$	.41	.9207 $_{15}$	.91	.9719 $_{7}$	.41	.99202 $_{22}$
.42	.6628 $_{36}$	.92	.8212 $_{26}$	.42	.9222 $_{14}$	.92	.9726 $_{6}$	.42	.99224 $_{21}$
.43	.6664 $_{36}$	.93	.8238 $_{26}$	.43	.9236 $_{15}$	.93	.9732 $_{6}$	.43	.99245 $_{21}$
.44	.6700 $_{36}$	.94	.8264 $_{25}$	.44	.9251 $_{14}$	.94	.9738 $_{6}$	.44	.99266 $_{20}$
0.45	0.6736 $_{36}$	0.95	0.8289 $_{26}$	1.45	0.9265 $_{14}$	1.95	0.9744 $_{6}$	2.45	0.99286 $_{19}$
.46	.6772 $_{36}$	.96	.8315 $_{25}$	.46	.9279 $_{13}$	.96	.9750 $_{6}$	.46	.99305 $_{19}$
.47	.6808 $_{36}$	.97	.8340 $_{25}$	.47	.9292 $_{14}$	.97	.9756 $_{5}$	.47	.99324 $_{19}$
.48	.6844 $_{35}$	.98	.8365 $_{24}$	.48	.9306 $_{13}$	.98	.9761 $_{6}$	.48	.99343 $_{18}$
.49	.6879 $_{36}$	.99	.8389 $_{24}$	.49	.9319 $_{13}$	.99	.9767 $_{5}$	.49	.99361 $_{18}$
0.50	0.6915	1.00	0.8413	1.50	0.9332	2.00	0.9772	2.50	0.99379

Table A1 Normal distribution function (continued)

z	$F(z)$	z	$F(z)$	z	$F(z)$
2.50	0.99379 $_{17}$	2.70	0.99653 $_{11}$	2.90	0.99813 $_{6}$
.51	.99396 $_{17}$	.71	.99664 $_{10}$	.91	.99819 $_{6}$
.52	.99413 $_{17}$	.72	.99674 $_{9}$	.92	.99825 $_{6}$
.53	.99430 $_{16}$	.73	.99683 $_{10}$	.93	.99831 $_{5}$
.54	.99446 $_{15}$	.74	.99693 $_{9}$	.94	.99836 $_{5}$
2.55	0.99461 $_{16}$	2.75	0.99702 $_{9}$	2.95	0.99841 $_{5}$
.56	.99477 $_{15}$	.76	.99711 $_{9}$	.96	.99846 $_{5}$
.57	.99492 $_{14}$	.77	.99720 $_{8}$	.97	.99851 $_{5}$
.58	.99506 $_{14}$	.78	.99728 $_{8}$	.98	.99856 $_{5}$
.59	.99520 $_{14}$	.79	.99736 $_{8}$	.99	.99861 $_{4}$
2.60	0.99534 $_{13}$	2.80	0.99744 $_{8}$	3.0	0.99865 $_{38}$
.61	.99547 $_{13}$	.81	.99752 $_{8}$	3.1	.99903 $_{28}$
.62	.99560 $_{13}$	.82	.99760 $_{7}$	3.2	.99931 $_{21}$
.63	.99573 $_{12}$	.83	.99767 $_{7}$	3.3	.99952 $_{14}$
.64	.99585 $_{13}$	.84	.99774 $_{7}$	3.4	.99966 $_{11}$
2.65	0.99598 $_{11}$	2.85	0.99781 $_{7}$	3.5	0.99977 $_{7}$
.66	.99609 $_{12}$	.86	.99788 $_{7}$	3.6	.99984 $_{5}$
.67	.99621 $_{11}$	.87	.99795 $_{6}$	3.7	.99989 $_{4}$
.68	.99632 $_{11}$	.88	.99801 $_{6}$	3.8	.99993 $_{2}$
.69	.99643 $_{10}$	.89	.99807 $_{6}$	3.9	.99995 $_{2}$
2.70	0.99653	2.90	0.99813	4.0	0.99997

The function tabulated is $F(z) = \dfrac{1}{\sqrt{(2\pi)}} \displaystyle\int_{-\infty}^{z} \exp(-\tfrac{1}{2}t^2)\,dt$.

$F(z)$ is the probability that a random variable, Normally distributed with zero mean and unit variance, will be less than z.

Table A2 Normal probability density function

z	$f(z)$	z	$f(z)$	z	$f(z)$	z	$f(z)$
0.0	0.3989	1.0	0.2420	2.0	0.0540	3.0	0.0044
0.1	.3970	1.1	.2179	2.1	.0440	3.1	.0033
0.2	.3910	1.2	.1942	2.2	.0355	3.2	.0024
0.3	.3814	1.3	.1714	2.3	.0283	3.3	.0017
0.4	.3683	1.4	.1497	2.4	.0224	3.4	.0012
0.5	0.3521	1.5	0.1295	2.5	0.0175	3.5	0.0009
0.6	.3332	1.6	.1109	2.6	.0136	3.6	.0006
0.7	.3123	1.7	.0940	2.7	.0104	3.7	.0004
0.8	.2897	1.8	.0790	2.8	.0079	3.8	.0003
0.9	.2661	1.9	.0656	2.9	.0060	3.9	.0002
1.0	0.2420	2.0	0.0540	3.0	0.0044	4.0	0.0001

The function tabulated is $f(z) = \dfrac{1}{\sqrt{(2\pi)}} \exp(-\tfrac{1}{2}z^2)$, the probability density function of the standard Normal distribution.

Table A3 Random numbers

20 17	42 28	23 17	59 66	38 61	02 10	86 10	51 55	92 52	44 25
74 49	04 49	03 04	10 33	53 70	11 54	48 63	94 60	94 49	57 38
94 70	49 31	38 67	23 42	29 65	40 88	78 71	37 18	48 64	06 57
22 15	78 15	69 84	32 52	32 54	15 12	54 02	01 37	38 37	12 93
93 29	12 18	27 30	30 55	91 87	50 57	58 51	49 36	12 53	96 40
45 04	77 97	36 14	99 45	52 95	69 85	03 83	51 87	85 56	22 37
44 91	99 49	89 39	94 60	48 49	06 77	64 72	59 26	08 51	25 57
16 23	91 02	19 96	47 59	89 65	27 84	30 92	63 37	26 24	23 66
04 50	65 04	65 65	82 42	70 51	55 04	61 47	88 83	99 34	82 37
32 70	17 72	03 61	66 26	24 71	22 77	88 33	17 78	08 92	73 49
03 64	59 07	42 95	81 39	06 41	20 81	92 34	51 90	39 08	21 42
62 49	00 90	67 86	93 48	31 82	19 07	67 68	49 03	27 47	52 03
61 00	95 86	98 36	14 03	48 88	51 07	33 40	06 86	33 76	68 57
89 03	90 49	28 74	21 04	09 96	60 45	22 03	52 80	01 79	33 81
01 72	33 85	52 40	60 07	06 71	89 27	14 29	55 24	85 79	31 96
27 56	49 79	34 34	32 22	60 53	91 17	33 26	44 70	93 14	99 70
49 05	74 48	10 55	35 25	24 28	20 22	35 66	66 34	26 35	91 23
49 74	37 25	97 26	33 94	42 23	01 28	59 58	92 69	03 66	73 82
20 26	22 43	88 08	19 85	08 12	47 65	65 63	56 07	97 85	56 79
48 87	77 96	43 39	76 93	08 79	22 18	54 55	93 75	97 26	90 77
08 72	87 46	75 73	00 11	27 07	05 20	30 85	22 21	04 67	19 13
95 97	98 62	17 27	31 42	64 71	46 22	32 75	19 32	20 99	94 85
37 99	57 31	70 40	46 55	46 12	24 32	36 74	69 20	72 10	95 93
05 79	58 37	85 33	75 18	88 71	23 44	54 28	00 48	96 23	66 45
55 85	63 42	00 79	91 22	29 01	41 39	51 40	36 65	26 11	78 32
67 28	96 25	68 36	24 72	03 85	49 24	05 69	64 86	08 19	91 21
85 86	94 78	32 59	51 82	86 43	73 84	45 60	89 57	06 87	08 15
40 10	60 09	05 88	78 44	63 13	58 25	37 11	18 47	75 62	52 21
94 55	89 48	90 80	77 80	26 89	87 44	23 74	66 20	20 19	26 52
11 63	77 77	23 20	33 62	62 19	29 03	94 15	56 37	14 09	47 16
64 00	26 04	54 55	38 57	94 62	68 40	26 04	24 25	03 61	01 20
50 94	13 23	78 41	60 58	10 60	88 46	30 21	45 98	70 96	36 89
66 98	37 96	44 13	45 05	34 59	75 85	48 97	27 19	17 85	48 51
66 91	42 83	60 77	90 91	60 90	79 62	57 66	72 28	08 70	96 03
33 58	12 18	02 07	19 40	21 29	39 45	90 42	58 84	85 43	95 67
52 49	40 16	72 40	73 05	50 90	02 04	98 24	05 30	27 25	20 88
74 98	93 99	78 30	79 47	96 92	45 58	40 37	89 76	84 41	74 68
50 26	54 30	01 88	69 57	54 45	69 88	23 21	05 69	93 44	05 32
49 46	61 89	33 79	96 84	28 34	19 35	28 73	39 59	56 34	97 07
19 65	13 44	78 39	73 88	62 03	36 00	25 96	86 76	67 90	21 68
64 17	47 67	87 59	81 40	72 61	14 00	28 28	55 86	23 38	16 15
18 43	97 37	68 97	56 56	57 95	01 88	11 89	48 07	42 60	11 92
65 58	60 87	51 09	96 61	15 53	66 81	66 88	44 75	37 01	28 88
79 90	31 00	91 14	85 65	31 75	43 15	45 93	64 78	34 53	88 02
07 23	00 15	59 05	16 09	94 42	20 40	63 76	65 67	34 11	94 10
90 08	14 24	01 51	95 46	30 32	33 19	00 14	19 28	40 51	92 69
53 82	62 02	21 82	34 13	41 03	12 85	65 30	00 97	56 30	15 48
98 17	26 15	04 50	76 25	20 33	54 84	39 31	23 33	59 64	96 27
08 91	12 44	82 40	30 62	45 50	64 54	65 17	89 25	59 44	99 95
37 21	46 77	84 87	67 39	85 54	96 37	33 41	11 74	90 50	29 62

Each digit is an independent sample from a population in which the digits 0 to 9 are equally likely, that is each has a probability of $\frac{1}{10}$.

Table A3

16 16	57 04	81 71	17 46	53 29	73 46	42 73	77 63	62 58	60 59
98 63	89 52	77 23	61 08	63 90	80 38	42 71	85 70	04 81	05 50
01 03	09 35	02 54	51 96	92 75	58 29	24 23	25 19	89 97	91 29
29 07	16 34	49 22	52 96	89 34	17 11	06 91	24 38	55 06	83 59
72 61	80 54	70 99	24 64	11 38	83 65	27 23	40 37	84 58	48 53
71 11	41 82	79 37	00 45	98 54	52 89	26 34	40 13	60 38	08 86
61 05	66 18	76 82	11 18	61 90	90 63	78 57	32 06	39 95	75 94
81 89	42 34	00 49	97 53	33 16	26 91	57 58	42 48	51 05	48 27
10 24	90 84	22 16	26 96	54 11	01 96	58 81	37 97	80 98	72 81
14 28	33 43	01 32	58 39	19 54	56 57	23 58	24 87	77 36	20 97
35 41	17 89	87 04	28 32	13 45	59 03	91 08	69 24	84 44	42 83
07 89	36 87	98 73	77 64	75 19	05 61	11 64	31 75	49 38	96 60
27 59	15 58	19 68	95 47	25 69	11 90	26 19	07 40	83 59	90 95
95 98	45 52	27 35	86 81	16 29	37 60	39 35	05 24	49 00	29 07
12 95	72 72	81 84	36 58	05 10	70 50	31 04	12 67	74 01	72 90
35 23	06 68	52 50	39 55	92 28	28 89	64 87	80 00	84 53	97 97
86 33	95 73	80 92	26 49	54 50	41 21	06 62	73 91	35 05	21 37
02 82	96 23	16 46	15 51	60 31	55 27	84 14	71 58	94 71	48 35
44 46	34 96	32 69	48 22	40 17	43 25	33 31	26 26	59 34	99 00
08 77	07 19	94 46	17 51	03 73	99 89	28 44	16 87	56 16	56 09
61 59	37 08	08 46	56 76	29 48	33 87	70 79	03 80	96 81	79 68
67 70	18 01	67 19	29 49	58 67	08 56	27 24	20 70	46 31	04 32
23 09	08 79	18 78	00 32	86 74	78 55	55 72	58 54	76 07	53 73
89 40	26 39	74 58	59 55	87 11	74 06	49 46	31 94	86 66	66 97
84 95	66 42	90 74	13 71	00 71	24 41	67 62	38 92	39 26	30 29
52 14	49 02	19 31	28 15	51 01	19 09	97 94	52 43	22 21	17 66
89 56	31 41	37 87	28 16	62 48	01 84	46 06	04 39	94 10	76 21
65 94	05 93	06 68	34 72	73 17	65 34	00 65	75 78	23 97	13 04
13 08	15 75	02 83	48 26	53 77	62 96	56 52	28 26	12 15	75 53
03 18	33 57	16 71	60 27	15 18	39 32	37 01	05 86	25 14	35 41
10 04	00 95	85 04	32 80	19 01	85 03	29 29	80 04	21 52	14 76
23 94	97 28	60 43	42 25	26 48	48 13	34 68	39 22	74 85	03 25
35 63	42 90	90 74	33 17	58 77	83 36	76 22	00 89	61 55	13 17
42 86	03 36	45 33	60 77	72 92	10 76	22 55	11 00	37 60	47 73
67 26	92 87	09 96	85 37	82 61	39 01	70 05	12 66	17 39	99 34
91 93	88 56	35 76	97 35	19 37	14 66	07 57	24 41	06 90	07 72
37 14	73 35	32 01	07 94	78 28	90 33	71 56	63 77	89 24	24 28
07 46	50 58	08 73	42 97	20 42	64 68	48 35	04 38	28 28	36 94
92 18	09 46	94 99	17 41	28 60	67 94	26 54	63 70	84 73	76 61
00 49	98 43	39 67	68 40	41 31	92 28	49 57	15 55	11 81	41 89
08 59	41 41	33 59	43 28	14 51	02 71	24 45	41 57	22 11	79 79
67 05	19 54	32 33	34 68	27 93	39 35	62 51	35 55	40 99	46 19
24 99	48 06	96 41	21 25	29 03	57 71	96 49	94 74	98 90	21 52
65 86	27 46	70 93	27 39	64 37	01 63	21 03	43 78	18 74	77 07
52 70	03 20	84 96	14 37	51 05	63 99	81 02	84 56	17 78	48 45
32 88	29 93	58 21	71 05	68 58	79 08	86 37	98 76	70 45	66 23
54 16	39 40	98 57	02 05	65 15	73 23	51 51	75 06	38 13	51 68
95 22	18 59	54 57	44 22	72 35	81 24	14 94	24 04	42 26	92 14
93 10	27 94	90 45	39 33	50 26	88 46	90 57	40 47	71 63	62 59
19 20	85 20	15 67	78 03	32 23	50 59	24 83	64 99	18 00	78 50

Each digit is an independent sample from a population in which the digits 0 to 9 are equally likely, that is each has a probability of $\frac{1}{10}$.

Table A4 Percentage points of the *t*-distribution

P	25	10	5	2	1	0.2	0.1
$v=1$	2.41	6.31	12.71	31.82	63.66	318.3	636.6
2	1.60	2.92	4.30	6.96	9.92	22.33	31.60
3	1.42	2.35	3.18	4.54	5.84	10.21	12.92
4	1.34	2.13	2.78	3.75	4.60	7.17	8.61
5	1.30	2.02	2.57	3.36	4.03	5.89	6.87
6	1.27	1.94	2.45	3.14	3.71	5.21	5.96
7	1.25	1.89	2.36	3.00	3.50	4.79	5.41
8	1.24	1.86	2.31	2.90	3.36	4.50	5.04
9	1.23	1.83	2.26	2.82	3.25	4.30	4.78
10	1.22	1.81	2.23	2.76	3.17	4.14	4.59
12	1.21	1.78	2.18	2.68	3.05	3.93	4.32
15	1.20	1.75	2.13	2.60	2.95	3.73	4.07
20	1.18	1.72	2.09	2.53	2.85	3.55	3.85
24	1.18	1.71	2.06	2.49	2.80	3.47	3.75
30	1.17	1.70	2.04	2.46	2.75	3.39	3.65
40	1.17	1.68	2.02	2.42	2.70	3.31	3.55
60	1.16	1.67	2.00	2.39	2.66	3.23	3.46
120	1.16	1.66	1.98	2.36	2.62	3.16	3.37
∞	1.15	1.64	1.96	2.33	2.58	3.09	3.29

For v degrees of freedom, $P/100$ is the probability that $|t|$ will exceed the tabulated value.

Table A5 Transformation of the correlation coefficient

r	z'	r	z'	r	z'	r	z'	r	z'	r	z'
0.00	0.000 $_{20}$	0.40	0.424 $_{24}$	0.80	1.099 $_{28}$	0.940	1.738 $_9$	0.960	1.946 $_{13}$	0.980	2.298 $_{25}$
.02	.020 $_{20}$	.42	.448 $_{24}$	.81	.127 $_{30}$	.941	.747 $_9$	.961	.959 $_{13}$	.981	.323 $_{28}$
.04	.040 $_{20}$	.44	.472 $_{25}$	.82	.157 $_{31}$	.942	.756 $_8$	.962	.972 $_{14}$	.982	.351 $_{29}$
.06	.060 $_{20}$	.46	.497 $_{26}$	.83	.188 $_{33}$	.943	.764 $_{10}$	.963	1.986 $_{14}$	.983	.380 $_{30}$
.08	.080 $_{20}$	.48	.523 $_{26}$	.84	.221 $_{35}$	.944	.774 $_9$	.964	2.000 $_{14}$	.984	.410 $_{33}$
0.10	0.100 $_{21}$	0.50	0.549 $_{27}$	0.85	1.256 $_{37}$	0.945	1.783 $_9$	0.965	2.014 $_{15}$	0.985	2.443 $_{34}$
.12	.121 $_{20}$	.52	.576 $_{28}$	.86	.293 $_{40}$	.946	.792 $_{10}$	.966	.029 $_{15}$	.986	.477 $_{38}$
.14	.141 $_{20}$	.54	.604 $_{29}$	.87	.333 $_{43}$	.947	.802 $_{10}$	.967	.044 $_{16}$	.987	.515 $_{40}$
.16	.161 $_{21}$	.56	.633 $_{29}$	.88	.376 $_{46}$	.948	.812 $_{10}$	.968	.060 $_{16}$	.988	.555 $_{44}$
.18	.182 $_{21}$	.58	.662 $_{31}$	.89	.422 $_{50}$	.949	.822 $_{10}$	.969	.076 $_{16}$	.989	.599 $_{48}$
0.20	0.203 $_{21}$	0.60	0.693 $_{32}$	0.90	1.472 $_{56}$	0.950	1.832 $_{10}$	0.970	2.092 $_{18}$	0.990	2.647 $_{53}$
.22	.224 $_{21}$	.62	.725 $_{33}$	.91	.528 $_{61}$	.951	.842 $_{11}$	.971	.110 $_{17}$	.991	.700 $_{59}$
.24	.245 $_{21}$	.64	.758 $_{35}$	.92	.589 $_{69}$	.952	.853 $_{10}$	.972	.127 $_{19}$	.992	.759 $_{67}$
.26	.266 $_{22}$	.66	.793 $_{36}$	.93	.658 $_{80}$	.953	.863 $_{11}$	.973	.146 $_{19}$	.993	.826 $_{77}$
.28	.288 $_{22}$	.68	.829 $_{38}$	.94	.738	.954	.874 $_{12}$	.974	.165 $_{20}$	.994	.903
0.30	0.310 $_{22}$	0.70	0.867 $_{41}$	0.95	1.832	0.955	1.886 $_{11}$	0.975	2.185 $_{20}$	0.995	2.994
.32	.332 $_{22}$	.72	.908 $_{42}$	.96	1.946	.956	.897 $_{12}$	.976	.205 $_{22}$	.996	3.106
.34	.354 $_{23}$	.74	.950 $_{46}$	.97	2.092	.957	.909 $_{12}$	.977	.227 $_{22}$	.997	.250
.36	.377 $_{23}$	.76	0.996 $_{49}$	.98	.298	.958	.921 $_{12}$	.978	.249 $_{24}$	.998	.453
.38	.400 $_{24}$	.78	1.045 $_{54}$	.99	2.647	.959	.933 $_{13}$	.979	.273 $_{25}$	.999	3.800
0.40	0.424	0.80	1.099	1.00	∞	0.960	1.946	0.980	2.298	1.000	∞

The function tabulated is $z' = \tanh^{-1} r = \tfrac{1}{2} \ln \dfrac{1+r}{1-r} = 1.1513 \log \dfrac{1+r}{1-r}$.

Table A6 Percentage points of the χ^2-distribution

P	99.5	99	97.5	95	10	5	2.5	1	0.5	0.1
$v=1$	0.0^4393	0.0^3157	0.0^3982	0.00393	2.71	3.84	5.02	6.63	7.88	10.83
2	0.0100	0.0201	0.0506	0.103	4.61	5.99	7.38	9.21	10.60	13.81
3	0.0717	0.115	0.216	0.352	6.25	7.81	9.35	11.34	12.84	16.27
4	0.207	0.297	0.484	0.711	7.78	9.49	11.14	13.28	14.86	18.47
5	0.412	0.554	0.831	1.15	9.24	11.07	12.83	15.09	16.75	20.52
6	0.676	0.872	1.24	1.64	10.64	12.59	14.45	16.81	18.55	22.46
7	0.989	1.24	1.69	2.17	12.02	14.07	16.01	18.48	20.28	24.32
8	1.34	1.65	2.18	2.73	13.36	15.51	17.53	20.09	21.95	26.12
9	1.73	2.09	2.70	3.33	14.68	16.92	19.02	21.67	23.59	27.88
10	2.16	2.56	3.25	3.94	15.99	18.31	20.48	23.21	25.19	29.59
11	2.60	3.05	3.82	4.57	17.28	19.68	21.92	24.73	26.76	31.26
12	3.07	3.57	4.40	5.23	18.55	21.03	23.34	26.22	28.30	32.91
13	3.57	4.11	5.01	5.89	19.81	22.36	24.74	27.69	29.82	34.53
14	4.07	4.66	5.63	6.57	21.06	23.68	26.12	29.14	31.32	36.12
15	4.60	5.23	6.26	7.26	22.31	25.00	27.49	30.58	32.80	37.70
16	5.14	5.81	6.91	7.96	23.54	26.30	28.85	32.00	34.27	39.25
17	5.70	6.41	7.56	8.67	24.77	27.59	30.19	33.41	35.72	40.79
18	6.26	7.01	8.23	9.39	25.99	28.87	31.53	34.81	37.16	42.31
19	6.84	7.63	8.91	10.12	27.20	30.14	32.85	36.19	38.58	43.82
20	7.43	8.26	9.59	10.85	28.41	31.41	34.17	37.57	40.00	45.31
21	8.03	8.90	10.28	11.59	29.62	32.67	35.48	38.93	41.40	46.80
22	8.64	9.54	10.98	12.34	30.81	33.92	36.78	40.29	42.80	48.27
23	9.26	10.20	11.69	13.09	32.01	35.17	38.08	41.64	44.18	49.73
24	9.89	10.86	12.40	13.85	33.20	36.42	39.36	42.98	45.56	51.18
25	10.52	11.52	13.12	14.61	34.38	37.65	40.65	44.31	46.93	52.62
26	11.16	12.20	13.84	15.38	35.56	38.89	41.92	45.64	48.29	54.05
27	11.81	12.88	14.57	16.15	36.74	40.11	43.19	46.96	49.64	55.48
28	12.46	13.56	15.31	16.93	37.92	41.34	44.46	48.28	50.99	56.89
29	13.12	14.26	16.05	17.71	39.09	42.56	45.72	49.59	52.34	58.30
30	13.79	14.95	16.79	18.49	40.26	43.77	46.98	50.89	53.67	59.70
40	20.71	22.16	24.43	26.51	51.81	55.76	59.34	63.69	66.77	73.40
50	27.99	29.71	32.36	34.76	63.17	67.50	71.42	76.15	79.49	86.66
60	35.53	37.48	40.48	43.19	74.40	79.08	83.30	88.38	91.95	99.61
70	43.28	45.44	48.76	51.74	85.53	90.53	95.02	100.4	104.2	112.3
80	51.17	53.54	57.15	60.39	96.58	101.9	106.6	112.3	116.3	124.8
90	59.20	61.75	65.65	69.13	107.6	113.1	118.1	124.1	128.3	137.2
100	67.33	70.06	74.22	77.93	118.5	124.3	129.6	135.8	140.2	149.4

For v degrees of freedom, $P/100$ is the probability that χ^2 will exceed the tabulated value.

Table A7 5% points of the F-distribution

$v_1 =$	1	2	3	4	5	6	7	8	10	12	24	∞
$v_2 = 1$	161.4	199.5	215.7	224.6	230.2	234.0	236.8	238.9	241.9	243.9	249.0	254.3
2	18.5	19.0	19.2	19.2	19.3	19.3	19.4	19.4	19.4	19.4	19.5	19.5
3	10.13	9.55	9.28	9.12	9.01	8.94	8.89	8.85	8.79	8.74	8.64	8.53
4	7.71	6.94	6.59	6.39	6.26	6.16	6.09	6.04	5.96	5.91	5.77	5.63
5	6.61	5.79	5.41	5.19	5.05	4.95	4.88	4.82	4.74	4.68	4.53	4.36
6	5.99	5.14	4.76	4.53	4.39	4.28	4.21	4.15	4.06	4.00	3.84	3.67
7	5.59	4.74	4.35	4.12	3.97	3.87	3.79	3.73	3.64	3.57	3.41	3.23
8	5.32	4.46	4.07	3.84	3.69	3.58	3.50	3.44	3.35	3.28	3.12	2.93
9	5.12	4.26	3.86	3.63	3.48	3.37	3.29	3.23	3.14	3.07	2.90	2.71
10	4.96	4.10	3.71	3.48	3.33	3.22	3.14	3.07	2.98	2.91	2.74	2.54
11	4.84	3.98	3.59	3.36	3.20	3.09	3.01	2.95	2.85	2.79	2.61	2.40
12	4.75	3.89	3.49	3.26	3.11	3.00	2.91	2.85	2.75	2.69	2.51	2.30
13	4.67	3.81	3.41	3.18	3.03	2.92	2.83	2.77	2.67	2.60	2.42	2.21
14	4.60	3.74	3.34	3.11	2.96	2.85	2.76	2.70	2.60	2.53	2.35	2.13
15	4.54	3.68	3.29	3.06	2.90	2.79	2.71	2.64	2.54	2.48	2.29	2.07
16	4.49	3.63	3.24	3.01	2.85	2.74	2.66	2.59	2.49	2.42	2.24	2.01
17	4.45	3.59	3.20	2.96	2.81	2.70	2.61	2.55	2.45	2.38	2.19	1.96
18	4.41	3.55	3.16	2.93	2.77	2.66	2.58	2.51	2.41	2.34	2.15	1.92
19	4.38	3.52	3.13	2.90	2.74	2.63	2.54	2.48	2.38	2.31	2.11	1.88
20	4.35	3.49	3.10	2.87	2.71	2.60	2.51	2.45	2.35	2.28	2.08	1.84
21	4.32	3.47	3.07	2.84	2.68	2.57	2.49	2.42	2.32	2.25	2.05	1.81
22	4.30	3.44	3.05	2.82	2.66	2.55	2.46	2.40	2.30	2.23	2.03	1.78
23	4.28	3.42	3.03	2.80	2.64	2.53	2.44	2.37	2.27	2.20	2.00	1.76
24	4.26	3.40	3.01	2.78	2.62	2.51	2.42	2.36	2.25	2.18	1.98	1.73
25	4.24	3.39	2.99	2.76	2.60	2.49	2.40	2.34	2.24	2.16	1.96	1.71
26	4.23	3.37	2.98	2.74	2.59	2.47	2.39	2.32	2.22	2.15	1.95	1.69
27	4.21	3.35	2.96	2.73	2.57	2.46	2.37	2.31	2.20	2.13	1.93	1.67
28	4.20	3.34	2.95	2.71	2.56	2.45	2.36	2.29	2.19	2.12	1.91	1.65
29	4.18	3.33	2.93	2.70	2.55	2.43	2.35	2.28	2.18	2.10	1.90	1.64
30	4.17	3.32	2.92	2.69	2.53	2.42	2.33	2.27	2.16	2.09	1.89	1.62
32	4.15	3.29	2.90	2.67	2.51	2.40	2.31	2.24	2.14	2.07	1.86	1.59
34	4.13	3.28	2.88	2.65	2.49	2.38	2.29	2.23	2.12	2.05	1.84	1.57
36	4.11	3.26	2.87	2.63	2.48	2.36	2.28	2.21	2.11	2.03	1.82	1.55
38	4.10	3.24	2.85	2.62	2.46	2.35	2.26	2.19	2.09	2.02	1.81	1.53
40	4.08	3.23	2.84	2.61	2.45	2.34	2.25	2.18	2.08	2.00	1.79	1.51
60	4.00	3.15	2.76	2.53	2.37	2.25	2.17	2.10	1.99	1.92	1.70	1.39
120	3.92	3.07	2.68	2.45	2.29	2.18	2.09	2.02	1.91	1.83	1.61	1.25
∞	3.84	3.00	2.60	2.37	2.21	2.10	2.01	1.94	1.83	1.75	1.52	1.00

v_1 is the degrees of freedom of the numerator and v_2 is the degrees of freedom of the denominator when F is calculated so that it is greater than 1. Table A7 gives the values which F exceeds with 5% probability and Table A8 gives the values which F exceeds with $2\frac{1}{2}\%$ probability.

Table A8 $2\frac{1}{2}\%$ points of the F-distribution

$v_1 =$	1	2	3	4	5	6	7	8	10	12	24	∞
$v_2 = 1$	648	800	864	900	922	937	948	957	969	977	997	1018
2	38.5	39.0	39.2	39.2	39.3	39.3	39.4	39.4	39.4	39.4	39.5	39.5
3	17.4	16.0	15.4	15.1	14.9	14.7	14.6	14.5	14.4	14.3	14.1	13.9
4	12.22	10.65	9.98	9.60	9.36	9.20	9.07	8.98	8.84	8.75	8.51	8.26
5	10.01	8.43	7.76	7.39	7.15	6.98	6.85	6.76	6.62	6.52	6.28	6.02
6	8.81	7.26	6.60	6.23	5.99	5.82	5.70	5.60	5.46	5.37	5.12	4.85
7	8.07	6.54	5.89	5.52	5.29	5.12	4.99	4.90	4.76	4.67	4.42	4.14
8	7.57	6.06	5.42	5.05	4.82	4.65	4.53	4.43	4.30	4.20	3.95	3.67
9	7.21	5.71	5.08	4.72	4.48	4.32	4.20	4.10	3.96	3.87	3.61	3.33
10	6.94	5.46	4.83	4.47	4.24	4.07	3.95	3.85	3.72	3.62	3.37	3.08
11	6.72	5.26	4.63	4.28	4.04	3.88	3.76	3.66	3.53	3.43	3.17	2.88
12	6.55	5.10	4.47	4.12	3.89	3.73	3.61	3.51	3.37	3.28	3.02	2.72
13	6.41	4.97	4.35	4.00	3.77	3.60	3.48	3.39	3.25	3.15	2.89	2.60
14	6.30	4.86	4.24	3.89	3.66	3.50	3.38	3.29	3.15	3.05	2.79	2.49
15	6.20	4.76	4.15	3.80	3.58	3.41	3.29	3.20	3.06	2.96	2.70	2.40
16	6.12	4.69	4.08	3.73	3.50	3.34	3.22	3.12	2.99	2.89	2.63	2.32
17	6.04	4.62	4.01	3.66	3.44	3.28	3.16	3.06	2.92	2.82	2.56	2.25
18	5.98	4.56	3.95	3.61	3.38	3.22	3.10	3.01	2.87	2.77	2.50	2.19
19	5.92	4.51	3.90	3.56	3.33	3.17	3.05	2.96	2.82	2.72	2.45	2.13
20	5.87	4.46	3.86	3.51	3.29	3.13	3.01	2.91	2.77	2.68	2.41	2.09
21	5.83	4.42	3.82	3.48	3.25	3.09	2.97	2.87	2.73	2.64	2.37	2.04
22	5.79	4.38	3.78	3.44	3.22	3.05	2.93	2.84	2.70	2.60	2.33	2.00
23	5.75	4.35	3.75	3.41	3.18	3.02	2.90	2.81	2.67	2.57	2.30	1.97
24	5.72	4.32	3.72	3.38	3.15	2.99	2.87	2.78	2.64	2.54	2.27	1.94
25	5.69	4.29	3.69	3.35	3.13	2.97	2.85	2.75	2.61	2.51	2.24	1.91
26	5.66	4.27	3.67	3.33	3.10	2.94	2.82	2.73	2.59	2.49	2.22	1.88
27	5.63	4.24	3.65	3.31	3.08	2.92	2.80	2.71	2.57	2.47	2.19	1.85
28	5.61	4.22	3.63	3.29	3.06	2.90	2.78	2.69	2.55	2.45	2.17	1.83
29	5.59	4.20	3.61	3.27	3.04	2.88	2.76	2.67	2.53	2.43	2.15	1.81
30	5.57	4.18	3.59	3.25	3.03	2.87	2.75	2.65	2.51	2.41	2.14	1.79
32	5.53	4.15	3.56	3.22	3.00	2.84	2.72	2.62	2.48	2.38	2.10	1.75
34	5.50	4.12	3.53	3.19	2.97	2.81	2.69	2.59	2.45	2.35	2.08	1.72
36	5.47	4.09	3.53	3.17	2.94	2.79	2.66	2.57	2.43	2.33	2.05	1.69
38	5.45	4.07	3.48	3.15	2.92	2.76	2.64	2.55	2.41	2.31	2.03	1.66
40	5.42	4.05	3.46	3.13	2.90	2.74	2.62	2.53	2.39	2.29	2.01	1.64
60	5.29	3.93	3.34	2.01	2.79	2.63	2.51	2.41	2.27	2.17	1.88	1.48
120	5.15	3.80	3.23	2.89	2.67	2.52	2.39	2.30	2.16	2.05	1.76	1.31
∞	5.02	3.69	3.12	2.79	2.57	2.41	2.29	2.19	2.05	1.94	1.64	1.00

Index